W9-ABR-913

PRACTICE OF PERFECTION AND CHRISTIAN VIRTUES

CHRIST IN THE TEMPLE

PRACTICE OF PERFECTION AND CHRISTIAN VIRTUES

By

ALPHONSUS RODRIGUEZ

of the Society of Jesus

Newly Translated from the Original Spanish

By

JOSEPH RICKABY

of the Same Society

IN THREE VOLUMES

VOLUME I

Authorized American Edition

LOYOLA UNIVERSITY PRESS

Chicago, Illinois

1929

Imprimi Potest

HENRICUS KEANE, S. J.

Praep. Prov. Angliae

11 Februarii, 1929

Imprimatur

✠ FRANCISCUS

Episcopus Menevensis

13 Februarii, 1929

Composed and Plated in the
United States of America

LIFE OF ALPHONSUS RODRIGUEZ*

Alphonsus Rodriguez was born at Valladolid in the year 1526, and in the twentieth year of his age he renounced the world to consecrate himself to God in the Society of Jesus at Salamanca. After having been engaged about thirteen years in teaching moral theology at Monterey, he was sent to Montille, in the province of Andalusia, to be there master of novices, and to deliver such spiritual exhortations as are delivered weekly in the houses of the Society. In these two employments he acquitted himself for thirty years together with all possible zeal and ability, and hereby evinced how skilled he was in the science of saints and in the direction of souls.

Being afterwards chosen to go to Rome, to the Fifth General Congregation, he there also gave marks of exemplary virtue and consummate prudence. At his return he was sent to Cordova, where for twelve years he had the direction of spiritual things, that is to say, the care of taking an account of the interior state of all the religious in the house, to help them to overcome and root out of their souls whatever opposed their advancement in perfection. As at Montille, so at Cordova his office was to make the weekly exhortations; and it was towards the end of the twelve years he remained here that, collecting together what he had written on various subjects, he compiled these volumes of the PRACTICE OF PERFECTION AND CHRISTIAN VIRTUES. He did not, however, publish them until a long time after, when he went to the Provincial Congregation held at Seville in the year 1606, where he was ordered to stay to take care of the novices and at the same time to publish this his work.

*Taken from the American edition of 1839.

After having applied himself for eight years together, without any relaxation, to the discharge of both these duties, he became so infirm that he had neither force to exercise any longer the painful function of master of novices, nor even to celebrate the holy Sacrifice of the Mass. Lest, however, he should be deprived of the precious body of Jesus Christ, he daily received it from the hand of another; and, having lived two years in this languishing condition, at length upon the twenty-first of February in the year 1616, in a good old age, full of merits, he happily rested in our Lord, in peace. His death was not less universally regretted than his sanctity was esteemed. He was a great lover of retirement, an exact observer of rules, and had a very great zeal for the salvation of souls. His self-abnegation was such that in all things he had but God in view. The time in which he was not engaged in the discharge of other indispensable duties, he spent in prayer and spiritual reading, adding to these pious exercises very frequent austerities, which he continued to the end of his life; and when it was once represented to him that he could not practise such penances without shortening his days, he answered: "An unmortified religious man is already dead."

Behold in short the life of this most excellent master of a spiritual life; but the reading of his works will still give you a better knowledge of him, for there was nothing he proposed to others to practise, of which he gave not first an example in himself, his life being nothing else than a constant practice of what in his writings he had taught others.

THE AUTHOR

to the

RELIGIOUS OF THE SOCIETY OF JESUS*

St. Gregory, being desirous to write some spiritual instructions for the conduct of certain religious houses, excuses himself in his Sixth Book and Twenty-seventh Epistle in these terms. "The exercises of mortification and prayer practised by religious produce such a source or fountain of wisdom in their hearts that they stand not in need of being watered with those few drops our aridity is able to impart to them. For, as the fountain in the midst of the terrestrial Paradise watered all parts thereof and kept it continually fresh and green without the help of rain, which it needed not, so those who are in the paradise of religion have no need of being watered from without, because prayer and mortification produce in them such a source or fountain of grace as is always sufficient to maintain their virtues in their full splendor and beauty."

I might, Reverend Fathers, upon this account, with far more reason than St. Gregory, excuse myself after the same manner he did to those faithful souls our Lord has planted in the garden of the Society of Jesus—souls He has cultivated and watered by the help of that mental prayer they daily make. But though this excuse would doubtless be a very just one if I imagined you expected anything new from me, yet I am prevented from making it, as I propose to myself nothing else in this work than to revive in your memories what you already know and daily practise. In

---

*Taken from the American edition of 1839.

doing this, I shall pay obedience to our holy founder, who in one of his constitutions ordains that "once a week, or at least once a fortnight, there shall be one appointed to lay before our eyes the obligations of a spiritual life, lest human frailty, which daily inclines us to relax in our duties, might cause us to forget, and to discontinue them." This constitution, God be praised, is exactly observed throughout the whole Society, and produces great fruit therein. Having, therefore, above these forty years been employed in the function of exhorting the novices or other religious, and having gathered divers things together for this purpose, my superiors and many other persons to whom I owe a deference were of opinion that I might render great service to God and to religion, and that the advantage drawn from my labors would be more lasting, if I should take care to review and put in order what I had already composed.

I considered, also, that in the constitution before cited, St. Ignatius puts this alternative:—"Let there be," says he, "one appointed to deliver these spiritual exhortations to the religious, or at least let the religious be obliged to read them." I was still more encouraged in my undertaking when I reflected that it is a practice established in the Society and very much recommended by saints, to read something every day that may promote our spiritual advancement. This being the principal design of the following work, I have for this reason laid before you, as clearly and briefly as I was able, such things as are more essential and more common to our profession. These, I trust, will serve as a mirror wherein, if we daily view ourselves, we shall be enabled to correct our imperfections and decorate our souls in such manner as will render them most pleasing to the eyes of His Divine Majesty.

Moreover, though my principal intention was to fulfil the particular obligation I have to serve those whom religion has constituted my fathers and brethren in Jesus Christ;

yet because we ought to extend as far as we can the effects of charity, and being particularly obliged to it by our institute, I have endeavored to dispose this work after such a manner as that it may be useful not only to our Society in particular, but to all other religious, and even to all persons in general who aspire to Christian perfection. Wherefore, that the title may correspond to the work, I have entitled it PRACTICE OF PERFECTION AND CHRISTIAN VIRTUES. I call it *Practice* because things are treated in it after such a manner as may render the practice very easy.

I hope by the mercy of our Lord that my labors will not be unprofitable; and that this grain of seed of the word of God, being sown in the good soil of souls aspiring to perfection, will render not only thirty or sixty, but even a hundred, fold.

TABLE OF CONTENTS

The First Treatise

On the Esteem and Affection We Ought to Have for Whatever Relates to Our Spiritual Advancement; and on Many Other Things Conducive to It

The Second Treatise

On the Perfection of Our Ordinary Actions

The Third Treatise

On the Integrity and Purity of Intention We Ought to Have in All Our Actions

The Fourth Treatise

On Union and Fraternal Charity

The Fifth Treatise

On Prayer

The Sixth Treatise

On the Presence of God

The Seventh Treatise

On the Examen of Conscience

The Eighth Treatise

On Conformity to the Will of God

FIRST TREATISE

ON THE ESTEEM OF SPIRITUAL THINGS

CHAPTER I

The Great Value We Ought to Set on Spiritual Things

I *WISHED,* says the Wise Man, *and there was given me sense; I asked it of God, and there came upon me the spirit of wisdom; and I preferred her before thrones and royal scepters; and I made no account of riches in comparison therewith, nor of precious stones; for all gold in comparison with it is as a little sand, and silver shall be counted as clay before it* (Wisdom vii. 7). The true wisdom on which we ought to set our eyes is perfection, which consists in union with God by love, according to the saying of the Apostle St. Paul: *Above all I commend to you charity, which is the bond of perfection* (Col. iii. 14), and joins and unites us with God. Now the esteem which Solomon says here he had of wisdom, we ought to have of perfection and of all that makes thereto. In comparison with that, all should appear to us as a little sand, a little clay and ordure, as the same Apostle said: *I count all things as ordure and refuse in view of gaining Christ* (Phil. iii. 8). This is a main means for gaining perfection: at the rate in which that esteem grows in our hearts, at the same will our perfection grow, and the whole house and the whole order. The reason is that such as is the value that we set upon a thing, such is the desire that we have of obtaining it; for the will is a blind power and follows what the understanding dictates and proposes to it: and according to the esteem and value that the understanding sets on a thing, so also is the will and desire to obtain it. And as the will is queen and commands all the other powers and energies of the soul, as well interior as exterior, it follows that according to the will and desire that we have of a thing, will be our contriving and taking means thereto and our efforts to obtain it. Thus it is very important to have a great esteem and appreciation of spiritual things and of what appertains to our spiritual progress, that so the will and desire of them may be great, and great also our effort to procure and gain them, for in all these things like goes with like.

A dealer in precious stones has need to know and form a right estimate of their value under pain of being deceived, for in default of such knowledge and such estimate he will exchange and sell a stone of great value for a thing of very little worth. Our trade is in precious stones and pearls. *The kingdom of heaven is like unto a merchant seeking in precious stones* (Matt. xiii. 45). We are merchants of the kingdom of heaven; we must know and form a right estimate of the price and value of the merchandise in which we deal, that we be not deceived, changing gold for clay and heaven for earth, which would be a huge mistake. And so says the Prophet Jeremy: *Let not the wise man glory in his wisdom, nor the strong man in his strength, nor the rich man in his riches; but let him that glorieth glory in this, in knowing and understanding me* (Jerem. ix. 23). This is the greatest of all treasures, knowing and loving and serving God, and this is the greatest business we can have on hand; or, rather, we have no other business than this; for this we were created and for this we entered religion: this is our end, our terminus, and our glory.

Would that this esteem and appreciation of perfection and of spiritual things appertaining thereto were deeply imprinted in the hearts of all, especially in religious, and that we helped one another and roused one another to this, not in words alone, after treating of it in our ordinary talks and conversations, but much more by the example of our deeds; that from them the beginner and the proficient and all might come to see that what counts in religion is spiritual things, much humility, much obedience, much devotion to recollection and prayer; not much learning, nor much fine preaching, nor any endowment of natural and human gifts—so says our blessed Father Ignatius in his Constitutions *(Reg. 16. Sum.)*. And it is necessary for all to understand this from the beginning and be nurtured on this milk, to the end that each one forthwith may set before his eyes and his heart that the thing to do is not to turn out a great scholar or a great preacher, but to become very humble and very mortified, since that it is which here in religion is esteemed and made much account of. That fact it is which they come upon and get to see, who have their eyes open to take a right view of things. These humble and mortified men are they who are sought after and held in high esteem by all. Not that we mean to say that we should give ourselves to virtue in order to be sought after and esteemed. But seeing that this it is which is esteemed and made much of in religion, everyone should bethink himself and come to say: "Doubtless this is the better thing, this it is that befits me, this is the right way; I mean simply to give myself to virtue and sincerely aim at my own spiritual progress, for all the rest without that is vanity."

Hence it will be understood what harm they may do who in their ordinary talk and conversation make it their whole business to discuss genius, abilities, and talents, and rate this man and that man accordingly. The consequence is that the younger members of the community, hearing this language of their elders, think that this it is that is current coin here and is valued, and this is the means they must take to thrive and grow to importance and be regarded. So they set their eyes upon this; and while the desire and esteem of learning, ability, and genius grows upon them, their desire and esteem of virtue, humility, and mortification decreases in proportion. So they come to make little account of the one in comparison with the other and choose to come short of virtue rather than of learning. Hereby many come to fall off and even afterwards to lose their vocation altogether. Better would it have been to have spoken to them of the importance and necessity of virtue and humility and how little learning and ability are worth—or, to say better, how harmful they are without virtue—instead of engendering in them by such conversations the desire of honor and of making a figure in the world, and being held for men of genius and great talents, which is apt to be their first step to perdition.

Surius, in his Life of St. Fulgentius the Abbot, supplies a very good example to this purpose. He says that, when this holy prelate saw any of his religious to be great workers, never ceasing all day long to serve and help the house, but saw on the other hand some not so diligent in spiritual things nor so interested in prayer, spiritual reading, and recollection, he had no great liking or esteem of them, and did not think they deserved it. But when he saw anyone much attached to spiritual things and very careful to make progress in them, although unable to do any work in the house or be of any service because of his weak and sickly condition, he had a particular love and esteem for such; and rightly so, for to what purpose is the possession of great parts and talents if the man is not obedient and submissive and the superior cannot do with him what he wills? Especially if he then takes occasion to take back a little of his free and easy ways and look for exemptions, much better in that case he had never had those abilities and talents at all. If the superior had to give an account to God whether he had in his house people who were good workers and of great parts, that would stand: but it is not so; it is not of that that he has to give an account, but of the care that he takes to get his subjects to advance in spirit and go on every day growing in virtue; and how, according to the abilities and talents which our Lord gives to each one, they busy themselves about their ministries and offices, not losing for that anything of their spiritual improvements. And of that same thing God will ask account of the subject. Certainly, says a holy man: "In the day of judgment we shall not be asked what we have read, but what we have done; nor how well we spoke, but how virtuously we lived."

Christ our Redeemer had sent His disciples to preach, and they returned very satisfied and pleased with themselves, saying: *Lord, we have done marvels and miracles: even the devils were subject and obeyed us in Thy name.* The Redeemer of the world answered: *Put not your satisfaction and joy in this, that ye do marvels and miracles and command the devils, and they obey you; but rejoice and be glad that your names are written in heaven* (Luke x. 20). We should put our satisfaction and joy in acquiring and gaining the kingdom of heaven, for without this all the rest will profit us nothing. *What doth it profit a man if he gain the whole world, and suffer the loss of his own soul?* (Matt. xvi. 26). Now if we say this, and Christ says the same, of the spiritual occupations and ministries of gaining and converting souls, that not on that account should we forget ourselves, because in that case it would profit us nothing though we converted the whole world, what is to be said of other occupations? It is not the right thing for a religious to be so absorbed and engrossed in studies or let himself be so carried away by external occupations as to forget his own spiritual progress, his meditation, his examen of conscience, his practice of mortification and penance; and to put spiritual things in the last place and take the worst time for them; and if anything has to be left out, to let *them* be the things left out is to live quite an unspiritual life, and not as a religious.

St. Dorotheus relates that he had for infirmarian and disciple, Dositheus, who was very diligent in his office, took great care of the sick, had their beds well made and their rooms in good order, all very clean and neat. St. Dorotheus went to visit the infirmary, and Dositheus said to him: "Father, there comes over me a thought of vainglory, saying to me: 'How well you keep everything! How pleased your superior will be with you!' " St. Dorotheus gave him an answer that quite cleared him of vainglory: "You have turned out a very knacky man, Dositheus, a very good infirmarian you have turned out, but you have not turned out a good religious." Let each one, then, take care that this may not be said of him: "You have turned out a very good infirmarian, or a very good porter, but you have not turned out a good religious; you have turned out a very good student, or a very good university man, or a very good preacher, but not a good religious." We have not come here for that, but to be good religious. That is what we ought to esteem and secure and keep ever before our eyes; and all other things we should take as accessories and additions to our spiritual progress, according to those words of Christ: *Seek ye first the kingdom of God and his justice, and all these other things shall be added unto you* (Matt. vi. 33).

Of those Fathers of the Desert we read that, since they could not be always reading, or meditating and praying, they spent their spare time in making baskets and in other manual works so as not to be idle, and some of them at the end of the year set fire to all that they had made, because they were not in need thereof for their support, but they worked only to occupy the time and not be idle. So we ought to fix our eyes principally upon our own spiritual progress, and as for other businesses and occupations, though they be with our neighbor, we ought to take to them as those holy Fathers took to making their baskets; not for that should we forget ourselves or neglect ourselves or lose on that account one point of perfection.

So we should always proceed on this foundation and hold it for a first principle, always to put in the first place the spiritual exercises which touch our own advancement, and never leave them off for anything, because this it is that must preserve and carry us forward in virtue; failing this, we shall soon see the falling off that will result. And we have abundant experience that, when we are not getting on as we ought, this always comes from our having grown slack in our spiritual exercises. *My heart hath withered, because I have forgotten to eat my bread* (Psalm ci. 5). If the upkeep and sustenance of our soul fails us, it is clear that we must become weak and languid. And so our holy Father much commends this to us and warns us of it many times. One time he says: "The aim of all those under probation, and of all others, ought to be what makes for their self-abnegation and their increase in virtue and perfection." Another time he says: "Let all give due time to spiritual things and try to increase their devotion so far as the grace of God shall impart it to them." Another time: "Let all give the appointed time to prayer, meditation, and reading, with all diligence in the Lord." And notice the phrase "with all diligence."

Hence it will be seen that, however many occupations of obedience and official duty one has, it is not the mind of superiors that on that account we should omit our spiritual duties, for there is no superior that wishes you to break your rules, and rules of such leading importance as these. So let no one endeavor to color and gloss over his imperfection and negligence in his spiritual exercises by a vest and cloak of obedience, saying: "I could not make my meditation, or examen, or spiritual reading, because obedience took me off." It is not obedience that stands in the way here, but the negligence of the individual and the little affection that he has for spiritual things. St. Basil says that we should take care to be very faithful in giving to God all the times that we have marked for prayer and spiritual exercises; and if at any time by some unavoidable occupation we are not able to make meditation or examen at the due time, we must remain with hunger and desire to supply and make it up forthwith as soon as we can. So when we miss our bodily allowance of food or of necessary sleep, for having been all night with an invalid, hearing his confession or helping him to die well, we take care to supply it forthwith and never fail to find time for that. This is the will of superiors when they occupy one of us in the time of his spiritual exercises, as is sometimes necessary; they do not mean us to omit them, but to put them off and make them up afterwards very completely, according to the saying of the Wise Man: *Be not hindered from praying always* (Eccles. xviii. 22). He does not say, *Do not hinder,* but *Be not hindered.* Let there be no hindrance or distraction to prevent you from ever holding fast to your prayer; and for the good religious there never is such hindrance because he always finds time to make it up and repair it. It is told of St. Dorotheus that, being guest-master and getting to bed very late, and sometimes rising in the night to give welcome to visitors, nevertheless he rose with the rest for prayer, and had asked someone to call him because the ordinary caller did not do so, knowing how he had been busied—and this though he was not yet quite recovered from a fever. This was desiring in good earnest not to fail in his spiritual duties, and not acquiescing in any excuse so as afterwards to go about out of sorts all day long. The same history tells also of a holy old man who saw an angel incensing all those who had gone with diligence to prayer, and also the vacant places of those who were not there for being hindered by obedience, but not of those who were absent through their own negligence. This is a great consolation for those whom the occupations of obedience prevent from coming up to time with the rest for spiritual duties, and a warning not to fail in them through our own negligence.

CHAPTER II

Of the Affection and Desire that We Should Have for Virtue and Perfection

BLESSED are they that hunger and thirst after justice, for they shall have their fill (Matt. v. 6). Justice is the particular name of one of the four cardinal virtues, distinct from the others, but it is also a common name for all virtue and holiness. We call a good and virtuous life, *justice (righteousness)*, and the holy and virtuous, *just (righteous)*. The Wise Man says: *The justice of the righteous shall deliver them* (Prov. xi. 6): that is to say, their holy life shall deliver them; and so the name is used in many passages of Scripture. *Unless your justice be greater than that of the scribes and Pharisees, ye shall not enter into the kingdom of heaven* (Matt. v. 20). So says Christ our Redeemer, meaning, "unless your virtue, religion, and holiness be greater." In the same manner is to be understood what Christ likewise said to St. John the Baptist when the latter made a difficulty of baptizing Him. *Thus it behooves us to fulfil all justice* (Matt. iii. 15), i. e., to give an example of obedience, humility, and all perfection. So, too, is the word to be taken in the phrase before us: "Blessed are they who have such a desire and affection for virtue and perfection that they are positively hungry and athirst after it, for they shall have their fill;" they shall gain it. And this is one of the eight beatitudes which He taught us and preached in that sovereign Sermon on the Mount. St. Jerome on these words says: "It is not enough for us to have a mind for justice, unless we suffer a downright hunger for justice"—*Non nobis sufficit velle iustitiam nisi iustitiae patiamur famem.* It is not enough to have some sort of desire of virtue and perfection; we must needs have a hunger and thirst after it so that we can say with the prophet: *As the hart, wounded and hard-pressed by the hunters, thirsteth after the fountains of waters, so doth my soul desire thee, O God* (Psalm xli. 1).

This is a thing of so great importance that, as we were saying in the last chapter, on it depends all our spiritual proficiency; and it is the beginning and only means of attaining to perfection, according to the saying of the Wise Man (Wisdom vi. 16): *The first thing necessary to gain wisdom*—which is the knowledge and love of God wherein our perfection consists—*is a true and heartfelt desire of it;* and the reason thereof is that, as philosophers say, in all things, and particularly in moral matters, the love and desire of the end is the first cause that moves and sets all the rest to work. Thus the greater the love and desire of the end, the greater the care and diligence that are employed to gain it. Thus it is very important that the desire and affection for virtue and perfection be great, since the care and diligence in securing and gaining it will be great in proportion.

So important and necessary is it that there should be in us this desire—springing from the heart and drawing us after it, without there being need of others going to look after us—that, where the desire of advancement in perfection is not found, there will be very little hope. Let us take an example in the case of a religious, and everyone will be able to apply the doctrine to himself according to his state. The care and vigilance of superiors over their subjects is good and necessary in religion, and necessary also are rebuke and penance; but when a man does things for this motive, there is not much trust to be put in him, because this motive at most may secure his going on well for some time while they are looking after him; but if this good behavior does not spring from the heart, from a true desire of his spiritual advancement, not much account is to be taken of it, for it cannot last.

This is the difference there is between things that move by a violent motion and things that move by a natural motion; those that move by violent motions—a motion proceeding from an external force and impression—the farther they go on, the weaker and feebler their course, as when you throw a stone up; but in things that move by a natural motion, as when a stone falls towards its center (the earth), the contrary is the case; the farther they go, the more lightly and rapidly they go. This is also the difference between those who do things for fear of penances and scoldings, or because people are looking at them, or for other human considerations, and those who are moved by love of virtue and pure desire of pleasing God. The good behavior of the former lasts only while the scolding continues and an eye is kept upon them; as soon as that is over, down they go. St. Gregory tells of his aunt Gordiana that, when her two sisters, Tharsilla and Aemiliana, rebuked her for frivolous conversation and for not observing the gravity which became the religious habit that she wore, she showed a serious countenance while they were rebuking her and seemed to take it well; but when the hour of rebuke and castigation was over, she lost all that seriousness which she had put on and wasted her time in the company of the secular young ladies who lived in the monastery. She was like a bow strung with a thick cord; as the cord relaxes, so also the bow relaxes and returns to its first position. Her serious demeanor, not coming from the heart, but being a thing put on, could not last.

This business of perfection is not strained; it is not a thing to be done on compulsion; it must come from the heart. So Christ our Redeemer said to that young man in the Gospel: *If thou wilt be perfect* (Matt. xix. 21). But if you do not will it, all the contrivances and methods that superiors can apply will never suffice to make you perfect. This is the solution and answer to the question which St. Bonaventure raises: How is it that in former times one superior sufficed for a thousand monks, and for three thousand, and five thousand (for so St. Jerome and St. Augustine say there used to be under one superior); and now one superior is not enough for ten monks and even less? The reason is that those monks of old had in their hearts a lively and ardent desire of perfection, and the fire that burned within made them greatly to take to heart their own advancement and press on their way with great fervor.

The just shall shine, and fly here and there like sparks in a bed of reeds (Wisdom iii. 7). By this metaphor the Holy Spirit aptly declares to us the swiftness and readiness wherewith the just travel on the road of virtue when this fire has caught on in their hearts. See with what swiftness and readiness the flame runs on in a dry reed-bed when it takes fire. In this way the just run on in the way of virtue when they are kindled and aglow with this divine fire. Such were those monks of old, and therefore they had no need of a superior to urge them on, but rather to govern them in their fervor. But in the absence of this desire, not only will one superior not suffice for ten monks, but ten superiors will not suffice for one monk nor be able to make him perfect if he does not want it. This is clear. For what is the use of visiting him at meditation? Can he not do as he likes as soon as the visitor has passed? And while he is there on his knees, he may be thinking of his studies, and of his business, and of other irrelevant things. And when he goes to give an account of conscience, can he not say what he likes and be silent about what is most to the point, and say he is getting on well when he is not getting on well, but badly? How idle it all is if he has no wish and no earnest desire!

Here comes in well the answer that St. Thomas Aquinas gave to a sister of his who once asked him how she might save her soul. He answered: "By willing it." If you will, you will be saved; if you will, you will improve; if you will, you will be perfect. This is the whole knot of the difficulty, that you should will and desire in sober earnest and your desire should spring from your heart, since God on His part is quite ready to help us. If this willing on your part is not done, all that superiors can do will be in vain. You are the person who must take to heart your own improvement, because that is your business, and on you it depends and on no one else, and for that you have come into religion. Let each one, then, make up his mind that on what day soever he relents on this point, and forgets himself and what regards his spiritual progress, and takes no further care to insure his spiritual duties' being well done, and keeps not up any ardent desire of improving and going forward in virtue and mortification, on that day he has missed his business. And so our Father, at the beginning of his Constitutions and Rules, lays down this foundation: "It is the interior law of charity and love which the Holy Ghost writes and imprints on hearts, that must preserve, guide, and advance us in the way of His divine service that we have entered upon." This fire of the love of God, this desire of His greater honor and glory, it is that must ever be exciting us to mount and go forward in virtue. When this desire really exists in the heart, it makes us diligent and careful to obtain what we desire, since our inclination is very industrious to seek and find what we desire, and means are never wanting thereto. Therefore the Wise Man says: *The first thing for gaining wisdom is a true and hearty desire thereof* (Wisdom vi. 18).

And, further, this virtue coming from the heart carries with it another advantage, which makes it so effectual as a means; it is that it renders things easy and sweet, however difficult they be in themselves. Else tell me, how came it to be so easy for you to leave the world and enter religion, except that it came from your heart to do so? The Lord gave you a strong will and affection for it; that was the grace of your vocation. He rid you of affection for the things of the world and set your affection on the things of religion, and with that He made it easy for you. And how comes this to be so difficult to those who remain there in the world? Because God has not given them this will and affection which He has given you; God "has not called them," as they say, nor done them this favor of the grace of a vocation. Now as to enter religion, God made the way easy for you by giving you a will and a great desire of it, so that not your parents and relations nor all the world besides were able to withdraw you from it; so also to make progress in religion and make its practices easy to you, it is necessary to continue that will and desire wherewith you first came to it. While that desire lasts, its practices will be easy to you; but when it drops, everything will be difficult and up-hill. That is why we find ourselves at times so heavy and lumpish and at other times so light and sprightly; let no one throw the fault on circumstances, nor on superiors, but on his own want of virtue and mortification. Father Master Avila says: "A healthy and strong man easily lifts a two-stone weight; but a sickly person or a child cries, 'Oh, dear, how heavy!'" That is the cause of our difficulty. Things are the same as they were: at another time they were easy to us, and we never boggled about them; the fault is in ourselves, that whereas we ought to be men and have grown in perfection, *in virum perfectum* (Eph. iv. 13), we are children in virtue; we have grown weak and slack in that desire of progress with which we entered religion.

CHAPTER III

That an Excellent Means and a Very Great Preparation to Receive Favors from the Lord Is to Keep Up a Great Desire of Spiritual Improvement

IT is every important to keep up this desire and this hunger and thirst after our spiritual improvement, since it is one of the chief means and best dispositions that we can have on our part for the Lord to give us the virtue and perfection that we desire. So St. Ambrose says that when a man has a great desire of his improvement and growth in virtue and perfection, God is so pleased therewith that He enriches and fills him with bounties and rewards; and he applies to this effect that which the most holy Virgin said in her canticle: *He hath filled the hungry with good things* (Luke i. 53); and the prophet in the psalm had said the same: *He hath satisfied the thirsty soul, and the hungry soul he hath sated with good things* (Psalm cvi. 9). Those that have such a strong desire of virtue and perfection as to hunger and thirst after the same, the Lord enriches with spiritual gifts because He takes great pleasure in the good desire of our heart. The angel Gabriel appeared to Daniel and told him that his prayers had been heard from the beginning, *because thou art a man of desires* (Dan. ix. 23). And to King David God confirmed the promise of the kingdom to go down to his descendants for the will and desire he had to build a house and temple unto the Lord—although He would not have him do so, but left it to his son Solomon. Nevertheless, He was well pleased with this desire and rewarded it as if he had put it in execution. And of Zacheus the holy Gospel says that he desired to see Jesus, and was seen first by Jesus, and He invited Himself and entered in by the gates of his house (Luke xix. 5).

Solomon in the sixth chapter of Wisdom enlarges on this point further. Speaking of Wisdom, which is God Himself, he says: *I easily let myself be seen by those who love me, and am found by those who seek me.* Do you know how easily? *She* (Wisdom) *herself goes before and anticipates them that desire her in earnest, to show herself first to them.* You have no sooner begun to desire than she is with you. *He that riseth early in the morning to seek her shall not have much labor in finding her,* going here and there, for on opening the door of his house *he shall find her sitting at his door* in expectation of his opening it (Wisdom vi. 13-15). The first object that he shall come across in opening will be this divine Wisdom, which is God Himself. Oh, bounty and infinite mercy of God! Not content with going to seek us and knocking at our door time after time for us to open—*See I stand at the door and knock,* He says in the Apocalypse (iii. 20), and in the Canticles, *Open to me my sister* (v. 2)—not content with that, as though weary of knocking, God sits at our door, giving us to understand that He would have come in long ago had He not found the door locked. Nevertheless He goes not away, but sits down there, so that on opening you may come upon Him at once. Though you have been slow in opening your heart to God and answering His good inspiration, He, notwithstanding, has not gone away, but is much more eager to come in than that: there He is, sitting at the door, looking for you to open to Him. *The Lord waiteth to have mercy on you* (Isaias xxx. 18). Never does friend desire to enter into the house of his friend as God desires to enter into your heart. He is more eager to impart Himself to us and do us favors than we can be to receive them. He is waiting for us to desire it and have this hunger and thirst for it. *Let him that thirsteth come to me and drink* (John vii. 37). *To him that thirsteth, I will give of the water of the fountain of life gratis* (Apoc. xxi. 6). The Lord wishes us to have a great desire of virtue and perfection, so that, when He gives us any of it, we may know how to esteem and preserve it as something very precious; for what is but little desired is commonly made little account of when it is attained. One of the chief reasons why we thrive so little in virtue and lag so far behind in perfection, is that we have no hunger and thirst after it; we desire it so feebly and languidly that the desires we have seem rather dead than alive.

St. Bonaventure says that there are persons who have good purposes and desires and never succeed in overcoming themselves or doing any violence to themselves to put them in execution, according to that word of the Apostle: *To will attends upon me, but to fulfil I do not see my way* (Romans vii. 18). These in many cases are not true purposes or desires, but velleities; you fain would will, but will you do not. *The sluggard willeth and willeth not,* says the Wise Man. *Desires are the death of the sluggard: his hands refuse to do any work: all day long he is yearning and desiring: it all goes in desires* (Prov. xiii. 4; xxi. 25). Father Master Avila compares such people to those who fancy in their dreams that they are doing great exploits, and when they awake from sleep find they do just the opposite, according to Isaias (xxix. 8): *The hungry man dreameth and eateth, but when he awaketh his soul is empty.* So these people at prayer fancy that they desire to suffer and be despised and made small account of; but when they go out from a prayer, and the occasion offers, their behavior is all to the contrary; the fact is, they were dreaming all the while and those were no true desires. Others liken them to figures of soldiers worked on embroidery that are always holding their swords over the enemy and never come to deliver the blow, according to that saying of the prophet: *Yea, a man passeth away like a shadow and apparition* (Psalm xxxviii. 7). So some pass all their lives in threatening without ever dealing a blow. The prophet Isaias likens them to the woman that is in the pains of childbirth and never succeeds in bringing the babe to light: *The children are come to the point of bringing forth, and there is no strength to bear them* (Isaias xxxvii. 3). St. Gregory on those words of St. Matthew: *Woe to them that are with child and are giving suck in those days* (xxxiv. 19), says: "Woe to them that have not brought to light the good desires that they have conceived," but have stifled within themselves the desires they had conceived, since never to bring our desires to the light of deeds is to stifle and slay them within the womb. Woe to them, for they pass all their life in desires, and death finds them without works; because hereafter not only shall the desires they had avail them naught, but they shall be chastised for not having carried into effect the good inspirations which the Lord gave them: their own children must turn against them, as they would have stood for them had they brought them to light.

Absalom was hung up by his golden and handsome tresses; so death shall come to many, and they shall be left hung up with their good and golden purposes. The Apostle and Evangelist St. John in his Apocalypse (xii. 2) says that he saw a woman that was near her bringing forth, and hard by a huge dragon ready to devour the child new-born. That is what the devil aims at to the utmost of his power when the soul conceives some good purpose; and so it is necessary that we should try to the utmost of our power to make our desires such, and so effectual, that we may come to put them in practice. This, says St. Bernard, is what the Prophet Isaias meant to say in these words so pithy and short: *If ye seek, seek* (Isaias xxi. 12). He means: Be not slack, since true desires and purposes ought to be effectual and persevered in, and such as to make us endeavor, with solicitude and care, more and more to please God, according to that saying of the Prophet Micheas (vi. 8): *I will show thee, O man, what is good, and what the Lord requireth of thee: truly it is to do judgment and love mercy, and to walk careful with thy God.* These fervent desires are what the Lord asks of us, to reward us and fill us with good things. Blessed are they who have this hunger and thirst after virtue and perfection, for they shall have their fill (Matt. v. 6); God will accomplish their desires. We read of St. Gertrude that the Lord said to her: "I have given to everyone of my faithful a tube and duct of gold wherewith to suck and draw from My deified heart as much as he shall desire"; the said tube and duct He explained as being a good will and desire.

CHAPTER IV

That the More a Man Gives Himself to Spiritual Things, the More Hunger and Desire He Has of Them

THEY that eat me shall yet hunger, and they that drink me shall yet thirst (Ecclus. xxiv. 29), says the Holy Ghost, speaking of divine wisdom; and St. Gregory says that there is this difference between the pleasures of the body and those of the soul, that the former we desire with great impatience when we have them not, and when we have got them, we make but little account of them. There in the world a man desires the headship of a college or a professor's chair; on gaining it, he at once reckons nothing of it and sets his eyes on a bigger thing. Give him a canonry or an auditorship; no sooner is he installed than he is weary of it and begins to desire something higher, a place in the royal council, and after that a bishopric; nor even with that is he satisfied, but at once has his eye on a higher post, and reckons nothing of what he has gained nor finds any satisfaction therein.

But with spiritual things it is just the other way; when we have them not, then they disgust and nauseate us; but when we have them and possess them, then we value them more and desire them more, and all the more, the more we taste them. And the saint gives the reason of this difference: When we gain and hold temporal goods and gratifications, then we better appreciate their insufficiency and imperfection; and when we see that they afford us no full satisfaction, nor the content that we expected, we make light of what we have attained and remain athirst and desirous of something greater, thinking to find there the satisfaction that we desired; but we are much mistaken, for the same will be our condition after having gained this thing or the other. Nothing in this world will be able to fulfil our aspirations, as Christ our Redeemer said to the

Samaritan woman: *Everyone who drinketh of this water shall thirst again* (John iv. 13). You may drink again and again of the water that is here; a little way farther on you will thirst again. The water of the satisfactions and gratifications that the world affords cannot quench or slake our thirst; but spiritual good things and delights, when they are attained, are then loved and desired more, because then their worth and value are better known; and the more perfectly we possess them, the more we shall hunger and thirst after them.

When a man has had no experience of spiritual things, nor has ever begun to taste them, it is no wonder, says St. Gregory, that he does not desire them; for who can love and desire what he does not know and has had no experience of what it tastes like? So the Apostle St. Peter says: *If ye have tasted how sweet the Lord is* (I Peter ii. 3). And the prophet: *Taste and see how sweet the Lord is* (Psalm xxxiii. 9). When you have begun to taste God and spiritual things, you will find in them such sweetness and delight that you will lick your fingers over them. That is what the Wise Man says in these words: He that eats and drinks of me, the more he eats, the more shall he hunger after me; and the more he drinks, the more shall he thirst after me. The more you give yourself to spiritual things and to God, the more hunger and thirst after them shall you feel.

But, someone will say, how does this agree with what Christ said to the Samaritan woman? Here Christ says: *He that shall drink of the water that I will give, shall no more thirst* (John iv. 13). In that other place the Holy Ghost says by the mouth of the Wise Man that the more we drink, the more we shall thirst. How does the one text agree with the other? The saint's reply is that what Christ said to the Samaritan woman must be taken to mean that he who shall drink of the living water which He there promises shall no longer thirst after sensual and worldly delights, since the sweetness of spiritual things and of God shall make them appear to him insipid. St. Gregory says: "As to one who has eaten honey all other things appear insipid, so when a man comes to taste of God and spiritual things, all the things of the world offend him and seem to him nauseous and sour"—*Sicut post gustum mellis omnia videntur insipida, ita gustato spiritu desipit omnis caro.* But what the Wise Man says in that other place—*They that eat of me shall still hunger and they that drink of me shall still thirst* (Ecclus. xxiv. 29)—is to be understood of those same spiritual things, meaning that the more one tastes of God and spiritual things, the more he will hunger and thirst after them, because he will better know their value and have better experience of their sweetness and deliciousness, and so will have more desire of them. Thus the saints reconcile these two passages.

But how make this agree with what Christ says in St. Matthew (v. 6): *Blessed are they that hunger and thirst after justice, for they shall have their fill?* Here He says that they who hunger and thirst after justice shall have their fill; that other passage from the Wise Man says that they who eat and drink thereof shall still hunger and still thirst; how are these two things compatible, to go on being still hungry and thirsty and to have their fill? To this there is a very good answer. This is the privilege and excellence of spiritual good things, that, while filling, they excite hunger, and while satisfying our heart, they excite thirst. It is a fulness attended with hunger and a hunger attended with fulness. This is the marvel, the dignity, and grandeur of these good things, that they satisfy and fill the heart, yet in such a manner that we always remain with hunger and thirst after them; and the more we go on tasting and eating and drinking of them, the more that hunger and thirst grows. But this hunger is not painful, but satisfying; and this thirst is not fatiguing or exhausting, but rather refreshing and causing in the heart a great satisfaction and joy.

In truth, fulness and satisfaction, perfect and complete, shall be in heaven, according to that word of the prophet: *Then, O Lord, thou wilt fill me completely,* and I shall be enraptured and satisfied, *when I shall see thee clearly in glory: then shall thy servants be inebriated with the abundance of the good things of thy house* (Psalm xvi. 15; xxxv. 9). But there in glory, says St. Bernard on these words, the sight of God will fill our souls in such a manner that we shall always remain hungry and thirsty. This glorious vision of God will never pall upon us; we shall feel ever a new joy in seeing and rejoicing in God, even as though that were our first day and our first hour in heaven. So St. John says in the Apocalypse that he saw the blessed standing before the throne of the Lamb with grand music and rejoicing; *and they sang as it were a new canticle* (Apoc. xiv. 3). This canticle and this divine manna will be ever new to us and will give us new relish, and we shall ever be in new wonderment, saying, *Manhu, what is this?* (Exod. xvi. 15). Such also are spiritual things on earth —inasmuch as they are a participation of those in heaven— that while they sate and satisfy and fill the heart, they do so in such a manner that we continue hungering and thirsting after them, a hunger and thirst that grows upon us; the more we give ourselves over to them and the more we taste and enjoy them, the more this very hunger is a repletion, and this very thirst is a great refreshment and satisfaction. All this should help us to have a high esteem and appreciation of spiritual things and such an inflamed desire and affection for them that, forgetting and despising all the things of the world, we come to say with St. Peter: *Lord, it is good for us to be here* (Matt. xvii. 4).

CHAPTER V

That a Desire of Growing and Going Forward in Self-Improvement Is a Great Sign of One's Being in the Grace of God

THERE is a consideration, very important and very consoling, that will be of much assistance in animating us to a great desire of self-improvement, a hunger and thirst after progress in virtue, and carefulness and solicitude to please the Lord daily more and more; it is that this is one of the greatest and surest signs of God's dwelling in the soul. So says St. Bernard: "There is no greater sign, no more certain evidence of the presence of God in a soul, than having a great desire of more virtue and more grace and perfection"—*Nullum omnino praesentiae Dei certius testimonium est quam desiderium gratiae amplioris.* And he proves it by what God says through the Wise Man: *He that eateth me shall have more hunger, and he that drinketh me shall have more thirst* (Ecclus. xxiv. 29). If you feel hunger and thirst for spiritual things, rejoice, for it is a great sign that God dwells in your soul. He it is that puts into you this hunger and excites in you this thirst; you have struck the vein of gold leading up to this divine treasure, since you follow it so well. And as the huntsman's dog goes feebly and lazily when he has not caught scent of the game; but when he has caught it he is excited to great activity, seeking the scent on this side and that, and never gives over till he finds the game, so he who has truly caught the odor of this divine sweetness runs in the odor of so precious an ointment. *Draw me, and we will run after thee in the odor of thine ointments* (Cant. i. 3). God, Who is within you, draws you after Him. But if you do not feel within yourself this hunger and thirst, fear lest perhaps God dwells not within your heart. This is the property of spiritual things and things of God, as St. Gregory says, that when we have them not we desire them not and have no care at all about them.

The glorious St. Bernard says that he trembled and his hair stood on end when he considered what the Holy Ghost says by the Wise Man: *Man knoweth not whether he be worthy of love or hatred* (Eccles. ix. 1). But if this reflection that we do not know whether we are in the grace of God or out of His grace, made holy men tremble who were as pillars of the Church, what effect should it have on us, who have reason for alarm for the many causes that we have given for it? *We have in ourselves the answer of death* (II Cor. i. 9). I know for certain that I have offended God, and I do not know for certain if I am pardoned: who will not tremble? Oh, how much would one give to get some pledge and security in a matter which touches him so nearly! Oh, if I knew that the Lord had pardoned my sins! Oh, if I knew that I was in the grace of God! But while it is true that in this life we cannot have infallible certainty of being in the grace and friendship of God without a particular revelation from Him, nevertheless we can form some conjectures which raise in us a moral probability thereof; and one of them, and a very chief one, is our being possessed with this hunger and thirst after spiritual progress and daily growth in virtue and perfection. And so this alone should suffice to move us ever to keep up this desire, in order to have so great a pledge and witness that we are in the grace and friendship of God, which is one of the greatest of consolations and satisfactions; aye, the greatest that in this life we can possibly have.

This is confirmed by what the Holy Ghost says in Proverbs iv. 18: *The way and path of the just and their manner of procedure is as the light of the sun that goeth forth in the morning and the further it goes, it goes growing and perfecting itself the more, until it arrives at the perfection of midday.* Thus the just, the farther they go, the farther they advance in virtue. St. Bernard says: "The just never cries, 'Enough'." *Nunquam iustus arbitratur se comprehendisse, nunquam dicit 'satis est,' sed semper esurit sititque iustitiam, ita ut si semper viveret, semper quantum in se est iustior esse contenderet, semper de bono in bonum totis viribus conaretur.* Of such it is said: *They shall go from virtue to virtue* (Psalm lxxxiii. 8), ever aiming at going further until they arrive at the height of perfection. But the path of the slothful, the imperfect, and the evil is as the light of evening, which goes decreasing and growing darker till it comes to the darkness and gloom of midnight. *The way of the wicked is darksome; they see not where they are likely to fall* (Prov. iv. 19). They come to such blindness that they see not where they stumble, nor have any eye for the faults and imperfections which they commit and no remorse of conscience for falling into them. Rather, they often take that to be no sin which is a sin, and that to be a venial sin which perhaps is mortal; such are their mental confusion and blindness.

CHAPTER VI

Showing How Not to Advance Is to Go Back

It is the common opinion of the saints that in the way of God not to advance is to go back: *in via Dei non progredi regredi est.* This we will explain here, and it will serve us for a good motive for advancing in perfection; for who would wish to go back upon what he has begun, especially seeing that that would be going against the sentence of our Savior in the Gospel: *He that putteth his hand to the plough,* entering on the way of perfection, *and turneth back, is not fit for the kingdom of God* (Luke ix. 62). Words that should make us tremble! The blessed St. Augustine says: "We don't *go back* so far as we make efforts to *go forward;* once we begin to stop, back we roll. Thus, if we wish not to go back, we must ever push on and endeavor to go forward"—*Ubi coepimus stare, descendimus: si volumus non redire, currendum est.* The same is said, almost in the same words, by St. Gregory, St. Chrysostom, Pope St. Leo, and many other saints, and they repeat it many times. St. Bernard pursues this theme at considerable length in two of his letters (254 and 341). He there addresses a lax and lazy religious who is satisfied with a common life and does not care to go further in his improvement, and argues with him in this manner: "You do not want to go forward? No. Then you want to turn back? Not that either. What, then, do you want? I want to stay as I am, neither better nor worse. Then you want what is impossible. For in this world there is nothing that can stay as it is; that is the attribute of God alone, *with whom there is no change, nor shadow of vicissitude*" (James i. 17). *O monache, non vis proficere? Non. Vis ergo deficere? Nihil minus. Hoc ergo vis quod esse non potest; quid enim stat in hoc saeculo?* All things in this world are in continual change. *The heavens and all things grow old, as a garment grows old; and as a vesture thou shalt change them, and they shall be changed: but thou art ever the self-same, and thy years shall not fail* (Psalm ci. 27-28). And particularly is it true of man, as Job says, that he never remains in one frame of being nor in one state. *He fleeth like a shadow, and never remaineth in the same state* (Job xiv. 2).

"Even Christ," says St. Bernard, "while he let Himself be seen on earth and conversed with men, was He at a standstill? No. St. Luke says of Him that *as He went on growing in age, so He went on also growing in wisdom and grace before God and men* (Luke ii. 52)"; that is, He showed in effect greater signs of wisdom and holiness. The prophet says that He prepared Himself to run this way: *He exulted as a giant to run his way* (Psalm xviii. 6). If, then, we wish to abide with Christ, we must go at the pace that He took, says St. John. *Whoever professeth to abide in him, must walk as he walked* (I John ii. 6). "But if, when Christ runs, you run not, but stand still, it is clear that you will get farther and farther away from Him, and remain far behind"—*Si illo currente tu gradum sistis, non Christo appropias, sed te magis elongas* (St. Bernard).

Jacob saw a ladder that reached from earth to heaven; and he saw on it angels, but none of them did he see sitting or standing still, but they either mounted up or went down: God alone was seated at the top of the ladder (Gen. xxviii. 12). This is to give us to understand, says St. Bernard, that in this life there is no intermediate way of virtue between mounting up and going down, between going forward and going backward, but by the very fact of a man's not going forward he goes backward. As when we work at the winch, the wheel flies back as soon as we stop it; so from the same moment you desist from going forward in virtue, you must of necessity go backward. Abbot Theodore puts the same thought in these terms, recounted by Cassian: "We must apply ourselves to the study of virtue without remissness, and seriously exercise ourselves in the practice of it, lest coming once to cease from growing better, we immediately begin to grow less perfect; for our souls cannot rest long in the same state, so as to grow neither better nor worse in virtue; for we lose what we do not gain, and whosoever flags in the desire of growing better will not be out of danger of falling away."

Still someone will say: "That is well said, and must be true, and so it will turn out, since saints say so; but all this has the appearance of talking in parables, figures, and enigmas; explain to us this parable" (Matt. xv. 15). That I will. The saints explain it at length. Cassian does so by an excellent comparison, which is also used by St. Gregory. As a man in midstream of a rushing river, if he tries to stop and does not labor to mount upstream, will run great risk of going with the current downstream, so they say it is with a man in the way of spiritual life. This way is so upstream and so difficult to our nature corrupted by sin, that if a man does not labor and force himself to go on, he will be carried away downstream by the current of his passions. Anyone steering his bark with tide and current against him, if he ceases to use his arms and row to make his way, finds himself thrown a long way back. *The kingdom of heaven suffereth violence, and the violent bear it away* (Matt. xi. 12). We need to go on continually using our arms and forcing our way against the current of our passions, otherwise we shall find ourselves decidedly deteriorated and thrown back.

St. Jerome and St. Chrysostom further declare this, along with another common doctrine of saints and theologians; and St. Thomas deals with it in speaking of the religious state (2a—2ae, q. 184, art. 5). St. Thomas says there that religious are in a state of perfection; not that they are perfect as soon as they are religious, but that they are bound to aspire and yearn after perfection; and whoever concerns himself not at all about being perfect, he says that he is a religious in pretence only, since he does not that for which he came into religion. I do not here go into the question whether a religious would sin mortally who should say: "I am satisfied with keeping the commandments of God and my essential vows; but as for those rules that do not bind under sin, I have no mind to observe them." On this point doctors speak differently. Some say that he would sin mortally; others say that it would not be a mortal sin unless there entered into it some sort of contempt. But what is certain and what all agree in is this, that a religious with that will and purpose would be a bad religious, a scandal, and an ill example, and that, morally speaking, he would be in great danger of falling into mortal sins; for *he that despiseth and maketh small account of small things, little by little will come to fall into great sins* (Ecclus. xix. 1). This is quite enough for our purpose, since it is a clear case of going back.

For the better understanding of this point, St. Chrysostom alleges some homely examples. If you had a slave, he says, who was neither thief, nor gamester, nor drunkard, but faithful and temperate and clear of all vice, who sat all day in the house doing none of the things that belonged to his duty, who doubts but that he would deserve to be severely chastised, though there were nothing else bad about him, because it is bad enough not to do one's duty. Again, if a laborer were a good man in all other respects, but simply folded his arms, and had no mind to sow or plough, or dress vines, that would be clear matter of rebuke, though he did no other harm, since we judge it bad enough for a man not to do what his duty demands. Further, in your own body, if you had a hand that did you no harm, but was idle and useless and served not the other members of the body, would you not reckon that evil enough?

In the same way in spiritual things the religious who here in religion stands idle with his arms folded, without going forward or troubling himself about perfection or making any advance in virtue, deserves a severe reprimand for not doing what is proper to his office and condition. His very not doing good is doing evil. His very not advancing is going back, since he fails in the duty of his profession. What worse thing could you look for in a piece of land than its being barren and bearing no fruit, especially if it has been well worked and cultivated! But a land like yours, cultivated with so much care, watered by so many showers of heavenly graces, warmed by such rays of the sun of justice, with all this bearing no fruit, but become an arid and sterile waste—what greater evil could you look for than such sterility! This is rendering evil for good to Him to Whom you owe so much and from Whom so many blessings have come to you.

There is another comparison often employed to the same purpose, which seems to put the matter well. As at sea there is a sort of heavy weather called "a calm," very dangerous for navigators, since they consume the provisions they had for the voyage and then find themselves without victuals in the midst of the sea, so it happens to those who are navigating the stormy sea of this world. They are becalmed in virtue, not caring to go on any farther therein; they consume and waste what they had acquired, run through what virtue they had, and then find themselves with nothing in the midst of the many waves and tempests of temptations that arise and the occasions that offer, for which they need more provision and more store of virtue. Woe to him that gets becalmed in virtue! *You were running well; who has hindered you from obeying the truth?* (Gal. v. 7). You began to run well when you entered religion, and now you are stranded and becalmed in virtue. *You are now full and in need of nothing* (I Cor. iv. 8). You play the senior and the man worn out with toil. You are rich, and have secured a competence. Consider that *you have still a long way to go* (III Kings xix. 7); that many occasions will arise requiring greater humility, greater patience, greater mortification and detachment; and you may find yourself unprovided and very behindhand in the hour of your greatest need.

CHAPTER VII

That It Is a Great Aid to the Attainment of Perfection to Forget Any Good Done in the Past, and Fix Our Eye on What Remains Still to be Done

LET him that is just aim at becoming more just, and him that is holy at becoming more holy (Apoc. xxii. 11). St. Jerome and St. Bede upon these words: *Blessed are they that hunger and thirst after justice, for they shall have their fill* (Matt. v. 6), say that Christ our Redeemer "clearly teaches us in these words never to think that what we have attained is sufficient, but every day to aim at becoming better"—*nunquam nos satis iustos aestimare debere, sed quotidianum iustitiae semper amare profectum.* That is what the glorious Evangelist St. John says in the words above quoted. The Apostle St. Paul, writing to the Philippians, gives a very suitable means thereto, which he says he made use of himself. *Brethren, I do not take myself to be perfect.* Who shall take himself to be perfect, if the Apostle says that he does not hold himself for such? *But I try to make haste to gain perfection.* And what do you do for that? Do you know what? *I forget the past, and put before me what has still to be done; and to this I animate myself and aim at securing it* (Phil. iii. 13). All the saints greatly commend this means, and no wonder, since it was given and practised by the Apostle. St. Jerome says: "Whoever wishes to be a saint, let him forget all the past good that he has done in the past, and rouse himself to secure what is still undone. Blessed is he who every day advances in virtue and perfection. And who is he? Do you know who? He who regards not what he did yesterday, but what it will be well to do today in order to make progress." *Felix ergo est qui quotidie proficit, qui non considerat quid heri fecerit, sed quid hodie faciat ut proficiat.*

St. Gregory and St. Bernard declare this more in detail. This practice has two principal parts. The first is to forget the good we have done hitherto and never set our eyes on it. It is necessary to give this warning in particular, because it is natural to turn our eyes readily on what pleases us and withdraw them from what may give us trouble. And because the sight of the progress we have made and the good that we think we have done pleases us, and the sight of our spiritual poverty and the amount that is still wanting to us saddens us, therefore our eyes rather turn to look at the good that we have done than at what remains undone. St. Gregory says: As the sick man seeks the softest part of his bed, and the freshest and most agreeable, to rest there, such is the infirmity of man and our frailty and imperfection that we find more joy and delight in looking at and thinking of the good that we have done than of that which remains for us still to make up. And St. Bernard further says: Understand that there are dangers here, for if you set yourself to look at the good you have done, what will come of that is that you will get proud, thinking that you are something; thence you will come at once to compare yourself with others and prefer yourself to them and even make light of them and much of yourself. Otherwise look at that Pharisee in the Gospel, what end came to him in this way. He set his eyes on the good that there was in him and applied his mind to reckoning up his virtues. *I thank thee, O Lord, that I am not as other men, robbers, unjust, adulterers, nor as that publican there: I fast twice a week, I pay punctually my tithes and first-fruits. Amen, I say unto you,* says Christ our Redeemer, *that that publican,* to whom he preferred himself, *went away just,* and he who took himself for just went out condemned as wicked and unjust (Luke xviii. 11-14). This is what the devil aims at in setting before you the good that you fancy you have done. His aim is that you should take yourself for somebody and become proud, and should despise others and make light of them, that so you may come to be condemned for a proud and bad man.

There is yet another danger, as St. Bernard says, in fixing your eyes on the good you have done and the labors you have undergone; it is that it will serve to make you careless of further progress, lukewarm and slack when there is question of going on, thinking that you have done enough work in religion and that you may now take your ease. Travelers, when they begin to grow weary of the road, turn their eyes back to see how much of it they have already gone; so when we are weary and lukewarmness is stealing over us, we begin to look at the work we have left behind; this makes us content with that, and apt more readily to settle down in our sloth.

To avoid these disadvantages and dangers it is highly expedient never to look at the good that we have done, but on the good we have still left undone: the sight of the former is an invitation to repose; the sight of the latter, an incitement to work. This is the second part of this prescription which the Apostle gives us, always to keep our eyes on what is wanting to our performances, thereby to animate and compel ourselves to make it up; this the saints declare by sundry examples and homely comparisons. St. Gregory says: As the debtor who is a thousand ducats in another man's debt does not rest or fold his arms upon having paid two hundred or four hundred, but keeps his eye ever fixed upon what still remains to pay—that it is that troubles him, and he is always in some solicitude until he has paid the whole debt—so we should not look at the good we have done hitherto, whereby we have paid part of the debt that we owe to God, but at the amount which remains to us to pay: this it is that should give us anxiety; this is the thorn that we should ever keep fixed in our heart. St. Gregory further says: As pilgrims and good travelers do not consider how far they have gone but how far they have yet got to go, and keep that before their eyes until they have finished their journey, so we, since we are travelers and wayfarers on the road to our heavenly country, should not look at the road we have gone over, but at the road that remains for us to go. Mark, he says, how for men on a journey, bound for a certain place, it avails little to have gone far if they do not complete the bit still to be gone. Mark again how the prize in a race, which is destined for the best runner, is not taken by him who runs a great part of the way nimbly and flags at the end. *So run that ye may attain,* says the Apostle (I Cor. ix. 24). Take care to run in such a way as to attain and compass what you are aiming at. Take no account of the run you have made up to this, but keep your eyes steadily on the goal of your journey, which is perfection, and see how much you come short of it, and so you will get along well. "He never ceases running," says St. Chrysostom, "who reflects that he has not reached the goal."

St. Bernard says that we should be like the merchants and traders of the world. You will see a merchant, a business man, taking such care and pains daily to increase his property as to reckon nothing of what he has gained and acquired hitherto nor of the labors that it has cost him; all his care and solicitude is for fresh gains and a daily increase more and more, as though hitherto he had done nothing and gained nothing; in this manner, he says, we should behave. All our care should be how daily to increase our store, how daily to make profit in humility, charity, mortification, and all other virtues, taking no account of how we have labored and what we have acquired hitherto. So says Christ our Redeemer that the kingdom of heaven is like a merchant, and He bids us do business: *Traffic till I come* (Luke xix. 13).

And to carry on further this comparison of a merchant, since the holy Gospel puts it before us, see how merchants and men of business in the world are so careful and solicitous as never to lose a point or miss an opportunity of increasing their store; and do you the like. Never lose a point nor let pass an opportunity of making progress without seizing it: "Let us all constantly endeavor to let slip no point of perfection that by God's grace we can attain," is the direction of our Father. Let slip no occasion of contriving to make some spiritual gain—from the biting little word that someone has said to you, from the command of obedience given against your will, from the occasion of humility that offers. All these are your gains, and you should go to seek and gather in these occasions; and on the day that the greatest number come in your way you should go to bed happier than usual, with the greatest satisfaction and cheerfulness, as does the merchant on the day that most occasions of gain present themselves, seeing that on that day his business has gone well. So also on that day your business as a religious has gone well if you have known how to profit by your opportunities. And as the merchant does not consider whether another man loses, nor is concerned about that, but the one thing he takes account of is his own profit, and in that he rejoices, so you should not look whether your neighbor does well or ill in giving you this occasion, nor whether he is right or not, nor be indignant against him, but rejoice in your own gain. How far should we be from worrying ourselves and losing our peace of mind when the like occasions offer if we proceeded in this way! If what might sadden us and disturb our peace is the very thing that we desire and go in search of, what will be able to trouble or upset us?

Consider again how the merchant is so absorbed in his profits that he seems never to think of anything else. In all cases and happenings that occur, his eyes and his heart at once turn to see how he can make some profit therefrom. When he is eating, he is thinking of this; and with this thought and care he goes to bed; with this he awakes at night, and rises in the morning, and goes thinking of it all day long. Now in this way we ought to proceed in the business of our souls; in all cases and happenings that occur, our eyes and heart should at once turn to see how we can make some spiritual profit thereof. This should be our thought when we sit at table; with this thought and care we should rise in the morning and go about all day long, and all our life long. For this is our business and our treasure, and there is nothing else for us to seek. St. Bonaventure adds that, as the merchant does not find all that he desires and needs in one market or fair, but in several, so the religious must seek to draw spiritual profit not only from prayer and spiritual consolation, but also from temptations, mean and lowly occupations, and from every occasion that offers.

Oh, if we sought and strove after virtue in this fashion, how soon should we find ourselves rich! *If thou seekest,* says the Wise Man, *after virtue and perfection, which is true wisdom, with the care and diligence wherewith men of the world seek after money and dig for mines and treasures, without doubt thou wilt light upon it* (Prov. ii. 4). And the Lord does not ask much of us in this, says St. Bernard, since to gain true wisdom and the true treasure, which is God Himself, He does not ask of us more care and diligence than men of the world employ in gaining perishable riches, which are liable to maggots and robbers, and tomorrow must come to an end; whereas the craving and desire of spiritual goods, and solicitude to attain them, ought to be greater in proportion as those goods are greater and more precious than the temporal. Hence St. Bernard's lamentation: "It is a great confusion and shame to us to see how much more diligent and careful worldly people are about worldly things, and even about their vices and sins, than we are about virtue; and with how much more promptitude and alacrity they run to their death than we to our life."

It is set down in ecclesiastical history that the Abbot Pambo, going one day to Alexandria and meeting with a worldly woman who was very finely dressed, began to weep bitterly, crying out several times: "Alas! What a miserable man am I!" And his disciples having asked him why he sighed and wept so bitterly, he answered: "Would you not have me weep to see this miserable woman taking more care and diligence to please men than I do to please God; and to see her at greater pains to lay snares for men, to drag them into hell, than I use endeavors to gain them for heaven?" Also, that apostolic man, Father Francis Xavier, was ashamed and extremely troubled to see that merchants had got before him into Japan, and that they had been more diligent to sail thither to sell their merchandise than he had been to carry thither the treasure of the Gospel, propagate the faith, and increase the kingdom of God. Let us conceive the same thoughts and be filled with a holy confusion to see *that the children of this world are wiser and more careful in the concerns of this life* than we are in our concerns for heaven (Luke xvi. 8). Let this be enough to draw us out of our tepidity and sloth.

CHAPTER VIII

That It Is a Great Aid to Perfection to Fix Our Eyes on Lofty and Exalted Things

OUR advancement in perfection will be greatly helped on by our fixing our eyes on lofty ideals that require great perfection to realize. So St. Paul advises, writing to the Corinthians: *Be ye emulous of the better gifts* (I Cor. xii. 31). Get yourselves ready for great things; meet and undertake things great and excellent. This is a determination of much importance, for our designs and desires must needs reach out very far if our performances are at least to come up to what is our strict duty. Where a bow or catapult is slack, then to hit the mark it is necessary to aim from three to six inches higher; otherwise, the string being loose, the missle will not go where you want, but by aiming it higher it comes to hit the mark. We are like a slack bow or catapult. We are so poorly strung that, to hit the mark, it is necessary to aim very high. Man was left by sin so miserable that to come to attain mediocrity in virtue it is necessary for his purposes and desires to travel far beyond. Someone says: "My only aim is to avoid mortal sin: I seek no further perfection." I greatly fear that you are not likely to attain even that, for the catapult is slack. If you aimed higher, you might reach that; but not aiming higher, I fear you must come short and are in great danger of falling into mortal sin.

The religious who makes it his endeavor to observe not God's commandments alone, but His counsels also, and to keep not from mortal sins alone, but from venial sins and imperfections, takes a good way to keep clear of mortal sin, since he aims much higher than that. And when through frailty he does not reach the height he proposed, but falls somewhat short, he will fail in a matter of counsel, in some small rule, and it will be an imperfection or at most a venial sin. But the other, whose only aim is not to commit mortal sin, when he falls short of that through the looseness of his bow and catapult, will fall into some mortal sin. And that is why among people of the world we see so many fall into mortal sins, while good religious, by the goodness of God, are so free and far removed from them. This is one of the greatest blessings that we have in religion, a blessing for which we owe many thanks to God, who has brought us thereto; though there were no other blessing in religion than this, that would be enough to make us live in great consolation and contentment, and to hold it for a great mercy and benefit of the Lord that He has drawn us to such a life, since here I trust in the Lord that you will pass your whole life without falling into mortal sin; whereas, were you in the world, I dare say you would not pass a year, or even a month, or perhaps even one week, without it.

Hence also will be understood the danger of the tepid and lax religious who thinks nothing of breaking the rules and will have no thought for things of perfection, since such a one is very near a fall in some grave matter. So, then, if you wish to advance, set your eyes on acquiring a most perfect humility, going so far as to receive with cheerfulness slights and affronts; and God grant that, after all that, you may come to endure them with patience. Set your eyes on acquiring a most perfect obedience of will and understanding; and you may be thankful if you do not fail sometimes in the execution of the thing commanded and in punctuality in fulfilling the same. Try to store up resignation and indifference as if to undergo great difficulties and trials that might occur; and, please God, you may be so afterwards in the ordinary and common accidents of daily life.

This, says St. Augustine, was the counsel of God, to put at the head of His commandments the highest and most perfect of them all: *Thou shalt love God with thy whole heart, with thy whole will, with thy whole soul, and with thy whole strength: this is the greatest of all the commandments and the end of them all* (Deut. vi. 5; Matt. xxii. 37). So great is the excellence of this commandment that theologians and saints say that its final perfection is not a thing of this life but of the next. Not to be occupied with anything else but God, and always to keep all our heart, all our will and understanding, and all our powers intent on loving Him, is the state of heavenly bliss; we cannot in this life attain so far as that, because we are forced to attend to the requirements of the body. And though this commandment is so high and involves so great perfection, nevertheless the Lord puts it in the front first of all, that we may know up to what point we are to extend our efforts and whither we should endeavor to arrive. Therefore, says St. Augustine, did God from the very beginning put before our eyes this so great and high commandment, that, having our eyes fixed on an end so high and requiring such great perfection, we should try to bare our arm and put the weight as far as ever we can. The higher we aim, the less shall we fall short.

On those words of the prophet: *Blessed is the man whom thou aidest, for he shall plan in his heart increases and ascensions in virtue* (Psalm lxxxiii. 6), St. Jerome says: The just and holy man ever has before his eyes the thought of ascending and going further in perfection; that is what he carries riveted in his mind, according to the saying of the Wise Man: *The thoughts and purposes of the robust man shall ever be in abundance* (Prov. xxi. 5). But the sinner and the imperfect man has no such thought; he contents himself with an ordinary life; at most he sets before his eyes a standard of mediocrity, and thence he comes to fall away and go down. Gerson says: This is the language of many people: "An ordinary life is enough for me; I want only to save my soul; as for those high and excellent heights of perfection, let them be for apostles and great saints: I don't pretend to fly so high, but to walk along a flat cart-road"—*Vox multorum est: sufficit mihi vita communis; si cum illis salvari potero satis est. Nolo merita apostolorum, nolo volare per summa, incedere per planiora contentus sum.* This is the language of the imperfect, who are many, since the perfect are few. Christ our Redeemer says in the Gospel: *The gate and way that leadeth to perfection and life is narrow and strait, and there are few that enter thereby, but the common way of sloth is very wide, and many there are that go therein* (Matt. vii. 13-14). St. Augustine says that these are they whom the prophet calls *beasts of the fields* (Psalm viii. 8) because they seek always to walk in the field, a wide, spacious place, and will never be confined to any rule or restraint. And Gerson says that by such language as this: "Enough for me an ordinary life; so I be but saved, it is sufficient; I aspire not to any higher perfection," a man plainly discovers his imperfection, since he makes no effort to enter in by the narrow gate. He adds further that these people who through their sloth and tepidity fancy that it is enough for them to gain the lowest seat in heaven, have great reason to fear lest they may come to be condemned with the foolish virgins who slumbered and slept, or with the slothful servant who buried the talent he had received and was therefore deprived of the one talent he had and cast into outer darkness; and we find not in the Gospel that he was condemned for anything else but for having neglected to improve the talent his master had endowed him withal (Matt. xxv.).

But to make it appear more clearly how shameful and deplorable a condition those men are in, the same Gerson uses this example. "Imagine," he says, "a father of a family, rich and highborn, who has many children, all of them quite capable of advancing the family and winning by their industry and abilities great honor to themselves and their lineage. All apply themselves with care to do their duty except one, who, while all the rest are doing what sons of such a sire should do, alone, out of sloth and laziness, chooses to sit idle at home enjoying himself, and cares not to do anything worthy of his ability and the rank of his father to increase the fortune of the family, though, if he would, he could do as well as any of the rest." Enough for him, he says, is a moderate competence; he has no mind for further honor or further augmentation, nor will he work for that end. The father calls upon him; begs and coaxes him to entertain higher thoughts; puts before him his ability, talents, and good parts, the nobility of his lineage, the example of his ancestors and of his brothers still living; but for all that he has no mind to leave his fireside or endeavor to be more of a man. Such a son clearly would give great annoyance to his father. In like manner, says Gerson, as we are sons of God and brothers of Jesus Christ, our heavenly Father is exhorting us and animating us to perfection: "My sons, be not content with an ordinary life." *Be ye perfect as your heavenly Father is perfect* (Matt. v. 48). Look at the generosity and perfection of your Father and behave as His sons whose sons you are, to show that you are *sons of your Father who is in heaven* (Matt. v. 45); look at the example of your brethren. If you will but fix your eyes on the example of your elder Brother, Jesus Christ! He it is that has honored all our race; and though it cost Him His blood and His life, He gave it as a good bargain for that exchange.

And if such an example is too dazzling for your eyes, fix them on your other brothers, men as weak as you are, born in sin as you were, full of passions and temptations and evil inclinations as you. It is for this that Mother Church puts before us the examples of the saints and celebrates their feasts. And if you wish to take examples that come nearer home, look at those of your brethren, born of the same mother, of the same religious order and Society. Fix your eyes on a Father Ignatius, on a Francis Xavier and Francis Borgia, on an Edmund Campion, and on others like them that you know. Try to imitate them; be not you a disgrace to your lineage and your order. And if with all this there is anyone not animated to do deeds of valor, but content with an ordinary and common life, is it not clear that, as far as in him lies, he will give displeasure and annoyance to God Himself, Who is our Father, and bad example to his brothers, and deserves that the heavenly Father should not own him for a son, nor his brothers know him for their brother?

Now this is what we are saying, that we should cherish high and generous thoughts and ever fix our eyes and heart on great and noble deeds, to the end that, supposing in our weakness we do not attain so high, at least we may not fall so far short nor be so much behind. Let us do in this matter as men who offer wares for sale; to start with, they usually ask more than the just price, to the end that buyers may come to give them what is just; and they who make bargains are wont at the beginning to demand more than is reasonable to bring the other party to reason, according to the proverb: "Ask what is unjust, or more than is just, that they may come to give you what is just." So it is here. I do not tell you to ask for what is unjust, but for what is most just. Fix your eyes on what is more just, that you may come at least to what is just. Ask and desire what is more precious, that so you may attain to mediocrity; for if you fix your eyes merely on mediocrity and do not reach out to more, even that you will not attain, but will fall far below.

By this it may be seen how important it is that in our spiritual conferences and exhortations we should treat of things of great perfection, exhorting to a profound humility, even to the furthest degree thereof; to a perfect mortification of all our passions and appetites; to an entire conformity with the will of God, so that it should not remain with us to will or not will aught else but what God wills or wills not, His will being our whole content and delight. And so in other virtues someone may say: "What is the use of talking and preaching such high doctrine to weak folk; aye, sometimes to mere beginners? If you proposed to us things proportionate to our weakness, plain and easy things, possibly we might embrace them; but in speaking of these points of perfection that reach to the third heaven you seem to be not speaking to us, but to an Apostle St. Paul and the like of him." You are mistaken; they are meant for you; it is to you we speak when we speak of these points of perfection; and the very reason that you allege for not speaking of them is our reason for speaking. You say you are weak and that I ought not to propose to you such high things. I say that it is just because you are weak that I must put these points of perfection before you, that setting your eyes on them you may come to mount reasonably high and not remain so low and limited in virtue.

For this end it is a great help to read much and hear read the lives of saints, and consider their excellent and heroic virtues; it being the intention of holy Church in proposing to us their heroic deeds, to invite us at least to get out of our sloth. And there is this other advantage in such reading, that it confounds and humbles us to consider the purity of life of these saints, and how far we come short of it. St. Gregory, on those words of Job: *He will look upon men, and say: I have sinned* (Job xxxiii. 27), says that, as a poor man is much more sensible of his own poverty when he considers the vast wealth and treasures of rich men, so the soul humbles herself more deeply and better knows her indigence, when she reflects upon those great examples the saints have left us and the glorious actions they have done. St. Anthony having been to visit St. Paul, the first hermit, and seen his great sanctity, his disciples went out to meet him on his return, saying, "Where have you been, Father?" "Alas," replied the holy man, "miserable sinner that I am,

I have no right to bear the name of a religious. I have seen Elias, I have seen John the Baptist in the desert, when I beheld Paul in paradise." We read also of the great St. Macarius that, having seen the sublime perfection of some monks whom he had visited, the blessed man wept, saying to his disciples: "I have seen monks; these are monks; I am no monk. Woe is me! I falsely bear the name of monk." What the saints said out of their deep humility, we may say with greater truth considering their examples. Thus by humility and shame we should make up what is wanting to us, and so on all sides aid ourselves much by this means.

CHAPTER IX

How Important It Is to Set Store by Little Things and Not Despise Them

HE that neglecteth small things shall fall by little and little (Ecclus. xix. 1). The lesson contained in this saying is of great importance, especially for aspirants to perfection. Great things of their own importance press upon our attention, but in smaller matters we are apt more easily to be careless and take little account of them as if they were of little value and importance, which is a great mistake, not without serious consequences. "They who fall into the greatest faults begin with the smallest"—*A minimis incipiunt qui in maxima proruunt,* says St. Bernard. He quotes a common saying: "No one goes to any extreme on a sudden"—*Nemo repente fit summus.* As a rule, no one ever comes to be on a sudden either very good or very bad, but good and evil grow little by little. Little by little great bodily ailments are developed, and spiritual ailments and great maladies of the soul in the same way. Thus when you see great falls of servants of God, think not, says the saint, that the evil began when it first came to your notice. One who has persevered a long time leading a good life, never comes to slip and fall all of a sudden; his fall comes of his first having become careless of tiny little things, by which carelessness, little by little, virtue was weakened in his soul and he deserved that God should withdraw His hand a little away from him, and so he was open to being easily overcome afterwards by a great temptation falling in his way.

Cassian illustrates this by a very appropriate comparison, a comparison used also by the Holy Ghost. Houses, he says, do not fall down of a sudden, but first the thing begins by some little leakages; then little by little the timbers of the building rot; the mischief gets into the walls and softens and imperceptibly ruins them till it reaches the foundations, and then the whole structure collapses in one night.

We are told, then, in the above words to beware of this danger, because he who makes no account of small things, little by little will fall into greater faults. This should be enough to convince us and put us on our guard, since it is the counsel of the Holy Ghost Himself. *By sloth and want of care,* says the Holy Ghost in Ecclesiastes, *the roof will come to fall, and for want of taking care to repair it, it will rain through* (Eccles. x. 18). Through neglect of repairing the house at the beginning when the damage was small; through not tiling it and stopping the leakages, some fine morning it comes to show itself a ruin. In like manner do men come to great falls and very evil ends. First come in our little affections and our passions like so many small leakages, and they go on little by little penetrating and softening and weakening the virtue of our soul, and so the whole building goes crash from mere neglect of repairs at the beginning when the mischief was small. From negligence in stopping those little leakages, from taking no account of small things, one fine morning a man finds himself under temptation; another day and he is out of religion. Would to God we had not so much experience of this! Truly it strikes one with great fear and dismay to see the first little cracks that were the beginning of the ruin of some who came to a very bad end. The devil is a clever fellow. He does not in the first instance assail God's servants in great matters—he is much too acute for that; but, little by little, imperceptibly, in small and minute things, he does his work better than if he tempted his man in great things. If he started with mortal sins, he would easily be perceived and packed off; but, entering by small and minute things, he is neither perceived nor packed off, but admitted.

Therefore does St. Gregory say that in some ways there is more danger in small faults than in great ones, because great ones are more clearly known and the evil of them accordingly is more in evidence, moving us to avoid them and to feel more alarm when we fall into them; but small faults are less known, less easily avoided, and made less account of; and as they are made nothing of, so they are repeated and continued, and men settle down to them and never make up their minds manfully to throw them off; and on the heels of small faults there come great ones. St. Chrysostom quite agrees. He says a thing which he calls a marvel: "I dare to utter a marvelous saying, which will appear to you new and unheard of; it is that sometimes we need take more care and pains over avoiding small sins than over avoiding great ones. For great sins of themselves strike us with horror, so that we abhor and fly from them; but the other sins, by the very fact that they are small, make us remiss and negligent; and as we make little account of them, so we never succeed in getting clear of them, and so they come to do us great harm"—*Mirabile quidem et inauditum dicere audeo: solet mihi nonnunquam non tanto studio magna videri esse peccata vitanda quanto parva et vilia; illa enim ut aversemur ipsa peccati natura efficit, haec autem hac ipsa re quia parva sunt desides reddunt, et dum contemnuntur non potest ad expulsionem eorum animus generose insurgere, unde cito ex parvis maxima fiunt negligentia nostra.*

This is the reason why the devil sets so much store by this means of approaching and assailing religious men and servants of God; and also because he knows right well that thereby he will gain a footing to succeed in making them afterwards fall in greater things. So St. Augustine says: "What matters it whether by a little or a great leak the water enters into the ship, so that in the end it founders? I care not for one more than the other, for it all comes to the same in the end." So the devil cares not whether he comes in by small things or by great things, so that he finally gains his end, which is to destroy and sink us. Of little drops of water multiplied, says St. Bonaventure, there come to be formed torrents and floods so great as to level to the ground high walls and buildings and strong castles. By a little leak and by a chink and crack the water silently and little by little makes its way into the ship until it sends it to the bottom. For this reason St. Augustine says that, as when a ship springs a leak, it is necessary to be always at the pump, pumping the water out that the ship may not founder, so by the help of meditation and examen we must be always ridding ourselves of the faults and imperfections that little by little are gaining upon us, that we may not founder and be drowned. This must be the exercise of the religious; we must be always at the pump, otherwise we run great risk. And elsewhere he says: "You have eschewed and escaped the waves and tempests and great dangers that there are in the stormy sea of the world; see that you do not come here in the harbor of religion to run aground on a sandbank; see that you do not come to danger and destruction by minute and small things; for at that rate it will profit you little to have eschewed and escaped those great dangers and tempests and rocks and cliffs, if afterwards in the harbor you come to stick fast in the sand."

CHAPTER X

Another Weighty Reason for Setting Great Store by Little Things

ANOTHER considerable reason why we should make account of little things is that, if we are careless and negligent in little things and take small heed thereof, it is to be feared that God will refuse us His particular and special aids and graces which we stand in need of to resist temptations and not fall into sin and to obtain the virtue and perfection which we desire; and so we come to great harm.

The better to understand this, we must presuppose a very good piece of theology taught us by St. Paul when writing to the Corinthians—that God our Lord never refuses to anyone that supernatural assistance and succor whereby, if he will, he will not be overcome by temptation but be able to resist and come out victorious. *God is faithful, who will not permit you to be tempted above your strength, but will give you such aid in temptation as that you may be able to suffer it with advantage* (I Cor. x. 13). God is faithful, says the Apostle; you may rest assured that He will not permit you to be tempted more than you are able to bear; and if He adds more trials and there come greater temptations, He will also add more succor and bounty that you may be able to come out of them, not only without loss, but with much profit and increase of good. But there is another aid and succor of God more special and particular. Man could resist and overcome temptation without this special aid if he availed himself as he ought of the first supernatural assistance, which is more general. But, oftentimes, with that first aid man will not resist temptation unless God give him that other aid more particular and special. Not that he could not, but that he will not; for if he willed, he might well resist with that first aid, since it is sufficient for the purpose if he would make the use of it that he ought. In that case his falling and being overcome by temptation will be his own fault, since it will be by his own will. And if God gave him then that other special assistance, he would not fall.

But to come to our point. This second aid and special superabundant and efficacious succor is not given by God to all, nor on all occasions, since it is a liberality and a most particular grace of His own bestowal; and so God will give it to whom He pleases; He will give it to those who have been liberal with Him. So the prophet says: *With the holy, Lord, thou wilt be holy; and with the benign, benign; and with the liberal and sincere, thou wilt be sincere and liberal; and with him that shall not be such, thou wilt pay him in the same coin* (Psalm xvii. 26-27). This is what our Father puts in his Rules: "The closer one shall bind himself to God our Lord, and the more liberal he shall show himself to His Divine Majesty, the more liberal he will find God to him; and the better shall he be disposed to receive every day greater graces and spiritual gifts." This is the doctrine of St. Gregory Nazianzen and other saints.

What it is to be liberal to God may be well understood from what it is to be liberal to men. In this world to be liberal to another is to give him, not his due and bonded right, but more than his due and bonded right. That is liberality; the other is not liberality, but justice and obligation. Now in the same manner, he who is very careful and diligent to please God, not only in matters of obligation, but also in those of supererogation and perfection, and not only in greater, but also in lesser things, he is liberal to God. Now to them that are thus liberal, God also is very liberal. These are God's favorites to whom He shows His bounties; to these He gives not only those general aids which are sufficient to resist and overcome temptations, but also those special and superabundant and efficacious aids wherewith they will nowise fall when they are tempted.

But if you are not liberal to God, how can you expect God to be liberal to you? If you are niggardly with God, you deserve that God should be niggardly with you. If you are so mean and close as to go sounding and measuring as with rule and compass—"Am I bound or not bound? Am I bound under sin or not bound under sin? Does it amount to a mortal sin or to no more than a venial?"—all this is being niggardly with God, since you want to give Him no more than you are obliged, and even in that possibly you fail. God then will be niggardly with you and give you no more than He is obliged by His word; He will give you those general and necessary aids which He gives to all, which are enough and sufficient to enable you to resist temptations and not fall in them; but you will have much reason to fear that He will not give you that special superabundant and efficacious aid which He is wont to give to such as are liberal to Him; and so you will come to be vanquished by temptation and fall into sin.

This is what theologians and saints commonly say, that one sin is often the punishment of another sin. That is to be understood in this way, that by the first sin a man loses, as punishment of his sin, all claim to that special and particular aid of God, and renders himself unworthy of it; and so he comes to fall into a second sin. They say the same of venial sins, and further of faults and negligences and general carelessness of life; for this also they say that a man may lose all claim and render himself unworthy of that special and efficacious assistance of God with which he will persevere and actually overcome temptation, and without which he will be overcome and fall into sin. So some saints explain the words of the Wise Man: *He that despiseth small things, shall fall little by little* (Ecclus. xix. 1). By despising small things and making little account of them one comes to render oneself unworthy of that special assistance of God, and so one comes to fall into great faults. In like manner is to be understood the saying of the Apocalypse (iii. 16): *Because thou art tepid, I will begin to vomit thee out of my mouth.* God has not yet vomited and thrown up entirely the tepid man, but He has begun to vomit and throw him up because by this negligence in which he lives, and these faults which he commits with advertence and of set purpose, he goes the way to make himself undeserving of that special and efficacious aid without which he will fall; and God will end by vomiting and throwing him up.

Let us consider how much reason we have to fear lest we should lose all claim and render ourselves unworthy of this special aid of God through our tepidity and sloth. How often do we see ourselves assailed with temptations and in great danger, and many times we find ourselves in doubt—"Did I dwell on it or not? Did I consent or not? Did it amount to a sin or not?" Oh, how well it would be worth our while for those critical moments to have been liberal to God and so made ourselves worthy of that special and liberal aid of grace whereby we should be quite secure of always keeping our footing, and without which we shall be in great danger and possibly be overcome!

St. Chrysostom assigns this means as one of the chief that we have for overcoming temptations. Speaking of the devil, our enemy, and of the continual war that he wages against us, he says: "You know well, my brethren, that we have in the devil a perpetual enemy who is always making war upon us, who never sleeps nor relaxes his efforts: you can have no truce with that cruel monster. So it is necessary always to be very wide-awake and very careful and watchful not to be overcome by him." How, then, shall we stand on our guard and prepare ourselves well not to be overcome, but always to get the better of this traitor and keep him under? Do you know how? St. Chrysostom says: "The only means to overcome him is to have gained beforehand this special assistance of God by our good life in the past. In this way we shall be always victorious, and in no other." Notice the expression, "in no other." St. Basil makes the same observation in these words: "He who wishes to be helped by the Lord never ceases doing what lies with him to do. He who does this is never left destitute of the divine assistance;" wherefore, he concludes: "We must make it our effort that our conscience shall not reproach us in anything." A sound conclusion is that we must be very careful in our spiritual exercises and in all our works to be worthy of this special aid from heaven.

Hence it will be seen how important it is to make much account of small things—if we can call those things small which bring us in so much good or so much harm. *He who feareth God, neglecteth nothing* (Eccles. vii. 19), because he knows full well that out of small things neglected one comes little by little to fail in greater; and he fears that, if he ceases to be liberal with God in these things, God will cease to be liberal with him.

In conclusion I say that this matter is so important, and we should make so much account of it, that we may take it as a general rule that, so long as a man makes much of little and minute things, all will go well, and the Lord will befriend him; and on the contrary, when he ceases to reckon much of little and minute things, he will incur great danger, because it is in this way that all evil enters into a religious. This Jesus Christ gives us to understand, saying: *He that is faithful in what is little, will be faithful also in what is much; and he that is unfaithful and evil in what is little, will be the like in what is much* (Luke xvi. 10). And therefore when one wishes to see how one is getting on in spiritual progress—and it is reasonable that we should often make reflection thereupon—let him examine himself by this and see whether he makes account of little things or whether he is getting into free and easy ways by taking small heed of them; and if he sees that now he does not trouble himself about small matters, nor does his conscience reproach him thereon as it used to do, let him look for a remedy with all care. The devil, says St. Basil, when he sees that he cannot drive us out of religion, applies all his powers to persuade us not to give ourselves to perfection and not to make account of small matters, deceiving us by a false assurance that one does not lose God for that. But we, on the contrary, should make it our effort that as he cannot drive us out of religion, so neither shall he hinder our perfection; but we will apply ourselves thereto with all our strength, setting much store by little and minute things.

CHAPTER XI

That the Business of Our Spiritual Advancement Is Not To Be Taken in General, but in Particular; and of How Great Importance It Is to Put Into Execution Those Good Purposes Wherewith God Inspires Us

IT will also be a great help towards our improvement—and it is a means commonly given by the masters of spiritual life—that we should not take this business of our improvement in general and in common, but in particular and little by little. Cassian says that the Abbot Moses one day in a spiritual conference asked his monks what it was that they aimed at by all their labors, abstinences, vigils, prayers, and mortification. They answered: "The kingdom of heaven." He said: That is the last end, but I ask now, what is the immediate and particular end you are aiming at whereby to arrive at your last end? Take the case of the laborer: his end is to gather much food and have wherewithal to spend his life in abundance; but all his care and diligence he expends in working at and cultivating the earth and clearing it of weeds, for that is the necessary means to the other end. And the merchant, though his end is to grow rich, applies all his thoughts to consider what businesses and what method of doing business will be most to the purpose for gaining this end, and there he applies all his industry and diligence. So the religious should act. It is not enough to say in general: "I intend to save my soul;" "I will be a good religious;" "I desire to be perfect;" but he must fix his eyes in particular on the passion or vice that stands most in his way and the virtue that is most wanting to him; and he must labor to gain that. In this way, advancing little by little and proceeding with care and diligence, now upon one thing, now upon another, he will come better to attain to what he aims at.

This is the means that another Father of the Desert proposed to that monk who, after being long very diligent and fervent, grew to be negligent in his spiritual exercises and generally very tepid. Desiring to recover his former state and finding the road closed and apparently very difficult, he did not know where to begin. The other consoled and animated him by this parable or example of a man who sent his son to clear the estate, which was full of thorns and weeds. The son, seeing the amount there was to do, lost heart and fell asleep and did nothing that day and the next. The father said to him: "You should not, boy, look at or take all the labor before you in a lump, but every day do a little, just enough to take in the body of a man." He did so, and in a short time cleared the whole estate.

Here it should be observed that one of the chief reasons why we get on slowly, and the Lord does not do us more favors, is that we do not put in execution the good purposes and desires which He gives us; and so because we do not give a good account of what He gives us, He does not bestow on us further gifts. A schoolmaster will not let a child go on to a higher style of letters or better copy until he has formed and copied well what has been given him; so the Lord is wont to deal with us in raising us to perfection. He is slower to give us greater things, the slower we are to put to good use what He has given us. And the more a man sets to work to realize and put in execution the desires that the Lord gives him in prayer, the more is God moved to grant him greater things.

Father Master Avila well says: "Whoever makes a good use of what he knows, will gain light to see what he does not know." Any other man cannot have the face to ask for that, since it may be well replied to him: "Why do you seek to know My will and good pleasure when what you know you do not carry out?" If you do not put into act the desires which the Lord gives you, how can you wish that He should give you greater things? With what face can you ask God in prayer to grant you this or that which you desire and find needful if you have no mind to amend or mortify yourself in point of a fault where you have great need of amendment, and God has given you many desires and inspirations about it? I do not know how you can raise up your eyes to beg of God other greater things, you who have no purpose of amendment even in the matter of an exterior fault that you have, but let yourself deliberately fall into it again and again. If, then, we wish to make progress in spirit, and that the Lord should do us great favors, let us be diligent in putting into execution the inspirations and desires which the Lord gives us.

It is the common doctrine of the saints that he who makes a good use of the benefits he has received renders himself worthy of fresh benefits; and, contrariwise, he who makes a bad use of them does not deserve to receive more. The Wise Man in Wisdom (xvi.) propounds this question: What is the reason why the manna melted away at the first ray of the sun and was of no further use; while if they put it in the fire it did not liquify, nor did the fire do it any harm, the heat of the fire being stronger than that of the sun? The same Wise Man answers at the end of the same chapter: *That it might be known to all that we must be beforehand with the sun to bless thee* (Wisdom xvi. 28)—that all might understand that it behooves us to be diligent in making our profit of the benefits that the Lord gives us and the blessings that we receive at His hand; and in punishment of the ingratitude and laziness that would not get up in the morning before sunrise to profit by the boon that the Lord had vouchsafed, God permitted the sun to spoil the provisions for the day. This is also what Christ our Redeemer marvelously declares in the holy Gospel (Luke xix.) in that parable of the nobleman who divided his substance among his servants that they might traffic therewith. When, after having taken possession of his kingdom, he asked them for an account, he made them governors or commandants of so many cities in proportion to the number of talents which each one had gained; him who had gained ten talents, he made governor of ten cities, and him who had gained five, of five—giving us to understand that as this king rewarded the industry and fidelity of his servants with such a step upwards as there is from ten talents to ten cities, so also if we put into execution the inspirations of God and are loyal and faithful in corresponding with them, very great also will be the abundant liberality wherewith the Lord will augment His divine gifts; and, contrariwise, if we do not correspond as we ought, not only will He deprive us of what He has given us, but we shall be further chastised, as was that servant who had not profited nor gained anything with the talent that he had received.

It is related of that most famous painter, Apelles, that, however numerous his occupations, he never passed a day on which he did not practise his art and paint something; and, stealing the time from other occupations that offered, he would say: "Today I have not drawn a line"—*Hodie lineam nullam duxi.* From that it became a proverb for any office when the day was let slip without practising or doing anything at it. That is how he came to be such a perfect and consummate painter. If, then, you desire to be a perfect and consummate religious, let no day pass on which you do not draw some line and make some mark in virtue. Go on overcoming and mortifying yourself every day in something; go on banishing every day some fault from the actions that you do, for in this way they will become daily better and more perfect. And when you come to the midday examen, see whether you have passed that half day without having drawn any line or marked any point in virtue, and say: "Today I have not drawn a line; oh, dear, today I have made no step forward in virtue, nor mortified myself in anything, nor made so much as one act of humility when I found occasions for it. I have spent this day to no purpose. It must not be so this evening; it must not be so tomorrow morning." In this way, little by little, we shall come to advance much.

CHAPTER XII

That It Will Be a Great Aid to the Attainment of Perfection Not to Commit Faults on Purpose, and Never Relax in Fervor

IT will also aid us much towards growth in virtue and perfection to try never to commit faults on purpose. There are two sorts of faults and venial sins; the one sort is that into which those who fear God fall through frailty, ignorance, and inadvertence, albeit with some carelessness and negligence. As to such faults as these, they who serve God and walk in His sight with an upright heart know by experience that they cause no bitterness of heart, but rather humility; nor do they find that on that account God turns away His face from them, but rather they experience new favor from the Lord and a new spirit by the humble recourse they have to God for them. Other faults and defects there are which they fall into with advertence and on purpose, who are tepid and remiss in the service of God; and these faults are an obstacle to the great blessings we should receive if we did not commit them. For these faults the Lord will often turn away His face from us in prayer, and withdraw many favors. Thus, if we wish to thrive and receive many favors of the Lord, we must take care not to commit faults on purpose. Enough the faults that we commit through our ignorance and inadvertence; let us not add to them more. Enough the distractions that we have in prayer through the fickleness of our imaginations; let us not distract ourselves voluntarily and on purpose. Enough the faults that we commit against the rules through our weakness; let us not break them of set purpose.

St. Basil lays down another means for gaining perfection, and says it is an excellent way to advance much in a short time; it is not to call halts on the road of virtue. There are those who make temporary efforts and then stop. Go on as you have begun and do not call these halts. On this road of spiritual life you will find yourself more wearied by making these halts than by not making them. In this there is a great difference from the bodily exercises; the more the body works and labors, the more it is worn out; but the more the spirit works, the more strength it gathers: *caro operando deficit, spiritus operando proficit* (St. Basil). And says the proverb: "The bow that is kept strung breaks, but the soul unstrung decays"—*Arcum frangit intentio, animum remissio.* St. Ambrose says that, as it is easier not to fall into sin but preserve innocence than after a fall to do true penance, so also it is easier to keep up the fervor of prayer and devotion than to return to it after being distracted for several days. The blacksmith who draws the iron red-hot from the furnace, in order that it may be soft and ready for him to make of it what he wishes with his hammer, does not let it go altogether cold, but before it goes cold he puts it back in the furnace so that he may readily deal with it as before. So we should never allow the heat of our devotion to die down; for once our heart has grown cold and callous, it will be hard to go back to our first fervor. Thus we see by experience that, however much a man may have advanced in virtue, yet if he grows careless for a season, in the little time that he surrenders to distractions and ceases to continue his pious exercises, he loses all that he had gained in a long time; scarce a trace is left of what he had before and it is with difficulty that he returns to it. Contrariwise, they who go on with fervor and persevere in their pious exercises, easily hold their own and in a short time advance much. The reason is that they lose no time and do not undo what they have done, unlike the tepid and slothful, who with their frequent halts do and undo, weave and unweave, and never finish their web. But the fervent, far from undoing, get on with their work and gather new strength daily by continual exercise, and new facility to do more and do it better; so they advance much. So says the Wise Man: *Hands slothful and remiss bring on poverty, but the hands of the strong gather riches* (Prov. x. 4). He who does not choose to work will grow poor, and he that puts his strength into his work will grow rich. *The soul of them that work shall grow fat* (Prov. xiii. 4).

A father of our Society, comparing tepid and slack religious with the diligent and fervent, used to say that the tepid and remiss who as they grow into seniors come to play the part of idlers and make it not their aim to get on with their perfection, are like old servants in the houses of our nobility, who render no service in the house, but make a show and sit by the gates of their masters' houses telling stories. They are given their keep as old servants, but they do not find favor or advancement with the master; indeed, he scarcely remembers them. You will see other young servants, youths so diligent and solicitous in the service of their master that they never think of pausing or sitting down all day long. Hardly has their master given them a hint of what he wants than the thing is done. These are they that find favor and advancement. Such are diligent and fervent religious.

CHAPTER XIII

Of Three Other Means That Will Enable Us to Advance in Virtue

A very good means to advance much is given by St. Basil and by the saints generally. It is that we should fix our eyes on the best members of the community, those whose virtue shines forth more conspicuously, and set about imitating them. The same counsel was given by the blessed Abbot St. Anthony; he said that the religious should go about like the busy bee, gathering from all flowers to make his honey—modesty from one, silence from another, patience from a third, from another obedience, from another indifference and resignation; in each one we should study that in which he shines most in order to imitate him. So we read that he did and thereby he became such a great saint. This is one of the chief blessings that we enjoy in religion, and therefore St. Jerome recommended community life rather than solitude, to the end that from one member you may learn humility, from another patience; this one will teach you to keep silence, the other, meekness. A philosopher named Chaerilas, a leading man of much distinction among the Lacedemonians, being asked what commonwealth he took to be the best in the world, said: "That wherein the citizens live together without any quarrels or seditions, and vie with one another who shall be most virtuous." This boon, among others, our Lord has given us in religion. May it please His Divine Majesty that it may always be so! There in the world, in almost all states, all men's contentions and rivalries turn on property and points of honor; scarcely will you find a man who has any emulation for virtue: but here, by the bounty and mercy of God, all the study of religious is in what touches on the renunciation of self, and how to grow more in virtue and perfection; and all their contentions and rivalries are on being every one of them more virtuous, more humble and obedient, and this without noise, without divisions, without detractions, but with a holy emulation and envy. It is no small favor and benefit, but a very great one, that the Lord has drawn us to religion, where virtue is favored and esteemed, where the professor or the preacher is not made more of for being a great professor or a great preacher but for being more humble and mortified; where the aim of all is to advance in virtue, and all by their example animate us to make progress. Let us, then, profit by so good an opening for practising this means.

Hence we can derive the second motive, which is the obligation we are under of giving good example to our brethren, "that considering one another all grow in devotion and praise of God our Lord," as our holy Father says. Or rather Christ Himself says so in the Gospel: *Let your light so shine before men, that they may see your good works, and glorify your Father, who is in heaven* (Matt. v. 16). Everyone well knows what force good example has to move others. A good religious in a house does more by his good example than any number of conferences and sermons can do, for men are more apt to believe what they see with their eyes than what they hear with their ears. They are persuaded that the thing is practicable which they see another put into act, and thereby are mightily moved and animated to do the like. This is that flapping of the wings of those holy living creatures which Ezechiel beheld (Ezech. iii. 13); when by your example you touch the heart of your brother and move him to compunction and devotion and desire of perfection.

St. Bernard avows that, at his entry into religion, the very sight of some spiritual and edifying religious—nay, even the very remembrance of them when they were absent or dead—brought him so great joy and comfort and filled his soul with such sweetness and devotion that oftentimes tears of joy came into his eyes. So says Holy Scripture in praise of King Josias: *The memory of Josias is as a box of sweet perfumes* (Ecclus. xlix. 1), comforting and strengthening and raising up the disheartened. Such we ought to endeavor to become, according to the words of the Apostle: *We are the good odor of Christ* (II Cor. ii. 15). We should be like a box of perfumes that freely communicates its sweetness, and comforts and animates all that come near. This should be a great motive to us to give ourselves earnestly to virtue and avoid giving any occasion of disedification to our brethren. For, as an exemplary religious is a great help and enough to edify and raise the tone of a whole house, so a religious who is not what he should be does a deal of harm, harm enough to disedify a whole community and draw them his way, the more so as example is more powerful for evil than for good, owing to our evil inclination to the one rather than to the other.

Almighty God commanded in Deuteronomy that, when the people of Israel were ready to join battle with their enemies, the captains should cause it to be proclaimed throughout the whole army: *Let the cowardly and faint-hearted return home*—and let the reason assigned be noted, as it makes for our purpose—*lest they make cowards of the rest, and infect them with their fear* (Deut. xx. 8). That is what a tepid and lax religious does in religion by his bad example; he makes cowards of the rest where there is question of making an effort and embracing things of perfection: sloth and tepidity are catching. That is how St. Eusebius of Emesa comes to say: "Those who have made up their minds to live in community are either diligent, to the great profit of the community, or negligent, to the great injury and peril of the same."

We may add a third means and motive to those we have already mentioned; it is the obligation we have of giving good example, not only to our brethren with whom we daily converse, but also to all the world, lest the whole order come to lose its good reputation by reason of the scandal given by some particular member; for men of the world often judge of all religious by the behavior of one, as if his fault were a sort of original sin, a talent of nature in them all, or were a sample of goods held in common stock. Thus people at once say: "Those of the Society also break rules, or do this or that," for one only whom they see breaking the rule and taking some liberty. Therefore everyone is bound to have an eye to edification, that by this means the reputation of the whole order may be preserved and increased. This obligation is more urgent upon us because we are still at our commencements, and all eyes are turned to us. *We are made a spectacle to the world, to angels, and to men* (I Cor. iv. 9); and although they have no reason to impute the fault of one man to a whole order, yet, after all, it is certain that the whole body consists of individuals, and consequently the growth or decay of that body depends upon the good or ill conduct of each individual. Let everyone, therefore, stand firm in his post like a good soldier. Let him take care lest a battalion so strong and well formed come to be broken through his fault; let not relaxation enter into the order through you.

It will be a good reflection for everyone to make account that religion, his mother, says to him those words in which the mother of the Maccabees spoke to her youngest son, encouraging him to suffer and to die for the observance of the law: *My son, have pity on me, who bore thee nine months in my womb, gave thee milk for three years, reared and bred thee to thy present age* (II Mac. vii. 27). "My son, I have borne you, not nine months, but nine years, and twenty years, and thirty years and more; I have given you milk for three years of probation and reared you in virtue and letters at so much cost to myself, till I set you in this state in which you now are. What I ask you in return for all this is to have compassion on me; let me not lose my honor in you, nor bring sorrow in my old age. Turn not against me, nor against yourself, the arms wherewith I have armed you for your own good and profit and that of your neighbor; let not what should have been an occasion and means of your being more thankful and more humble and mortified become an occasion of your being more vain, unrestrained, and unmortified."

CHAPTER XIV

That It Will Help Us Much Always to Behave As We Did the First Day We Entered Religion

ONE of those ancient monks once asked Abbot Agatho how he should behave in religion. He answered: "See what you were the first day you left the world and were received into the cloister, and such remain always." If, then, you desire to know how to be a good religious and how to advance much in virtue and perfection, this is a good means. Consider with what fervor and fortitude you left the world and all that you had in it—kindred, friends and acquaintance, property, riches, comforts, and amusements—and persevere in that contempt of the world and that forgetfulness of parents and relations, and that casting off of comforts and conveniences; and in that manner you will be a good religious. Consider also with what humility you asked to be received into religion and with what entreaty; and how, the day they granted your request, you thought that heaven was opened to you, and you felt a deep sense of gratitude to God and to your order for so great a boon and benefit; and go on now with this gratitude and humble acknowledgment. Feel now as much obliged and as much indebted as on the first day they received you; and in this manner you will advance in religion. Consider also, after your reception, with what devotion and modesty you behaved at the commencement, with what obedience, with what humility, with what promptitude, with what indifference and resignation in all things; and persevere always therein, and in this way you will go on thriving and growing in virtue and perfection.

This means is much commended by the saints, as we shall presently see; but it is necessary to understand it well. We do not mean to say that you ought not now to have more virtue than on the first day you entered religion. The veteran should never be content with the virtue of a novice, because it is clear that the veteran should have more virtue and be more advanced than the novice who began yesterday, as in study he who has been at his studies ten years ought to be more advanced and know more than the beginner. Religion is a school of virtue and perfection, and so he who has gone further in the school ought to have learned and advanced more. But just as, speaking to one who began to study with much fervor and great energy and afterwards has grown lazy and slack, we tell him to return to his first fervor and to the care and diligence with which he started at the beginning, and that in this way he will get on with his studies, so what we say now is that you should return to those first fervors with which you started on the way of virtue the very first day that you entered religion. See with what courage and spirit you began then to serve God, so that no obstacle could stand in your way and you made no difficulty about anything, and go on now with that fervor and with that same iron determination and strong resolution, and in this manner you will make great progress in religious life. That is what the saints mean to say of this method.

The blessed St. Anthony, when his disciples asked him to give them some spiritual advice for their improvement, began his discourse with this, as St. Athanasius relates in his Life; "Let this be the first thing of all that I charge you, that none should begin to abate the fervor with which he undertook the journey; but, as if starting afresh, let every one ceaselessly increase what he has begun." And besides many other repetitions of the same, when he was near death, by way of last will and testament, to impress it more on their hearts, he inculcated it once more in moving words, as the last words of a father: "I, my sons, in Scripture language am going the way of our fathers, since now the Lord calls me, and I desire to see Him in heaven; but you, sons of my heart, I exhort not to lose in a moment the labor of so many years; consider that this day you are starting religious life, and go on ever increasing in the firmness of this resolution." If you desire to progress in virtue and perfection, put this before your eyes every day; and make account that every day you are starting afresh and ever behave as though this was the first day that you had begun, and in this way you will be good religious. St. Augustine also puts this means: "Forget entirely everything that you have done up to this, and make account that every day you are starting anew."

St. Anthony used to explain this by a household example. As the servants and domestics of noblemen, however much they have served their masters and however much they have worked, fail not to put their hands to any new business that offers and stand ever as ready and prepared to do what they are bidden as they were the first day they entered service, as though they had done no service or work up to this; so, he said, we ought to serve God our Creator and Lord. We have a good example of this in the glorious St. Bernard. Surius relates in his Life that he reckoned others for saints and perfect men, and thought that as people advanced and moved far ahead in perfection they might be allowed sundry indulgences and licenses in sundry things. This is an excellent way not to make rash judgments of others when we see them doing anything of that sort. But for himself, he said that he always held himself for a beginner and novice, and that these licenses and exemptions did not befit him, and so he missed no point of the rigor of religious life nor of the common labors and exercises of humility. He was the first in all works of obedience and the first to put his hand to the broom and the dish-cloth. In no point did he seek exemption or excuse from doing as others; but when others were doing any manual work, and he did not know how to do it, then not to lose the occasion he managed to do something else instead and busied himself in some still more humble and lowly occupation. Sometimes he would take a pickax and set himself to turn up the ground, or a hatchet, and would cut wood and carry the pieces on his back to the kitchen; and he greatly rejoiced to occupy himself in such exercises, and thought that he had need of all this for his improvement! He was not like some who, when they do these things, say: "Just for example's sake;" because they think that they do not need them, nor that this does any good in their case. It is well that you do it for the sake of example and edification, but it would be better for you to consider that you also have need of it, since St. Bernard thought that he had such need.

St. Anthony here adds another good point that further explains what has gone before. The saint is not content with our not going back upon those first fervors with which we commenced, but wishes us always to be going on and advancing and growing more and more. As he who begins anew to serve God makes it his care every day to advance and grow in that service, seeing that hitherto all has been offences and sins, thereby to make up for the past and render himself worthy of the reward and prize; so we ought always to proceed like one who has attained nothing up to this, but has been a spendthrift and a squanderer.

This means, says St. Gregory, is suitable to all, even though they be very perfect; for the Prophet David was a perfect man and yet he said, like a beginner, *Today I have begun* (Psalm lxxvi. 11). He went on with as much fervor and diligence in the service of the Lord in extreme old age as though he would then begin anew to serve Him, according to the saying of the Wise Man: *When a man shall have finished, then he shall begin* (Ecclus. xviii. 6). The true servants of God, the farther they go and the nearer they approach to the goal and to perfection, make their way with greater care and fervor, *like men digging out a treasure,* as Job says (iii. 21). As those who are seeking a treasure by digging, says St. Gregory, the more they dig and the deeper they go, give themselves to the work with greater diligence because, understanding that the hidden treasure they seek is getting nearer and that they want but a little to strike upon it, they are thereby animated to labor more vigorously, and dig with greater zest and eagerness; so those who are really working at their own improvement and perfection, the farther they go on and the nearer they come to the end, throw themselves into the work with greater energy: "Oh, since the treasure is now near, let us animate ourselves and make an effort, since now little is wanting to reach it." *And that the more, as you see the day coming nigh,* as the Apostle says (Heb. x. 25); meaning, as St. Gregory says, that we should work harder, the nearer the reward and the prize. When a stone is moving in a downward direction, the nearer it approaches its center, the greater becomes its velocity and speed till it arrives; so when a man goes on advancing in virtue and perfection and is getting nearer and nearer to God, Who is his center and last end, the more energy he puts forth finally to arrive. These, St. Basil says, are they whom St. Paul calls *in carefulness not slothful, fervent in spirit, serving the Lord* (Rom. xii. 11). There are some who in their commencements, when they enter religion, start with fervor, and on leaving the novitiate at once slacken off and play the ancient; these are not *fervent in spirit,* but tepid and lazy. The fervent in spirit are they who go on ever as on the first day, with an ardent desire and an insatiable hunger, never glutted nor weary with the service of God, but ever desirous of serving Him more and more, according to the word of the prophet: *In thy commandments he shall delight exceedingly* (Psalm cxi. 1).

CHAPTER XV

That It Will Be a Great Help for Everyone to Ask Himself Frequently: "What Did You Enter Religion for?"

ANOTHER practice also will help us very much to grow in virtue and attain perfection; it is that which St. Bernard used, as Surius relates in his Life. He carried it ever in his head and often spoke to himself, saying: "Bernard, Bernard, for what hast thou come into religion?"—*Bernarde, ad quid venisti?* We read the same of the holy Abbot Arsenius, who often asked himself the same question: "Arsenius, Arsenius, for what hast thou come?" He often took account of himself. "Arsenius, why hast thou left the world? What was thy end and intention in leaving it and betaking thyself to religion? Was it not that therein thou mightest succeed in pleasing God entirely, and not trouble thyself about pleasing and satisfying men nor about standing high in their esteem? Take care of this, then, and make no account of the opinion and esteem of men. That would be going back to the world which thou hast left. Do not return to it in heart; little will it avail thee to be here in religion in body, if in heart thou art in the world, desiring the applause and esteem of men." With these thoughts those saints aroused and animated themselves greatly. We, too, should arouse and animate ourselves with the same, to go forward and overcome all difficulties that we meet with in religion. When you feel difficulty in any order of obedience, arouse yourself with these words: "For what purpose have you come into religion? Was it, perchance, to do your own will? Certainly not, but to follow the will of another. Why, then, do you wish to do your own?" When you feel any effect of poverty, you should animate yourself with this: "Did you, perchance, come here to seek your own conveniences, to have everything completely to your satisfaction, and to want nothing? Know you not that you have come to be poor, and to suffer need like a real poor man? Why have you to complain of then?" When you think that people do not make enough of you, animate and console yourself with this reflection: "Did you, perchance, come to religion to be regarded and esteemed? Certainly not, but to be forgotten of men, and to despise the opinion and esteem of the world. Why do you refuse what you have come for, and seek to return to what you have left?" This it is to be a religious—not to do your own will, to be poor, to suffer need, to seek to be forgotten and disregarded. This it is to be dead to the world and live to God.

For this we came into religion, and little will it profit us to be therein if we do not that for which we came; for it is not the place that makes saints, but a religious and perfect life. St. Augustine says this very well in a sermon that he gave to the religious who dwelt in the desert: "You see, brethren, here we are in solitude; we have left the world and are in religion. But it is not the place that makes holy the inhabitants, but good works—a religious life that will make the place holy and us also. Alas, holy as the place may be, and however strict the enclosure of religion, still you may sin there, and this means damnation. Trust not in that," says St. Augustine, "since the angel sinned in heaven, and Adam in paradise, and there was no place holier than those. The place does not make people holy; if the place were sufficient for that, neither the angel would have fallen from heaven, nor man from paradise." So do not think that you have done your business and are master of the field when you can say: "I am a religious; I am a member of the Society." That is not enough unless you do that for which you came to religion. See that you did not come to be a good student, or a learned graduate, or a good teacher but to be a good religious and aim at perfection. Oh, how very little it matters whether you turn out more or less of a scholar, or whether you turn out a great or a middling preacher! What does matter, what makes all the difference, is that you turn out a good and perfect religious. What *are* we doing, if we are not doing that? And what have we done all this while, if we have not done that? To what have we applied our minds if we have not applied them to that for which we came hither? My friend, my brother, whereunto art thou come? *Amice, ad quid venisti?* (Matt. xxvi. 50).

Take account of yourself and often ask yourself this question: "Ah, my God, what art or trade might I not have learned all these years I have been in the Society, and come out well in it by this time! If I had set myself to a painter, I should by this time have painted well; if to an embroiderer, I should know how to use my needle so cleverly as to gain my livelihood thereby. I have set myself to be a good religious and have not succeeded at that. So many years I have been going to the school of virtue and I have not yet learned the A B C of it. I have not yet attained the first degree of humility. Others become good philosophers and good theologians in seven years' time; and I, after so many years, have not become a good religious." Oh, if we sought and aimed at true virtues with as much care and diligence as we aim at learning!

St. Bernard says: "Many look to science, but few to conscience. If a good conscience were looked to with as much zeal and solicitude as vain and secular science is sought, it would be at once more speedily attained and more usefully retained"—*Multi quaerunt scientiam, pauci vero conscientiam. Si vero tanto studio et solicitudine quaereretur conscientia quanto quaeritur saecularis et vana scientia, et citius apprehenderetur et utilius retineretur.*

It were only fair that we should take as much care and pains over our spiritual progress as we do over our studies. St. Dorotheus says that he found this consideration a great help: "When I was a student in the world, I took my studies so much to heart that I remembered and thought of nothing else, not even of my dinner, and it seemed I had no time to think of what I had to eat, so much so that had it not been for my companion and very dear friend who took care to provide me with something to eat and to call me at dinner-time, often I would have forgotten to eat. The vehement desire that I had to learn went so far that, when I was at table, I had my book always open before me, that I might eat and study at the same time; and at night, when I came from school, I at once lit my candle and studied till midnight; and when I lay down to sleep, I took my book to bed, and after I had slept awhile, I fell to reading again, and was so wholly taken up with this passion for study that I could take no delight in anything else. Since I came to be a religious man, I have often reflected and said to myself: 'If thou wert hereto so ardent in thy desires to acquire eloquence and human letters, what great pains and care oughtest thou not to take now in order to acquire true virtues and true wisdom, seeing that thou art come here for no other purpose?' And from this thought I gathered no little strength."

Let us, then, rouse and animate ourselves also with this consideration, that it is of greater concern for us to be good religious than to be good students and good men of letters. All our solicitude and diligence ought to be how to attain to this divine wisdom; that should be our business. The Son of God had no other business on earth but to occupy Himself in loving us and seeking our advancement and greater good, and that at so much cost to Himself. And shall we think it much to have no other business here but to occupy ourselves in loving and pleasing God and seeking and procuring His greater glory? *Wherefore lift up your hands that hang down as if tired, and brace up your loose knees* (Heb. xii. 12). Abandoning tepidity and sloth, let us put trifles aside and quicken our pace. *Let us make haste to enter into that rest* (Heb. iv. 11). Let us push on and cover the ground to climb the mountain of perfection and glory, *even to the mountain of God, Horeb* (III Kings xix. 8). And as a traveler that has slept till late in the morning makes haste to repair the time he has lost, by mending his pace till he overtake his company that has gone ahead, so should we make haste and never stop in our course till we have recovered the time we have lost by our negligence. Oh, how my companions and brothers have gone ahead, and I alone am left behind, notwithstanding that I began my journey first and entered into religion before them! Oh, that we regretted so much the time we have lost hitherto, and felt it so much that it might serve us as a spur to run henceforth with great ardor!

Denis the Carthusian relates an incident taken from the lives of the ancient Fathers. There was a youth who wanted to enter religion, but his mother endeavored to thwart his good purpose and brought up many reasons, to all of which the young man simply answered: "I want to save my soul" —*Salvare volo animam meam.* At last, as she could do nothing with him, she let him go and he entered religion. But after a while his fervor cooled down and he began to live very carelessly. Then it came to pass that his mother died, and he fell dangerously ill. In a trance he was carried before the judgment seat of God and saw his mother, with many others, expecting sentence of condemnation. His mother, turning her eyes, saw her son in the ranks of those who were to be condemned, and in amazement cried out: "Son, hast thou come to this? What has become of those words: 'I want to save my soul'?" He felt so ashamed that he did not know what to answer. He came out of the trance, and it pleased God that he should get better. He took the vision as a warning from God, and changed so much that he was wholly given over to bewailing the past and doing penance. Many people endeavored to persuade him to moderate and abate some part of his austerities, lest he should destroy his health by them, but he rejected all their advice, saying: "If I could not suffer the reproaches of my mother, how shall I suffer those of Christ and His holy angels on the day of judgment?"

CHAPTER XVI

Of Some Other Things That Will Help Us to Go On in Self-Improvement and Gain Perfection

BE ye perfect as your Heavenly Father is perfect (Matt. v. 48), says Christ our Redeemer in that sovereign Sermon on the Mount. St. Cyprian on these words says: "If to men it is matter of exultation and glory to have sons like themselves, and then they rejoice, more and more glad at having become fathers when they see that in features, air, and demeanor and in all things their children are in the likeness of their parents, how much more will our heavenly Father be glad and rejoice when He sees that His spiritual sons are coming out like Himself! What a palm of victory, what a reward, what a crown, what a glory, think you, will it be that you should be such that God may not have to complain of you: *I have begotten sons, and reared them and exalted them, and they have dishonored me* (Isaias i. 2)"—but that you should be such that your works may redound to the great glory and honor of your heavenly Father! This is the great glory of God, to have sons so like Him that through them He comes to be known, honored, and glorified.

But how shall we be like our heavenly Father? St. Augustine tells us: We shall be like God in proportion as we partake of His justice and holiness; the more just and perfect we are, the more we shall resemble our heavenly Father. Therefore does the Lord so much desire us to be holy and perfect, and reminds us of it and repeats it frequently—sometimes by St. Paul: *This is the will of God, your sanctification* (I Thess. iv. 3); sometimes by St. Matthew: *Be ye perfect as your Heavenly Father is perfect* (Matt. v. 48); at other times by the Apostle St. Peter: *Be ye holy, because I the Lord your God am holy* (I Pet. i. 16;

Levit. xi. 44). This is the will of our heavenly Father. It is a great satisfaction to parents to have good, wise, and holy children. *A wise son,* says Solomon, *is the joy of his father;* and, contrariwise, *a foolish and worthless son is the sorrow of his mother* (Prov. x. 1). For this reason, if there were no other, we should endeavor to give ourselves to virtue and perfection, to give satisfaction to God. This should ever be the principal motive of all our actions, the satisfaction of God and His greater honor and glory.

Besides this, we will mention sundry other motives to aid and animate us thereto. St. Augustine says that the reason why Holy Scripture calls us so many times *sons of God—I will be your Father, and you shall be my sons*—and why the prophets so often repeat it, and the Apostle St. Paul: *Be ye imitators of God, as most dear sons* (Eph. v. 1); and the Apostle St. John: *See what great love the Father hath for us, granting us to be called and to be sons of God* (I John iii. 1), and in many other places—the reason, he says, of this frequent repetition is to induce us, seeing and considering our dignity and excellence, to value ourselves and watch over ourselves with greater care and diligence. A rich dress is kept with much solicitude, and great care is taken that no stain fall upon it. A precious stone and other rich articles are kept with greater care. We should keep with great care what we have received and call ourselves to great account for it. That is why, as St. Augustine says, Holy Scripture so often puts before us the fact that we are sons of God and that God Himself is our Father, to the end that we may behave as His sons whose sons we are and not fall away or degenerate from the high and generous thoughts of sons of God.

Pope St. Leo agrees, saying: "Recognize your dignity; remember that you are a son of God and do nothing unworthy of the nobility and high birth of such a son"—*Divinae consors factus naturae noli in veterem vilitatem degeneri conversatione redire: memento cuius capitis et cuius cor-*

poris sis membrum. St. Paul in the Acts of the Apostles sets this before the Athenians to animate and raise them to higher things: *for we are of divine lineage, being of divine lineage, etc.* (Acts xvii. 28). To apply that to ourselves, and keep up the example which St. Augustine gives of the dress: as any stain looks very ugly on a rich dress, and the richer the stuff, the more unsightly does it appear—on brocade or gold lace a stain is a great disfigurement, but on sackcloth it is not seen and no account is taken of it—so in them who live there in the world the stain of a venial sin is not noticed, and oftentimes even of a mortal sin, and no account is taken of it, sad to say; but in religious, who are the cherished and petted sons of God, any stain and any imperfection is conspicuous and strikes the eye—a want of modesty, a slight murmuring, an impatient and angry word, gives great offence and disedification here, whereas among men of the world it is taken no notice of. Dust on the feet is no consideration, but on the eyes and in the pupils of the eyes it is a considerable matter, and very much so. Worldly people are as the feet of this body of the Church; religious are as the eyes and pupils of the eyes; thus any fault in a religious is very considerable, because it takes off the gilding and causes great unsightliness in him, and therefore he is bound very carefully to guard against anything of the sort.

Another helpful means of self-improvement we have touched on above; it is to understand that we have still a long way to go and that what we hold and have gained hitherto is as nothing. This means also is suggested to us by the text quoted before. Why, think you, does Christ our Redeemer say: *Be ye perfect as your Heavenly Father is perfect?* (Matt. v. 48). Can we possibly attain to the perfection of our heavenly Father? *Can man possibly appear just in comparison with God?* (Job iv. 17). No, certainly, not by thousands of miles; how ever much we advance, there will always be an infinite distance between us and

Him. Yet He tells us to be perfect as our heavenly Father is perfect, to give us to understand that on this road of virtue we must ever be moving on and never be content with what we have got, but labor for what is still wanting. Saints commonly say, and very rightly, that there is no surer sign of a man's being far from perfection than his thinking that he has already attained it; for on this marvelous road, the farther a man journeys, the more ground he sees still before him to cover, and how much is wanting to him.

St. Bonaventure says that, as the higher a man climbs a mountain, the more ground he sees, so the nearer a man approaches the summit of this mountain of perfection, the more it opens out upon him for further exertion. It is a common experience, in looking at a high mountain from afar, to fancy that it reaches the sky and that from thence we could touch the sky with our hand; but as we go on with our journey and reach the top, we find that the sky is much higher than that. So on this road of perfection and knowledge and love of God, *Man shall ascend to a high heart, and God shall be exalted still higher* (Psalm lxiii. 7-8). So St. Cyprian explains this passage, that the higher we mount in the knowledge of God, the higher God remains. However much you know of God, there is much more to know; and however much you love Him, there is much more to love. There is always room to mount on this road of perfection; and if anyone thinks that he has reached and gained perfection, it is because he is far off and so fancies that he could touch the sky with his hand.

This may be also understood from what we see in earthly sciences. The more a man knows, the better he appreciates the shortcomings of his knowledge. And so that philosopher said: "The only thing that I know is that I know nothing." And a great musician used to say sadly that he knew nothing, because he seemed to himself to descry such vast fields of knowledge as he could never attain or understand. So is this knowledge of God. The servants of God who have studied and made much progress therein know well how much is wanting to them for the attainment of perfection. And this is the reason why the farther a man advances, the humbler he is, partly because as one grows in other virtues, one grows also in humility and self-knowledge and self-contempt, all these things going together; and again because the more light and appreciation a man has of the goodness and majesty of God, the deeper becomes his knowledge of his own misery and nothingness. *Abyss cries to abyss* (Psalm xli. 8), the great abyss of the knowledge of God and of His goodness and infinite majesty discovers to us the depths of our own misery; and by the beams of this divine light we come to see the specks and motes of our imperfections and how much we still want of being perfect. The novice and the beginner sometimes fancies that he has now got virtue; that is because he does not know how much he is wanting in it. A man that has little or no skill in painting, when he sees a picture, admires it at once and discovers no fault; a good painter comes along, looks at it attentively, and discovers many faults. The same falls here; you are not master of the art of self-knowledge, and therefore fail to see the faults there are in this picture of your soul; whereas another, who is better skilled in that art, sees them very well. Let all this serve to inflame us with a desire of acquiring that virtue we still want, for *blessed are those who hunger and thirst after justice* (Matt. v. 6); that is to say, as St. Jerome explains it, they who, however just they are, are never satisfied and never think their present estate enough, but hunger continually after more virtue and perfection, as did the Prophet David when he said and begged of God: *Lord, wash me yet more and more from my iniquity, and cleanse me from my sins.* I am not content with being cleansed and washed of my sins; I am not content with being white, but I would fain that Thou wouldst make me white as snow and whiter even than snow. *Thou shalt sprinkle with hyssop, and I shall be cleansed: Thou shalt wash me, and I shall be made whiter than snow* (Psalm l. 9). Thus we should cry and raise our voices to God: "Lord, give me more humility, more patience, more charity, more mortification, more indifference and resignation!" *Wash me yet more.*

CHAPTER XVII

Of the Perseverance We Ought to Have in Virtue, and What Will Aid Us Thereto

ST. AUGUSTINE, on the words of St. Paul: *No one is crowned, but he who lawfully fighteth* (II Tim ii. 5), says that to fight lawfully is to fight with perseverance to the end, and that he it is who deserves to be crowned who does this. St. Jerome also says: "Many enter on the way of virtue and perfection, but few persevere in it to the end"—*Coepisse multorum est; ad culmen pervenisse paucorum.*

There went out of Egypt, says Holy Writ (Num. i. 1-47; xiv. 29-30), six hundred thousand men, besides women and children, and of all that number two only entered the Land of Promise. Thus it is no great thing to begin well; the difficulty is not there, but in persevering and ending well. St. Ephrem says that as when you build a house, the difficulty is not in laying the foundation, but in raising the building to its perfect height; and the higher the building is raised, the more the labor and expenses increase: so in the spiritual building, the hardest task is not to lay the foundation, but to carry your work on to perfection; it will avail us nothing to have begun well, unless we also end well. "In Christians," says St. Jerome, "we consider not how they begin, but how they end. St. Paul began ill, but ended well; Judas began well, but ended ill." What did it avail him to have been an apostle of Christ and to have worked miracles? What will your good beginnings profit you if you come to a bad end? It is to perseverance alone that the crown is promised. *He who shall persevere to the end, he shall be saved* (Matt. xxiv. 13). Jacob saw Almighty God not at the foot, nor in the middle, but at the top of the ladder; to let us know, says St. Jerome, that "it is not enough to begin well, nor yet to go on doing well only for a time, unless we hold on and persevere to the end." St. Bernard says: "Put the term of your journey and perseverance where Christ put it, of whom St. Paul says: *He was obedient unto death* (Phil. ii. 8); because however far you run, if it be not unto death, you will not gain the crown."

Christ our Redeemer gives us a special warning of this in the holy Gospel: *Whosoever setteth his hand to the plough, and looketh back, is not fit for the kingdom of heaven* (Luke ix. 62). As also when at another time He bids us *remember Lot's wife* (Luke xvii. 32). What was it she did? God having brought her out of Sodom in order to save her from the fire that consumed the city, she stopped upon the way and turned to look behind her, and immediately, in the very place where she turned her head, she was changed into a statue of salt. What does that signify? Do you know what? St. Augustine says: "Salt seasons and preserves things; and therefore our Savior would have us remember Lot's wife to the end that, looking upon what happened to her, we may preserve ourselves with that salt, and take warning therefrom to persevere in the way of goodness that we have entered upon, and not turn back, for fear lest we also be turned into statues of salt, from whence others may take salt for their preservations and perseverance, seeing our fall. How many do we see nowadays who serve us only for statues of salt, for our preservation! Let us, then, be wise at other men's cost and do nothing to make other men wise at ours.

St. Augustine and St. Jerome further add that to begin well and end ill is to make monsters, since those works and actions which begin by being good according to reason and end in evil and sensuality, are grotesque figures, as if a painter to the head of a man should add the neck of a horse; such a thing it is to begin well and end badly. With this St. Paul reproaches the people of Galatia who had gone back: *Are ye so senseless that, having begun in the spirit, ye are ending in the flesh? Who hath bewitched you?* (Gal. iii. 3).

That we should be able to persevere and obtain this reward from the Lord, it is necessary to take care to establish ourselves well in virtue and mortification, lest for want of solid foundation we come to deteriorate and fall. Worm-eaten apples quickly fall and never ripen, but the good and sound ones remain on the tree until they come to maturity. In the same manner, if your virtue be not solid and your heart be vain; if there be within it some little worm of presumption, or pride, or impatience, or other irregular passion, that worm will by degrees gnaw away and consume all the pith of it and weaken the substance and rigor of your virtue and endanger your perseverance. The Apostle says: *It is very important to confirm and fortify your heart by grace* (Heb. xiii. 9) with true and solid virtues.

Albertus Magnus well explains how we should be well grounded in virtues so as to be able to continue and persevere in them. He says that a true servant of God ought to be so grounded in virtue and have it so deep fixed in his heart, as to have it always in his power to practise it and not depend upon what others may do and say. There are a sort of people that seem to be humble and very peaceable so long as nothing thwarts them and all things happen to their liking; but upon the least cross accident that occurs, this peace vanishes and they come out in their true colors and show what they are. In this case, says Albertus, this virtue of peace and humility is not in them, but in the people about them. It is the virtue of others and not yours, because they take it away and make you a present of it when they please. This is being good by the virtue of another, as people in the world say when they are praised:

"So it shall be by our favor, sir." And they say true. [*Eso será para virtual de vuestra merced;* i.e., "My merits are your kindness;" i.e., "It is very kind of you to make me out so."] You ought to be good, not by another's virtue but by your own virtue, the virtue that is in yourself and does not depend on others. These people are well compared to still cesspools; if you let them alone, they emit no bad smell: but if you stir them up, they are unendurable. Thus people, so long as you do not touch them but let them go on according to the taste of their own palate, seem clear water; but stir them up a little, and you will see what an odor they send forth. *Touch the mountains, and they will smoke* (Psalm cxliii. 5).

CHAPTER XVIII

Of Another Means to Advance in Virtue; Namely, Spiritual Exhortations and Conferences, and How to Profit by Them

AMONG other means which a religious order and our Society in particular provides to aid and animate its subjects to advance in virtue and perfection, spiritual conferences and exhortations, concerning which we have a rule, hold a chief place. Accordingly we shall say something of the way how to profit by them, which may serve to help all the world to profit by the sermons which they hear. In the first place, it will help much to this end not to go to exhortations by routine and for form's sake, but with a sincere desire of profiting and getting good by them. Let us consider with what eager longings those Fathers of the Desert met for those spiritual collections and conferences which they held, and what good store of provision they took from thence back to their cells. With the like eagerness and desire should we go to exhortations, and then they will turn to our profit; as, when a man goes to dinner with a good appetite, it then appears that what he eats is likely to do him good. St. Chrysostom observes that, as hunger is a sign of the body's being in good health, so a longing desire of being nourished with the word of God is a sign of a good and happy disposition of the soul. But if you do not hunger after the divine word nor find any relish in it, it is a bad sign, and shows that you are sick, since you have lost your appetite and your soul loathes this spiritual food. If for no other reason, the mere thought of hearing a little speech and discourse of God should be enough to make us go to these conferences with great relish and delight, for naturally a man is glad to hear another speak well of one he loves, as a father to hear of his son. If you loved God, you would delight to hear Him spoken of. So Christ our Redeemer says: *He who is of God, heareth the Word of God, and the reason why ye desire not to hear it, is because ye are not of God* (John viii. 47).

Secondly, if we intend to draw benefit from these discourses, we must not hear them in a spirit of curiosity, marking the good language, the graceful action and pronunciation, the quaint and new conceits of the preacher. It is this that with great reason we blame in secular persons, and this is why nowadays many profit so little by sermons. We should turn away our eyes from that and fix them on the substance of what is said. What should we say of a sick man whom the barber-surgeon comes to bleed, and he, instead of letting himself be bled, takes to admiring the instruments. "Oh, what a neat lancet!" "Oh, what a pretty razor!" "Oh, what an elegant sheath; where was it made?" Leave that alone, and let yourself be bled: that is your business; the rest is no affair of yours.

The like do they who neglect the substance of what is said, which is what they stand in need of, and occupy themselves with the words, the plan and artifice of the discourse. Such people may aptly be compared to a sieve or bolter, which retains only the chaff and bean and lets all the corn and meal pass through. The Second Book of Esdras says that, when Esdras read the law of God to the people of Israel, such was their emotion and so loud their lamentations and groans, comparing their doings and life with the law which they heard, that the Levites had to go about pacifying them and proclaiming silence, to enable the reader to continue. It is in this way that exhortations and sermons should be heard, with confusion and compunction of heart, considering how different we are from the standard they put before us and how far we are from the perfection there proposed.

In the third place, and by way of confirmation of what has gone before, all should understand that these exhortations are not for the saying of new and extraordinary things, but to bring to mind common and ordinary things, things that we have daily in hand, and to warm our hearts to them. We should go to them on this understanding; and thus casting aside all curiosity, we shall profit more by them. To this end our Father expressly orders that these discourses be given in our Society. "Let there be someone," he says, "who every week, or at least every fortnight, shall deliver these and the like admonitions, lest by the weakness of our nature things be forgotten and their execution dropped." By the way, Father Master Nadal notes here in his Observations on the Constitutions, that though the Constitution uses the disjunctive, "every week, *or* at least every fortnight," nevertheless it is the universal custom of the Society that this is not put off for a fortnight, but is done every week. The Society has taken the better course, and no one could say this better than Nadal, since he had visited almost the whole Society and knew well the universal custom of the same. These discourses are to refresh the memory of what we know, because we easily forget what is good and need to have it told to us again and again. And even though we hold it in memory, yet we must have it cried out to us to quicken our will and desire, telling us of our obligation and profession and what we have come to religion for. True is that saying of St. Augustine: "The understanding flies before, but little or no movement of the heart follows"—*Praevolat intellectus; sequitur tardus vel nullus affectus.* Therefore it is necessary to say the same thing many times over, as did St. Paul to the Philippians: *For the rest, brethren, rejoice in the Lord: to write to you the same thing is no trouble to me, and is necessary for you* (Phil. iii. 1). The Apostle was in no want of things to say—he who had been raised to the third heaven could tell them things new and exquisite; but he felt himself obliged to say and repeat the same things that he had already said, because that was more necessary for them. And this should be the particular aim of him who gives these exhortations and of him who preaches sermons, not to say what promises to make him appear more learned and erudite—for that would be to preach of himself—but what promises best for the benefit of his hearers; and this is what the hearers also themselves should look for. Thus they will not wax weary of hearing common things that they know, for they will see that they do them not, or anyhow do them not with such perfection as they ought.

Fourthly, it will be of very great profit that whatever is said in exhortations be received by each one as particularly addressed to himself and not as a thing said for the benefit of others. Let us not act herein as worldly persons ordinarily do when they hear a sermon. A great teacher used to say: "All you who hear me are like carvers, for all the business of the carver is to cut up for others and take nothing for himself. So you, when you hear me, say: 'Oh, what a good point for Dick! Oh, how that will come home to Harry! Oh, if that neighbor of mine were here, how it would meet his case!' and you keep nothing for yourselves. I want guests, not carvers of the word of God." *Every wise word that the prudent man shall hear,* says Ecclesiasticus (xxi. 18), *he will approve and take to himself; but the vicious and vain is displeased with it, and throweth it over his shoulders.* Let us, then, be wise and let everyone take what is said as said for him, as if it were said for him alone and he alone were being spoken to and no other. Possibly, what seems to come home well to another will come home better to yourself; we often see the mote in our neighbor's eye and see not the beam in our own (Matt. vii. 3). This especially because, though at present you feel not that the point touches you, you should store it up for afterwards, when you will find the need of it, and that perhaps very soon. Thus you should always take what is said as said for you alone.

In the fifth place, better to clear up what we have said, it is highly proper that all should understand and always take for granted that, when a thing is mentioned or reprehended in these addresses, it is not as implying that the mischief is already in the house, but simply that it may never come to be there. Preventive and preservative medicine is much better than what is given for the cure of a malady already broken out. And this is what we do in these exhortations, according to the counsel of the Wise Man: *Apply the medicine before the illness* (Ecclus. xviii. 20). We apply the medicine and the remedy before the sickness comes, exhorting to what is good and censuring what is evil, that no one may come to fall into what he knows already for a thing evil and dangerous. Thus it would be a great fault to form such a judgment as: "This is said for our friend John," and still more to utter it. The speaker does not intend to note any one in particular—for that would not be prudent nor profitable, but would rather do harm. So to pass such a judgment would be to condemn the giver of the exhortation of doing a thing that would be very ill done.

But, although this circumspection and care should be observed on the part of him who preaches or gives the conference, yet on the part of the listener it will be very well for everyone to take what is said as said for himself and for himself alone. Not that he should understand that it was the speaker's purpose to point to him and mark him out, for that would be wrong, as we have said, but that everyone in the audience should begin listening with his hand on his breast; and, comparing his actions and life with what he hears, should say: "Truly all this is addressed to me; I stand in great need of it; God has put it into his mouth for my benefit;" for from this much fruit will be gained. From the conversation that Christ our Redeemer held with the Samaritan woman the holy Gospel says that she went away crying out and saying: *Come and see a man who hath told me all that hath befallen me* (John iv. 29). When the preacher speaks to his audience and tells them what passes in their souls, then the sermon and conference is a good one, and it is that which satisfies them and does them good.

Sixthly, it is necessary that we should understand the word of God to be the food and sustenance of the soul; and so we should always contrive to gather something from conferences and sermons to keep and preserve in our heart, to strengthen and sustain us for subsequent action. On these words of Christ: *The good soil on which the seed falls are they who with a good heart and good disposition hear and receive the word of God, and bear fruit of good works in patience,* St. Gregory says that, as it is a grave and dangerous infirmity for a man not to retain in his stomach the bodily food which he eats, but cast it up at once, so is it not to retain in one's heart the word of God that one hears, but it comes in at one ear and goes out at the other. The prophet says: *I have hidden away, O Lord, and guarded thy words in my heart, not to sin* (Psalm cxviii. 11), to resist temptations, to rouse myself to virtue and perfection. How often does it happen that one is under temptation and in some danger, and one remembers some text of Holy Scripture or some other good thing that one has heard and thereupon one is strengthened and animated and feels much benefit! With three texts of Holy Scripture Christ our

Redeemer overcame and routed the three temptations with which the devil assailed Him (Matt. iv. 4, 7, 10).

From what has been said it will be seen how reprehensible they are who go to conferences and sermons for form's sake, or are there sleeping, or distracted and thinking of other things, which comes to the same as sleeping. The holy Gospel says: *The devil cometh and taketh the word out of their heart, that they may not be saved* (Luke viii. 12) or profit thereby. These are the birds of prey that devour the grain that it may not spring up. Possibly that word which you lost when you were asleep or distracted was a means to your improvement; and the devil, for the envy that he bears to your good, contrives in all the ways that he can that it may not take root in your heart. St. Augustine says that the word of God is like a fishhook, that takes when it is taken. As when the fish takes the hook it is caught and held thereby, so when you take and receive the word of God, you are taken and held by it. That is why the devil labors so much to draw off your attention, that you may not apprehend what is said, that you may not be held by it, and that it may not gain any hold on your heart. Let us, then, make it our endeavor to go to conferences and sermons with due dispositions and so to hear the word of God that it may take hold on our heart and bear fruit. The Apostle St. James says: *Be ye not hearers only of the word of God, but doers.* Do not deceive yourselves by thinking that you fulfil all you ought by listening, for *he that heareth the word of God and doeth it not is like a man who looketh at his own face in a looking-glass, and presently goeth away and forgetteth his form and figure* (James i. 22-23). They alone shall be justified who put things into execution; for, as St. Paul says, *it is not the hearers of the law that shall be accounted just before God, but the doers of the law shall be justified* (Rom. ii. 13).

In the "Spiritual Meadow," which was composed by John Eviratus, or according to others, by St. Sophronius, Patriarch of Jerusalem, and was approved in the Second Council of Nicaea, [and Theodoret has the story in his "Religious History," which see] it is related that one day a holy man named Eusebius was sitting with another named Amianus, reading a book of the Gospels. Amianus read and the other explained as he went on. Now it happened that some laborers were working on the land in a field. Eusebius was distracted by looking at them, and did not attend to the reading. Then Amianus, having a doubt about a passage he was reading, asked Eusebius to explain it. Eusebius, as he had not been attending, asked him to read it again. Amianus saw he had been distracted and reproved him, saying: "No wonder you did not notice, as you should have done, the words of the Gospel; you were amusing yourself, watching those laborers." When Eusebius heard this reproof, he was so ashamed of himself that he gave command to his eyes that at no time should they find satisfaction in looking at any sight, not even at the stars of heaven. Thence he took a narrow path homewards and shut himself up in a hut and never went out of it again for all the rest of his life. In this strait prison he lived for forty years and more, until he died. And that necessity as well as reason might compel him to keep quiet, he bound himself by the loins with a girdle of iron, and with another heavier cincture about his neck. To these cinctures of iron he fastened a chain, and the chain he fastened to the ground, so that he was forced to remain bent and could not go freely, nor look on any sight, not even on the stars of heaven. In this way the servant of God punished himself for one inadvertence and distraction that happened at the exposition of the word of God—to our confusion who make so little account of the many distractions that we have.

SECOND TREATISE

ON THE PERFECTION OF OUR ORDINARY ACTIONS

CHAPTER I

That Our Advancement and Perfection Consists in Doing Ordinary Actions Extraordinarily Well

THOU shalt go justly about what is just, says the Lord to His people (Deut. xvi. 20) : what is good and just, do it well, justly, and in knightly fashion. The business of our advancement and perfection does not consist in doing things, but in doing them well; as neither does it consist in being a religious, but in being a good religious. Paulinus made much of St. Jerome's living in the Holy Places, where Christ our Lord wrought the mysteries of our redemption; and St. Jerome wrote back to him: "It is not the living in Jerusalem that is praiseworthy, but the living well in Jerusalem." Which saying afterwards became a proverb to warn religious not to be content with being in religion, because, as the habit does not make the monk, so neither does the place, but a good and holy life. The point is not being a religious, but being a good religious; not doing the exercises of religious life, but doing them well. All our good consists in what the Evangelist St. Mark relates that the people said of Christ: *He hath done all things well* (Mark vii. 37).

It is certain that all our good and all our evil depends on our works according as they are good or evil, for we ourselves shall be such as our works have been. They tell what each man is made of, for by the fruit the tree is known. St. Augustine says that the man is the tree, and the works the fruit that it bears; and thus by the fruit of works it is known what each man is. And therefore Christ our Redeemer said of those hypocrites and false preachers: *By the fruit of their works ye shall know what they are* (Matt. vii. 20). And, contrariwise, He says of Himself:

The works that I do give testimony of me; if ye will not believe me, believe my works, for they tell who I am (John x. 25, 38). And our works tell not only what each one is in this life, but also what he must be in the next; for we shall be such forever in the life to come as our works have been in this; for God our Lord will recompense and reward everyone according to his works. As is often said in Holy Writ, as well in the Old as in the New Testament: *Thou, O Lord,* says the psalmist, *wilt render to everyone according to his works* (Psalm lxi. 13); and St. Paul: *What a man soweth, the same shall he reap.*

But let us descend to particulars and see what those works are upon which all our good and all our advancement and perfection depend. I say these are no other than our common and ordinary actions, such as we go through every day. In holding to it that that ordinary meditation which we make be well made, in making those examens that we make well made, in hearing mass and saying it as we ought, in reciting our hours and other devotions with deference and attention, in exercising ourselves continually in penance and mortification, in doing our office and the duty laid upon us by obedience so that it be well done, in this rests our advancement and perfection. If we do these actions perfectly, we shall be perfect; if we do them imperfectly, we shall be imperfect. And this is the difference between a good and perfect religious and an imperfect and tepid one; the difference lies not in the doing of more or different things in this case and in that, but in doing what one does perfectly or imperfectly. For this reason is the one a good and perfect religious, that he gets these things well done; and for this, is the other imperfect, that he does them with much tepidity and negligence. And the more a man lays himself out and goes forward in this particular, the more perfect or imperfect will he be.

In that parable of the sower who went out to sow his seed, the holy Gospel says that even the good seed, sown on good soil, yielded here thirty-fold, there sixty-fold, and there a hundred-fold (Matt. xiii. 23). Whereby, as the saints explain, are denoted the three different degrees of those that serve God—beginners, proficient, and perfect. We all sow the same seed, because we all do the same actions and observe the same rule; all of us have the same hours for meditation and examens and from morning till night we are all occupied by obedience; yet, for all that, how one man excels another—*homo homini qui praestat!* What a difference, they say, between Peter and Peter, between one religious and another! The reason is that in one the works that he sows yield a hundred-fold, inasmuch as he does them with spirit and perfection, and these are the perfect; in another they yield increase, but not so much, only sixty-fold, and these are they who go on improving; in another they yield only thirty-fold, and these we are saying are beginners in God's service. Let everyone, therefore, see to which of these degrees he is arrived. See if you be not amongst those who yield only thirty-fold; and God grant that none of us find ourselves of the number of them of whom the Apostle St. Paul says that on the foundation of faith they have built wood and straw and chaff to burn in the day of the Lord (I Cor. iii. 12-13).

Take care, therefore, you do nothing out of ostentation, out of human respect, to please men, or to gain their esteem; for this were to make a building of wood, straw, and chaff, to burn at least in purgatory; but endeavor to do all your actions with the greatest perfection you are able, and that will be to *erect a structure all of silver, gold, and precious stones.*

The fact that herein lies our advancement and perfection will be well understood from this consideration. All our advancement and perfection consists in two things: in doing what God would have us do, and in doing it as He would have us do it; nothing more can be asked, nothing more can be desired than this. As to the first, the doing of what God would have us do, by the mercy of God we have already secured that in religion; and this is one of the greatest advantages and greatest comforts that we enjoy; that we are sure that in the occupations given us by obedience we are doing what God would have us do. This stands for a first principle in religion, drawn from the Gospel and the doctrine of the saints. *He that heareth you, heareth me* (Luke x. 16). In obeying the superior, we obey God and do His will, for that is what God requires us to do there and then. There remains the second point, which is, doing things as God would have us do them; that is, with all possible perfection, because so God would have us do them. And that is what we are going to speak of. It is recounted in the Chronicles of the Cistercian Order, that St. Bernard, being with his religious at matins, saw a multitude of angels who noted and wrote down what the monks did and how they did it. They noted the doings of some in letters of gold, of others in silver, of others in ink, of others in water, according to the attention and fervor with which each one prayed and sang. But of some they wrote nothing at all, who, being present in body but absent in spirit, let themselves be carried away with vain and unprofitable thoughts. He saw also that chiefly at the Te Deum the angels were much concerned that it should be sung very devoutly, and that from the mouths of some, when they intoned it, there came out as it were a flame of fire. Therefore let everyone see what his prayer is like; whether it deserves to be written in gold, or in ink, or in water, or not to be written at all. See whether, when you are at prayer, there come forth from your heart and mouth flames of fire, or yawns and expressions of disgust. See whether you are there in body only, but in spirit at your studies or your office or business, or other things not to the point.

CHAPTER II

That It Ought Greatly to Animate Us to Perfection, That God Has Put It in Something That Is Very Easy

FATHER MASTER NADAL, a man distinguished in our Society for his learning and virtue, when he came to visit the provinces of Spain, made this one of the chief recommendations that he left behind him, that our advancement and perfection consisted in doing well the particular ordinary and daily things that we have in hand. Thus our progress and improvement does not lie in a multiplication of other extraordinary works, nor in filling high and exalted offices, but in doing perfectly the ordinary duties of religion and filling those offices in which obedience places us, though they be the meanest in the world, because that is what God requires of us. On this we should fix our eyes if we wish to please Him and attain perfection. Let us, then, consider at what a little cost we may be perfect, since we may be that by doing what we actually are doing without adding further works, which should be a great consolation for all and animate us much to perfection. If we demanded of you for your perfection exquisite and extraordinary things, elevations and lofty contemplations, you might excuse yourself, saying that you could not venture so high. If we demanded of you daily disciplines to blood, or fasting on bread and water, or going barefoot with a perpetual hairshirt, you might say that you did not feel strong enough for that; but that is not what we demand of you, nor in that does your perfection lie, but in doing the very thing that you are doing, taking care that it be well done. With the same works that you are doing, if you like, you can be perfect: the cost is already paid; you need not add more works. Who will not be animated hereby to be perfect, when perfection comes so ready to his hand and lies in a thing so familiar and so feasible?

God said to His people, to animate them to His service and the observance of His law: *The commandment that I give thee this day is not a thing very far and very exalted above thee, nor is it set there on the horn of the moon, that thou shouldst be able to say: which of us can mount up to heaven to reach it? Nor again is it a thing on the far side of the sea, that thou shouldst take occasion to say: who shall be able to cross the sea, and bring it hither from such a distance? No, it is very near and very ready to thy hand* (Deut. xxx. 11-14). We may say the same of the perfection of which we now speak. So with this consideration the blessed St. Anthony exhorted and animated his disciples to perfection. "The Greeks," he said, "to attain to philosophy and the other sciences, take great journeys and long voyages with great labor and risk to themselves; but we, to attain virtue and perfection, which is the true wisdom, have no need to put ourselves to such labors and perils, not even to stir out of our house, since within the house we shall find it, and even within ourselves. *The kingdom of God is within you* (Luke xvii. 21)"—*Graeci studia transmarina sectantur; regnum autem coelorum intra vos est.* In these ordinary and daily things that you do your perfection lies.

An ordinary question at spiritual conferences at a time of devotion, such as Lent, Advent, Whitsuntide, or renovation of vows, is what means will help us to dispose and prepare ourselves for this renovation, or this Lent, or to receive the Holy Ghost or the Child Jesus newly born. You will see given such and such means and such and such considerations, all good. But the principal means, and that on which we ought to insist, is that of which we speak now; namely, to perfect ourselves in our ordinary actions. Go to work ridding yourself of the faults and imperfections which you commit in these ordinary and daily things; contrive daily to do them better and with fewer faults, and that will be a very good, or rather the best, preparation for all that you seek. Fix your eyes on this principally and let all other means and considerations go to help this.

CHAPTER III

In What the Goodness and Perfection of Our Actions Consists, and of Some Means to Do Them Well

LET us now see in what the goodness of our actions consists, to the end that thereby we may better come to know the means of doing them well. I say briefly that it consists in two things, of which the first and chiefest is that we act purely for God. St. Ambrose asks the reason why God in the creation of the world, after He had created the corporeal things and the animals, praised them at once. God created the plants and trees, and Scripture says at once that *He saw that it was good* (Gen. i. 10-25). He created the beasts upon the earth, the birds also and fishes; and He saw that it was good. He created the heavens and stars, the sun and moon; and He saw that it was good. He praised everything He created as soon as He had created it. But man He seems to leave alone without praise, because He added not presently: *He saw that it was good,* as He said of the rest. What mystery is this? And what can be the cause of this difference? The cause, says the saint, is this, that the beauty and goodness of beasts and corporeal things consists in their outward appearance and there is nothing perfect in them besides what at once strikes the eye, and therefore they may be praised as soon as they are seen. But the goodness and perfection of man consists, not in the exterior, but in what lies inwardly hid. *All the glory of the king's daughter is from within* (Psalm xliv. 14). It is this which is pleasing in God's sight. *For man seeth what outwardly appeareth, but the Lord seeth the heart* (I Kings xvi. 7). He sees with what intention everyone does each action, and it is upon this account that

He did not praise man, as He did all other creatures, as soon as He had created him. The intention is the foundation of the goodness of all our actions. Foundations are not seen, and yet they sustain the whole edifice. Our intention also does the same. The second thing required for the perfection of all our actions is that we do what we can on our part to do them well. It is not enough that your intention be good, nor to say that you do this for God, but you must contrive to do it in the best way you can, the better to please Him. Our blessed Father Ignatius once asked a brother who was somewhat negligent in his office: "Brother, for whom do you do that?" "For the love of God," answered the brother. Said our Father: "Then I assure you that if hereafter you do it in that way, I shall take care to give you a right down good penance; for if you did it for men, it were no great fault to do it with so little care; but doing it for so great a Lord, it is a great fault to do it in that style."

The second means which the saints set forth as very efficacious to this end is to walk in the presence of God. Seneca says that a man desirous of virtue and of doing things well should imagine that he is in presence of some personage for whom he has a great respect, and do and say all things as he would do and say them if he really were in that person's presence. *Sic vive tanquam sub alicuius boni viri ac semper praesentis oculis.* Now if this be sufficient for doing things well, how much more effectual will it be to walk in the presence of God and keep Him ever before our eyes, considering that He is looking at us—especially as this is no imagination, like the other, but a reality and fact, as Scripture so often repeats. *The eyes of God are clearer than the light of the sun: they see all the ways and steps of men, and the depths of the abyss, and the hearts of mortals and the most hidden things there* (Ecclus. xxiii. 28).

Hereafter we shall consider the presence of God in a treatise expressly dealing with the subject; for our present purpose it is enough to point out how important the exercise of the presence of God is for doing our ordinary actions well. If, indeed, through attention to the presence of God we were to be careless over our work and make mistakes in it, that would be no devotion, but an illusion. The exercise of the presence of God that the Scriptures and the saints recommend to us consists in doing our actions in such fashion that they may well appear before God and contain nothing unworthy of His sight and presence. St. John seems to remind us of this in the Apocalypse when, speaking of the four living creatures he saw before the throne of God, he says that *within and without, they were full of eyes* (Apoc. iv. 6): eyes in their feet, eyes in their hands, eyes in their ears, eyes in their lips, eyes in their very eyes; to signify that those who would perfectly serve God and be worthy of His presence, ought to be very circumspect to do nothing whereby they may render themselves unworthy to appear before Him.

You ought to be full of eyes within and without, so as to see how you work, and see how you walk, and see how you talk, and see how you hear, and see how you see, and see how you think, and see how you want, and see how you desire, that in all these things there may be nothing to offend the eyes of God, in whose sight you are.

Let the just, says the Royal Prophet, *eat and drink*— there is no harm in that—*and feast and rejoice in due season* (Psalm lxvii. 4), but *before God,* so that all may appear before the eyes of God, and there be nothing in it unworthy of His presence.

Let us take notice that, instead of these words in Genesis; *Henoch walked with God, and was seen no more, because the Lord took him* (Gen. v. 24), Ecclesiasticus and St. Paul say: *Henoch pleased God, and was translated to paradise* (Ecclus. xliv. 16; Heb. xi. 5), giving us hereby to understand that it is all one to walk with or before God, and to please God, because they explain the one by the other. Origen and St. Augustine give the same explanation to what is said in Exodus, where, when Jethro came to see his son-in-law Moses, Aaron and the chief of the people of Israel assembled to *eat bread with him before the Lord* (Exod. xviii. 12). The Scripture says not that they assembled to eat bread before the Tabernacle, or before the Ark, for they were not then in being; but they met together to rejoice and divert themselves with him by entertaining and feasting him, and kept the same moderation and decency during their mirth and feasting as they would have done had they eaten in God's presence, taking care that there should be nothing that might offend His sacred eyes. It is after this manner that the just and perfect walk before God in all things, even in the most indifferent actions necessary for the preservation of life.

In this way also many saints say that we accomplish what Christ our Redeemer says in His Gospel: *One must always pray and never desist* (Luke xviii. 1), and what St. Paul says to the Thessalonians: *Pray without ceasing* (I Thess. v. 17). They say that he prays always who is always doing good. So St. Augustine on the verse, *all day long thy praise* (Psalm xxxiv. 28), says: "Would you find a good means of being all day long praising God? Do well all that you do, and so you will be ever praising God." *Quidquid egeris bene age, et laudasti Deum.* The same says St. Hilary: "By this we succeed in praying without ceasing, when by means of actions pleasing to God and done always to His glory, all our life is converted into prayer. *Sancti cuiusque viri vita omnis oratio fit.* And in this way, living according to the law day and night, that very life will come to be a *meditation on the law day and night* (Psalm i. 2)." And St. Jerome on that verse: *Praise ye him, sun and moon, praise ye him all ye stars, and thou light, praise the Lord* (Psalm cxlviii. 3), asks how can sun and moon and light and stars praise God, and answers: "Do you know how they praise Him? In that they never cease doing their duty well; they are always serving God and doing that whereunto they were created, and this is to be always praising God." Thus he who does his duty well, he who does very well the daily and ordinary things of religious life, such a one is always praising God and always in prayer. We may confirm this from what the Holy Ghost says by the Wise Man: *He who observeth the law multiplieth prayer; it is a wholesome sacrifice to keep the commandments and stand aloof from all sin* (Ecclus. xxxv. 1). Hereby is well seen how much value and perfection attaches to doing the ordinary things that we do, taking care that they be well done; and how this is living ever in prayer and in the presence of God, and is a sacrifice very wholesome and very pleasing to God.

CHAPTER IV

Of Another Means to Do Our Actions Well, Which Is to Do Them as if We Had Nothing Else to Do

THE third means to do our actions well is to do each of them apart, as though we had nothing else to do; to make our meditation, to say mass, to recite our beads and divine office, and to do all the rest of our actions as if really we had no other business but just this that we are about. What gets in our way? Let us not mix up our works; let not one hinder the other; let us keep ourselves always to that which we are doing at present. While we are at prayer, let us not think of our studies nor of our office nor of business; all that serves only to hinder prayer, so that we do neither the one nor the other well. You have all the rest of the day left to study in, to do the duties of your office, to fulfil your ministry. *All things have their time* (Eccles. iii. 1); let us give to each thing its proper time: *Sufficient for the day is the evil thereof* (Matt. vi. 34).

This is a means so just and so conformable to reason that even the pagans, who had not the faith, taught it as the proper way to deal more reverently with those beings whom they took for gods. Hence sprang that old proverb, *Adoraturi sedeant*—"Let them who are to deal with God settle down to do it," in attention and repose, not cursorily and distractedly. Plutarch, speaking of the regard and reverence with which priests in his time approached their gods, says that, whilst the priest offered sacrifice, a herald ceased not to cry out and say in a loud voice: *Hoc age, quod agis.* "Do what you are doing, put your whole self into this business, do not turn aside, look well to the business on which you are engaged this hour." Think what you are about, stand to that, put all your care and energy into that which is now present, never mind for the time being the whole of the rest of things, and in that way you will do everything well.

A philosopher went about to prove that we should attend only to what we are doing at present and not to the past nor to the future, and he gave this reason: the present alone is that which is in our power and not the past nor the future, for what is already past is no longer in our power, and as for the future, we do not know whether it will come. Oh, if a man could succeed with himself and be so far master of his thoughts and imaginations as never to think of anything else but what he is at present doing! But such is the instability of our heart and on the other hand so great the malice and cunning of the devil that, availing himself thereof, he brings before us thoughts and solicitudes of what we are to do next, to hinder and disturb us from doing what is before us at present. This is a very common temptation of the devil and a very harmful and ingenious one, his aim being therein that we should never do anything well. For this purpose, in meditation the devil brings in thoughts of business, study, the duties of your office, and represents to you how you might do this or do that well, to the end that you may not make the meditation well, which is your present concern; and in return for that he does not hesitate to put before you a thousand ways and manners of doing that other thing well in the future, to the end that you may do nothing well now; and afterwards, when you come to the doing of it, he will not fail to find something else to put before you, that you may not do that well either. And in this way he goes on playing tricks upon us, that we may never do anything well. *But his intentions are not hidden to us* (II Cor. ii. 11) ; we understand them well. Leave alone what is to come and just at present take no care of it; for though that be a good suggestion for afterwards, it is not good to think of it now. And when there comes to you this temptation under pretense that afterwards you will not remember the suggestion that then occurred, by that very fact you will see that it is not God, but a temptation of the devil, because God is not a friend of confusion, but of peace and tranquility, order and agreement. Thus what disturbs your peace and tranquility and the order of things, is not from God, but from the devil, who loves confusion and perturbation. Let it alone and trust in God that, on your doing what you ought to do, He will suggest to you in due time all that will make to your purpose, and with advantages. And even though the reason and the good point, and the good argument and solution occur to you at the time of your spiritual duties, give it up and believe that you will lose nothing thereby, but rather gain. St. Bonaventure says that the science which is set aside for virtue's sake is found afterwards more amply by that same virtue. And Father Master Avila says: "When a care comes to you out of due time, say: 'My Lord gives me no orders about this just now, and I have no business to think about it. When my Lord shall command me, then I will deal with it.' "

CHAPTER V

Of Another Means, Which Is to Do Every Action as if It Were to Be the Last of Our Life

THE fourth means which the saints give for doing our actions well is to do every action as though it were to be the last of our life. St. Bernard says, directing a religious how to do his actions: "Let each one ask himself over every action: 'If you were to die at once, would you do this? Would you do it in this manner?'" And St. Basil says a thing, which another holy man also says, to put it in plain English, thus: "You should conduct yourself in every action as if you were to die at once. In the morning think that you will not live till night; and when the night comes, do not dare to promise yourself that you shall see the morning, for many die suddenly" (Ā Kempis). This is a very efficacious means of doing everything well. And so we read of the blessed Abbot St. Anthony that he often gave this reminder to his disciples, to animate them to virtue and to doing things with perfection. Another author says: "Think that every day is your last"—*Omnem crede diem tibi diluxisse supremum.* If we did things each in turn, as if we were to die at once and as though this action were to be our last, we should do them in another manner and with other perfection. Oh, what a mass should I say, if I understood that that was to be the last action of my life, and that there was now no time left me to work or gain merit! Oh, what a meditation should I make, if I understood that that was my last, and that now I had no more time to beg God's mercy and pardon for my sins! Hence the proverb: "If you want to know how to pray, go to sea." Prayer is made in another manner with death before one's eyes.

They tell of a religious, a priest and servant of God, that he had the custom of going to confession every day to prepare for saying mass. At the end of his course he fell sick, and the superior, seeing the sickness to be mortal, said to him: "Father, you are very ill; make your dying confession." The sick man answered, raising his hands to heaven: "Blessed and praised be the Lord, that now for thirty years and more I have made my confession every day as if I were to die at once; and so there will be no need now but to get ready for absolution as I would if I were about to say mass." That man went on well, and so we should go on. Every confession we should make as though it were our dying confession, and every communion as though it were our dying communion, and so do all our other actions; and thereby at the hour of our death it would not be necessary to tell us to confess so as to be ready to die, but only to dispose ourselves for absolution as though we were going to communion. If we lived always in this way, death would find us well prepared and never come upon us as a surprise. And this is the best prayer and the best devotion to guard against a sudden death. *Happy,* says Christ our Redeemer, *is that servant whom his master, at his coming, shall find thus watching* (Matt. xxiv. 46). And so lived holy Job: *All the days of this life,* he says, *I am looking for the other life* (Job xiv. 14). Every day I make account that this is the last for me. Call me, O Lord, on the day that Thou pleasest, since I am disposed and prepared to answer Thee and to meet Thy call at any time and hour that Thou wishest to call.

One of the best means to know whether we walk well and rightly before God is to consider whether we are in a state to answer Him at what time soever He calls and in what occupation soever we are engaged. I speak not here of an infallible certainty, for such is not to be had in this life without a particular revelation; but I speak only of probable and moral conjectures, which is all we can pretend unto. A great and main means to attain is to see whether in the condition and present conjuncture you are in and in the very action you are about, you would not take it ill that death should come upon you. Think whether you are as ready to answer to God as Job was in case He should call you at this moment. Try yourself often in this manner and ask yourself many times this question: "If death were to come upon you now, would you have reason to be glad?" When, reflecting and examining myself, I find that I should be glad if death were to come upon me at this instant and in the very action I am doing, I fancy I am going on well and feel some satisfaction. But when I find that I should not like death to come just at present and catch me in this office, occupation, and conjuncture, but had rather he would wait a bit until the schemes I have on hand which distract my thoughts were brought to an issue, that is not a good sign, but rather I take it for a clear indication that I am neglecting my spiritual welfare and not living as a religious should do. For as that holy man says: "If you had a good conscience, you would not much fear death;" and if you do fear it so much, it is a sign that you have some remorse of conscience and your accounts are not in good order. Better fear sin than death. The steward whose accounts are in good order desires that they should come and take them; but he who has them in bad order is afraid of their coming and sets up all the excuses and delays in his power.

Father Francis Borgia used to say that a good exercise for a religious was four and twenty times a day to put himself in the condition of a dying man; and he added that a man might then think of himself in a good state when, often repeating these words: "I must die today," he found nothing that troubled him. Let everyone, then, enter into an account with himself and examine himself many times on this point. And if it appears that you are not today in a state and condition to die, take care to put yourself in good condition for this final crisis. Reckon that you beg of the Lord to grant you a few days of life for this purpose and that He does grant them, and profit by the time and endeavor to live as if you were presently to die. Blessed is he who lives in the disposition that he desires to be found in at the hour of death. This is one of the most profitable things that we can preach to our neighbor, that they should live in such a disposition as they desire to be found in at the hour of death and not put off their conversion and repentance to the future; for tomorrow is uncertain and who knows if you shall have tomorrow? "God, who has promised pardon to the sinner if he repents," says St. Gregory, "has never promised him that he shall have tomorrow" —*Qui poenitentibus veniam spopondit, crastinum diem non promisit.* It is a common saying that nothing is more certain than death, nor more uncertain than the hour of death.

But Christ our Redeemer says yet more. *Be ye ready,* says He, *because the son of man will come at the hour ye think not* (Luke xii. 40). For though He speaks in this place of the general Day of Judgment, yet this may be understood also of the hour of death because then each one shall receive his particular judgment and such a sentence as, being once pronounced, will never be revoked, but confirmed at that great and general day. Christ does not content Himself with saying the hour is uncertain and that you know not when it will come, but He says it will come just when you least expect it and perhaps when you are least of all prepared for it. St. Paul tells the Thessalonians that *the Lord will come like a thief in the night* (I Thess. v. 2); and St. John in the Apocalypse, speaking in God's name, says: *I will come to thee as a thief, and thou shalt not know at what hour I mean to come* (Apoc. iii. 3). A thief gives no notice, but waits for the hour when all are least upon their guard and even asleep. And along with this same comparison Christ our Redeemer teaches us how we should behave, to the end that death may not catch us on a sudden and off our guard. *Know ye that if the father of the family knew at what hour the thief would come, he would surely watch, and would not suffer his house to be broken open* (Luke xii. 39). If he knew the hour, it would be sufficient to be awake just then; but because he cannot foresee the hour, or whether it will be in the beginning, towards the middle, or at the end of the night, he continually stands upon his guard to save himself from being robbed. Thus you must ever be watchful, for death will come at the hour you think not.

It is a very great mercy of God that the hour of death should be uncertain, to the end that we may always be prepared for it; for if we knew the time, this assurance would give us occasion to become more lax and sin with greater confidence. If, uncertain as we are of the hour of death, we live, notwithstanding, with so great negligence, what should we do if we were assured we should not die for some time! *Fool,* says the Son of God to the rich, covetous man, *this night they are requiring thy soul of thee, and what will become of those riches thou hast gathered together?* (Luke xii. 20).

Now what we preach to others, we should take also to ourselves, as the Apostle warns us: *What thou teachest to others, thou dost not teach thyself* (Rom. ii. 21). One of the temptations the devil most commonly makes use of to deceive men is to hide as much as he can from them so clear a truth as this; to divert their eyes and their thoughts from it and make them believe that there's time enough for this world and the next, and that one day they will grow better and live after another manner than they do now. It is not only worldlings he abuses after this manner, but he also deceives many religious after the same fashion, persuading them to defer their spiritual advancement from one day to another, till they have done their studies, till they are out of this office and got this business off their hands: then I will get to rights my spiritual duties and my penances and mortifications. Unhappy you, if you die in your studies! What will then the learning serve you for which you have relaxed your efforts after virtue, but as *straw and wood,* for you to burn the more thereon in the next life! (I Cor. iii. 12). Let us, then, profit ourselves by what we say to others. *Physician, cure thyself* (Luke iv. 23). Apply this remedy to yourself, since you have need of it.

CHAPTER VI

Of Another Means of Doing Our Actions Well, Which Is to Take No Account of Anything beyond Today

THE fifth means that will greatly aid and animate us to do ordinary things well and to perfection is to take no account of anything farther than the present day. And though at first sight this means seems not at all different from the last, yet it really does differ, as we shall see in the sequel. One of the things which is wont to discourage and enfeeble many in the way of virtue, one of the temptations which the devil puts into their heads, consists of such reflections as these: "Can you manage to go on for so many years in such recollection, such punctuality, such exactness, mortifying yourself continually, denying your appetite, and setting aside your own will in all things?" The devil represents this as very difficult, and that it is not a life that can be carried on for such a long time. We read of our blessed Father Ignatius that, when he retired to Manresa to do penance, amongst other temptations wherewith the devil assailed him this was one: "Can you suffer a life so austere as this for the seventy years of life that still remain to you?" Against this temptation this means is directed. There is no question of many years, nor of many days, but only of today. It is a means very proportionable to our weakness. For one day, who will not animate and force himself to live well and do all that in him lies that his actions may be well done? This is the means that our Father sets before us in the particular examen, where he bids us make our resolution from half-day to half-day.

"From now till dinner-time at least I propose to be modest in my gait, to keep silence, and practise patience." In this way that becomes easy which possibly might be too hard, if you took it absolutely: "I propose never to talk, and always to go about with restraint on myself in great composure and recollection."

This was that means the monk made use of, of whom we read in the lives of the Fathers, that, being so much tempted to gluttony that even at break of day he found himself ready to faint for hunger, yet he resolved not to break the holy custom of his order in eating before three in the afternoon; and to this end made use of this artifice. In the morning, talking to himself, he said: "Hungry as thou art, is it much to wait till nine o'clock? Then thou mayest eat." At nine o'clock, "Verily," said he, "I ought in something to do violence to myself, and not eat till noon. As I have been able to wait till nine o'clock, so shall I be able till twelve;" and so he entertained himself that time. At twelve he put his bread in water and said: "While the bread soaks, I must wait till three o'clock as I have waited till this hour; and I will not for a gain of two or three hours break the monastic custom." Three o'clock came and he ate, after saying his prayers. This he did for many days, beguiling himself with these short terms, till one day, sitting down to eat at three o'clock, he saw a smoke rise out of the basket where he kept his bread and go out by the window of his cell, which must have been the wicked spirit that tempted him. From this time forth he never felt those false fits of hunger and faintness that he used to have; on the contrary, he had no trouble in passing two days without eating. Thus our Lord rewarded the victory he had gained over his enemy and the conflict that he had endured.

But it is not without reason we said that this means was very proportionable to our weakness, for after all it treats us as men are wont to treat infirm and feeble folk, helping us on little by little, that the work may not frighten us. But if we were strong and fervent and had much love for God, it would not be necessary to help us on in this way, so little by little, to hide from us the labor and difficulty; since the true servant of God does not put before him the length of time or the number of years, but all time seems short to serve God and all labor little, and so it is not necessary to help him on in this way, little by little. St. Bernard says this well. "The truly just man is not like the hireling or day laborer, who binds himself to serve for one day or one month or for one year, but forever without limit and without term he offers himself to serve God with hearty good will. *For ever and aye I will never forget, O Lord, thy law and thy commandments and counsels* (Psalm cxviii. 93). And because he offers himself and determines to serve God absolutely and without limit and does not fix a term, saying: "For a year, or for three years, I will do this," therefore his reward and recompense shall also be without limit for ever and aye"—*Non enim ad annum vel ad tempus instar mercenarii, sed in aeternum divino se mancipat famulatui. Non igitur ad tempus; proinde iustitia eius manet non aliquanto tempore, sed in saeculum saeculi. Sempiterna igitur iusti esuries sempiternam meretur refectionem.* In this way St. Bernard explains the saying of the Wise Man: *Being made perfect in a short space, he fulfilled a long time* (Wisdom iv. 13). The true just man in a short time and in a few days of life lives many years, because he loves God so much and has such a desire to serve Him that, if he lived a hundred years or even a thousand, he would be ever busying himself in serving Him more and more. And for this desire and determination it is as though he did live all that time in this manner, because God will reward him according to his desire and determination. These are men indeed, lusty, strong men, like Jacob, who for the great love that he bore Rachel thought it a little thing to serve for seven years and then for seven years more. *All this time seemed to him short for the great love he bore her* (Gen. xxix. 20).

CHAPTER VII

Of Another Means to Do Our Actions Well, Which Is to Get into a Way of So Doing Them

THAT fine old philosopher Pythagoras gave very good advice to his friends and disciples, how to be virtuous and make to themselves the practice of virtue easy and sweet. Let everyone, said he, choose a good course of life, and in the beginning not mind its seeming hard or painful, for custom will afterwards render it quite easy and agreeable. Behold here a very important means whereby to help ourselves, not so much because it comes from that philosopher, but because the Holy Ghost Himself suggests the same, as we shall see afterwards, and because it is most proper to attain our end. We have already chosen an excellent way of living, or, to say better, the Lord has chosen one for us, *because it is not you that have made choice of me, but it is I that have made choice of you* (John xv. 16); blessed and glorified be He forever for that. Notwithstanding, there may be a more or a less in this state of life in which God has put us; for, according to the works that you do therein, you may become either a good or a tepid religious. If, then, you desire to advance and gain perfection therein, accustom yourself to do all your duties well and perfectly; accustom yourself to make your meditation well and your other spiritual duties; accustom yourself to be very exact in obedience and the observance of rules and to make account of little things; accustom yourself to recollection, to mortification and penance, to modesty and silence; and do not leave off because at the beginning you find some difficulty therein, for afterwards by custom it will become to you very sweet and pleasant and you will never feel that you can sufficiently render thanks to God for having accustomed you thereto.

The Holy Ghost teaches us this doctrine in many passages of Holy Scripture. In Proverbs (iv. 11) He says: *I will show thee the way of wisdom*—I will teach thee to find a sweet savor in the knowledge of God, because this is the meaning of wisdom *(sapientia)* in Holy Scripture, says St. Bernard. Wisdom is savory *(sapida sapientia):* wisdom is a sweet and savory knowledge of God. I will teach thee, then, he says, the way whereby thou mayest come to find savor and a sweet taste in the knowledge, love, and service of God. *I must take thee by the narrow paths of virtue*—he calls them *narrow* because at the beginning they are made difficult to us by our evil inclination and we think it a narrow path—*but after thou hast passed these narrow entrances, thou shalt find the way very wide, roomy, and to thy liking, and thou shalt run without tripping up or being brought to a standstill anywhere* (Prov. iv. 12). The Holy Ghost teaches us gracefully by this metaphor that, though at the beginning we find difficulty in this way of virtue and perfection, we must not be alarmed at that, for afterwards we shall not only find no difficulty, but much relish, content, and mirth, and shall come to say: *I have labored a little, and have found much rest to myself* (Ecclus. li. 35). The same is repeated in Ecclus. vi. 20: *Thou shalt labor a little and presently shalt eat and enjoy the fruit of thy labor.* The Apostle St. Paul also teaches us the same: *Every training and every good exercise in the beginning appeareth difficult and painful and sad; but afterwards, as one groweth used to it, it not only becometh easy, but very pleasant and enjoyable* (Heb. xii. 11). Thus we see in all the arts and sciences. How difficult is study when one first enters upon it! How often is it necessary for one to be brought to it by force! Hence they say: "Letters draw blood at first entrance." But afterwards by practice, as one improves and learns, one develops such a taste as to find all one's entertainment and recreation in study. So it is in the way of virtue and perfection. St. Bernard declares this very well on those words of Job: *The things that formerly my soul could not bear to touch, now of necessity have become my food* (Job vi. 7). "How great is the effect of exercise and custom and what power it has! In the beginning you think a thing very difficult and insupportable; but if you accustom yourself to it, it will not appear so difficult nor so burdensome as that. A little after you will think it light and easy and feel it almost as nothing; a little after that you will not feel it at all; and in a short time you will not only not feel it, but it will give you so much delight and contentment that you will be able to say with Job (vi. 7) as above"—*Primum tibi importabile videbitur aliquid; processu temporis, si assuescas, iudicabis non adeo grave; paulo post et leve senties; paulo post nec senties; paulo post etiam delectabit.*

Thus it all goes according to the way in which one has got accustomed to act. The additions and instructions for meditation and examen are difficult for you to observe because you are little accustomed to do so. You find such difficulty in fixing your imagination, so that it may travel where you wish immediately upon awaking and in times of meditation; that is because you never have done violence to it, nor accustomed it to being brought to order and restrained, and not go thinking of anything but the matter of meditation. The reason why silence and recollection makes you silent and melancholy is because you practise it little. *Cella continuata dulcescit, et male custodita taedium generat*—"A quiet corner is sweet when you stay there, and wearisome when you keep it badly" (Ā Kempis). Worldly people find prayer and fasting difficult because they are not accustomed to it.

King Saul clad David in his armor, seeing that he was to fight with the Philistine; and, as he was not used to bear such arms, he could not walk under their weight; he afterwards got used to armor and fought good battles in it. And what I say of virtue and goodness, I likewise say of vice and evil. If you allow a bad habit to arise, the evil thing will grow and gather strength and afterwards it will be very difficult to cure it, and so you will remain with it all your life. Oh, if from the beginning you had accustomed yourself to do things and do them well, how well off would you find yourself now, seeing virtue and goodness having become so sweet and easy to you! See how satisfied he is who has a habit of not blaspheming, and with what ease and comfort he avoids so many mortal sins. Begin, then, to form a good habit from this hour, for better late than never. Take to heart the doing well of these ordinary actions that you do, since that goes for so much in you; and apply thereto the particular examen, one of the best examens you can make, and in this manner it will become to you sweet and easy to do them well.

CHAPTER VIII

Of How Great Importance It Is for a Religious Not to Slow Down in the Way of Virtue

BY all that we have said it is easy to comprehend of how great consequence it is for a religious to keep up his devotion and always to go on with fervor in the exercises of religion and never let himself fall into tepidity and weakness, for afterwards it will be very hard for him to get out of it. God certainly can make you return afterwards to a life of fervor and perfection, but it will be a miracle and a prodigy. St. Bernard perfectly well treats this point, writing to Richard, Abbot of Fountains, and his religious, in whom God had wrought this wonder, that, whereas hitherto they had led a tepid and loose kind of life, God had now changed and brought them to great fervor and perfection; whereat the saint marvels much and sends his congratulations: "The finger of God is here. Who will grant me to come over and see this marvel? For a marvel it is, no less than that which Moses (Exod. iii. 2) beheld of the bush that burned and was not consumed. It is a most rare and very extraordinary thing for anyone to advance and raise himself afterwards beyond the level to which he has once settled down in religion. It will be easier to find many seculars converted from a bad to a good life than to meet even one religious passing from a tepid and lax life to a fervent and perfect one." *Rarissima avis in terra est qui de gradu quem forte in religione semel attigerit vel parum ascendat.* And the reason of this is that persons in the world have not the remedies that their souls need so constantly at hand as religious have; and so, when they hear a good sermon or see a neighbor and friend carried off by a sudden and unhappy death, the novelty of the thing causes in them alarm and astonishment and moves them to amend and change their lives. But the religious who has these remedies so constantly at hand, such frequentation of sacraments, so many spiritual exhortations, such exercise in meditating the things of God and dealing with death, judgment, hell, and heaven, and for all that is tepid and slack—what hope can there be of his changing his life? His ears are inured to it, and so these considerations cannot aid or move him; and what moves others does not move him nor make any impression on him.

This is also the reason of that celebrated pronouncement of St. Augustine: "Since I have begun to serve God, as I have not known any better men than those who had done well in religion, so I have not known worse than those who have fallen from it"—*Ex quo Deo servire coepi, quomodo difficile sum expertus meliores quam qui in monasterio profecerunt, ita non sum expertus peiores quam qui in monasteriis ceciderunt.* St. Bernard says that very few of those who have fallen and failed in religion return to the state and degree that they held before, but rather go on getting worse. Over such, he says, the Prophet Jeremy weeps: *How has the purest gold lost its luster, how has that color so brilliant faded,* how has that former beauty changed? *They who were reared in purple* and laid on costly couches, they who were regaled with divine delights in prayer, and all their discourse and conversation was in heaven, *have come to embrace dung* and revel in mud and *filth* (Lam. iv. 1-5).

Thus, ordinarily speaking, there is little hope of those who begin to go backward and take a turn for the worse in religion—a thing that ought to strike great fear into us. And the reason is that which we have mentioned, since they fall sick under the very medicines and remedies under which they ought to improve and get well. But if that which improves and cures others only makes them sick and worse than they were, what hope can there be of doing them any good? When you find a sick man on whom medicines have no effect, but rather he feels worse for them, you may well take him for one undone. That is why we take so much account of sin and a fall in religious and fear it so much, while we do not give so much thought to it in people of the world. When a physician sees a fainting-fit or a great feebleness of pulse in a sickly and weak subject, he is not much concerned; but when he sees it in a robust and very healthy man, he takes it for a very bad symptom, because such a mischance cannot happen in that case without the predominance of some malignant humor, prognosticating death or serious illness. So it is here: if a secular falls into sins, they are not mischances very inconsistent with the careless life of one who goes to confession once or twice a year and lives in midst of so many occasions of sin; but in a religious, sustained by such frequentation of sacraments, so much prayer, so many pious exercises, when he comes to fall, it is a symptom of a great decay of virtue and a deep-seated infirmity, and there is reason to fear.

But I do not say this, says St. Bernard, to drive you into discouragement, especially if you seek to rise immediately; for the more you put it off, the harder it will become. *I say this that ye may not sin,* nor fall nor grow weak, *but if anyone hath fallen, we have a good advocate in Jesus Christ* (I John ii. 1), Who can do what we cannot do. Therefore let none be discouraged, since if he heartily returns to God, without doubt he will obtain mercy. If the Apostle St. Peter, having attended the school of Christ for so long a time, and been so much favored by Him, fell so grievously, and after so grievous a fall as that of having denied his Master and Lord returned to so lofty and eminent estate, who will be discouraged? "You have sinned in the world," says St. Bernard; "was it more than St. Paul? You have sinned here in religion; was it more than St. Peter?" But they, since they repented and did penance, not only gained pardon, but very high sanctity and perfection. Do you the like, and you will be able to return not only to your former state, but to much greater perfection.

CHAPTER IX

How Important It Is for Novices to Make Progress during the Time of Their Novitiate, and Accustom Themselves to Do the Exercises of Religion Well

THIS instruction for novices may also serve all those who are entering on the way of virtue. The first rule of the master of novices in our Society says the thing well in a few words, which are addressed not to us only, but to all religious. "Let the master of novices understand well that he has given over to his charge a thing of the highest importance." And the rule gives two very solid reasons to make the master of novices open his eyes and understand the weightiness and importance of his charge. The first is that on this first training and formation of the novices there usually depends all their future progress. The second is that all the hope of the Society pivots on this, and on this depends the well-being of the order. Coming down to explain these things more in particular, I say first that on this first training given and the attitude taken up by each novice in his novitiate, depends all growth or decay for the time to come. Commonly speaking, as we said in the last chapter, if in the time of his novitiate an individual is tepid and careless of his spiritual progress, tepid and careless he will remain. It is not to be supposed that afterwards he will act with greater care and fervor; there is no reason to believe that he will effect this change and improvement afterwards, but very much reason to believe that he will not.

To make this better appear, let us address our discourse to the novice himself, weighing the reasons and convincing him therewith. Now you are in your noviceship, you have a great deal of time to apply to your spiritual advancement and different means that may contribute thereto, your superiors thinking of nothing else but this and making it their chief endeavor. Now you have many examples before your eyes of others who are bent on no other purpose than this. It is a thing that animates and encourages one much, to live with companions who have in view this object alone and nothing else; and the sight of others going ahead obliges one, however heavy and lumpish he be, to get out of his sloth. Now you have a heart disengaged and free and seemingly desirous of virtue, with nothing to withdraw you from it, but much to aid you. But if now that you are here for this purpose alone, and have nothing else to think of, you do not improve nor gain any virtue, how will it be when your heart is taken up and divided in a thousand different ways? If now with so much freedom from business, such advantages and aids at hand, so much leisure, such conveniences, and so many helps, you make not your meditation and examen well, nor take pains to observe your additions and do your other spiritual duties properly, what will become of you when the care of your studies shall take up your thoughts, and, in later life, business, confessions, and sermons? If with so many conferences, so many exhortations, so many examples, and so many solicitations, you do not profit, what will become of you when you shall meet with impediments and obstacles on all sides? If in the beginning of your conversion, when novelty should increase your fervor and zeal, you are, notwithstanding, slack and listless, what will become of you when your ears shall be inured and hardened to all things that may touch or do you any good? And further, if now while passion is but beginning to stir and the evil inclination is not strong, being only at its commencements, still you have not the courage to resist it, how will you resist and overcome it afterwards, when it shall have taken deep root and gathered strength by habit, so that it will be like a very death struggle for you to change it?

St. Dorotheus illustrated this very well by an example which he recounts of one of the Fathers of the Desert, who, being one day in a place full of cypresses of all sorts, great and small and of medium size, bade one of his disciples pluck up a little one he pointed at, which his disciple presently did without any difficulty. Then he pointed to another, somewhat bigger, which he in like manner plucked up by the roots, but with greater difficulty than the former, being forced to take both hands to it. To pluck up another, which was yet stronger, he had to call in the help of one of his companions. And, lastly, all of them together labored in vain to pull up another which was much bigger still. "Behold," said the ancient Father, "how it is with our passions. In the beginning, when they are not yet rooted, it is easy to master them if you take but ever so little pains. But afterwards, when by long habit they have taken deeper root, it will be very hard; much force will have to be used, and I do not know if you will succeed."

By what I have said, we may perceive that it is a very grave abuse and a very dangerous temptation to defer from day to day our amendment, thinking we shall be better able to mortify and overcome ourselves another time, because at present we have not the courage to do it by reason of the great difficulty. If, whilst this difficulty is yet small, you cannot bring yourself to surmount it, what will you be able to do when it shall become greater? And if at present, whilst your passion is but like a lion's whelp, you have not the courage to attack it, how will you be able to do it when it shall be grown a great and furious beast? Hold it, therefore, for a certain truth that if now you are tepid and remiss, tepid and remiss you will be in the time to come. If you now are not a good novice and a good apprentice, you will never hereafter be a good senior nor a good workman. If at present you are neglectful of obedience and the observance of rules, you will be more so afterwards. If now you are careless over your spiritual duties and botch them, a botcher you will remain all your life. The whole point lies in the established attitude which you take up now. They say that the business of kneading dough lies in the first putting in of the yeast.

St. Bonaventure says: In the attitude which one takes up at the beginning, in that he remains. It is very difficult for an old man to bend himself to that to which he was not accustomed in his youth. It is a proverb of the Holy Ghost: *A proverb it is,* says Solomon: *train the youth to go his way, and when he is old he will not depart from it* (Prov. xxii. 6). Hence St. John Climacus came to say that it is a very dangerous thing and matter of much apprehension, when one enters on his course with tepidity and faintheartedness, because, he says, it is a clear indication of a fall to come. For this reason it is of supreme importance to accustom oneself to virtue from the outset and do one's spiritual duties well. The Holy Ghost warns us of this by the Prophet Jeremy: *It is a good thing for a man to accustom himself to bear the yoke from his youth* (Lam. iii. 27), because he will hold to it afterwards, and thereby render to himself the way of virtue and goodness easy; otherwise he will find it very difficult. *What thou hast not gathered in the time of youth, how thinkest thou that thou shalt find it afterwards in the time of old age?* (Ecclus. xxv. 5).

From this first reason follows the second, because if all the progress of a religious in future depends on his first formation, then all the good of the order depends likewise thereon; for an order does not consist of the walls of its houses and churches, but of the assembly of the religious, and they who are in the noviceship are they who have to be afterwards the whole order. For this reason the Society was not satisfied with establishing seminaries and colleges where Ours are reared in letters and virtue together, but established seminaries of virtue alone, where attention is paid to abnegation and mortification of self and to the practice of true and solid virtues, as being more of a main foundation than letters. For this the houses of probation exist, being, as our Father Francis Borgia says, for the novices a Bethlehem, that is to say, "the House of Bread," because there are made the biscuit and provisions for the voyage, against the great risks that await us. This is harvest time, this the season of abundance; these are the years of fertility, in which your business is to take in supplies, as Joseph did, against coming years of hunger and sterility. Oh, if the people of Egypt had understood, and cast up their account, and carefully considered what they were doing, they would not have been in such a hurry to empty their houses of the wheat which Joseph was gathering and locking up in his barns! Oh, if you would take account how important it is for you to come out well provisioned from the house of probation! In that case, certainly, you would not be eager to get out of it quickly, considering how ill you are off for virtue and mortification. And therefore Father Francis Borgia says that such as aim or are glad at shortly going out of the novitiate show signs of want of judgment and lack of understanding of their need of good preparation; they make light of the day's work that is before them, since they so lightly take the risk of rushing into it unprovided.

Oh, how rich and laden with virtues does our Father take us to be, when we are to leave the house of probation! He appoints two years of probation and experiment, wishing the novice during that time to think of nothing else but his spiritual advancement, seeing no other books and studying nothing else but what may forward him in self-denial and growth in virtue and perfection. He is supposed to go out at the end of that time so spiritual and fervent, such a lover of mortification and recollection, so devoted to prayer and spiritual exercises as to need even to be restrained therein. He therefore advises such persons, when they go to the colleges, to abate somewhat of their fits of fervor during the time of their studies; not to make such long prayers nor do so many mortifications. Our Father supposes one to leave the noviceship with so much light, so much knowledge of God and contempt of the world, so fervent and devout and inwardly lifted up to spiritual things as to need these cautions. Do you, then, endeavor to go out such. Make the most of this time, so precious that perchance never in your life will you have such a time again for gathering spiritual riches. *Let not so good time pass in vain, nor lose any part of it* (Ecclus. xiv. 16).

One of the great favors that the Lord does to those whom He draws to religion in their tender age, and for which they owe Him infinite thanks, is that it is then very easy for them to apply themselves to virtue and religious discipline. A tree, while it is tender at the beginning, may be easily shaped so as to grow into a very beautiful tree. But afterwards, when you have let it grow in its own way and become crooked and awkwardly spreading, you will break sooner than guide it into the shape you want; and such it will remain as long as there is life left in it. So it is easy to shape and direct one of tender age and turn him to what is good; and by accustoming him to it from the time that he is small, it will be rendered very easy for him afterwards and so he will go on and ever persevere in it. It is a great thing for stuff to be dyed in the wool, because then it never loses its color. Who can restore to its whiteness, says St. Jerome, the wool that has drunk in a purple dye? And another says: "An earthern jar long retains the odor of the first liquor poured into it." The Scripture praises King Josias for that, *when yet a boy, he began to seek the God of his father David* (II Chron. xxxiv. 4).

Humbertus, a person of note and Master General of the Order Preachers, relates that a certain religious after his death appeared some nights to another religious, his companion, all in glory; and, leading him out of his cell, he showed him a great number of men, clad in white and encompassed with light, who carried very fair crosses upon their shoulders as they went in procession towards heaven. A little after, he beheld another procession, fairer and more resplendent than the former, each member of which carried a far richer and a more beautiful cross in his hands, and not on his shoulders as the former did. After that, a third procession passed, still more glorious and admirable than the two former, for all their crosses were of a surprising beauty, and they carried them neither on their shoulders nor in their hands, but an angel going before, each carried his cross for him, so that they followed with much alacrity and joy. The religious, astonished at this vision, asked an explanation. His companion answered that the first, who carried their crosses upon their shoulders, were those who had entered religion at a mature age; the second, who held their crosses in their hand, were those that entered in early youth; and the last, who marched with so much freedom and cheerfulness, were those who when they were small children had renounced the world and embraced a religious life.

THIRD TREATISE

ON PURITY OF INTENTION

CHAPTER I

That in Our Actions We Ought to Shun the Vice of Vainglory

ONE of the things most recommended and repeated in our Constitutions and Rules is to keep a right intention in all our actions, seeking in them ever the will of God and His greater glory. At every step our Rules repeat to us these words: "To the greater glory of God," or "Looking ever to the greater service of God," which is the same thing. Our blessed Father had so engraven on his heart this desire of the greater glory and honor of God and was so used to the practice of doing all things for this end, that from thence he came to bring it out and utter it so frequently. *From the abundance of the heart the words come forth* (Luke vi. 45). This was ever, as it were, his coat of arms and the soul and life of all his actions. With much reason do they put on his pictures this lettering, A.M.D.G., *Ad maiorem Dei gloriam*—"To the greater glory of God." These are his arms, this his motto and coat; this is the summary of his life and exploits. Such also ought to be our arms, our motto and coat, that as good children we may resemble our Father.

With reason does he inculcate this so forcibly upon us, since all our progress and perfection turn on the actions which we do; and the better these are and the more perfect, the better and more perfect shall we ourselves be. But our actions will be more fraught with goodness and perfection in proportion as our intention is more right and pure and our end and aim higher and more perfect, for this it is that gives life and being to our works, according to the text of the holy Gospel: *The light of thy body is thine eye: if thine eye be pure and simple, all thy body will be bright and lightsome; but if it be evil and double-minded, all thy body will be dark and in the shade* (Matt. vi. 22). By the *eye* the saints understand the intention, which sees and first forestalls what it seeks; and by the *body* they understand the action, which follows the intention as the whole body follows the eyes. Christ our Redeemer, then, says that what gives light and brightness to our actions is the intention and so, if the end and intention of the action is good, the action will be good, and if evil, evil; and if the end be high and perfect, the action will be so likewise.

It is this also which the Apostle St. Paul says: *If the root be holy, so too are the branches* (Rom. xi. 16). As is the root, so will be the tree and the fruit thereof. Of a tree the root of which is injured, what can be expected but unpleasant and sour and worm-eaten fruit? But if the root is healthy and good, the tree will be good and bear good fruit. So in actions the goodness and perfection thereof lies in the intention, which is the root. And to the same account it is said that the purer they are, the better and more perfect they will be. St. Gregory on that text of Job, *Whereon are its supports firmly fixed?* (Job xxxviii. 6), says that, whereas the whole structure of a material building rests on certain pillars and the pillars on their bases and pedestals, so the whole spiritual life rests on the virtues, and the virtues are founded on the right and pure intention of the heart.

But to proceed with this subject in an orderly manner, we will speak first of the evil end which we have to shun in our actions, not doing them for vainglory or for other human considerations, and then we will speak of the right and pure intention which we ought to have, because the first thing to do must be to withdraw from evil, and after that to do good, according to those words of the prophet: *Depart from evil, and do good* (Psalm xxxiii. 15).

All the saints admonish us to be much on our guard against vainglory, because, say they, it is a cunning thief which often steals from us even our best actions, and which insinuates itself so secretly that it has even robbed and despoiled us before we perceive it. St. Gregory says that vainglory is like a robber in disguise, who insinuates himself into the company of a traveler, pretending to go the same way that he goes, and afterwards robs and murders him when he is least upon his guard and thinks himself in perfect security. "I confess," says the saint in the last chapter of his "Moralia," "that when I go about to examine my own intention in writing these books, methinks my sole aim is to please God therein; but, notwithstanding, when I am off my guard, I find that some desire of satisfying and pleasing men intermixes itself, and some vain self-complacency. I know not how nor in what manner, but at the end of a little while I come to see that this business goes not in its later course so free from dust and chaff as it was when I began. I know I began with a good intention and desire simply of pleasing God, but since then I see it is not so pure as that. The same thing happens here as in eating; we begin to eat of necessity, and gluttonous delight steals over us so subtly that what we began of necessity to sustain nature and preserve life, we continue and conclude for the mere pleasure of the palate." Thus here in religion we often take up the duty of preaching and the like for the advancement and profit of souls; and then vanity gains an entrance and we desire to please and satisfy men and to be taken notice of and esteemed; and when things fall out otherwise, our wings evidently droop, and we do the work with a bad grace.

CHAPTER II

In What the Malice of Vainglory Consists

THE malice of this vice consists in this, that the vainglorious man endeavors to walk off with the glory and honor that belong to God alone, according to the words of St. Paul: *To God alone be honor and glory* (I Tim. i. 17), which He has no mind to give to another, but reserves to Himself. *I will not give any glory to another* (Isaias xlii. 18). So St. Augustine says: "Lord, he who would be praised for Thy gifts and seeks not Thy glory but his own in the good he does, is a robber; he is like the devil himself, who endeavored to rob Thee of Thy glory."

In all the works of God there are two things; the profit of the work, and the honor and glory thence resulting, which consists in the doer's of the work being praised, esteemed, and honored for it. Now God has ordained in this life, and wishes it to be so carried out, that all the profit of His works should go to man, but all the glory should be for God Himself. *God hath wrought all things for himself* (Prov. xvi. 4) *for his praise and glory and honor* (Deut. xxvi. 19). And all things preach to us His wisdom, goodness, and providence; and therefore it is said that the heavens and earth are full of His glory (Psalm xviii. 1: Isaias vi. 3). Thus, when in your good actions you seek the glory and honor of men for yourself, you pervert the order which God has established in good works and do an injury to God, seeking and endeavoring that men, who should ever be occupied in honoring and praising God, should be taken up with praising and esteeming you—seeking that the hearts of men, which God has made as vessels to be full of His own honor and glory, should be full of your honor and glory and high renown, which is tantamount to stealing away those hearts from God and, as it were, casting God out of His own house and home. What greater evil can there be than to steal away God's honor and glory and the hearts of men? With your mouth you bid them look to God, but at heart you wish them to turn their eyes away from God and fix them on you. The truly humble man has no wish to live in the heart of any creature, but in that of God alone; he would not have one take thought of him, but of God alone, nor busy himself about him, but about God, and that Him alone all men should entertain and keep in their heart.

The malice of this sin may be further gathered from this example and comparison. A married woman would clearly be doing her husband wrong, if she were to dress and adorn herself to please any other man but him. Good works being the apparel wherewith we adorn and array our soul, we do God great wrong if we put them on to please anyone but God, Who is the spouse of our soul.

Or again, see what a foul shame it would be for a knight to plume himself much on the score of some slight labor undertaken for the love and service of his prince, when that prince had first exposed himself to great affronts and labors on behalf of that same knight. What bad form it would be for that knight to boast and brag of some petty service, a mere nothing, that he had rendered his master! What a sorry figure he would cut before all the company! And what if the prince had done and undergone all that hard work without any help from the knight, while the knight was indebted to the prince's aid and countenance for the little that he had done, for which, moreover, he had been promised and had received high reward! All this we may apply each one of us to himself, to make us ashamed of having a high conceit of ourselves for anything we have done for God, still more of boasting of it, since in comparison with what God has done for us and what we ought to do for Him, it is miserably little.

The malice of this sin further appears in this, that theologians and saints reckon it among the seven vices commonly called *deadly,* or more properly *capital,* because they are the heads and principles of the rest. Some enumerate eight *capital vices,* and say that the first is pride and the second vainglory; but the common opinion of the saints, and that received in the Church, puts seven capital vices; and St. Thomas says that the first of these is vainglory, and that pride is the root of them all, according to the Wise Man: *The beginning of all sin is pride* (Eccles. x. 13).

CHAPTER III

Of the Loss That Vainglory Entails

CHRIST OUR LORD clearly warns us in these words of the Gospel: *Take care not to do your good works before men, or to be seen and praised by them; otherwise ye shall have no reward with your Father who is in heaven.* Be not as those hypocritical Pharisees, who do all their works to be seen by men and honored and esteemed by them. *In truth I tell you, these have already received their reward* (Matt. vi. 1-2). You had a desire to be regarded and esteemed; that moved you to do what you did, but that also shall be your reward and crown; expect none other in the next life. Unhappy you, you have already received your wages and have nothing further to hope for! *The hope of the hypocrite shall perish,* says holy Job (viii. 13), the hypocrite being he who does things to be regarded and praised. St. Gregory shows this very well; human esteem and praises were what the man desired, and it shall end with his life. *The fool shall find no pleasure in his folly* (Job viii. 14). Oh, what a mockery and deceit shall you find when your eyes are opened and you see that with that wherewith you might have gained the kingdom of heaven, you have gained only a vain applause of men, a "Well said," or a "Well done." He who seeks the esteem and praises of men in payment of his virtuous acts, offers for sale at a low price a thing of high value; for that whereby he might have merited the kingdom of heaven, he seeks an idle praise. What greater delusion and what greater folly can there be than this, to have worked hard, done many good works, and find yourself afterwards left with nothing! This is what the Propheth Aggeus says: *Advert and see what ye are doing in this matter. Ye have sown much, and have reaped little; ye have eaten, and not been filled; ye have drunk and not quenched your thirst; ye have clothed yourselves, and not got warm; all that ye do hath profited you nothing, because ye put it into a sack full of holes, so that ye have scarce put it in on one side than it goes out on the other* (Agg. i. 5-6). Another text says: *He who gathereth riches is as one who pours wine into a cask or barrel full of chinks and holes,* so that to pour it in and pour it out is one and the same thing. This is the doing of vainglory: to gain and to lose is one and the same thing; the loss is conjoined with the gain. *Why do ye give your silver for what is not bread, and spend your labor on what cannot satisfy your hunger?* (Isaias lv. 2). Now that you do things, now that you labor and weary yourself, do the things in such a way that you may get some return from them and not lose them entirely.

St. Basil gathers three losses that this vice of vainglory entails upon us. The first is that it makes us weary and afflicts our body with labor and good works. The second, that it robs us of these good works after they are done, making us lose all the reward and recompense of them. It does not keep us from learning, says St. Basil—that were no such great loss, to rob us of a reward we had not worked for; but it takes care to make us weary ourselves in doing good works and then robs and despoils us of them, depriving us of the reward. It is, he says, like a pirate that lurks in ambush, watching for a ship to come out of harbor well-laden with merchandise, and then delivers his attack. It is not the way of pirates to chase a vessel when she comes out of harbor empty to go for a cargo of merchandise. They wait till she returns with her cargo; so this robber, called vainglory, waits till we are laden with good works and then assaults and despoils us of them.

Further, it not only deprives us of the reward, but makes us deserve chastisement and torment instead thereof; it converts good into evil and virtue into vice by the vain and evil end that it sets before us. And thus of good seed there is reaped an evil crop and pain and chastisement is merited by that whereby we might have merited heaven. And all this vainglory does so sweetly and pleasantly that the man not only does not feel his loss—as he does lose all that he does—but actually enjoys it, so much so that, however much you tell him and he sees himself that he is losing all, nevertheless he seems bewitched by this desire of being praised and esteemed, inasmuch as it quite carries him away. Therefore St. Basil calls vainglory "a gentle despoiler of our spiritual gifts and a pleasant enemy of our souls"—*dulcem spiritualium exspoliatricem, incundum animarum nostrarum hostem.* It is a very endearing enemy; it is a pleasant impoverisher. Thus it is, says the saint, that this vice infatuates so many by the sweetness and pleasantness that it carries with it. This human praise, he says, is a thing very sweet and delicious to simpletons, and thereby it infatuates them. *Dulce quid humana imperitis gloria est.* And St. Bernard says: "Fear this arrow of vainglory; it enters pleasantly and seems a light thing, but I tell you of a truth it inflicts no slight wound on the heart" —*Time sagittam; leviter volat leviter penetrat; sed dico tibi non leve infligit vulnus; cito interficit.* Like corrosive sublimate, it is a small powder, but deadly poison.

Surius relates how, when the great Pacomius was sitting in a certain place of the monastery with other grave Fathers, one of his monks brought out two little mats that he had made that day and put them hard by his cell, in front of where St. Pacomius was, that he might see them, thinking that he must surely praise him for being so industrious and careful, inasmuch as, while the rule only ordered him to make one mat a day, he had made two. The saint, understanding that he had done this out of vanity, heaving a great sigh, said to the Fathers who were with him: "See how this brother has worked from morning to night, and all his labor he has offered to the devil, and has loved rather the esteem of men than the glory of God." He called the monk and gave him a good scolding and enjoined him for penance that, when the monks should assemble for prayer, he should go there with his mats at his sides and say in a loud voice: "Fathers and brothers, for the love of the Lord do you all pray for this wretched sinner, that He may have mercy on him for having set more store by these two little mats than by the kingdom of heaven." And he further enjoined that, when the monks were at dinner, he should stand in like manner in the middle of the refectory with his mats at his sides all the time that the meal lasted. And his penance did not stop there; after that was done, the abbot ordered that they should shut him up in a cell, and nobody was to visit him, but he was to be there alone for the space of five months, and they were to give him nothing to eat but bread, salt, and water, and every day he was to make two mats, unseen and fasting. Hence we may learn for our instruction what severe penances those ancient Fathers gave for slight faults, and the humility and patience wherewith their subjects took them and profited thereby.

CHAPTER IV

That the Temptation to Vainglory Assails Not Only Beginners, but Also Those Who Are Well-Advanced in Virtue

ST. CYPRIAN, speaking of the second temptation with which the devil assailed Christ our Lord, when he took Him to the pinnacle of the Temple and said to Him: *If thou be the Son of God, cast thyself down* (Matt. iv. 6), exclaims: "O execrable malice of the devil! The malignant fiend thought to overcome by vainglory Him Whom he had not conquered by gluttony!" He wanted Him to fly through the air, to be a spectacle of admiration to all the people. He thought to succeed with Him as he had with others. He knew by experience and had proved it many times, that he had overcome by the temptation of vainglory and pride those whom he had not been able to overcome by other temptations, vainglory being a harder thing to overcome than gluttony. It is hard not to take delight in hearing oneself praised. As there are few who like to hear themselves ill-spoken of, so there are very few who do not take satisfaction in others' thinking and speaking well of them. Hence we see that this temptation of vainglory touches not beginners and novices alone, but even the most ancient in eligion, men well versed in perfection; indeed, it is more properly their temptation.

The holy Abbot Nilus, who was a disciple of St. John Chrysostom, relates of those old and experienced Fathers that they brought up and instructed novices differently from seniors. On novices they enjoined great attention to temperance and abstinence, because they said that he who lets himself be carried away and overcome by the vice of gluttony will easily be vanquished by the vice of lust; for how shall he resist the greater enemy, who does not know how to stand out against the less? But the seniors they advised to be very watchful to defend and guard themselves against vainglory and pride, as seamen have to take precaution against sunken rocks at the mouth of the harbor. It often happens that after a prosperous voyage vessels come to shipwreck in the harbor; so many who have voyaged well through the whole course of their life, overcoming and mastering all the temptations they met with, at the end, when nearing the harbor, confident in their past victories and taking themselves to be secure, have waxed proud and careless and so come to a miserable fall; and the vessel that had not sprung a leak nor in any way behaved ill on so long a voyage over the open sea, has come to mishap and shipwreck in port. That is the doing of vainglory, and so the saints call it a storm in harbor; others compare it to one who goes on board a ship, well-provisioned and laden with merchandise, and scuttles and sinks it.

Therefore those ancient Fathers did not instruct beginners and novices to be on their guard against vainglory, for they thought it was not necessary. Just come in from the world, running with blood and with the wounds of their former sins still unclosed, beginners carry with them matter enow of humility and confusion; to these their instructors preached abstinence, penance, and mortification. It was the seniors who had deeply bewailed and lamented their sins and done much penance for them, and had had long exercise in the practice of virtue, that needed these warnings against vainglory. But as for beginners, who were void of virtue and full of passions and evil inclinations, and who had not yet done with duly lamenting their sins and their past forgetfulness of God, these gave no ground for attacks of vainglory, but much for sorrow and shame. That treatment was quite right. Hence they may gather occasion of great confusion who, having many things to humble themselves for, yet for one point in which they shine and think they do very well, vaunt themselves and give themselves airs. Here we are much mistaken; one single defect ought to be enough to confound and humble us, but with us it is the other way about—all the many faults and defects we have are not enough to humble us, but one good point that we fancy we find in ourselves is enough to make us proud, and desire to be honored and esteemed on the strength of that. Herein well appears the malice and subtlety of vainglory, since it lets nobody off, but assails people who present no grounds for it. As St. Bernard says: "It is the first sin we fall into, and the last we overcome." Therefore, brethren, says St. Augustine, let us all arm ourselves and forestall the attacks of this vice, as did the Prophet David, saying: *Turn away my eyes that they behold not vanity* (Psalm cxviii. 37).

CHAPTER V

Of the Special Need That There Is to Beware of the Vice of Vainglory in Those Who Have the Office of Helping Their Neighbor

ALTHOUGH, as we have said, all need to be watchful against this temptation of vainglory, yet we whose office it is by our institute to help to the salvation of souls, need more particularly to be forearmed against it. For our ministries are very exalted and open and manifest to the whole world; and the greater and more spiritual they are, so much greater on the one hand is our danger, and the greater our offense on the other, if we seek ourselves therein and want to be regarded and esteemed by men. This would be exalting ourselves with that which God most prizes and esteems; namely, His graces and spiritual gifts. So St. Bernard says: "Woe be to them to whom it has been given to conceive and speak well of God and spiritual things and understand the Scriptures and preach eloquently, if that gift which has been given them to gain souls and extend and spread the honor and glory of God, they turn to the purpose of seeking themselves and being regarded and esteemed by men! Let them fear and tremble at what God says by the Prophet Osee: *I have trusted them with my riches; I have given them my silver and gold and the precious jewels that I most valued, and they have made of them an idol of Baal* (Osee ii. 8)." They have fabricated with it an idol of honor. *Vae qui bene de Deo et sentire et loqui acceperunt, si quaestum aestiment pietatem, si convertant ad inanem gloriam quod ad lucra Dei acceperunt erogandum, si alta sapientes humilibus non consentiant.* St. Gregory applies to this purpose what St. Paul says to the Corinthians: *Let us not be as many who adulterate the word of God* (II Cor. ii. 17). He gives two explanations of this passage. The first is when one understands and explains Holy Scripture in another manner than what it really means, engendering and extracting therefrom by one's own spirit false and adulterous senses, the lawful husband and author thereof being the Holy Ghost, and the true and lawful sense that which He has declared to His Church through her saints and doctors. The second explanation of adulterating the word of God is what makes to our purpose. There is this difference between the true and lawful husband and the adulterer, that the former intends to beget and have children, while the latter intends only his own lust and satisfaction. In the same way he who by the word of God and the office of preaching which he holds does not intend so much to beget spiritual children to God —which is the end for which preaching is ordained, according to the saying of St. Paul, *I have begotten you by the Gospel* (I Cor. iv. 15)—as his own gratification and satisfaction, seeking to be regarded and esteemed, such a one adulterates the word of God. And therefore also the saints call vainglory a spiritual lust because of the great delight that is taken in it, as greater than the other carnal delight and lust as the soul is greater than the body. Let us not, then, adulterate the word of God; let us not in our ministries aim at anything else than the honor and glory of His Divine Majesty, according to what Christ our Redeemer says: *I seek not my own glory, but the honor and glory of my heavenly Father* (John viii. 56).

Holy Scripture relates an action of Joab, Captain General of the Army of David, an action worthy of being recounted and imitated by us. It says that Joab with his army was besieging the city of Rabath, the capital city of the Ammonites, where their king resided with his court. When he was pushing the siege with advantage and was on the point of entering and taking the city, he dispatched couriers to King David letting him know how the matter stood, that he might come and enter and take it. And he gives this reason: *That the honor of the victory may not be attributed to me, if I enter and take it* (II Kings xii. 28); and so it was done. This is the loyalty that we should observe with God in all our ministries, never seeking to have the fruit and conversion of souls or the good success of enterprises attributed to us, but all to God. *Not to us, O Lord, not to us, but to thy name give glory* (Psalm cxiii. 1). All the glory should be given to God Who is in heaven, as the angels sang: *Glory be to God on high* (Luke ii. 14).

Of St. Thomas of Aquin we read in his Life that never in his career had he any vainglory amounting to a fault. He never took any complacency or satisfaction in the great learning and angelic understanding and other gifts and graces that God gave him. And of our blessed Father Ignatius we read that for many years before he died he never had so much as a temptation to vainglory; so illuminated was his soul by light from heaven and so great his knowledge and contempt of himself, that he used to say there was no vice that he feared less than vainglory. There is the model that we should imitate; we should blush and be ashamed when we allow vanity to arise in us even in mean things. How would you be if you saw yourself a great doctor and preacher, gaining great fruit of souls and highly valued by princes and prelates and all the world? We need to accustom ourselves in small things to make no account of the praises and esteem of men, nor regard human considerations, that so we may be competent to do the same in great things.

CHAPTER VI

Of Sundry Remedies Against Vainglory

ST. BERNARD in his fourteenth sermon on the psalm *Qui habitat,* on that verse, *Thou shalt walk upon serpents and basilisks, and trample underfoot lions and dragons,* declares at length how some of these animals do hurt with their teeth, biting; others with their breath; others with their claws; others terrify by their roaring; and so the devil invisibly does hurt and makes mischief for men in all these ways; and he applies the properties of these animals to various temptations and vices whereby the devil makes war on us. Coming to the basilisk, he says: "Of the basilisk there is told a portentous thing, that by even his look he infects men so grievously as to kill them." And the saint applies this to the vice of vainglory, according to those words of Christ: *Take heed that ye do not your good works before men to be seen by them* (Matt. vi. 1), as though He would say: "Take heed of the eyes of the basilisk." So the saint says that there is this about the vice of vainglory, that it kills only the blind and the careless, who display themselves and put themselves forward for the vice to see them and do not take care themselves to look at it first, considering what a vain and useless thing this vainglory is; for if in this way you first catch sight of the basilisk of vainglory, it will not kill you nor do you any harm—rather you will kill it, undoing it and turning it all to smoke.

Let this be the first remedy against vainglory, to try to get the first look at this basilisk by setting ourselves to consider and examine attentively how the opinion and esteem of men is all a puff of wind and vanity, giving us nothing and depriving us of nothing, so that we shall be neither better for men's praising us and setting store by us, nor worse for their disparaging us and persecuting us. St. Chrysostom, commenting on the verse of the Fifth Psalm, *For thou wilt bless the just,* treats this subject well. He says that these words are used by the prophet to animate the just man who is persecuted and hears hard words said of him by men, not to be alarmed at that or make much account of it. What harm will the contempt of all mankind do him, if the Lord of angels blesses and praises him? On the contrary, if the Lord does not bless and praise him, nothing will avail him aught, not though all the world praises and publishes his merits. He quotes the example of holy Job, who, sitting upon a dunghill, covered all over with leprosy, ulcers, and worms; persecuted and scoffed at by his friends, by his own wife, and by the whole world, yet was, notwithstanding, more blessed than them all because, while men loaded him with insult and spoke ill of him, God spoke well of him, saying that he was *a man simple, upright, fearing God, and keeping aloof from evil, and persevering in innocence* (Job ii. 3). Here was a man truly great, and the unfavorable judgments of men and the poor opinion that the world entertained of him lost him nothing. St. Chrysostom further says that all our care and diligence should be to be regarded and esteemed before God, because to be so before men takes nothing away from us and brings us nothing in and there is no reason why we should take account of it. The Apostle St. Paul said: *I care nothing for being judged and made light of by men;* I have no mind to satisfy men; it is God that I seek to satisfy, since He is my judge: *He that judgeth me is the Lord* (I Cor. iv. 3). St. Bonaventure adds another point. "Be not angry," says he, "with those that speak ill of you, for what they say is either true or false; if it be true, you must not wonder they dare say what you durst do; if it be false, their detraction can do you no harm." But if, notwithstanding, some stirrings of sensitiveness should arise, suffer, he says, all with patience, as one suffers a cautery if fire is applied to a wound; for as the cautery cures the wound, so the detraction that you suffer will perhaps cure you of some secret pride lurking in your heart.

The second means that will help us very much for the obtaining of this end, is that which St. Basil, St. Gregory, St. Bernard, and generally all the saints recommend to us; which is to take very great care to let no expressions slip out of our mouths that may turn to our own praise. "Never say anything of yourself that may redound to your praise," says St. Bernard, "though the person you speak to should be one of your most familiar friends; but, on the contrary, endeavor to hide your virtues with more care than you take to hide your vices." Father Master Avila used so great a circumspection in this matter that, when it seemed necessary for the instruction of his neighbor to say something of edification that had happened to himself, he recounted it as of a third person, so that the other might not understand that he was the man. Concerning our Father Ignatius, we were told by a prelate of Spain who had known him at Paris that, when he was treating of prayer and persuading others to it, some asked him how he himself got on in prayer, to which he answered: "I shall only tell you what it befits you to know; that is charity and necessity, the other is vanity." We read in like manner of St. Francis that he was so reserved in this matter, that he not only never discovered to others the favors and particular graces God had communicated to him in prayer, but, when he went from it, he endeavored so to compose himself in his words and comportment that none should be able to perceive what he had in his heart.

In the third place, not content with never saying a word that might redound to our own praise, we should go further and do all we can to keep secret the good works that we do, as we are told in the Gospel: *When thou prayest, enter into thy private room and shut the door and there pray to thy heavenly Father in secret. And when thou givest alms, let not thy left hand know what thy right hand doeth* (Matt. vi. 6), as though to say: "Don't let even yourself know." *And when thou fastest, anoint thy head and wash thy face, that thou mayest not appear to men to be fasting* (Matt. vi. 17). Show then more cheerfulness than usual; make a feast of it, because in that province of Palestine, St. Jerome says, they used to anoint their heads on feast days.

Great is the subtlety of this vice, and therefore the Redeemer of the world recommends us so strongly to be on our guard and hide away from it, doing our works in secret, that we may not lose them nor be robbed by this thief. This is the precaution taken by travelers, says St. Gregory, to conceal the money they carry with them; for if they showed and made a display of it, the thief would catch sight of it and rob them. He cites to this effect what befell King Ezechias, who showed the treasures of his house to the ambassadors of the King of Babylon, and the Babylonians afterwards made booty of them and carried them off to Babylon. They also bring into this effect the comparison of the hen, who cackles when she lays an egg and thereupon loses it.

The true servant of God, says St. Gregory, is so far from this that he is never satisfied with stopping short at any good deed that may possibly come to be known, thinking that he has been already rewarded for that, but endeavors to heap up thereupon other good deeds that cannot possibly be known of men. St. Jerome tells of St. Hilarion that, perceiving the concourse of people that followed him and the reputation that his miracles had occasioned, he was much afflicted and wept every day very bitterly; and his disciples asking him what was the occasion of his sadness and tears: "Methinks," said he, "seeing the esteem that men have of me, that God is paying me in this life for the service which I endeavor to render Him." This is another consideration and another very good means to aid us against this vice. Be on your guard and do not aspire after the praises of men, for fear lest God should pay you therewith for any good that you may happen to have done in this life. For so He is wont to do, as He Himself tells us in saying to the rich glutton: *Remember, son, that thou hast received thy good things in this life* (Luke xvi. 25). It is also for the same reason that the saints do counsel us to avoid all sorts of singularity in devotion, because what is unusual most attracts notice, and it is a common saying that he who does what no one else does draws the eyes of all the world upon him. These things are wont to foster in your soul vainglory and pride, whence arises contempt for others.

But because we cannot always hide our good works, especially when we are called upon to contribute by our example to the edification of our neighbor, let this stand for the fifth remedy, to take care to rectify our intention, raising our heart to God and offering Him all our thoughts, words, and actions, to the end that, when vainglory comes to claim a part in them, we may say to it according to the advice of Father Master Avila: "You come too late; all is already given to God." It will also be very good to make use of the answer St. Bernard made to a thought of vainglory that came to his mind while he was preaching: "I did not begin for you, and I won't leave off for you." For we ought not to let the fear of vainglory make us desist from our good undertakings; we must only stop our ears and thereby render ourselves deaf to the praises of men. St. Chrysostom says we ought to behave to the world as a father behaves towards his son while he is yet in his infancy, for whether the child fondle his father or show himself peevish to him, it is all the same thing to the father; he laughs as well at the one as at the other because he looks upon him as a baby, who knows not what he says nor what he does. Let us look upon the world in the same manner and take it for a baby, not having sense to know what it is saying. Father Francis Xavier, Apostle of the East Indies, used to say that whoever would enter into himself and consider what he really is before God, would think that men were making game of him when they praised him and would take their praises for real insults.

Let us conclude hereupon, and make our final remedy against vainglory, self-knowledge, which is directly opposed to it. If we would plunge and sink deep into this, we should quite understand that we have no ground for any approach to vainglory, but much for self-abasement and humiliation; and this, not only looking at our evil deeds and sins, but even looking at the works which seem to us very good and righteous: on examination we should find therein abundant matter for humiliation and shame. St. Gregory often repeats: "All human righteousness, that which we commonly hold and have on our part, is convicted of being unrighteousness if it is judged strictly; kind indulgence apart, our work, from which we look for reward, is often worthy of punishment." And so holy Job said: *I feared for all my works* (Job ix. 28), because of the defects and faults that are usually mingled with them when one does not walk cautiously keeping guard over oneself. When vainglory approaches, let us attentively examine and take account at night what the day has been like; we shall find in ourselves a depth of miseries, evils, and faults that we have fallen into in thought, work and word, and omission; and if in aught by favor of our Lord there has been any good done, we shall commonly find that we have failed by pride and vainglory or by laziness and negligence, and by many other faults that we know, and by many others that we do not know, but may well believe that they are there. Let us, then, enter into ourselves, let us take refuge in knowledge of ourselves; let us look at our feet, that is, at the foulness of our works, and that will at once put a spoke in the wheel of vanity and pride rising in our heart.

CHAPTER VII

Of the End and Good Intention That We Ought to Have in Our Actions

WE have considered how vanity and regard for the opinion of men are to be avoided in the actions that we do if we would keep aloof from evil. Now we will consider the end and intention that we ought to have in them, which is the greater honor and glory of God. The blessed St. Ambrose applies to this purpose what naturalists tell of the eagle, that the test that he uses to know his young, whether they be legitimate or spurious, is to take them in his talons and expose them hanging in mid-air to the rays of the sun; and if they look fixedly at it without winking, he takes them for his own and returns them to the nest and rears them; but if he sees that they cannot look fixedly at the sun, he takes them for no offspring of his and lets them fall to the ground. Now in this it shall be known if we are true sons of God, if we look fixedly at the true Sun of Justice, that is, God; directing to Him all that we do, so that the end and aim of all our actions is to please and satisfy God and do in them His most holy will. This agrees well with what Christ our Redeemer says in the Gospel: *Whoever shall do the will of my Father who is in heaven, he is my brother and my sister and my mother* (Matt. xii. 50).

We read of one of those ancient Fathers that at every action which he wished to set about he paused a little while; and when asked what he was doing, he answered: "Look you, our actions of themselves are worth nothing if we do them not with a good end and intention; and as the marksman, to hit the mark, stops, pausing a little while, looking and taking aim, so I, before I do any good work, ordain and direct my intention to God, Who ought to be the end and aim of all our actions; and that is what I am doing at the time of my pause." Now that is what we ought to do. *Put me as a seal on thy heart* (Cant. viii. 6). And as the marksman, better to make sure of his mark, shuts his left eye and looks only with his right, that his sight may be more collected and not distracted nor end by looking in many directions, so we ought to shut the left eye of human and earthly considerations and open only the right by a good and right intention, and in this manner we shall hit the mark and come home thereby to the heart of God. *Thou has wounded my heart, my sister, my spouse, thou hast wounded my heart with one of thine eyes* (Cant. iv. 6).

To speak more clearly and descend more to particulars in this matter, I say that we should endeavor to refer and direct all our actions to God. And in this there is greater and less. In the first place, at rising we should offer to God all the thoughts, words, and actions of that day and beg Him that all may be for His glory and honor, so that afterwards, when vainglory comes, we may answer with truth: "You come too late; that is already given away." And further, we should not be satisfied with offering and referring actually to God, when we rise, all that we are to do that day, but we should try to accustom ourselves as far as we can never to start anything that is not actually referred to the glory of God. And as the stonecutter or mason at work upon a building is wont to hold the plummet or rule in his hand and to apply it to every stone or brick that he lays, so we ought to regulate and direct every action that we do by this rule of the will and greater glory of God. And further, as the workman is not content with applying the rule or plummet once at the beginning, but applies it again and again until the stone is well and completely laid, so we must not be content with referring to God once for all at the beginning the actions which we do, but also during the time of doing them we should do them in such manner as to be always offering them to God, saying: "Lord, it is for Thee that I do this, because Thou commandest it, because Thou willest it."

CHAPTER VIII

In Which It Is Explained How We May Do Our Actions with Great Rectitude and Purity of Intention

TO explain how we may do our actions with greater perfection and purity, the masters of spiritual life bring a good comparison. As mathematicians abstract from the matter, and deal only with the quantities and figures, of bodies, making no account of the matter in which they are, be it gold or silver or any other substance, since that is no concern of theirs, so the servant of God in the actions that he does must fix his eyes chiefly on doing the will of God, abstracting from all matter, not looking to see whether it is gold or clay, not minding whether they put him in this office or that, since our progress and perfection lie not therein, but in doing the will of God and seeking His glory in what we do. The glorious St. Basil says this very well, and it is founded on the doctrine of the Apostle St. Paul. All the life and actions of a Christian man have one end and aim, which is the glory of God, for *whether you eat or drink or do any other thing,* says the Apostle, *you should do all to the glory of God* (I Cor. x. 31).

The Apostle St. John relates how Christ our Redeemer was talking with the Samaritan woman, being very tired and weary with His journey, and the disciples had gone into the town to look for something to eat, as the hour was late. When they came with the food, they said to Him: *Master, eat. But he answered them: I have meat to eat ye know not of. And when they asked one another: Hath any man brought him something to eat? My meat, he answered, is to do the will of him that sent me* (John iv. 32). See here what ought to be our meat in all things we do. When you study, when you hear confessions, when you lecture or preach, your meat must not be the satisfaction of knowing or studying or preaching, since that would be to make clay of gold, but all your meat and nourishment and satisfaction should be the fact of your doing the will of God, which requires you there and then to be doing those things. And the same also should be your meat when you serve in the domestic offices of the house. Thus one and the same is the meat, and one and the same the diet, of porter and infirmarian as of preacher and lecturer. So you should be as content in your office as he is in his, since you have the same ground of contentment that he has, which is doing the will of God. Thus we should ever aim at having in our mouth and in our heart these words: "For Thee, O Lord, I do this, for Thy glory, because so Thou willest;" and we must not stop in this exercise until we come to do things *as serving the Lord and not men* (Eph. vi. 7), as St. Paul says, and until we do them in such a way as to be always in them actually loving God, and rejoicing in them inasmuch as therein we are doing the will of God, so that when we are at work it seems that we are rather loving than working.

Father Master Avila makes here a good and very homely comparison. When a mother is washing the feet of her son or husband who has come off the road, she is at once serving and loving and rejoicing, and taking particular pleasure and satisfaction in the comfort she is giving. Oh, if we could succeed in doing our actions in this manner! Oh, if we could hit on this treasure hidden in the field, a treasure so manifest and open in one way and yet so hidden and concealed in another, what spiritual and interior and advanced men should we be! This is true alchemy, most certain to make out of copper and iron the finest gold; for though the work be in itself very humble, hereby it is made very exalted and of immense value. Let us, then, from now onwards aim at turning whatever we do into the finest gold, since the thing can be done so easily. In the Holy of Holies in the Temple of Solomon, everything was either of gold or covered with gold (III Kings vi. 19-22); so everything in us should be love of God or done for love of God.

CHAPTER IX

That the Reason Why We Find Ourselves Sometimes Distracted and Thrown Back in Our Spirituality by Exterior Occupations Is Because We Do Them Not as We Should

FROM what has been said it will be understood that the reason why we find ourselves at times distracted and spiritually enfeebled by exterior occupations does not lie in the occupations, but in our own selves, inasmuch as we know not how to profit by them and do them as we ought. And so let no one throw the blame on his occupations, but on himself, in that he does not know how to profit by them. Crack the nut; since it is not what is on the outside that is eaten, but what is in the inside. If you stop on the exterior of the work and this outer shell, that will harass and break your body and dry up your spirit. The inside, the kernel, which is the will of God, ought to be your food. So crack with the teeth of consideration this shell, and leave this bark outside and pass on to the marrow, like Ezechial's great eagle (Ezech. xvii. 3), that made its way inside and drew out the marrow of the cedar, not stopping at the bark. *I will offer thee holocausts of marrow* (Psalm lxv. 15). That it is on which we ought to rest, and offer it to God, and in this manner your soul will thrive and grow.

Martha and Mary are sisters; they do not disturb nor hinder one another, but aid one another. Prayer helps to do action well, and action, done as it ought to be done, helps prayer, like good sisters. If you feel yourself troubled and disturbed in action, it is because Mary, that is, prayer, does not help you. *Martha, Martha, thou art solicitous, and troubled over many things* (Luke x. 41). Martha is troubled because her sister Mary does not help her. *Tell her, Lord, to help me* (Luke x. 40). Endeavor to procure the aid of Mary, that is, of prayer, and you will see how the trouble will cease. Ezechiel (viii. 1) says of those holy living creatures that each held its hand under its wing, to give us to understand that spiritual men keep the hand of action under the wing of contemplation without removing the one from the other, since in action they contemplate and in contemplation they act. Cassian also says of those monks of Egypt that while working with their hands they ceased not on that account to contemplate God, doing with their hands the office of Martha and with their heart that of Mary.

St. Bernard puts this very well. "Those engaged in spiritual life and prayer take much care so to occupy themselves in exterior works and occupations that the spirit is not stifled nor devotion quenched. Thus exterior occupations are no hindrance to recollection and interior devotion, for they do not occupy the understanding, but leave it free to be able to think of God"—*Hoc maxime curant spiritualibus exercitiis dediti, taliter se circa exteriora occupare ut devotionis spiritum non exstinguant: unde licet extrinsecus bonorum operum exercitiis fatigentur in corpore, intrinsecus tamen reficiuntur in mente.* Thus a very ancient and very spiritual father, Father Master Nadal, used to say that there were two sorts of person that he greatly envied in religion—novices, because they did not mind nor spend their time on anything else than their spiritual progress; and lay brothers, because, having their understanding unpreoccupied and disengaged, they are able to pass the whole day in prayer.

St. John Climacus relates that there was in a monastery a cook, a very busy man, owing to the great number of religious—he says there were two hundred and thirty, besides guests; and in the midst of all his occupations he kept up a very great interior recollection, and had further attained to the gift of tears. St. John Climacus wondered, and asked him how he had attained it in the midst of so great and continual occupation. After much importunity he answered at last: "I never think that I am serving men, but God, and always hold myself unworthy of quiet and repose; and the sight of this material fire makes me always weep, and think of the bitterness of the everlasting fire."

It is told of St. Catherine of Siena in her Life that she suffered much persecution from her parents, who heaped ill treatment upon her to compel her to marry. The persecution went so far that they ordered that no private room or cell should be allowed her in which to collect her thoughts, but occupied her in housework. Further, they took out of the kitchen a slave they had and put her in the place, so that she should have no time to pray nor do her other spiritual exercises. But, taught by the Holy Ghost, the history says, she built there within her heart a very retired spiritual cell and purposed never to go out of it, and succeeded in so doing. Thus as for the first cell, which she occupied before, sometimes she was within, sometimes outside; but out of this other holy spiritual cell, which she had built within herself, she never stirred. They turned her out of her former cell, but they could never turn her out of this. She pictured to herself that her father represented Jesus Christ; her mother, our Lady, her brothers and the rest of the family, the apostles and disciples of the Lord. Thus she went about her work with great alacrity and diligence, for though she was in the kitchen and busy serving, she was ever thinking of her Spouse, Jesus Christ, Whom she made account that she was serving; she ever enjoyed the presence of God and was with Him in the Holy of Holies. And she often told her confessor, when he had any exterior occupations and was forced to go on a journey: "Father, make within yourself a cell and never go out of it." Let us do the like, and exterior duties and occupations will not distract us, but rather aid us to be always in prayer.

CHAPTER X

Of the Great Benefit and Gain to Be Found in Doing One's Actions in the Manner Aforesaid

ACTIONS done in the manner aforesaid are called full actions, and they who live in this manner, according to St. Jerome and St. Gregory, are said in Holy Writ to live *full days* and to be *full of days* (Job xlii. 16: Psalm lxxii. 10) ; and that, though they have lived but a short time and died young, according to the saying of the Wise Man: *Being made perfect in a short time, he fulfilled many years* (Wisdom iv. 13). How is it possible in a short time to live a long time and fulfil many years? Do you know how? By doing full works and living full days. *Full days shall be found in them* (Psalm lxxii. 10). This second passage explains the first. From morning till night and from night till morning live as a good religious and servant of God; the servant of God lives a full day of twenty-four hours, since he occupies it all in doing the will of God. His very meals, recreation, and sleep are not empty and useless hours for him, since he directs and refers them all to the greater honor and glory of God and does them because it is the will of God that he should do them. He does not eat for appetite like beasts, nor seek his satisfaction and amusement in these things; rather he would be glad to do without any of them if such were the Lord's good pleasure. O Lord, that we could go without eating, without sleep, and without these recreations and amusements! O Lord, that one could be always loving Thee and have no need to meet and supply these miseries of the body! *Deliver me from my necessities* (Psalm xxiv. 17) that I may be eternally taken up with Thee.

I see that such is not the state and condition of this life; but the just man bears that with patience, though not without pain, saying to himself with Job and David: *I sigh before I eat* (Job iii. 24); *I mingled my drink with my tears* (Psalm ci. 10); *Every night I will water my couch with my tears* (Psalm vi. 7). So should we do, shedding tears when we go to take our rest, saying: "Ah, Lord, what a misery that I have to lie here such a long time without remembering Thee! *Woe is me that my sojourning is prolonged!* (Psalm cxix. 5). When wilt Thou take me, O Lord, this poor exile? Woe is me; how long is this captivity to last? *Lead my soul out of prison* (Psalm cxli. 8). When wilt Thou draw me, Lord, out of the prison of this body, that I may be able to give myself entirely to Thee? Oh, when shall that be? Oh, how long is that hour in coming!" These are full works and full days. In this manner, the just lives long in a short time, and a few days of his life make many years of merits. But he who has not done good work, nor well employed the days of his life, though he has lived a long time and attained many years, is said to die void of days because he has spent his days and his years in vain, and he may say *that his years are few and evil* (Gen. xlvii. 9).

On those words of Isaias that King Ezechias spoke on recovering from his sickness: *I said, In the midst of my days I will go down to the gates of the grave* (Isaias xxxviii. 10), St. Jerome observes that just and holy men fulfil their days, as did Abraham, of whom Holy Writ says that *he died full of days and in a good old age* (Gen. xxv. 8); but the wicked always die in the midst of their days, and even do not get so far, according to the saying of the prophet: *Men of blood and contrivers of evil shall not live out half their days* (Psalm liv. 24), since they have let their years pass by to no purpose. So Holy Writ calls the sinner of a hundred years a child of a hundred years, and says that such a one shall be accursed. *The child of a hundred years shall perish, and the sinner of a hundred years shall be accursed* (Isaias lxv. 20), because he has not lived like a man, but like a child. Hence it is that in the case of the wicked, death always takes them unseasonably, without their being ripe or ready for it. So, when it comes, they cry: "Oh, that I could have at least another year of life to do penance!" In the same way it happens to tepid and slack religious that, though they have been many years wearing the habit, they can count but few days in religion.

We read in the Chronicles of St. Francis that one of these holy religious was asked how long he had been a friar and he answered: "Not for one minute." The other did not understand and was much surprised at the answer; whereupon the servant of God said to him: "I know it is for seventy-five years that I have worn the habit of a Friar Minor; but for how much of that time I have been a friar with my works, I do not know." Please God that none of us may be able to say with truth what this holy man said out of humility. The matter does not lie in many years of religion nor in a long life, but in a good life. "Many count the years of their conversion, but often there is little fruit of amendment," says Thomas à Kempis. A few days of a good life are worth more than many years of a tepid and slack one. Before God there are not counted the years of life, but the years of a good life; nor the years of religion, but the years in which one has lived as a good religious. In the Book of Kings it is said: *A son of one year old was Saul when he began to reign; and he reigned two years over Israel* (I Kings xiii. 1). Yet it is certain that he was king for forty years, as St. Paul says: *God gave them for king Saul, son of Cis, for forty years* (Acts xiii. 21). Why, then, is it said that he reigned only two years? Because in the annals and chronicles of God they count only the years of good life; and it is said that he reigned for two years, because it was only for that time that he reigned as a good king. And in the Gospel (Matt. xx. 8) those who had come last to labor in the vineyard, though they had labored only one hour, were preferred to those who had come in the morning, because in that hour they had earned as much as or more than the others all the day long. Do you reckon up at this rate how long you have lived in religion.

All this is said very well by St. Eusebius Emesenus: "We are wont to reckon up our years, and the periods of time that we have now lived; be not deceived, whoever you are, by the number of days that you have spent here since you bodily left the world; reckon that you have lived that day only on which you denied your own will, resisted your passions and appetites, kept your rules, and did your meditation and your spiritual duties well." Make up years of these days, if you can, and measure thereby the time that you have been a religious; and fear lest that be said of you which is said in the Apocalypse of the Bishop of the Church of Sardis: *I know thy works, that thou hast the name of being alive, and thou art dead: wake up, for I find not thy works full before my God* (Apoc. iii. 1-2). I know your works, says God; though men know them not, I know them well. You have the name of being alive, and you are dead; you have the name of Christian, and not the works of a Christian; the name of religious, and not the works of a religious; your works agree not with the name you bear, since your works are not full, but vain and empty. They are not full of God, but void of God and full of yourself. All that you seek is yourself in them, your own conveniences, your own honor and esteem. Let us, then, watch over ourselves; let us strive to make our actions full and our days full, that in a short time we may live long and be very deserving before God.

CHAPTER XI

A Further Declaration of the Rectitude and Purity of Intention Which We Ought to Have in Our Actions

THERE is a very good piece of advice ordinarily given to those who deal with their neighbor, telling them how they ought to be disposed in the works and ministries that they do; and this same advice declares very well how pure should be our intention in our actions and with what detachment and simplicity we should seek God in them; the same is the teaching of those glorious Fathers and doctors of the Church: Jerome, Gregory, and Chrysostom, as we shall see. When you take in hand any work to the end that some good, general or particular, may thence accrue to your neighbor, have not chiefly in view the fruit and good success of the work, but the doing therein of the will of God. Thus, when we hear confessions, preach, or lecture, we must not have chiefly in view the conversion or amendment and profit of those with whom we speak or whose confessions we hear or to whom we preach, but the doing of the will of God in that work, and doing therein the best we can to please God. The success of such work, the amendment of our neighbor and his actually drawing fruit from the sermon—that is not our affair, but God's. *I planted, Apollo watered, but God gave the increase* (I Cor. iii. 6). To plant and water, says the Apostle, that is what we can do, as the gardener does; but the plants' growing, and the trees' bearing fruit, that is not the work of the gardener, but of God. The fruit of souls, their rising out of sin and being converted and growing to perfection, is all to be laid to God's account. The value and perfection of our work does not depend on that. This purity of intention, then, we must strive to have in our actions, and in this manner our intention will be very pure and we shall enjoy great peace. He who does his works in this spirit is not troubled when somehow the success and fruit that he aimed at in his good work is hindered or rendered impossible, since he does not make this his end nor set his heart on that, but on doing therein the will of God and making the best job of it that he can to please God. But if, when you preach, hear confessions, or do business, you are much wedded to the result and fruit of your good work and make that your principal end, and then in some way your design is thwarted, you are sure to be troubled and come to lose sometimes not only peace of heart, but patience also and even suffer further loss still.

Our blessed Father Ignatius used to illustrate this by a very good example or comparison. Do you know, he says, how we ought to behave in our ministrations to our neighbor? As the Guardian Angels behave to those whom they receive in charge from the hand of God, to advise, defend, direct, enlighten, move, and help on to good so far as they can; but if their charges make an ill use of their liberty and prove rebellious and obstinate, the angels do not distress themselves on that account, nor are they pained, nor lose one jot or tittle of the blessedness they enjoy in God, but rather say with Jeremy: *We have treated Babylon and she is not healed, let us leave her* (Jer. li. 9)—so we should take all possible means to draw our neighbors out of sin and do them good; and after we have done our duty diligently, we must remain in much peace of soul and not lose heart because the patient holds on to his malady and has no mind to be cured.

When the disciples returned from preaching, mightily pleased with themselves because they had worked miracles and cast devils out of men's bodies, Christ our Redeemer answered them: *Rejoice not in that, but rejoice that your names are written in heaven* (Luke x. 20). Our joy must not depend on our success, even though it be as good success as that; but see whether you are doing works such as to merit thereby that your name be written in the kingdom of heaven; see if you are doing the duties of your office. It is in that that you should put your joy and satisfaction; as for those other successes and conversions and marvels, they stand not to your account, and the reward and glory to be given to you will not be in proportion to them, but in proportion to your labors, whether men be converted and improved or not. This is seen clearly, taking the thing the other way about. Supposing great fruit gained and all the world converted by your sermons and ministrations, and you have not gone on as you ought, what will it profit you, as Christ our Redeemer says in the Gospel? So in like manner, if you do what you ought, though not a soul be converted, not on that account will your reward be less. In a fine plight certainly would the Apostle St. James be if his reward depended on that, and he were to set up his rest on that, since they say he converted only seven or nine persons in the whole of Spain; but not for that did he merit less, or please God less, than the rest of the apostles.

Furthermore, we find another great consolation in this fact, that not only will God not ask of us an account whether we have gained much fruit or not, but He will not even demand an account whether you have preached a fine sermon or given a grand lecture. That is not what God commands us, nor does in that our reward lie; but what God commands and requires of me is that I do that which shall be possible and be in my power according to the talent that I have received—if little, little; if much, much; and with that He rests satisfied. *Of him to whom they have given much, much shall be required; and little of him to whom little has been given* (Luke xii. 48).

St. Chrysostom explains this very well. Treating of the parable of the talents, he asks what is the reason why the servant who gained two talents receives the same reward as he who gained five? When the master came to ask an account of the talents he had divided among his servants, the holy Gospel says that he came who had received five, and said: *Lord, thou gavest me five talents; thou seest that I have gained an increase of other five.* And the master says to him: *Well done, good and faithful servant; because thou hast been faithful in a little, I will set thee over much.* He comes who had received two talents, and says: *Lord, thou didst entrust me with two talents. See here, I have gained an increase of other two* (Matt. xxv. 20-23). And the master answers in the same words, promising the same reward to him as to the other who had gained five talents. What is the reason of this? A very good reason, answers the saint, since the gain of five talents in the one case, and of not more than two in the second, was not a matter of greater or less diligence, but because they gave five talents to the one, wherewith he was able to double the amount and gain an increase of another five, while to the other they gave only two; yet the one showed as much diligence as the other, and worked as hard as the other in making the best of what he had received, and so was able to merit and receive the same honor and recompense.

This point is very profitable and very consoling, being applicable to all things and to all offices and duties. If one man works and takes as much pains as another in the charge committed to him, he may merit as much as the other, although he does not do so much. For example, if I labor as much over preaching a sorry sermon as you over preaching a good one, it may be that I merit as much as you and even more. In the same way in studies; though your neighbor be but a poor scholar and you a good one, though he knows little while you know much, it may be that he merits more with the little that he knows than you with the great deal that you know; and the same in all occupations. Though I do not do my job to such a nicety as you do yours and my abilities and talent do not go so far as that, yet it may be that I merit more with the little that I do than you with the great results that you achieve. This consideration will help much to keep the one party from vainglory, the other from discouragement.

This is also the doctrine of St. Jerome on the same parable. "The master receives with like good grace and honor him who brought in four talents as him who brought in ten; for God regards not so much the amount gained as the good will, diligence, and charity with which the work is done." "God is more pleased with the affection shown than with the value of our offerings," says Salvian. As also says St. Gregory: "God does not regard what is given, but out of how much love it is given"—*Deus non respicit quantum, sed ex quanto.* God regards the heart rather than the gift. Thus one with fewer works may please God better than another with more, if he does them with greater love. Herein clear shines forth the greatness of God, since no service, however great it be, is great before Him if it proceed not from great love, since God has no need of our goods and cannot increase in riches nor in any other good thing. *If thou beest just, what wilt thou give him thereby, or what shall he receive at thy hand?* (Job xxxv. 7). What He does look for and value is being loved, and our doing what is in our power. We see this literally laid down in the matter of the two mites which that widow in the Gospel offered. Christ our Redeemer was sitting hard by the treasury, or charity box, of the Temple, where people threw in their alms; and there came those Pharisees or those rich men, and some threw in silver coins, others perhaps gold. Then came a poor widow and threw in two mites. Christ turns to His disciples and says to them: *Verily I say to you, this widow hath offered more than all; because the others have given out of their superfluity,* and even so have not given according to their condition, *but she of her poverty hath given all that she had* (Mark xii. 43-44). So, says St. Chrysostom, in the same way God will regard those who preach, study, labor, and do other ministries and offices; He will not look so much to what they do as to the good will, love, and diligence with which they do it.

CHAPTER XII

Of Some Signs Whereby It Will be Known When One Goes After Things Purely for God, and When One Goes After Them for Oneself

THE blessed St. Gregory notes a good sign whereby to know whether in our ministrations to our neighbor we are seeking purely the glory of God or are seeking ourselves. See if, when another preaches very well and stirs up the whole world and gathers much fruit in souls, you are as pleased as when you do the like. If you are not pleased, but seem rather smitten with sadness or envy, it is a clear sign that you are not seeking purely the glory of God. And he quotes to this effect the Apostle St. James: *If you have a bitter jealousy, and nourish in your heart feelings of contention and envy, your wisdom cometh not from above, but is earthly, animal, diabolical* (James iii. 14). This is not zeal for the glory and honor of God, but zeal for your being honored and esteemed as that other is. For if you desired the glory of God, and not your own, you would be glad that there should be many such men and that others should do what you had not the capacity nor knowledge to do. So the Scripture tells us of Moses, when Josue would have had him hinder several persons from prophesying in the camp, he answered, showing himself much annoyed: *Why are you zealous on my account? Would to God that all the people might prophesy, and that God would impart His Holy Spirit to them all* (Num. xi. 29). A servant of God ought in like manner to say: "Would to God that all were great preachers and that the Lord would give them much of His spirit, that thus the honor and glory of God might be spread wide and His holy name known and hallowed all over the world!"

We have a very good example of this in Father Master Avila. It is said of him that, when he learned that God our Lord had brought into the world the Society of Jesus by means of our holy Father and understood the end and institute thereof, he said that he had aspired for many years to bring this to pass, but could never compass it; and that the same thing had happened to him as might happen to a little child who, being on the slope of a mountain, should try with all his strength to roll a heavy burden to the top and could not do so by reason of the smallness of his strength; and then a giant should come along who took up the burden which the child could not lift, and carried it whither he would with the greatest ease. By this comparison, in his humility, he made himself out a little child and our Father Ignatius a giant. But what makes to our purpose is that he remained as satisfied and pleased as if the Society had been instituted by his means, since he desired therein nothing but the glory of God and the salvation of souls. These are God's good and faithful ministers, who seek not themselves but Jesus Christ.

The true servant of God should have such a pure desire of the glory and honor of God and of the profit and salvation of souls that, when God would have this effected by means of some other person, he should be as well satisfied as if it had been done by himself. Wherefore it is a very laudable practice that some servants of God, who are zealous for the conversion of souls, do observe in praying after this manner: "Lord, let this man be converted; let this soul be gained to Thee; let the profit and the estate be made by means of whomsoever Thou shalt please; I don't want anything attributing to me." This is walking in truth and purity, desiring not our honor and reputation, but the greater honor and glory of God.

We may say the same concerning our own and our brethren's spiritual advancement. Whoever is pained or disheartened because he sees his brother growing and advancing in virtue while he lags behind, seeks not purely the greater glory of God. For though it be true that a faithful servant of God ought to have his heart pierced with sorrow to see that he serves not so great a Master with such diligence as he ought, yet it does not therefore follow from thence that he needs must fret himself or repine because another makes greater progress than he does. On the contrary, in the great sorrow he has that he serves God no better, it should be a comfort and relief to him to see that, though in his weakness he falls below standard, there are others who come up to what he would desire, glorifying and greatly serving the Lord. That discouragement and distress which some feel is born of self-love and some pride or secret envy; for if you really desired the greater honor and glory of God, it is clear that you would receive much pleasure and content from seeing others growing greatly in virtue and perfection, although on the other hand you would feel sorrow and confusion for your not serving Him so well.

Secondly, when a religious does his duty and the things commanded him in such sort as not to mind whether they command him this or that, whether they put him in this office or that, it is a very good sign that he does things purely for God, since he maintains this equanimity and entire indifference by the fact of his seeking only to do the will of God, resting not at all on the matter of the actions he does. But if he does not do what is humble and laborious with the same good grace as what is easy and honorable, it is a sign that he does it not purely for God, but is seeking himself and his own taste and convenience. And so that holy man says very well: "If God were the motive of thy desire, thou wouldst rejoice in whatever way He ordered the affair."

Thirdly, it is a sign that you are not doing things purely for God, but for human considerations, when you expect your superior to thank you for what you do and the labor you undergo, giving you to understand by his words that you have done the thing well, or at least showing some sign of satisfaction, and are disheartened when he does nothing of the sort. If you did things purely for God, you would not wonder at that, nor take account of it; rather you would be confounded and ashamed when the superior gave you any indication, taking it to come of your imperfection and weakness, and you would complain of yourself and say: "Sorry and wretched creature that I am, am I such a child and so tender in virtue that it is needful to nourish me and keep me up with these things!" It is told in the "Spiritual Meadow" of the abbot, John the Younger, a monk of the Thebaid, who was the disciple of Abbot Amon, that for twelve years he served one of the ancient Fathers who was infirm; and though this Father saw that the task was so heavy and so engrossing, he never spoke to him one kind or loving word, but on the contrary treated him rudely. Finally, the old man finding himself near his death, and a great many hermits coming to visit him and being all gathered round him, he called this humble and patient disciple and, taking him by the hand, he said to him three times: "Stay with God! Stay with God! Stay with God!" and commended him to the assembled Fathers, to treat him as a son, saying: "This is not a man, but an angel; for these many twelve years that he has served me in my sickness, he has never had a good word from me, yet, notwithstanding, he has never failed to serve me with great diligence and affection."

CHAPTER XIII

How We Ought to Go on Growing and Mounting in Rectitude and Purity of Intention

OUR blessed Father Ignatius says in greater detail how we ought to mount in this rectitude and purity of intention: "Let all strive to have a right intention, not only about their state of life, but about all particular details; ever sincerely looking in them to serve and please His Divine Majesty for His own sake, and for the singular benefits wherewith He forestalls us, rather than for the fear of punishment or the hope of reward, though they should be aided by these motives also; and in all things let them seek God, stripping themselves, as far as possible, of the love of all creatures, to bestow their whole affection upon the Creator thereof, loving Him in all things, and all things in Him, according to His most holy and divine will."

There are several ways of seeking and serving God. To serve God out of fear of punishment is to seek God, and is a good thing; because that fear, though it be servile, ceases not to be good and to be a gift of God, and therefore the Royal Prophet begged it of God when he said: *Pierce my flesh, O Lord, with Thy fear* (Psalm cxviii. 120). But if we should say to ourselves and have in our hearts this sentiment: "If there were no hell and I were not afraid of being punished, I would offend God," divines hold that such an act as this would be evil and sinful and show a will very ill disposed. Notwithstanding, to help ourselves with the fear of punishment, with the apprehension of death and judgment, thereby to excite ourselves the better to serve God and to abstain from offending Him, is good; and it is upon this account that the Holy Scripture frequently puts these things before us and threatens us with them.

Secondly, to serve God for the reward which we hope for in glory, is also to seek God, and that in a better way than the former, because there is more perfection in doing our actions for the motive of reward in glory than for that of fear of hell: this is to go increasing in perfection. Moses acted after this manner, as St. Paul teaches us, when he says: *By faith, Moses, after he came of age, made nothing of being the son of Pharaoh's daughter, who had adopted him: he despised that, and sought rather to be humbled and despised for God than to enjoy all the treasures and riches of Egypt, because he had his eye on the recompense and reward that he hoped for* (Heb. xi. 24-25). And the Royal Prophet said: *I have disposed my heart, O Lord, to observe thy law, looking at the recompense thou hast promised* (Psalm cxviii. 112). This motive is good also, and we should aid ourselves with it; but our holy Father will have us go further, and desires that we should still elevate our hearts and entertain higher thoughts. *Aspire to better gifts, and I will show you a still more excellent way* (I Cor. xii. 31). He is not content that we should seek and serve God in any ordinary manner, but he would have us seek and serve God for Himself, for His infinite goodness, and for His being what He is, which is the highest of all titles.

The glorious Fathers of the Church, Basil, Chrysostom, and Gregory, treat this point excellently well. They liken those who serve God for reward to Simon of Cyrene, who took up Christ's Cross for a price reckoned as the hire of his day's work. So these people serve God for the price and day's wage to be given them. They say that we should not be solicitous and careful about remuneration, reckoning up at so much the remuneration and pay; for this is the part of hirelings and day laborers who seek their own interest. We should not serve God in this manner, but as true sons for pure love. There is a great difference, say they, between the service of a slave, the service of a servant, and the service of a son. The slave serves his master for fear of chastisement and the whip. The servant, or vassal, serves his lord for the pay and reward that he hopes from him; and if he is diligent in serving him, it is because in that way he hopes to thrive and be handsomely rewarded. But the son serves his father for love and is most careful not to offend him, not for fear of chastisement, which the son fears no more when he is grown up, nor for hope of getting anything from him, but for pure love. Thus a good son, though his father be poor and has nothing to leave him, serves and honors him on the ground that he deserves it for being his father, and takes it for sufficient reward of his service and labor that his father is pleased. So other saints tell us we should serve God, not for fear of punishment, like slaves, nor for hope of pay and remuneration, like hired servants and day laborers, but as true sons of God, since God has done us the favor of making us such. *See what charity the Father hath for us, in that we are called and be sons of God* (I John iii. 1); and with truth we call God, *Father,* and His Son, *Brother.* Since we are sons of God, let us love and serve Him as sons, and honor Him as a Father, and such a Father—for pure love, to give satisfaction to our heavenly Father as He deserves for being what

He is, for His infinite goodness alone, even though we had hearts and bodies without end to employ in loving and serving Him.

St. Chrysostom says very well: "If you have been found worthy to do something for God and then go seeking some other reward besides the mere fact of your having been found worthy to please Him, it shows that you do not know what a good thing it is to please God; for if you knew it, you would never seek any other external reward or remuneration." For what greater good can we desire or propose to arouse ourselves than to please and give satisfaction to God? *Imitate God as dearly beloved children, and love him as Christ hath loved us,* says St. Paul (Eph. v. 1). Consider, says St. Bonaventure, how liberally and without any interest of His own God has loved us and done us so many favors, and not only without self-interest, but to His own heavy cost, since we have cost Him His lifeblood. In this manner, then, we should love and serve God purely and without any manner of self-interest. Our very virtues and supernatural gifts we should desire, not for our own advancement and satisfaction, but purely for God and His greater glory, to have wherewith to thank God and give Him greater satisfaction. And the glory of heaven itself we should also desire after this manner. When we put before our soul the reward of the good that we do, to animate us to do well, that should not be the ultimate end on which our desire should finally rest; but our ultimate end should be the greater service and glory of God, since the more glory we attain, the better shall we be able to honor and glorify the Lord. This is true love of charity and true and perfect love of God. This is pure seeking of God and of His greater glory, all else is seeking ourselves and loving ourselves. This is the distinction which theologians and moral philosophers draw between perfect love, which they call love of friendship *(amor amicitiae)*, and love of desire *(amor concupiscentiae)*, in that the former loves its friend for love of the friend and the good of virtue, whereas the love of desire is when I love another, not so much for his own sake as for the interest and advancement which I think will accrue to me from him, as when one serves the rich and the powerful in expectation of favors to be received from them. It may well be seen that this is not perfect love, but a love full of self-love, not so much loving your friend as loving for yourself and your own conveniences and interests. Thus we say that you love bread and wine with the love of desire, since you do not love it for itself, but for yourself and as something to come in to yourself; that is loving yourself. In this way they do love and serve God who serve Him for fear of punishment or hope of the reward which He is to give them. This love is largely mingled with love of self; you do not seek God purely and disinterestedly therein. This Christ our Redeemer gives us to understand when, after He had worked the famous miracle of feeding five thousand men, not to count women and children, with five loaves and two fishes, much people followed Him, to whom He said: *Amen, amen, I say to you, ye seek me and come to me, not because ye take me for God, as having seen the signs and wonders I have wrought, but because ye have eaten of the loaves and had your fill. Seek not for the meat that perisheth, but for that which endureth unto life everlasting* (John vi. 26-27), which is Christ and doing purely the will of God. Oh, what a good answer was that of the servant of God, of whom Gerson relates that he was greatly given to penance and prayer, and the devil, envious of so many good works, tried to divert him from them, and so assailed him with a temptation about predestination: "Why weary and fatigue yourself so much? You are not to be saved; you are not to go to glory." He answered: "I do not serve God for the glory of heaven, but for His being what He is." Thereat the devil stood abashed.

The glorious St. Bernard goes even further still. He would have us so forgetful of self-interest in the works that we do as not to be content with loving and serving as sons, but go beyond that. The love of sons is all very well, nevertheless they sometimes have an eye to the estate and the inheritance, and think of that; sometimes, too, they love and serve their parents that they may not disinherit them, or that they may leave them an extra portion. "I hold in suspicion that love which is kept up by hope of gaining some other object besides the object loved; and when that other object drops from view, vanishes or falls off. That is no pure nor perfect love; true and perfect love is not mercenary. Pure love does not borrow strength from hope (of gain), gather strength, nor feel the depression of failing hope." He means to say that the true lover does not need to keep himself up with extrinsic considerations to serve God, or labor for what he expects they have to give him; nor would he be discouraged or cease to labor though he knew they had nothing to give him, for he is not moved thereto by self-interest, but by pure love.

But what shall be the love so high and perfect as to exceed and supersede the love of sons? Do you know what? says the saint. It is the love of the bride for the bridegroom, for true and perfect love is content with itself alone. It has a reward, but its reward is that which it loves; loving the beloved, that is its reward. Now such is the love of the bride, that seeks not nor aims at anything else than loving and, on the part of the bridegroom, to be loved by him; that is all its concern. Now in this way, says St. Bernard, we should love God, Who is the Bridegroom of our souls, so that we should stop and rest on this love for His being what He is, and that should be all our satisfaction and joy. True and perfect love is content with itself alone; the lover is content and satisfied with this love. This should be our merit and this should be our reward; we should not seek or aim at anything else than loving. The motive of our loving God should be to love Him; the fruit of our loving God should be to love Him; and the end of our loving Him should be to love Him. I love because I love, and I love to love. *Is per se sufficit, is per se placet et propter se: ipse meritum, ipse praemium sibi est amor, praeter se non requirit causam, non fructum: fructus eius usus eius; amo quia amo, amo ut amen.*

St. Chrysostom takes up this subject and goes on with it very well. Think not, he says, that because you have not an eye to any reward or interest, your recompense and reward shall be less on that account; nay, it will be greater. The less you think of gaining, the more you will gain. It is certain that the more a work is stripped of all self-interest, the purer and more perfect it will be, inasmuch as there is no admixture of your own in it, and so it will be more meritorious. The more you turn your eyes away from all manner of self-interest and the more purely you aim at pleasing God, says St. Chrysostom, the greater shall your reward be. The further you are removed from the spirit of a day laborer, the greater shall be your daily wage, because God will not pay you as a hireling servant, but as a son, the heir of the treasures of his father. We shall be sons and heirs of God, and brothers of Christ, inheriting jointly with Him; we shall enter with Him into our share, inheriting and enjoying the goods of our Father Who is in heaven (Rom. viii. 17). The mother of Moses had hire and salary paid her by Pharaoh's daughter for her to rear her own son (Exod. ii. 9); but she did not do it for hire and salary, but for the love she bore her child.

CHAPTER XIV

Of Three Degrees of Perfection Whereby We May Ascend to Great Purity of Intention and Great Love of God

THESE three degrees are gathered from the doctrine of the saints and especially of the glorious St. Bernard. The first is when one intends solely and seeks the glory of

God in such sort that, in the things that he does, all his contentment is in God, in fulfilling and doing the will of God, forgetful of all things in the world. St. Bernard says: "Would you know, so far as can be known here on earth, a good sign, whether you love God much and are growing in that love? See whether there is anything outside of God that can afford you consolation and satisfaction." His words are: "Certainly, so long as I can reap consolation or delight from any extrinsic object whatsoever, I dare not say that our Beloved yet occupies the innermost fold of my affections and most ardent love." And this is what St. Augustine also says (Confess. x. 29): "He loves Thee less, who along with Thee loves anything that he loves not for Thy sake"—*Minus te amat, qui tecum aliquid amat, quod non propter te amat.* A singular and excellent love was that of the holy queen, Esther, who in the midst of her pomp and royal splendor could say: *Lord, thou knowest that thy handmaid, from the time that she was brought here even to this very day, hath never rejoiced in anything except in thee, Lord God of Abraham* (Esther xiv. 18). That is a perfect and singular love.

St. Gregory on the text, *Who build themselves solitudes* (Job iii. 14), says: "This is to build oneself a solitude, when one is so unseated and detached from all creatures and has lost love and affection for all things of earth in such sort that, though his position sets him in the midst of as many recreations and amusements as the world contains, for all that, he finds himself alone by himself, because those things yield him no contentment nor consolation. Such a man has built a solitude for himself, since all his satisfaction is fixed in God and so he finds no company nor comfort in aught else." Even here we find experience of this, when we have a friend in whom all our affection is centered, away from whom, even in a great company of other people, we feel ourselves in a solitude and altogether lonely because it was in him that all one's delight lay. In like manner, he who has placed all his love and contentment in God and has cast off from him all affection for creatures, though he be much in company and in the midst of all the recreations and amusements in the world, finds himself alone because he has no taste for all that, but only for Him Whom he loves. They who have arrived at this, says St. Gregory, enjoy great quiet and tranquillity of soul; there is nothing to disturb them or give them pain; they are neither troubled with adversity nor vain and petulant in prosperity, since they have no love nor affection for anything in the world, nor fret themselves, nor change as things about them change, nor depend on such things, because they reckon nothing of them. Do you know, says St. Gregory, who has reached this point, or built himself such a solitude? He who said: *One thing I have asked of the Lord; this will I seek, that I may dwell in the house of the Lord all the days of my life* (Psalm xxvi. 4). *And now what is my expectation? Is it not the Lord?* (Psalm xxxviii. 8). This point, also, the holy Abbot Silvanus had reached, of whom we read that, when he came forth from his prayer, the things of earth seemed to him so mean and shrunken that he lifted up his hands and covered his eyes, not to see them, saying to himself: "Shut yourselves, my eyes, shut yourselves, and see not any things of the world, for there is nothing in it worth looking at." The same we read of our blessed Father Ignatius, that when he raised his heart to God and looked at the sky, he would say: "Ah, how mean is earth when I look at heaven!"

The second degree may be that which the glorious Bernard assigns in his Treatise on the Love of God, when a man not only forgets all outward things, but himself also, not loving himself for himself, but in God and for God and in view of God. We must be so forgetful of ourselves and of all our advancement and interest, and love God so purely and perfectly, that in the good things which we receive at His hands, as well of grace as of glory, all our contentment and rejoicing should be not for our own good and advancement, but because therein is fulfilled the will and good pleasure of God. Thus do the blessed in heaven, where they rejoice more in the fulfilment of the will of God than in the greatness of their own glory. They love God with a love so intense and pure, and are so transformed and united with His will, that the glory which they have and the happy lot which has befallen them, they do not cherish so much for the benefit and profit thence ensuing to them, nor for the satisfaction which they receive, as because God is pleased with it, and such is His will. So we should love God, says St. Bernard, as he did who said: *Confess to the Lord, because he is good* (Psalm cxvii. 1). He does not say, *because he is good to me,* but *because he is good.* He does not love as that other loved of whom it is said: *He will confess to thee, when thou shalt have done him good* (Psalm xlviii. 19); but he loves and praises God because He is good in Himself.

The third and last degree of perfection and love of God, says St. Bernard, is this: "When one is so forgetful of self that in what he does he does not look to see, *is God pleased with me?* but *how can I give pleasure and satisfaction to God, and God be pleased, satisfied, and take delight in the work that I am doing?* Thus all that he takes account of is the approval, contentment, and good pleasure of God, not remembering himself, nor setting any more store by himself than if he did not exist and were not in the world at all. This is the purest and most perfect love of God. This love is truly a mountain, a mountain of God, high, fertile, plentiful: *mons coagulatus, mons pinguis* (Psalm lxvii. 16); a thing of great and exquisite perfection, for that is the meaning of "mountain of God," a thing very grand and excellent.

But who shall be able to ascend this mountain so high? (Psalm xxiii. 3). *Who will give me wings as of a dove to fly and rest upon it?* (Psalm liv. 7). "Woe is me," says that glorious saint, "that in this exile I cannot wholly forget myself." *Unhappy man that I am, who will deliver me from this captivity!* (Rom. vii. 24). *Lord, I suffer violence, answer for me* (Isaias xxxviii. 14). When shall I die, O Lord, to myself, and live for Thee alone! *Woe is me that my exile is prolonged!* (Psalm cxix. 5). *When shall I come and appear before the face of God!* (Psalm xli. 3). When shall I be, O Lord, united and transformed into Thee by love, wholly denuded and forgetful of myself and made one spirit with Thee, so that now I love nothing in myself, nor for myself, nor to myself, but all in Thee and for Thee? So St. Bernard tells us: "To lose yourself in a manner as though you were not and not to be conscious of yourself at all and to be emptied out of self, as it were reduced to nothingness, that is having your conversation in heaven, and not the affections of earth." This perfection is of heaven rather than of earth, as the psalmist says: *I will enter into the powers of the Lord: Lord, I will be mindful of thy righteousness alone* (Psalm lxx. 16). When the good and faithful servant shall enter into the joy of his Lord and shall be inebriated with the abundance of His love, then we shall be so absorbed and transformed into God as not to remember ourselves. *When he shall appear, we shall be like him, because we shall see him as he is* (I John iii. 2). Then shall the creature be in complete accord with its Creator, as the Scripture says: *The Lord hath created all things for himself* (Prov. xvi. 4). Then we shall love God purely, and not love ourselves for ourselves, nor any other creature except in God. "Our delight will be not so much our desires crowned to the full or the happiness that is fallen to our lot, as the seeing God's will fulfilled in us and about us" [St. Bernard]. All our joy will be not in our own joy, but in the joy and satisfaction of God. This it is to *enter into the joy of the Lord* (Matt. xxv. 21).

"O holy and chaste love!" cries St. Bernard: "O sweet and delicious affection! O pure and high-refined intention of the will! All the higher-refined and purer, I say, inasmuch as there is no longer left in it any admixture of anything of our own; all the more delicious and sweeter inasmuch as all that is felt is of God. To be thus affected is to be deified and transformed into God." *We shall be like him,* as St. John says. St. Bernard alleges three comparisons to explain how this deification and transformation into God shall be. As a drop of water thrown into a great quantity of wine loses all its properties and qualities and takes the color and taste of the wine; and as iron, kindled and made red-hot in the forge, appears no longer iron, but fire; and as the air, receiving the brightness of the sun, is transformed in a manner into brightness, so that it seems the brightness is all one; so, he says, in our final state of bliss we shall lose all our own tastes, and all that we shall love there shall be God and for God. "Otherwise, how shall God be *all in all* (I Cor. xv. 25), if in man there remains still something of man?"—*Alioquin quomodo erit Deus omnia in omnibus, si in homine de homine quidquam supererit?* Our own shall have no part there; my glory and my satisfaction will be the satisfaction and glory of God, not my own. *Thou art my glory and the lifter up of my head* (Psalm iii. 4). Now though we cannot here reach so high, we should make it our endeavor to fix our gaze on this height; for the farther we advance and approach to it, the greater will be our perfection and union with God. And so St. Bernard concludes: "This, eternal Father, is the will of Thy Son in our regard; this His prayer for us to Thee, His God and Father: *I will that as I and thou are one, so also they may be one in us* (John xvii. 21); that is to say, that they love Thee for Thine own sake and themselves only in Thee. This is the end, this the consummation, this is perfection, this peace, this the joy of the Lord, this *silence in heaven* (Apoc. viii. 1)." This is the end and furthest perfection to which we can attain.

FOURTH TREATISE

ON UNION AND FRATERNAL CHARITY

CHAPTER I

Of the Merit and Excellence of Charity and Fraternal Union

BEHOLD, says the Prophet David, *how good and pleasant a thing it is, for brethren to dwell together in unison!* (Psalm cxxxii. 1). St. Jerome speaks of this psalm as applying properly to religious. "Lo," he says, "what a good thing, what a subject of great joy it is, that for one brother we have left there in the world, we find so many gathered here in religion," who live and cherish us better than our brothers in the flesh. "My brother in the flesh," the saint goes on to say, "does not love me so much as my fortune." That is what our relations are after. It is all self-interest. For that, they go after us; for that, they trouble us; and when that motive does not exist, they care nothing about us.* This is not true love, but self-interest. But your spiritual brothers, who have already left and spurned all they had of their own, do not come here to seek after other people's property. They love not your fortune, but your soul. That is true love. So says St. Ambrose: "The brotherhood of the spirit is greater than that of the flesh; for the brotherhood of flesh and blood makes us like one another in body, but the brotherhood of the spirit makes us all have one heart and one soul, as was said of the first believers" (Acts iv. 32).

St. Basil insists very well on this great union of religious. "What thing more agreeable, what thing more happy and

---

* *Note to American Edition.*—The author is here no doubt thinking of the bitter family disputes over titles and inheritances so common in his day. No one had a truer appreciation of the beauty of family affection than Rodriguez. Elsewhere he says (Volume II, Treatise I, Chapter 19): "What makes the mother not feel the continual labors she has in rearing her child but love? What makes the wife tend night and day her sick husband but love?"

blessed, what thing more marvelous and admirable can be imagined?—to see men of so many different nations and countries so conformable and alike in their customs and mode of procedure that they seem to be but one soul in many bodies, and many bodies the instruments of one soul" —*Homines ex diversis nationibus ac regionibus profectos in unum veluti coaluisse, ut in pluribus corporibus per exactam morum ac disciplinae similitudinem adeo in unum veluti coaluisse, ut in pluribus corporibus unus modo esse animus videatur, vicissimque plura corpora mentis unius instrumenta cernantur."* That is set down in the Life of our blessed Father Ignatius for a great marvel and almost a miracle that God has wrought in the Society, to see a union and conformity so great and so well set between men of such different nations, so different and unequal either in natural character or in rank or in inclination or in individual bent and disposition. Though our natures differ, yet grace and virtues and supernatural gifts make us mutually conformable and one. *God it is who maketh men of one manner to dwell in a house* (Psalm lxvii. 7). That is the sense of the text.

And so great is the favor that the Lord in His goodness and mercy does us herein, that not only we who are here in religion enjoy it, but the odor thereof spreads and diffuses itself also to those outside in the world, to their great edification and profit and the great glory of God our Lord. Thus we see in the case of many of those who enter the Society that, when they are asked what moved and inclined them thereto, they say it was this union and brotherly spirit which they saw in it. This agrees very well with what St. Augustine says on these same words: *Behold what a good and pleasant thing it is for brethren to dwell together in unity:* "At this sound so pleasant, at this voice so sweet, men have been roused to leave their parents and properties and band together in religious life. This is the trumpet that has called them together and united them from various quarters of the world, taking this union and mutual charity to be a heavenly life. Thus it is that has brought forth monasteries and peopled religious houses: this the lodestone that has attracted hearts."—*Iste dulcis sonus, ista melodia etiam monasteria peperit.* Thus, of the three things that the Wise Man mentions as very pleasing to God, the first is *concord and union among brethren* (Ecclus. xxv. 1).

We have two precepts of this charity. The one is the first and principal commandment, to love God with our whole heart, with our whole soul, and with all our strength. The second is to love our neighbor as ourselves. It is of this second precept that we have to treat here; since that it is that makes the union and brotherhood of which we purpose to treat. This union of souls and hearts is the effect and property of this charity and love, which, as St. Denis says, has the power to unite and draw things to one another. So St. Paul calls it *the bond of perfection* (Col. iii. 14), the perfect tie and bond which binds together things that were apart and makes of many wills one. It makes me seek for others what I seek for myself; it makes me seek it as for myself; it makes my friend a second self; it makes us be as one thing. So St. Augustine approved the saying of him who called his friend, "the half of my soul"—*dimidium animae meae*—one soul divided among two bodies. That we may see the value and excellence of this charity and love of our neighbor and what a store the Lord sets by it, let us begin with these last words of Christ. St. Chrysostom here calls attention to the fact that, when Christ our Lord has laid down this first and greatest commandment of loving God, He proceeds at once to the second commandment of loving our neighbor and says that it is next to the first. See, says the saint, the goodness and bounty of the Lord, that notwithstanding the infinite distance there is between man and God, He requires us to love our neighbor with a love so near and so like to the love with which we love God.

He fixes in a manner the same measure to the love of our neighbor as He fixed to the love of God, since of God He says that we should love Him with our whole heart and with our whole soul and of our neighbor He says that we should love him as we love ourselves. As when here on earth we wish well to a person and would fain commend him to another, we are wont to say: "If you love him, you will be loving me," so, says St. Chrysostom, that is what Christ our Redeemer wished to tell us in saying *the second is like to the first* (Matt. xxii. 39); if you love your neighbor, you will be loving God. And so He said to St. Peter, *Feed my sheep* (John xxi. 17), as though He would say: "If you love me, take care of them who are mine, and in that it will be seen that you love me in right down good earnest."

But further, the Lord wishes us to love our neighbor with the same love wherewith we love Him. This is the new commandment that He gives us. *A new commandment I give you, that ye love one another as I have loved you* (John xiii. 34). As Christ has loved us purely for God and for God's sake, so He wishes also that we should love our neighbor for God and for God's sake. He calls it a new commandment, says St. Augustine, not only because He has newly explained and newly commended it to us by word and example, but because it is really something new that He is asking of us. Natural love is a love very old and very ancient, founded as it is on flesh and blood; it is a love that not only the good but the wicked also feel; and not only men, but dumb animals. *Every animal loveth his own like* (Ecclus. xiii. 19). But the love wherewith Christ would have us love our neighbors and brethren is a new love, because it must be a love spiritual and supernatural, loving our neighbor for God with the same love of charity wherewith we love God. And so theologians and saints observe that the love wherewith we love God for God and that wherewith we love our neighbor for God, is one and the same charity and virtue. They call it a theological, that is to say, a divine, virtue; a virtue that has God for its aim and object, because the infinite goodness of God is worthy of being loved for its own sake, and for it at the same time we also love our neighbor.

Finally, in the whole of Holy Writ we shall find no point more strongly urged nor more frequently recommended and repeated, than this union and fraternal charity. And Christ our Redeemer at the time of His leave-taking, in that last discourse at the Supper, harks back upon it to commend it to us once and again. *This is my commandment, that ye love one another as I have loved you.* And again He says: *This I command you, that ye love one another* (John xv. 12, 17). This I command you as My last will and testament. He would have us thereby see how much He desired that this should be stamped and rooted in our hearts, knowing of what importance it was for us, and that thereon depended the whole law and the fulfilment of all the rest of the commandments, according to the saying of the Apostle: *He that loveth his neighbor hath fulfilled the law* (Rom. viii. 8). And thence His beloved disciple took this doctrine; he seems to treat of nothing else in his canonical epistles, having sucked it in from the breasts of his Master. St. Jerome tells of him that, when he was very old and could scarcely go to church, but it was necessary for his disciples to carry him in their arms, his only preaching was this: "My sons, love one another." His disciples, wearied and tired of his always repeating the same thing, said to him: "Master, why do you always tell us that?" He replied, says St. Jerome, in a sentence worthy of St. John: "Because it is the Lord's commandment; and if you fulfil it, that alone is sufficient." *For all the law is fulfilled in one saying: thou shalt love thy neighbor as thyself* (Gal. v. 14). If you keep this commandment, you keep all.

St. Augustine here reflects on the weight and stress that the Lord laid on this commandment, wishing it to be the sign and device by which the world should know us and take us for His disciples. *In this shall all men know that you are my disciples, if ye have love one for another* (John xiii. 35). Christ our Redeemer does not stop here, but in the prayer which He made to His eternal Father (John xvii.), He not only wishes that hereby men should know us for His disciples, but also that there should be such a union and brotherhood amongst us as to be enough to convince the world of the truth of our faith and religion, and that Christ is the Son of God. *I ask thee, Eternal Father, not only for these my disciples, but also for all those who by means of them are to believe in me, that they may all be one among themselves, as thou in me and I in thee, that the world may believe that thou hast sent me* (John xvii. 20). Could He have said more to heighten the excellence of this union and brotherhood, since it is enough and should be enough for the world to trust it to be the work of the coming of the Son of God into the world, and yield itself up to receive the Christian doctrine and religion?

The truth and force of this is well seen in what happened to Pacomeus, who, being a soldier in the army of Constantine the Great and a heathen, had no rations to give to his soldiers; and they were dying of hunger. In this plight they came to a town where they met with a kind reception, and the townsmen banded together to bring them all things needful in such plenty and with such good will that Pacomeus was amazed and asked who these people were that they were so inclined to do good. They answered him that they were Christians, whose institute it was to harbor all and help all and do them good. He lifted up his hands to heaven and, calling God to witness, he pledged himself to the Christian religion. That was his motive for becoming a convert and believing that this was the true faith and religion.

The Redeemer of the world adds another thing that is very consoling: *I ask thee, Eternal Father, that they may be one with one another, that the world may know that thou lovest them for themselves as thou lovest me for myself* (John xvii. 23). One of the chief signs whereby is seen a love of special predilection borne by God to a congregation—a privileged and singular love on the model and likeness of the love that He bears to His own Son—is His giving them this grace of union and brotherhood with one another, as we see He gave and imparted it to the primitive Church, to those people who enjoyed the first-fruits of the Spirit. And so says St. John: *If we love one another, God abideth in us, and his charity is perfect in us* (I John iv. 12). If we love one another, it is a sign that God dwells in us and loves us much. If *where two or three are gathered together in my name, there am I in the midst of them,* so He says (Matt. xviii. 26), what shall it be where so many are united and gathered together in His name and for His love? In order, then, that we may enjoy these so many good things and hold this so great assurance of God's dwelling in us and loving us with a special love, let us endeavor to maintain ourselves always in this charity and union.

CHAPTER II

Of the Need We Have of This Charity and Union, and of Some Means to Preserve Us in the Same

BUT above all things have charity, which is the bond of perfection (Col. iii. 14). The Apostle St. Paul teaches and recommends to us many virtues, but above all, he says, I recommend charity, which is the tie and security of the life of all. The same does the Apostle St. Peter say: *Before all things I recommend to you charity and unbroken union one with another* (I Pet. iv. 8). Hence we can gather of how much importance this virtue is since these holy apostles and princes of the Church recommend it so much as to say that it is to be *above all* and *before all,* so that of this we should always make greater account than of all other things.

In the first place it is easy to see the general necessity of this charity, for what religious order could exist without union and conformity? And to say nothing of a religious order, no gathering or community of men could continue without some sort of union and order. Take away from a multitude any vestige of association and order, and what will be left but a Babylon, a City of Confusion, a pandemonium? The proverb says: "Where there is a multitude, there is confusion." Understand this if the multitude be without order and union, because when well ordered and united, it is nothing short of a hierarchy. So all gatherings of men and commonwealths, however barbarous they be, always contrive to get some union and order, depending all on one head or on a number who stand for one government. We see this even in animals, not only in bees—for in them wonderful is the instinct which nature has given them in this respect—but even in wolves and lions and other wild beasts, for by the very instinct of self-preservation they contrive some union, since by division they would come to an end and perish. Even of the devils themselves, though they are spirits of division and sowers of tares, Christ Himself says that we must not believe that they are divided among themselves for the very reason that *if Satan be divided against himself, how shall his kingdom stand?* (Luke xi. 18). And to this same purpose He alleges there that principle so certain and so proved by experience: *Ever kingdom divided against itself shall be laid waste, and house upon house shall fall* (Luke xi. 17). A kingdom divided against itself needs no enemies to destroy and lay it waste; the inhabitants themselves will go about destroying and leveling down one another, and things will go tumbling over one another. So Plato comes to say that there is nothing in a commonwealth more pernicious than discord and disunion, nor anything more useful and profitable than peace and mutual union. St. Jerome says this of religious life, and says it more forcibly. It is this unity and charity, he says, which makes religious be religious; without it, a monastery is a hell and its inmates, devils. For what greater hell can there be than for people who must be always in bodily conjunction with one another and deal with one another daily, to hold different wills and opinions? But if there be union and charity, religion will be a paradise on earth and they who live therein will be angels, beginning here on earth to enjoy the peace and quiet which angels enjoy. And St. Basil confirms this statement. Men living in religion, he says, are in that peace and charity and union which makes them like angels, among whom there are no lawsuits nor contentions nor dissensions. St. Lawrence Justinian says that there is not here on earth any so lively presentiment of the society of heaven and the heavenly Jerusalem as the society of religious united in love and charity. It is a life of angels, a life of heaven. *Truly God is in this place; this is none other than the house of God and gate of heaven* (Gen. xxviii. 16-17).

But to leave generalities and come to the particular need that we have of this union and fraternal charity, our Father, treating of the means whereby the Society will be preserved and augmented in its spiritual good, says that one of the principal means that will aid much thereto will be this union and mutual charity. And besides general reasons, which show the necessity of this union in any order and community, there are particular reasons making it more necessary for us. The first is because the Society is a squadron of soldiers whom God has newly sent to support His Church, aid her in the war that she wages against the world and the devil, and gain souls for heaven. It is this that the patent of our Institute sets forth; this is the proclamation made in the bull of erection of our Society: "Whoever desires to enlist under the standard of the cross and give in his name for this service, and so forth." And this it is that is meant by the name of "Company" which we have taken. We are a company of soldiers; we beat our drums, we show our colors, we gather recruits to fight against the enemies of the cross. If the squadron be compact and in good order, all acting with one accord, they will break through rocks and none will put them to the rout. A very strong thing that! So the Holy Ghost likens the Church to *an army terrible in battle array* (Cant. vi. 3), a squadron well drawn up in camp. When a squadron is well drawn up and linked together man with man, it leaves no opening for anyone to break through, since all support one another. But, disunited and disordered, it is a very weak thing, easily broken up, readily put to rout. In the Second Book of Kings, David by way of saying that he has overcome his enemies says: *The Lord hath divided mine enemies before me, even as waters are divided* (II Kings v. 20). And the mountain where this happened was called *Baalpharasim;* that is, the place of division, which shows that to divide and to vanquish is one and the same thing, and the place of division is taken for the place of victory. Writers on war say that an army in confusion and disorder marches to a butchery rather than to a battle; and there is nothing more inculcated in military discipline than not to break or disorder the squadron, but make sure that it shall always be well united and in order, unit in touch with unit and every man at his post. Not only the common good, but the particular good of each individual soldier, depends on this order's being kept, since with the loss of the squadron the individual will be lost also.

So it will be in our company and squadron. If we are united and back one another up and all agree together, we shall break through our enemies and by none shall we be overcome or routed. *Brother holpen by brother is as a strong city* (Prov. xviii. 19). *A triple-trilled cord is hardly broken* (Eccles. iv. 12). When many strings are joined together and make one, the result is very strong. In the cord of the crossbow, those threads of which it is composed have singly little or no strength at all; but, many together, we see that they are strong enough to bend strong steel. So shall we be, if we are united and all go together.

St. Basil, animating religious hereto, says: "Consider with what union and unanimity these Maccabees fought the battles of the Lord." And of those large armies of more than three hundred thousand men Holy Scripture says in the Books of Kings that *they marched out as though they were one man* (I Kings xi. 7), since they all went with one and the same will and mind, and in this way they struck fear and terror into their enemies and gained great victories. In this spirit we must fight the spiritual wars of the Lord; and so we shall gather great fruit of souls by our ministries and amaze and confound our enemies. The devil himself, says St. Basil, will be afraid and not dare to attack us, seeing us so united against him, and will lose all hope of doing us any harm.

Our Father puts this for one of the chief reasons why this union is particularly necessary for us: "Let union and mutual conformity," he says, "be most diligently secured, and nothing to the contrary permitted, to the end that, united to one another by the bond of fraternal charity, they may be able better and more effectually to employ themselves in the service of God and assistance of their neighbor." And in another place he says that without this union the Society cannot be preserved nor governed nor gain the end for which it was instituted. It is certain that, nourishing divisions, parties, or dissensions within our own body, not only shall we never attain the end of our institute, which is to gain souls to God, but we shall not be able to govern or preserve our own selves. If soldiers, who ought to be united to fight against the enemy, were to turn to fighting one another, it is clear that not only they would not win the war, but they would destroy and overthrow themselves; they are lost (Osee x. 2). *If ye bite and devour one another, see that ye be not eaten up by one another* (Gal. v. 15). If discords, envies, and murmurings come in among you, beyond doubt you will devour and destroy one another. This is what we have to dread in religion, not enemies from without nor persecutions and contradictions that the world may raise against us—they will do us no harm, St. Bernard says very well, speaking on this point to his religious: "What thing from without can come and supervene upon you, that can possibly disturb and sadden you, if here within all goes well and you enjoy brotherly peace and charity?" And he quotes that saying of the Apostle Peter: *Who shall be able to harm you, if ye are zealous for good?* (I Pet. iii. 13). So long as we are what we ought to be, very united and brotherly with one another, no contradiction or persecution from without shall be able to do us any harm or prejudice; rather it will help and serve for our greater good and improvement, as we read in ecclesiastical history of the persecutions which the Church suffered from without, that they no more did her harm than the pruner harms the vine; for one twig that they cut off, there spring up others more fruitful. And therefore it was a very good thing that one of those holy martyrs said to the tyrant, that what he did in shedding the blood of the Christians was to lay out the ground for the wheat to grow and increase the more. In the Book of Maccabees Holy Scripture praises the Romans for their great union and conformity among themselves. *They entrust their magistracy every year to one man, and all obey this one, and there is no envy nor jealousy among them* (I Macc. viii. 16). So long as the Romans remained united in this manner among themselves, they were lords of the world and brought their enemies under; but when they started civil wars among themselves, they were destroyed. Hence the proverb: "By concord small powers grow; by discord the greatest fall to pieces"—*Concordia res parvae crescunt; discordia maximae dilabuntur.*

Apart from this there is a particular reason why we are in greater need in the Society of aiming at this union, as our Father shows forth in the eighth book of his Constitutions. That is because in the Society there are special difficulties and obstacles in the way of securing this union, and therefore it is necessary to prop it up more and find remedies against these obstacles. The difficulties that there are in the Society in this respect our Father reduces to three. The first is the fact that, the Society being so scattered and poured out all over the world among believers and unbelievers and its members being so remote and separate one from another, mutual knowledge and intercourse and union become more difficult; the more so since, embracing, as the Society does, such different nations, among many of whom there is opposition and contrariety, it is no easy thing to get rid of an aversion with which one is born and which grows as one grows, and to regard a stranger, not as a foreigner, but as a son and brother of the Society. The second difficulty is that the men of the Society must be for the most part men of letters, and knowledge puffs up, and creates in a man a high opinion of himself and small opinion of others, and engenders also hardness of heart. St. Thomas says that learned men are not usually given to devotion so much as the simple and unlettered. Hence there is reason to fear that this may cause them to be less loving and brotherly with one another, each one following his own opinion and judgment and laying himself out in his own line and seeking to procure honor and reputation for himself, which is apt to be the root of great disunion and division. The third difficulty and impediment, and that not a small one, is that these same persons will be men of mark, hobnobbing with princes and lords, with city magnates and cathedral chapters; and from these intimacies there are apt to follow various party attachments, as also a disposition to seek singularities and privileges and exemptions and not live like the rest—a great prejudice to union and brotherhood.

Since for greater resistances greater preventives are necessary, our Father there lays down means to meet these difficulties. The first and most fundamental of all is not to admit and incorporate into the Society men who have made no effort to get their vices and passions well under, since unmortified folk will not endure discipline, order, or union. The learned man will be puffed up, will want privileges beyond the rest, will seek for the first place and take no account of others, will court the favor of prince and lord, will want someone to wait upon him; hence will follow at once coteries and divisions. The more learned and capable a member of the Society be, if he has no great fund of virtue and mortification, the more is disunion to be feared and his giving trouble in religion. They say very well that letters and high talents in an unmortified man are like a good sword in the hands of a madman, to the hurt and harm of himself and others. But if learned men are mortified and humble, *not seeking themselves but the things of Jesus Christ,* as St. Paul says (Phil. ii. 21), then much peace and union will ensue, since their example will be of great benefit to the rest and will draw them to follow in their path. This is the chief means of prevention against this and other evils and will of itself suffice if well observed. Beyond this, our Father goes on to propose other particular means to meet these obstacles. To supply the want of mutual intercourse and knowledge, owing to our people's living so remote and distant from one another, he proposes frequent communication by edifying letters, such as are usual in the Society. By such letters people keep up a good acquaintance with one another and animate one another to a common method of action, so far as the diversity of nations will allow; and that is a great aid to union.

Another very main means our Father lays down to maintain us in this union, and that is an exact observance of obedience, since obedience binds and unites religious one with another, making of many wills one and of many judgments one judgment. Give up self-will and private judgment, as it is given up by obedience, and there remains one will and judgment common to the superior and to all his subjects. So united with their superior, subjects are united among themselves according to the rule: "Things that are equal to a third thing are equal to one another." And the more united subjects are with their superior, the more they will be among themselves. Obedience and religious discipline and observance of rules is a leveling line that smoothes down and levels all and causes great order and union. The ancients, to signify union, were wont to use the hieroglyphic of a lyre with many strings, which by reason of their being in tune and concord with the first make a most sweet melody. So a community with so many strings attuned to the first, which is the superior, makes a most sweet consonance and harmony. And as on a lyre, if there be a single string out of tune or strained, it goes for nothing and undoes the whole of that attunement and harmony; so also in religion, one member out of tune and not in concert with his superior will make all the consonance and harmony of that union go for nothing. Hence some have ventured to say that the word *concord* comes from *chord;* but they say better who hold that it comes from *cor* (heart), since all have one heart, according to that text in the Acts of the Apostles: *The multitude of believers had one heart and one soul* (Acts iv. 32).

St. Bernard says that as the cause of a ship's leaking is the fact of the timbers' not being well joined together or well caulked, so also the ruin and destruction of a religious order comes of the members' not being well joined and united one with another by the bond of union and fraternal charity. And our Father General Claude Aquaviva, in the letter he wrote on this subject, says that we should make as much account of this union and charity and guard it with as much care as though the whole good of the Society depended thereon, as indeed it does. And Christ our Redeemer, in the farewell prayer that He made on the night of His Passion, asked of His eternal Father for us as a thing necessary for our preservation: *Holy Father, guard them in thy name, that they may be one as I and thou are* (John xvii. 11). And, by the way, let us consider in these words the comparison that He makes; as the Son is one with the Father by nature, so He would have us be one by love, and that shall be our guard and preservation.

CHAPTER III

Of Some Reasons from Holy Scripture Binding Us to Keep Charity and Union with Our Brethren

DEARLY beloved, if God hath so loved us, so we ought to love one another (I John iv. 11). The glorious Evangelist St. John, having declared the great love that God has borne us and shown us in giving us His only-begotten Son, infers and concludes from thence that we also ought to love one another. Here one might raise a doubt and ask with reason how from the fact of God's having loved us so much the apostle draws an inference and conclusion to the love of our neighbor, since it seems that he ought only to have inferred and concluded that we should love God for having loved us so much. To this there are many good answers. The first is that the apostle did this to show us the excellence of the love of our neighbor and the esteem that God has of it; as also it is said (Matt. xxii. 36-39) that when a doctor of the law asked Christ our Redeemer: *Master, what is the greatest commandment of the law?* He answered: *Thou shalt love God with thy whole heart and with thy whole soul and with all thy strength: this is the greatest and first of the commandments;* and He immediately adds: *And the second is like to this, Thou shalt love thy neighbor as thyself.* They were asking Thee, O Lord, only about the first; why dost Thou speak of the second?

All to show the excellence of the love of our neighbor and the great regard God has for it.

The second answer is that the love of God and the love of our neighbor are as two rings linked together and put upon the finger so that it is impossible to leave off one without drawing off the other; they must go together. So the love of God and the love of our neighbor are always conjoined; the one cannot be without the other, because it is by one and the same love of charity that we love God and our neighbor for love of God. Thus we cannot love God without loving our neighbor and we cannot love our neighbor with the love of charity without loving God at the same time, since God is our reason for loving our neighbor. And so to show that in loving our neighbor we also love God, the apostle immediately goes on: *If we love one another, God also is in us by love, and his charity is perfect in us* (I John iv. 12). And to show us that in the love of God there is included also the love of our neighbor, he said: *This commandment we have of God, that he who loveth God must also love his brother* (I John iv. 12). The love that God bears to men and the desire that He has and the store that He sets by our also loving Him, is shown in a strong light by the fact that we cannot love God without loving our neighbor nor offend our neighbor without offending God.

If a king were to love a courtier of his so much as always to put himself in front of him when any sought to injure or murder him, so that they could not touch nor hurt the courtier, nor attack him with musket or sword, without wounding and hurting the king first, would not that be an extraordinary love? Now this is what God does for men; He puts Himself ever in front of them, so that you cannot offend your neighbor without offending Him, to the end that you may beware of offending your brother for fear of offending God. *He who toucheth you*, says the Lord, *toucheth the apple of mine eye* (Zach. ii. 8). Thus, offending our neighbor, we offend God; and loving our neighbor, we love God; and loving God, we love our neighbor. Since, then, the love of God and the love of our neighbor always go together and the one is included in the other and they never can be divided or separated, St. John was able to infer and conclude to either of these loves because, in asking that, he asked the other. But the reason why he inferred and concluded expressly to the love of our neighbor and not to the love of God, was that the debt of loving God is a principle *per se notum,* manifest and known of itself, and principles are known and not proved, only conclusions. And so he landed in the conclusion of love of our neighbor and stated it expressly, because one would not be certain to draw it.

The third reason is because St. John in his epistle is not speaking of a love bare and dry, but of a fruitful and profitable love, accompanied with benefits and good works. So he says: *My little children, let us not love in word or tongue only, but in deed and truth* (I John iii. 18), for that is true love. And to give us to understand that God requires these good works on behalf of our neighbors and brethren according to that saying of Osee quoted in the holy Gospel: *I would have mercy and not sacrifice* (Osee vi. 6; Matt. xii. 7), for this reason did he draw expressly the conclusion of loving our neighbor. Thus an absent creditor writes a letter to his debtor: "What you owe me, I shall be glad if you will give it to So-and-So, who is there with you, for it is one thing whether you give it to him or me, and I take it as received." In this way St. John says in the name of God, our creditor, to Whom we are indebted for so much love and so many benefits: *If God hath so much loved us, we also ought to love one another* (I John iv. 11). Since God has loved us so much and we owe Him so much, let us love our neighbors and brethren, since God has transferred to their credit the debt that we owe Him.

The charity and good work which you do to your neighbor, you do it to God, and He takes it as done to Himself.

Verily I say to you, that when ye have done this thing to one of these my least brethren, ye have done it to me, says Christ Himself (Matt. xxv. 40). This is another motive, and a very powerful one, for loving and doing good to our brethren, since in this way it will come about that, though looking at them we seem to owe nothing to any of them, yet looking at God and the great debt we owe Him, wherein He has yielded and made over His right to our neighbor, we shall recognize ourselves as bound to that neighbor even to being his bond slaves. And so Father Master Avila says very well: "When your flesh uses this language to you: 'What do I owe to that man to do him any good, and how ever shall I love him, seeing he has done evil to me?' answer that perhaps you would listen if the motive of your love was your neighbor himself; but since it is Christ, Who takes as done to Himself the good or evil done to your neighbor, on what side can there be anything to bar the course of love and good works, be my neighbor whoever he may be or do me whatever evil he will, since I keep no account with him, but with Christ?" Hence that is quite a good inference of the apostle, putting in the premise the great love that God has borne us and thence concluding to our duty of loving our neighbor. And to move us and persuade us more to this love, he puts into the same premise the mystery of the Incarnation: *Because God hath sent His only Son into the world* (I John iv. 9) to remind us and make us reflect that God has allied Himself with mankind, and so we should look upon our fellow men as akin to God and brothers of Jesus Christ, and love them as such.

CHAPTER IV

Of the Manner and Character of the Union Which We Ought to Have with Our Brethren

THE glorious saints and doctors of the Church, Basil and Augustine, declare to us very well what should be the union that we should keep with our brethren by the comparison and metaphor which St. Paul draws from the human body and the conformity and union of its members one with another. See, they say, the union and conformity that obtains between the members of our body and how they help and serve one another, the eye the foot, the foot the hand; how the hand defends the head; and how, when they tread on your foot, the tongue says: "See how you are treading on me!"; how they all rush to the help of the weaker part, as may be seen if you have any wound or any other necessity. Each takes to itself what it needs for its sustenance and gives to another what is over. And what sympathy, as the doctors call it, there is, so that if the stomach is out of order, the head suffers; and when one member recovers its health, the whole body is glad and rejoices. *God hath so tempered the body that the members are solicitous for the good estate of one another*, says St. Paul, *so that if one member is suffering, all the rest suffer with it; and if one is whole, all the rest rejoice* (I Cor. xii. 25). St. Augustine reflects on this very well: "What is there in the whole body farther from the eyes than the foot? Yet, when the foot treads on a thorn, thrusting it in, at once the eyes look for the thorn, the body stoops down, and the tongue asks, 'Where is it?' At once the hand applies itself to draw it out. The eyes are all right, the hand is all right, the body, head, tongue, and even the foot is all right everywhere else except in one little point painful, where the thorn is, and yet all the members are full of compassion, and rush to the rescue with great solicitude;

and when it is put right, all rejoice." Now in this way we should behave towards our brethren, one looking after another as after himself, and one rejoicing at the good of others and compassionating the troubles of others as his own.

In these two things, says St. Basil, there is chiefly seen the love and charity that we bear to one another—if we are distressed and full of compassion at the afflictions and spiritual and corporal troubles of our neighbor, and rejoice in his good, according to the saying of the Apostle: *Rejoice with them that rejoice, weep with them that weep* (Rom. xii. 15). And so says St. John Climacus: "If anyone wishes to examine the charity and love he has for his neighbor, let him see if he weeps over his faults and is glad of his graces and spiritual progress." This is a very good sign of our love of our neighbors. St. Angela of Fulgino used to say: "My soul received more grace of God when I wept and grieved for the sins of my neighbor than when I wept for my own;" not that a man ought not to feel and grieve more for his own sins than for the sins of his neighbor, but to give us to understand by this exaggeration how grateful to God is this exercise of charity towards our neighbor. St. Bernard says that these two exercises are the two breasts of Christ's spouse between which He rests (Cant. i. 12); both the one and the other has its own milk, sweet and savory as honey, the one of congratulation and exhortation, the other of consolation.

There is further to be considered in this comparison of St. Paul, on the one hand the diversity of members and their differences in condition and quality, since some are eyes, some feet, others hands, each holding his own distinct office; and on the other hand we are to consider the union and brotherhood there is among them in so high a degree, each being content with the same office that he holds, without envy of any other, though higher. So we must behave; each one must be content with the office that he holds and not envy those who have higher offices and ministries.

Further, never did a superior member despise an inferior, but valued it, aided and defended it all in its power. So those who hold higher ministries must not despise those who hold lower ministries and offices, but value them, aid them, and have great consideration for them as for members whereof we have need. *The eye cannot say to the hand, nor the head to the foot, I have no need of you:* rather God has in such manner tempered and ordered the members of the body that *those which seem the lowest and feeblest are the very ones of which we stand in greatest need* (I Cor. xii. 21-22). Otherwise, consider the feet, and what a breakdown would be ours if they were to fail us. The Lord has ordained all this, says St. Paul, in His high wisdom and providence, *that there be no schism* or division between the members of the body—*ut non sit schisma in corpore* (I Cor. xii. 25), but great union and conformity. So it is here in this body of religion, that some hold the office of head, others of eyes, others of feet and hands; nor can the head say that it has no need of the hands, nor the eyes that they have no need of the feet; rather it seems that they are just the component that we need most, to be able to live and do anything in religion: so we are wont to say that they are our feet and hands, because without them it seems we can do nothing. And this has been a high providence of God that there should be no schism amongst us, but much union and conformity.

This is the portrait of true union and charity; and hence we must learn how we are to aid and serve one another, which is a thing that goes a long way to the preservation and augmentation of union; and so the Apostle St. Paul much recommends it to us: *By charity of spirit serve one another* (Gal. v. 13). Thus it is great praise in religion to be an obliging person, ready to serve and aid and give satisfaction to all; it shows charity and humility and mortification, and not to be as some are, who for want of mortification and readiness to take a little trouble and go a bit out of their way have no idea of giving pleasure and satisfaction to their brothers. In that so heroic act of Christ our Redeemer in washing the feet of His disciples, no doubt He meant to give us an example of humility, but of humility conjoined with the exercise of charity and brotherly love. *If I have served you and washed your feet, I your Lord and Master, it will be reasonable that you should do the same for one another* (John xiii. 14). I have given you an example how you are to behave to one another and how you are to serve and aid one another in humility and charity.

CHAPTER V

Here We Begin to Declare in Particular What It Is That Union and Fraternal Charity Requires of Us, and What Will Help Us to Keep It

CHARITY is patient and kind, charity envieth none, worketh no evil, is not puffed up, seeketh not her own interest (I Cor. xiii. 4). Union and fraternal charity requires the exercise of all the virtues; for what hinders and makes war on it is envy, ambition, impatience, self-love, want of mortification, and the like. Thus, to preserve it in us, there is needed the exercise of the contrary virtues. That is what St. Paul teaches us in these words, and so the only thing needed will be to declare them further.

Charity is patient, charity is kind. These two things, to suffer and to do good to all, are very important and necessary to preserve this mutual union and charity. For as we are men and full of defects and imperfections, we all give occasion enough for others to suffer at our hands; and as on the other hand we are so weak and so needy, we need others to help us and do us good. And so the Apostle says that in this way charity will be preserved and the commandment of Christ accomplished by our aiding one another and overlooking one another's failings. *Bear ye one another's burdens, and so ye shall fulfil the law of Christ* (Gal. vi. 2). St. Augustine on these words makes a good comparison to this purpose. Naturalists write, he says, that stags, when they want to swim across a river or an arm of the sea, to go in search of pasture on some island, dispose and arrange themselves in this way. Since their heads are so heavy by reason of their horns, they all draw up in single file and each one to lighten his fatigue rests his head on the haunches of him before him, and so they help one another. Thus they are all eased by resting their heads on someone else. Only the first stag has his head in the air, suffering this fatigue to lighten that of his companions. And that he may not be so very much fatigued either, when he gets tired, he drops from first to last and the one behind him takes his duty for another little while, and so they go on changing until they reach the shore. In this way we must aid and succor one another; each must make it his aim to ease another's burden and lighten his fatigue so far as is possible. This is what charity requires; and to withdraw one's own person from fatigue and leave the burden to another shows a want of charity. The more you do, the more you merit; you are really doing something for yourself.

St. Augustine says there that one of the things in which charity is proved and becomes most apparent is in suffering and bearing the ill humors and imperfections of our neighbors. *Supporting one another in charity, solicitous to preserve the unity of the spirit in the bond of peace* (Eph. iv. 2-3). *Charity suffereth all, and taketh all upon herself* (I Cor. xiii. 7) and thereby is preserved. If you do not know how to suffer and have patience with and support your brethren, be sure that your charity cannot last, for all your multiplied considerations and methods and remedies. If natural love and fleshly love suffer the importunate demands of a sick man, as we see in the case of a mother attending her son or husband in sickness, more reason is there that the spiritual love of charity should be able to suffer and support the importunities and weaknesses of our brethren. And remember, says St. Augustine, that this office and exercise of charity is not to last forever, for in the other life there will be no occasion of suffering or overlooking the failings of our brethren; therefore let us suffer them and overlook their failings in this life, to deserve to gain the life that is everlasting. Let us not consider the lengthening out of time, for the work after all will last but a short time and the reward we shall receive will last forever. So important are these two things, to suffer and to succor our brethren, and aid them and do them good, that St. Augustine goes so far as to say that Christian life is summed up in these two things; and with reason, since Christian life exists by charity, and in this is included all the law, as Christ our Redeemer says (Matt. xxii. 5); and so what sums up charity, sums up Christian life.

Again, the Apostle St. Paul says: *Charity is not puffed up nor proud.* Love and friendship knows no such thing as pride and haughtiness; rather they cause a great equality among those who love one another. Hence the saying of the Wise Man: *I will not be ashamed of saluting a friend* (Ecclus. xxii. 31). With a friend we keep no ceremonies; we stand on no points of honor—friend does not look at friend to see whether he is the first to show courtesy. No one is ashamed of doing honor and an act of courtesy to a friend, and doing it first, because among friends there is great equality and straightforwardness; love knows nothing of these precedences. And so Aristotle said that friendship must be among equals. And another said: "Majesty and love go not well together"—*Non bene conveniunt nec in una sede morantur maiestas et amor.*

To sit on a throne and wield great authority, that is not compatible with friendship. You have to abase yourself and humble yourself and put yourself on an equality with your friend if you are to have true friendship, for a friend is a second self.

Even in God the love that He bore to men had such power as to make Him abase Himself and put Himself on an equality with them. *Thou hast made him a little less than the angels* (Psalm viii. 6). Thou hast made Him man as we are; and so He says to us: *I will not now call you servants, but friends* (John xv. 15), which implies some manner of equality. See the tenderness of the love of Christ! Even here we do not say: "So-and-So is a friend of the king," though he be a great personage, a marquis or a duke; but "So-and-So is very intimate with the king," since to say "friend" implies a sort of equality. A God of infinite majesty has been pleased to make Himself so thoroughly man amongst men and has loved us so much, that He calls us not "servants," but "friends" in so many words. So here in religion charity has no idea of anything like haughtiness, but must needs cause a great equality and straightforwardness amongst all. This same equality, which is an effect of love, helps much to preserve and augment charity and union. One helps the other, and hence it is that where there is humility and straightforwardness among all, it is a sign of great union and brotherly affection. And so we see by the goodness of the Lord in the Society that as charity shines forth, so also there shines forth this equality and straightforwardness amongst all, "everyone desiring and seeking to yield the preference to others, esteeming all in his heart as if they were better men than himself" (Rule 29). And he who was somebody in the world feels more honored and rejoices more, as St. Augustine says, in the company of his poor brothers than in the dignity and nobility of his wealthy parents, for what he values and esteems is virtue, and all the rest he counts for nothing.

St. Ambrose observes very well what a help this is to the preservation of charity. These are his words: "It goes a long way towards strengthening charity, when, according to the Apostle's teaching (Rom. xii. 10), men try to gain ground on one another, who shall get the start at honoring one another and giving another the advantage; when one man takes every other man for his superior; when subjects love to serve and superiors know not what it is to be haughty; when the poor man makes no difficulty of the rich being preferred before him and the rich man delights in putting the poor on a level with himself; when men of rank are not proud of their quality and lineage and men of meaner origin do not vaunt themselves on being men as much as the noble; lastly, when not more deference is paid to great wealth than to good character, nor do the power and decorations of the unjust go for more than the unhonored honesty of the upright."

CHAPTER VI

Of Two Other Conditions of Charity and Union

CHARITY, says the Apostle, *is not envious* (I Cor. xiii. 4); rather he who really loves another desires his good and his prosperity as much as if it were his own. The glorious St. Augustine declares this by the example of Jonathan and the great love that he bore to David. Holy Writ says: *The soul of Jonathan was joined and united with the soul of David: one heart and one soul was made of both, because Jonathan loved David as his own soul* (I Kings xviii. 1). And the consequence thereat was that, though he was the son of the king, he sought the kingdom rather for David than for himself. *Thou shalt be King of Israel, and after thee I will be second* (I Kings xxiii. 17). Jonathan rejoiced in the good of David as though it were his own. The saints allege another example, which shows more the property and effect of charity, the example of the blessed in heaven. There in heaven there is no envy of others' being greater than oneself; rather, if so it might be, each would wish his neighbor greater glory and would share his own with him, and that his inferior should be his equal or greater than he, because each one rejoices in the glory of another as though it were his own. And this is not so very difficult to understand; for if here on earth the natural love of mothers makes them rejoice as much in the good of their children as if it were their own, how much more will that heavenly love do, being so much more excellent and perfect? Let us, then, rejoice in the good of another as much as if it were our own, for that is the proper effect of charity.

To invite and animate us thereto, St. Augustine observes that charity and love make their own the good of others, not by despoiling anyone of it, but simply by being glad and rejoicing over it. And there is not much to wonder at in what he says; for if by loving another's sin and rejoicing therein a man makes that sin his own, because *God sees the heart* (I Kings xvi. 7), what wonder is it that by loving another's goodness and rejoicing therein he also makes that his own, especially as God is more ready to reward than to punish? Let us, then, consider and weigh this truth—on the one hand what an excellent thing charity is and what great gain and profit we make thereby, since in that way we can make our own all the good works of our brethren by merely rejoicing and taking complacency therein, and that even with greater security than in the case of our own good works, since no vainglory can arise from them as from our own; and on the other hand let us consider what an evil thing envy is and how pernicious, since it turns a neighbor's good to our own evil. Thus we are led to make it our effort to shun the one and embrace the other.

Hence follows the second particular, which the Apostle adds at once: *Charity is not ambitious, nor seeketh her own interests* (I Cor. xiii. 13). Anyone must be far removed from that who takes his neighbor's good for his own and rejoices therein as though it were his own. One of the things that make the greatest war on charity and most hinder this union is self-love, or self-seeking, the looking after one's own conveniences and interests. For this reason our Father calls self-love a most grievous and deadly enemy of all order and union. Humbert in the Rule of St. Augustine calls it the bane of common and religious life, infecting and ruining everything. And although it is true that this self-love is the general enemy of all the virtues, yet it is particularly the enemy of this. Indeed, the very name tells us this; for if it is the love of self, it is not the love of the community, which is the love of charity. Self-love is division; it is something private and particular; it wants everything for itself; it seeks itself in all, which is directly contrary to charity and union.

Upon what the Scripture tells us of Abraham and Lot, that *the land could not hold them living together* (Gen. xiii. 6)—each owning so many head of cattle that the land was too narrow to afford them pasture, and so the shepherds of the one quarreled with the shepherds of the other and it was necessary for peace sake for the two to go apart—St. Chrysostom observes: "Where there is *mine* and *thine,* at once there are lawsuits and occasions of contention and discord even among kinsmen and brothers; but where this is not the case, peace and concord are safe"—*Ubi est meum et tuum, ibi omnium litium genus et contentionis occasio; ubi autem haec non sunt, ibi secura versatur pax et concordia.* So we see, says the saint, that in the primitive Church there was great union and concord among the faithful; they had all one soul and one heart because there was no *mine* and *thine* amongst them, but all things were in common (Acts iv. 32). That is the reason why there was among them so much harmony and union. And therefore all religious orders, inspired by God and founded on Scripture, have laid down poverty for their first and principal foundation. Of this we make our first vow, that there being no *mine* or *thine,* and self-love finding nothing to settle upon, we may all have one heart and one soul.

No doubt it is a great help to preservation of charity and union amongst us to have divested and despoiled ourselves of all the goods of the world. But it is not enough to have no *mine* and *thine* in these temporal things; it is necessary that we should not have them in other things either, for if we have them, that will make war on us and be an obstacle to this union and charity. If you seek honor and reputation for yourself; if you desire the higher post; if you go about in quest of your own gratifications and conveniences, thereby you will come to disunite yourself from and disagree with your brethren: that is what commonly makes war on charity. Thence it comes that you are smitten with a sort of envy at seeing your brother display talent, shine and receive praise, be looked up to and made much of, because you will want that honor and estimation for yourself and think that the other robs you of it. Hence also arises joy, or at least an indescribable feeling of satisfaction, when another does not succeed in some affair, because you fancy that thereby he is being humbled and marked as inferior to you. Hence it befalls you at times to seek to throw your brother into the shade directly or indirectly, sometimes in an argument, sometimes by sundry little words that slip out unbidden and spring from the abundance of what you have in your heart. All this sort of thing is disorderly self-love, ambition, pride, and envy, which are the maggots apt to destroy union and mutual charity. *Charity,* says the Apostle, *rejoiceth not in evil, but rejoiceth in truth* (I Cor. xiii. 6). Charity takes no delight in the depreciation of others, but wishes them to rise and win and advance to greater things, and the greater the better. You are our brother; may you go on with a blessing upon you a thousand and a thousand times; that shall be my joy and my contentment (Gen. xxiv. 60). A merchant trading for a company is nowise distressed at the gains that his partners make, nor at the good industry wherewith they make them; rather he rejoices greatly thereat because it all turns to his own profit and to that of the whole company. So we should rejoice at any good done, or talent displayed, or forward step taken by our brothers, since it all comes to turn and redound to the good and profit of the whole of that body of the Society, a member and part whereof I am and the good things whereof I enjoy.

CHAPTER VII

Of Another Thing That Charity Requires, and Which Will Help Much to Preserve It, Which Is to Have and Show a Great Esteem for Our Brothers and Always Speak Well of Them

CHARITY and love of one another must not be only interior, in the heart, but must show itself also in works, according to that text of Scripture: *Whoever seeth his brother in need, and nevertheless closeth his heart to shut him out, how shall we say that the charity of God is in him?* (I John iii. 17). When we are in heaven, as we shall have no wants, says St. Augustine, these works will not be necessary for the preservation of charity. Fire there, being in its own sphere, has no need of fuel and wood to keep it in; but here below without them it quickly dies out; so also here in this miserable life charity will readily die out in the absence of works to maintain and preserve it. St. Basil here applies to this purpose what the Apostle and Evangelist St. John says in his first canonical epistle: *In this we know the great love that God has borne us, in that he has given his life for us; and so ought we to give our life for our brethren* (I John iii. 16), if it be necessary. St. Basil very well infers from thence: "If the love that Christ asks us to bear to our brethren must go so far as to give our life for them, with much more reason should it be extended to other things which commonly offer and are of less difficulty than giving our life for them."

One of the principal things which this union and charity requires, and a thing that will help much to preserve it and carry it on further, is to have a high esteem of our brethren. Rather, this is the foundation on which this whole structure of charity is founded and planted. It is not a love of fancy, which goes blindly, nor a love of mere tenderness and sentiment, arising from this heart of flesh which we carry, but a love of reasons, a spiritual love of the higher part of the soul, which regards higher and eternal reasons. It is that love which we call appreciative, which springs from the love that we bear to God, Whom we set above all things, and leads us to value our neighbor as a thing belonging to God. From the esteem and good opinion that we have of our brethren it comes to pass that we love them and honor them and reverence them, and do all other offices and practices of charity. So far as this esteem goes, so far also will go our love and all that follows upon love. So says St. Paul, writing to the Philippians: *Let us at heart esteem all as if they were our betters* (Phil. ii. 3) : that is the root and foundation of all this business. And writing to the Romans he says: *Let us vie with one another for the first turn in honoring one another* (Rom. x. 12). The glorious Chrysostom observes that he did not say that we should honor one another, but that we should get the start of one another in this office. It is not my policy to wait until the other man shows courtesy to me and takes notice of me first; everyone should aim at getting the start of his neighbor and winning the first turn. This is what our holy Father commends to us in his Rule: "In all things endeavoring and desiring to yield the better share to others." This is winning the first turn in honoring one another.

To come now more to details, one of the things by which we ought to endeavor to show a high opinion of our brethren is by always speaking of them well and respectfully, and in words that witness the appreciation and regard we have of them. Of our blessed Father Ignatius we read that everyone was convinced that he had a good opinion of him and loved him as a father. The result was that all also had for him much love and respect. There is nothing that so kindles charity and preserves it as the knowledge that our brother loves us and wishes us well and feels and speaks well of us. How many good effects spring therefrom! And so says Seneca there: "If you wish to be loved, love." There is no more efficacious means to be loved, since love cannot repay but by other love.

St. Chrysostom notes this well on those words of Christ: *What you wish other men to do to you, do it you to them* (Matt. vii. 12). The saint says: "Would you receive benefits? Do benefits to others. Would you obtain mercy? Show it to your neighbor. Would you be praised? Praise others. Would you be loved? Love. Would you that men should yield you the preference and the better thing and the place of greater honor? Be you the first to yield it, and contrive to give it to others"—*Vis beneficia capere? Confer beneficium alteri. Vis misericordiam consequi? Miserere proximi. Vis laudari? Lauda alium. Vis amari? Ama. Vis partibus primis potiri? Cede illas prius alteri.*

Besides, this speaking well of others is a thing that gives great edification, and the reason why it edifies is because it is a sign of the presence of great love and great union. And, contrariwise, any little word which directly or indirectly may throw another into the shade and take the shine out of him—the least breath of such a thing felt amongst us would be matter of great disedification, since people would at once gather that there was there some rivalry and envy; and consequently anything redolent of this should be far from us. Suppose your brother has his defects; it is hard if he has not some good point about him. Take hold of this and leave that. Imitate the bee, which lights upon flowers only, not minding the thorns that surround them, and follow not the example of the beetle, which goes straight for the dunghill.

CHAPTER VIII

That We Ought Much to Beware of Telling Another, "So-and-So Has Said This and That of You," Where It May Give Him Any Offense

MY intention is not at present to speak of detraction, because I shall treat of it in another place; here we shall only notice one thing of great importance which serves our purpose. As one ought to take particular care not to speak ill of another, so when we hear anything said of another that may give him any displeasure or resentment, we ought also to take care not to tell him: "Such a one has spoken thus and thus of you," for this serves only to exasperate minds and sow discord amongst brethren, a thing very pernicious and much abhorred of God. *Six things the Lord hateth, and the seventh He heartily detesteth and abominateth, the sower of discord amongst brethren* (Prov. vi. 16-19). As we say we abhor a thing with all our heart, so the Scripture uses the like human language of God, to signify the height of His displeasure against such men. But if God detests such as these, men abhor them also. *The talebearer,* says the Wise Man, *shall defile his own soul, and shall be hated in all company; and he that dealeth with him shall also be hated* (Ecclus. xxi. 31). These are they who get the name of talebearers; this it is to go in for talebearing, a thing unworthy of men of probity, much more of religious. *Never give occasion to anyone,* says Ecclesiasticus (v. 16), *to be able to say that you are a talebearer.* What can be a more pernicious and prejudicial thing in a community than to be a scandal-monger and to go about making your brethren fall foul of one another? That is doing the devil's work, for that is his office.

And be it observed here that to set one person against another, it is not necessary that the things told be grave; very small and minute things, things that at times do not amount even to venial sins, are enough for that. So it is this that we must make account of, not merely whether the thing said or related be of itself grave or light, but whether it is a thing that can upset or sadden your brother and cause in him some disgust or disunion with the other party. Someone has been thoughtless in saying a little word that gave others to understand something that was less to the credit of another in point of learning, or capacity, or virtue, or talent, or something like that, and you with still greater thoughtlessness go off to tell it to the other party; you see now what resentment you may have excited in him; you thought you were doing nothing and you stabbed him to the heart. *The words of the talebearer seem simple, and they penetrate to the inmost bowels* (Prov. xxvi. 22). There are some things that some people are wont to make nothing of because they look at them from I know not what point of view—or the fact is that they do not look at them at all; but looked at from the point of view from which they should be looked at they present such a different appearance that there is much fear and doubt that they amount to mortal sin, for the inconveniences and evil effects that follow from them; and this is one of those things.

Now if to say these things and sow these discords amongst brethren is a thing so prejudicial and pernicious and so much abhorred of God, what must it be to sow these tares between subjects and their superior and cause disunion between the members and the head, between parents and children! How much more abominable is this in the sight of God! Now this is done also when similar language is used of the superior. Great was the love and obedience that King David's subjects paid him, and quite united they were with him; but when they heard evil spoken of him and his government maligned by a wicked son of his, Absalom, they refused obedience and rose up against him (II Kings xv.). Oh, how many times does it happen that, when one is living in right down good faith and putting much trust in his superior and judging well of all that he does and trusting to him his soul and discovering to him his whole heart, by some light word that another says all this edifice is thrown down, and in its place there succeed a thousand sleights of malice and duplicity, rash judgments, fits of reserve, murmurings; and sometimes this plague spreads so far that it infects this one and that one, and that one and another, and another and another! It is beyond belief what harm is done by a few light words like these.

But someone will say: "It is a good thing at times for a person to know what is remarked and said of him that he may tread warily and not give occasion." That is true; then you may tell him the thing but without letting him know who has said it, and that though it has been said in public, that none may excuse himself by saying that another would have told him before long. Let everyone look to himself. *Woe to him by whom the scandal cometh* (Matt. xvii. 7). And though the other importune you much to let him know who said it and you know the information would be a great gratification to his curiosity, still you must not tell him; it is a mistake sometimes to give such satisfaction to a friend. That is no good friendship, for you do him harm by telling him and do the other harm as well, and still more harm to yourself because you are left with a scruple about the harm that you have done to the one and the other.

The harm and bad consequences of such a disclosure may be well understood by this, that, when one makes known anyone's fault to the superior, that by his fatherly care and providence he may be able to apply a proper remedy, according to the rule we have on this matter, he does not want the culprit to understand that it was he who made it known; and the superior does his best, and ought to do his best, to make sure of this secrecy as his rule recommends, that this may not be the cause of any bitterness or dislike among the brethren. Now if, when this is done lawfully and according to rule and with charity and desire of greater good, there still are these fears and it is needful to proceed with caution, with how far greater reason are these awkward consequences to be apprehended when one discovers to another who it was that spoke of his fault, doing this not lawfully nor according to rule, but carelessly and indiscreetly and in a bad way and perchance sometimes with some emulation or envy, or on other considerations not good, or at least which the other might imagine to be not good! St. Augustine highly praises his mother St. Monica upon this account, that when she heard often on one side and another complaints and words of resentment and rancor, she never told anything she had heard of one to the other, but only what might smooth them down and remove their rancor and go to unite and reconcile them. So we ought to act, being ever angels of peace.

CHAPTER IX

That Good and Fair Words Help Very Much to Preserve Charity, While Their Contraries Have a Contrary Effect

AMONG the things that contribute much to preserve and augment fraternal charity are soft and fair words. *A sweet word multiplieth friends and appeaseth enemies,* says the Wise Man; and, on the contrary, *A harsh word raiseth up fury* (Ecclus. vi. 5; Prov. xv. 1). Hard, rough, and bitter language awakens ill will and causes disunion, for we are men and feel such language and are disgusted and stung thereby: hence we look not upon our brother as we did before; we view his conduct in an evil light and perhaps speak ill of him. This being so, it is of very great importance that our discourse be always so seasoned with sweetness and affability that thereby we may gain the good will of our brethren, according to the saying of Ecclesiasticus: *A prudent man maketh himself amiable in his words* (Ecclus. xx. 13). In the first place we must observe as the foundation of all that is to be said, that none should deceive himself herein by saying: "My brothers are very virtuous men and will not be shocked nor tried by one light word, be it a trifle haughty or ungracious; they will not mind that." The question is not what your brothers are or ought to be, but what you ought to be and how you should behave to them. If you say they will not be angry for so small a thing, "The smaller it is," answers St. Bernard, "the easier it is for you to abstain from it." St. Chrysostom says this rather aggravates your fault, that you did not take means to overcome yourself in so light a matter. You should not be naughty because your brother is good. *Is thy eye evil,* says our Savior, *because I am good?* (Matt. xx. 15). I say, then, that we ought to have a good opinion of all our brethren and not believe they are so thin-skinned as to be angry for any small matter; but this does not exempt us from using as much caution and moderation in dealing with them as if they were more brittle than glass and the weakest creatures in the world, not giving them on our part any occasion of annoyance or irritation, however weak or imperfect they may be. And this caution we should keep for two reasons. One reason touches ourselves; it is that, however much virtue another has, that does not make our action cease to be our fault; and again for a second reason, touching our neighbor, that not all people on all occasions are so well disposed, or so well in form, as not to be sensible of the offenses we commit against them. Everyone may know by himself what words or manner of saying them may please or displease his brother, following the rule which the Holy Ghost gives us by the mouth of the Wise Man: *Judge of thy neighbor by thyself* (Ecclus. xxxi. 18). Let everyone consult himself and see whether he be content that they should speak coldly of him, that they should answer him sharply and command him after a haughty and imperious manner; and if he finds this will touch him to the quick, let him abstain from speaking in that manner, because his neighbor is a man like himself and may have the same feelings as he has.

Humility, also, is a very proper means to make us never speak but as we ought; for if we be humble and account ourselves the least of all, we shall need no other safeguard than this. This alone is sufficient to teach us how to behave so that we shall never speak a hasty word at which anyone may be offended, but always speak to everyone with respect and esteem. It is clear that no one would say to his superior: "Your reverence does not understand what I say," for he is speaking as an inferior to one whom he respects. If, then, anyone says these or the like words to his brother, it is because he does not take himself for his inferior, and so speaks to him without respect. Let us therefore be humble and, following the counsel of the Apostle (Phil. ii. 3), reckon ourselves the least of all; and we shall soon learn the words that we ought to utter and the manner in which we ought to utter them. But apart from these general rules and remedies, we will go on to mention in particular some sorts of words that are contrary to charity, that we may avoid them.

CHAPTER X

That We Ought to Be Much on Our Guard Against Biting Words That May Offend Our Brother or Give Him Any Displeasure

THERE are little remarks that bite and wound another, covertly reflecting on his social condition or intelligence, not so keen as it might be, or any other defect, natural or moral. Such remarks are very much against charity; and the wittier and smarter they are, the worse they are and the more harm they do, for they strike the hearers more and stay longer in their memories. And the worst of it is that he who speaks them is sometimes very much pleased with himself, thinking that he has said a clever thing and shown discernment; whereas in reality he very much deceives himself, and instead of showing discernment, he has only shown a poor understanding and a worse will, since he employs the understanding which God gave him for His service, in making pointed remarks that wound and scandalize.

Albertus Magnus says that, as when one has bad breath it is a sign of something wrong in liver or stomach, so when one speaks evil words, it is a sign of some illness at heart. And what would the glorious St. Bernard say of the religious who gave vent to biting witticisms? If any display of wit on the part of a religious he called a blasphemy and a sacrilege, what name would he give witty remarks at the expense of our brethren? All these things are very alien to religious life; and, accordingly, all that touches thereon should be very far from the mouth of a religious, such as the use of nicknames and poking fun at others and mocking them and the making or repeating of facetious couplets on the fault or absent-mindedness of another, and the like things. Neither in jest nor in earnest can they reasonably be tolerated, of which let each one judge by himself. How would you take it that anyone should give you a nickname and that all the world should laugh, seeing how well the name fitted? Since, therefore, you would not like it done to yourself, do you not do it to another, for that is the rule of charity. Should you be pleased, supposing you had a slip of the tongue, that people should at once make a point not to let it fall to the ground, as they say, but make a story of it? Certainly you would not. How, then, do you will for another what you would not will for yourself—nay, what you would resent and angrily complain of if it were done to you?

Even the very mention of mocking and scoffing and calling nicknames is offensive and ill-sounding in the mouth of a religious; how much more the doing of such things! We should so much abhor them as not even to take their very names in our mouth, as St. Paul says of the vice of impurity: *As for fornication and all manner of uncleanness, let it not be so much as named among you, as becometh saints* (Eph. v. 3). And so it should be as regards this vice, and St. Paul goes on accordingly joining it with the other: *Nor foul or foolish talking, nor jokes that are unbecoming.* The very mention of such things is not in accordance with the holiness that we profess. St. Bernard says well: "If for idle words we have to give an account to God at the day of judgment, what shall it be of words that are more than idle?" What of words that wound the feelings of my brother? What of words that do harm?

CHAPTER XI

That We Ought to Beware of Wrangling, Contradicting, and Reprehending

WE must also avoid any wrangling with another or contradicting him, it being a thing very contrary to union and fraternal charity; of which St. Paul gives us warning when, writing to Timothy, he says: *Do not contend in words, for it serves for nothing else but the disedification of the hearers.* And a little after, he adds: *A servant of God must not be contentious, but gentle and peaceful in his behavior to all men* (II Tim. ii. 14, 24). The saints much recommend this to us, and from them our Father has borrowed it and inserted it in his Rules. St. Dorotheus says that he had rather things should be left undone than see any disputes or contests arise amongst brethren in doing them, and adds he would repeat this a thousand times. St. Bonaventure also declares that there is nothing more unworthy or misbecoming God's servants than to insist on getting their own way and to wrangle with one another as market women are wont to do. And St. John Climacus goes on to say that obstinacy in maintaining one's own opinion, though it be true, is certainly instigated by the devil; and the reason is that that which usually moves men thereto is the excessive desire they have of human honor. To that end they aim at getting their own way, appearing wise and intelligent and coming out conquerors, or, at least, not seeming inferior to others; and thus it is always the devil of pride who is the occasion of this obstinacy.

Now in this, two sorts of faults may be committed. The first and greatest is his who first contradicted the other, because it is his obstinacy that began the dispute and kindled the fire, and so his fault is greater. And though for the most part the subject they dispute about is in reality of so small consequence that it is no matter whether the thing in debate be the one way or the other, yet the loss of peace and charity, which ordinarily are greatly impaired by these disputes, is of much consequence. The other says this in good faith, and understands the matter so. Let him alone in his good faith. There is nothing in it. *Dispute not about what does not concern thee,* says the Wise Man (Ecclus. xi. 9). Even though the thing in hand be of consequence and you imagine that your brother may indeed receive some prejudice by adhering to his opinion, yet it is a good plan, they say, to bear with him for the present instead of contradicting him, but take him apart and tell him the truth afterwards, that he may not remain in error. Hereby the end is gained and unpleasant consequences avoided.

The other fault to observe here is, when it happens that someone contradicts you, you should not insist upon your point nor seek to push your opinion and get the better of him; but as soon as you have laid down once or twice what you take to be the truth, if others do not believe you, let them think what they please. This is done by lapsing into silence as though you knew no more—not, however, with the affected air which some take up as though they did not yield, but desired their opinion to stand and the blame to rest with the other party. *He that avoideth contention, gaineth honor,* says the Wise Man (Prov. xx. 3). And with reason does he say so. It is the property of noble hearts to bate one's right in season, and let oneself be beaten in the like contentions and wrangles. He who acts thus, does an act of charity to his neighbor by avoiding the bitterness and irritations that usually follow upon these disputes. He does an act of humility within himself, vanquishing the desire of coming out with the honors of victory. Likewise an act of love of God, cutting off the occasion of many sins that are almost inseparable from a war of words; as the Wise Man says: *Abstain from contention, and thou wilt diminish sins* (Ecclus. xxviii. 10). On the other hand, he who maintains his view obstinately, besides the disedification that he gives, is the cause of the loss of peace and charity with many unpleasantnesses and rancors that follow therefrom. And instead of gaining honor and esteem, as he thought to do, he loses it because they take him for a "swollen head," a man who likes coming out "top dog" and will never bate an inch to anybody.

It is said of St. Thomas Aquinas that in scholastic disputations he never peremptorily contradicted anyone, but said what he thought with incredible mildness and temperance of language, throwing no scorn on anyone, but rather paying honor to all, as one whose object was not to come victorious out of a dispute, but to get the truth recognized. The instance is also well known of those two old monks who dwelt together in one cell and never had contention or wrangle between them—how they wished to make trial to see if they could get up a dispute about a brick as to whose it was, and they did not succeed. That is how we should succeed in our disputations.

You should also beware of undertaking to reprehend and correct your brother, though you fancy you could do it with all charity and in the handsomest manner. That is the office of the superior. Now men take it with more or less of good will to have one superior or two to admonish and rebuke them, but they do not take it at all well for one who is not their superior to usurp that office. Men commonly have no mind to be corrected and reproved by their equals. We have also a rule forbidding anyone to command or rebuke another without authority from the superior to do so. As one cannot give an order without authority from the superior, so neither can one give correction. This is not a business to entrust to all. Even the superior himself, when he has to correct another and admonish him of his fault, must first look well about him and wait for his opportunity and measure his words, what he has to say and how he is to say it, in order that the correction and admonition may be well taken, and profit the delinquent, all of which points are necessary. And here is a man who will take upon himself without further ado to tell his brother of his fault on the spot, and often in the act itself, under color of zeal. This is not the zeal of charity, but often a thing very contrary to charity and more likely to do harm than good. Nay, even though there be much justification for what you do, the other is readily tempted to say within himself—and it is a mercy if he does not say it out loud: "Who has made you superior and why do you meddle in the office of another?" *Who hath made thee prince and judge over us?* If you tell the other that what he is doing is against the rule, he may tell you that your reprehending of him is also against the rule.

It is related of Socrates that one day when he was at dinner with some friends in the house of a leading citizen who had invited them, he smartly took to task one of the company for some fault that he saw him commit at table. Whereupon Plato, who was also present, said: "Would it not have been better to have left this till afterwards and reprehended him in private?" Socrates replied: "And would it not also have been better for you to have told me this afterwards in private?" He cleverly cast back his reprehension in his face, observing that he was doing the very thing that he found fault with in another. That is what these reprehensions serve for. And not only is this no zeal of charity, but often it is bad humor on the part of him who gives the rebuke, and his impatience and lack of self-control, which makes him so offended at the fault of his brother and sometimes with what is no fault of his own at all. He cannot contain himself till he has come out with it, and therein he thinks to have found relief and satisfaction. He cannot, or he will not, mortify himself, and he wants to mortify the other. The spirit of mortification and rigor is very good for each one to maintain with himself, but with his brother he should always maintain a spirit of love and gentleness. This is what the saints teach by word and example, and it helps much to union and fraternal charity. Hence it follows that, if it is not good to rebuke and correct your brother even when you think you are doing it excellently well and with charity and kindness, much less will it be good if you point out to him his fault not so excellently well nor with such excellent reserve.

Thus we should be much on our guard against the practice, and generally against all words that may mortify our brethren.

Cassian relates that one day Abbot Moses, in dispute with Abbot Macarius, happened to say a word to mortify him and somewhat discompose him, and at once God chastised him, permitting a devil to enter into him, and such a foul and filthy devil, too, as to drive him to put into his own mouth ordure and dirt, until by the prayer of Macarius he was delivered therefrom. This shows how much God abhors this fault, since He so chastised it in one who was such a great servant of His and a man of such approved sanctity as we know the Abbot Moses to have been. A chastisement something like this we read of in the chronicles of the Order of St. Francis. An aged friar in presence of a nobleman of Assisi addressed another friar in some rough and harsh words showing some anger. But in the act of saying them he entered into himself, and seeing his brother troubled by the words and the secular disedified, he was kindled to take vengeance upon himself. So taking some dung, and putting it into his mouth and chewing it, he said: "Let the tongue chew dung that has poured out against his brother poison of passion." And it is said then that that nobleman was greatly edified and almost out of himself, seeing with what zeal and fervor the religious atoned for his fault. In consequence he was more devoted than ever to the friars, offering himself and all his goods to serve the order.

CHAPTER XII

Of the Good Grace and Good Words with Which an Office of Charity Should Be Exercised

THE blessed St. Basil, in a sermon exhorting to monastic life, gives an admonition and instruction very good for those who are occupied in outward offices of charity, how they should behave in exercising them. When you have, he says, to do these offices, you must not be content with the mere bodily exertion, but you must take care to do what you do with a good grace and show mildness and gentleness in your words, that the others may understand that you do this out of charity, and so your service may be pleasing to them. And the same says Ecclesiasticus: *Son, in thy good deeds give no motive of complaint, nor in thy gifts cause sadness by evil words. Shall not a fall of dew temper heat? So too is the word better than the gift. Seest thou not that a good word is worth more than the thing given?* (Ecclus. xviii. 15). This is the salt which St. Paul says must give a relish to all that you do. The gracious air with which you serve and the kind terms in which you answer are worth more than all that you do. And, contrariwise, know that however much you labor and fatigue yourself, if you do not do it with a good mien, using kind words and answers, it will not be valued or go for anything, but will seem all lost. *Let your words and answers,* say the Apostle, *always be seasoned with the salt of graciousness and gentleness* (Col. iv. 6), with such phrases as "Delighted," "Most willingly." Even if you are busy and have a great deal to do and cannot do what you are asked, do not on that account return your brother a dry and disagreeable answer; even then you must see that your answer be so good that the other may go away as contented and happy as if you had done the thing, in view of your kindness. Say such things as this: "Certainly I should be much pleased to do it if I could, but just now I can't. Will it do afterwards?" And if the obstacle is that you have not leave, say: "I will go and ask leave for it." Make up in good words for what you cannot do in deed; thus your good will is understood. This is also what Solomon says: *A gracious tongue aboundeth in a good man* (Ecclus. vi. 5). Words spoken with graciousness and breathing tenderness and love must always abound in a good and virtuous man, that being a great means to the preservation of charity and mutual union.

St. Bonaventure says that we ought to be ashamed to utter a harsh and disagreeable word that could possibly offend or displease our neighbor, even though it be spoken offhand and on the spur of the moment, and though the word in itself be very slight. And if at any time it shall happen that we are off our guard in this particular, we should be careful to confound and humble ourselves and offer satisfaction to our brother by begging his pardon.

It is related of St. Dositheus that when he was infirmarian he took particular care not to run foul of anyone, but to speak to all very peacefully and charitably. Still it did happen sometimes that, having to deal with so many persons—now with the cook, as to whether that pot should be put in this place; at other times with the dispenser, because he did not give him the better portion for the sick, or because he did not give it him at once; at other times with the refectorian, because he took away some things from the refectory—he raised his voice, and spoke some rough and offensive word; and when this happened, he was so ashamed of himself that he went to his cell and, prostrate on the ground, had his fill of weeping, until St. Dorotheus, his master, went there, who understood the situation. "What's this, Dositheus? What have you been doing?" He at once told his fault with many tears: "Father, I have spoken disdainfully to my brother." St. Dorotheus scolded him well. "Is this humility? Are you still alive?" After scolding him, he said: "Rise now, God has forgiven you; let us start afresh." And the story goes that he got up as cheerfully as if he had heard his pardon from the mouth of God, and made a new resolution never to speak to anyone disagreeably and harsh.

For the common profit of those who do services of charity as also of those who receive them, St. Basil gives two short and solid pieces of advice. How, he asks, shall we render well this service of charity to our brothers? And he answers: If we reckon that in serving our brother we are serving Christ, Who said: *Verily I say to you, that what ye have done to the least of my brethren, ye have done it to me* (Matt. xxv. 40). Do things as one serving God and not men, and in that way you will do them well, in good style and with a good grace. He goes on to ask: And how am I to receive the service that my brother does me? He answers: As when the master serves his servant—*velut servus ab hero;* and as St. Peter behaved when the Lord offered to wash his feet: *Lord, dost thou wash my feet?* (John xiii. 6). Thus there is preserved on the one hand humility in both parties concerned, inasmuch as the one will not disdain nor be weary of the service he renders to his brother, regarding him as a son of God and brother of Christ and reckoning that in serving him he serves Christ Himself; and the other will not flatter himself upon seeing all people at his service, but rather will be confounded and humble himself more at that, considering that it is not done for him but for God. And on the other hand mutual charity will be preserved and much augmented for the same reason.

CHAPTER XIII

Of What We Are to Do When We Have Had Any Passage of Arms or Disagreement with Our Brother

BUT since, after all, we are men, and not all of us always so much upon the alert but that one may be taken some day by surprise to the extent of saying a harsh or disagreeable word or giving some occasion of offense to his brothers, it will be well to see how we are to behave after that. When that happens, we are not to answer in the same harsh and disagreeable tone, but should have in us virtue and humility enough to take the thing well and know how to dissemble it. The fire of our charity should not burn so low that a few drops of water will extinguish it. For this reason it is, says St. Basil, that St. Paul calls it *fraternal charity,* to signify that it must not be a light and accidental love, but well-marked and strong. *Let fraternal charity last ever between you* (Heb. xiii. 1), *loving one another as brethren* (Rom. xii. 10). It were greatly to be desired that none should ever give occasion to his brother, either in deed or word, for the least displeasure in the world; but it is also to be desired that none should be so brittle as glass, such a tender babe in virtue, as for a mere nothing to be put out and talk loud and break the peace. It were better that none should find fault with anyone, nor meddle in the office of another; but when it does happen that someone breaks the law in this, it is not reasonable and proper that the other party should at once throw this in his face, asking if he has got leave, or saying that there is a rule that none should meddle in the office of another; that only serves to make something of what was nothing, if you had only kept quiet and taken no notice. When one hard body strikes another hard body, it sounds and makes a noise; but if the hard body strikes a soft one, it is neither heard nor felt. We see that a hard ball discharged from a culverin shatters a tower of very good masonry with a great crash, but striking on sacks of wool its force is deadened by that soft material. So Solomon says on this subject: *A soft answer turneth away wrath, but hard words awaken fury* (Prov. xv. 1), for that is throwing fuel on the fire, contrary to what the Wise Man advises: *Throw not fuel on the fire of a man in a violent passion* (Ecclus. viii. 4). You should not feed his fire with your replies, but have so much softness and virtue in your composition that, though at times they say a hard and rough word to you, it makes no noise, it is not felt, it nowhere appears, but is deadened and drowned where it fell.

St. Dorotheus teaches us a very humble way of answering on such occasions. He says that, when others speak roughly and reprehend us and even accuse us of having done what we have not done, we should still answer with humility, asking pardon as if we had really given occasion for the rebuke, though we have given none, and say: "Pardone me, brother, and pray to God for me." He got this from one of those ancient Fathers, who advised him so. With this store of supplies on board, on the one side being very careful not to offend or give any occasion of displeasure to our brothers, and on the other being wide-awake for occasions of suffering and taking in good part any annoyance that may be offered us, we shall live in great peace and union.

But when some day you fail in this, and it happens that you have had a passage of arms with your brother because he has broken out and you have not had virtue and humility enough to bear it and take no notice, but one hard body has hit another and there has been a noisy collision, so that you remain offended and full of resentment against your brother and he also against you for the reply and retort with which you met him—then, says St. Bonaventure, this feeling of resentment must not be suffered to endure either on the one side or on the other; but you must seek to make it up and be reconciled to your brother before dinner or at least before going to bed. *Let not the sun go down upon your anger* (Eph. iv. 26); put an end to it before nightfall. Now the way to satisfaction and reconciliation, he says, must be by the one's asking pardon of the other. And our Father gives us the same recommendation in his Constitutions. He says: "It must not be allowed to give place for any irritation or disagreement to exist amongst Ours; but if anything of the sort comes about through our weakness and the instigation of the enemy, who is ever seeking to fan and kindle the fire of discord amongst brethren, means must be taken that they return at once by due satisfaction to their former brotherhood and kindliness." And among other spiritual admonitions that are found in the manuscripts of our Father, there is one to this effect, that, when anything of this sort occurs, the parties should at once ask pardon of one another, and this is the due satisfaction that the Constitutions require. With this humility the breach of charity will be repaired, as St. Bernard well observes: *Sola humilitas est laesae caritatis reparatio.* We should all be very ready to ask pardon and to give it, according to the word of the Apostle: *Bearing with one another, and pardoning one another, if anyone hath matter of complaint against another* (Col. iii. 13). Nay, each one should try to get the start in this transaction and not wait for or allow the other to take away his crown therein—*that none may take thy crown* (Apoc. iii. 11)—for whoever is the first to make advances by humbling himself and going first to beg pardon, that one gains a great crown. Thus the senior in religion, and he who has or ought to have a better hold on virtue and mortification, should aim at being the first in this transaction and abate his right and not stand on points, as to whether he has been the injured party or most in the right. When the shepherds of Abraham and Lot, his nephew, quarreled about the feeding-ground of their flocks, at once Abraham yielded his right and gave Lot the choice. *I pray thee, let there be no disagreement between me and thee, and between my shepherds and thine, since we are brothers. Here thou hast all the land in sight: go apart from me, I pray thee. If thou takest the left, I will take the right. If thou choosest the right, I will go to the left* (Gen. xiii. 8-9).

In the chronicles of the Cistercian Order there is a story of a monk who, every time he communicated, had this favor done him by the Lord, that it seemed as though he were receiving a honeycomb, and this delightful sweetness lasted three days. It happened one day that he rebuked another and went a little beyond bounds in doing so, and then he went to communion without being reconciled to his brother. That day, the story says, he felt in his mouth a bitterness greater than that of gall because he had not complied with what Christ our Redeemer commands in His Gospel: *If thou art offering thine offering at the altar, and there thou rememberest that thy brother hath some complaint against thee, leave thine offering at the foot of the altar, and go first to be reconciled to thy brother, and, that done, thou canst return and offer thy gift* (Matt. v. 23-24). Hereby we see what store the Lord sets by one's being reconciled with one's brother at once, since, though he be at the foot of the altar, He requires him to go back and be reconciled to him before making his offering to God.

CHAPTER XIV

Of Three Directions to Be Observed When Another Has Given Us Some Occasion of Annoyance

FROM what has been said, we may gather three directions to be observed when our brother has offended us or given us some occasion of annoyance. The first is that we must be very far from desiring any revenge. We are all brethren and members of the same body, and no member wounded by another member takes vengeance on it, nor was ever boy so senseless as, because he had bitten his tongue, to pull out in his vexation the teeth that did the mischief. They are of the same household; now that one harm has been done, let not there be done two. Thus we should say, when a neighbor offends us: "He is of my body; let us pardon him; let us not do or wish him any evil: now that one harm is done, let there not be two in this body of religion." *Rendering no man evil for evil* (Rom. xii. 17). I am not speaking of revenge in a grave matter, for here in religion we are very far, and all should be very far, from that; but I speak of lighter things such as one thinks he may desire and do without sin. One will say: "I do not wish any harm to befall my brother, but certainly I should like to say to him two words that he would feel and come to see the mischief he has done in this matter." Another is glad at the rebuke and penance given to him with whom he has some matter of animosity. Another feels a strange satisfaction and complacency in the man's not succeeding well in some undertaking and coming out of it disappointed and humbled. This is revenge; this is an evil thing; this is not having forgiven with all your heart. In this state of mind one may well have some scruple over the words of the Paternoster: *Forgive us our trespasses as we forgive them that trespass against us.* In some sort this would mean more amongst us in religion than in those of the world desiring a grave vengeance on their enemies. *Say not: As he hath done unto me, so will I do unto him* (Prov. xxiv. 29). Desire not for your brother a return of what he has done to you, since that would be to desire vengeance.

Secondly, we must not only be far from desiring any sort of vengeance upon him who has offended us, but we must also beware of another thing which people in the world think lawful. Those in the world are wont to say: "I wish no evil to Jones, but I shall never be able to stomach him any more." These people keep up in their heart a dislike and aversion for him who has injured them, and they cannot swallow any more from that quarter, as they say. We consider such action in these worldly people to be wicked, and we sometimes doubt whether they have fulfilled in rigor the obligation of the precept, since this sometimes leads to their refusing to speak to the person, and giving some scandal thereby. But how much greater a fault would it be if here amongst us there were anything of the sort, and there remained in your heart any bitterness or dislike against your brother and you did not look upon him *as yesterday and the day before* (Gen. xxxi. 2)! This is a thing very alien to religious life. *Let all bitterness of heart, all anger and indignation be removed from you* (Eph. iv. 31). We ought to be very bountiful to one another, very merciful, and ready to forget injuries, and that altogether from the heart. Do you know how much "from the heart" means? St. Paul tells you: "As God pardons us"—*As the Lord hath condoned to you, so do ye also* (Col. iii. 13). See how much from the heart God pardons us when we repent and beg pardon of our sins! God keeps no ill-will nor grudge against us nor shows us a sour face, but makes us friends as before. He cherishes and loves us as if we had never offended Him, and throws not our sins in our teeth nor remembers them anymore: *I will not remember any more their sins and iniquities* (Ezech. xviii. 22). *He will cast into the depths of the sea all our sins* (Micheas vii. 19). In this way we ought to forgive and in this way to forget injuries. There should remain in us no aversion or grudge against our brother, but it should be as though he had never offended us and nothing had passed between us. If you wish God to forgive you in this way, do you also forgive your brother; otherwise, take heed and be afraid, lest you become like that servant who had no compassion for his fellow servant, and whom his master delivered over to the sword of justice. *So shall my heavenly Father do to you* as ye have done to your brother, *unless you forgive everyone his brother from his heart* (Matt. xviii. 35). *Forgive and ye shall be forgiven: with the same measure wherewith ye have measured out to others, so shall it be measured unto you* (Luke vi. 37-38).

The third thing, which better explains what has gone before, St. Basil says, is that, as we should not keep up any particular affection for anybody, since these affections give rise to many bad consequences, as we shall say hereafter, so neither should we keep up an aversion for anyone, since these aversions also give rise to many bad consequences. What worse consequence could there be than this, if (which

God forbid) such language were heard amongst us: "Raphael does not get on well with Gabriel; since so-and-so happened, they have not been on the same footing as before; they do not hit it off with one another; they are at loggerheads." Encounters of this sort are enough to bring religious life to the ground. If Christ our Redeemer willed us to be known for His disciples by our loving one another (John xiii. 35), and it is not so with us, but quite the contrary, there will be there no disciple of Christ, no good religious.

Now for a remedy to all this. As when you feel a particular affection for anyone, you should diligently endeavor to cast it off, that it may not take root in your heart nor become dominant there—and the masters of spiritual life particularly advise us that it is necessary then to make great account of not letting this particular affection and inclination of the will come to light nor show itself in deeds nor let it be possibly understood or seen by anyone, because such a thing is apt to give great scandal and offense—so also, when you feel an aversion and dislike for anyone, you must be careful at once with all diligence to throw it off, that it may take no hold upon your heart nor any root there. And you must be particularly careful not to let it be in any manner visible in your actions that you have this aversion or temptation, for that might give great offence and lead to many evil consequences.

And not only must you be careful that others may not come to see it, but also that the party concerned may not be able to see it either. This is readily understood by the very example that we have before us. There are some people who endeavor that others should not come to see the particular affection they bear to some individual, wishing to avoid the censure and scandal that might occasion; but as for the person to whom they bear that affection, they give him to understand it in many things; sometimes by declaring it openly, at other times covertly, which is a great and very pernicious evil. So there are those who, while they are careful that others shall not come to see how ill-disposed they are towards their brother, for the sake of avoiding the censure and scandal that might arise therefrom, nevertheless show it to him in outward appearance and behavior, cutting him and not treating him as before, looking glum and severe on every occasion of meeting him and purposely letting him see that they resent what he has done. This also is very wicked, since it is a kind of vengeance taken upon one's brother. Of all these things we should very much beware.

For this as for any other temptation the saints advise us by reason of the danger to walk with great precaution and circumspection, that the temptation may not run away with us and make us do something in accordance with it. Therefore, when you feel any aversion or dislike or rancor against another, you must be very much on your guard not to let this aversion or dislike carry you off and cause you to say something or do something in evidence of it and so give occasion of offence to your brother. Rather you should then make an effort to do him good turns, praying to God for him and speaking well of him and aiding him upon occasions, according to the counsel of the Gospel (Matt v. 44), and what St. Paul says: *Be not overcome by evil, but overcome evil by good; for, doing this, thou shalt heap coals of fire upon his head* (Rom. xii. 20-21).

Thomas à Kempis tells of a priest and servant of God, a companion of his in the same monastery, that, having to go on business to another convent, he met on the way a layman, with whom he engaged in familiar conversation. They came to speak of the things of God, and in the course of this conversation the layman went on to tell him that he wished to tell him a certain thing had happened to him at another time, which was that for a long time when he heard mass he could never see the Blessed Sacrament in the hands of the priest. Thinking that this was because he was too far off and his sight too weak to be able to see it, he went up to the altar where the priest was celebrating, and for all that he could see no more in one place than in the other, and this lasted for more than a year. In his perplexity and confusion, not knowing the cause of it, he bethought himself and determined to lay open the matter in confession to a good priest. This priest after discreet examination found that this man was at enmity with a neighbor for a certain injury that he had received, which he had no mind on any account to forgive. The good confessor, considering his malice and hardness of heart, partly scolded him, partly admonished him, giving him to understand the great danger in which he lay; and that, if he did not from his heart pardon the injuries done him, it was in vain for him to ask pardon for his own sins, and that this was the reason why he could not see the Blessed Sacrament. Hearing this, he was struck with compunction of heart and, obeying the counsel of his good confessor, he pardoned his enemy. When the confession was over and he had received penance and absolution, he entered the church, heard mass, and without difficulty saw the Blessed Sacrament. In thanksgiving he was never wearied with blessing the Lord for this benefit and for the others that He marvelously works among His creatures.

CHAPTER XV

Of Rash Judgments, Explaining in What Their Malice and Gravity Consists

AND thou, says St. Paul, *how darest thou judge thy brother, and despise him and undervalue him in thy heart?* (Rom. xiv. 10). Among other temptations wherewith the devil, the enemy of our good, is wont to make war upon us, one of the chief is by intruding upon us judgments and suspicions against our brethren to the end that we may give up the esteem and good opinion that we have of them and along with it our love and charity for them, or at least that that charity may become lukewarm and cool down. For the same reason we should do our best very diligently to resist this temptation, and reckon it a very grave one; for it strikes a chord coming so close home to us as does charity. So St. Augustine advises us: "If you wish to maintain yourself in love and charity with your brethren, before all things it is necessary to be greatly on your guard against judgments and suspicions, which are the poison of charity." St. Bonaventure says: "A pestilence hidden and secret, which drives away God and destroys charity among brethren." The malice and gravity of this vice consists in its defaming your neighbor in your own thoughts, depreciating and making less of him, giving him an unjustly low place in your heart, and that on indications slight and insufficient. Herein you aggrieve and wrong your brother; and the fault will be the greater, the more serious the matter on which you pronounce judgment and the more frivolous the evidence. The gravity of this fault will be understood from another like it. If you were to ruin another in the good estimation of your brother, defaming him and depriving him of the esteem and good opinion which your brother had of him, that would be clearly a grave sin. But this same offence and injury you do him in abandoning without cause and without sufficient evidence the esteem and good opinion that you had of him, for your brother sets the same value in having a good name with you as with another man. Hereby one may well see the injury and offence done in this fashion to your neighbor. Would not you take it ill that another should conceive such a mean opinion of you without your having given any sufficient cause for it? Measure him by yourself, which is the measure of charity with our neighbor, and of justice also.

It is to be observed here that it is one thing to have a temptation to form rash judgments and another thing to be overcome by that temptation. So we are wont to say in other temptations, that it is one thing to have temptations to impurity and another thing to be overcome and consent to them; and we say that the evil is not in the first, but in the second of these two things. In this case, likewise, it is not wicked to be troubled with thoughts of rash judgment—though it would be better if we were so full of love and charity for our brethren, and had such a high opinion of them and such a deep knowledge of our own faults that it never entered into our heads to look at or consider the faults of other people. But after all, as St. Bernard says, "the fault is not in the feeling, but in the consent" and in being overcome by the temptation. *Non nocet sensus, ubi non est consensus.* A man is then overcome by the temptation to rash judgment when he makes up his mind and consents thereto and thereby loses the high opinion and good repute that he had of his brother and thinks less of him. In such a case, when he goes to confession, he must not say that there occurred to him judgments against his brother, but that he consented to them and was overcome by that temptation.

Theologians here warn us that we must be very careful not to specify to anyone else the judgment and suspicion that has occurred to us against our neighbors, lest the person we tell it to comes also himself to have the same judgment and suspicion, or possibly be confirmed in the idea that had already occurred to him; for our inclination is so evil that we are readier to believe evil than good of another. Even in confession, they observe that we must not name the person against whom the judgment has occurred nor the person at whom offence is taken for such and such a thing that he has done, not thereby to engender in the mind of the confessor any evil suspicion or disesteem of him. So great is the caution and care which they require us to have concerning the honor and good repute of our neighbor. And are you ready on slight and ill-founded conclusions to surrender the esteem and reputation which your neighbor had with you, a reputation to which he has a natural right with all men, so long as his deeds do not bear direct witness to the contrary?

Besides the injury and offence hereby done to your neighbor, this vice contains in itself other malice and grave injury to God, by usurpation of the jurisdiction and judgment which properly belong to God. Against this our Savior says in the Gospel: *Judge not, and ye shall not be judged: condemn not, and ye shall not be condemned* (Luke vi. 37). St. Augustine says that He here forbids rash judgments, which consist in judging the intention of the heart and other things uncertain and hidden, because God has reserved to Himself the cognizance of this case and so forbids us to meddle therein. The Apostle St. Paul declares this more in particular when writing to the Romans: *Who art thou that darest judge another man's servant? In view of his master he standeth on his feet or falleth* (Rom xiv. 4). To judge is the act of a superior. This man is not your subject: he has a Master; namely, our Lord; leave him to Him to judge and take not on yourself the jurisdiction of God. *Judge not before the time until the Lord cometh, who will light up the hidden things of darkness and manifest the intentions of hearts; and then shall every man have his praise from God* (I Cor. iv. 5). This is the reason which the Apostle gives why we should not judge, because there are uncertain and hidden things which belong to the judgment of God, and so he who meddles in judging these things usurps the jurisdiction and judgment of God. In the Lives of the Fathers there is a story told of one of those monks, who, upon sundry indications that he saw or heard spoken of, judged ill of another monk; and immediately he heard a voice from heaven that said to him: "Men have taken away My judgment, and meddled in the jurisdiction of another."

And if we say this, and the saints say it, of things that wear some appearance of evil, what shall be said of those who put a bad construction even on things in themselves good, judging that they are done with an evil intention and for human motives? This is most properly to usurp the jurisdiction and judgment of God, these people seeking to enter even into the hearts of men and judge of intentions and hidden thoughts, a thing peculiarly proper to God. *Ye have made yourselves judges, giving unjust sentences,* says the Apostle St. James (ii. 4). And the Wise Man says that they seek to make themselves diviners, judging what they know not and cannot know. *In the likeness of a diviner and conjecturer he judgeth of what he knoweth not* (Prov. xxiii. 7).

CHAPTER XVI

Of the Causes and Roots Whence Rash Judgments Proceed, and Their Remedies

THE first root whence rash judgments proceed is that which is the root of all evils and sins, which is pride, but particularly so in this case. St. Bonaventure notes here a thing worthy of consideration. He says: "People who take themselves to be spiritual men are usually more tempted than others in this particular of judging and marking down others, as if they were so to fulfil what the Apostle says in another sense: *The spiritual man judgeth all things* (I Cor. ii. 15)." They fancy they see in themselves gifts of God, and whereas they ought to be more humble, they grow vain of them and take themselves for somebodies, and in comparison with themselves they make little of others, seeing them less recollected and more occupied and diverted with exterior things. Hence they turn reformers of other people's lives, forgetting their own.

The saints say that simplicity is the daughter of humility, since he who is truly humble keeps his eyes open only upon his own faults and closed upon those of his neighbor, and ever finds in himself so much to consider and deplore as never to raise his eyes or his thoughts to the study of other people's faults; and thus once a man is truly humble, he will be far removed from these judgments. To this end the saints assign this remedy as very important, as well for this as for other failings, that we should keep our eyes open solely to see our own faults, *ut sciam quid desit mihi* (Psalm xxxviii. 5), and closed against the sight of the faults of our neighbors. Thus we shall not be like hypocrites whom Christ censures in the holy Gospel, who *see the mote in the eyes of their neighbor, and not the beam that they have right across their own eyes* (Matt. vii. 3). The keeping of our eyes ever on our own failings carries with it great and high benefits. It carries humility and self-abasement; it carries fear of God and recollection of heart; it carries peace and tranquillity. But to go prying into your neighbor's defects carries with it great evils and ill consequences, such as pride, rash judgments, indignation against my brother and ill opinion of him, troubles of conscience, fits of indiscreet zeal, and other things that disturb the heart. Thus, if ever you do see some defect in your neighbor, the saints bid you draw fruit from it. An excellent way of doing this is laid down for us by St. Bonaventure, who says: "When you see in your brother something that displeases you, before you judge him, turn your gaze within and see if there be in you anything worthy of reprehension; and if there be, turn your sentence against yourself and condemn yourself in that in which you were minded to condemn another, saying with the prophet: *It is I who have sinned, I who have done evil* (II Kings xxiv. 17). I am the evil and perverse creature, who do not deserve to kiss the ground on which the other treads, and do I dare to judge him? And what has that which I see in my brother to do with what I see in myself?" St. Bernard teaches another good rule, which we may adopt in this matter: "When you see anything in another that displeases you, turn your eyes at once upon yourself and see if you have the same fault; and if so, give it up. And when you see anything in your brother that pleases you, turn your eyes also upon yourself and see if you have that good point; and if you have it, take means to keep it; and if you have it not, take means to attain it." In this way we shall profit by everything.

St. Thomas assigns other reasons of these judgments. They come sometimes of an evil heart, whereby a man judges of others from what he has done or would do himself, according to the saying of the Wise Man: *The fool walking in the road, being himself void of sense, reckons all men to be fools* (Eccles. x. 3); which in plain English is what the proverb says: "The robber fancies all the world to be thieves." As when you look through a blue glass, all the world seems blue; and if you look through a pink glass, all seems pink; so to the evil and imperfect man everything seems evil; he sees all things in a bad light because he looks through a glass of the same hue. Because he does things for these ends and on these motives, he thinks that everybody else does the same. To him well applies that saying of St. Paul: *You condemn yourself in these judgments, because you do that very thing which you judge* (Rom. ii. 1). A good and virtuous man always takes things on the better side, even though there be some indications that make the thing doubtful; to take them on the worse side is not a good sign. St. Dorotheus says that as a man with a good constitution and a good stomach turns into good nourishment even inferior food, and, contrariwise, a man with a bad constitution and a bad stomach turns good food into peccant humor, so also herein—a man who has a good and upright heart and aims at virtue turns everything to good, takes everything on the better side; whereas he who does not aim at virtue turns all into peccant humor, taking things on the worse side.

The saints go further and say that even when what one sees is clearly bad, though it is not sin to judge that for evil which certainly is so, yet then virtue and perfection show themselves in efforts made to excuse one's neighbor as far as possible. "If you cannot excuse the deed, excuse the intention," says St. Bernard; "think that it was some piece of inadvertence or ignorance; think that it must have been natural forgetfulness; think that it was some sudden burst of impulse"—*Excusa intentionem, si opus non potes; puta ignorantiam, puta subreptionem, puta casum.* If we loved our neighbor as we love ourselves, if we regarded him as a second self, since a friend is a second self, there would never be wanting to us modes and manners of excuse. Oh, how a man excuses himself! How he defends himself! How he diminishes and lightens his faults! So should we do to our neighbor if we loved him as we love ourselves. And when the fault is so evident and culpable as to leave no room for excuse, then, says St. Bernard, think that the occasion and temptation was very grave and vehement, and say within your heart: "What would have become of me if that temptation had assailed me with as much force as it assailed him, and the devil, the tempter, had as much power to tempt me as he had to tempt him?" We read of our blessed Father Ignatius that, when a deed was so evidently bad as to leave no room for excuse and there was no other way out of it, he suspended his judgment and laid hold of a text of Scripture and said: *Judge not before the time* (I Cor. iv. 5); and that saying of the Lord to Samuel: *God alone it is that seeth hearts* (I Kings xvi. 17); and that of St. Paul: *In the eye of the Lord every man keepeth his footing or falleth* (Rom. xiv. 4).

St. Thomas mentions another main root of this habit. He says that rash judgments often arise from some aversion or envy or rivalry on the part of him who judges; this strongly inclines him to think ill of all the doings of the person judged and view them in the worst light on very slight indications, for everyone readily believes what he desires. This is seen by the contrary, for when one has great love for another, he sees at once all his doings in a good light and is so far from putting a bad construction on them or taking them in ill part that he rather excuses and makes light of them, even when he sees them not such as he would wish. *Charity thinketh no evil* (I Cor. xiii. 5). One and the same fault and one and the same evidence, how different they appear in one whom you love and one for whom you have an aversion! Every day we experience this, that one man's goings on shock us, while another perhaps goes further, and we are not offended nor take any heed of it. Both the one and the other fact is well stated by the Wise Man: *Hatred raiseth up quarrels, but love on the contrary covereth all up and putteth faults out of sight* (Prov. x. 12). Thus the passing of judgment on others is for want of loving them. Hence also it is that even what is no fault in our brother oftentimes offends us—his demeanor, his conversation, his way of going on, and sometimes even what in him is virtue. Hence it follows that, as simplicity is a great help to the preservation of charity, so also charity is a great help to simplicity; those two virtues go hand in hand like good sisters.

It will also help us much to consider attentively the cunning and malice of the devil, who seeks to rob us of the esteem and consequently of the love that we should bear to our brethren by little trifles that sometimes are not faults, or if they are, are so trivial that men cannot be free from faults of that sort, since in this life there is no man who does not commit faults and venial sins. The Apostle and Evangelist St. John says: *If we say we have no sin, we deceive ourselves and speak not the truth* (I John i. 8). And the Wise Man says: *Seven times shall the just man fall* (Prov. xxiv. 16); he means to say, he shall fall many times and not cease to be just on that account. Now it is not fair that anyone should lose your good will for that for which he ceases not to be just, nor forfeits one point of the grace of God. True love of charity is not so strait pinned up, not such a house on sticks, as are the friendships of this world, which are dissolved by any trumpery accident, even by failure to pay a salute to your friend. The love of charity is founded in God, Who cannot fail. Let us, then, copy the tender ways of God, Who ceases not to cherish and love us, full of faults and imperfections and venial sins as we are; not for that does He diminish one point of His love. God suffers in me so many faults and imperfections, and I cannot suffer one small fault in my brother without at once throwing it in his teeth and showing annoyance and remaining embittered and in ill humor against him! You show therein that your love is not pure love of charity for God's sake; for if it were, what does not make God angry would not make you angry nor raise your displeasure. What does not make God angry ought not in all reason to make His servants and creatures angry. This man you are angry with is a child of God, His much cherished and well-beloved child; now if God loves and esteems him, it is reasonable that you also should love and esteem him. *Dearly beloved, if God hath loved us so much, we ought also to love another* (I John iv. 11).

Add to this a doctrine of St. Gregory, and it is a common opinion of the saints; they say that sometimes God our Lord denies His lesser gifts to those to whom He gives great gifts and by a secret dispensation of His providence leaves them with sundry faults and imperfections. This to the end that, seeing how for all their desires and efforts to rid themselves of an evil way and an unhappy propensity that they have about them they never succeed, but with so many good purposes they still fail in this point, they may walk ever in humility and self-abasement and understand that, as they cannot compass these lesser things, still less can they achieve those greater things of themselves. Thus a person may in one way be very perfect, very virtuous, a saint; and yet on the other hand along with that have sundry faults and imperfections which God has left to try him and to keep him in humility in the midst of the gifts that he enjoys. Hence we should draw this conclusion, apt to our purpose, that we ought not to pass an unfavorable judgment on anyone for his having some of these faults, nor esteem or prefer ourselves before him because we think we have not such faults. Remember what St. Gregory says, that this man with this fault may be perfect, and you without it may be imperfect. In this manner you will guard humility in yourself on the one hand, and on the other hand esteem and love of your brother and will not judge him nor hold him in less regard on that account.

CHAPTER XVII

In Which the Above Is Confirmed by Sundry Examples

IN the lives of the Fathers it is told of the Abbot Isaac that he came one day from the solitude in which he lived to a company of monks and judged ill of one of them, thinking him worthy of punishment because he saw in him some signs of small virtue. Afterwards he returned to his cell and found at the door an angel standing, who barred his entrance; and when the holy man asked the reason, the angel answered that the Lord had sent him for an answer, where he wished or commanded them to cast this monk whom he had judged and condemned. Then the abbot recognized his fault and begged pardon of the Lord. The angel told him that the Lord forgave him that once, and bade him for the future greatly beware of playing the judge or passing sentence on anyone before the Lord, the Judge of all, judged him.

St. Gregory relates of Cassius, Bishop of Narnia, a great servant of God, that his nose was naturally very red and fiery. Totila, King of the Goths, seeing it, judged that it came of his being a great toper. But the Lord was careful to strike in at once for the honor of His servant by permitting the devil to enter of a sudden into one of Totila's courtiers, his sword bearer, and torment him in the sight of the king and of all the army. They took the possessed person to the saint and he, praying and making the sign of the cross over him, delivered him at once from the devil, whereat the king changed his judgment and held him in great honor ever after.

In the lives of the Fathers it is related that there were two monks, very holy and brotherly together, on whom the Lord had bestowed this favor, that each saw in the other the grace of God that dwelt in him by some visible sign—what it was the history does not say. One of them went out one Friday morning from his cell and saw a monk eating; and as soon as he saw him, without further examination of the necessity or cause he had for eating so early, said to him: "How comes it that you are eating at this hour, today being Friday?"—taking that to be a fault in the other. When he returned to his cell, the monk, his companion, was greatly afflicted, not seeing in him the customary sign of the grace of God, and said to him: "Brother, what is that thou hast done since thou wentest out?" And he answered that he did not know he had done anything bad. His companion answered: "Perhaps thou hast spoken some idle word." At once he remembered what he had said and the judgment he had passed on the other monk. He told him what had passed and they both fasted a fortnight in penance for this fault. When that was over, he saw the sign as usual.

In the chronicles of St. Francis there is related a marvelous vision that the Lord showed to Brother Leo, one of the companions of St. Francis. He saw a great number of Friars Minor in procession, very shining and fair, among whom he saw one more glorious, from whose eyes flashed rays brighter than those of the sun; so bright and fair they were that he could not look him in the face. Holy Brother Leo asked who this friar was whose eyes shone so bright, and was answered that it was Brother Bernard de Quintaval, first companion of St. Francis, and that the light shone from his eyes so brilliant because he always judged on the more favorable side whatever he saw in others, and took all others to be better than himself. When he saw the poor in their rags he used to say: "These people observe poverty better than you," and judged them as if they had voluntarily promised and chosen that poverty. When he saw the rich and well-dressed, he used to say with much compunction: "Maybe these wear haircloth under their clothes and secretly chastise their flesh and outwardly dress in this manner to shun vainglory, and so it may be that they are better than you." For this simplicity in his eyes the Lord gave him that particular glory in them. This is the example we should copy. St. Dorotheus says: "When you enter another's cell and see it all in disorder, say in your heart: 'O happy and blessed brother, who art so absorbed in God as not to see these things!' And when you see it well-arranged and tidy, say: 'That is the way he keeps his soul.' "

In the same chronicles it is related how, when St. Francis was going about Italy preaching, he found on the road a poor and very infirm man, on whom he took pity and compassion, and began to talk to his companion in words expressive of his compassion for the infirmity and poverty of this poor man; and his companion said to him: "Brother, it is true that this person looks very poor but maybe he is richer in desire than all that there are in the land." St. Francis scolded him at once very severely for this speech and rash judgment, and said to him: "Brother, if you wish to stay in my company, you must do the penance I shall give you for this sin against your neighbor." The brother submitting himself with great humility and acknowledgment, ready to do any penance, St. Francis commanded him to cast himself naked at the poor man's feet, and confess that he had sinned against him by detraction, and beg his pardon and prayers. His companion entirely accomplished on the spot the penance laid upon him.

We read also in another place of the same chronicles that the same saint, having for a time almost quite lost his sight by profuse and continual weeping, went to look for Brother Bernard to find comfort in conversing with him of God, of which he had special gift, so that they often spent the whole night together talking of spiritual things and heaven. When he came to his cell, which was in a remote part of the mountain, Brother Bernard was wrapt in prayer; and the holy man Francis called from hard by his cell, saying: "Brother Bernard, come to talk to this blind man." But he, all entranced as he was in God, heard nothing and made no answer to the saint. After a little interval he repeated his call once more: "Brother dear, Friar Bernard, come to console this poor blind man." As Friar Bernard did not answer him, St. Francis turned away, very sad and murmuring within himself that Brother Bernard, though called many times, had not taken the trouble to answer. The saint thus went his way, lamenting on the road and abashed. Then he went apart from his companion, and put himself in prayer on this doubt, how it was that Brother Bernard would not answer him, and at once heard God's reply, Who reproved him and said to him: "Why art thou troubled, little man? Can it possibly be reasonable that a man should leave God for a creature? Brother Bernard, when thou didst call, was with Me and not by himself, and therefore could not come to thee nor answer thee a word because he did not hear thee." The holy father at once returned to Brother Bernard in a great flutter, to accuse himself and receive from him penance for this thought; and finding that he had got up from his prayer, he threw himself at his feet, telling his fault and relating the rebuke which the Lord had given him, and bade Brother Bernard under obedience to inflict on him the penance which he should command him to inflict. But Brother Bernard, suspecting that the saint would command something extreme in the way of humility, as he was wont to do in contempt and chastisement of himself, sought means to excuse himself, and said: "I am ready, father, to do what you command provided you promise me on your part that you will do what I tell you." The holy father was content to agree to this, being readier to obey than to command. Then the saint said: "I command you under holy obedience that in punishment of my presumption, when I am lying my length upon the ground, you put your feet one on my breast and the other on my mouth, and thus step three times over me, treading on my breast and my mouth, saying the words that I deserve: 'Lie there on the ground, caitiff son of Peter Bernardon; whence came upon thee such pride, seeing thou art so base and vile?'" Brother Bernard, hearing this, was in doubt what to do; but for obedience sake, and not to distress the holy father, he did it with as much reverence as he could. That done, St. Francis said: "Now do you command what you wish under holy obedience." Said Brother Bernard: "Under holy obedience I command you that, whenever the two of us are together, you chide me very severely for my faults." Father St. Francis was much pained at this, for he held him in his great reverence for his holiness; and from that time forth the saint never stayed any long time with Brother Bernard, not to have occasion to scold so holy a soul; but when he went to see or hear him speak of God, he brought the interview shortly to a close.

Surius relates that one day the priest of the church came to visit the holy Abbot Arsenius, who was ill. He found him lying on a carpet, and at the head of the bed a pillow. There came with the priest an aged monk who, finding Arsenius thus, began to take scandal, thinking that these were comfortable quarters enough for a man who they said was so holy, not knowing who Arsenius was. Then the priest, who was a sagacious man, took the aged monk a little apart and questioned him: "Pray tell me, father, what you were before you became a monk." He answered that he was very poor and had no property nor means of livelihood to speak of. Then the priest replied: "But know that Arsenius, before he was a monk, was a person very well off and in a high station, a tutor to princes, and gold rolled in his house; and for a man like that to have left all things and come to this poverty and humility, see whether there is not something to admire there and whether the carpet and pillow that he has is an excess of comfort for a man reared in such abundance and now aged and infirm." The old man stood abashed and convinced.

Cassian relates of the Abbot Machetes that, discoursing and teaching on this subject that we must not judge anyone, he told of himself that he had judged his monks particularly on three things. The first was that some monks had abscesses formed inside their mouths which gave them much pain, and to be rid of it they put themselves under treatment and had it lanced, which he judged to be a fault and a mark of want of mortification. The second was that some others, enfeebled somewhat by the rigors of the rough life they led, under necessity made use of a coverlet of goats' hair to lie upon and cover themselves withal, and he judged this to be an excess of comfort and a departure from the austerity that monks should practise. The third was that secular persons came and were moved by devotion to beg blessed oil of the monks, and they blessed and gave it them; and he thought this great presumption on their part, giving themselves out as though they were saints. He further acknowledged that in punishment for these blameworthy judgments, God had let him fall in all three particulars and that he had done the same thing which he condemned in others. For first of all an abscess formed in his mouth, and, compelled by the great pain and torment it gave him, and the advice of his elders, he had put himself under treatment and got it lanced. And under stress of this same infirmity he made use of the aforesaid coverlet; and constrained by the earnest entreaties and importunity of secular persons, he had given them blessed oil. He concluded by admonishing all to take warning by his example, and to dread and carefully shun this vice, saying that they would come to fall into the same case on which they pronounced judgment, as had happened to himself.

Anastasius, Abbot of the Monastery of Mount Sina, who flourished at the time of the Sixth General Council, relates that there was in his monastery a monk who did not pay so much attention to the practices of the community, choir, disciplines, and the like, and was not taken to be such a good religious. The hour of his death came, and they found him in great joy. Anastasius reproved him: "How now, can a monk who has taken life so easily be so cheerful at this hour?" The monk replied: "Be not astonished, father; the Lord has sent me an angel to tell me that I am saved because I have accomplished His word: *Judge not, and ye shall not be judged: forgive, and ye shall be forgiven* (Luke vi. 37). And though it is true that I have not been so faithful to the exercises of the community, partly through negligence, partly through my want of health, yet I suffered them to illtreat me and forgave them from my heart and judged them not, but rather excused what they did or said; for this I am full of joy."

CHAPTER XVIII

Of Other Manners of Union and Friendships Not Good

WE have treated of the union and love that is good and spiritual; now we shall proceed to treat of three manners there are of union and love, not good nor spiritual, but evil and hurtful. St. Basil in his Monastic Constitutions says that religious ought to have great union and charity one with another, but in such sort that there be no particular friendships nor affections whereby two or three band themselves together to keep up such affections, for this would not be charity, but division and sedition, even though such friendship seemed just and holy. And in his fine sermon *De Institutionibus Monachorum,* going into this point more in detail, he says: "If there be anyone found to have more affection for one religious than for another, even if it be for his own brother according to the flesh, or on any other consideration, let him be punished as one wronging common charity." And he gives the reason there, and more expressly in the following sermon, how it is that herein he does an injury to the community; the reason being that he who loves one more than another shows clearly that he does not love the others perfectly, since he does not love them all as he does this one, and thus he offends the others and wrongs the whole community. And if to offend one individual is a matter so grave the Lord says it is to *touch the apple of His eye* (Zach. ii. 8), what shall it be to offend a whole community, and such a community? And so St. Basil then strongly charges religious in no manner to love some individuals more particularly than others nor have special dealings with some more than with others, so as not to aggrieve anyone *nor give offense to anyone* (II Cor. vi. 3), but to have a common and general love of charity of God, Who sends His sunshine and rain upon all equally (Matt. v. 45). The saint goes on to say that these particular friendships in religion are a great seed plot of envy and suspicion, and hatreds and enmities; and further cause divisions, private meetings, and cliques, which are the pest of religious life, for there one discovers his temptations, another his judgments, another his complaints, and other secret things that ought to be hushed up. There go on detractions and criticisms of one another and sometimes of the superior. There people infect one another with their mutual faults in such sort that each catches the fault of the other in a few days. Finally, these friendships are the cause of much breaking of rules and of the doing of many things that ought not to be done, to suit one's friend, as they experience too well who form such friendships.

St. Ephrem says: "Familiarities and conversations of this sort do no little damage to the soul." Thus it is necessary that we should avoid and stand greatly on our guard against them and always hold this for a fundamental principle, that here in religion we must not have particular friends, intimacies, and exclusive dealings that may offend the community. Our friendship should be spiritual, not founded on flesh and blood, nor on long acquaintance and familiarity, nor on other human titles and foundations, but on God our Lord, Who embraces all. Thus there should be an equality of love with all, as with sons of God and brothers of Christ. Let us never in any way consent to our heart's being captivated by any creature; let it be the captive of God alone.

In the chronicles of the Order of St. Francis it is related of a holy man, Brother John of Lucca, that he withdrew from and greatly shunned familiar conversations; and one who was fond of and desired to profit by his conversation complained one day, asking why he was so shy and dry in treating with those who wished him well. The servant of God answered: "It is for your good I do it, since the more I am united with God, of the more profit shall I be to those who wish me well; whereas these your soothing friendships separate me in some degree from God and so do harm to you and me."

CHAPTER XIX

Of the Second Manner of Friendships and Associations That Are Not Good

THERE is a second manner of particular friendship, different from the first inasmuch as it has a different end, but not less harmful to the community and to union and fraternal charity, nay, rather more: it is when one desiring advancement and influence and reputation unites and attaches himself to those whom he thinks likely to forward him thereto. Cassian says that severe bodily ailments develop little by little, and spiritual ailments and great evils of soul alike develop little by little. Let us, then, describe the gradual development of this particular malady, and along with it we will tell the ordinary way in which a religious student comes to deteriorate and go to ruin.

Such a one comes out of the noviceship having made good progress there by the grace of God, and entertaining a high esteem of spiritual things and much affection for them, as it is reasonable he should come out. He goes to the colleges, and there in the ardor of his studies he begins to fall off in his spiritual exercises and either leaves them out in part or does them by routine or for form's sake, without drawing fruit from them, which comes to the same thing. He goes on further, and as now on the one hand his spiritual aims are failing him because he does not do his spiritual duties as he ought, and on the other *knowledge puffs him up* (I Cor. viii. 1) and makes him vain, he comes little by little to set great store by genius and talents and lose his esteem of virtue and humility. This is the gate whereby ordinarily all the undoing and loss of students enters and commences, and thus much heed should be taken to prevent it. Steadily there decreases in them the appreciation and esteem of the quality of virtue, humility, mortification, and all that regards their advancement in spiritual things; while their admiration and esteem of the quality of learning and ability steadily increases because they fancy that thereby they are destined to thrive and come out strong men, regarded and esteemed. Thus they begin to fix their gaze upon this, and desire to be taken for men of fine genius and talent, and to that end they desire to come out well in disputations and the maintaining of theses; they solicit with much eagerness whatever may lead to that and seek occasions to shine and show off and perchance to cast others into the shade and undo them, that they may not get the start of them. Going on further, they begin to aim at ingratiating themselves with some master and grave Father and with all who they think can help and support them with superiors, and they strike up a friendship with them, all in order to mount up and win consideration and be regarded and esteemed, and that these authorities may be favorable to them in their progress.

This is one of the most harmful and pernicious things that can be found in religion and most contrary to union; for what greater evil can enter into religion than the entering in of ambition and self-seeking? And what greater pestilence could enter in here than to have language of this sort coming in amongst us, that now it is necessary for a man to look to himself and get others to back him; and that if he does not, he will be forgotten and thrust into a corner and no account made of him; and that that is how things go nowadays even here? God deliver us from such evil language, and much more from there being anyone found to begin to instill this poison into the heart now of one guileless man, now of another, who was ever so far removed from it, and open his eyes to his perdition. Very different from this is the truth which the Society professes. Our Father in the Tenth Part of his Constitutions says: "Let all who are of the Society give themselves to solid and perfect virtues and to spiritual things, and make more account of them than of learning and other natural and human gifts." This is what the Society esteems and values; therefore let not the old serpent with his cunning and venom deceive you, persuading you that by breaking the commandments of your elders and eating of the forbidden fruit, *you shall become as gods* (Gen. iii. 5). Let him not make you believe that there you will grow and be honored and esteemed, for he lies, liar as he is, the fact being that you will come in for nothing but loss of character; whereas if you go by the other way of virtue, making always greater account of spiritual things and of what makes for your spiritual progress, in that way you will thrive and the Lord will lift you up both in the one and in the other. He will give you the virtue that you desire, and honor and esteem also; you will be regarded and esteemed before God and before men.

We have in confirmation of this a history very much to the purpose in the Third Book of Kings. Holy Scripture tells how God bade Solomon to ask whatever he would and He would give it to him. Solomon set his eyes on wisdom and asked it of God, and Scripture says: *God was so pleased that Solomon had set his eyes on wisdom that he said to him: Since thou hast asked me for this, and not for long life, nor riches, nor victories and vengeance on thine enemies, I give thee wisdom, and that in such sort that thou shalt be called the Wise, eminently so, since there hath not been before thee, nor shall be after thee, anyone the like* (III Kings iii. 10-12). And further, and this is what makes to our purpose, so greatly was God pleased with what Solomon had so happily resolved upon choosing and asking, that, not content with giving him the wisdom that he asked for and which was given him so abundantly, as has been said, He gave him also what he had not asked for; God gave him both the one and the other. *Since thou hast asked so fitly, I will give thee also what thou hast not asked for, riches and honor, and that in such abundance as never had any other King anything like it* (III Kings iii. 13). So also will God deal with you if you do the right thing in choosing and setting before your eyes true wisdom, which consists in true and solid virtues. He will give you the virtue that you desire, on which you set your eyes, because that is very pleasing to God; and He will give you also the honor and esteem on which you did not set your eyes; God will give you both the one and the other. And so we see by experience that these are they who are regarded and esteemed both before God and before men. For we have God's word for it, that *he who humbleth himself shall be exalted* (Luke xiv. 11); and the more you humble yourself and give yourself to virtue, the more you shall be exalted and esteemed; and the more you fly from honor and esteem, the more it will persist in following you, as the shadow follows him who flies from it. But as for those other ambitious people who go like chamelons swallowing air to be swollen out and seem great, the more will honor fly from them; for where they think to mount up, they go down; and where they think to be regarded and esteemed, they lose caste. In fact they come to be taken for proud people, restless, and disturbers of religion; and so there is nothing needed but to cut them off from it as unsound and rotten members, that they may not infect others.

But to come back to our point I say that here in religion, as we ought to be very far from ambitions and pretensions, so also we ought to be far from forming those friendships which are directed thereto. We ought to be tied to nobody, nor should it be the word here: *I am of Paul, I of Apollo, I of Cephas* (I Cor. i. 12). I am not of this man or of that, but of my superior; with him I aim at being united and with no one else in particular. We have no need in the Society of patrons or supporters, nor of standing upon compliments, nor of forming a connection with anyone, for we are not office-hunters, nor have we come here on the hunt for anything but our salvation. Be you a good religious and attend in earnest to the business on which you have come into religion, and you will have no need of anyone but God. This is he who has peace and comfort in religion: the others will never have it, as they themselves experience and confess. A religious should be ashamed to be taken for one who goes about looking for patrons, gaining good wills, and flattering perhaps with others that they may support him and shelter him, for this argues great imperfection and great weakness. The house that needs props is weak; it is in the way of falling: the tree that must be supported by stays is tender, not strong, not well rooted. So you, if you have to go about looking for stays and props, are tender, ill rooted in virtue and even in religion. This is the warning that our Father General Aquaviva gives particularly to students, and says that they must be in no way allowed to attach themselves to older Fathers nor have them for patrons; and he warns those same Fathers to beware of such patronage, and much more to beware of trying to get the young ones to make up to them and want to have them for a refuge, and again of making offers to young men to help them in all their needs, and still more of any senior's taking it for an honor and a badge of authority to have young men for clients and resenting their not applying to him, taking such reserve on their part for a proof that they undervalue him and make little account of him, and perhaps going so far as to tell some young man that he is very stiff and shows too much gravity. This is not showing too much gravity, but showing oneself a good religious, for this is religious life and the other thing is not, but a thing smacking much of the world and very worldly. And if anyone complains of you on that account, he will be complaining of your being virtuous, and like a good religious keeping so far apart from this familiarity, so redolent of the world and so contrary to religion. May the Lord grant that no other complaint may ever be made of us!

CHAPTER XX

Of a Third Sort of Union and Association Very Harmful to Religion

THE third sort of associations and particular friendships is worse and more contrary to union and fraternal charity than the preceding; it is when sundry individuals unite and ally themselves to alter the institute of a religious order and the established rule and holy enactments thereof. St. Bernard on the words of Canticles (i. 5), *The children of my mother have fought against me,* writes: "Not that the spouse, the Church, forgets what she has suffered from Gentiles, Jews, and persecutors, but this she more expressly laments and feels with peculiar keenness, I mean the war that is waged by enemies within our own house, a war far direr and more deadly than anything that foreign enemies can do." We may apply the same saying to a religious order, as a chief member of the Church. The children of my mother have fought against me, those whom I have reared, given them their studies and their degrees at so much cost and labor to myself; these arms that I gave them to fight against the world and convert souls to God, they have turned against me and with them make war upon their mother; see if this is not a grief to feel. Still, deplorable as it is, we ought not to be surprised at such a persecution. Blessed St. Francis experienced it in his days in his order; and the Catholic Church even in the lifetime of the apostles suffered this persecution at the hands of her own children, who rose up against her with the errors and heresies that they invented. The members follow in the wake of their Head, Who is Christ, Who traveled by this road of labors and persecutions, because thereby the elect are purified as gold in the crucible. So says St. Paul: *There must be factions and divisions, that those who are truly good may be made manifest among you* (I Cor. xi.

19); and Christ our Lord: *It needs must be that scandals come, nevertheless woe to that man by whom scandal cometh* (Matt. xviii. 7). Scandals in the Church, scandals in religion, for we are men. But that is no excuse; woe to him that causes the scandals; it were better for him if he had never been born.

The glorious St. Basil speaks gravely and severely against these combinations. "If any of their own accord cut themselves off from the rest of the community and seek to make a society within the Society, this is a vicious society and these are evil associations. It is a sedition and a division." A malicious machination it is in religion when people go about to alter and adulterate the established customs of their first institute, and all the worse the more they color it with pretence of improvement and reform. St. Basil says that such persons are first to be admonished and corrected in private and afterwards before others, according to the order laid down in the Gospel; and if they are none the more amended by that, *let him be to thee as the heathen and the publican* (Matt. xviii. 17). Such a one should be counted excommunicate and separated from the rest, like the sick of a contagious malady, that he may not infect the others. And our Father recommends the same in his Constitutions, according to the Apostle: *Would that they were cut off that trouble you* (Gal. v. 12). Cut off the rotten member that it may not infect the rest.

It is easy to see how great this evil is and how harmful to religious, since by the mere exposition of it, its poisonous nature is shown, and so it should not be necessary to take the trouble of opening it out further. But the matter of itself is so grave that we will here enlarge upon it and show cause sufficient for us not only to abhor, but to detest and abominate so great an evil, and remain rooted in attachment to our institute. Religious life is not an invention of men, but of God; and so the things laid down for the preservation and increase of a religious order must not be taken for human inventions, as though they were the contrivance of some particular individual; they are the contrivances and inventions of God. As God took and chose the blessed St. Francis for the founder of his order, and the blessed St. Dominic for the founder of his, and our blessed Father Ignatius for the founder of the Society, and so of the rest; He gave them and showed them the means and so the particular manner of going about the work that was most suitable for the well-being and progress of the order, beyond what they could have discovered for themselves, because *God's works are perfect* (Deut. xxxii. 4), and in any other way this work of God would have remained mutilated and imperfect.

So in the Life of our Father, from an answer he gave, meeting something said by Father James Laynez, we may gather that the more substantial things of our institute—what we may call its sinews and foundations—were revealed and inspired by God our Lord to our blessed Father Ignatius. God Himself being author and source of this order, took Ignatius for its head and His principal instrument in the work of foundation. This may likewise be gathered from the method he is said to have observed in making and writing the Constitutions and the abundant prayers and tears which every word cost him of those words which he has left us in writing. Thus, to determine whether it was fitting or not that the churches of our professed houses should have any revenue for the upkeep of the fabric—a point which is not the most substantial of our institute—he said mass for forty consecutive days and gave himself to prayer with more fervor than usual. Hence we may see how much communication and consultation he had with God over the Constitutions, and the light that our Lord gave him to choose and determine that which would be most agreeable to His Divine Majesty. And that we may not seem to pitch our voice too high or to be crying our own wares—although the reason already given is sufficient of itself—*we have other testimony stronger than this* (John v. 36), and it is well that we should allege it, for it is very important for us to be well grounded on this principle.

It is recounted in the chronicles of the Order of St. Francis that the saint retired with two companions to Mount Caynerio, near Reate, to compose and write his rule for presentation to the sovereign pontiff, so that he might obtain the apostolic bull of its confirmation, since hitherto it had not been confirmed by bull, but only by word of mouth, *vivae vocis oraculo,* by Innocent III. On that mountain he fasted forty days on bread and water, persevering day and night in continual prayer; so he composed his rule as the Lord inspired and revealed, as is said there and as actually was the case, as will appear presently. Taking the rule written on the mountain, he gave it to keep to Friar Elias, his vicar general, a prudent man according to the world and a learned man. Elias, seeing it founded on greater self-contempt, humility, and poverty than seemed to him expedient, lost the rule on purpose, that it might not be confirmed, but another more to his liking. Father St. Francis, who sought rather to follow the will of God than that of man and made small account of the opinions of the wise men of this world, returned to the mountain to keep another forty days' fast, and by fasting and prayer to ascertain the will of God and compose another rule. Friar Elias, knowing this, set himself about to thwart what was going on, and assembled some superiors and doctors among the friars and told them how Father St. Francis wanted to make a rule so strict that it was impossible to keep it. They required him as vicar general to go to St. Francis and tell him on the part of them all that they had no mind to be bound by this rule. Friar Elias did not dare to go alone with this message, but said that he would go with them. They all went to the mountain where the holy Father was praying in a lonely cell and, coming near it,

Friar Elias called for St. Francis. The saint, knowing his voice, came out of the cell and, seeing so many friars with him, asked what these friars wanted. Friar Elias answered: "They are superiors of the order, who, having heard tell of the new rule that you are making and fearing that you are making it too severe, protest that they have no mind to be bound by it, that you are making it for yourself and not for them." The saint, hearing these words, fell on his knees and raising his eyes to heaven, said: "Lord, did I not tell Thee that these people would not believe me?" And suddenly there came a voice from heaven which said: "Francis, there is nothing of thine in this rule; all that is in it is Mine, and I want the rule kept to the letter, to the letter, to the letter, without gloss, without gloss, without gloss. I know how much human weakness can stand and how much I intend to aid it; let them that have no mind to keep it leave the order and leave it to the rest to observe." Francis turned to the superiors and said: "Have you heard? Have you heard? Have you heard? Do you want me to get it said to you a second time?" And Friar Elias and the superiors, out of themselves, trembling and dumbfounded, recognizing their fault, turned on their heels without uttering another word. The holy patriarch returned to compose his rule, neither more nor less than what the Lord had revealed to him; and, having finished the composition, he took it to the sovereign pontiff, who was Honorius III. The pope reading the rule and remarking on its severity and poverty, which seemed very strait and difficult to observe, St. Francis replied: "I, holy Father, have not put one single word into this rule out of my own opinion and judgment; but our Lord Jesus Christ has compiled and composed it, Who alone knows very well all that is necessary and profitable for the salvation of souls and the good estate of the friars and the preservation of this, His order. To Him all the things to come in the Church and in this order are manifest and present; and that being so, I neither ought nor can change anything." And the pope, moved by the inspiration of God, gave the bull and apostolic confirmation of the rule, *ad perpetuam rei memoriam.*

In this manner God is wont to inspire and give the rule to the founders of religious orders; and in this manner He inspired and gave it to our holy Father Ignatius. And of this we have another account, even more authentic than the preceding, since we have the apostolic bulls with their leaden seals that say so. Gregory XIII, of happy memory, in the bull and constitution which commences *Ascendente Domino* and in another which he gave before, commencing *Quanto fructuosius,* having first set down all the points of our institute and in particular those that seemed to raise some difficulty and about which he had been informed that some both within and without the Society called for investigation, declares and says expressly these formal words: "Wherefore the said Ignatius by divine inspiration *(divino instinctu)* so considered that the body of the Society should be organized in its members, orders, and grades." What clearer language could have been used?

This being presupposed, let us come to the point and enter into a reckoning with those who seek to form private associations for the altering of a religious institute and of the things established by its founder. Don't you think it is great pride to have such a high idea of oneself and of one's judgment and opinions as to dare to say, the road that Ignatius has left us laid down in his Constitutions is not a good one; it would be better for us to go by the road that pleases me? What greater folly and wrong-headedness could there be? The greatness of this infatuation can be seen from another similar to it; one well exemplifies the other. One of the greatest evils and sins there are in the Church of God is heresy. I do not dispute now whether there can be any other sin greater, since it is clear that a greater sin would be the express hatred of God: but those sins are not commonly committed here on earth; there in hell is their place. But I say that of the sins that commonly find place here on earth, they say that heresy, whereby one separates oneself from the Church, is the greatest; and with reason, for besides its destroying the foundation of the whole Christian religion, which is faith, and other reasons that there are, does it not strike you as an excessive and extreme pride? To think that anyone should be so confident in himself and hold so fast to his own judgment as to come to believe and rather take for true what seems good to him and suits his fancy, in preference to what the Catholic Roman Church has settled to be believed, what has been approved in so many councils, where has been assembled the cream of all the good there was in the world as well in learning as in sanctity, and has been confirmed by the blood of so many thousands of martyrs who have died for it, and by innumerable miracles that have been wrought in confirmation of it! To think that a man should come to say: "But I rather believe in my last night's dream or in what a Martin Luther tells me"—a bad man and a perverse, an apostate, immoral and living in sacrilegious concubinage! What greater pride and folly, what greater blindness and absurdity could there be! But this is the way they go and this is what in their own measure they do, those persons we are speaking of who prefer their own judgment and opinion to his whom God our Lord has taken for head and founder of this religious order, and think that the way they have dreamt of and invented is better than that which God our Lord has inspired and revealed to him whom He was pleased to take for His principal instrument in the foundation of the Society. It is a pride and presumption like that of Lucifer. What? Has God hidden from our Father Ignatius, whom He chose for head and founder, the right way that was proper for the well-being of the order, and has revealed it to you? Is not this enough to make you understand that it is a deceit and delusion of the devil, who wishes to take you for his means and instrument to make war on the Society, which he so much abhors, and trouble the peace and union of the order, as he took that other, the heretic, to trouble the peace of the Church? "Oh," you say, "but I am aiming only at the reform of the order." You deceive yourself; the devil, the father of lies, is blinding you with this false and lying phrase, for this is not to reform the Society, but to destroy and undo the Society. And observe that this is no exaggeration, but a plain and very clear truth. To reform an order is, when the order has fallen and departed from its primitive institute, to take measures for its return to its first principles and keep the rule and arrangement which its first founder bequeathed to it. This is a good and holy work, and many religious orders have gone through it in the desire to maintain themselves in their first institute and rule. But to change the institute and primitive way of life that our first founder has left us, inspired by God, and to seek to introduce another way, different from that, is not to reform the order, but to seek to destroy and undo it and create another order, different from the first, of your own design and fashion and to your own taste, as Friar Elias wanted to do with the order of St. Francis; and so this is not the spirit of God, but of the devil.

The holy Council of Trent dealing with the reformation of religious orders and making some very holy decrees to that effect, our Father General James Laynez laid this supplication before those fathers: "Most holy fathers, these decrees of reformation do not seem applicable to our Society of Jesus, seeing that it is at this day a new order, distinct from other orders, and as such has its own distinct methods of procedure, approved by the apostolic see; and by the goodness of God we have not departed from our first institute and rule; and so if these decrees shall be applied to it, it will not be reformed, but destroyed." The holy council fell in with this reason and replied: "Hereby, however, the holy synod does not intend to make any innovation or prohibition to hinder the order of clerks of the Society of Jesus from being able to serve the Lord and His Church according to their pious institute approved by the holy apostolic see" (Trid. Sess. 25, de reform. cap. 16). The holy Council of Trent does not wish nor venture to change the institute and mode of procedure which the Lord gave to the Society by means of our blessed Father Ignatius, as approved by the apostolic see, but on the contrary approved and confirmed it; and have you the hardihood to seek to alter and change it for I know not what human regards and reasons that occur to you?

Quite other esteem, and other regard and reverence did he pay to our institute and its founder—that cardinal of whom there is related in the Life of our Father a thing very much to our purpose. It is related there that the Cardinal of the Holy Cross, Marcellus Cervini, who came afterwards to be pope and took the name of Marcellus II, a little before he was raised to the see of the sovereign pontiff, had a long argument with Father Doctor Olave, a distinguished theologian of the Society, upon that constitution which we have that none of the body can accept any dignity outside of the Society unless compelled thereto by obedience put upon him by one who can command him under pain of sin, and that even the General cannot issue such a command except by order and mandate of the sovereign pontiff, and of this all the professed make a special vow. The cardinal said that the Society would render a greater service to the Church of God by providing it with good bishops than by giving it good preachers and confessors and that the fruit would be all the greater inasmuch as a good bishop can do more than a poor clerk. He alleged many reasons to this effect, to which Father Olave replied, giving him to understand that the greatest service that the Society could render to holy Church was by keeping itself in its proper purity and lowliness, thereby to serve it for a longer period and in greater security. And since in the end the cardinal, thinking his own reasons the better, stuck to his opinion, Doctor Olave said to him: "If reasons are not enough to convince your illustrious lordship and make you change your mind, the authority of our Father Ignatius, who thought so, is enough to make us believe that that is the better arrangement." Thereupon the cardinal said: "Now I give in and say that you are right, for supposing I thought that reason was on my side, nevertheless the authority of Father Ignatius in this matter would weigh with me more than all the reasons in the world. And even reason itself says the same; for since God our Lord chose him to plant in His Church an order like yours and to spread it all over the world with such fruit of souls and to rule and govern it with such a spirit of prudence as we see has been done and is done, it is also to be believed, and it would seem that it cannot be otherwise, that the same God has revealed and disclosed the manner in which He wishes this order to serve Him and preserve itself for the future." With how greater reason should we ourselves who are religious and should be children of obedience, subject ourselves and submit our judgment when we see that a thing is a rule and constitution of the Society, ordained by him whom our Lord has given us to be its head and founder. And this especially, seeing that it has been since so much approved and confirmed by all the sovereign pontiffs who have been, from then up to this time, and by the holy Council of Trent; and that on this score the Lord has blessed and made such use of the Society, producing such fruit by its means for these sixty years and more! *Trespass not over the ancient boundaries which thy fathers have set,* says the Wise Man (Prov. xxii. 28).

An so to repress such presumption and venturesomeness, His Holiness Gregory XIII in his bull and constitution, *Ascendente Domino,* after having approved and confirmed anew the Institute and manner of life of the Society and in particular the things which some might wish to amend, commands in virtue of holy obedience, and under pain of excommunication *latae sententiae* and of incapacity for any office or benefice *ipso facto* without further declaration, that no one of any state, rank, and pre-eminence whatsoever shall presume in any manner to impugn or contradict any point of the Institute or Constitutions of the Society, either directly or indirectly, not even under color of disputation or wish to know the truth; and if any doubt arises on these points, he says that it is well that the apostolic see be consulted thereupon or the General of the Society or other persons to whom the matter shall be committed, and that none other shall dare to meddle therewith. The same, even at greater length, is enacted by his successor Gregory XIV in another constitution made on this head, which commences *Ecclesiae Catholicae,* in very grave words. "Considering," he says, "that it would be to the no small prejudice of religious discipline and detriment of all religious life, if what has been in holy fashion laid down by founders of orders and received and approved many times by the same order in its general congregations and, what is more, established and confirmed by this holy apostolic see, should be, not to say changed, but even altered or impugned under any pretext whatsoever, We command in virtue of holy obedience all persons of whatsoever state and condition they be, ecclesiastical or secular or religious, even though they be of the same Society, under pain of excommunication *latae sententiae* and of being held disqualified and incapable of any office and dignity and of privation of active and passive voice, which penalties are incurred *ipso facto* without further declaration, absolution therefrom reserved to the apostolic see; and renewing the constitution of Gregory XIII, our predecessor, and all the penalties therein contained, [We command] that none shall presume to impugn or contradict any point of the Institute or Constitutions or decrees of the Society, either directly or indirectly, or under color of greater good or zeal or any other pretext whatever." And he adds another thing very special and substantial, that none is to propose or give in any memorials on the said subject, for anything to be added or struck out or changed except to the sovereign pontiff immediately, or intermediately through his nuncio or apostolic legate, or to the General of the Society or to the general congregation. And our present Holy Father Paul V, in the bull that he issued in the year 1606 confirming the Institute and privileges of the Society, makes special mention of these two constitutions of Gregory XIII and Gregory XIV and approves and grants them anew. Hence it appears what pitfalls there are about this matter, since none can transgress herein without the gravest penalties and without incurring the greater excommunication *ipso facto*, whether he be of the Society or out of it, religious, cleric, or layman, of whatsoever state, rank, condition, and pre-eminence he be.

Let us, then, conclude with the conclusion of St. Paul writing to the Corinthians: *For the rest, brethren, rejoice, be perfect, exhort one another, be of one mind, have peace* (II Cor. xiii. 11). Let us rejoice, my Fathers and brothers, and be glad that the Lord has drawn us to an order so holy and professing such perfection; and let us speak ever of this perfection and how to keep ourselves in great peace and union, exhorting and animating one another thereto; and in this way the Lord, Who is the author and fountain of peace and love, will ever be with us.

FIFTH TREATISE

ON THE EXCELLENCY OF PRAYER

CHAPTER I

Of the Value and Excellence of Prayer

THE glorious Apostle and Evangelist St. John, in the fifth and eighth chapters of the Apocalypse, expresses admirably well the excellency and merit of prayer. *There came an angel and stood before the altar, having in his hand a thurible of gold, to whom was given much incense, to the end he should offer up of the prayers of the saints upon the golden altar which was before the throne of God. And the smoke of the incense of these prayers went up from the hand of the angel to the presence of God* (Apoc. viii. 3-4). St. Chrysostom says that one proof of the merit of prayer is that in the Holy Scripture it alone is compared to thymiama, which was a composition of incense and of many other admirable perfumes; for as the smell of well-composed thymiama is very delicious, so prayer also, when well made, is very acceptable to God and gives great joy to the angels and all the citizens of heaven. Thus St. John, speaking in such human language as we can speak, says that those heavenly beings hold in their hands pouncet-boxes full of admirable perfumes, which are the prayers of the saints, and these they apply again and again to their most pure nostrils to enjoy that sweet odor (Apoc. v. 8).

St. Augustine, speaking of prayer, says: "What more excellent than prayer? What more useful and profitable? What sweeter and more delicious? What higher and more exalted in the whole scheme of our Christian religion?" The same says St. Gregory of Nyssa: "Nothing of the things of this life that are esteemed and valued has the advantage of prayer." St. Bernard says that, though it is quite an ordinary thing for the angels to assist God's servants by their invisible presence, to deliver them from the deceits and machinations of the enemy, and to raise their desires to serve God with greater fervor, yet it is especially when we are occupied in making our prayer that these angelic spirits assist us. He quotes to this effect many passages of Holy Scripture, as that of the psalmist: *In the sight and presence of the angels I will praise thee* (Psalm cxxxvii. 1); and again: *There went forward the princes along with the singers in the midst of the young maidens sounding their timbrels* (Psalm lxvii. 26), which he interprets, saying that the angels join with those who make prayer; and again what the angel said to Toby: *When thou didst pray with tears, I offered thy prayer to God* (Tob. xii. 12). In the instant that prayer goes out from the mouth of him that prays, at once the angels, who are hard by, catch it up and present it to God. St. Hilary says the same: "The angels preside over the prayers of the saints and offer them each day to God." Thus, when we are at prayer, we are surrounded by angels, in the midst of angels, doing the office of angels, exercising ourselves in what we are to do forever in heaven, praising and blessing the Lord; and for this we are specially favored and loved by the angels as being their companions now and destined to be their companions hereafter, filling up the seats of their former companions who fell.

St. John Chrysostom, speaking of the excellences of prayer and wishing to say great things of it, says that one of the greatest of great things that it is possible to say of it is that whoever is at prayer is dealing and conversing with God. "Consider the height, dignity, and glory to which the Lord has raised you, in that you can speak and converse with God, hold conversations and colloquies with Jesus Christ, desire what you would, and ask for what you desire"—*Considera quanta est tibi concessa felicitas, quanta gloria attributa orationibus, fabulari cum Deo, cum Christo miscere colloquia, optare quod velis, quod desideras postulare.* No tongue, he says, sufficies to declare the dignity and height of this intercourse and conversation with God or its utility and profit for ourselves. If in those who here on earth ordinarily converse with prudent and wise men, in a short time there is felt a notable improvement, and it is recognized that they have advanced in prudence and wisdom, and to those who converse with good men virtue and goodness is communicated—hence the proverb: "Deal with the good and you shall be one of them"—what shall be said of those who speak and converse again and again with God? *Approach to the Lord and ye shall receive light from Him* (Psalm xxxiii. 6). What light and knowledge, what blessings and benefits shall they receive from such dealing and conversation! And so St. John Chrysostom says that there is nothing that makes us grow so much in virtue as frequent prayer and dealing and conversing repeatedly with God, because thereby there comes to be formed the heart of a generous and high-souled man, a heart ready to despise the things of the world and to soar above them, uniting and transforming itself in a manner unto God and becoming spiritual and holy.

CHAPTER II

Of the Need in Which We Stand of Prayer

OF the need in which we stand of prayer we have abundant experience; would to God we had not so much! For man, being in such need of the favor of God by reason of his being liable to so many falls, surrounded by so many dangerous enemies, and wanting so many things for soul and body, has no other resource but constant recourse to God, begging with his whole heart divine favor and aid in all his dangers and necessities. So King Josaphat said, coming to be surrounded by enemies: *As we are so weak and so poor and so needy and know not what to do, we have no other resource but to raise our eyes to God, and ask in prayer for what we want and stand in need of* (II Chron. xx. 12). So Pope Celestine in a decretal letter to teach the importance of prayer, says: "I know nothing better to say to you than what my predecessor, Zozimus, said: 'What time is there in which we have not need of God?' None. Then in every time, in all cases, in all affairs we need to have recourse to Him by prayer and crave His favor; great pride it is for a weak and miserable man to presume anything of himself"—*In omnibus igitur actibus, causis, cogitationibus, motibus, adiutor et protector orandus est Deus.*

St. Thomas, treating of prayer, gives one very good and substantial reason for its necessity, and it is the teaching of Saints Damascene, Augustine, Basil, Chrysostom, and Gregory, that what God by His divine providence and disposition has determined from eternity to give to souls, that He gives them in time by this means of prayer, and on this means depends the deliverance, salvation, conversion, and cure of many souls and the progress and perfection of others. Thus, just as God has determined and arranged that by means of matrimony the human race should be multiplied, and by means of ploughing and sowing and cultivating the earth there should be abundance of bread and wine and other fruits, and by means of craftsmen and building materials there should be houses and buildings, so He has determined to work many effects in the world and impart many graces and gifts to souls by this means of prayer. So Christ our Redeemer says in the Gospel: *Ask and it shall be given you, seek and ye shall find, knock and it shall be opened unto you; for everyone that asketh receiveth, and he that seeketh findeth, and the door shall be opened to him that knocked* (Matt. vii. 7). Thus this is the means and this the conduct whereby the Lord wishes to supply our needs and enrich our poverty and fill us with good things and graces. Hereby is well seen the great need that we have of having recourse to prayer. And so the saints make a good comparison in saying that it is a chain of gold attached to heaven and reaching right down to earth, whereby all good things are lowered and let down to us and whereby we must mount up to God. Or they say that it is the ladder of Jacob, that reached from earth to heaven, whereby angels ascended and descended. The glorious St. Augustine says that prayer is the key of heaven that fits all the gates of heaven and all the coffers of the treasures of God, and nothing hidden from it. And elsewhere he says that what bread is to the body, prayer is to the soul. The same says the holy martyr and abbot Nilus.

One of the chief reasons whereby the saints declare on the one hand the value and worth of prayer and on the other the great need in which we stand of it, is that prayer is a chief and most efficacious means to attune and put in order our whole life and to overcome and smooth down all the difficulties that present themselves in the way of virtue. And so they say that on it depends the government of our whole life; and that, when prayer is well in order, life is well in order; and when prayer gets out of order, everything else gets out of order. "He knows how to live well, who knows how to pray well"—*Recte novit vivere, qui recte novit orare,* says St. Augustine. And St. John Climacus says that a servant of God once spoke a memorable word to him, which was this, that from early morning he knew what was to be the order of the whole day; meaning that, if he made his morning prayer well, all the rest went well, and contrariwise when he did not make his morning prayer well. And it is the same with all the rest of life. And so we ourselves very commonly experience that when we make our prayer well, we go on in such good order, so cheerful, so vigorous, so full of good purposes and desires, that it is something to praise God for; and, contrariwise, when we are careless at prayer, everything goes amiss. St. Bonaventure says: "Where prayer fails, thereupon everything goes forlorn;" thereupon tepidity sets in, thereupon little by little the spirit begins to grow feeble and to wither and to lose that vigor and heartiness which it once had; thereupon, I know not how, all those holy purposes and thoughts of first fervor disappear and all our passions begin to awake and revive; thereupon the man comes out a lover of vain mirth, a lover of talking, laughing and enjoyment, and such like other vanities; and what is worse, thereupon there bursts into new life the appetite of vainglory, of anger, of envy, of ambition, and the like, which before seemed to be dead.

The Abbot Nilus says that prayer should be the looking-glass of the religious. In it we should look and look again every day for a long time to see and recognize our faults, to go on getting rid of anything ugly that we find in ourselves. In this looking-glass we should look and study the virtues that shine forth in Christ, in order with them to adorn and beautify our soul. The glorious St. Francis says: "One of the things most desirable in a religious is the grace of prayer: without it there is no hope of fruit or improvement; with it everything may be hoped for." St. Thomas Aquinas, among other grave utterances related in his Life, said that a religious without prayer was a soldier in battle naked and without arms. That holy archbishop of Valentia, Friar Thomas of Villanova, said that prayer was like the natural heat of the stomach, without which it is impossible for the natural life to be preserved, or for any food to do good; whereas with it everything is well digested and assimilated, the man is nourished, and all the members are supplied with virtue and strength enough to do their work. So, he says, without prayer the spiritual life cannot be preserved; with it, it is preserved; with it, the man revives and recovers spiritual strength enough for all the works of obedience that he has to do and for all the occasions and afflictions that may offer; with prayer, all those things are digested and made light, and all converted to the profit of the soul. Finally, if we use prayer as we ought, we shall find therein a remedy for all our faults and a means of preserving ourselves in virtue and religion. If perchance you become careless in obedience and observance of rules, if you begin to grow disorderly on any point, if passion and evil habit begin to revive, all this will be checked and remedied, by favor of the Lord, at once when we betake ourselves to prayer. And if you grow remiss in prayer itself and careless therein, you must cure and recover yourself by that same means. In prayer we have a universal remedy even for a falling off in prayer itself. Thus they make an excellent comparison who say that prayer is as the hand in the body, which is an instrument for all the body and even for itself, since the hand works for the sustenance and clothing of the whole body and for all other things necessary for body and soul and even for itself; for if it is ailing, the hand waits on the hand; if it is dirty, the hand washes the hand; if it is cold, the hand warms the hand; in short, the hands do everything. So it is with prayer.

CHAPTER III

That We Owe Much to God for Having Made So Easy for Us a Thing at Once So Excellent and So Necessary

IT will be reasonable for us to consider and ponder here the great and singular favor that the Lord has done us. Prayer being in itself a thing so high and excellent and on the other hand so necessary for us, God has made it so easy for all that it is always in our power to take to it in every place and at every time. *With me is prayer to make to God who giveth me life,* says the Prophet David (Psalm xli. 9). The gates of God's mercy are never closed; they are wide open to all at every time and at every hour. We shall always find Him disengaged and desirous to do us good, and even soliciting us to ask. There is an excellent reflection that is often made to this effect. If God were to give leave once a month only for all who would to go in and address Him, promising to give them an audience willingly and to do them favors, it would be a boon highly valued, as it would be if a temporal king made a similar offer. How much more reasonable is it that we should value the offer and invitation that God makes us herein, not merely once a month, but every day and many times a day! *At night and at morning and at midday and in the afternoon,* says the prophet, embracing all times, *I will tell and put before God* (Psalm liv. 18) my labors and miseries, in full confidence that every time and at whatever hour I approach Him He will hear me and do me favors. God is not like men, annoyed at being asked, for, unlike them, He is none the poorer for giving. A man has so much the less, by how much he bestows on another; he robs himself of that which he gives and is the poorer for his liberality. It is for this reason, then, that men are annoyed at being asked; and if they give once or twice with good will, they are tired of it the third time, and give nothing or give in such a way that they are never asked again. *God,* as St. Paul says, *is rich and liberal to all who call upon him* (Rom. x. 12). He is infinitely rich; and as He makes Himself none the poorer by giving, so He is not angry nor weary at people asking of Him, though it be every minute and He have the whole world begging at His door. He is rich enough for all and to enrich all, without ceasing to be as rich as before; and as the fund of His riches is infinite, so also the source of His mercy in inexhaustible, to meet the needs of all; and He desires that we should beg of Him and have recourse to Him very frequently. It will be reasonable, then, for us to acknowledge and be grateful for so great a favor and benefit and to make the best of so large and advantageous a licence, taking care to be very assiduous in prayer. For, as St. Augustine says upon these words of the psalmist: *Blessed be our Lord, who has not deprived me of my prayer nor of his mercy.* We must believe for certain that if God withdraw not from us the spirit of prayer, neither will He withdraw His mercy. Wherefore, that His mercy may never forsake us, let us never leave off the exercise of prayer.

CHAPTER IV

Of Two Sorts of Mental Prayer

LEAVING apart vocal prayer, a thing so holy and in such common use in the Church of God, we will for the present treat only of mental prayer, of which St. Paul writes: *I will pray, sing, and cry to God in spirit and with my heart* (I Cor. xiv. 15). There are two sorts of mental prayer, one common and easy, the other very special, extraordinary, and advanced, something received rather than made, according to the saying of ancient saints well versed in prayer. St. Denis the Areopagite says of his master, Hierotheus, that *erat patiens divina,* that is to say, he rather received what God gave than did things for himself. There is a very great difference between these two sorts of prayer; the former may in some measure be taught by words, the second we cannot so teach because no words are able to express it. It is *a hidden manna, which no man knoweth but him that receiveth it* (Apoc. ii. 17). Even the receiver cannot explain how it is nor even properly understand how it is, as Cassian well observes, quoting to this effect what he calls a divine and heavenly saying of the blessed St. Anthony Abbot: "Prayer is not perfect so long as the monk at prayer is aware of the very fact that he is praying." This high and exalted prayer does not leave room for the person to bethink himself, nor reflect on what he is about, "suffering," we should say, rather than "doing." It happens not unfrequently that a man has his mind so taken up and absorbed in some business that he remembers not himself, nor where he is, nor reflects upon what he thinks, nor observes how he thinks. It is the same in this perfect prayer, wherein man is so ravished and lost in God that he thinks no more of himself, nor understands how this is, nor what way it goes, nor what way it comes, nor keeps any account of methods, preambles, or points, nor how he must now do this and now that. This is what happened to St. Anthony himself, of which Cassian makes mention, that oftentimes having set himself to prayer overnight, he remained in it till the next day, when, the light falling upon his eyes, he complained that the sun rose too soon to deprive him of those lights which God interiorly communicated unto him. St. Bernard, speaking of this kind of prayer, says that we very seldom find it, and when we do, its stay is very short. *Rara hora, parva mora;* so that how long time soever it lasts, it seems to us all to have been done in a moment. St. Augustine, experiencing in himself the effects it produces, says: "Lord, Thou leadest me on to a tenderness very unusual, and a strange sweetness, such that if it were to go on, I know not where it would stop." Even in this most special prayer and contemplation St. Bernard marks three degrees. The first he compares to eating; the second to drinking, which is easier and pleasanter than eating because there is no labor for the teeth; the third in inebriation. And he quotes the saying of the spouse in the Canticles: *Eat, my friends, and drink and be inebriated, my dear ones* (Cant. v. 1). All this is a case of receiving rather than of doing. Sometimes the gardener draws water from his well by force of his arms; at others, standing with folded arms, he sees the flood from heaven soaking the earth without his doing anything else but receive it and guide it to the roots of the trees to make them more fruitful. So there are two kinds of prayer: the one is sought with industry, aided by God; the other is found ready made. By the first you go toiling and begging, and living on what you beg; the second sets before you a full table, which God has spread for you to satisfy your hunger, a rich and abundant table, signified by those words of the spouse: *The king hath led me into his cellars*

(Cant. i. 3). And again: *I will gladden them in the house of my prayer* (Isaias lvi. 7).

This prayer is a particular gift of God, a gift which He bestows upon whom He pleases; sometimes in reward of services done and much mortification practised and suffering borne for His love; at other times as a gracious gift of sheer liberality irrespective of previous merits, as it is said in the Gospel: *Is it not lawful for me to do what I please?* (Matt. xx. 15). Anyhow, it is not a thing that we can teach. And so certain authors have been reproved and prohibited for having undertaken to teach what cannot be learned nor taught, making a matter of art what is above all art, as though in their way one could infallibly arrive at becoming a contemplative. Gerson severely reprehends this in a book he composed against Ruysbroek, in these words: "You have torn the flower from the root." As the flower cut from the root and taken in hand soon withers and loses its beauty, so these intimate communications of God to the soul in this high and lofty prayer are of such a nature that in the attempt to take them out of their place and explain and share them with others, they lose their luster and splendor. So do they act who try to explain and teach what cannot be explained or understood. These analogical acts, these transformations of the soul, this silence, this self-annihilation, this immediate union, this depth of Tauler—what is the use of talking of such things if you understand them not, nor know what you are talking about? Nay, some say, and say well, that there is this difference between this divine science and other sciences, that in other sciences, before you learn them, you must learn their terms, whereas in this you cannot understand the terms till you perfectly possess and are master of the science. In others, the theory precedes the practice; in this, the practice goes before the theory.

I say still further that not only we cannot express what this prayer is, nor teach it to others, but you must not seek to apply yourself to it nor raise yourself to it if God does not raise you, apply you, and lift you up to it. That would be great pride and presumption, and you would deserve to be deprived of the grace of prayer that you have and be left without any. *He hath led me,* says the spouse, *into his cellar* (Cant. ii. 4). This entry which God gives to the soul into His privacy and into His wine cellar, to sate and inebriate her with His love, is a most particular gift of the Lord; the bride did not go in by herself, no, not until her Beloved took her by the hand and led her in. That lifting of yourself up to the kiss of His mouth is not a thing that you can or ought to do unless He Himself lifts you up. It would be great impertinence and audacity. Even the bride does not dare do that—she is too bashful and humble for that—but she begs of her Beloved to give her this kiss: *Let him kiss me with the kiss of his mouth;* meaning, as St. Bernard says: "I cannot of my own strength attain to such love and such high union and contemplation as this unless He give it me." It is His goodness and gracious liberality that must raise us to this kiss of the mouth, to this so high prayer and contemplation, if He be pleased that we should reach it. It is not a thing that we can teach or that we can or ought to lay ourselves out for.

CHAPTER V

How Holy Writ Lays Before Us These Two Sorts of Prayer

THESE two sorts of prayer that we have spoken of are marvelously set before us by the Holy Ghost in the thirty-ninth chapter of Ecclesiasticus. He says there of the wise man, by whom the Church understands the just: *He will set his heart to watch at break of day to the Lord who made him, and will pray in the sight of the Most High* (Ecclus. xxxix. 6). He puts first the ordinary prayer. The man must rise in the morning, which is the time suited for prayer and is often spoken of in Scripture. *In the morning I will present myself before thee. Let me anticipate the dawn and cry out. Mine eyes have opened early in the morning unto thee, O Lord, to meditate thy words. To thee I watch from break of day* (Psalm v. 5; cxviii. 148; lxii. 2). The text says to *watch* because he is going to be wide-awake, not to sleep and meditate on a pillow. What more? *He will set his heart,* hand it over to prayer. He is not there in body only while his heart is on business. That is what the saints call "sleepiness of heart." Faintness and sloth of heart are great obstacles to prayer because they hinder the reverence which one should observe in dealing with God. And what is it that causes this reverence in the just? The consideration that I am in the presence of God and that I am about to speak to a Majesty so high—that makes me stand in reverence and at attention. This is the preparation and disposition wherewith we should go to prayer.

But let us see what prayer it is that the just man makes. *He will open his mouth in prayer, and begin by begging pardon for his sins* (Ecclus. xxxix. 7), moving himself to shame and repentance for them. This is the prayer that we should make on our side, bewailing our sins and begging God's mercy and pardon for them. We must not content ourselves with saying: "I made my general confession at the beginning of my conversion and after that I spent some days in bewailing and repenting of my sins." It is not right that we should forget our sins upon confessing them, but we should endeavor to keep them ever before our eyes, according to the saying of the prophet: *My sin is always before me,* that is, before my eyes. On the words, *Our bed is strewn with flowers* (Cant. i. 15), St. Bernard says: "Your bed, that is, your heart, is still malodorous because you have not quite got rid of the vices and follies that you brought in from the world; and have you the audacity to invite the Bridegroom to come to it? Do you wish now to practise other exercises, high and exalted, of love and union with God, as if you were perfect?" Make it your first care to cleanse and wash your bed well with tears. *Every night I will wash my bed, and moisten my couch with my tears* (Psalm vi. 7). Then you have to adorn it with the flowers of virtues, and so invite the Bridegroom to come to you as he did to the bride. Busy yourself with the kiss of the feet, humbling yourself and grieving much for your sins; and with the kiss of the hands, which is offering your good works to God and seeking to receive at His hands true and solid virtues; and as for that third kiss of the mouth, that high and exalted union, leave that till such time as the Lord shall please to raise you to it.

It is told of a very ancient and spiritual father (Father Araoz) that he spent twenty years in these exercises of the purgative way. And are we to get tired of it at once and seek to ascend to the kiss of the mouth and the exercises of the love of God? We need a good foundation to raise so high a building. Besides many other good and profitable things that there are in this exercise, of which we shall speak hereafter, there is this about it, that it is a great remedy and efficient preservative against falling into sin. He who is continually abhorring sin and making acts of shame and sorrow for having offended God, is very far from committing sin anew. And, contrariwise, the saints observe that the reason why some have fallen who seemed to be very spiritual men and men of prayer, and possibly were so, is for want of this exercise; they gave themselves over in such manner to other exercises and considerations, sweet and to their taste, that they forgot the exercise of self-knowledge and consideration of their sins and so came to an unmeasured sense of security, not walking in such fear and reserve as they ought, and thereby they came to fall into what they ought not; they too quickly forgot their low estate and fell from the height they thought to have attained. It is fitting, then, that for a long time our prayers should consist in bewailing our sins, as the Wise Man says, until such time as the Lord takes us by the hand and says, *Friend, go up higher* (Luke xiv. 10).

Now let us see what this high and very special prayer is, which the Lord gives when He pleases. The text goes on: *If the great God and Lord please, he will fill him with the spirit of understanding* (Ecclus. xxxix. 8). *If he please,* because this is no hereditary right, but a grace and mere effect of His liberality. You are at prayer, and on a sudden there comes a light from heaven, like a flash of lightning, whereby you are set thinking and see the point and get an appreciation and high notion of what you never understood before. That is the gift of prayer. How many times you have traveled over the same ground, and your attention was never arrested on it as now! He calls that *the spirit of understanding* because nothing appears in it but a simple apprehension, upon which the man becomes tranquil and at rest, with that light shed upon him. It happens in this world sometimes that a man comes across a very perfect and highly finished picture, and he stands regarding it for a long time, with his eyes fixed, without moving about, wrapt in mighty admiration, so that he cannot have enough of looking at it; such is this prayer and high and exalted contemplation. Or, to speak better, this is the way in which the blessed in heaven see God. Heavenly bliss consists in the sight and contemplation of God. In it we shall be absorbed and penetrated through and through with the vision and love of God for ever and ever, with one simple vision of that Divine Majesty, rejoicing in His presence and in His glory, without any wandering of the mind and without ever being weary of looking at Him; or rather, as the text says, *and they sang as it were a new song before the throne* (Apoc. xiv. 3), that song and that divine manna will always be something new to us and we shall be ever in new admiration.

In this way, then, there is carried on here on earth this high and perfect prayer which is called contemplation when the Lord is pleased to give it, so that the person is never sated or cloyed with seeing and contemplating God, without play of the mind hither and thither, without fatigue, all by one simple look. The text says, *He will fill him,* because His grace is so copious and so abundant that it overflows and cannot be contained in so narrow a vessel. And so the text goes on at once with the following: *And he will pour out the words of his wisdom like rain, and in prayer he will praise the Lord* (Ecclus. xxxix. 9). Thence immediately follow colloquies; this is the proper time to converse with God, when the soul is moved, instructed, and lifted up by this heavenly light and wisdom.

And so our Father marks this time for making colloquies. "When a spiritual movement comes over us, we will make colloquies." Be this saying well taken note of. After we have helped ourselves by the use of our reasoning powers, meditating and considering, when the meditation now has inflamed our heart and we feel moved thereby, then is the time for colloquies and treating familiarly with God by petitions and determinations, because this is the prayer that God hears, and that leads to a happy settlement with His Divine Majesty. As St. Augustine says, when God moves one to ask, it is a sign that He intends to give what is asked. This is the very special kind of prayer that God gives to whom He pleases. *For if the great Lord willeth, he will fill him with the spirit of understanding* (Ecclus. xxxix.). If He wills, we shall easily be able to reach this high and singularly excellent prayer.

But if the Lord is not pleased to raise us to such a high prayer as this, St. Bernard says we must not be afflicted nor discouraged, but be content with the practice of virtues and with the fact that the Lord keeps us in His friendship and grace and does not let us fall into sin. He says: "Oh, that the Lord may be pleased to give me peace, goodness, and joy in the Holy Ghost, mercy, simplicity and charity to my neighbor; with that I am content! As for those other high contemplations, in heaven's name let them be kept for apostles and great saints"—*Utinam detur mihi pax, bonitas, gaudium in Spiritu Sancto, misereri in hilaritate, tribuere in simplicitate, gaudere cum gaudentibus, flere cum flentibus, et his contentus ero. Cetera sanctis apostolis virisque apostolicis relinquo. High mountains for stags, the rock the refuge of urchins* (Psalm ciii. 18). Those high mountains of contemplation are for such as run to perfection with the nimbleness of stags and deer; but I, who am an urchin, or hedgehog, full of thorns and faults and sins, betake myself to the *holes* of that *rock, which is Christ* (I Cor. x. 4), and wash away my faults and sins in the blood that flows from them, and that shall be my prayer.

But if the glorious Bernard was content with the practice of the virtues and grief and contrition for his sins, and left that other very special prayer to apostolic men and great saints to whom the Lord is pleased to impart it, it will be right for us also to be content therewith, and to make this our exercise in prayer—to conceive sorrow and shame for our sins and attend to the mortifying of our passions and the rooting up of our vices and the overcoming of all the repugnances and difficulties that may confront us in the way of virtue. As for that other very special and eminently high prayer, let us leave it till the time that the Lord shall be pleased to call and raise us thereto. And even then, when we think that we are called to it, there is need of great caution and of much sober deliberation, for there are apt to be in this matter many delusions. Sometimes a man thinks that God calls him to this prayer because of a certain sweetness and pleasantness and facility which he feels in the exercise of the love of God; and God does not call him, but it is he himself that mounts up and meddles with it, the devil deceiving and blinding him, that he may leave what is necessary and do nothing and profit nothing either way or the other.

A great master of spirit says very well that as it would show little sense of propriety for a man unceremoniously to seat himself at the king's table without his command and licence when the king himself had commanded that man to assist and wait upon him; so he does very ill and very rudely who seeks to deliver himself up entirely to the sweet repose of contemplation not being evidently called thereto by God Himself. St. Bonaventure gives a good admonition here, that a man should exercise himself in the line that is safer and more profitable; that is, in the extirpation of vices and evil inclinations and in the acquisition of true virtues. That is a very plain and safe road, on which there can be no delusions. The more a man busies himself with mortification, humiliation, and resignation, the more he will please God and will merit more of Him than by those other exquisite and extraordinary ways, in which, St. Bonaventure goes on to say, there are apt to be many deceits and many illusions of the devil, the man taking that to be God which is not God and that to be something great which is nothing. For this reason extraordinary kinds of prayer must be examined in the light of the rules governing ordinary prayer, and not the latter by the former, which is the common doctrine of the saints, as we shall see presently.

CHAPTER VI

Wherein This Doctrine Is Further Explained and Confirmed

FOR the greater confirmation and explanation of this doctrine, the saints and masters of spiritual life here observe that, to arrive at this high prayer and contemplation that we spoke of, there is necessary great mortification of our passions and a thorough grounding to begin with in the moral virtues and much time spent in their exercise;

otherwise they say it will be vain to pretend to enter upon this contemplation or make profession of it. It is proper, they say, to be Jacob wrestling before being Israel, *who sees God face to face* (Gen. xxxii. 30)—*Oportet ut prius sis Iacob luctans quam Israel Deum videns* (St. Bernard). You must first be a strong wrestler and vanquish your passions and evil inclinations before arriving at this intimate union with God. Blosius says that whoever seeks to arrive at a very excellent degree of divine love without first applying himself with great diligence to the correction and mortification of his vices and the casting off from himself of the inordinate love of creatures, is like a man who, laden with lead and iron and bound hand and foot, were to climb a very high tree. Wherefore they advise masters of spirit that, before treating with their disciples of this contemplation, they should first make them busy themselves with thorough mortification of all their passions and the formation of habits of virtue—patience, humility, obedience—and long exercise in the practice thereof. They call this the "active" life, which should go before the "contemplative." Failing to observe that, many who have not proceeded by these steps, but have sought to rise to contemplation without due order, are found after many years of prayer very devoid of virtue, impatient, passionate, proud, so that, once you touch them on the sore point, they burst out into unmeasured words of impatience, clearly showing how far they are from perfection and mortification.

Our Father General Everard Mercurian declared this very well in a letter that he wrote on this matter in these words. "There are many who, rather from lack of discretion than from desire of improvement, when they hear tell of another, and that a very high, practice of prayer, of love of God, of anagogical acts, and a certain indescribable silence, have sought to ascend to the practice of the unitive way before their time. Thus they have lost much time and have covered very little ground; and at the end of many years they find themselves with their passions as lively, with their affections as uncontrolled, as great lovers of their comfort as if they had never dealt with nor had had any communication with God. They are as wedded to their own will, as backward in submitting their own judgment, when superiors have wished to make some arrangement about them that did not please them or was not to their mind, as they were on the first day. The reason of this is that they wanted to fly before they had wings. They skipped and scampered over the ground and did not go by the measured steps that they should have taken; they did not first ground themselves in mortification and the practice of the virtues; and so without foundation they could not set up a good building. They built on sand, and so they fail in the hour of emergency."

Hence we may see how true, how common and general is this doctrine; it is what the saints commonly say when they assign three parts or three manners of prayer, according to the three ways called respectively purgative, illuminative, and unitive. Such is the holy doctrine drawn out by St. Denis the Areopogite, and after him by St. Gregory Nazianzene and by all the rest who treat of spiritual things. They say, and all agree in this, that before dealing with this so high and lofty prayer that belongs to the unitive way, we must occupy ourselves with what belongs to the purgative and illuminative. First it is necessary to exercise ourselves in sorrow and repentance for our sins and to root out from ourselves vicious and evil inclinations and to acquire true virtues, imitating Christ, in Whom they shine forth; because if we sought to pass on further without that, it would be without foundation, and so we should always remain imperfect and unformed, as he who should try to pass into the class of the seniors without being well grounded in that of the juniors, and to mount the second step of a ladder without going on the first.

CHAPTER VII

Of Ordinary Mental Prayer

LEAVING aside the very special and extraordinary prayer, since we can neither teach nor explain what it is nor how it is, nor does it depend on our will to have it, nor does God bid us attain it, nor will He ask us any account of it, we will treat now of the mental prayer which is ordinary and common and can in some sort be taught and attained by labors and counsels with the aid of the grace of the Lord.

Amongst the other favors and benefits that the Lord has done us in the Society, this is a very particular one, that He has given us a method of prayer to go by, approved by the apostolic see, in the Book of Spiritual Exercises of our blessed Father Ignatius, as appears by the brief which is at the beginning of them, in which His Holiness Paul III, after having had them strictly examined, approved and confirmed them, saying they were very useful and wholesome, and strongly exhorted all the faithful to go through the practice of them. Our Lord imparted to our Father this method of prayer, and he imparted it to us in the same order in which our Lord imparted it to him. And we must have great confidence in God that by this way and method which He has given us, He will help us and do us favors, since with it He gained our Father and his companions, and after them many others, and therein He made known to him the method and plan of the Society, as he said. We must not seek other ways and other extraordinary methods of prayer, but do our best to mold ourselves upon what we have, like good and true sons.

In the Exercise of the Powers, which is the first of the Exercises, our Father teaches us the method to be followed in prayer in all the rest of the exercises. It is that in each point that we take in hand, we must go exercising the three powers of our soul, memory, understanding, and will—first, by memory putting before the eyes of the understanding the point or mystery on which we wish to make meditation; and then the understanding comes in, reasoning, meditating, and considering the things that will better aid us to move our wills; and thereupon must follow the affections of the will. This third is the principal exercise in which we should dwell, since it is the end of the meditation and the fruit to be drawn from all the considerations and reasonings of the understanding. That is all ordained to move the will to the desire of good and abhorrence of evil. On this account he gave this exercise the name of the Three Powers because it is the first exercise in which he teaches us this method of prayer; although in all the exercises that follow, the three powers must also be exercised as in the first.

This method of prayer which our Father here teaches and the Society practises, is not singular, nor has it any contrivances apt to issue in illusions, as is the case with some others. Rather it is a method very common and much in use among the ancient Fathers, and very conformable to human nature, which is argumentative and rational, governed by reason and by reason is persuaded, convinced, and brought over, which makes this method easier, safer, and more profitable. Thus we must not be in prayer after the manner of persons languishing or dazed with light, without doing anything, which would be a great delusion and error; but we must cry therein to God by means of the exercise of our powers and co-operate along with Him; for God requires the co-operation of His creatures, and that is what our Father teaches us in the Book of Exercises. Other methods there are of prayer by giving up reasonings, employing negations and certain silences, taken from mystical theology. These methods commonly should not be taught, nor sought either, as we have said before. Young people, who are no great hands at the knowledge of their passions and the practice of virtues, if they are set to these particular methods, are liable to illusions and deceits; and when they think they have gained some advantage, they find themselves with their passions all vigorous and unabated, passions which were lulled to sleep by this food and bait of prayer, and now wake up and prove very dangerous. Moreover, in these choice and particular methods there is engendered a hardness of judgment, a disposition that lends itself to any delusion; and so our blessed Father Ignatius apprehended, saying that such people generally have something of that about them.

I say, then, that the first thing we have to do in meditation, in whatever point we take in hand, is to put before us by memory the point on which we wish to meditate. The second is to enter on the meditation, which is to be done by reasoning with the understanding, considering and reflecting on the particular aspects of that mystery; and thereupon must follow the affections of the will. Thus the memory proposes the subject, and forthwith the reasoning and meditation of the understanding must find place, for this is the source from whence must flow all the acts and exercises which we make in our prayer, and everything else that is done in the prayer is done in virtue of this. The reason whereof is clear in sound philosophy; for our will is a blind power, which cannot take a step without the understanding's going before: *nihil volitum quin praecognitum.* This is a common maxim of philosophers; the will cannot will a thing that has not first passed through the understanding. The understanding is the linkboy that goes before, lighting the path of the will and guiding it, and showing it what to go for and what to shun. So St. Augustine: "A thing may be loved that is not seen by the eyes, but not a thing that is not known"—*Invisa diligi possunt, incognita nequaquam.* And St. Gregory: "None can love what he is absolutely ignorant of." We may well love things that we do not see; but what we have no knowledge of at all, we cannot love, for the object of the will is good understood as such. We love and go after a thing because we apprehend it as good and worthy of being loved; and, contrariwise, we abhor a thing and shun it, because we judge and apprehend it to be evil and worthy of abhorrence. So when we wish anyone to change his mind and purpose, we try to persuade him with reasons and convince his understanding that what he is bent on doing is not fitting or good and that the other course is the better and proper for him, so to lead him to abandon the one and embrace the other. Thus the act and reasoning of the understanding is the foundation of all the other acts and exercises that we do in prayer, and that is why meditation is so necessary.

CHAPTER VIII

Of the Necessity of Meditation

HUGH OF ST. VICTOR says that no prayer can be perfect which is not preceded or accompanied by meditation. This is the doctrine of St. Augustine, who says that prayer without meditation is lukewarm. They prove it very well, since if one does not exercise himself in knowing and considering his misery and weakness, he will fall under delusion and will not know how to ask in prayer for what befits him, nor with the fervor that is befitting. Many through not knowing and studying their faults become the prey of delusions, and presume upon themselves in a way that they would not presume if they did know themselves; and so they treat in prayer of other things than those that are necessary. But if you want to know how to pray and ask God for what befits you, exercise yourself in considering your faults and miseries, and in that way you will know what you ought to ask; and considering and understanding your great need, you will ask for it with fervor and as you ought to ask, as does the poor needy man who knows and understands well his necessity and poverty.

St. Bernard, arguing that we are not to mount to perfection by flying but by walking, says that walking and mounting to perfection must be done with two feet, meditation and prayer; since meditation shows what is wanting to us, and prayer obtains it; meditation shows us the way, and prayer carries us along it; lastly, by meditation we know the dangers that encompass us, and by prayer we escape and are delivered from them. Hence St. Augustine comes to say that meditation is the beginning of all good, since whoever well considers how good God is in Himself, and how good and merciful He has been to us, how He has created us, how much He has done and suffered for us, is at once fired with love for this good Lord; and whoever knows well his faults and miseries, comes to humble and make little account of himself; and whoever considers how badly he has served God and how much he has offended Him, feels himself worthy of any penalty and chastisement; and thus by meditation the soul comes to be enriched with all virtues.

Therefore it is that Holy Scripture so much recommends to us meditation: *Blessed is the man that meditateth day and night on the law of the Lord; he shall be as a tree planted near streams of water, that shall yield much fruit* (Psalm i. 1-3). *Blessed are they who search his commandments, and seek him with all their heart* (Psalm cxviii. 2). These are they who seek Him with all their heart, and by this they seek Him. And so the prophet asks God for grace to keep His law. *Give me understanding, and I will search into thy law, and keep it with all my heart* (Psalm cxviii. 34). And, contrariwise: *If it were not for the regular meditation that I make on thy law, perhaps by this time I should have perished in my humility* (Psalm cxviii. 82), that is, in my difficulties and dangers, as St. Jerome explains. Thus one of the greatest praises that the saints bestow on meditation and consideration, or even the greatest, is that it is a great helper to all the virtues and to all good works. Gerson calls it "the sister of reading, the nurse of prayer, the guide of action, the perfection and withal the consummation of all things."

But because contrary comes to be better known by contrary, one of the principal causes of all the evils in the world is want of consideration, according to the saying of the Prophet Jeremy: *With desolation is all the earth laid desolate, because there is none who considereth in the heart* (Jerem. xii. 11), none who stops to think attentively. The principal cause of the spiritual desolation of the earth and of the multitude of sins in the world, is that there is hardly anyone who will enter into himself and stop to think and turn over in his heart the mysteries of God. For who would dare to commit a mortal sin if he reflected that God died for sin and that it is so great an evil that it was necessary for God to make Himself man to satisfy in all rigor of justice for it? Who would dare to sin if he reflected that for one mortal sin God chastises in hell for ever and ever? If one set himself to think over and weigh well that sentence, *Depart from me, ye cursed, into everlasting fire* (Matt. xxv. 41)—that eternity! that for ever and ever!—and that so long as God is God he must burn in hell, who would there be who for the pleasure of a moment would choose everlasting torments?

St. Thomas Aquinas used to say it was a thing he could not understand how a person in mortal sin could laugh and make merry. And he had much reason to say so, because the man knows for certain that, if he were to die, he would go to hell forever, and he is not sure of one moment of life. There was that man [Damocles] in feastings and fine music and rejoicings; and all because he had over his head a naked sword, hanging only by one hair, he trembled every moment lest it should fall, and nothing gave him any pleasure. How should it be with him who is threatened not merely with temporal but with eternal death, hanging upon one little thread of life? He may drop down dead suddenly where he is; and going to bed in good health may open his eyes in hell! A servant of God used to say to this effect that he thought that in a Christian commonwealth there ought not to be more than two prisons; one that of the Holy Inquisition, the other the lunatic asylum: for either the man believes that there is a hell lasting forever for the sinner, or he does not: if he does not, let them take him to the Inquisition for a heretic; if he does believe it and nevertheless has a mind to remain in mortal sin, let them take him to the lunatic asylum; for what greater lunacy can there be than that! Doubtless, if anyone would attentively consider these things, it would be a great check upon him against sinning. That is why the devil is so diligent in trying to keep us from this meditation and consideration.

The first thing the Philistines did when they caught Sampson was to put out his eyes; and so it is the first thing that the devil contrives to do to the sinner. Now that he cannot get him to abandon the faith, he contrives that he shall believe as though he did not believe: he contrives that he shall not consider what he believes nor dwell upon it any more than as if he believed it not; he shuts his eyes, which comes to the same thing for him. As it is no use, says St. Augustine, to open your eyes if you are in the dark, since you will see nothing; so it is no use to be in the light if you keep your eyes shut, since you will see nothing that way either. This is why meditation and mental prayer are of such importance—they make you open your eyes.

CHAPTER IX

Of One Good Result and Great Advantage That We Should Draw from Meditation, and of the Method to Adopt in Order to Profit Thereby

IT is well to exercise ourselves in meditation, in affections and desires of the will; of this we shall treat presently; but it is necessary that these affections and desires be well founded on reason, because man is rational and requires to be carried by reason and by way of understanding. Thus one of the principal objects to which meditation should be ordered and directed is that we may be finally disabused and well informed as regards facts, and quite convinced and resolved in point of what it is right for us to do. They are wont to say here, when one is brought back to a good and well-ordered life: "This man is disabused." This disabusing should be one of the principal fruits that we ought to endeavor to gather from meditation. This fact should be carefully noted, since it is primary in this matter. It is at one's commencements above all that one needs to exercise oneself more particularly in this, in order to be well grounded in and thoroughly convinced of these truths.

That we may be better able to gather this result from meditation, and that it may be very fruitful, it is needful that it be not done superficially, nor at a gallop, nor in a dead-alive and feeble manner, but with much attention and tranquil consideration. You have to meditate and consider in a very leisurely way and great quiet of mind the shortness of life and the frailty and vanity of the things of the world, and how death is the end of all, that thus you may come to despise all things here below and put your whole heart in what must last forever. You have to consider and ponder many times over how vain is the esteem and opinion of men, that makes such war upon us, since it takes nothing from you and adds nothing to you, nor can it make you either better or worse than you are, that thus you may come to despise it and not make any account of it, and so of the rest. In this way a man gradually rids himself of illusions, convinces himself and makes up his mind to do what for him is the right thing; and all this goes to make a spiritual man of him. *He shall sit in solitude and be silent, because he hath raised himself above himself* (Lam. iii. 28). He is getting a courageous heart, a contempt of all the things of the world, and is coming to say with St. Paul: *What I counted gain before, I now count as loss, something absolutely to cast out, that I may gain Christ* (Phil. iii. 8).

There is a great difference between meditating and meditating, and between knowing and knowing. A learned man knows a thing in one way, a simple and ignorant in another; the learned man knows how the thing is in truth, but the simple man knows only the outward appearance. Thus if a simple person finds a precious stone, he covets it for its luster and outward beauty and for nothing else, because he does not know its value; but a skillful jeweler, finding such a stone, covets it much, not for its luster and outward beauty, but because he knows well the value and virtue thereof. This is the difference there is between him who knows how to meditate and consider divine mysteries and spiritual things, and him who has no such knowledge; the latter takes a superficial and outside view of things, and, though they make a good impression on him by the luster and radiance that he sees in them, he is not much moved to desire them: but he who knows how to meditate and ponder these things, clears his mind of illusions and makes firm resolves. Knowing well the value of the hidden treasure and of the precious pearl which he has found, he despises all else and makes little account of it in comparison. *He went and sold all he had and bought it* (Matt. xiii. 46).

This difference is declared to us by Christ our Redeemer in the Gospel, in the story of that woman who suffered from a flux of blood. The holy evangelists relate how the world's Redeemer was on His way to heal and raise up the daughter of the ruler of the synagogue, and such a crowd of people went with Him that they pressed on Him, when a woman caught sight of Him that had been suffering from a flux of blood now for ten years. She had spent all her money on doctors and they had been unable to cure her; rather she found herself worse than before. With the desire that she has to gain her health, she breaks through the crowd of people with great faith and confidence: *For she said within herself, If I touch but the hem and edge of his garment, I shall be healed* (Matt. ix. 21). She goes up and touches, and at once the running flow of blood dries up and stops. Christ our Redeemer turns round and says: *Who hath touched me?* St. Peter says to Him, and the other disciples: *Master, so many people are pressing on thee, and sayest thou, who hath touched me?* I do not mean that, says Christ, but *someone hath touched me,* not in the manner of the rest of people, but in a particular manner, *because I feel that virtue hath gone out from me* (Luke viii. 46). There is the point, that it is to touch Christ, and this it is that He asked about; for as for that other indiscriminate touching, as the populace and the rest of the folk touched Him, no account is to be taken of it.

This, then, is all the business of meditation, to touch Christ and His mysteries in such sort as to feel in ourselves the virtue and fruit thereof. To this end it is of great importance that we go about our meditation with great attention, ruminating and breaking up things in very leisurely fashion. That which we do not chew is neither bitter nor savory; that is why a sick man swallows his pill whole, that he may not taste the bitterness. For the same reason neither does the sinner taste the bitterness of sin or death or judgment or hell, because he swallows them whole, taking them at a gulp and all in one volley. For the same reason neither do you taste nor relish the mystery of the

Incarnation and Passion and Resurrection and the other benefits of God, because you do not break them up nor ruminate them nor ponder them as you ought. Do you chew and break up the grain of mustard seed or pepper and you will see how it burns and draws tears from the eyes.

CHAPTER X

Of Other Good Things and Advantages That There Are in Meditation

ANOTHER good thing and great advantage, says St. Thomas, that there is in meditation, is that from it there springs true devotion, a thing so important in spiritual life and so desired by all who journey that way. Devotion is nothing else than a promptitude and readiness of will for all that is good; and thus the truly devout man is he who is prompt and disposed for all good: such is the common doctrine of the saints. Now St. Thomas says there are two causes of this devotion, the one extrinsic and principal, which is God; the other intrinsic on our part, which is meditation; for this promptness and readiness of the will for the things of virtue arises from the consideration and meditation of the understanding, the understanding being that which, after the grace of God, starts and kindles this fire in our heart. Thus true devotion and fervor of spirit does not consist in the sensible sweetness and relish which some experience in prayer, but in keeping a will prompt and disposed for all points of the service of God. This is the devotion that lasts and endures; that other soon comes to an end, consisting as it does of affections of sensible devotion, coming of a sudden desire of something attractive and lovable, and being often the result of natural constitution, a soft and affectionate character and an impressionable heart. Such a one is quickly moved to sentiment and tears; and when this devotion is run out, the good purposes often dry up also. This is a sentimental love, founded on tastes and consolations; while the taste and consolation lasts, this person will be very diligent and punctual, a lover of silence and recollection; and when the wind ceases, all is over. But take those that are founded on truth by means of meditation and consideration, convinced and disabused by reason—these are they that persevere and hold out in virtue; and even when sweetness and consolations fail them, they are still the same as before, because the cause endures, that is, the reason that convinced and moved them. This is a strong and manly love, and in it, not in sweetnesses and consolations, are seen the true servants of God and they who have made real progress. It is often said that our passions are like little dogs that go on barking, and in time of consolation have their mouths stopped: God throws to each of them his morsel of bread, which keeps them quiet, and they ask nothing; but when this bread of consolation is gone, this and that and the other one start barking, and there you see what each man is good for. They likewise compare these tastes and consolations to articles of personal property that are soon worn out, and solid virtue to landed property that is lasting and permanent, and therefore more valuable.

Hence arises a thing that we often experience, and which is worthy of consideration. We see some persons on the one hand who have great consolations in prayer, and afterwards in occasions of temptation we see them weak and even falling; and on the other hand we see others who suffer great aridities in prayer and know not what consolation or sensible sweetness is, and yet we see them very strong under temptation and far from falling. The cause is that which we have been saying, that the one were founded on tastes and feelings, while the others are founded on reason, and so remain free from illusions, convinced and firm set in truth, and thereby continue and persevere in what once they have been persuaded of and resolved upon. And so one of the methods that are usually prescribed, and a very good one, to persevere in the good resolutions made in prayer and put them in execution, is to try to keep in mind the motive that then caused in us that good resolution and desire, because what then moved us to desire it will afterwards help us to keep and carry it out. And there is even more in it, and it is this—that by going about to undeceive and convince oneself in this way, even if one afterwards forgets the motive and reason that formerly moved him, nevertheless in virtue of that reaction against error and the resolution then taken under conviction of truth and of reason, the man stands firm and strong enough afterwards to resist temptation and persevere in virtue.

Gerson set such store by meditation that, being asked what exercise was most useful and profitable for a religious recollected in his cell, reading, or vocal prayer, or manual labor, or application to meditation, he said that, saving obedience, the best would be application to meditation. And he gives this reason, that though in vocal prayer and spiritual reading one may possibly feel for the time greater devotion and profit than in meditation, yet leaving off the book you were reading before, or in ceasing your vocal exercise, your devotion also is apt to come to an end. But meditation improves a man and disposes him better for what is to come and therefore he says that we must accustom ourselves to meditation, so that though books fail, meditation may be our book, and thus true devotion may not fail.

CHAPTER XI

Of the Conduct to Be Held in Meditation, and the Fruit to Be Gathered from It

MY heart hath grown warm within me, and in my meditation fire shall be enkindled (Psalm xxxviii. 4). In these words the Prophet David, according to the explanation of many doctors and saints, points out the method we should observe in prayer. They explain this passage of the fire of charity and love of God and our neighbor, which the meditation of heavenly things lit and made to burn in the breast of the Royal Prophet. My heart, he says, gathered heat and was enkindled there within me. This is the effect of prayer. But how did this heat gather? How came it to be kindled there within him? Do you know how? By meditation. *And in my meditation this fire shall be enkindled.* This is the means and instrument to enkindle this fire. Thus, says St. Cyril of Alexandria, meditation is like the strokes of the steel on the flint to make fire come forth. By the exercise and meditation of the understanding you must strike blows on the hard flint of your heart until the flame bursts forth of love of God and desire of humility and mortification and the other virtues, and you must not stop until you have drawn forth and enkindled in it this fire.

Although meditation is very good and necessary, yet all our prayer must not be let go in reasonings and considerations of the understanding, nor must we stop there, for that would be rather a study than a prayer; but all the meditations and considerations that we make, we must take as means to awaken and kindle in our heart affections and desires of virtue. For the goodness and holiness of Christian and religious life does not consist in good thoughts and understanding of holy things, but in solid and true virtues and especially in the acts and operations thereof; such activity being, according to St. Thomas, the last perfection of virtue. Thus it is on this that we should principally dwell and occupy ourselves at prayer. This we must take for a first principle in this matter. Even the philosopher there in heathendom said it, and Gerson quotes him: "We go inquiring and investigating what manner of thing virtue is, not for the knowledge, but to be good and virtuous men." Though a needle is necessary to sew, yet it is not the needle that sews, but the thread; he would be very silly who spent the whole day in putting in and drawing out a needle without thread, for that would be labor in vain; yet that is what they do whose prayer is all understanding and meditating, with little of loving. Meditation should be as the needle, which goes in first, but only goes in that through it there may go in the thread of love and affection of the will, wherewith we are to unite and conjoin ourselves to God.

Our Father warns us of this point much in particular and repeats it to us many times in the book of the Spiritual Exercises. After having set down the points which we are to meditate, with some brief reflections, he says at once: "And refer all this to myself to draw some fruit." In this lies the fruit of prayer—in each one's knowing how to apply to himself and to his own improvement what he meditates, according to his wants. The glorious Bernard says well: As the sun does not warm all to whom it gives light, so knowledge and meditation, though it teaches us what we have to do, does not move and stir the wills of all to do what it teaches. It is one thing to have knowledge of great wealth, and another thing to possess it; so he says it is one thing to know God, and another thing to fear and love God: it is not the knowing many things of God that makes us truly wise and rich, but the fearing and loving of God. He brings in also another good comparison to this effect. As a hungry man would benefit little by having set before him a table plentifully laid with exquisite dishes if he did not eat them, so it will little profit him who practises prayer to have before him a rich and splendid board of many excellent considerations if he does not eat thereof, applying them to himself by his will so as to make profit out of them.

Descending herein more into particulars, I say that what we ought to draw from meditation and prayer should be holy affections and desires, formed first interiorly in the heart, that afterwards in due time they may come out in action. The blessed St. Ambrose says that the end of meditation is action. Of those holy and mysterious living creatures whom the Prophet Ezechiel saw, he says, among other particulars, that they had wings and under the wings the hands of a man, to give us to understand that the flight and play of the understanding should be subservient to action. We ought, then, to draw from prayer affections and desires of humility, disparaging ourselves and desiring to be disparaged by others—desires of suffering pains and labors for the love of God, and rejoicing in those that at present fall to our lot—affections of poverty of spirit, desiring that the worst of the house be for us and that something may be wanting to us even of necessaries—grief and contrition for our sins, and firm purposes rather to fall asunder than to sin—thanksgiving for favors received—true resignation into the hands of God—and finally, desire to imitate Christ our Redeemer and Master in all the virtues that shine forth in Him. To this our meditation should be directed and ordained, and this is the fruit that we should draw from it.

Hence it follows that, since meditation and the exercise of the understanding are taken up as a means to move the will to these affections, and this is the end and purpose of the whole business, we ought to use meditation and the exercise of the understanding so far as is necessary to this end and no further, since the means should be proportionate and commensurate with the end. Thus, when we feel our will excited and moved to desire of some virtue, as to sorrow for sin, contempt of the world, love of God, desire of suffering for His sake, or the like, we should at once cut short the thread of the activity of the understanding—even as a mason removes the wooden scaffolding of arches and bridges when the masonry is set—and stop and dwell on this affection of the will till we are satisfied and have drunk it well into our soul. This is a very important direction, and our Father puts it in the book of Exercises, where he says that on the point whereon we find the devotion and feeling that we desire, we should there stop and occupy ourselves upon it, without anxiety to pass to anything else until we are quite satisfied. As a gardener watering a seed plot, when the water begins to work its way into the earth, stops the flow of the stream and lets the water thoroughly soak and be drunk in by the bowels of the dry earth, and passes not on till it is well soaked and irrigated; so when the water of good affections and desires begins to enter into our soul, which is as earth without water, as the prophet says: *My soul, O Lord, is as earth without water before thee* (Psalm cxlii. 6), we should stop the flow of reasoning of the understanding and enjoy this irrigation and affection of the will as long as we can, until the whole heart is saturated and soaked and we can rest satisfied.

The blessed St. Chrysostom brings another comparison pat to our purpose. Have you not seen, he says, when a lambkin goes to suck the breasts of its mother, it does nothing but turn now here now there, and now sucks at the teat and then at once quits; but when the milk begins to flow, it immediately holds fast and quietly enjoys it? So in prayer, before the dew descends from heaven, man goes discoursing and reasoning from one point to another; but when the heavenly dew comes, we must at once stop and taste that sweetness and delight.

CHAPTER XII

How Important It Is to Dwell on the Acts and Affections of the Will

IT is so important to dwell and rest on the acts and affections of the will, and the saints and masters of spiritual life attach such value to this, that they say that this it is that makes a good and perfect prayer, and even what they call "contemplation," when the man no longer seeks incentives to love by meditation, but rejoices in love found and desired and rests in it as in the term of his search and desire, saying with the spouse in the Canticles: *I have found him whom my soul loveth, I have held him and will not let him go* (Cant. iii. 4). And this is what there the same spouse says: *I sleep, but my heart watcheth* (Cant. v. 2); because in perfect prayer the understanding is, as it were, asleep, having given over reasoning and speculation, and the will is watching and melting away in love of the Spouse. And so pleased is the Bridegroom with this sleep of his spouse, that he gives orders that they are not to awaken her until she wishes. *I adjure you, daughters of Jerusalem, by the she-goats of the mountains and by the stags of the plains, that ye awaken not nor bring back to consciousness my beloved until she herself will* (Cant. iii. 5). Thus meditation and all the other parts of prayer which they assign, are ordained and directed to this contemplation, and are as it were steps whereby we are to mount to it.

So says St. Augustine in the book that he calls the "Ladder of Paradise": "Reading seeks, meditation finds, prayer petitions, but contemplation relishes and enjoys what it has sought and asked for and found"—*Lectio inquirit, meditatio invenit, oratio postulat, contemplatio degustat.* And he quotes the saying of the Gospel: *Seek and ye shall find, knock and it shall be opened unto you* (Matt. vii. 7). St. Augustine says: "Seek by reading, and you shall find by meditation; cry out by prayer, and it shall be opened to you by contemplation." And so the saints remark, and Albertus Magnus says it, that this is the difference between the comtemplation of faithful Catholics and that of heathen philosophers—that the contemplation of philosophers is wholly directed to the perfection of the understanding by the knowledge of known truths, and so stops at the understanding, because that is its end to know and understand more and more; but the contemplation of Catholics and saints of which we now treat, does not stop at the understanding, but passes on to refresh and move the will and inflame and kindle it to the love of God, according to the saying of the spouse: *My soul melted away when my beloved spoke* (Cant. v. 6). And St. Thomas has noted this well in treating of contemplation. He says that, though contemplation essentially lies in the understanding, yet its ultimate perfection is in the love and affection of the will. Thus the chief aim and end of our contemplation should be the affection of the will and the love of God.

Thus, says St. Augustine, Christ our Redeemer taught us in the Gospel when He said: *When ye pray, do not speak much* (Matt. vi. 7). St. Augustine says: It is one thing to speak much, and reason and conceive many things with the understanding, and another thing to dwell long on love and affections of the will. The first is a thing that we must try to get out of in prayer, consisting as it does of much speech and talk, whereas this business of prayer, says the saint, is not a business of many words. We do not deal with God in prayer by rhetoric or by abundant discourses and quips and conceits of happy thoughts and reasonings, but by tears and sighs coming from the heart, and this is according to what Prophet Jeremy says: *Let not the pupil of thine eye be silent* (Lam. ii. 18). St. Jerome says hereon: "It is the tongue that speaks; how can the pupils of the eyes speak?" He replies: "When we shed tears before God, it is then that the pupils of our eyes utter cries to God." Though we do not speak with the tongue, we can cry to God with the heart, as St. Paul says: *God hath sent the Spirit of his Son in your hearts, crying, Abba, Father* (Gal. iv. 6). And in Exodus (xiv. 15) God said to Moses: *Why dost thou cry to me?* Moses had not spoken a word, but in his heart he was praying with such fervor and efficacy that God said to him: *Why dost thou utter me these cries?* In this way we ought to utter cries to God in prayer, with our eyes—*Let not the pupil of thine eye be silent*—with tears and groans and sighs and desires of the heart.

CHAPTER XIII

Satisfying the Complaint of Those Who Say They Are Unable, and Have No Idea How, to Meditate and Reason with the Understanding

HEREIN lies the answer to a complaint very common with some, who make themselves miserable, saying that they have no ability nor any idea how to reason with themselves in prayer; no considerations occur to them whereby to enlarge and extend the points of meditation, but their thread comes to an end at once. No reason for them to afflict themselves on that account, for, as we have said, this business of prayer consists rather in desires and affections of the will than in reasonings and speculations of the understanding. Nay, the masters of spiritual life observe that it is necessary to take care not to let the meditation of the understanding run to excess, for that would much impede the motion and affection of the will, which is the main thing—and the impediment is greater, the more subtle and refined are the considerations on which one dwells. And naturally so, for in a reservoir containing only a certain measure of water, with many outlets, the more runs by one outlet, the less will run by another. Now the soul's power is finite and limited; and the more is drained off by the outlet of the understanding, the less runs by that of the will. Thus we see by experience that, when the soul is full of devotional feeling, and then the understanding strays into some speculation or curiosity, the heart at once dries up and the devotion stops; the reservoir has been dried up by that other outlet of the understanding, and so the outlet of the will is dry.

So Gerson says that hence it comes that oftentimes and very often the unlearned are the more devout, and prayer goes better with them than the learned, because they are less run away with by the understanding; they do not occupy or distract themselves with speculations and curiosities, but proceed at once by plain and simple considerations to stimulate and move the will to affection: these humble and homely considerations have more effect on them than those high and dainty thoughts have on the others. We see this in that saintly cook of whom we spoke above (Treatise III, Chapter 8), who from the material fire that he dealt with took occasion to remember everlasting fire, and that so devoutly as to keep the gift of tears in the midst of his occupations.

And this is to be well taken notice of, that, provided the affection and desire be very high and very spiritual, it does not matter about the thought and consideration being lowly and common. We have many examples of this in Holy Writ, where the Holy Ghost conveys to us very high and lofty matter in the guise of very plain and common comparisons. On the text: *Who will give me the wings of a dove, that I may fly and rest?* (Psalm liv. 7), St. Ambrose asks why the prophet, desiring to fly and mount on high, asks for the wings of a dove and not of other birds, since there are many better flyers than the dove. He answers it is because this prophet knew very well that the wings of a dove are better apt to fly high in perfection, sustain a good flight in prayer; that is to say, the simple of heart pray better than people of acute and subtle understanding; as the text has it: *His dealing is with the simple* (Prov. iii. 32). God communicates Himself to the simple and humble of heart.

Hence there is no reason why a person should be sad or torment himself because he cannot reason or find considerations wherewith to enlarge upon the points of the meditation. Nay, they tell us, and very reasonably, that they are better off to whom God closes the vein of soaring speculation and opens the vein of affection, in order that, with the understanding tranquilized and quiet, the will may repose in God alone, occupying herself wholly in loving and delighting in the Sovereign Good. If God does you the favor that, from some plain and simple consideration, as that God became man, that He was born in a stable, that He laid Himself on the Cross for you, you are inflamed with the love of God and with desire to be humbled and mortified for that love, and you keep to that for the whole hour and many hours, that is a more precious prayer than if you attained to many reasonings and many high and dainty reflections, because you have been occupied in the better and more substantial part of prayer, and that which is the end and fruit of it all. Hence will be understood the mistake of those who, when no reflections occur on which they can rest, think they are not making a good prayer, and that they are making a good prayer when many such reflections occur.

In the chronicles of St. Francis it is related that, one day, holy Brother Giles said to St. Bonaventure, who was Minister General of the order: "Many thanks to the Lord do you doctors owe, that you can serve and praise Him; but we ignorant and unlettered people who have no competence, what can we do to please God?" St. Bonaventure answered: "If our Lord gave no other grace to a man but that of being able to love Him, that would be enough for him to do God greater services than all other graces put together." Brother Giles said: "And can an unlettered man love our Lord Jesus Christ as much as a doctor?" "One little simple old woman," said St. Bonaventure, "can love our Lord more than a master in theology." Brother Giles at once got up in a great heat and betook himself to the part of the garden that was nearest to the city, and there with loud cries called out: "Poor little old woman, unlettered and simple, only love our Lord Jesus Christ and you may be greater than Brother Bonaventura!" Thereupon he fell into ecstasy, as was his wont, and remained rooted to the spot for three hours.

sacrifices will be acceptable on my altar.

Communion:
I have chosen you from the world that you should bear fruit, and that your fruit should remain.

CHAPTER XIV

Two Pieces of Advice Calculated to Aid Us Much in Making Our Meditation Well and Drawing Fruit Therefrom

TO make meditation well and draw the due fruit from it, it will aid us much, in the first place, to understand, as the first principle upon which we proceed, that meditation is not an end, but a means taken towards our advancement and perfection. Thus we ought not to stop at meditation as at a terminus and final end; our perfection consists not in the enjoyment of great consolation and great sweetness of contemplation, but in attaining to a perfect mortification and victory over ourselves and our passions and appetites, bringing them back, so far as is possible, to that blessed state of original justice in which we were created, when flesh and appetite were altogether subject and conformable to reason, and reason to God; the meditation we make should be a means to arrive at this.

As the iron in the forge becomes soft with fire, so that they can work it, bend it, do what they will with it, so it should be in meditation. If we find mortification and the breaking of our own will very hard and difficult, we must have recourse to the forge of meditation and there, with the heat and fire of devotion and the example of Christ, soften our heart that we may be able to work it and mold it to all that is necessary for the greater service of God. This is the function of meditation, and this the fruit that we ought to gather therefrom; and therefore the sweetnesses and consolations which the Lord is wont to give therein are not for us to rest in them, but to make us run more readily and nimbly in the way of virtue and perfection.

This the Holy Ghost would give us to understand by what happened to Moses, descending from the mountain where he had conversed with God. The sacred text says that, coming from thence, his face was resplendent with the rays of light, and this light took the shape of horns, in which the strength of animals is wont to dwell; showing us that we ought to gather from prayer strength and vigor for well-doing. Christ our Redeemer taught us the same thing by His example, on the night before His Passion putting Himself in prayer once, twice, and thrice, to prepare Himself for the suffering that was now so near; not that He had need of it, as St. Ambrose observes, but to give us an example. The holy Gospel (Luke xxii. 43) says that there appeared to Him there an angel comforting Him, and He came forth from His prayer so comforted that He said to His disciples: *Arise, let us go to meet our enemies, for now he draws nigh who is to give me up* (Matt. xxvi. 46). And He Himself offers and gives Himself up into their hands: *He was offered, because himself willed it* (Isaias liii. 7). All this to teach us that we ought to take prayer as a remedy to overcome the difficulties that meet us on the way of virtue.

St. Chrysostom says that prayer is an attuning of the lyre of our heart to make sweet music to God. Thus we go to meditation to tune our heart, to bring to harmony the chords of our passions and affections and all our actions, that all may accord with reason and with God. This is what every day we say or hear said in spiritual conferences and exhortations, that our meditation should be a practical meditation, that is to say, directed to action, since it has to serve to smooth down the difficulties and overcome the repugnances that present themselves in the way of spirit. Therefore the Holy Ghost calls it prudence: *The science of the saints is prudence* (Prov. ix. 10); because prudence is directed to action, differing from the science of the learned, which is only to know. Thus the saints say that prayer is a general and most efficacious remedy for all our temptations and for all sorts of necessities and occasions that may come in our way; and one of the principal praises of prayer is this.

Theodoret, in his Religious History, tells of a holy monk who was wont to say that physicians ordinarily treat each corporal disease with a particular and proper remedy, and frequently apply many remedies to the cure of one disease, because all remedies fall short and have only a limited virtue in them; but prayer is a universal remedy and is very efficacious in all our necessities, to repel and resist the attacks of the devil and to gain all sorts of virtues, because it applies to the soul an infinite good, which is God Himself, on Whom it rests for support. They also call prayer omnipotent; prayer alone, they say, can do all things. And Christ our Redeemer gives us this remedy of prayer against all temptations: *Watch and pray that ye enter not into temptation* (Matt. xxvi. 41).

The second advice is that, before we put ourselves in meditation, we should have fixed beforehand the points upon which we are to meditate, as also the fruit we are to gather therefrom. But some may say: "How shall we know beforehand what fruit to draw from the meditation we are about to make? Please tell us that?" Certainly I will. Have I not just now said that, when we have recourse to meditation, it is to find out a remedy for our spiritual infirmities and to gain the victory over ourselves and over our passions and bad habits; and that meditation is a means whereby we help ourselves for the amendment and reformation of our lives? This being so, we must consider for some time before we begin our meditation and ask ourselves, what is the greatest spiritual necessity I have? What is it that most hinders my progress in virtue and makes most war on my soul? This is what I must bring ready thought of, and hold before my eyes to insist on it, and draw from meditation a remedy for it. Let us take an example. I feel in myself a great inclination to be held in honor and esteem and to have much notice taken of me;

and that considerations of what men will think about me take a great hold of me; and when occasion offers of my being made small account of, I am troubled and feel it much, and haply sometimes I show it. This, I think, it is that makes most war upon me, hinders my advancement and the peace and tranquillity of my soul, and makes me fall into my greatest faults. This, then, being your greatest need, your cure consists in overcoming and rooting this tendency out, and that is what you should bring ready prepared and keep before your eyes and take it to heart, to gather this good from your meditation.

Thus it is a mistake to make a practice of going to meditation to take what luck you find and pick up there anything that offers, like a sportsman who fires at random to hit where he may hit and let come of it what will come —leaving what is most necessary. The sick man who goes to the dispensary does not take the first drug that comes to hand, but what he needs for his ailment. Here is a man full of pride even to the depth of his heart; another of impatience, another of self-opinionatedness and self-will, as is clearly seen whenever occasion offers—in fact he is taken red-handed in the fault every day—and the fellow goes to meditation to pick flowers and quips and conceits, laying hold of the first that comes and is most to his taste, picking now this and now that. That is not the way to get on. One should always take account of one's greatest need and contrive something to meet that, since it is for that that one goes to meditation.

St. Ephrem alleges to this purpose the example of the blind man in the Gospel, who approached Christ with loud cries that He should have mercy on him. Christ asked him what it was that he would have Him do for him. He at once represented his greatest necessity and that which gave him most trouble, which was his loss of sight, and asked for a remedy for that. *Lord, that I may see* (Luke xviii. 41). Do you think that he asked for any other of those things of which in good sooth he stood in need? Do you think he said: "Lord, give me a garment, because I am poor?" He does not ask for that, but, leaving all the rest aside, he comes to his greatest necessity. So then, says the saint, we should do in prayer; we should come to our greatest necessity, and insist and persevere in that until we get what we want. That there may be no excuse or demur in this matter, it is well to observe that, though in truth, when one goes to meditation, one should aim at gathering from thence desires of the particular virtues that are wanting to him, and ordinarily take care that the points and matter taken for meditation be suitable and proportionate thereto—to the end that the will may be moved more readily and with greater firmness and fervor to those desires, and so gather more easily the desired fruit—yet it is also needful for us to understand that any exercise or mystery that we meditate may be applied to that necessary purpose. Prayer is like the manna from heaven, in which everyone found the flavor that he desired: if you desire the flavor of humility, the consideration of your sins and of the death and Passion of Christ and of the benefits you have received from God, will yield that flavor; if you desire grief and shame for your sins, any of those subjects will yield that flavor; if you desire patience, you will find that flavor also, and so of the rest.

CHAPTER XV

How It Is to Be Understood That in Meditation We Should Take to Heart One Thing, That of Which We Have Greatest Need, and Insist Thereon Until We Get It

WE do not mean by this to say that we should always have our mind fixed on one thing in meditation. Though humility, or something of that sort, be our greatest need, still we may well occupy ourselves at meditation in the acts and exercise of the other virtues. There strikes you an act of conformity to the will of God for whatever He shall wish and arrange to make of you: dwell on that as long as you can; it will be a very good prayer and time well spent, and will not blunt your lance for humility, but rather sharpen it. There strikes you an act of gratitude and hearty recognition of all the benefits you have received from God, as well general as particular: dwell on that as long as you can: it is very reasonable every day to return God thanks for benefits received, and especially for that of our having been brought into religion. There strikes you a great horror and sorrow for your sins and a firm purpose to die a thousand deaths rather than offend God; dwell thereon, for it is one of the best and most profitable acts you could make in prayer. There strikes you a great love of God, a great zeal and desire for the salvation of souls, and of offering yourself to any labor whatever for their sake. Dwell thereon. We may also dwell on asking favors of God as well for ourselves as for our nearest and dearest, and for the whole Church, which is a part and a very principal part of prayer. On all these things and the like we may dwell at prayer, and it will be a very good prayer. Thus the Psalms, which are a very perfect prayer, we see are full of an infinity of different affections. Therefore Cassian said, and the Abbot Nilus, that prayer is a field full of flowers, or as a wreath woven of many various sweet-smelling herbs. *The odor of my son is as the odor of a full field which the Lord hath blessed* (Gen. xxvii. 27). There is another advantage in this variety, that it is apt to aid us and render our prayer the easier, so that we can stay and persevere in it the longer, since to be always repeating one and the same thing is apt to cause weariness, whereas variety delights and entertains.

What we mean to say is that it is very important for our spiritual advancement to take for some time one thing, and that should be the thing that we feel most needful for our soul. On this we should principally dwell at meditation, asking it much of our Lord and stirring ourselves to acts upon it once and again, one day and another, one month and another, and this should be our principal concern, and this we should keep ever before our eyes and have it fixed in our heart. This is the way in which business is done here in this life. Hence the saying: "God keep me from the man of one business."

The glorious St. Thomas, treating of prayer, says that desire is greater and more effectual, the more it is reduced to one thing; and he cites the saying of the prophet: *One thing I have asked of the Lord, for this I will entreat and aim ever until I attain it* (Psalm xxvi. 4). He who aims at knowing any science or art well, does not start learning one one day and another another, but he goes on for some time until he compasses it. So also he who aims at compassing any virtue does well to exercise himself for some time chiefly in that virtue, directing his meditation and all his spiritual duties to the gaining of it. This especially since, according to the doctrine of St. Thomas, all the virtues are connected together; that is to say, they are united and dovetailed into one another in such fashion that he who has one of them perfectly will have them all. Thus, if you gain true humility, you will gain therewith all the virtues. Uproot from all your heart pride and plant therein a most profound humility; if you have that, you will have great obedience and great patience; you will complain of nothing, any labor will seem to you little enough, all will seem to you very easy in comparison with what you deserve; you will have much charity for your brothers because you will hold them all to be good and yourself only wicked; you will have much simplicity and not judge anyone because you will have such a sense of your own defects as not to mind those of others, and so we might run through the rest of the virtues.

To this end it is a very good plan to apply the particular examen to the same point as meditation and make the two conjointly, for in this way all our exercises tending in one direction, much profit is made. Cassian goes further. Not only at time of examen and set meditation would he have us insist on that of which we stand in greatest need, but many times during the day we should lift up our spirit to God in ejaculatory prayers, with sighs and groans from the heart; and he would have us add penances besides, and mortifications and special devotions for this end, as we shall say elsewhere more at large. For if this be my greatest need, if this is the vice or passion or evil inclination that reigns most in me and makes me fall into most faults; if on the rooting out and vanquishing of this vice and gaining this virtue, then, depends the vanquishing and rooting out of all vices and the gaining of all virtues, whatever labor and diligence is spent on it will be well employed.

St. Chrysostom says that prayer is like a fountain in the midst of a garden or orchard, inasmuch as away from it everything is dry, and by it everything is green, fresh, and fair. All depends on using this fountain of prayer for watering; this it is that must ever keep all the plants of virtues in their bloom and beauty—obedience, patience, humility, mortification, silence, and recollection. But as in an orchard or garden there is wont to be some tree or floweret more dainty and cherished, to which the watering is chiefly applied, and though water run short for the rest it must never run short for this; so it should be in the garden and orchard of our soul—everything must be done to water and preserve it by the irrigation of prayer. You must always keep an eye on one main thing, which is that of which you stand in greatest need; to this you must chiefly apply yourself, for this you must never fail to find time. And as in going out of the garden you put your hand on the flower that pleases you most, cut it and go out of the garden with it, so in prayer you must lay your hand on what you find most necessary, and that you must take out of it.

This is a sufficient answer to the usual question, whether it is good to gather fruit at prayer in conformity with the exercise that makes the matter of meditation. We have said that, though one should always take account of what one finds most necessary, yet it is also good to exercise oneself and elicit affections and acts conformable to the mystery meditated. But here we must notice a very important point touching these acts and affections that we form at meditation bearing upon virtues that present themselves in accordance with the things meditated: they must not be done superficially, nor at a racing pace, but in very leisurely style, dwelling on them with long pauses and great restfulness, until we are satisfied and feel that that truth is fixed and sunk into our hearts, even though it take the whole hour to do so. One act and affection of this sort, kept up in this manner, is worth more than many acts of various virtues done and got through at top speed.

One of the reasons why some people make not so much profit out of prayer is that they go at a racing pace through acts of virtues; they go skipping and flying from one thing to another. Here comes a happy thought of an act of humility, and they make an act of humility, and forthwith pass on; there comes the thought of an act of obedience, and they make an act of obedience, forthwith another of patience; and so they go at a run like a cat over hot coals, so that, though there were fire under their feet, they would not burn. The consequence is that, when they come out of meditation, everything is forgotten and at an end and they remain as tepid and unmortified as before.

Father Master Avila reprehends those who, when they are on one subject and another occurs, at once leave that and pass to the other. He says that this is a usual artifice of the devil, to the end that, jumping from one branch to another like a magpie, they may lose the fruit of their meditation. It is very important that we should dwell on affections and desires of virtue until they soak in and find thorough entrance into our soul. Thus, if you wish to elicit acts of contrition and sorrow for your sins, you must dwell thereon until you feel in yourself a great horror and abhorrence of sin, according to the saying of the prophet: *I have abhorred iniquity and abominated it* (Psalm cxviii. 163). This will make you come forth with firm purposes to die a thousand deaths rather than commit one mortal sin.

Thus St. Augustine well observes that for the horror that men have of certain sins, as blasphemy or parricide, they do not fall into them except on rare occasions. Of other sins he says on the contrary that by practice they come to be made small account of; by custom men have lost by this time their fear and horror of them, and so they fall easily into them. In like manner, if you wish to elicit acts and exercise yourself in humility, you must dwell on that affection and desire of being despised and made little account of until this affection and desire comes to soak in and gain full entry into your soul, and all the fumes and spirits of pride and haughtiness fall away and come to an end, and you feel yourself moved to be despised and depreciated; and so of the rest of affections and acts of other virtues. Hence it will be seen what a help it will be to our advancement to take to heart one thing, and insist and persevere in that as we have said. If there be deep-seated in us the affection and desire of being despised and made small account of, or any other similar affections, and we hold to that an hour in the morning and another hour in the evening, and the same the day after that, and the day after, it is clear that quite another effect will be produced in our heart, and the virtue will remain stamped and soak down into our heart in quite another manner than if we had gone over it at a gallop.

St. Chrysostom says that, as one rainy day or one irrigation is not enough for the lands, however good they are, but many such rainy days and many waterings are needed, so also many irrigations of prayer are needed for our soul to be saturated and soaked through with virtue; and he quotes to this effect the saying of the prophet: *Seven times in the day I praised thee* (Psalm cxviii. 164). Seven times a day did the Prophet David water his soul with the water of prayer, and dwelt on one and the same aspiration, repeating it many times, as we see frequently in the Psalms. In one psalm alone he repeats twenty-seven times, *For his mercy endureth forever* (Psalm cxxv. 1-27), proclaiming and giving thanks for the mercy of God. In another psalm, which consists of only five verses, he eleven times rouses and invites us to praise God (Psalm cl). And Christ our Redeemer taught us also by His example this method of prayer and perseverance in one thing in His prayer in the Garden. Not content with having once made this prayer to His eternal Father, He went back upon it and repeated a second and a third time the same prayer, *eundem sermonem dicens* (Matt. xxvi. 44), and at the end, says the holy Gospel, at greater length than at the beginning. He dwelt more on this prayer, *prolixius orabat* (Luke xxii. 43), to teach us to insist and persevere in prayer on one thing, backwards and forwards again and again; for in this way and by this perseverance we shall come to attain the virtue and perfection which we desire.

CHAPTER XVI

How We May Dwell Long in Meditation on One and the Same Thing; and a Very Profitable, Practical Method of Meditation by Descending to Particular Cases

IT remains for us to describe the method which we shall be able to use in order to continue a long time aspiring after the same virtue, since it is so important, as we have said. The common and ordinary means usually given for this is to endeavor to continue the same act and affection of the will, or return to reiterating and repeating it anew, as one gives a new tap to a hoop that it may not stop running or as one flings fresh fuel into the furnace, aiding ourselves to this end by the same first reflection that originally moved us to this affection and desire, repeatedly rousing the will therewith when we see that it is growing cold, saying with the prophet: *Turn thou, my soul, unto thy rest, since the Lord hath blessed thee* (Psalm cxiv. 7). Awake, my soul, and turn to thy repose; see how much thou art concerned in this, and how right and reasonable that thou shouldst do much for the Lord, to Whom thou owest so much. When the first consideration no longer suffices to move us, we must make use of another new consideration or pass on to another point. For this we should always bring different points ready prepared, so that when we have finished one which seems no longer to make any impression on us, we may pass to another and another that may move us afresh and prompt our aspirations to what we desire.

Furthermore, as here on earth, to avoid the repugnance that may be caused by continuing again and again the same dish, we are wont to dress it in different manners till it seems new and gives us a new appetite, so also to persevere a long time on one and the same thing in prayer, which is the food and sustenance of our soul, it is a good plan to dress it in different ways. This we can do sometimes by passing to another point and another consideration, as we just now explained; for every time that a person moves and actuates himself by a different motive or consideration on the same thing, it is like dressing the dish in another manner, and so it becomes as it were new. And even without any new motive or new consideration, the aspiration after the same virtue may be dressed in many ways. Thus, in dealing with humility a person may sometimes dwell on his self-knowledge of his own miseries and weaknesses, rousing shame and self-abasement for them; at other times he may dwell on desires to be despised and held in small account by others, making no account of the opinion and esteem of men, but taking it all for vanity; at other times he may be ashamed and blush to see the faults that every day he heaps up, and beg of God pardon and remedy for them; at other times he may return thanks that he has not been left to fall in other and graver matters. By this variation and difference we escape the loathing that is often caused by continuance of the same thing and are able readily and with relish to last out and persevere in exciting affections of one and the same virtue, whereby the virtue takes root and gets a better hold on the heart. For as every time the file passes over the iron, it takes off something, so every time we make an act of humility or of any other virtue, something of the contrary vice is worn away and got rid of.

Besides this, there is another way of persevering in meditation on one subject for many days—a very easy and profitable way; and that is by coming down to particular cases. The masters of spiritual life here observe that we must not be satisfied with drawing from meditation a general desire or purpose of serving God or of advancing and being perfect in general, but we must come down to that in which we know that we shall be able to serve and please God better. Neither must we be content with eliciting a general desire of any particular virtue, as to be humble, obedient, patient, or mortified—for this desire or velleity of virtue even vicious people have, since virtue is a fair and honorable thing, of much profit both for this life and the next. It is easy enough to love and desire it in general, but in whatever virtue we desire, we must come down to particular cases. Thus, if we wish to attain a great conformity to the will of God, we must come down and conform ourselves to His will in particular cases: as in health, so in sickness; as in life, so in death; as in consolation, so in temptation. If we aim at attaining the virtue of humility, we must come down to the particular, imagining particular cases, likely or possible to turn up, of our being despised and losing caste; and so of other virtues; for these occasions are more felt, and in them the difficulty of virtue lies; here virtue is proved and made to appear, and these are the means to gain it.

Our first instances should be taken from lesser and easier things; thence we may go on to things more difficult, things that we should feel more if they did occur. Thus we should go on and face them little by little, eliciting acts thereupon as if they were actually present till we find no obstacle in the virtue we are after, but have courage for everything, and the field is won. And when actual occasions present themselves, in these we should exercise ourselves first of all, disposing ourselves to bear them courageously and with profit, each according to his condition. A servant of God adds that in meditation we should always put before us something to do that very day; so far even as this do they wish us to descend to particulars in our meditation. This is one of the most profitable exercises that we can go through in meditation; for, as we have said, our meditation ought to be practical, or directed to action, to gain the virtue we desire and overcome all repugnances thereto. This is what soldiers do, who, before war, are wont to engage in jousts, tournaments, skirmishes, and the like exercises to be prepared and skillful for real war.

Cassian greatly commends this practice; so also do Plutarch and Seneca. They say it is very profitable to have your mind always engaged on the thought of trials and troubles; for as he who will think of nothing but pleasant eventualities weakens himself and has no staying-power and is quite upset when disagreeable things befall him, and turns to think of other things pleasant and agreeable; so he who is accustomed ever to be picturing to himself sicknesses, exiles, prisons, and all other adversities that can happen, will be more ready and wide-awake when they do come, and will find that such things strike more terror in the beginning than they do harm in the end. St. Gregory says well: "The missiles that are foreseen hit you less." A blow does not hurt you so much when you were expecting it, and in thought had half got it down already, as when it catches you suddenly. It is clear that enemies frighten you more when they spring upon you suddenly than when you were on the lookout for them.

In the Life of our blessed Father Ignatius we read a marvelous example to this effect. One day that he was unwell, the doctor told him not to give way to sadness or any gloomy thoughts. Thereupon he began to think attentively within himself what occurrence could possibly happen to him so disagreeable and hard as to affect the peace and tranquillity of his soul; and having turned the eyes of his reflection over many things, one thing alone presented itself that he would most take to heart, and that was if by any chance our Society were broken up. He went on reflecting how long this affliction and pain would last, in case it happened; and he thought that, if it happened without any fault on his part, within one quarter of an hour of recollection and prayer he would be rid from that grief and recover his ordinary peace and cheerfulness, although the Society were dissolved like salt in water. This is a very good and very profitable prayer.

The Apostle St. James says in his canonical epistle: *Is anyone sad among you? Let him pray* (James v. 13). When you feel any sadness or discouragement, have recourse to prayer and you will find there comfort and remedy. This is what the Prophet David did: *My soul refused to be comforted: I had recourse to God, and I found comfort* (Psalm lxxvi. 3-4). When he felt himself destitute of comfort, he had recourse to God and raised his heart to Him, and forthwith his soul was filled with joy and consolation: "This is the will of God; He wills it so. If God is satisfied, we are all satisfied." As after the coming of the occasion and the distress it is a very good remedy to have recourse to prayer in order to bear it well and with advantage, so also it is very important to take this remedy by anticipation beforehand, so that the trouble may not afterwards strike us as something new, but as something easy and bearable.

St. Chrysostom says that one of the reasons why holy Job was so brave and constant in his adversities and afflictions was because he had anticipated them in the manner we have said, thinking of them beforehand and presenting them to his imagination and rousing himself to meet them as something that might well happen, as he himself says: *The fear that I feared hath befallen me, and what I was afraid of hath come true.* But if you are not fortified beforehand on this point and if even in desire you feel difficulty, what will it be in act? If, when you are at prayer and far from the occasion, you do not feel courage and strength to embrace this office or that practice or that hardship and affront, what will it be when you are away from prayer and confronted by the difficulty of the occasion and the work, and without the consideration and meditation of the example of Christ supporting and animating you? You much desired something at prayer, and afterwards when the occasion offered, you broke down; what would it have been if you had not anticipated it, and even at prayer had had no desire of it? "If he who makes resolutions often fails, what shall become of him who rarely or never makes any resolution?" (Ā Kempis.)

Herein we present abundant matter to enable one to last out and persevere in meditation on one subject and in the same affection many hours and many days, since the particular occasions that may offer and to which we may descend are countless, and there is much to do to bring yourself to face them all. And when you have come to that pitch that you fancy you feel in yourself courage and strength for everything, think not that all the work is done, but rather there is a long way to go, since there is a great gap between word and deed and between desire and execution. It is plain that execution is harder than desire, for in practice the object in present, but in desire, only the imagination. Thus it often befalls us that we are very fervent in prayer and fancy that there is no obstacle in our way, and afterwards, when the occasion offers, we find ourselves very far from what we thought.

Thus it is not enough that you feel in yourself those desires, but you must manage to make those desires so strong and so effectual as to reach to execution, for that is the proof of virtue. And if you see that your performances agree not with your desires, but that, when the occasion offers, you find yourself other than at meditation you thought you were, be confounded to think that your whole being goes out in desires; or to say better, that they cannot be true desires, but delusions and imaginations, since a very slight thing troubles and upsets you and makes you turn back. And as the smith, when the work does not turn out well, puts it back a second time into the fire to forge it anew, so you must go back to the furnace of meditation to forge those desires better, and stop not till the work agrees well with the desire and there is no fault to find with it.

But even when you have come to this, that you seem to take up well the occasions that offer, think not that the whole work is done; for in the same work there are many degrees and steps to mount, to reach the perfection of virtue. For the first degree it is necessary to practise yourself in taking up with patience all the occasions that offer. This is the first degree of virtue; suffer with patience, if you cannot with joy; and in this you will find enough to occupy your intention for some days, and even a good many. And when you have got so far as to suffer with patience all the occasions that offer, you have still a long way to go to arrive at the perfection of virtue; for, as philosophers say, the sign of one's having gained the perfection of virtue is when one does the works thereof with promptitude, facility, and delight. See, then, whether you do the works of the virtue of humility, of poverty, of patience, and of the other virtues, with promptitude, facility, and delight; and thereby you will see if you have gained the virtue. See whether you rejoice as much under contempt and dishonor as worldly people do under honor and marks of respect, which is the rule laid down for us by our holy Father, drawn from the Gospel. See if you relish and rejoice in poverty of food and clothing and lodging, and in the worst things' in the house being given you, as much as the covetous man in riches and abundance. See whether you rejoice in mortification and suffering as much as people of the world in ease and comfort. If we are to attain to this perfection in every virtue, we shall have plenty to think about, even over one virtue, for many days and perhaps years.

CHAPTER XVII

That in the Consideration of the Divine Mysteries We Should Also Proceed Leisurely, and Not Pass Over Them Superficially; and of Some Means to Help Us to Do This

IN the consideration of the divine mysteries it is again very important to dig deep in one subject and not pass over things hurriedly; for one mystery, well considered and pondered, will do us more good than many superficially glanced at. To this end our Father, in the book of Spiritual Exercises, makes so much account of repetitions, that for every exercise he further bids us make one or two repetitions thereof; thus what is not found the first time over is found by further perseverance: *He that seeketh findeth, and the door shall be opened to him that knocketh* (Matt. vii. 8). Moses struck the rock with his rod, and no water came; he struck a second time, and there was a flow of water (Num. xx. 11). Take the case of that blind man in the Gospel; Christ our Redeemer did not cure him all at once, but wrought the cure little by little. First He put spittle on his eyes and asked him if he saw anything. He said he saw certain shapes, but did not know what they were: *I see men walking like trees* (Mark viii. 24). He took the men for trees. The Lord then proceeded to put His hands on his eyes and healed him entirely, so that he saw clearly and distinctly. So it is wont to happen in meditation, that by returning once and again to the same subject and persevering in it, one comes to find out more. Even so when one enters a dark room; to start with, one sees nothing, but comes to see something by staying there. And in particular we must take care always to dwell on the consideration of things until we are quite disabused of error and penetrated with truth, and convinced, and resolved to do the right thing, for this is one of the chief fruits that we have to draw from meditation, and we need to be well grounded in it.

Now to come to the means that will help us to consider and ponder the mysteries in this manner, when the Lord sends His divine light and opens the eyes of the soul, she finds so much to consider and so much to dwell upon that she can say with the prophet: *Rouse mine eyes from slumber, O Lord, and I will consider the marvels of thy law* (Psalm cxviii. 18). *I will rejoice over thy works, as one who findeth much spoil* (Psalm cxviii. 162). The second passage explains the first. I will rejoice in the abundance of mysteries and marvels that I have found in Thy law, as one rejoices who finds much booty after gaining a victory.

The blessed St. Francis and St. Augustine spent whole days and nights over those two short ejaculations: "Who art Thou and who am I? May I know myself and may I know Thee, my God and my all!" This is a method of prayer very akin to that which the Prophet Isaias says the citizens of heaven observe, who, wrapt in contemplation of the Divine Majesty, are perpetually singing, saying, and repeating, *Holy, holy, holy* (Isaias vi. 3). St. John the Evangelist says the same, speaking of those mysterious living creatures who stood before the throne of God:*And they rested not either day or night saying, Holy, holy, holy, Lord God omnipotent, who was and who is and who is to come* (Apoc. iv. 8).

But to arrive at this, it is necessary that we ourselves should do our part, accustoming ourselves to dwell on the mysteries, pondering and sounding the depths of their particular details, and that we should practise ourselves much in this. Gerson says that one of the chief means that we can apply, and one that will help much to enable us to make this meditation well, will be to exercise ourselves continually upon it. It is not a business that is taught by rhetorical phrases, or can be learned by the hearing of many discourses or the reading of many treatises on prayer, but only by putting our hand to the work and exercising ourselves much therein. When a mother goes about teaching her son to walk, she does not spend an hour in giving him instructions on the method he must observe in walking, telling him to move his feet now one way now another, but she makes him walk, and in that way the child finds out and comes to know how to do it. This, then, must be the method whereby we are to learn this science. And though it is true that to obtain the gift of prayer or of anything else supernatural, no exercise of our own in sufficient, but it must come from the gracious and liberal hand of the Lord—*For the Lord giveth wisdom, and from his mouth proceedeth prudence and knowledge* (Prov. ii. 6); yet His Majesty wishes that we should exercise ourselves therein as though we had to attain it by this means alone; for *he disposeth all things sweetly, and reacheth from end to end strongly* (Wisdom viii. 1). And so He disposes the works of grace conformably to those of nature; and as other sciences and arts are attained by practice, so He wishes to teach us this science also in that manner. By fiddling one learns to fiddle; by walking one learns to walk; and by praying one learns to pray.

Gerson says that the reason why there are so few contemplatives today is for want of this exercise. Of old, as we see, there were in those monasteries of monks ever so many men of high prayer and contemplation, and nowadays you will scarcely find one man of prayer; and when one speaks of contemplation, it sounds like talking Arabic or metaphysics—one of those things that nobody understands. The reason of this, he says, is that formerly those holy monks practised much prayer themselves, and when youths entered the monasteries, they at once imposed this duty on them and exercised them much in it, as we read in the Rule of St. Pacomius and other monastic fathers. So Gerson counsels what he takes to be very important for the good of monasteries, that they should have spiritual men, learned and well versed in prayer, who, when youths enter the monasteries, should at once from the first instruct them in the exercise of prayer. And our Father took this advice so seriously and left it so strongly inculcated in his Constitutions, that not only in the beginning, in the houses of probation, he would have someone to instruct newcomers therein, but in all the colleges and houses of the Society he would have appointed a prefect of spiritual things to attend to this and see how everyone got on in prayer, for the great importance that he attached to it.

Another thing, also, that will help us much to continue this exercise of prayer and persevere much in it, is to have a great love of God and spiritual things. So spoke the Royal Prophet: *How I love, O Lord, thy law: all day long it is matter of my meditation* (Psalm cxviii. 97). I am never wearied of thinking of it day and night; it is all my delight and recreation; *and I recreated myself over thy commandments, which I loved* (Psalm cxviii. 47). If we had a great love of God, we should willingly think of Him days and nights and never want matter of thought. Oh, how willingly does a mother think of a son whom she tenderly loves! How little need has she of arguments and considerations to refresh herself in the memory of him! In speaking of him her heart is at once touched and tears start from her eyes, without further arguments or considerations. Begin to speak to a widow of her deceased husband, whom she dearly loved, and you will see how she begins at once to sigh and weep. Now if natural love can do this—and why do I speak of natural love? If the frantic love of one who is over head and ears in his passion often keeps him so absorbed and swallowed up, as we see, in the object of his passion, that seemingly he can think of nothing else—how much more shall the supernatural love of the infinite beauty and goodness of God be able to do, since grace is more powerful than nature and perversity! If God were all our treasure, our heart would at once go out to Him; *for where thy treasure is, there is thy heart also* (Matt. vi. 21). Everyone willingly thinks of that which he loves and in which he takes delight: therefore Holy Scripture says: *He tasted and saw* (I Kings xiv. 27; Prov. xxxi. 18) : *Taste and see that the Lord is sweet* (Psalm xxxiii. 9). Tasting goes before seeing, and seeing gives increase of yearning and love. So says St. Thomas, treating of this matter, that "contemplation is the daughter of love," because from loving God one is moved to think of and contemplate Him; and the more one looks and contemplates, the more one loves, because good things looked upon invite us to love them; and the more we delight in going on looking and loving.

CHAPTER XVIII

Showing in Practice How It Is in Our Power Always to Make a Good Meditation and Gather Fruit from It

THE very special and extraordinary prayer of which we spoke above is a very particular gift of God, which He gives not to all, but to whom He pleases; but as for that ordinary and plain mental prayer of which we are treating now, God refuses it to none. Some make the mistake of thinking that, because they cannot attain to that high prayer and contemplation, they cannot pray at all and are not made for it; whereas the other and lower is a very good and profitable prayer and by it we can attain to perfection. Of this, then, we will now speak, since with the grace of the Lord it is in our power always to make it well and draw fruit from it, which is a very consoling fact.

By two ways we may gather this conclusion very well from what has been said. In the first way, because this method of prayer that our Father teaches us is to exercise therein the three powers of our soul, putting with the memory before the eyes of the understanding the point or mystery on which we wish to meditate, and thereupon setting to work with the understanding, reasoning, meditating, and considering those things which will better help to move our will; whereupon must follow our affections and desires of the will; and this last is the principal fruit that we should draw from meditation. Thus meditation does not consist in those sweetnesses and sensible relishes that we sometimes feel and experience, but in the acts that we make with the powers of our soul. Now to make these acts is always in our power, however dry and disconsolate we may be. For though I be drier than a stick and harder than a stone, it is in my power with the favor of the Lord to make an act of abhorrence and grief for my sins, an act of the love of God, an act of patience and an act of humility, an act of desire to be contemned and slighted in imitation of Christ, Who was contemned and slighted for me. We must allow that this affair of making a good meditation and drawing fruit from it does not consist in eliciting these acts with relish and sensible consolation, nor in feeling much what one does; not in this does the goodness and perfection of those acts consist, nor the merit of them. And this is to be noted, because many are much mistaken who are heartbroken, thinking they can make nothing of meditation because they do not feel all the sorrow for their faults and sins or all the aspiration after virtue and desire of it that they could wish. These feelings belong to the sensitive appetite; the will is a spiritual power and independent of that; thus it is not necessary to feel one's acts in this manner, but it is enough to seek it with the will.

So all divines and saints, dealing with contrition and sorrow for sin, advise penitents who are disconsolate because, taking into account the gravity of mortal sin, they cannot burst out into tears nor feel in themselves that sensible grief that they would have wished, so that their very hearts should have broken with grief. They tell them, true contrition and sorrow for sin is not in the sensitive appetite, but in the will. Be grieved for your having sinned because it is an offense against God, worthy of being loved above all things, for that is true contrition. As for that feeling, when the Lord gives it, receive it gratefully; and when He does not, be not distressed, for it is not that that God asks of us. Clearly He cannot ask of you what is not in our power. Now this feeling that you would like to have is a taste of sensible devotion which is not in our power; and thus God does not ask it of us, but only what is in our power, which is grief of the will, a thing quite independent of that feeling. And the same with acts of love of God; love God with your will above all things, for this is a strong and appreciative love, and what God asks of us; that other is a love of tenderness, which is not in our power. The same with acts of other virtues and all the good purposes that we form.

This truth may be well seen by what is true on a contrary supposition; for it is certain that if a man with his will embraces and consents to a mortal sin, he will certainly sin mortally and go to hell for it, even though he have no feeling nor sensible relish for it whatsoever. Therefore, when a man embraces what is good, though he have no feeling nor sensible relish in the matter, he will please God and merit heaven, especially as God is more ready to reward than to punish. Nay, oftentimes these acts are more meritorious and pleasing to God when they are done in dryness without taste of sensible consolation, because they are purer and stronger and more lasting, and a man puts more of his own into them then than when he is carried off his feet by devotion. Thus it is a sign of a more solid virtue and of a will firmer in the service of God, for whoever makes these acts without these side aids of spiritual delights and consolations, what would he do were such aids at hand to him? Father Master Avila says very well: "The one is carried in arms like a baby; the other walks on his own feet like a grown-up person." Blosius says that such persons are like men who serve a master at their own cost. It is very important that we should accustom ourselves to make our meditation in this manner, because the more ordinary course of meditation with many is apt to be dryness; these others are extraordinary comforts. As those who voyage on the high seas in galleys do it by force of their arms in rowing, when the wind drops; so those who seek to practise meditation, when the fair wind of lights and consolations from the Lord drops, must contrive to carry on their voyage by the oars of their own faculties, helped by the favor of the Holy Ghost, though it be not so copious and superabundant.

Secondly, we may draw this conclusion in another way. Meditation, as we have said, is not an end, but a means to our spiritual progress and our gaining the victory over our passions and bad inclinations, and so smoothing the way and removing obstacles that we may give ourselves over entirely to God. When the scales fell from the eyes of St. Paul's soul with that light from heaven and that divine voice, *I am Jesus, whom thou persecutest* (Acts ix. 5), what a changed man he was, how convinced, how resolved and given over to do the will of God! *Lord,* he cried, *what wouldst thou have me to do?* That is the fruit of a good meditation. And we were saying that we must not be content with drawing from meditation general purposes and desires, but we must descend in particular to that of which we have most need, and prepare ourselves and be on the lookout to surmount well the occasions that may present themselves that day, and go our way with all edification.

To apply this to our purpose, by the grace of the Lord this is always in our power; it rests with us always to put a hand to what we have the greatest need of. Put one hand to humility, another to patience, another to obedience, another to mortification and resignation; and take care always to come out of meditation very humbly, very resigned and indifferent, very desirous to mortify yourself and conform yourself in all things to the will of God; and especially always take care to come away from meditation determined that day to live well and with edification, according to your particular condition. So you will have made a very good meditation, and a better one than if you had shed many tears and enjoyed much consolation.

This being so, there is no need for anyone to be distressed at being unable to find many reflections and considerations or feelings of devotion, for meditation does not consist in this, but in the other. Nor again should one make much account of distractions and thoughts that usually give trouble at meditation without our wanting them, a thing that we are apt very commonly to complain of. Try, when you notice this and come back to yourself, to lay hold of what is necessary for you and of the fruit that you have to gather, and hereby supply and make up for the time that has gone over the distraction; so you will have your revenge on the devil, who has made you so distracted with irrelevant thoughts. This is a very profitable direction for meditation. As it is with one who, traveling in company with others, has fallen asleep, and his companions have gone on ahead, when he wakes, he makes ever so much effort to catch them up, and covers as much ground in a quarter of an hour as he would in a whole hour had he not fallen asleep; so you, upon advertence and coming to yourself after the distraction, must manage so well as to do in the last quarter of an hour what you would have done in the whole hour if you had been very attentive. Take account of yourself and say: What was it that I intended to get out of this meditation? What was the fruit that I came prepared to gather from it? Humility? Indifference? Resignation? Conformity to the will of God? Know, then, that I mean to get it all the same out of this meditation, just to plague the devil. And when it seems to you that you have done badly the whole meditation through and gathered none of the fruit that you desired, then at the examination of the meditation, of which we shall speak afterwards, you must do this and thereby make up for the faults that you have committed in the meditation, and so you will always gather fruit from it.

CHAPTER XIX

Of Some Other Easy Means and Methods How to Make a Good and Profitable Meditation

THERE are other easy methods that will help us much to make meditation, and which, being easily practised, evince that it is always in our power to make mental prayer and that there is no one but may make it so as to derive advantage from it.

On the first head, that is very good for this purpose which some masters of spirit observe. They say that we must not make meditation a fiction or an artificial thing, but that we must act in it as men act in matters of business; they pause to think of what they are doing and how their business goes and how it may be expected to go better. Thus the servant of God should deal with himself in meditation, simply and without artifice. How goes it with me in the matter of my spiritual progress and salvation?—for this is our business and we are in this life for nothing else than to transact this affair. Let the religious, then, take account of himself and set himself to consider very leisurely: How am I getting on with this business? What have I profited by these ten, twenty, thirty, or forty years that I have been in religion? What have I gained and acquired in the way of virtue, humility, and mortification? I want to see the account that I shall give to God of these so great advantages and means that I have enjoyed in religion to augment and increase the capital and talent that He has given me. And if hitherto I have made bad use of the time, I desire to make it up from now henceforth, that my whole life may not pass as it has gone hitherto. In the same way, every individual according to his state may set himself to think in detail, plainly and simply and without any artifice, how he does his office, how he ought to do it well and in conformity to the will of God, how he shall carry on his business in a Christian manner, how he shall govern his house and family so that all may serve God, how he shall bear well the occasional annoyances which his state and office carries with it; and in all this he will find matter enough to consider, deplore, and amend. And this will make a very good and very profitable meditation.

John Gerson tells of a servant of God who used often to say: For forty years I have studied this matter of prayer with all the care I could, and I have found no better means, no shorter and more compendious method of making a good meditation, than to present myself before God as a little child and as a poor beggarman, blind, naked, and forlorn. This is a manner of prayer that we see the Prophet David used frequently, calling himself sometimes a sick man, sometimes an orphan, sometimes blind, sometimes poor and begging; the Psalms we find full of this. And we know by experience that many who have practised and habitually used this kind of prayer, have come thereby to attain to a very high prayer. Do you, then, adopt this practice and, please God, by this means you will come to attain what you desire. The prayer of a poor man is a very good prayer. See, says Gerson, with what patience and humility the poor man stands waiting at the gate of the rich, hoping for a small alms, and with what diligence he repairs to where he knows alms are given. And as the poor man, naked and forlorn, is before the rich, begging alms, and expecting of him with great humility and reverence a remedy for his necessity, so should we stand before God in prayer, representing to Him our poverty, our need, and our misery and hoping for remedy from His liberality and goodness. *As the eyes of the handmaid are fixed on the hands of her mistress, so should our eyes be fixed and hanging on God, till we obtain mercy of Him* (Psalm cxxii. 2).

It is told of the Abbot Paphnutius that, living in the interior of the desert and hearing tell of that bad woman Thais, how she was a snare of perdition to many souls, besides being the cause of many quarrels and murders, he conceived within himself a desire of converting her and bringing her to God. For this end he put on secular clothes, took money with him, and went to the city where she lived. And so he did convert her, taking occasion of some words which she let fall. For when he asked for a more secluded place, she said to him: "Make yourself quite easy about men, that they will not see you here, albeit from the eyes of God you cannot hide yourself in any place, how secluded soever." It is a long story, but, coming to what makes for our purpose, he converted this woman, took her to the desert and shut her up in a cell, sealing the door with a seal of lead, leaving only one little window through which they could give her every day a small pittance of bread and a little water. When Paphnutius was taking leave of her, she asked him how she was to make prayer to God. To this the holy abbot answered: "You deserve not to take into your filthy mouth the name of God. Your prayer shall be to go on your knees, look to the east, and say many times over these words: *Thou who hast made me, have mercy on me.*" And so she remained for three years without ever taking into her mouth the name of God; always keeping before her eyes her many great sins, asking God's mercy, and saying those words that the saint had taught her. And with this prayer God was well pleased. At the end of three years, Abbot Paphnutius went to consult the blessed St. Anthony as to whether God had pardoned this woman her sins. Anthony called his monks together and bade them all sit up that night in prayer, each by himself, in order that the Lord might declare to some one of them the solution of the case on which Paphnutius had come. While then they were all at prayer, Paul, the chief of the great Anthony's disciples, saw a bed in heaven, adorned with rich hangings and upholstery and guarded by four virgins. At sight of this rich display, he thought and said within himself: "This reward and gracious welcome is kept for none other than my Father Anthony." While he was thinking this, he heard a heavenly voice which said: "This bed is not for thy Father Anthony, but for the sinner Thais." And fifteen days after, it pleased the Lord to take her to enjoy the glory and repose of heaven. Be you, then, satisfied with holding to this prayer and make up your mind that you do not deserve any other, and I dare say you will please God more than by that prayer which you fancy.

In a spiritual treatise, "On Spiritual Communion," left in manuscript by a Carthusian monk, the author recounts a story of our holy Father and his companions, which he assures us he received from a person worthy of credit. Ignatius and his companions were going one day to Barcelona on foot, as ordinarily they were wont to do, each one carrying his knapsack upon his back. They met upon the way a good man who saw them, had compassion on them, and pressed them extremely to give him their knapsacks to carry, alleging that he was stronger and better able to carry them than they. After much demurring they gave in to his importunities, and so continued their journey. When they arrived at the inn, the Fathers contrived each one to seek out his corner, there to recollect himself and commend himself to God. The good man, seeing them do this, also contrived to seek out his corner and put himself on his knees as they did. Pursuing their journey, they asked him one day: "Brother, what do you do there in that corner?" He answered that what he did was to say: "Lord, these are saints, and I am their beast of burden; what they do, I desire to do, and I offer that then to God." The man made such progress by this prayer that he came to be a very spiritual man and had the gift of a very high prayer. Now who is there that cannot, if he will, make this prayer?

I knew an ancient Father of the Society, a very great preacher, whose prayer for a long time was to say with great humility and simplicity to God: "Lord, I am a beast. I know not how to make my prayer. Teach me Yourself to make it." And by this means he made great progress and came to an eminent degree in prayer, fulfilling in himself what the prophet said: *I am become as a beast before thee, and am always with thee* (Psalm lxxii. 23). Humble yourself, then, as a beast of burden before God, and the Lord will be with you. Much is arranged and gained in this way with His Divine Majesty. So the saints take note here of a thing of much importance, that, as humility is a means to attain the gift of prayer, so also prayer should serve as a means to attain humility and keep us and make us advance in it. And they add that from a good prayer one should always get up with a sense of humiliation and confusion. Whence it follows that, when you come from your meditation highly pleased with yourself, with an indescribable vain complacency and a secret esteem and good opinion of yourself, saying to yourself that now you are getting on and becoming a spiritual man, you should hold that prayer in grave suspicion. So if you say that you cannot find many considerations nor high contemplations, humble yourself and draw that good from your meditation. None can excuse himself from doing this, and it will make a very good prayer.

Father Master Avila, in one of his letters, gives a very good means to adopt when one cannot get on at meditation, but is a prey to divers thoughts and temptations. Throw yourself, he says, at the feet of Christ, and say: "Lord, inasmuch as this is my own fault, I am certainly very sorry for the fault I am in and the occasion I have given; but inasmuch as it is Thy will, and the punishment and chastisement that I have justly deserved for my great faults in the past, and my present negligences and defects, I accept it with all my heart and am glad to receive at Thy hand this cross, this dryness and distraction, this desolation and spiritual dereliction." This patience and humility will be a very good prayer and please God more than the prayer you desired to make, as we shall say more at large farther on.

It is told of our Father Francis Borgia that, when he thought he had not done his meditation well, he took care that day to mortify himself more and go about all his duties with greater attention and diligence, thus to make up for the failure of the meditation, and so he counseled us to do. This a very good way of making up the defects of meditation and will serve also to bring us to make our meditation well. The holy Abbot Nilus, speaking of prayer, says that, as when we fall out of order and go amiss during the day and commit some fault, we seem to feel at once the chastisement of God in prayer, because He shows us then a severe countenance; so also, when we have mortified and overcome ourselves in something, we seem at once to feel it at prayer, God seeming to will to pay us there in money down. "If you suffer in patience hard and rough things, you will find the fruit of your labor in time of prayer." (St. Nilus.) The saint mentions for making prayer, quite in accord with what we have just been saying: "If you want to pray well, do nothing contrary to prayer; in this way God will draw nigh to you and do you many favors."

And in general let all understand that the chiefest care of the servant of God should be to cleanse and mortify his heart, to keep himself from all sin, and be ever quite firmly resolved not to commit a mortal sin for anything in the world. In this resolve he should found himself right well in prayer, and dwell upon it, and again and again move himself thereto, for there is nothing more necessary for us so long as we are in this miserable life; and on this foundation everyone should build all the rest of his contemplated edifice of perfection. And you should not repine at this, but be very grateful to God even though He grants you no other and higher prayer; for holiness consists not in meditation, but in doing the will of God. *Fear God, and keep his commandments, for this is all man* (Eccles. xii. 13), so Solomon concludes the discourse of Ecclesiastes; that is to say, in this consists all the well-being of man and fulfilment of his duty, and with this he will be holy and perfect.

I wish to conclude with a method very consoling for all. When you do not feel at meditation that entry into things, that attention and devotion, that intimate union which you desire, exercise yourself in having a great will and desire of it, and thereby you will make up for what you think is wanting to you; since God our Lord, as the saints say, is not less content and satisfied with this good will and desire than with high and lofty prayer. God taught this to the holy virgin Gertrude, as Blosius relates. He says that one day this saint was complaining that she could not keep her heart so elevated to God as she desired and thought herself obliged to do; whereupon she was taught from heaven that with God it is enough for man to wish for and sincerely desire to have a great desire, when at heart he feels little or nothing. Before God his desire is as great as he would fain have it to be. In a heart that has the like desire—you must understand, a will and desire to have it—she was told that God dwells more willingly than any man could among fresh and delightful flowers. God has no need of your high prayer; He seeks only for your heart; *that* He looks to, and *that* He takes for the deed. Offer yourself entirely to God in prayer, give Him your whole heart, and desire to be there in heaven praying with the fervor of the highest seraphs; and this good will God will regard and take for the deed. Accordingly, it will be a most pious devotion and profitable reflection, when we find ourselves tepid and dry at meditation, to consider how many servants of God are there at prayer—perhaps shedding tears and even their blood—and join ourselves in spirit to them; and not to them alone, but to the angels and heavenly spirits also, putting ourselves in relation with what they are doing and so supplying what we cannot do, saying in our heart, and often with our lips, those words of the canon of the mass: "Deign, O Lord, to receive, along with the prayers of the angels and saints in glory, our voices also, who in humble confession cry out to Thee, 'Holy, holy, holy.'" Lord, what they say, I say; what they do, I also wish to do; and as they praise and love, I also would fain praise and bless and love Thee. And sometimes it will be well to fall back upon ourselves, when at any time we seemed to have made a good meditation, and say: "Lord, what I wished then, I wish now; as then I offered myself entirely to Thee, so I offer myself now; in that manner in which I then grieved for my sins and desired humility, patience, obedience, in that same manner now, O Lord, I desire and ask for them."

Above all, it is a marvelous good practice to unite our actions with the actions of Christ and supply our faults and imperfections by the merits of Christ and of His sacred Passion. And this we should do not only as regards prayer, but in all other actions, offering to the eternal Father our prayers in union with the love and fervor with which Christ prayed and praised Him on earth: our fasts in union with His fastings; begging the Father to be pleased to supply our impatience by the patience of Christ, our pride by His humility, our evil doing by His innocence. This practice, Blosius says, our Lord revealed to some of His special friends that so we may make our actions to be of value and merit and by this method may eke out our poverty by the infinite treasure of the merits of Christ.

CHAPTER XX

That We Must Be Content with the Prayer Described, and Not Repine or Complain at Not Reaching Anything Higher

ALBERTUS MAGNUS says that a truly humble man does not dare to lift up his heart to desire that high and exalted prayer and those extraordinary favors which the Lord sometimes bestows on His friends. He has such a mean opinion of himself that he thinks himself unworthy of all favor and spiritual consolation; and if ever, without his desiring it, the Lord visits him with some consolation, he receives it with fear, thinking that he does not deserve these comforts and bounties and knows not how to profit by them as he should. So if we had humility in us, we should be quite content with any manner of prayer of those that we have described; or rather, we should take it for a particular favor of the Lord that He takes us by the road of humility, for by this we are safe, and in any other way possibly we might fall into vanity and perdition. St. Bernard says that God deals with us as parents on earth do with their children of tender age. If the child asks for bread, they give it willingly; but if it asks for a knife to divide the bread, they will not give it, for they see that it is not necessary, but rather might do the child harm by its cutting itself with it; so the father takes the knife himself and divides the bread, that the child may have no trouble nor run any risk. In this way the Lord acts; He gives you bread already divided into portions, but has no mind to give you the sensible sweetnesses and consolations that there are in high prayer, because perchance you might cut yourself therewith, taking yourself for a spiritual man and preferring yourself to others. The Lord does you a greater favor in giving you your bread already cut than if He gave you a knife to cut the bread. If God by this your present prayer gives you strength and fortitude so great that you would rather burst asunder than sin and keeps you all your life without falling into mortal sin, what better prayer do you want or what better fruit?

This is the answer which the father of the prodigal son gave to the elder brother, who was indignant at seeing his brother received with such festive rejoicings and would not go into the house, saying: "I have served thee so many years and have been subject to thy command and have always been obedient, and thou hast never given me so much as a kid to make merry with my friends; but for this other, who has wasted his property and been disobedient, thou hast killed the fatted calf and made a splendid feast with ever so much music and great doings." The father answered: "Son, see that I do not this because I cherish that other rather than thee. Thou art always in my house with me; still, it will be well for thee to know and duly value what I am doing for thee; do I not always show thee favors and bounty enough in keeping thee always with me?"

(Luke xv. 28-31). And so in your case do you think it a small thing that the Lord should keep you always with Him in His house? It is a better gift that the Lord should give the gift of perseverance and keep you always by Him, not letting you depart from Him and fall into sin, than that He should reach you a hand after a fall, as He did to the prodigal son; just as it is a better gift not to let you break your head than to cure you after it is broken. Now if God, with this prayer that you have, gives you this, what have you to complain of? If with this prayer He gives you a great readiness for all things that form part of the service of God, indifference and resignation for all orders of obedience, what more do you want? If God with this prayer keeps you in humility and in His fear and in the habit of going cautiously, shunning occasions and dangers of sin, why should you sigh for more? This is the fruit that you should draw from any prayer, however high and exalted, that you reached; and were the Lord to give you many spiritual sweetnesses and consolations therein, to this you should refer them all. Now this is what God is doing for you with that plain and ordinary prayer; He gives you the end and fruit of prayer otherwise than by means of those extraordinary elevations and spiritual sweetnesses and consolations, as they experience who persevere in that prayer. So we ought to render God twofold thanks, for that on the one hand He delivers us from the danger of vanity and pride which we might fall into if He took us by the other road; and on the other hand that He gives us the fruit and profit of meditation in full abundance. Holy Writ tells us of the holy patriarch Joseph that he spoke to his brethren in harsh and severe words, and on the other hand he filled their sacks with corn and told his steward to see them well treated. So the Lord often deals with us.

We do not sufficiently understand in what meditation consists; or rather, we do not sufficiently understand in what our spiritual progress and perfection consists, which is the end and fruit of meditation. Thus, many times when things are going badly with us, we think they are going well; and when they are going well, we think they are going badly. Draw from your meditation the fruit we have described, especially to live that day well and with edification, as we have said above, and you will have made a good meditation, though, when you were at it, you were drier than a stick and harder than a stone. And if you do not gather this fruit, you have not made a good meditation, though you were shedding tears the whole time and thought yourself lifted to the third heaven. Henceforth, then, do not complain of meditation, but turn all your complaints against yourself, and say: "I'm getting on badly in mortification. I'm getting on badly in humility, in patience, silence, and recollection." That is a good complaint, since you are complaining of yourself, that you do not do what you ought to do and is in your power. On the other hand, when you go complaining of meditation, it looks like complaining of God for not giving you the facility and consolation and repose you would like. That is not a good complaint; it is not a speech to move God to mercy, but rather to anger and indignation, as holy Judith said to the people of Bethulia: *That is not a speech to call down mercy, but rather to excite anger and kindle indignation* (Jud. viii. 12). It is a wonderful thing to see how we go the wrong way about things in this business, not seeing that what we ought to complain of is our not being forward in mortifying, humbling, and correcting ourselves, which is in our power; and instead of that we go complaining of that which is not in our power, but stands to God's account. Busy yourself in mortifying and overcoming yourself and do your part therein, and leave to God what stands to Him to do, seeing He is more desirous of our good than we are ourselves; and if we do what is on our part, we may be quite sure that He will not fail in giving us on His part what is proper for us. Of this we will speak at greater length in treating of conformity to the will of God, where more of set purpose we will meet this complaint and temptation.

CHAPTER XXI

Of the Causes of Distraction at Prayer, and Remedies for It

THIS is a very common complaint, and so the saints commonly treat of it, Cassian in particular. They say that distraction in prayer may come of three causes or roots. The first is our own carelessness and negligence in pouring ourselves out during the day with little guard of our heart and little custody of our senses. He who lives in this way has no need to inquire whence it comes that he is distracted in prayer and can make no way in it, since it is clear that the images, shapes, and representations of things that have been allowed to enter therein must needs afterwards molest and disturb one in prayer. Abbot Moses in the Collations of Cassian says very well that, though it is not in the power of man not to be assailed with importunate thoughts, still it is in his power to refuse them admittance and cast them out when they come. He goes on to say that it is largely in a man's power to correct and amend the quality of these thoughts and make them good and holy, and consign to oblivion those others that are vain and irrelevant. If a man gives himself to spiritual exercises of reading, meditation, and prayer, and occupies himself in good and holy works, he will have good and holy thoughts; but if he deals with nothing of the sort during the day, but lets his senses browse on idle and irrelevant objects, such also will be his thoughts. And Cassian makes a comparison, which is also that of St. Anselm and St. Bernard. They say that the heart of a man is like a millstone which is always grinding; but it is in the power of the miller to make it grind wheat, or barley, or rye; what you put under it, that it will grind. So the heart of man cannot go without thinking of something; it must always grind, but by your industry and care you may make it grind wheat, or barley, or rye, or earth; what you put into it, that it will grind.

According, then, to this, if you wish to be recollected at prayer, you must take care during the day to keep your heart recollected and guard the gates of your senses; the Lord loves to converse with souls that are as enclosed gardens. This was a maxim of the ancient Fathers, and Cassian quotes it. You must take the current of your thoughts higher upstream, and keep yourself during the day in such condition as you would wish to find yourself in prayer; since from the state and temper of the mind out of prayer is formed and determined what it is to be in prayer. St. Bonaventure says: "As is the liquid that you pour into a vessel, such will be the odor; and as are the herbs which you plant in the garden of your heart, such will be the fruit and seed that they will produce."

And since it is quite a common and natural thing to think often of what one loves, if you wish to keep your heart steady and firm at prayer, and that thoughts of vain and irrevelant things may be forgotten and put an end to, you must mortify your affection for them, despise all the things of earth and fix your heart on those of heaven. And the more you advance and grow in this, the more also you will advance and grow in firmness, steadiness, and attention at prayer.

Secondly, these distractions are wont to arise from the temptation of our enemy, the devil. St. Basil says that, as the devil sees that prayer is the means whereby all good comes to us, he endeavors by all ways and means he possibly can to hinder it and put a thousand obstacles in our way, that, finding us bereft of this help, he may gain readier entrance into our soul for his deceits and temptations. He acts with us as the general, Holofernes, did with the city of Bethulia, which was standing a siege against him. He cut the aqueducts whereby water came into the city (Judith vii. 6); in like manner the devil does all in his power to break and dismantle in us this aqueduct of prayer, whereby the water of grace and of all spiritual blessings finds its way into our soul. St. John Climacus says that, as at the sound of the bell the faithful and religious visibly assemble to pray and praise God, so our enemies, the devils, unite at that time invisibly to tempt us and hinder us from prayer. In the "Spiritual Meadow" it is told of one of the Fathers of the Desert, the Abbot Marcellus, that, rising one night to pray and sing psalms according to his custom, he heard the sound of a trumpet, sounding what seemed like a battle-charge. The old man was much puzzled to imagine where such a sound could come from in such a lonely place, where there were no soldiers nor any war. Then the devil appeared to him and told him that, though he thought there was no battle going on, there was a battle, and that trumpet roused the devils to attack the servants of God; and that, if he wanted to escape the combat, he had better go back to bed and sleep, otherwise he would see it. But he, trusting in the Lord, started his prayer and went on with it.

One of the things that go far to let us see the great importance of prayer is the great spite that the devil has against it and the continual war that he makes upon it, as the holy Abbot Nilus well observes. Other good works the devil suffers and can get on with, as fasting, discipline, and haircloth; but an allotted time of prayer he cannot endure and tries by all ways in his power to hinder and put obstacles to it. Hence it is that, when we are at prayer, we are apt occasionally to feel more temptations than at other times. Then there seems to come upon us the whole troop of thoughts, thoughts at times so evil and foul that it looks as though we had come here for no other purpose than to be tempted and molested with all manner of temptations. Things that never have occurred to us, never entered our mind in the whole course of our life, then present themselves at meditation; everything seems to have been kept for then. That is because the devil knows that prayer and meditation is the remedy for all our ills, the source and origin of all spiritual blessings; therefore he takes great pains and calls out all his powers to hinder it. That is why the saints call prayer the torment and scourge of the Evil One. The same should be to us a reason and motive for esteeming it all the more and giving ourselves all the more to it, the more we see the devil for envy trying to stop us. St. Thomas, Abulensis, and other grave authors say that this is the reason why holy Mother Church, guided by the Holy Ghost and understanding well the wont of the devil to tempt and make all the war he can upon people at their prayers, has ordained that at the beginning of every canonical hour there should be repeated the verse: *Incline unto my aid, O God: O Lord, make haste to help me;* whereby we implore the Lord's gracious aid to pray as we ought, and His assistance against the snares and temptations of our enemies.

Thirdly, these thoughts and distractions sometimes come, without any fault of ours, from our own infirmity and weakness; for we are so weak and miserable, and our nature is so maimed and depraved by sin, our imagination especially, that we cannot say an Our Father without sundry incongruous thoughts' coming into our mind, as St. Bernard complained. For this it will be a good remedy to take for matter of our meditation the very distress that we suffer, humbling ourselves, considering and recognizing how great our weakness is, for this humility and self-knowledge will be a good meditation. Besides this, we will mention other remedies that the saints and masters of the spiritual life give us.

CHAPTER XXII

Of Other Means of Keeping Up Attention and Reverence at Meditation

THE blessed St. Basil asks how one can keep one's heart firm, attentive, and undistracted in prayer, and says that the most efficacious means is to consider that one is in the presence of God, and that He is looking to see how one prays. Here on earth, in the presence of a sovereign, conversing with him, one stands with great respect and reverence, paying great attention to what he does and to the manner and style of doing it. We should take for great discourtesy to turn our back on his majesty and bring in a medley of remarks not to the point. What shall he do who shall attentively consider that he is in the presence of the majesty of God, that God is looking at him, not only at his outer man that is visible exteriorly, but into the innermost recesses of his heart! Who is there that shall dare to take off his eyes and his thought from what he is doing, to turn his back on God and go thinking of other irrelevant things? The great monk James, as Theodoret relates, made use of this consideration to show what a great piece of rudeness that is. St. Augustine also says the same. If I were the domestic servant, he says, of a man of the same nature as myself, and at the time that I ought to be serving him I omitted bringing him his meat and drink to go talking with another servant, he would have just reason to rebuke and chastise me. And if I went before a judge to complain of someone who had done me wrong, and then left him in the midst of the proceedings and stayed chatting with some one of the lookers-on in court, think you not that the judge would take me for an ill-mannered man and bid such as ill-bred suitor be off from his tribunal where he was sitting in judgment? But this is what they do who go to prayer to speak with God and then give way to distractions, thinking of other things quite out of place there. Our Father also sets down this means in one of the "additions," or notices, which he gives for meditation, where he says that, a little before starting the meditation, for the space of one Our Father we should raise up our heart to heaven and consider that God is there present and is looking at us, and so with great reverence and humility we should enter on the meditation. And we must take care that this presence of God is not to be lost sight of all the time of the meditation, according to the saying of the prophet: *The meditation of my heart is in thy sight always* (Psalm xviii. 15).

St. Chrysostom says: When you go to prayer, reckon that you are entering the heavenly court, where the King of Glory is seated under a starry canopy, surrounded with innumerable angels and saints, and that they are all looking at you, according to that saying of St. Paul: *We are a spectacle to God, and to the angels and to men* (I Cor. iv. 9). St. Bernard advises us what we ought to do in such surroundings: "When you enter the church to betake yourself to prayer, put your hand on your mouth and say: 'Stay ye here at the door, ye evil thoughts and desires, and do thou, my soul, enter into the joy of thy Lord, that thou mayest see and do His holy will' "—*Veniens ad ecclesiam pone manum tuam super os tuum et dic: Expectate hic, cogitationes malae, intentiones et affectus cordis et appetitus carnis: tu autem, anima mea, intra in gaudium Domini Dei tui.* St. John Climacus says: Let him who prays consider that he is really before God; let him be like a firm and steady pillar that moves not. And he relates how once, seeing a religious more attentive than the others at the chanting of the psalms, and especially at the beginning of the hymns, with his mien and look quite changed, as though he were speaking to someone, he asked him afterwards to tell him what it meant. The monk replied: "At the beginning of the divine office it is my practice with great care to gather together my heart and thoughts, and call them before me and say: *Come let us adore, and fall down, and weep before the Lord that made us, because he is the Lord our God, and we are the people of his pasture and the sheep of his hand* (Psalm xciv. 6-7). All these are very good and profitable considerations for securing attention and reverence at prayer.

Others give for a remedy to meditate in presence of the Blessed Sacrament, if we are in a place where we can do so; or to look towards the nearest place where the Blessed Sacrament is kept, and fix our heart there: also to look at pictures and images. Others again aid themselves by looking up to heaven. It is also a good means to enliven oneself under distractions and dryness at meditation to say some ejaculatory prayers and speak orally to God, representing our weakness and asking a remedy for it. *Lord, I suffer violence, answer thou for me* (Isaias xxxviii. 14). That blind man in the Gospel, when Christ our Redeemer seemed to take no notice of him and was passing him by, and the company were bidding him hold his peace, still ceased not to cry out, lifting up his voice higher and higher, saying, *Jesus, Son of David, have mercy on me* (Mark x. 47). So we should do when the Lord makes as though He did not hear us and seems to pass us by without attending to us; and though the crowd and rout of thoughts and temptations impels us to be silent, not for that should we be silent, but cry out louder and louder: *Jesus, Son of David, have mercy on me. Strengthen me, O Lord God, in this hour* (Judith xiii. 9), that I may be able to think of Thee and be firm and constant in prayer. A holy woman used to say: If you cannot speak to God with your heart, cease not to speak to Him by word of mouth repeatedly; for what is thus said over and over again, readily communicates heat and fervor to the heart. And this same saint confessed that sometimes, for not having used these vocal prayers, she had lost her mental prayer, weighed down and hampered by sloth and sleep. And this sometimes befalls us; it comes to pass that we neglect to use our voices at meditation out of sloth and weakness and being half asleep; whereas, if we did speak, we should be awakened and roused to meditation.

Gerson also says that it is a good remedy against distractions to bring the exercise well prepared, and have several points fixed as matter for meditation, because thereby, when we are distracted and notice the same, we have ready our fixed and determined point to have recourse to; and if we make no way with that, we pass on to another point of those which we have ready prepared, and so recover more easily the thread of our meditation. And we ourselves find, when we examine ourselves, that oftentimes the cause of our distractions and mind-wandering was our not having brought well prepared and known the points on which we were to meditate, nor having had any definite and fixed resolves to bring ourselves to. Besides, this admonition and the one that follows it are necessary for us to come well prepared to meditation; accordingly our Father commends them to help us in these emphatic words: "It will be a great help, before starting meditation, to call to mind the points that are to be meditated on, and have marked out a definite number of them." And we read of him that not only at the beginning of his conversion, but afterwards also, when he was old, he would read and prepare his exercise at nightfall and retire to rest with that on his mind; so that none may think that this is a business for novices. And though you know the exercise very well from having meditated several times before, yet it is an excellent thing to prepare it afresh; especially since, as these are the words of Holy Scripture, dictated by the Holy Ghost, the reading of them with a little quiet and repose arouses new attention and devotion to meditate and profit by them better.

It will also help us very much to this purpose, immediately on awakening, not to give place to other thoughts, but think of the exercise we have to make and prepare ourselves for our meditation by some consideration adapted to the matter thereof. Cassian, St. Bonaventure, and St. John Climacus hold this admonition to be of great importance. They say that thereon depends the guidance of the meditation and, consequently, the good order of the whole day. St. John Climacus observes that the devil, seeing this to be so important, keeps a sharp watch for our first waking, to the end that he may at once seize upon the lodging and thus gather the first-fruits of the whole day. He says, also, that among the wicked spirits there is one they call Precursor, whose charge it is to assail us by night at the time that we awake out of sleep; or, even before we are quite awake or come perfectly to ourselves, to put before us foul and filthy fancies or, at least, idle ones, and thereby take possession of us for the whole day, figuring to himself that all will be his who first occupies the heart. Wherefore it is important that we also be greatly on the alert to give no place to this, but immediately on our awakening, when we have scarcely opened our eyes, there should be already planted in our heart the memory of our Lord before any strange thought comes to occupy the lodging. Our Father also gives us the same recommendation, and adds that the same practice should be kept up, in such manner as is possible, when meditation is made at another hour. We should in that case pull ourselves together beforehand, thinking, "Where am I going? And before whom am I to appear?" So we should briefly call to mind the matter of the meditation, as one tunes a violin before playing. And generally our Father used to say that on the observance of these and other like directions, which he calls "additions," depend in great measure the success of the meditation and the fruit to be drawn from it. And it is our ordinary experience that, when we go well prepared and observe well these directions, things go well with us at meditation, and badly when we do not.

The Holy Ghost says by the Wise Man: *Before prayer prepare thy soul, and be not as a man who tempteth God*

(Ecclus. xviii. 23). St. Thomas and St. Bonaventure observe on these words that to go to prayer without preparation is in a manner to tempt God because to tempt God, as theologians and saints say, is to seek to gain an end without taking the ordinary and necessary means thereto, as if one were to say: "I will not eat, because God can easily sustain me without eating; He will sustain me." That would be tempting God and asking for a miracle without necessity. When the devil carried Christ our Redeemer to the pinnacle of the Temple, and tried to persuade Him to cast Himself headlong, since God would command His angels to receive Him and bear Him up in their hands, He answered: *Thou shalt not tempt the Lord thy God* (Matt. iv. 7). "I can come down by the stairs; that other way would be to tempt God to work a miracle without necessity." Now preparation is so principal and necessary a means to meditation that the Wise Man says that to seek to make meditation without preparation is to tempt God and want Him to work a miracle on your behalf. Our Lord certainly wishes us to make a good meditation, with great attention and reverence, but by the ordinary means, that is to say, by disposing and preparing ourselves for it in the manner we have said.

CHAPTER XXIII

A Great Comfort for Those Who Are Troubled with Distractions at Prayer

FOR the comfort of those who are troubled with this temptation, St. Basil observes that God is offended by these thoughts and distractions only when they are voluntary, when a man is distracted with advertence and seeing what he is about, with scant reverence and respect. He who at prayer sets himself on purpose to think of his studies, of the duties of his office, or of business, well deserves that God should not listen to him, but rather chastise him.

Here comes in well what St. Chrysostom says: "How can you expect God to hear you if you do not hear yourself?" But when a man honestly does what is in his power, and is distracted through weakness, and unable to keep up such attention as he would wish—his thought failing him and flying in other directions, as the prophet says, *My heart hath abandoned me* (Psalm xxxix. 13)—then the Lord is not offended at that, but rather is moved to compassion and commiseration, knowing well as He does our infirmity and weakness. *As a father hath compassion on his children, so the Lord hath compassion on them that fear him, for he knoweth the clay of which we are formed* (Psalm cii. 13-14). As a father who has a son liable to fits of insanity, has compassion on him and feels it much when the boy begins to converse in his right mind and then comes out with some absurdity; so our most compassionate Father in heaven pities and compassionates us when He sees that such is the weakness and infirmity of our nature that at the nick of time, when we are conversing with Him in our right mind, we break out into a thousand incongruous thoughts. And thus, though one never feels any sap or moisture of devotion at meditation, but very great dryness, and is assailed by thoughts and temptations and passes all the time in this way, not for that does the meditation cease to be very pleasing to God our Lord and of great value and merit in His august divine presence; nay, often it is more pleasing and meritorious than if the time had passed in much devotion and consolation, because the person has suffered and borne more labor and difficulty in it for the love of God. And he does not fail, either, in gaining by that meditation grace and favors to enable him to serve the Lord better and grow in virtue and perfection, although he does not feel it. So it happens to a sick man when he eats some nourishing food; though he has no appetite and finds no relish in it, but only pain and torment, yet he gathers strength thereby and is kept up and becomes better.

From what has been said it will be seen what a great error it is to give up meditation because in it one finds oneself a prey to many thoughts and temptations. Only we need to be well warned and take care lest on this occasion, under the plea that we can do no more, we give entry to tepidity and remissness, getting into easy-going ways and letting things slide, carried away by every wind that blows, carelessly letting thought and imagination go where it will. No; we must do what is on our part; we must with great care and diligence have an eye to and drive away those thoughts as the holy patriarch Abraham drove away and kept an eye on the birds that were swooping down on the sacrifice (Gen. xv. 11). While in this matter we do honestly what is in our power, there is nothing to deserve punishment.

We read of St. Bridget that, when she was much wearied with many distractions at prayer, our Lady one day appeared to her and said to her: "The devil, envious of the good of men, does all in his power to put impediments and obstacles in their way when they are at prayer; but do thou, daughter, take care to persevere as best thou canst in thy good will and holy desires, whatever temptation may trouble thee, how evil soever it be, and unable as thou mayest feel to throw it off; and that will be a very good and profitable prayer, and of great merit before God." We have mentioned above (Chapter 18) a very good means to recover what we think we have lost by distraction.

CHAPTER XXIV

Of the Temptation to Sleep, Whence It Comes, and the Remedies to Meet It

ANOTHER kind of distraction is the temptation to sleep. That may arise sometimes from natural causes, as want of sleep, heavy fatigue and labor, the hour, the person's age, excessive eating and drinking, though it be only of water. At other times it comes from a temptation of the devil, as those holy Fathers of the Desert related that God showed in vision that there were some devils who settled on the cowls and heads of monks and made them sleep and others who put a finger in their mouths and made them yawn. At other times it comes from our remissness and negligence and our taking a posture in prayer that occasions sleep.

The principal remedy is that already mentioned; namely, attention and remembering that we are in the presence of God. One would not dare to sleep in presence of a great sovereign, neither should we dare if we reflected that we are in presence of the majesty of God regarding us; so reflecting, we should be much ashamed to sleep at meditation. It is also a good remedy to stand up, not to lean against anything, to wash the eyes with cold water; and some are in the habit of carrying a wet handkerchief for that purpose when they are molested with this temptation. Others help themselves by looking up to the sky, by opening the window to the light, or by going to make their meditation in presence of the Blessed Sacrament in company with others; or again by taking a discipline before meditation, which keeps them wide-awake and devout. Others, likewise, at meditation inflict on themselves some pain, which keeps them awake; or, if they are alone, they extend their arms for some time in the form of a cross. It is also helpful to recite some vocal prayers—a great help to keeping awake and lively, as we have said above (Chapter 22). There are these and other like remedies, besides begging our Lord to heal us of this infirmity.

Caesarius in his Dialogues tells of a religious of the Cistercian order who often used to sleep over his prayer. One day Christ our Redeemer appeared to him, crucified with his back turned to him, and said: "Because you are remiss and tepid, you deserve not to see My face." He tells of another who came in for a more severe castigation; for, he being at prayer in choir and sleeping as usual, there came to him a crucifix from the altar and gave him such a blow on the jowl that two days after he died. All this gives us well to understand how displeasing to God is such remissness and tepidity. *Because thou art lukewarm I will begin to vomit thee out of my mouth* (Apoc. iii. 16).

Of St. Romuald, abbot and founder of the Camaldolese, St. Peter Damian relates that he took it for such a grave fault for any of his religious to sleep in time of prayer that he would not allow the delinquent to say mass the day he had fallen into this fault, for the little respect he had shown in presence of the Lord Whom he was to receive.

CHAPTER XXV

How Proper It Is to Take Some Extraordinary Times to Give Ourselves More to Prayer

As men of the world besides their daily meals have their extraordinary feasts and banquets, in which they are wont to go beyond their ordinary fare; so also it is proper that besides our daily prayer we should have our spiritual feasts and banquets, where our souls shall not feed by pittance as on other days, but have their fill of the abundance of the sweetness and grace of the Lord. And nature herself teaches us the same practice; for we see that, not content with the dew that falls every night on the earth, it will also at times rain a whole week or two without stopping; and all that rain is necessary that so the earth may be thoroughly soaked with water, and no days of sunshine and wind coming after may avail to dry it up. So, then, it is also proper that our souls, besides the common dew of every day, should have some well-marked times in which they may wax so full of virtue and the sap of devotion that neither their occupations, nor the winds of the temptations and vicissitudes of life, may be able to dry them up. So we read of many holy men and prelates of the Church that many times, leaving their occupations and affairs, they would often recollect themselves for a time in places set apart to give themselves more to prayer and contemplation. We read of the holy Abbot Arsenius that it was his custom to take one day a week for this purpose, and that was the Saturday, on which day he remained in prayer from the afternoon to the morning of the next day.

And this is a very important expedient, not only for our advancement and growth in virtue and perfection, but also to prevent our falling back. For such is the weakness and misery of man and the inclination we have to evil that, though we begin sometimes our spiritual exercises with fervor, we afterwards come little by little to grow lax and fall off from the fervor with which we commenced. We return to our tepidity and remissness as easily as water, however much it is heated, afterwards returns little by little to its natural coldness when it is taken off the fire. Indeed, tepidity seems more ingrained and connatural to us than coldness to water. As the Holy Spirit says: *The senses and thought of a man's heart are inclined to evil from his youth, for wicked is their race and connatural their malice* (Wisdom xii. 10). As we are of nothing, we return to our nothingness.

Add to this that in a busy life like ours, taken up as some of us are with studies, others with the work of the ministry, others in offices and exterior employments, we stand in more particular need of these intervals of recollection because, good and holy as our occupations are, yet as a knife is blunted by daily use and from time to time must be sharpened again because the steel has lost its edge, so we come to be blunted and lose the care of our spiritual advancement from having to help others. Even there in the world philosophers say: *Omnis agens agendo patitur*—"An agent suffers and loses something of his own." And everyone knows this well by his own experience. On this account it imports much to recollect ourselves from time to time, disengaging ourselves from all other occupations to make up this loss and replace the daily waste and gather new strength to go forward, since we are more bound to ourselves than to our neighbor, and well-ordered charity begins at home.

Especially so, since for the very end of aiding and advancing our neighbor this care of ourselves is of great importance; for it is certain that on our own greater spiritual advancement depends the greater spiritual advancement of our neighbor. Thus the time is not lost to our neighbor that we take for ourselves, but rather is gained; it is like letting land lie fallow for a year that it may bear a better crop afterwards. Father Master Avila says that it is like taking the millstone off to pick it anew that it may grind better. Thus one's being a very busy man is not only no reason for not doing this; but, rather, the busier a man is and the more charged with ministrations and business affairs, the greater need he has of having recourse to this remedy. Those who voyage by sea need often to come into port to take refreshment; so those who are charged with business affairs and occupations and ministrations to their neighbor, in the midst of so many dangers and occasions of sin, need often to take refuge in the harbor of solitude and recollection, to refresh themselves and make themselves up anew and increase their store of the goods they require. We read in the holy Gospel a very good example of this. The Evangelist St. Mark tells how the apostles were very much taken up with ministrations to their neighbor, so much so that they had hardly time to eat, such was the crowd of people that had recourse to them. They went to make a report to Christ our Redeemer of what was happening, and He said to them: *Come apart to a desert place and rest ye awhile* (Mark vi. 31). Now, if the apostles had need of this relaxation and recollection, and the Savior of the world advised them to it, how much more need have we?

Writers on prayer say well that as sleep is to the body, so is prayer to the soul. So Holy Scripture calls it a sleep: *I sleep, but my heart watcheth. I adjure you, daughters of Jerusalem, by the goats of the mountains and stags of the plains, not to awaken my beloved until she herself wishes it* (Cant. v. 2; viii. 4). They say in explanation of this that as the body is set at ease by bodily sleep and gathers new strength, so the soul is relieved by this sleep of prayer and gathers new vigor of mind to labor for God. And, further, as a man eating the best food, if he has not the repose of necessary sleep, becomes listless and infirm and is in danger of going out of his mind, so also he who is much taken up with external works, however good and holy they may be, if he loses the necessary sleep and repose of prayer, will grow listless and infirm in spirit and will be in danger of losing his soul. That is why the Bridegroom bids them not to awaken His beloved till she herself wishes. When one is awakened from sleep by the noise that they make, it is disagreeable; but when one wakes because the body is now satisfied and the humors that ascend to the brain have been dissipated, that is very soothing. So God wishes for the soul that none may disturb or hinder her prayer, but that, when she has had what is necessary, then she may awake and occupy herself in works of charity, since in this way she will do them well.

Though for all of us, at all times, it is very important to apply ourselves to these spiritual exercises and devote more time to prayer, and the more we make use of it the better, yet it is more necessary in certain particular occasions and conjunctures. Thus, when one sees himself going tepid and slack in the spiritual exercises of meditation, examen, and spiritual reading, not doing them as he ought nor gathering from them the fruit that might reasonably be expected; when he sees that he is weak and negligent in the observance of rules and makes no account of small things; when he seems to be not getting on in spirit, but is turned inside out, carried away by business and the affairs he has on hand; also when he descries some point on which he does not succeed in overcoming and mortifying himself as he ought—in all these cases it is an excellent thing to recollect oneself for some days over these exercises, to arrive at a proper resolution of self-conquest; for it may be that in one period of these he will gain more grace of the Lord and more strength to mortify himself and gain the victory over himself than by the ordinary labor of many days. It often happens that a man goes halting on his way, falling and rising again, and by one course of these exercises he is disenchanted and gets thoroughly in earnest and resolves to do the right thing; he changes his tone and takes another line of action. For, after all, the being for such a time alone, dealing with oneself and with God, is a great preparation for the Lord to speak to the heart and do great favors there. *He shall sit in solitude and be silent, for he is lifted above himself* (Lam. iii. 28)—lifted above himself and made another man. We have seen extraordinary changes brought about in this way, and *the hand of the Lord is not shortened* (Isaias lix. 1). We should never lose heart, but always do what is in our power. Who knows what God will work in your soul by means of this preparation? It may be that God has attached your improvement and perfection to one of these exercises.

Besides, after any long journeys and businesses and occupations that involve much distraction, this recollection seems as important as the comfort and good treatment of the body after a long illness, that one may come back upon oneself and recover what one has lost. And for the same reason also it is a very good thing to prepare ourselves beforehand by these exercises, when we are going to be taken up with the like occupations, so as to do things in a more spiritual way and without injury to oneself. Preservative medicine is better than the medicine that cures you after you have been ill. That is why our Father recommends all superiors before entering on their office to recollect themselves first by some days of retreat. And it is a good thing to do the same when we are going to undertake a long and important mission; of this Christ our Redeemer gives us the example, Who before commencing to preach recollected Himself for forty days in the desert. Also a time of tribulation and distress, whether private or particular, or general distress of the whole Church or of the whole order, is a very good occasion for this; for to put in more prayer and more penance and mortification has always been a usual practice in the Church to appease God and obtain His mercy.

All these are good occasions to recollect oneself in these exercises. But it is not necessary to go seeking occasions. Our own need and interest should urge us to desire and bring this about many times; at least no year should be let pass without our taking these spiritual vacations. And when it is done, it should be done in earnest and with all our heart; for a thing of such consequence as this should nowise be done for form's sake or as a compliment to others or to save appearances. The Lord has given this means very particularly to the Society, not only for our own advantage, but also for the aid and profit of our neighbor; so the bulls of our institution set this down as one of the principal means which the Society has to aid its neighbor. And this is another chief reason why our Father wishes that we should make much use of these exercises, and puts it into the Constitutions and into the Rules of Priests that we should be very dexterous in the use of this kind of arms so profitable for the gaining of souls. These are his words: "In giving the Spiritual Exercises to others after having had experience of them in himself, let each one have practice and know how to give an account of them and aid himself with this arm, since we see that God our Lord makes it so effectual for His service." By this means our Lord gained our blessed Father Ignatius; by this He gained his companions; by this since then so many others have been gained as well within as outside of the Society: and in both the one and the other we have seen that the Lord concurs with marvelous effect to their end, as with a means given so directly from His hand. Thus we should have great confidence that thereby He will help us also and bestow on us great blessings.

Another main consideration to help and animate us to this is the singular favor and grace which His Holiness Paul V has done in this particular to all religious in the bull and constitution which he published on the twenty-third of May in the year 1606, the first of his pontificate, declaring the indulgences that religious enjoy; where he grants a plenary indulgence and remission of all sins to all religious, of whatsoever order they be, who recollect themselves for the space of ten days to make these spiritual exercises, every time they make them. In this is seen the esteem which His Holiness has of this practice, and which we should have. And for the consolation of all I will set down the pontiff's very words: "To those who by permission of their superiors shall put away their other business and for ten days remain in their cells, or separated from the conversation of others, and attend to the reading of pious books and other spiritual things apt to lead the mind to devotion and spirituality; adding frequent considerations and meditations on the mysteries of Catholic faith, on the benefits of God, on the four last things, on the Passion of our Lord Jesus Christ, and other exercises of ejaculatory or vocal prayers; exercising themselves in mental prayer for at least two hours day and night; making at the same time a general confession or an annual confession or an ordinary confession and receiving the most holy Sacrament of the Eucharist or celebrating mass; every time they make these said Exercises, We mercifully grant in the Lord a plenary indulgence and remission of all sins."

CHAPTER XXVI

Of the Fruit That We Should Gather When We Betake Ourselves to These Exercises

ON three things particularly we should set our eyes, to gain them from the Exercises. The first is to renew ourselves in the ordinary things that we do every day and perfect ourselves in them, since all our advancement and perfection consist in doing these ordinary things and getting them well done. Let no one think that making the Exercises consists merely in recollecting oneself for eight or fifteen days, spending much time in prayer. All *that* is only that one may come out of retreat with a habit established of making one's meditation better, of observing the additions and instructions given to make it well, of making one's examens well, of saying or hearing well mass and divine office, of making one's spiritual reading with fruit, and so of all the rest. To this end does a man disengage himself for a time from other occupations to exert and practise himself in doing these things well, that he may come out renewed and accustomed to do them so and ready so to do them in the future. Thus our Father says that during the whole time of the Exercises, which is a month when they are made in their entirety, the particular examen should be kept on the observance of the additions and the diligent and exact fulfilment of the Spiritual Exercises, noting the faults that are committed regarding the one and the other, that so the exercitant may become habituated and accustomed henceforth to do all these things right well. And he repeats this many times, as understanding well the great means of self-improvement therein contained. And not only in regard of spiritual duties, which are the mainspring that should give force to all the rest, but in all duties and occupations, the exercitant should come forth improved by the Exercises, drawing from them support henceforth to do his office better and his ministries, and to keep the rules.

Thus the fruit of the Exercises is not for those days of retreat, but mainly for the time that follows. It is when a man comes forth from the Exercises that we are to see the benefit of them in his works.

The second thing that we are to aim at gaining from the Exercises is to overcome ourselves and mortify ourselves in regard of certain evil tendencies and imperfections that we have. Let each one set his eyes on those things in which he is prone most ordinarily to go wrong or to be the cause of others' going wrong by the offense and disedification that he gives them, and contrive to come forth from the Exercises amended on this point; and then he will have made the Exercises right well, for that is what they are particularly for, and that is their end. The title which our holy Father prefixes to the Spiritual Exercises is the following, in the original Spanish: "Spiritual Exercises, for a man to overcome himself, and order his life without being determined by any affection that is inordinate." *Exercicios espirituales para vencer à si mismo, y, ordenar su vida, sin determinarse por afeccion alguna que desordenada sea.* This means that one should aim at coming out of the Exercises altered and transformed into another man. *And thou shalt be changed into another man,* said Samuel to Saul (I Kings x. 6)—*into a perfect man,* says St. Paul. (Eph. iv. 13). It should be seen in a man's subsequent proceedings that he has made the Exercises. If before he was a lover of talking and losing time, let it be seen that now he is a lover of silence and recollection; if before he was a lover of comfort and his own ease, let it be seen that now he is a lover of mortification and penance; if before he spoke biting words, that henceforth he speaks them no more; if before he was lax and careless in the observance of rules and made no account of little things, that from this time forth he is very obedient and very exact and takes account of things quite small and minute and by the grace of the Lord does not fall into any deliberate fault. For if a man is to continue exhibiting the same evil propensities and faults and come out just as he went in, what is the good of the Exercises?

St. Ambrose (De Poenitentia ii. c. 10) has a story of a young man; and as he tells it, we may tell it also. This young man had gone wrong. He had occasion to take a long journey, and during that time he changed his mind. He came back to his native town and, meeting his former companion, he gave her a wide berth. She was surprised; and thinking that he had not recognized her, she went up to him and said: "I am Harriet." He replied: "But I am not Harry." He was a changed man. In this way we should change and transform ourselves so as to be able to say with the Apostle: *I live, now not I,* not I that lived of old under the Law, and persecuted the Church, *but Christ liveth in me* (Gal. ii. 20). And this, says St. Ambrose, is what Christ our Redeemer means by saying: *If anyone will come after me, let him deny himself* (Matt. xvi. 24); let him change himself into another man and contrive not to be what he used to be. Of our Father Francis Borgia it is related in his Life how he conveyed the body of the empress to Granada, how the Lord there gave him great light and opened his eyes to the vanity of the world by that spectacle of death which he had before him, and how on his return to court, as he says, he seemed to find the court quite changed. It was himself that had been changed and transformed by the knowledge and enlightenment that God had given him. In this way, then, we should come out of the Exercises with the new light and awakening to reality that the Lord is wont to impart in them.

The third thing that we should set our eyes on to gain from the Exercises follows from the former; it is the gaining of some virtue and some point of perfection, particularly that which we are in greatest need of; for the rooting out of vices is done to plant virtues in their stead. "Two things," says that holy man (Thomas à Kempis), "aid much to advancement; the one is to turn away with a vigorous effort from what one's nature is viciously inclined to"—here you have the former thing insisted on—"and to labor earnestly for the virtue that is most wanting to us"—which is this third thing. So the Directory to the Exercises, treating (Chapter 6) of the way in which we of the Society should make use of them, observes that we should not spend all the time on the first week, two or three days being sufficient for that, but should pass on to the other meditations which involve greater perfection.

Among other suggestions there made is this, that from time to time we should take up some leading rules in which are contained all the perfection we could desire; as the rule that says that, as worldly men love and seek with great diligence honors, fame, and the repute of a great name upon earth, so we should love and intensely desire the contrary. Take to heart in retreat the gaining of this perfection and the attainment of this degree of humility, that you rejoice as much under ignominies and affronts, under injuries and false testimonies, as worldly men rejoice in honor and reputation. If you do that, you will remain master of many strivings and foolish impulses that usually come in our way, to being held in honor and repute, one man for his learning, another in the discharge of his office, another in his ministrations and management of business—trifles that get in the way and greatly impede our spiritual perfection. Take to heart another time the rule that says: "Let all in all things endeavor to serve and please the Divine Goodness purely for Itself, rather than for fear of punishments or hope of rewards." Try to attain to this purity of intention, that you seek not your own interest in anything, neither little nor great, neither temporal nor eternal, but in all things desire purely the will and glory of God, that being your satisfaction, forgetful of yourself and of your own advancement and convenience. Take to heart another time the gaining of a most perfect conformity to the will of God, taking all things that occur, great and small, in whatever manner and by whatever way or means they come, as coming from the hand of God. On these and the like points of perfection we should fix our gaze when we go into retreat to make the Exercises, and not stop till we do gain them.

CHAPTER XXVII

Some Directions That Will Help Us to Profit More by These Exercises

TO make better profit of the Spiritual Exercises and gather from them the fruit that we have said, it is to be observed, first, that, as we have said above, when a man sets about meditation, not only should he have arranged beforehand the points that he is to meditate on, but also the fruit that he is to gather therefrom. So, also, on being about to make the Exercises, a man must bring prepared in detail what he is to gather from them. Before going into retreat he must look and consider with himself very leisurely and attentively: "What is the greatest spiritual necessity that I have?" "What is that to which my vicious nature or my passions or my evil habits most incline me?" "What is it that makes war on my soul?" "What is there in me that may offend and disedify my brothers?" And this is what he must keep before his eyes to get from the Exercises and to resolve effectually to amend. This is a very good preparation for entering on the Exercises. And it must be observed that, when one goes into retreat, one should not fix one's eyes on the attainment of a very high prayer, nor think that by shutting himself up in retreat he is to have at once easy access to God with much quiet and attention; for it may be that he will have more distractions, more disturbances and temptations, than he had in his offices and ministries; but he must put before his eyes the gaining of what we have said, and make a resolution thereon in all earnestness. That gained, he will make a good retreat, though he may not have the devotion that he desired; and if that is not gained, though from the beginning to the end he melted in tears and devotion, he will not have made a good retreat, for that is not the end of retreat, but the other.

That direction also will be a great help which our Father gives us and wishes us always to observe in meditation; that as soon as the hour of meditation is over, the exercitant, for the space of a quarter of an hour or thereabouts, sitting or walking up and down, should make an examination of his meditation and take account how he has succeeded in it; and if it has gone badly, let him look into the cause thereof; let him look and see whether he had the exercise well prepared beforehand, whether he gave way to strange and irrelevant thoughts, whether he let himself be overcome by sleep, whether he dwelt excessively in speculation of the understanding, whether his heart was languid and remiss at meditation, whether he took no pains to exercise affections of the will, whether his intention was not as pure as it should have been, seeking rather consolation than the divine will. And if he finds he has been at fault, let him repent thereof and purpose amendment henceforth; but if he finds that the thing has gone well, let him return thanks to God our Lord and contrive to do things in the same manner in the remaining meditations.

This instruction is of great importance because, in the first place, by means of this examination and reflection on how one has got on at meditation, a person gains experience how things go badly and how they go well, to avoid the one and follow the other; thus spiritual discernment is acquired, and that mastery of the subject that springs from experimental knowledge. On this account our Father set much store by this examination and reflection as a means to make us masters, not only in this, but also in our other exercises and ministries. So he says in the Fourth Part of his Constitutions that it will be a great help to a confessor to do his office well if, after he has heard a confession, he makes reflection to see and consider if he has committed any fault in that confession, especially if he is a beginner, to correct himself another time and by dint of blundering learn to hit well. For this end, also, is made the examination of meditation. Meditation is so valuable, and it so much behooves us to get into the way of making it well, and steadily to banish the faults that we commit in it, that our Father, not content with the examen that we are wont to make every day at noon and night, would have us examine our meditation on the spot immediately after concluding it.

The second thing that we have to do in this examination of our meditation, and a very important thing, must be to see what was the fruit that we have drawn therefrom and apply ourselves to drive it home anew, as when people repeat a lecture and draw out in black and white its conclusions and truths and make a sort of epitome of them. So much account must be made of this examination that, when one cannot find time to make it after the meditation, it should be made in the meditation itself at the end of it.

We may add here another point, which is this, that it will be a good plan for a man to note down what he gathers from the meditation, putting in writing, not at length, but briefly, the desires and purposes that he draws from it and also some truths and illustrations or discoveries of error which the Lord is wont to give therein, sometimes concerning certain virtues, sometimes concerning the mysteries meditated. Such we read to have been the practice of our first Fathers, our blessed Father Ignatius and Father Peter Faber, and we have some things of theirs that they wrote thereon. Father Francis Xavier also was accustomed to do the same, as we read in his Life; and in the Directory to the Exercises this advice is also given. Also our Father General Claudius Aquaviva recommends it to us in the "Industriae" that he wrote, treating of meditation. And besides the fact that thereby our purposes and desires are brought more to a head, we find by experience how profitable it is for a man to read these things long afterwards; for, being his own, and he having felt them as they stand, they make more impression on him than other things, and he readily comes to appreciate them again; and seeing that since that time he no longer comes up to that point he had then attained and instead of advancing is going back, he is ashamed at no longer being what he once was. Thus either he is animated to go back to the old standard of perfection or at least to make up by shame for his falling short of perfection. So this practice will always be profitable, particularly at the time of the Exercises.

Lastly, I say that if ever there is a time when it is good to give an account of one's conscience and of one's prayer to some spiritual man, as we shall say afterwards, it will be at this time particularly; and for not humbling themselves to this some do not gather the fruit that they should gather from the Exercises.

CHAPTER XXVIII

Of Spiritual Reading, How Important It Is, and of Sundry Means That Will Help Us to Make It Well and Profitably

READING is the sister of prayer and a great aid thereto. So the Apostle Paul advises his disciple Timothy to attend to it. *Attend to reading* (I Tim. iv. 13). Of such importance is this spiritual reading for anyone who is trying to serve God that St. Athanasius says in an exhortation to his religious: "You will find none in earnest about his spiritual progress who does not give time to spiritual reading." St. Jerome in his letter to Eustochium strongly recommends her to give herself to this holy reading: "Let sleep creep over you," he says, "holding a book, and let the sacred page receive your drooping face"—*Tenenti codicem somnus obrepat, et cadentem faciem pagina sancta suscipiat.* All the saints greatly recommend this spiritual reading, and experience well shows us how profitable it is, since histories are full of the great conversions which the Lord has wrought by this means.

Because this reading is such a chief and important means for our advancement, the founders of religious orders, resting on the doctrine of the Apostle and the authority and experience of the saints, have ordained that their religious should make spiritual reading every day. Of the blessed St. Benedict, Humbertus says that he ordered that every day there should be a set time for this reading; and along with that he ordered that at that time two of the most ancient monks should go round visiting the monastery to see if there was anyone who left the duty out or hindered the rest. Thereby will be seen what importance he attached to it; and, by the way, it will also be understood that these visits, which it is customary to make every day here in religion during spiritual duties, are founded on the teaching and experience of the saints of old. For the first and second time St. Benedict ordered that the delinquent should be corrected mildly; but if he did not amend, that they should correct him and give him such a penance that the rest should fear and take warning. In the Society we have a rule for this spiritual reading, which says: "Let all twice a day give the time that is appointed for examen of conscience, prayer, meditation, and reading with all diligence in the Lord;" and the superior and prefect of spiritual things take care that everyone should always set aside some time for this. And speaking generally, this is a means commonly used by all who aim at virtue and perfection; and so that all may practise it with greater fruit, we will mention some things that will help thereto.

St. Ambrose, exhorting us to give to prayer and spiritual reading all the time we can, says: "Why do you not fill up with reading or with prayer all the spare time you have?

Why do you not go to visit Christ our Lord and converse with Him and hear Him? For when we pray, we converse with God; and when we read, we listen to God"—*Deum alloquimur cum oramus: illum audimus cum divina legimus oracula.* Let this, then, be the first means to make profit of spiritual reading, to make account that God is speaking to us and telling us that which we read there. St. Augustine also assigns this means: "When you read you should make account that God is telling you what you read, not merely that you may know it, but that you may fulfil and put it in execution." And he adds another very good and devout consideration. "Do you know," he says, "how we should read Holy Scripture? As when a person reads letters that have come from his native country, to see what news we have of heaven. We should read to see what the Scriptures have to tell us of our native land, where we have our parents and brethren, our friends and fellow citizens, and where we are desiring and sighing ourselves to be."

St. Gregory says that Holy Scripture—and the same may be said of any other spiritual reading—is as a looking-glass put before the eyes of the soul that therein we may see our interior, the good and evil about us, the progress we are making, or how far we are from perfection. These good books tell us sometimes of the admirable doings of the saints to animate us to imitate them, that seeing their great victories and triumphs we may not be discouraged at our own temptations and trials. At other times they recount to us not only their virtues, but their falls, that by the one we may know what we have to imitate and by the other what we have to fear. So they put before us at one time a Job who rose like the crest of a wave to temptation, at another time a David who was overthrown thereby, that the one may animate us to confidence in the midst of trials and the other may make us humble and afraid in the midst of successes and consolations, that we should never have a secure confidence in ourselves, but walk always with great caution and reserve. So says St. Augustine: "You will, then, read Holy Writ to the best advantage if you use it as a mirror to see therein the image of your soul, striving to correct and remove whatever is there reprehended as unsightly and evil and to adorn and beautify it with the examples and virtues that you read of there."

But, coming down more into detail as to the manner we should adopt herein, it is to be observed that for this reading to be profitable, it must not be done hastily or at a gallop, as when one reads stories, but very leisurely and attentively; for as an impetuous flow of water and a heavy shower does not penetrate or fertilize the earth, but gentle small rain; so for reading to enter and be drunk in by the heart, the reading must be done with pausing and pondering. And it is good, when we find any devout passage, to dwell on it a little and make there a sort of station, thinking over what is read and trying to move the affections of the will in the way that we do at meditation. At meditation, indeed, this is done more leisurely; we dwell more on things and ruminate and digest them more; but it should also be done in its way at spiritual reading. So the saints advise, and say that spiritual reading should be like the drinking of a hen, that drinks a little and then lifts up its head, and once more again drinks a little and again lifts up its head.

Hereby is seen how reading is sister and companion to meditation; so much so that, when we wish to start a person at mental prayer and would go with him little by little according as the disposition of the person requires, we counsel him first of all to read devout books, making in the reading proper stations and pauses, as has been said; for thereby the Lord is often wont to raise a person to mental prayer. And also in the case of others, who cannot get into meditation and fancy they can make nothing of it, they are usually advised to take some book and join prayer with reading, reading a little and meditating and praying thereupon and then again reading a little; for in this way the understanding being, as it were, tied to the words of the reading, it finds no room to pour itself out in divers imaginations and thoughts as it did when it was free and loose. Thus we may combine meditation with reading. This is why the saints so much recommend spiritual reading, giving it almost the same praises and commendations that they give to meditation. They say it is the spiritual food of the soul, making her strong and steady against temptations; that it engenders in her good thoughts and desires of heaven; that it gives light to our understanding and inflames and kindles the will; that it drives away worldly sadness and causes true cheerfulness, spiritual and according to God, and other such things.

The blessed St. Bernard gives another admonition, how to make profit of spiritual reading. He says: "He who applies himself to reading should seek not so much science as savor"—*Non tam quaerat scientiam quam saporem.* Mere knowledge of the understanding is a dry thing if it does not reach the will, feeding the affections and nourishing devotion; for that is what makes reading juicy and fruitful, and is the end and purpose thereof. This is a very important admonition, since there is a great difference between reading for knowledge and reading for spiritual advancement, between reading for others and reading for oneself; the former is study, the latter is spiritual reading. If in reading you set your eyes on knowing things or on gathering matter for subsequent preaching or talking to others, that will be studying for others, and not spiritual reading for your own advancement. There will be other times for that. *Everything has its time* (Eccles. iii. 1). The time of spiritual reading is not for that, but for what we have said.

The saints also recommend us not to read much at one sitting, nor get through many pages, not to weary the spirit with lengthy reading instead of refreshing it; very good and necessary advice for certain persons who seem to place their happiness in reading much and getting through many books. As the body is not nourished by much eating, but by good digestion of what one does eat; so neither is the soul nourished by reading much, but by ruminating and well digesting what is read. For the same reason they say also that spiritual reading should not be of difficult things, but of plain things, rather devout than difficult, since difficult things are apt to fatigue and dry up devotion. Hugo of St. Victor quotes an example of a servant of God who was admonished by revelation to drop the reading of those things, and read the lives and martyrdom of the saints and other plain and devout things, whereby he profited much.

St. Bernard goes on again to say: "Something of our daily reading should every day be taken down into the stomach of memory, there to be more minutely digested, and thence again brought up and ruminated again and again—something to our purpose, something that makes for the end we have in view, something to engage our attention so that it may have no inclination to wander away to strange ground." As we do not eat our daily meals simply for pastime, but that on the strength of the sustenance we take we may be able to work all that day and all our life long; so our reading, which is the food and spiritual sustenance of the soul inasmuch as it is the words of God, is not meant merely to give us good occupation for the time of reading, but to profit us all the day after. To this end it will be a good practice, before we begin to read, to raise our heart to God and beg this grace that we may drink in and well take to heart what we read, thereby to become more earnest in pursuit of virtue, more disabused of error, more determined to do what behooves us. So we read that blessed Gregory was wont to prefix prayer to his reading and say: *Depart from me, ye malignant, and I will search into the commandments of my God* (Psalm cxviii. 115).

That we may set a higher value on this reading and animate ourselves the more to it, the saints compare spiritual reading with hearing the word of God and say that, though reading has not the liveliness of the living voice, it has other advantages which sermons have not. In the first place, a preacher cannot be at hand at all times like a good book. Secondly, a happy saying of a preacher passes off into the air and so cannot have so great an effect upon me; but a good thing said in a book may be turned over again and again, ruminated and pondered, and so take greater effect. Thirdly, in a good book I find a good and outspoken counselor; for, as a philosopher said well, what at times a friend or adviser dare not tell me, a book will tell me fearlessly, and warn me of my vices and defects, scold me and exhort me. Fourthly, by reading I enter into conversation with those who have written the book; at one time I can go and have a period of conversation with St. Gregory, at another time with St. Basil, at another with St. Chrysostom, hear them and listen to what they say, as if I were then their disciple. So they say, and with good reason, that good books are a public treasure for the great benefits and riches that we can draw from thence.

Finally, such are the advantages and profits that follow from spiritual reading that St. Jerome, treating of the inward fire of the soul, asks: "Where is this fire?" and answers: "Doubtless, in the Holy Scriptures, by the reading whereof the soul is set on fire with God and purified from all vices." And he quotes to this effect what the disciples said, when Christ our Redeemer had appeared to them on the road to Emmaus: *Was not our heart burning within us, while he spoke to us on the way, and laid open to us the Scriptures?* (Luke xxiv. 32). And to the same effect the psalmist: *The utterances of the Lord are holy utterances, silver tested by fire* (Psalm xi. 7). And St. Ambrose: "That the reading of Holy Writ is life, the Lord Himself witnesses, saying: *The words that I have spoken to you are spirit and life* (John vi. 64)." Therefore, that we may live a spiritual life and walk always in the spirit, inflamed with the love of God, let us give ourselves much to spiritual reading and practise it in the manner that has been said.

Hence it follows that they do ill who, once having read a good book, throw it into a corner and say: "I have done with that." A good book is not meant to be read once over only; the second time over it will do you more good, and the third time more, and so you will ever find it new, as they find by experience who have a desire to profit. That is a very good thing also which some do; when they find anything in a book that moves them much and gives them particular satisfaction they take a note and mark it, to have always at hand some arguments of greater weight and cogency, matter wherein they are more likely to find some marrow of devotion and consolation suitable to the several times and occasions that occur.

Out of many examples of the good of spiritual reading, I will borrow one from St. Augustine that is very instructive. St. Augustine, then, tells the story how an African knight named Poticianus came one day to pay him a visit and gave him news of the wonders that were publicly related of the blessed St. Anthony. He went on to say that one afternoon, when the emperor was in the city of Treves, taken up with witnessing certain public games which were being celebrated there, himself and three friends belonging to the court went out for a stroll in the country. Two of them, apart from the rest, went into the cell of a monk and found there a book in which was written the life of St. Anthony. One of them began to read it; and suddenly, his heart set on fire with holy love and disgusted with himself, he said to his friend: "Tell me, I pray, what is it that we aim at gaining with all our labors that we undergo, fighting so many years in so many wars? Can we possibly come to any better fortune in the palace than to be what is called within the inner circle of the emperor? But in that state what is there that is not precarious and fraught with great danger? And is it to this so great danger that we are making our way through heaven knows how many other dangers? But if I want to be a friend of God, I can be so at once." Saying these words, in labor with the birth of a new life within him, he cast his eyes once more on the book, and underwent an inward change and was detached from all the things of the world, as appeared at once; for, after he had done reading, great waves of emotion rose in his heart, and he said with a deep sigh to his friend: "Now I am quiet and at ease; I have renounced our hopes and expectations and am determined to serve God, and from this hour I mean to stay in this place; if you do not care to imitate me, do not try to divert me from my purpose." The other answered that he could not separate from him, nor cease to bear him company in the hope of such a reward. So they both began to raise the spiritual edifice and follow Christ at the due cost, which was the abandonment of all things. And what was no less wonderful, both were married, and their wives, when they heard of the case, consecrated themselves to God and made a vow of virginity. St. Augustine relates this story, and it was to him a very moving example, so much so that on the spot he cried out to a friend in great excitement of mind, saying: "What are we doing? What is this that you have heard? The unlearned rise up and carry off the kingdom of heaven, and we with all our learning are being plunged into the abyss!" So complaining and so feeling, the saint says that he went into a garden that he had there and threw himself under a fig tree and gave free vent to his tears. With great anguish and trouble of heart he began to say: "How long, O Lord, how long art Thou going to be displeased with me? Is there to be no end to Thy anger? Remember not, O Lord, our former iniquities!" And he went on repeating time after time these words: "How long? How long?

Tomorrow, tomorrow. Why not today? Why not today put an end to my turpitudes?" And saying this with great emotion, he heard a voice which said to him: "Take and read; take and read." Then he says he rose to take up a holy book that he had by him to read in. For he had heard of that same Anthony, that upon one reading of the Gospel which he happened to hear, which said: *Go, sell all that thou hast and give to the poor, and come follow me, and thou shalt have treasure in heaven* (Matt. xix. 21), he had determined to leave all things and follow Christ. Moved by this example and still more by the voice that he had heard, he says he took the book and began to read in it; and there and then God poured upon him such a great light that he left all things in the world and gave himself entirely over to the service of God.

SIXTH TREATISE

ON THE PRESENCE OF GOD

CHAPTER I

Of the Excellence of This Exercise and the Great Benefits That It Contains

SEEK *the Lord with strength and perseverance,* says the Prophet David; *seek his face ever* (Psalm civ. 4). The face of the Lord, says St. Augustine, is the presence of the Lord. Thus to seek the face of the Lord ever, is to walk ever in His presence, turning the heart to Him with great desire and love. St. Bonaventure says that to walk always in this exercise of the presence of God is to enter on the bliss of heaven here on earth, since the bliss and happiness of the saints consists in seeing God continually without ever losing sight of Him. Since in this present life we cannot see God clearly as He is—that is proper to the blessed—let us at least imitate them in such way as we can and our frail nature allows, by striving to be ever regarding, looking up to, and loving God. As God our Lord has created us to stand eternally before Him in heaven and enjoy His presence there, so He would have us here on earth attain to some first sketch and outline of that blessedness by ever walking in His presence, looking up to Him and reverencing Him, albeit in the twilight. *Now we see in a glass darkly, but then face to face* (I Cor. xiii. 12). That clear vision is the reward and glory and blessedness that we hope for; this dim twilight apprehension is the meritorious means whereby we are to arrive thither. But, after all, we do imitate the saints in such fashion as we can, trying never to lose sight of God in the actions which we do. The saints and angels who are sent to our aid to guard and defend us, discharge these ministries in such a way as never to lose sight of God. So said the Angel Raphael to Toby: *I seemed to eat and drink with you, but I used another invisible food, and another drink that cannot be seen by men*

(Tob. xii. 19), being sustained by God. *The angels ever see the face of my Father who is in heaven* (Matt. xviii. 10). We in like manner, though we eat and drink, converse and deal with men, and seemingly are altogether taken up therewith, ought to contrive that that should not be our food and entertainment, but another invisible food that men see not, which is ever to be regarding and loving God and doing His most holy will.

Great was the exercise which the saints and those holy patriarchs found in walking ever in the presence of God. *I kept the Lord ever before my eyes, because he is ever at my right hand that I may not slip* (Psalm xv. 8). The Royal Prophet was not satisfied with praising God seven times a day, but he aimed at keeping God ever before him. This exercise was so continual with those holy men that their common manner of speech was: *As the Lord liveth, in whose presence I stand* (III Kings xvii. 1). Great are the benefits and advantages which follow from walking ever before God, considering that He is looking at us; and therefore the saints made such efforts in that direction, since that is enough to secure a man's behaving in a very orderly and very proper manner in all that he does. Otherwise, tell me, what servant is there whose behavior is not quite correct in presence of his master? What servant so bold as in presence of his master not to do what the master bids him, or dare to offend him to his face? What thief would dare to steal, seeing the judge looking on hard by? But God is looking at us: He is our Judge, He is all-powerful, He can make the earth open and swallow down to hell the man who offends Him; who shall dare to offend such a God? And so St. Augustine: "When I consider, O Lord, that Thou beholdest me always and watchest over me night and day with as much care as if in heaven and on earth Thou hadst no other creature to govern but myself alone; when I consider well that all my actions, thoughts, and desires lie open clearly before Thee, I am all full of fear and covered with shame." Certainly we are under great obligation to live justly and righteously from the consideration that we do all things under the eyes of a Judge Who sees all things and from Whom nothing can be hidden. If here the presence of a grave personage puts us on our good behavior, what should the presence of God do!

St. Jerome, on the saying of God to Jerusalem by the Prophet Ezechiel, *Thou hast forgotten me* (Ezech. xxii. 12), says: "The remembrance of God banishes all sins." St. Ambrose says the same. And in another place St. Jerome says: "The remembrance of God and the walking in His presence is such an efficacious motive that we should never do anything to displease God if we remembered that He is present and beholds us." For Thais, the sinner, this thought was enough to make her give up her evil life and go into the desert to do penance, as we have said above (Treatise V, Chapter 16). Holy Job said: *Are not all my ways under his eyes, and does he not count all my steps?* (Job xxxi. 4). God is looking at me as an eyewitness, and is counting my steps; who should dare to sin or to do any duty badly?

On the other hand, all the disorder and perdition of the wicked come from their not remembering that God is present and is beholding them; this is what Holy Scripture goes repeating many times, speaking in the person of the wicked: *There is none that seeth me* (Isaias xlvii. 10): *He will not see our ways* (Jerem. xii. 4). St. Jerome has noted this in the twenty-third chapter of Ezechiel, where the prophet reproaches Jerusalem with many vices and sins, and sums up the cause of them all in the fact of her having forgotten God. And the same cause is assigned in many other passages of Scripture. As a horse without a bridle, and a ship without a rudder, goes upon rocks and destruction; so when this bridle is removed, man is carried away by his disorderly appetites and passions. *He keepeth not God before his eyes,* says the Prophet David, *nor sees him present before him, and therefore his ways,* that is, his works, *are stained with faults at all time* (Psalm ix. 5).

As for the blessed St. Basil, the remedy that he gives in many places for all temptations and troubles and for all untoward events and occasions that may occur, is the presence of God. Thus, if you want a brief and compendious method of attaining perfection, a method that contains and embraces in itself the strength and efficacy of all other methods, here it is; and therefore God taught it to Abraham: *Walk before me, and be perfect* (Gen. xvii. 1). Here as in other places of Scripture the imperative is taken for the future, to emphasize the infallibility of success. It is so certain that you will be perfect, if you live always looking at God and observing that He is looking at you, that from that point you may give yourself out for such. For as the stars from the aspect of the sun, which they have present and to which they look, draw light to shine within and without themselves, and virtue to influence the earth; so just men, who are as stars in the Church of God, from the aspect of God, from seeing Him as present and turning their thought and desire to Him, draw light whereby they shine with true and solid virtues in their interior, which God sees; and on the exterior, which men see, they shine with all decency and comeliness and draw virtue and force to edify and advance others. There is nothing that illustrates so well the need that we have of keeping ever in the presence of God as this comparison. Mark the dependence that the moon has on the sun and the need that it has of keeping ever before it. The moon of itself has no light, but only what it receives from the sun according to the aspect wherewith it regards it. It works on sublunary bodies according to the light which it receives from the sun, and so the effects wrought on them wax and wane according to the waxing and waning of the moon. And if any object gets in front of the moon, so as to disturb the aspect and sight of the sun, in that instant at once the moon is eclipsed and loses its light and splendor, and withal a great part of its efficacy to work, which it holds by means of the light. The soul stands in the same relation to God, Who is its sun.

This is why the saints so much recommend to us this practice. St. Ambrose and St. Bernard, speaking of the constancy and perseverance which we should have in it, say that, as there is no instant or moment in which man does not enjoy the bounty and mercy of God, so there should not be any instant or moment in which he does not keep God present in his memory. *Sicut nullum est momentum quo homo non utatur vel fruatur Dei bonitate et misericordia, sic nullum debet esse momentum quo eum praesentem non habet in memoria.* And elsewhere St. Bernard says: "In all his actions and in all his thoughts the religious should endeavor to remember that he is in the presence of God; and all the time that he is not thinking of God he should hold for lost. God never forgets us; it would be right that we should try never to forget Him." St. Augustine on the verse, *I will fix mine eyes upon thee* (Psalm xxxi. 8), says: "Lord, I will not turn my eyes away from Thee, since Thou never turnest Thine from me." And the prophet: *Mine eyes are ever fixed on the Lord* (Psalm xxiv. 15). St. Gregory Nazianzen says our remembrance of God should be as often and as frequent as our breathing, and even more: *Non tam saepe respirare quam Dei meminisse debemus.* For as we need to breathe to refresh the heart and temper the natural heat, so we need to have recourse to God in prayer to restrain the disorderly ardor of concupiscence, which keeps stimulating and exciting us to sin.

CHAPTER II

In What This Practice of Walking Always in the Presence of God Consists

THAT we may be able better to profit by this practice, it is necessary to explain in what it consists. It consists in two points, that is, in two acts, one of the understanding, the other of the will. The first act is that of the understanding, which is always required and presupposed for any act of the will, as philosophy teaches. The first thing, then, must be to consider with the understanding that God is here and in every place, that He fills the whole world, that He is whole in the whole, and whole in every part and in every creature, how small soever it be. Of this we should make an act of faith, since this is a truth that faith proposes for our belief. *He is not far from each one of us, since in him we live and move and have our being* (Acts xvii. 27-28). You must not imagine God as far from you or outside of you, since He is within you; "I sought, O Lord," says St. Augustine, "outside of me Him Whom I held within me." He is within you. God is within me with a more intimate and inward presence than that whereby I am in myself; in Him we live and move and have our being. It is He Who gives life to all that lives, and strength to all that has power, and being to all that has being. But for His sustaining presence all things would cease to be and fall back into nothing. Then consider that you are in God, surrounded and encompassed by God, swimming in God. Those words, *Heaven and earth are full of thy glory* (Isaias vi. 3), are very good words to express this.

Some may help themselves further herein by considering the whole world full of God, as indeed it is, and imagining themselves in the midst of this infinite sea of Godhead, surrounded and encompassed therewith as a sponge would be in the midst of the sea, all soaked and full of water within and all surrounded and encompassed with water on all sides without. And this is not a bad comparison for our limited understanding, though it falls far short and wants much of declaring what we mean. For this sponge in the midst of the sea, if it rises up, strikes the surface and if it sinks down, strikes the bottom and if it is carried to one side or the other, it strikes the shore; but in God there is nothing of that. *If I ascend into heaven, thou art there; if I go down into hell, thou art there; if I take wings in the morning, and fix my abode on the furthest verge of the sea, there also thy hand shall guide me and thy right hand shall hold me* (Psalm cxxxviii. 8-10). There is no end or boundary to God, for He is immense and infinite. And, further, as the sponge after all is a body, it cannot be entirely penetrated by the water, which is another body; but we are entirely and all throughout penetrated by God, Who is a pure spirit. But, after all, these and other like comparisons, though they fall short, are helpful and good to give us to understand in some sort the infinite immensity of God and His intimate presence within us; and therefore St. Augustine alleges them.

Nevertheless, it is to be observed on this practice that, to realize this presence of God, it is not necessary to form any idea or representation of God by means of the imagination, fancying that He is here at our side or in any other definite place, or to imagine Him as having such or such form and figure. There are those who imagine Jesus Christ our Redeemer in front of them or by their side, and that He goes with them and is ever looking at them in all that they do, and in this manner they walk always in the presence of God. And of these, some imagine they see before them Christ crucified, others as bound to the pillar, others in the prayer in the Garden, sweating drops of blood, others in some other stage of the Passion or in some joyful mystery of His most holy life, according to what strikes each of them most; or at one time they imagine Him in some stage, at another in another. And although this is very good, if it can be done, yet commonly speaking it is not what is best for us, since all these figures and imaginations of bodily things are wearisome and fatiguing and go far to break people's heads. A St. Bernard and a St. Bonaventure must have known how to do this sort of thing differently from us, and find in it much ease and relief. Thus they entered into those gaping wounds of Christ and found their way into His side, and that was their fortress and their refuge and their place of repose, thinking they heard those words of the spouse in the Canticles: *Arise, my love, my beautiful one, and come, my dove who dwellest in the holes of the rock and in the hollow of the wall* (Cant. ii. 13-14). At other times they imagined the foot of the Cross planted in their heart, and received in their mouth with the greatest sweetness some drops of the blood that ran and streamed from the fountains of the Savior. *Ye shall draw waters with joy from the fountains of the Savior* (Isaias xii. 3). It was all very well for these saints to do this, and they found much good in the exercise; but if you were to try to spend the whole day in these considerations and in this presence of God, you might carry on in this manner for one day or one month, but you would lose a whole year of prayer because you would break your head over it.

The reasonableness of this remark will well appear from this fact. Even for making the composition of place, which is one of the preludes to meditation whereby we try to render present to ourselves the subject of our meditation, imagining the event actually to be happening before our eyes, writers on prayer observe that the imagination must not be drawn on too much in representing the shape of these corporeal things thought of, lest you break your head and come in for other awkward consequences and illusions that may happen thereby. Now if for a prelude to meditation, which is done in so short a time, calmly and at leisure, without involving anything else that requires attention, so much wariness and caution is necessary, what must it be to endeavor all day long and in the midst of other occupations to preserve this composition?

But this presence of God which we speak of here, excludes all these imaginations and considerations and is very far removed from them, since in the first place it is not necessary to feign that He is here, but to believe it, since such is the truth. Christ our Redeemer, inasmuch as He is man, is in heaven and in the Blessed Sacrament of the altar, but He is not in every place; and so when we imagine Christ present as man, it is an imagination that we frame to ourselves; but as God He is present here and in me and in every place; He fills it all. *The Spirit of the Lord hath filled the round of the earth* (Wisdom i. 7). We have no need to imagine what is not, only to rouse ourselves and believe what is. Secondly, the humanity of Christ our Lord may be imagined and figured by the imagination, since He has a body and a figure, but God as God cannot be imagined or figured as He is, for He has neither body nor figure, but is a pure spirit. Even an angel we cannot imagine as he is, nor our own soul either, for it is a spirit; how much less can we imagine or visualize God as He is!

But how are we to consider God as present? I say that we can do no more than make an act of faith, presupposing that God is here present without seeking to know how or in what manner, as St. Paul says Moses did: *Invisibilem tanquam videns sustinebat*—"God being invisible, he considered and held him present as if he saw Him (Heb. xi. 27), without seeking to know or imagine the way in which He is. It is as when one converses with a friend at night, without dwelling on the manner of his presence nor remembering that at all, but simply rejoicing and delighting in the conversation and presence of such a friend. In this manner we must consider God as present; it is enough to know that God is here as our friend to rejoice in Him. Stay not to look how He is present, a thing that you will never make out, because it is now nighttime for us. Hope for the day dawning; and when the morrow of the next life comes, then

God will discover Himself, and we shall be able to see Him clearly as He is. *When he shall appear, then we shall be like him, because we shall see him as he is* (I John iii. 2). Therefore did God appear to Moses in the cloud and shade, that you may not see Him, but only believe that He is present.

All that we have said so far belongs to the first act of the understanding, which must be presupposed. But we need to observe that the main part of this exercise does not consist in that; for not only must the understanding be occupied in beholding God present, but the will also must be occupied in desiring and loving God and uniting itself with Him; and in these acts of the will this exercise chiefly consists, of which we shall speak in the following chapter.

CHAPTER III

Of the Acts of the Will, in Which This Exercise Chiefly Consists, and How We Are to Practise Them

ST. BONAVENTURE in his "Mystical Theology" says that the acts of the will whereby we are to raise up our hearts to God in this holy exercise are ardent desires of the heart, wherewith the soul desires to unite herself to God in perfect love. They are inflamed affections; they are lively sighs which we heave from our innermost being, crying thereby to God; they are pious and loving affections of the will, spiritual wings, as it were, by which the will takes flight, extending itself upwards, rising farther and farther to union with God. These vehement and inflamed desires and affections of the heart are called by the saints "aspirations" because by them the soul lifts itself up to God, which is the same thing as to aspire after God; and also, as St. Bonaventure says, in the same way as by breathing we heave out breath from the interior of our body without thinking about it, so without thinking or almost without thinking, we heave out these inflamed desires from the interior of our heart. A man gives expression to these aspirations and desires by short and frequent prayers, which are called ejaculations, "thrown out rapidly"—*raptim iaculatas,* says St. Augustine, because they are as fiery darts and arrows coming forth from the heart and in an instant shot out and sent up to God. The monks of Egypt, as Cassian says, made great use of these prayers and set great value on them, partly because, being short, they do not tire the head, and again because, being made with fervor and elevation of spirit, they find their way in an instant into the presence of God and leave no room for the devil to disturb him who makes them, nor raise any obstacle in the heart. St. Augustine says some words worthy of the consideration of authors who treat of prayer: "That watchful and lively attention, which is necessary to pray with due reverence and respect, is not here relaxed and lost, as commonly happens in long prayers." By means of these ejaculatory prayers those holy monks succeeded in continually keeping up this exercise, lifting up their hearts very frequently to God, treating and conversing with Him.

This method of walking in the presence of God is commonly more appropriate for us, easier, and more profitable; but it will be needful to explain more at length the practice of this exercise. Cassian puts it in this verse: *Come unto my aid, O God; O Lord, make haste to help me* (Psalm lxix. 2), which the Church repeats at the beginning of every canonical hour. At the beginning of every business that has any danger in it, beg God to help you to come well out of it, using these words. In all things we need the Lord's favor and therefore we should be always asking it. Cassian says that this verse is marvelously well suited to express our sentiments in whatsoever state or occasion or happening we see ourselves. By it we invoke the help of God; by it we humble ourselves and acknowledge our need and misery; by it we brace ourselves up and trust in being heard and favored by God; by it we kindle in ourselves the love of the Lord, Who is our refuge and protector. For all the combats and temptations that may come in your way, you have here a strong shield, an impenetrable coat of mail, an impregnable wall. Thus you should ever have this ejaculation on your mouth and in your heart; it should be your perpetual and continual prayer and your means of walking ever in the presence of God. St. Basil puts the practice of this virtue in taking occasion of all things to remember God. Do you eat? Give thanks to God. Do you dress? Give thanks to God. Do you walk out into the field or the garden? Bless God, Who has created it. Do you look up to the sky? Do you look at the sun and all the rest? Praise the Creator of it all. When you sleep, every time you awake, bless God.

Others, seeing that in the spiritual life there are three ways—one purgative, for beginners; another illuminative, proper to those who are making progress; a third unitive, proper to the perfect—assign three sorts of aspirations and ejaculatory prayers. The first is for those whose object is to obtain pardon for their sins and to rid their soul of vices and earthly affections; and they belong to the purgative way. The second is for those who are aiming at gaining virtues and overcoming temptations and embracing difficulties and labors for virtue's sake; and they belong to the illuminative way. The third is for those who aim at attaining to the union of their soul with God by the bond of perfect love; and they belong to the unitive way. These authors wish each one to practise this exercise according to the state and condition in which he finds himself. But, as for that, however perfect anyone may be, he may well exercise himself in sorrow for his sins and begging God's pardon for them and grace never more to offend Him, and that will be a very good exercise and very pleasing to God. And he who is engaged in cleansing his soul of vices and disorderly passions and gaining virtues, may all the same exercise himself in love of God in order to gain that same end with greater ease and sweetness. And all may practise this exercise, sometimes with these acts: "O Lord, would that I had never offended Thee;" "Never permit me, Lord, to offend Thee;" "To die, yes, but not to sin;" "May I rather die a thousand deaths than fall into mortal sin." At other times one may raise up one's heart to God, giving Him thanks for benefits received, general and particular, or begging for sundry virtues, now a profound humility, now obedience, now charity, now patience. At other times one may raise one's heart to God with acts of love and conformity to His most holy will, as by saying: *My beloved to me, and I to him* (Cant. ii. 16); *Not my will, but Thine be done* (Luke xxii. 42); *What is there for me in heaven, and away from thee what have I desired on earth?* (Psalm lxxii. 25). These and the like are very good aspirations and ejaculatory prayers to enable one to walk always in this exercise of the presence of God. But the best and most effectual are generally those that the heart conceives of itself when moved by God, though they be not couched in words so well composed and orderly as those that we have quoted. Nor is it necessary, either, to have a multitude and variety of these prayers, since one single ejaculation repeated frequently and with great affection may suffice for one to carry on this exercise many days and even for a whole lifetime. If you find you get on well with ever saying those words of the Apostle: *Lord, what wouldst thou have me to do?* (Acts ix. 6), or those of the spouse, *My beloved to me, and I to him* (Cant. ii. 16), or those of the prophet, *What have I, O Lord, to desire in heaven or earth but thee?* (Psalm lxxii. 25), you need no more; stay and entertain yourself therein, and let that be your continual exercise of walking in the presence of God.

CHAPTER IV

Further Explanation of This Exercise, and a Method of Walking in the Presence of God Very Easy and Profitable and Leading to Great Perfection

AMONG other aspirations and ejaculatory prayers that we may use, the chiefest and most suitable for the practice of this exercise is that which the Apostle teaches: *Whether ye eat or drink, or whatever else ye do, do all for the glory of God* (I Cor. x. 31). Now you eat, now you drink, now you do something else—do all for the glory of God. Contrive in all things that you do, as frequently as you can, to lift up your heart to God, saying: "For Thee, O Lord, I do this, to satisfy and please Thee, because Thou so willest it; Thy will, O Lord, is my will, and Thy satisfaction my satisfaction; I will nothing and reject nothing but what Thou willest or rejectest; this is all my joy and all my satisfaction and delight, the accomplishment of Thy will, to please and satisfy Thee; I have nothing else to wish or desire, or set my eyes on, in heaven or on earth." This is an excellent way of living ever in the presence of God, very easy and profitable and carrying high perfection, since it is living in the continual exercise of the love of God. Here I will only add that this is one of the best and most profitable methods there are, of all that we can take up, of living in perpetual prayer. Nothing else would seem to be wanting to conclude and canonize and extol this exercise but to say that thereby we shall practise that continual prayer which Christ our Lord asks of us in the Gospel: *We must always pray, and never give up* (Luke xviii. 1). For what better prayer can there be than to be ever desiring the greater glory and honor of God, ever conforming oneself to His will, willing nothing and rejecting nothing but what God wills and rejects, and placing all one's joy and satisfaction in the joy and satisfaction of God?

Therefore a doctor says, and with good reason, that he who shall persevere diligently in this exercise of these inward affections and desires will derive such benefit from them that in a short time he will feel his heart vastly altered and changed and will find in himself a particular aversion for the world and a singular affection for God. *Ye are no longer strangers and foreigners, but fellow citizens of the saints and domestics of the house of God* (Eph. ii. 19). This is beginning to be citizens of heaven and henchmen of the house of God. These are those lords in waiting that St. John saw in the Apocalypse, who had the name of God written on their foreheads, that is, the continual memory and presence of God. *And they shall see his face, and have his name written on their foreheads* (Apoc. xxii. 4), for all their dealing and conversation is now no longer on earth, but in heaven. *Fixing our gaze not on the things that are seen, but on the things that are not seen, for the things that are seen are temporal, but the things that are unseen are eternal* (II Cor. iv. 18).

It is to be observed in this exercise that when we make these acts, saying: "For Thee, Lord, I do this, for Thy love, and because Thou so requirest," and the like, we should make them and say them as speaking to God present and not as lifting up our heart and thought far away from ourselves and out of ourselves. This observation is of great importance in this exercise, because this is properly walking in the presence of God, and this it is that makes this exercise sweet and easy and moves and profits us more. Even in other prayers, when we meditate on Christ on the Cross or at the pillar, writers on prayer advise us not to imagine this taking place there in Jerusalem, a thousand or so many years ago, because that is more wearisome and not so impressive; but we must imagine it in the present, going on there before our eyes, and that we hear the blows of the whips and the hammering in of the nails. And if we meditate the exercise on death, they say that we should imagine that we are now to die, given up by the doctors, and with the blessed candle in our hand. How much more reason will there be in this exercise of the presence of God to make the acts that we have said, not as speaking with one absent and away from us, but as speaking with God present, because the exercise itself requires it, and in sober truth it is so.

CHAPTER V

Of Some Differences and Advantages Which This Particular Exercise of Walking Always in the Presence of God Has over Others

TO evidence the perfection and profit of this particular exercise and further to declare the same, we will mention some points in which it differs, and differs for the better, from other methods. In the first place, in other methods which some are wont to bring forward of walking in the presence of God, all seems to be an act of the understanding and all seems to end in imagining God present; but in our method the act of understanding and of faith in God's presence is presupposed, and the soul passes on to make acts of the love of God, wherein our exercise principally consists; and it is clear that this is better and more profitable than the former. As in prayer we have said that we should not dwell on the act of the understanding, that is, the meditation and consideration of things, but on the act of the will, which consists in affections and desires of virtue and of the imitation of Christ, and this should be the fruit of the prayer; so here the principal thing in this exercise, and the best and the most profitable, lies in the acts of the will, and that is the thing we ought to lay stress on.

The second conclusion that follows is that this act is easier and pleasanter than the others because in the others there is need of discussion and labor of the understanding and imagination to set things forth and represent them—

a thing that is apt to weary people and break their heads, and so cannot be kept up so long; but in this exercise there is no need of such discussion, but solely of affections and acts of the will, which are made without fatigue. For, though it is true that there is here also some act of the understanding, yet that is presupposed by faith without our fatiguing ourselves over it; as, when we adore the Blessed Sacrament, we presuppose by faith that Christ our Savior is there, yet all our attention and occupation is in adoring, reverencing, loving, and asking favors of the Lord Whom we know to be there. So it is in this exercise. And by reason of its being easier one can hold on and persevere in it a longer time. So even with sick people who cannot otherwise make their prayer, we are wont to counsel them to raise their heart to God repeatedly with some acts and affections of the will, because that they can do with ease. Thus, though there were no other advantage in this exercise but this of our being able to hold on and persevere in it longer than in others, we should value it much; how much more, seeing that there are in it so many other advantages.

The third and principal thing, and a thing much to be taken notice of, is that the presence of God is not merely for us to dwell upon, but a means for us to do our ordinary actions well. If we were to content ourselves with merely paying attention to God as present, and thereby grow negligent in our duties and commit faults in them, that would be no good devotion, but an illusion. We must always make up our minds that, though with one eye we deal with His Divine Majesty, we are to fix the other on doing our works well for Him. The reflection that we are in the presence of God should be to us a motive for doing well and with greater perfection all that we do; and this is done much better by this exercise than by others. In other exercises the understanding is much occupied with those corporeal figures which we endeavor to set before us and by the thoughts that we seek to draw from what is before us. Now to draw out a good thought, a man often does not look well at what he is doing and so does it badly; but this exercise, involving no occupation of the understanding, nowise hinders the doing of our duties, but rather is a great aid to our doing them well, because we are doing them for the love of God and before God, Who is looking at us. So we endeavor to do them in such manner and so well that they may be fit to appear before the eyes of His Divine Majesty and have nothing in them unworthy of His presence.

SEVENTH TREATISE

ON THE EXAMEN OF CONSCIENCE

CHAPTER I

The Importance of Examination of Conscience

ONE of the principal and most efficacious means for our spiritual advancement is examination of conscience, and as such the saints recommend it. St. Basil, who was one of the earliest instructors to give rules for monks, commands them to make this examination every night. St. Augustine in his rule commands the same. St. Anthony Abbot taught and commended it much to his religious; so do St. Bernard and St. Bonaventure and Cassian and commonly all. The blessed St. Chrysostom, on those words of the Royal Prophet David: *Have compunction and shame for your sins upon your beds* (Psalm iv. 5), treats of this examination and advises its being made every night before we go to bed, for which he gives two good reasons. The first for the day following, that we may find ourselves better disposed and prepared not to sin nor to fall into the faults into which we have fallen today, because today we have examined ourselves and repented of them and made a purpose of amendment, which clearly will be a check upon us not to commit them again on the morrow. The second for the day itself; even today it will be some check upon us to have to examine ourselves at night, for the consciousness that we have to render an account and have our conduct overhauled that same day, will make us behave advisedly and live with greater reserve. As a master, says St. Chrysostom, does not allow his steward to fail to give in his accounts day by day, that there may be no chance of his being careless and forgetful and his reckoning's thereupon going wrong, so also it will be reasonable for us to call ourselves to account every day, that negligence and forgetfulness may not throw the accounts out.

St. Ephrem and St. John Climacus add a third reason, and say that, as diligent merchants every day make a computation and reckon the losses and gains of that day and if they find any loss, are very careful to make it up; so we should every day examine and take account of our losses and gains, that the loss may not go on increasing and swallow up the capital, but may be made good and remedied at once. St. Dorotheus adds another great advantage, which is that by dint of examining ourselves and pulling ourselves up every day for our faults, the vice and passion does not take root in us and grow into a habit and evil custom. On the other hand, they say of the soul that is not careful to examine herself that she is like the vineyard of the sluggard, of which the Wise Man says: *I passed by the field of the sluggard and the vineyard of the fool, and lo, it was all full of nettles, and the ground covered with thorns, and the stone wall was broken down* (Prov. xxiv. 30). Such is the soul that makes no account of examining her conscience; she is like an uncultivated vineyard, full of brambles and briers. This evil earth of our flesh never ceases to send up sundry evil weeds, and so it is ever necessary to go, hoe in hand, hoeing and rooting out the weeds and tares that are sprouting. The examen serves this purpose of a hoe, to make a clearance and root out the vice and evil propensity that was beginning to sprout, and not let it go farther or take root.

Not only the saints but even the heathen philosophers knew by the light of natural reason the importance and efficacy of this means. That great philosopher Pythagoras, as St. Jerome and St. Thomas relate, among other instructions that he gave to his disciples, gave them this as a main point, that everyone should have two times marked out, one in the morning and one at night, at which to examine himself and take account of three things—What have I done? How have I done it? And what have I left undone of what I ought to do?—rejoicing over what was good, and grieving over what was evil. Seneca, Plutarch, Epictetus, and others recommended the same.

Our blessed Father Ignatius, resting on the doctrine of the saints and on reason and experience, recommends to us examination of conscience as one of the chiefest and most effectual means that we can employ on our part for our improvement. And he gave us a rule thereon: "Let it be their practice every day to examine their consciences." And elsewhere he says that this should be done twice a day. And in some sort he esteemed this examination more than meditation because by the aid of examen we put in execution the resolutions we drew from meditation, to the mortification of our passions and the extirpation of our vices and defects. And so much account is made of it in the Society that we are called to it twice a day by sound of the bell, once in the morning and again at night, and we are visited at examen as at meditation, that none may omit making it either in the morning or at night. And our Father was not content that we ourselves should practise this examination, but he would have us persuade those with whom we deal to do the same. So the good workmen of the Society, in dealing with anyone, at once teach him to make the general examination of conscience and also the particular examen in order to get rid of any bad habit —such as swearing, lying, cursing, or the like. Such was the practice of our first Fathers, as we read of Father Peter Faber that this was one of the first devotions that he gave to those with whom he dealt. And we read of our blessed Father that, not content with giving this method of the particular examen to anyone whom he wished to cure of any vice, he took means not to let him forget to put it in practice. He made him before dinner and before bedtime give an account to some confidential agent whom he assigned to him, and tell him if he had made the examen, how he made it, and whether he had made it in the manner appointed. And we know also that he kept his first companions for a long time with no other support than that of examinations of conscience and frequentation of the sacraments, thinking that, if that was done, it would be quite enough to preserve them in virtue.

Hence we should gather great esteem and appreciation of this practice of examining our consciences twice every day, as being a most important and efficacious means towards our spiritual progress. We should accordingly practise it every day, and the day that we fail therein we should consider that we have failed in one of the chiefest points of our religion. We should hold no occupation sufficient to justify our omitting this examen; and if through any unavoidable occupation we have not been able to make it at the appointed hour, we should take care to make it as soon as possible, say, the first thing of all after dinner. Even sickness and indisposition, which is sufficient to excuse us from any long prayer, should not excuse us from making our examens. Thus it is right for all to hold as a first principle that the examens must never be omitted, neither the general nor the particular. An invalid has plenty of matter on which to make his particular examen; for instance, on conforming himself to the will of God in the sickness and pains that He sends and the remedies ordered by the doctor, which sometimes are more painful than the illness itself; or on bearing with patience the neglect that he fancies people have of him; or on being indifferent and resigned to live or die as God pleases.

CHAPTER II

On What Subjects the Particular Examen Should Be Made

WE have two examens in the Society, one particular, the other general. The particular examen is made on one subject only; the general is made on all the faults that we have committed that day in thought, word, and deed; and that is why it is called general, because it embraces all. We will speak first of the particular examen and then say briefly what is to be added concerning the general, because many things have to be done alike both in general and in particular, and what shall be said of the particular will serve also for the general. We will deal with two things concerning this examen: first, on what subjects it should be made; secondly, how it should be made.

Touching the first point, that we may understand to what subjects we should principally apply this examen, there is to be carefully noted one rule and direction that our Father gives in his book of Spiritual Exercises, and he has it from St. Bonaventure. He says that the devil conducts himself towards us like a commander who is minded to attack and capture a city or fortress. He goes about with all diligence to reconnoiter first of all the weakest point of the fortification, and there he concentrates all his artillery and employs all his forces, though it be at the risk of great loss of life; because if he can batter that part down, he is sure to gain an entrance and take the city. So the devil takes measures to reconnoiter in us the weakest part of our soul, to assail and overcome us there. This, then, should serve as a warning to us to be beforehand and on our guard against our enemy. We must look at and recognize attentively the weakest part of our soul, the part most destitute of virtue, which is that to which natural inclination or passion or bad custom or evil habit most carries us, and there we must keep better watch and ward. The saints and masters of spiritual life say that this should be our chief endeavor, with special care and diligence to root out from within us this vice, because this is where our want is greatest, and chiefly to this we should apply the particular examen.

Cassian gives two reasons for this; the first is that this weakness it is that generally puts us into the greatest dangers and makes us fall into the greatest faults, and therefore it is reasonable that we should apply there our greatest care and diligence. The second is that once we have conquered and subdued our strongest enemies, that make the most serious war upon us, we shall easily overcome and strike down the rest. The soul is braced up and strengthened by the sense of triumph and victory, and the enemy proportionately weakened. Cassian quotes to this effect the example of certain games that formerly took place in Rome in presence of the emperor, where they brought out many wild beasts for men to fight with; and they who wished to signalize themselves more and give pleasure to the emperor, made first for that animal which they saw to be the strongest and most ferocious, reckoning that when that was conquered and dead, they should have an easy triumph over the rest. So he says we should act. We see by experience that commonly each one has a sort of "King Vice" that carries him away for the great inclination that he has to it. There are certain passions that are called predominant, which seem to lord it over us and make us do what otherwise we would not do. So you hear some people say: "If I had not this, I think there is nothing that would embarrass me or give me trouble." This, then, we should attend to most in our particular examen.

In the war that the king of Syria waged against the king of Israel, Holy Scripture tells us (I Chron. xviii. 30) that he gave command to all the captains of his army not to fight against anyone, great or small, but only against the king of Israel, thinking that in overcoming the king he overcame his whole army. And so it turned out; for, when King Achab was struck with an arrow, shot at random on the chance of hitting someone, the battle was over. That is what we have to do; overcome this "King Vice," because thereupon all the rest of his crew will readily give in; cut off the head of this giant Goliath and at once all the other Philistines will be routed and fly. This is the best general rule for everyone to understand on what he ought to make this examen.

But in particular one of the best pieces of advice that can be given in this matter is for everyone to confer with his confessor and spiritual father, having first given him an entire account of his conscience, of all his inclinations, passions, affections, and bad habits, without there remaining anything that he does not lay open; for in this way everyone's need and particular circumstances being seen and understood, it will be easy to determine on what point it will be proper to make the particular examen. And one of the principal things that are to be mentioned in giving an account of conscience is on what the particular examen is made and what profit is derived from it, as is laid down in the Rules of the Prefect of Spiritual Things, and the instruction we have on this subject. It is very important for everyone to succeed in making the particular examen on what is most suitable for him. As a physician has effected not a little, but a great deal, when he has diagnosed the root of the illness, because then he will hit upon the right remedies, and the medicines will take effect; so we have achieved not a little, but a great deal, if we hit upon the root of our infirmities and ailments, because that will be to hit upon the cure of them by applying the remedy and medicine of the examen. One of the reasons why many make little profit of their examen is because they do not apply it where they ought to apply it. If you cut the root of the tree and tear up the weed by the roots, all the rest will soon wither and die; but if you go for the branches and leave the root, it will soon sprout and grow again.

CHAPTER III

Of Two Important Pieces of Advice How to Hit Upon and Choose the Right Subject for Particular Examen

COMING down more to particulars, two principal things are to be noted here. The first is that, when there are exterior faults that offend and disedify our brethren, that is the first thing that we should try to abolish by means of the particular examen, even though there be other interior things of more importance. Thus, if one has a fault in conversation, either by talking too much, or speaking impatiently and angrily, or uttering words of detraction that may give one man a bad opinion of another, or the like, reason and charity require that we should first get rid of these faults that are apt to offend and disedify our brethren and contrive to live and converse with them in such manner as to give no one cause of complaint against us. So the holy Gospel says of the parents of the glorious Baptist: *They were both just before God, living in the observance of all the commandments and ordinances of the Lord without blame* (Luke i. 6). They were just before God and lived blamelessly before men. This is great praise of a servant of God, and one of the things that a religious living in community should endeavor to make sure of. It is not enough to be just before God, but you must try to make sure that your way of going on in religion be such that none may have any ground of complaint against you. *Without blame;* so that none may have to say of you: "A very good fellow but for so-and-so." So, if there is anything that may give offense, it is there that the particular examen should start.

But in the second place it is to be observed that we must not go our whole life making particular examen on these exterior things, for they are easier and more in our power than the interior. St. Augustine says very well: "I command my hand, and it obeys me: I command my foot, and it obeys me; but I command my appetite, and it obeys me not." It is clear that hand and foot are more obedient than appetite, since they have no proper motion of their own to the contrary such as appetite has. So we must endeavor to get clear of these exterior things as soon as we can, and have done with them, that we may have time over for other and greater things, as to gain some main virtue or some higher perfection—a most profound humility of heart, not only to the extent of thinking meanly of oneself, but going so far as to rejoice that others think meanly of one and hold one of small account; doing things purely for God, so far as to come to say what that holy cook said: "I never think that I am serving men, but serving God" (Treatise III, Chapter 9); a great conformity to the will of God in all, and so of the rest. For, though it is true that the particular examen is properly and directly for the getting rid of faults and imperfections—and there is always in us store enough of matter for that, since so long as life lasts we cannot be without faults and venial sins—yet we must not go all our life at that. The time is very well spent that is taken up in weeding the flower garden, yet it must not be all spent in clearing the soil of noxious and evil growths, but rather the purpose of this clearance is to plant good flowers. So the time is very well spent that is taken up during examens in rooting up the vicious and evil inclinations of our soul, but the purpose of all that is to plant therein good and fragrant flowers of virtues. *Behold, I have set thee up today to root up and destroy, to plough over and eradicate, and to build and plant,* said God to Jeremy (Jer. i. 16). The first thing must be to break up and root out, but after that to build and plant.

Especially, since even for getting rid of these same faults and imperfections it is sometimes well to make the particular examen on some higher virtue or perfection; this is often a more effectual means thereto, as well as a shorter and more pleasant. Have you the fault of speaking to your brethren in an offhand manner and too freely? Make your examen on taking all to be your betters and yourself for the least of all. That will tell you how you should address them and how you should reply to them; you may rest quite assured that you will not speak to them any rough or biting word if you attain to this humility. In the same way, do you feel repugnance and difficulty in trying circumstances that occur? Make your examen on taking all things that happen as coming from the hand of God and by a particular arrangement and providence of His, and that He sends them to you for your greater good and profit; and in this way you will do well under them. Do you fail in modesty, lightly rolling your eyes about and turning your head from one side to another, or being curious in wanting to know the news and inquiring into everything that passes? Make your examen on walking in the presence of God and doing all things in such sort as they may appear to His august countenance, and you will soon find yourself modest, recollected, and spiritual; and that without any fatigue or seeming to lay much stress on the point. Otherwise look how, when you come out from a devout prayer, you have no mind to talk or look about you, because dealing and conversing with God makes you forget all that sort of thing. But if you wish to take and remedy all these exterior faults one after another, besides its being a very long and roundabout way, you will find that, when you want to make examen, say, on modesty of the eyes, you will not be able to make it and your head will ache in trying to put such restraint on yourself. So a doctor finds fault with those spiritual directors who spend all their energies in warning you against those exterior faults; he says that the chief care of a good master and pastor of souls should be to reform the heart and make his disciple enter into himself, as Holy Scripture says of Moses: *He led his flock into the interior of the desert* (Exod. iii. 1). Busy yourself in reforming the heart, and everything else will soon be reformed.

CHAPTER IV

That the Particular Examen Must Be Made on One Thing Only

THE particular examen must always be made on one thing only, as the name itself implies. And the reason why it is proper to do so is that in this way the method is more effectual than if we made it on many things together; for it is clear, and natural reason teaches, that a man can do much more against one vice by itself than by taking many together, for he who clutches at much, grasps little. This manner of overcoming our enemies, that is, our vices and passions, Cassian says, was taught us by the Holy Ghost instructing the children of Israel how to behave against those seven tribes and nations opposed to them, to overcome and destroy them. *Thou canst not overcome them all together, but little by little God will give thee victory over them all* (Deut. vii. 22). Cassian observes, as though answering a tacit objection, that there is no fear lest, when a man turns his attention against one vice alone and gives his chief care to that, the rest may do him much harm. First, because this very care taken to correct one particular vice will cause in his soul a great horror and abhorrence of all other vices for the common motive on which they all agree; thus going forearmed against them all. Secondly, because he who goes about his particular examen with care to root out that one evil thing, thus cuts at the radical tendency there is in the heart to all other evil things, which is the license of letting oneself go after anything and everything that one likes. Thus the making of the particular examen against one vice is fighting against all vices, since this check and vigilance employed on one particular serves also for the rest. We see in the case of a wild horse how drawing the bridle and giving him the check, that he may not be unruly and run disorderly down one way, serves also that he may not run disorderly down other ways. Add to this a third consideration, that every day also we make another examen, a general examen, which embraces all the rest.

So far must the principle be carried of not making the particular examen except upon one thing alone, that even in dealing with one vice or one virtue it is many times, and indeed most commonly, better to divide it into parts and degrees, and to go little by little applying the particular examen first to one part or degree and then to another, so to be able better to attain the end desired; for if we were to take it in general, all in a heap, we should effect nothing. Thus, if one wishes to apply the particular examen to the rooting out of pride and vanity and the gaining of humility, he must not take it in general thus: "I intend to be proud in nothing, but humble in all things," for that comprises much; indeed, it would be attempting more than if you were to make your particular examen on three or four things together, and so there would be little gained for your clutching at too many things. What you have to do is to divide it into parts or degrees. In this way the enemies, being divided and taken one at a time, will be better overcome and we shall come to gain more expeditiously what we desire.

For the better putting of this in practice, we will set down here some main things on which the particular examen may be made, dividing them into parts and degrees. And though for some virtues we have done this in special treatises, yet, that it may be found all together in this its proper place, we will gather it together here; and we may also use it as a pattern and mirror in which we may look and see whether we are getting on and what is wanting to us to gain perfection.

CHAPTER V

How to Divide the Particular Examen According to the Parts and Degrees of Virtues

Of Humility

I. To utter no words that may redound to my own praise and reputation.

II. Not to take pleasure in hearing myself praised and well spoken of, but rather thence to take occasion to humble and confound myself more, seeing that I am not such as others think or such as I ought to be. To this may be added rejoicing when another is praised and spoken well of. And when I feel any resentment at this, or any movement of envy, to note it for a fault; as also when I take any vain complacency or satisfaction at others' speaking well of me.

III. Never to act from human respect or to gain the good opinion of men or to be seen and esteemed by men, but purely for God.

IV. Never to excuse myself, much less throw the blame on others, whether in outward word or in my own mind.

V. To cut off and lop away at once all vain, arrogant, and proud thoughts that occur to me from things that touch my honor and reputation.

VI. To take all others for my betters, not speculatively merely, but practically and in act, behaving to all with that humility and respect which I show to superiors.

VII. To take well the occasions of humility that come in my way. In this I should go on growing and advancing by these three steps: (1) taking such occasions patiently; (2) taking them readily and promptly; (3) taking them cheerfully and with joy. And I must not stop until I come to be glad and rejoice in being disparaged and held in small account, to resemble and imitate Christ our

Redeemer, Who chose to be disparaged and held in small account for me.

VIII. In this matter and in others like it the particular examen may be applied to making acts and doing practices of humility—or of any other virtue on which the particular examen is made. These acts and practices may be either interior or exterior. We should rouse ourselves to these acts so many times in the morning and so many times in the afternoon. We should begin with fewer and gradually add more until the habit or custom is gained of this particular virtue we are in quest of.

Of Fraternal Charity

I. To shun detraction or any mention of the fault of another, even though it be slight and public. Not to pull to pieces his doings or show any sign of undervaluing him either in his presence or in his absence, but try to let it be that for anything that proceeds from my mouth all men are good, honorable, and estimable.

II. Never to tell another, "Jack says so-and-so of you," when the matter is such as might cause annoyance, however small it may be; for this were to sow discord and tares among brethren.

III. Not to utter sarcastic words or harsh and peevish words that might give pain to another. Not to be obstinate in maintaining a point, nor contradict another, nor rebuke him, unless you have charge of him.

IV. To treat all with love and charity and show it in act, trying to meet others' wants, assist and give them satisfaction so far as you can. This especially when you are in an office that obliges you to meet people's wants; to this you should give great attention, and whatever you cannot do in deed, make it up by a gracious manner and kind answers and words.

V. To avoid any aversion for another and still more to avoid showing it, as it would be by refusing to speak to him for some displeasure you had conceived against him, or by refusing to meet his need when you might, or by giving any other sign that you have a grudge against him.

VI. Not to behave to any particular person as you would not behave to anyone else; to avoid familiarities and particular friendships that give offense.

VII. Not to pass judgment on anyone, but rather try to excuse your neighbor's faults, in your own thoughts and in company having a high opinion of all.

Of Mortification

I. To mortify myself in things and occasions that offer without my going to seek them, whether they come immediately from God or come by means of superiors or by means of neighbors and brethren or in any other way, trying to bear them well and profit by them.

II. To mortify myself and overcome myself in everything that is likely to hinder me from keeping my rules and doing my ordinary and daily duties well, spiritual as well as external; because all the faults that we commit therein come of our not overcoming and mortifying ourselves in a matter which takes some trouble, or of not abstaining from some pleasure and gratification.

III. To mortify myself in conducting myself with the modesty that is to be expected of a religious, especially as regards the eyes and tongue, when there might be any fault therein.

IV. To mortify myself in sundry things that I might lawfully do, as by not leaving my room, by not seeing some curious sight, by not asking about or seeking to know what is no affair of mine, by not saying things that I have a mind to say, and the like. I am to apply the examen to making these acts of mortification, so many in the morning and so many in the afternoon, beginning with fewer and gradually adding more, for the practice of these voluntary mortifications, though it be in little things, is very profitable.

V. To mortify myself even in things that I am obliged to do, in this way: When I go to meals, to study, to lecture, to preach, or any other duty that I have a liking for, mortify first my appetite and will, saying in my heart: "I have no mind to do this, O Lord, for my own satisfaction, but because Thou willest it."

Of Abstinence or Gluttony

I. Not to eat anything before or after the common hour nor away from the refectory.

II. To be content with what is given to the community, not seeking other dishes nor the same dishes differently dressed, not accepting special food except for some known necessity.

III. In these common things not to exceed the rule of temperance in point of quantity.

IV. Not to eat with great eagerness nor very hurriedly, but with modesty and decency, not letting appetite run away with me.

V. Never to speak of food, much less grumble or complain about it.

VI. To cut short and stop all thoughts of gluttony.

Of Patience

I. Not to give any outward sign of impatience, but rather to show great tranquillity in word and action and in the cast of my countenance, repressing all impulses and emotions to the contrary.

II. Not to give place and entry into my heart for any perturbation or resentment or indignation or sadness; much less any desire of revenge, though it be in a matter quite trifling.

III. To take all events and occasions that occur as sent by the hand of God for my good and profit, in whatever manner or by whatever means or channel they come.

IV. To go on exercising myself and bringing myself to act in this matter, first, by taking all things as they come with patience; secondly, with promptitude and readiness; thirdly, with delight and joy, as being the will of God.

Of Obedience

I. To be exact in outward obedience, leaving the letter of the alphabet just begun; meeting also the signification of the will of the superior without waiting for an express command.

II. To obey in will and heart, having one and the same wish and will as the superior.

III. To obey also with the understanding and judgment, adopting the same view and sentiment as the superior, not giving place to any judgments or reasonings to the contrary.

IV. To take the voice of the superior and the sound of the bell as the voice of God, and obey the superior, whoever he be, as Christ our Lord, and the same for subordinate officials.

V. To follow blind obedience, that is, obedience without inquiry or examination or any seeking of reasons for the why and wherefore, it being reason enough for me that it is obedience and the command of the superior.

VI. To go on to acts of the will, exciting myself to believe, when I obey, that I am therein doing the will of God, and make that all my joy and satisfaction.

Of Poverty

I. Not to give or receive from another, either within or without the house, anything without leave.

II. Not to borrow or take anything from the house or the room of another without leave.

III. Not to keep anything superfluous, stripping myself of all that is not necessary to me, as well in books and the furniture of my room as in dress and food and everything else.

IV. Even in the necessary things of which I have the use, I must make a point of showing myself a poor man, because such I am; contriving that my things be the poorest, the plainest, and of least value. Thus, in my room, in my dress, in my food, and in all the rest, the virtue of poverty is ever to shine out and I am to let it be seen that I am a poor man; desiring and rejoicing that the worst of the house be ever for me for my greater abnegation and spiritual profit.

V. To rejoice that even in necessary things something is wanting to me, because this is to be a true and perfect poor man in spirit and an imitator of Christ our Redeemer, Who, being so rich and powerful (II Cor. viii. 9), made Himself poor for love of us. So do I wish to feel want even of necessary things, suffering hunger, thirst, cold, weariness, and nakedness.

Of Chastity

I. To practise modesty of the eyes, not looking at persons or things that may be an incentive to temptation.

II. Not to utter or listen to words touching on this matter or that may awaken movements or evil thoughts, nor read such like things.

III. To give no place to any thought bearing on this matter, though it be very remotely, casting them off with great diligence and promptness from the very beginning.

IV. Not to touch another person on his hands, and much less on his face or head, nor allow myself to be touched.

V. To observe with myself much decency and modesty, not looking at myself, uncovering or touching myself without absolute necessity.

VI. To have no particular friendships, neither giving nor receiving little presents or things to eat. And with persons who appeal to me and with whom I feel this affection and inclination, to go with great reserve, honestly shunning their intimacy and conversation, which is usually the only thing to be done in such cases.

Of Doing Ordinary Actions Well

I. Not to fail any day to do my spiritual duties completely, giving them the full time allotted to them; and when at that time there is some unavoidable occupation to claim me, to make it up at another time.

II. To make my meditation and my general and particular examens well, observing the additions and dwelling in my examens on sorrow and confusion for faults and purpose of amendment, rather than on examining how often I have fallen, for in this is the force and fruit of the examens, and for want of this some usually profit little thereby.

III. To do any other spiritual duties well, as mass, office, spiritual reading, and penances, as well public as private, taking care to gather from them the end and fruit for which they are severally ordained, not doing them out of custom, perfunctorily, and for form's sake.

IV. To do my office and discharge my ministries well, doing all that I can and all that rests with me that they may go well, as one who does things for God and in presence of God.

V. Not to commit any deliberate fault.

VI. To make great account of little things.

VII. And because my progress and perfection turns on doing well and perfectly these ordinary duties that we do every day, I mean to be very careful from time to time, when I feel myself going slack upon this point, to make my particular examen on the same for some days, to renew myself and rehabilitate myself in doing them well.

Of Doing All Things Purely for God

I. Not to do anything for any human respect or to be seen and esteemed by men or for my own comfort or interest or simply to my own taste or satisfaction.

II. To do all my actions purely for God, accustoming myself to make actual reference of them all to God: first, in the morning when I awake; secondly, at the beginning of each action; thirdly, also during the action itself, often in it raising my heart to God, saying: "For Thee, O Lord, I do this, for Thy glory and because Thou so willest it."

III. To go on applying this particular examen and exciting myself to the same so many times in the morning, so many times in the afternoon, beginning with fewer and then adding more, until I come to gain a habit and custom of very frequently in my work raising my heart to God, and my eyes do not turn therein to regard anything but His Divine Majesty.

IV. I am not to stop in this examen and exercise until I come to do all my actions as one serving God and not men; and until I come to do them in such manner as to be always actually loving God in them, rejoicing that I am there doing His will, and all my joy and satisfaction is in that, so that, when I am at work, I seem to be rather loving than working.

V. This must be the presence of God in which I endeavor to walk, and the continual prayer which I seek to carry on; since it will be very good and very advantageous for my soul and will enable me to do things right down well and in perfection.

Of Conformity to the Will of God

I. To take all things and all occasions that offer, whether great or small, in whatsoever way and manner they come, as coming from the hand of God, Who sends them with the affection of a father for my greater good and profit; conforming myself therein to His most holy and divine will as if I saw Christ Himself saying to me: "Son, I wish that just now thou shouldst do or suffer this."

II. To contrive to go on growing and mounting in this conformity to the will of God in all things by these three steps: (1) to receive things with patience: (2) with readiness and ease: (3) with joy and gladness, this being the will and good pleasure of God.

III. I must not stop in this examen and exercise until I find in myself a sensible satisfaction and joy that the Lord's will is fulfilled in me, though it be with afflictions, contumelies, and pains, and until all my joy and satisfaction is the will and satisfaction of God.

IV. Never to omit doing a thing that I take to be the will of God and His greater glory and service, endeavoring therein to imitate Christ our Redeemer, Who said: *I ever do that which is most pleasing to my Eternal Father* (John viii. 29).

V. To walk in this exercise is a very good way to walk in the presence of God and in continual prayer, and very profitable.

VI. The examen on mortification that we have set down above may be better applied by way of conformity to the will of God, taking all events and occurrences as coming from the hand of God in the manner that has been said; and in this way it will be easier and of a better relish and more profitable, since it will be an exercise of the love of God.

It must be observed that we do not mean hereby to say that the particular examen is to be made in the order in which the virtues are here set down, or by the degrees or parts that are assigned under each virtue. The rule to be observed here is that each one should choose the virtue of which he stands most in need and begin therein by that part or degree which is now necessary for him; and when he has done with that, he should proceed to select out of the rest what is most proper for him until he comes to the perfection of that virtue by the grace of the Lord.

CHAPTER VI

That the Matter of the Particular Examen Should Not Be Lightly Changed, and for What Length of Time It Is Well to Keep It on the Same Subject

IT is to be observed here that we must not lightly change the matter of the examen, taking now one thing, now another, for this is, as they say, to beat about the bush and get no forwarder. Our policy must be to follow up one thing right to the end and after that take up something else. One of the reasons why some people make so little profit by their examen is very often this, that they do nothing but by fits and starts, making the particular examen on one thing for a week or a fortnight or for a month and then getting tired and passing on to another thing without having gained the first, and then make another new start, and then another. One who takes it into his head to raise a stone up the slope of a mountain right to the top and, after lifting it some way, gets tired and drops it and lets it roll down to the bottom, will never succeed, however much he labors, in getting the stone to its place. So it is with those who begin to make their examen on one thing and, before bringing it to a head and gaining what they sought, abandon it and take another and then another. This is to tire yourself out without result, *always learning, and never arriving at knowledge of the truth* (II Tim iii. 7). In the business of perfection success is not won by fits and starts, but by long perseverance. It is necessary to persist and take one thing to heart and hold to it until you have got it, though it be at great cost. St. Chrysostom says: As those who are digging for a treasure or mining for gold or silver cease not to hollow out and extract earth and remove all obstacles that come in the way and sink ten or twenty shafts until they strike on the treasure which they seek, so we, who are in quest of true spiritual riches and the true treasure of virtue and perfection, must not grow weary until we strike upon it, overcoming all difficulties, so that nothing may stand in our way. *I will pursue my enemies,* says the prophet, *and catch them up, and not be weary or turn back until they give in and I gain the victory over them* (Psalm xvii. 38). This holy persistance it is that overcomes vice and gains virtue, not fits and starts.

But let us now come to a reckoning. On how many subjects have you made your examen since you took the matter up? If you had succeeded in all, you would be a perfect man by this time. But if there is one in which you have not succeeded, why did you give it up? You will say that you were not getting on well with it. Now it is just for this reason that you do not get on well, because you keep changing and have not the perseverance to carry on any one thing to the end. If, making your examen and taking particular care over that thing, you say that you were not getting on well with it, you will get on worse when you do not make your examen on it. If he who makes resolutions often fails, what will become of him who seldom or never makes a resolution? Anyhow, this making a resolution morning, midday, and night, will be some check to prevent your falling so often. And though you fancy that you do not succeed in amending yourself and are doing no good, be not discouraged on that account and do not give it up, but humble yourself and be ashamed at examen time and turn to make new resolutions and start afresh.

For to this purpose God permits these failings, and suffers the Jebusite to remain in the land of your soul, that you may come to understand that you of your own strength can do nothing, but all must come from the hand of God, and so you may have recourse to Him and ever live attached to and dependent on Him. Under this trial a man is often more fervent and diligent in improving himself than he would be if God gave him at once what he desired.

But someone will ask: For how long a time will it be good to keep the particular examen on one thing? St. Bernard and Hugo of St. Victor treat this question: For how long a time will it be good to struggle against one vice? And they answer: Until the vice becomes so enfeebled that, as soon as it rises up in rebellion, you can at once easily put it down and reduce it to reason. Thus it is not necessary to wait until one no longer feels the passion or the repugnance, for that would be never to finish. Hugh of St. Victor says: That is more for angels than for men. It is enough that now this vice or passion is no longer very troublesome to you nor gives you much to think about, but that, as soon as it arises, you meet it and cast it from you with facility; then you may well stop the struggle and make the particular examen on something else. Even Seneca teaches us: "We fight against vices, not to overcome them entirely, but not to be overcome"—*Contra vitia pugnamus, non ut penitus vincamus, sed ne vincamur.* It is not necessary that we should not feel the vice at all; enough that it is now a beaten foe, so as to give us no more trouble nor disturb us in our course of well-doing.

To hit the mark better in this matter, it is well that everyone should talk it over with his spiritual father, for this is one of the chief things on which we need counsel. For some things it is enough to apply the examen for a short time, as we have said above. There are other things in which the examen may be well employed for a year or even many years; for "if every year we rooted out one vice, we should soon be perfect men" (Thomas à Kempis). And there are things such that a whole lifetime would be well spent over one of them, for that would be sufficient for some particular man to attain perfection. Thus we have known persons who have taken to heart one thing and applied their particular examen to it as long as they lived, and so came to signalize in it and do it to perfection—one in the virtue of patience, another in a most profound humility, others in great conformity to the will of God, others in doing all things purely for God. In this manner, also, we should endeavor to come to perfection in some virtue, insisting and persevering in it until we gain it. This does not hinder our interrupting this examen sometimes; nay, it is well that so it should be done, turning to make the examen for a week on silence, on doing our spiritual duties well, on speaking well of all, of speaking no word that could in any way offend anyone, and on other such like things as are apt at times to sprout up within us and show their heads above ground. After that we may return at once to our post and follow out our principal purpose until we entirely succeed in our aim.

CHAPTER VII

How the Particular Examen Is To Be Made

THE second principal topic that we proposed to treat was how to make this examen. The particular examen embraces three times and an examination of oneself twice repeated. The first time is in the early morning at rising; everyone should then form a resolution to be on his guard against this or that particular vice or defect of which he wishes to correct and amend himself. The second time is at midday, at which the first examen should be made, which contains three points. The first is to ask grace of our Lord to remember how many times I have fallen into this defect on which I am making my particular examen; the second, to take account of my soul touching this defect or vice, going over my conduct from the hour at which I arose and made my resolution to the present hour, and see how many times I have fallen therein, and make as many dots on a line of a little book, kept for that purpose, as shall answer to the number of times I find I have fallen; the third is to be sorry for having fallen, asking God's pardon for the same and purposing not to fall that afternoon into that fault, with the grace of God. The third time is at night before going to rest; then the examen must be made a second time, neither more nor less than at midday, by these three points, going through the time from the last examen until the present moment and making on the second line as many dots as shall answer to the number of times I find I have fallen. And to extirpate more easily and more readily this defect or vice on which we are making the examen, our Father puts three notices, which he calls "additions": the first, that every time the man falls into this particular vice or defect, he should repent, putting his hand to his breast, which can be done even in the presence of others without their noticing what is done; the second, that at night time, after having made the examen, he should compare the afternoon's dots with those of the morning, to see whether there is any improvement; the third and fourth, that he should also compare today with yesterday and this week with last week in reference to the same defect.

All this teaching is drawn from the saints. St. Anthony advised the writing down of the faults discovered by the examen, for the doer's greater shame and as an admonition to him to labor at their amendment. St. John Climacus would have us, not only at night and examen time, but at all hours, to note down immediately upon committing it any fault into which we fall, that thus the examen may be better made, as the good man of business and the good steward puts down in his day book at once anything that he sells or buys so that nothing may be forgotten and that he may be better able to make up his account at night. St. Basil and St. Bernard expressly lay down the counsel to compare one day with another, in order to get a better idea of one's advancement or falling back, and diligently to aim at growing better every day and more like the holy angels. St. Dorotheus advises us to compare week with week and month with month.

The method that our Father lays down of taking the amendment of a fault time by time and little by little, half a day at a time and no more, is a method set down by St. Chrysostom, St. Ephrem, and St. Bernard, as most efficacious for the uprooting of any vice or fault. Even in the heathen world, Plutarch also prescribes it and gives the example of a man of a very choleric temperament, who had great difficulty in keeping his temper and took for his task not to get angry for one day; so he spent one day without getting angry, and another day he said: "Well, I don't mean to get angry today, either, not today at least." He did the same another day and another, until he came to make himself of a very sweet and agreeable disposition. Well, this is the way our Father instructs us in the particular examen, to make the effort easier for us. Dealing with an invalid who has lost his appetite, they give him his dinner little by little, that he may be able to eat it. If you put a whole chicken before him, he would think it impossible to have to eat all that and could not eat a mouthful; but cut off a little bit and give it him, and keep the rest there, hidden between two plates; in this way, little by little, morsel by morsel, you make him eat all that he needs. Our Father wishes in this way to help us with the particular examen, as they do with infirm and weakly people, little by little, half a day and half a day at a time, that we may be able to get on. If we took it all together—"All the year long I am not to talk;" "All my life I am to walk with my eyes cast down, under such control and with such modesty"

—the mere thought, perchance, would weary us and we should think it impossible to carry through. It would be a sad and melancholy life. But just for one half day, for one morning, till dinner-time, who would not be willing to go about with propriety and restrain his tongue? After midday you will make your resolution only for the afternoon; as for tomorrow, God has not pronounced what it shall be; and how do you know if you shall get as far? And if you do live so long as that, that is not more than one day either and you will not be sorry tomorrow to have spent today in such recollection; rather you will find yourself very glad of it and more disposed today to do it better and with greater facility and delight. I sometimes think that some people fail by not making a strenuous effort in this practice of making their resolution that half day only, and it would be a great help towards rendering their resolution more effectual.

In the chronicles of St. Francis it is related of Brother Juniper that, though he always spoke very little, yet one time he kept perpetual silence for six months together, in this way. The first day he purposed to keep silence in honor of God the Father; the second, in homage to God the Son; the third, in homage to the Holy Ghost; the fourth, for the love of our Lady; and so he ran through all the saints, each day observing silence with new fervor and devotion in honor of some one of them. Following this plan, a man is more encouraged to correct himself on that particular point on which he is making his particular examen and is also more ashamed and confounded for the faults that he commits, since even for so short a time he could not carry out his purpose. Thus in every way this method will be a great help to us.

CHAPTER VIII

That in the Examen We Should Insist and Dwell Principally on Sorrow and Purpose of Amendment

WHAT is to be particularly very much observed as regards the method of making the examen, is the matter of the three points which it contains. The two last are the most important; that is, grief and repentance for our faults and negligences and a firm purpose to correct them, according to that text of the prophet, *Have compunction in your beds* (Psalm iv. 5). In this sentiment of compunction and repentance and in this firm purpose not to fall again, all the force and efficacy of the examen as a means of self-amendment lies; and, therefore, on this most time should be spent. One of the chief reasons why many get little profit and amendment out of their examens is that they let the whole time slip away in searching out the times in which they have fallen into faults; and scarcely have they done with this point when examen time is over, and they do the rest superficially. They do not dwell on sorrow and repentance for their faults, nor on being ashamed and begging pardon for them, nor on making firm purposes of amendment for that afternoon or the day following, nor in begging God's grace and strength to that end. Hence it comes that, as many times as you have fallen today, so many you fall tomorrow, because the only thing you have done in the examen is to remember and call to mind the number of times that you have fallen. That is not the way to correct yourself; it is only the first point of the examen and the foundation on which the other principal points must be built. The effectual way to correct yourself is to grieve and repent in all sincerity for your faults, with a firm purpose of amending them, and to ask our Lord for grace to that end. You will never amend yourself if you do not that. These two things, grief for the past and purpose of amendment for the future, are so akin to one another that the one goes on at the same rate as the other, for it is certain that, where we really abhor a thing, we take care not to plunge into it.

Every day we say and preach this to seculars; it is only reasonable that we should take it to ourselves. What is the reason, we say, why people in the world fall back again so easily into the same sins after so many confessions? Do you know what it is? The reason commonly is that they did not detest them in good earnest, nor did they come to confession with firm purposes never to sin again. Thus, since their heart was never fully determined to return wholly to God, but they only turned round half-face, as they say, they easily went back to what they had never entirely quitted; whereas, if they had been really sorry and detested their sin and had a firm purpose never to sin again, they would not have gone back to it at once so easily on leaving the confessional, just as if they had not confessed at all. For this reason also it is that you fall into the same faults in the afternoon as in the morning and the same today as yesterday, because you were not sorry for them in good earnest, nor detested them from your heart, nor had any firm purpose of amendment, nor dwelt upon this. Had you done so, you would not have relapsed into them so readily and so easily, since we are not wont so easily to do what we have once detested and what we are grieved and pained at having done. Sorrow and repentance for our sins, when it is real, not only rids us of past sins, but is a medicine preservative for the future; for he who steadily abhors sin is far from falling into it anew.

Even that heathen philosopher knew the efficacy and force of this means for not falling into sin, for, when a bad woman asked him an excessive price for sinning, he answered: "I do not buy repentance at so dear a rate." Let this answer be noted, for it is worthy not only of a philosopher, but of a Christian and a religious. Sometimes I set myself to consider the folly of those who make up their minds to sin by saying: "I will repent afterwards and God will pardon me." But how can you be so foolish as to choose just now to gratify your appetite and gather a brief thrill of pleasure that passes in a moment, bargaining with it to keep up afterwards for life a perpetual sorrow and repentance for having allowed yourself that gratification? For, though it is true that God will pardon you that sin afterwards, if you repent of it, yet, after all, to obtain pardon, it is necessary to repent and be sorry afterwards for having done it. There is much force in this argument, even if we think only of earthly considerations—apart from the motive of the love of God, which should always be our principal motive—and look merely at our own satisfaction and self-love. I have no mind to do that which I know must give me afterwards much pain and much grief for having done it. The thrill of pleasure in doing it is over in a moment, while the grief and pain of having done it must last all my life, so that I can never afterwards take satisfaction or complacency therein. Great folly it is to choose so much pain at the price of so little pleasure.

St. Paul says the thing better: *What fruit did ye gather from that whereof ye are now ashamed?* (Rom. vi. 21). What show can that small satisfaction that you get make in comparison with the sorrow that you must feel afterwards? This should be considered beforehand before a fall. When the temptation comes, you should make this calculation and say: "I have no mind to do that of which I must afterwards be ashamed and repent as long as I live." Even here, when you want to persuade a man not to do a thing, you say to him: "See how you will repent afterwards of having done it." And he says: "No, I shall not repent;" for, if he thought that he would repent, he sees well what madness it would be to do what he knows must afterwards make him sorry and give him much pain.

I have said this that it may be seen what an efficacious means true sorrow and repentance is, to prevent our falling into our faults again; hence we may understand how important it is to dwell on this in our examens. It is true that one may have true sorrow and purpose of amendment and withal relapse again into sin, for we are not angels, but weak men, vessels of earth, which may break and fall to pieces and once more be made up again. Nevertheless, when a man, after finishing his confession, returns at once to the same oaths and to the same desires and sins that he has just confessed, we are wont commonly to say that he cannot have had true contrition or sorrow for that sin, nor any firm purpose of amendment, seeing that he relapses so quickly. In the same way it is a great indication and argument that you were not really sorry and had not any firm purpose of amendment when you made your examen at midday or at night on having broken silence, to see how that same afternoon or the very next day you break silence just in the same way as if you had not made any examen; and I say the same of other faults on which you are making examen. Even before your brethren you are ashamed to tell a fault or have it told you when you have told it already three or four times. How much more should you be ashamed before God, if you have really told your fault before Him, repenting of it from your heart and begging pardon and purposing amendment, not thrice or four times, but more than three or four dozen times! No doubt we should amend ourselves and make progress in quite another way if we repented and were sorry in good earnest and made firm purposes of amendment.

CHAPTER IX

That It Is a Very Helpful Thing to Add Some Penances to the Examen

OUR Father was not satisfied with sorrow and repentance and inward purposes, but we read in his Life that, for the better composing of the end desired, he recommended the addition of some penance to the particular examen, marking out for ourselves a certain penalty to exact of ourselves every time we fall into the fault which is the matter of our particular examen. Fra Louis of Granada gives instances of some servants of God whom he knew, one of whom, when he found at his night examen that he had exceeded in some ill-spoken word, would bite his tongue in penance for the same; and another would take a discipline for this and any other defect he fell into.

It is said of the holy Abbot Agatho that for three years he carried a pebble in his mouth to gain the virtue of silence. As we here wear a haircloth to mortify the flesh and to serve us as a caller to chastity, so this saint carried a pebble below his tongue that it might be, as it were, his haircloth and serve him as a reminder and caller not to speak more than necessary. And of our blessed Father Ignatius, we read that at the beginning of his conversion he was much tempted to laughter and that he overcame the temptation by free use of the discipline, giving himself as many strokes each night as there were times that he had laughed during the day, however slight the laugh had been. And it is usually a great help, this adding of some penance to the examen, for with the penance the soul feels chastened and afraid to commit that fault another time. The spur makes the beast go, however lazy it be. Such an aid is the spur that no sooner does the creature feel that there is one there, though it does not prick it, than it makes it go. If every time that a man broke silence he had to take a public discipline or dine on bread and water for three days, which was the penance of old, marked in the Rules for those who broke silence, of a surety it would greatly restrain us from talking. Besides this, and the merit and satisfaction there is in it, there is another very great advantage, which is that God our Lord, seeing the penance wherewith a man chastises and afflicts himself, is wont to hear his petition and desire. And this is one of the effects of penance and exterior mortification that the saints set down, and our holy Father sets it down in the Book of the Exercises. The angel said to Daniel: *From the first day that thou didst set thy heart to understand, and to afflict thyself in the sight of thy God, thy prayer was heard* (Dan. x. 12). The Prophet Daniel added to his prayer fasting and mortification of the flesh, and so obtained the deliverance of his people and moved God to reveal to him great mysteries and do him other very particular favors. And we see that in the Church of God this means has always been very commonly used to obtain and gain the favor of God in distresses and necessities.

When an infant asks of its mother the breast that it needs, and asks it only by expressing its desire by signs, the mother often refuses or puts it off; but when it asks by weeping and wailing, the mother cannot refrain from giving it at once. So when a man asks of God the virtue of humility, of patience, of chastity, or the victory over some temptation, or any like thing, and asks only by desire and word, oftentimes he does not gain what he asks, or is long put off; but when to prayer we join penance and mortification of the flesh and afflict ourselves before God, then we gain our petition much better, with greater certainty, and in shorter time. God has a great love of men and, seeing them putting themselves to pain and affliction to gain what they ask, He is moved to compassion and uses greater mercy with them. We read in Holy Writ that the patriarch Joseph could not contain himself when he saw the affliction and tears of his brethren, but discovered himself to them and made them partakers of all his goods: *Joseph could no longer contain himself, and said to his brethren, I am Joseph* (Gen. xlv. 3). What will not He do, Who loves us more than Joseph and is our Brother, when He sees our affliction and grief? In every way this means will avail us much.

This agrees very well with what Cassian says, treating of the care and diligence with which we should proceed in the warfare and particular examen. If the struggle and particular examen ought to be, as we have said, on that point of which we have most need; if it ought to serve to uproot that passion or inclination which reigns more in us than others, which more particularly upsets us and puts us in greater dangers and makes us fall into most faults; if it be to overcome that vice, the overcoming of which will carry victory over all the rest, and the gaining of that virtue with which we shall have gained all other virtues, with how much solicitude and diligence will it be reasonable for us to act in a matter of so much importance to us! Do you know with how much? Cassian tells us: "Against this predominant passion let him employ his man's force, devoting all his care and solicitude to attacking and watching it; against it let him direct the daily arrows of his fasts; against it let him heave every moment the sighs of his heart and hurl the darts of his groans; against it be the labors of his watchings and the meditation of his heart; against it let him ceaselessly pour out before God the wailings of his prayers, begging Him especially and continually to put an end to the assaults of that vice."

We must not rest content with taking this care about our examen alone, but also about our meditation; and that not only in the time set aside for meditation, but frequently in the day we must raise our heart to God with ejaculatory prayers and sighs and groans of the heart: "Lord, humility; Lord, chastity; Lord, patience." For this we should often visit the Blessed Sacrament, asking with much earnestness of the Lord to give us grace to gain a thing so important to us; we must have recourse to our Lady and the saints to be our intercessors. To this end we must direct our fasts, haircloths, disciplines, and subjoin certain devotions and offer certain particular mortifications. If in this manner and with this care and diligence we went to work with our particular examen, we should quickly feel the better for it because the Lord would see our affliction and hear our prayer and fulfil the desire of our heart. And all this must be well observed to aid us also therewith in other temptations and grave needs that occur. St. Bonaventure says that our Lady told St. Elizabeth of Hungary that no spiritual grace comes to the soul, regularly speaking, otherwise than by prayer and afflictions of the body.

CHAPTER X

Of the General Examination of Conscience

THE general examination of conscience contains five points. The first is to give thanks to God for benefits received. This calling to mind of benefits received is put first in order that, contrasting therewith the faults and sins that we have committed in return for so many benefits, we may thence take occasion better to enter into sentiments of confusion and heartfelt sorrow. Thus, the Prophet Nathan first recounted to David the favors that God had done him in order to show the deformity and magnitude of the sin that he had committed. The second point is to ask of our Lord grace to know the faults and sins into which we have fallen. The third, to take account of our soul, going through our conduct from the hour at which we made our resolutions, first for thoughts, secondly for words, thirdly for actions. The fourth point is to beg God's pardon for the faults that we find we have committed, grieving and repenting for the same. The fifth, to purpose amendment by the grace of the Lord, with an Our Father.

This general examen should be made always along with the particular; for immediately in the morning on rising we should offer to our Lord all that we are going to do that day. So our Father says, speaking of the particular examen, that immediately on rising we should purpose to be on our guard against that particular vice which we wish to correct; and this is the first time for the particular examen. We should also at the same time offer to God all the thoughts, words, and actions of that day, that all may be for His glory, purposing at the same time not to offend Him and begging His grace to that end. It is reasonable that all should have the custom of doing this. Afterwards, twice a day, at midday and at night, we must make the general examen along with the particular. Such is the custom of the Society founded on our Constitutions, and we find it expressed in the first of the Common Rules: "Let all twice a day give the time marked out to them for the examination of their conscience." Thus, as the clock is regulated and the weights wound up twice a day, at morning and at night, that it may keep time, so we ought to regulate the clock of our conscience by the morning and night examen that it may always keep time. Thus at noon, when we go through and take account of the times that we have failed in the matter of our particular examen, from the hour at which we made the purpose, which was when we rose, down to then, so also we must run through and take account of the faults we have committed in thought, word, and deed from the time that we rose till then; and after that we must move ourselves to shame and repentance for the faults committed in the matter of our particular and general examen together, and purpose amendment for the afternoon as well in the one as in the other. And at night we must make in like manner the particular and the general examen together, going through and taking account only of the time since our previous examen at midday.

The main thing to notice about the manner of making this general examen is the same as we said of the particular, that all its force and efficacy lies in these two latter points, that is, in repentance and shame for the faults we have fallen into and a firm purpose of amendment for the afternoon or for tomorrow morning; in that consists our making our examen well and drawing fruit from it. Father Master Avila says of this examen: "You should make account that you have entrusted to you a prince's son to take continual care of, to see after him and set him in the way of good habits and clear him of bad ones, and that every day you call him to account." Now if you had such a charge, it is clear that you would not lay the main stress of his amendment on his telling you how many times he has fallen and failed today, but in making him acknowledge his fault, in rebuking him and giving him admonitions and drawing from him purposes of amendment; and you would tell him plainly, in so many words, that being the son of him whose son he is, he must mend his ways. So, then, in this manner you ought to regard your soul as a thing entrusted to you by God and in this manner you ought to deal with it in the account that you ask of it. And on this you ought to lay the stress of your examen and self-amendment—not on calling to mind the faults that you have committed, but on shame and repentance for having committed them and on rebuking yourself as you would rebuke another person of whom you had the charge, and on making firm resolutions not to fall again into these faults.

And we ought to be aided hereto by the consideration that the general examen is the proper and legitimate preparation for confession; and this is the title that our Father gives it in the Book of Spiritual Exercises: "A general examination of conscience for a man to cleanse his soul and better prepare for confession." And the reason is manifest. For two principal things are required for confession; the first is examination of one's faults, the second is sorrow for them. These things are done completely in the examen of conscience and so, if we make this examen well, we shall make our confession well. And it is to be observed that the sorrow necessary for confession, as the Council of Trent and that of Florence says, includes two things: regret and repentance for sin, and purpose not to sin any more. Where either of these two things is wanting, there will be no sufficient disposition for confession. Some think that then only is their confession null and void, when they leave out some sin through shame; but I believe that there are many more cases of confessions' being bad, sacrilegious, and null, for want of true sorrow and purpose of amendment than for want of due acknowledgment of sins.

Hereby may be seen how necessary this preparation is and how important it is to accustom ourselves in our examen to excite ourselves, and take time over exciting ourselves, to sorrow for our faults and purpose never to fall into them again. And so I say that of the three principal points that there are in the examen—the other two being what we may call preludes—the chief part of the time should be spent on the two last, that is, on begging God's pardon and moving ourselves to repentance and shame for our faults, and on making purposes of amendment. The lesser portion of the time should be spent in running through and calling to mind the faults into which we have fallen. For this latter point, albeit it is one of those three principal points, the third part of the examen time is sufficient. The other two parts should be kept for the other two points, since they are the principal points and on them the force and efficacy and fruit of the examen depends.

But someone will say: "How shall we be able in such a short time as the third part of a quarter of an hour to go through all the times that we have fallen in the matter of the particular examen, besides the faults that we have committed in that of the general examen by thought, word, and deed? Why, even the whole quarter of an hour would seem too little for this." The best means for this is to bring the first point already done when we go to examen. It is told of our blessed Father Ignatius that every time he failed in the matter of his particular examen he tied a knot on a shoe-string that he carried on his girdle for this express purpose, and afterwards by the knots he knew the number of times without stopping any more on it. And as for what regarded the general examen, he did not let an hour of the day pass without recollecting himself, leaving all else alone to examine his conscience. And if perchance some business came in upon him, so grave and so urgent an occupation as not to allow him that hour to fulfil his devotional practice, he made it up the next hour or as soon as the occupation gave him a vacant moment.

This would be a very good devotion, every time the clock struck to cast a glance at our conscience. Some even have the practice of examining themselves over every action they do. And if it seems much to you to do this every hour or over every action, it will be good to do it at least over every one of the principal actions of the day; and of some we have special directions that on finishing them we should make examen of them, as we have said above. St. Bonaventure says that a servant of God should examine himself seven times a day. And if in the particular examen we keep that addition of putting our hand to our breast every time we fall, we shall easily remember thereby the number of times that we have fallen. Although our Father does not appoint this addition to enable us to remember our faults, but to make us repent of them at once, and therefore he prescribes this gesture of putting the hand to the breast, as though to say, "I have sinned"; yet, after all, if we keep this addition, it will be a great help to us afterwards to remember easily the times we have fallen. Add to this that, when one keeps a reckoning with oneself and lives with a careful eye to making progress, whenever one falls into a fault such a person at once feels remorse of conscience, which is the best awakener to make him remember it.

This is the final answer to two sorts of persons. For some there are to whom a whole quarter of an hour seems little time enough to remember the faults into which they have fallen, and to these we have already given a method how to bring the first point as it were already done, that so they may have time over to busy themselves with the two following. Others there are on the contrary whom the quarter of an hour of examen leaves much at large, and they do not find anything to spend it on; these we may more easily satisfy. We have already said that alike at midday and at night the general examen must be made along with the particular, and after having seen the faults into which we have fallen in the one examen and in the other, we should occupy ourselves in sentiments of shame and repentance for them and in begging pardon and in firm purposes of amendment and in asking of our Lord grace thereto; on which occupation the more we dwell, the better.

St. Dorotheus adds to this a piece of advice very helpful. He says that at examen we should not only take account of the faults into which we have fallen, but much more of the roots of those faults, examining the causes and occasions that led to our fall, that so we may be forewarned and on our guard against them from this time onwards. Thus, if by going out of my room I have broken silence or murmured, I must resolve not to go out of it henceforth without necessity, and then to go forewarned, and so of others the like things. Otherwise, it will be like a man stumbling over a stone and, for not paying attention to the occasion of his stumbling, stumbling there the next morning also; or as a man wanting to set a blighted tree right by merely cutting off some branches and the rotten and worm-eaten fruit. If we make our examens in this way, the time prescribed for them will not seem too ample, but short.

CHAPTER XI

That the Examen of Conscience Is a Means of Putting into Execution All Other Spiritual Methods and Directions, and the Reason Why We Do Not Profit by It Is That We Do Not Make It As We Ought

THE blessed St. Basil, after having given his monks many spiritual directions, concludes with this, that every night before going to bed they should make examen of conscience, thinking that this will be sufficient to secure the observance of all that he has said and hold them to it. With this also I wish to conclude this treatise, much commending this examination to all, since by the grace of the Lord it will be enough to put all other spiritual directions into execution and remedy all our faults. If you are growing slack at prayer, careless of obedience, uncontrolled in talking, beginning to take back a little of your free and easy worldly ways, all that will be stopped and cured at once by this examen. He who makes this examination of conscience every day may reckon that he carries with him a governor, a master of novices, a superior, who every day and every hour will ask of him an account, advise him what to do, and rebuke him on any point on which he fails.

Father Master Avila says: "Your faults cannot go on long if this examination of conscience goes on," and this squaring of your accounts and rebuking yourself every day and every hour. And if your faults do go on, and at the end of many days, and perhaps years, you are as unmortified, your passions as full and lively as at the beginning, it is because you do not use as you ought these means that we have for our spiritual progress. For if you had really taken to heart the getting rid of one fault and the gaining of one virtue and had gone about it with care and diligence, purposing amendment three times a day at least, morning, midday, and night, comparing every day the faults of the evening with those of the morning, and the faults of today with those of yesterday, and those of this week with those of the week past, repenting and being ashamed so many times for having fallen and begging support of our Lord and of His saints to correct yourself—at the end of so much time you would have come out with some result.

But if a man goes on making his examen out of routine and for form's sake, without any true sorrow for his faults and any firm purposes of amendment, that is no examen, but a vain ceremony and a Christmas game. Hence it is that the same evil propensities and the same bad habits and inclinations that a man brought from the world, he keeps after many years of religion. If he was proud, proud he is today; if he was impatient and haughty, the same he is today; if he used to utter sharp and stinging words, he utters them today: he is as unmannerly today as he was the first day, as self-willed, as greedy, as great a lover of his own comforts. And God grant that, instead of advancing and growing in virtue, they have not grown in ill-nature and in free and easy ways as they became seniors in religion; and that, while they ought to be more humble, they are not more uppish and presumptuous and fall not into that false position of which St. Bernard speaks: "Many there are who there in the world would have been held in small account, and here in religion want to be great people; and who there would not have found necessaries, but here seek comforts"—*Quodque perversum est, plerique in domo Dei non patiuntur haberi contemptui, qui in sua nonnisi contemptibiles esse potuerunt.*

From what has been said it will appear also what a bad excuse it is that some make for their faults, saying: "Oh, that is my way." Rather he is all the more to blame who, knowing that he has this or that bad way and being bound to bestow all his care and diligence in fortifying that weak side of his character, not to come to ruin thereby, lets himself be at the end of so long a time as passionate and unrestrained as he was the first day he came. Let him, then, who makes it his business to serve God—for to all such persons we are speaking here—enter into himself and begin anew, trying henceforth to get his examination of conscience well done, so that the fruit thereof may appear. We are men, and we have our faults and shall have them so long as we are in this life; but we should try to realize three things by aid of the examen. In the first place, if our faults were many, let them henceforth be few; secondly, if they were great, let them be smaller; thirdly, let them not always be the same, for to repeat the same fault time after time argues great carelessness and negligence.

Evagruis, in a book which he wrote on the life and bodily exercises of monks, mentions one holy monk who said: "I do not know that the devils have ever caught me twice in the same fault." This man must have made his examen of conscience well; this man repented in earnest and made firm purposes of amendment. In this way, then, we should make our examens. By this means God raised and elevated our blessed Father Ignatius to such perfection. We read in his Life a notable and very special thing. Comparing yesterday with today and his present state of progress with his past, he found that every day he had advanced and gained ground, or, rather, had gained not earthly ground but heaven. So much so that in his old age he came to say that the state in which he was at Manresa—which in the time of his studies he used to call his "primitive Church"—had been like a noviceship; and daily God went on adorning his soul and filling in with odors of perfection the portrait of which at Manresa He had sketched only the outlines. Let us, then, use as we ought the means which the Lord has so specially given us, and let us have great confidence that thereby He will raise us to the perfection which we desire.

EIGHTH TREATISE

ON CONFORMITY TO THE WILL OF GOD

CHAPTER I

In Which Two Fundamental Principles Are Laid Down

NOT as I will, but as thou willest (Matt. xxvi. 39). For two ends, the saints tell us, the Son of God descended from heaven and clothed Himself with our flesh, making Himself true man. The one end was to redeem us by His precious blood, the other to teach us by His doctrine the way to heaven and instruct us by His example. For, as it would profit us nothing to know the way if we remained shut up in the prison, so, says St. Bernard, it would not profit us to deliver us from prison if we did not know the way. And as God was invisible, that we might see Him and be able to follow and imitate Him, it was necessary that He should make Himself man and clothe Himself in our human nature, as the shepherd clothes himself with the shepherd's smock frock, which is the skin of a sheep, that the sheep may follow him, seeing their own likeness. St. Leo says: "If He were not true God, He would bring us no remedy; if He were not true man, He would give us no example." He did the one and the other in all completeness for the excess of love that He bore to men. As His *redemption was copious* (Psalm cxxix. 7), so also was His teaching; for it was not only given by words, but much more abundantly by the example of His deeds. *Jesus began to do and to teach* (Acts i. 1). He first began *to do,* and that all His life long, and afterwards *to preach* for the last three years of His life, or two and a half.

Now, among the things that Christ our Redeemer taught us, one of the chiefest was that we should have an entire conformity with the will of God in all things. He taught us that, not only in words—instructing us how to pray, He set down for one of our principal petitions, *Thy will be done on earth as it is in heaven* (Matt. vi. 10)—but He also confirmed this doctrine by His example: *I came down from heaven, not to do my own will, but the will of him that sent me* (John vi. 38). And at the time of accomplishing the work of our redemption, that Thursday of the Supper, in that prayer in the Garden, though His body and sensible appetite naturally shrank from death—and so to show that He was true man He said: *Father, if it be possible, let this chalice pass from me* (Matt. xxvi. 42)—yet His will ever remained quite ready and desirous to drink the chalice which His Father was sending Him, and therefore He added at once: *Yet not my will, but thine be done.*

To go to the root of the matter and establish ourselves well in this conformity, we must suppose two brief but very substantial fundamental principles on which all this matter must turn as upon two hinges. The first is that our advancement and perfection consist in conformity to the will of God; and the greater and more perfect this conformity, the greater will be our perfection. This foundation lends itself to being readily understood, for it is certain that perfection consists essentially in charity and love of God, and a man will be more perfect the more he loves God. Full of this doctrine is the holy Gospel, full the epistles of St. Paul, full the writings of the saints. *This is the greatest and first commandment* (Matt. xxii. 38). *Charity is the bond of perfection* (Col. iii. 14). *The greatest of these virtues is charity* (I Cor. xiii. 13). The highest and most perfect is charity and the love of God. But the highest and most exalted and purest point of this love, and what we may call the acme of it, is conformity in all to the will of God, so as to have one will of acceptance and one will of refusal with His Divine Majesty in all things. St. Jerome says, and he has it from a pagan philosopher: "To have the same *I will* and *I will not* with him whom you love; that is true friendship"—*Eadem velle et eadem nolle, ea demum firma amicitia est.* It follows that, the more conformable and the more united to the will of God a man is, the better will he be. Further, it is clear that there is nothing better or more perfect than the will of God. Therefore, the more a man seeks and conforms himself to the will of God, the better and more perfect will he be. So that other philosopher argued: "If God is the most perfect being there is, the more perfect any other being will be, the more it is assimilated and made like to God."

The second fundamental principle is this, that nothing can happen or come about in this world but by the will and ordinance of God—always understanding, *except fault and sin,* for of that God is not cause nor author, nor can He be; for as it is repugnant to the nature of fire to freeze and to that of water to warm and to that of the sun to darken, so it is infinitely more against the goodness of God to love evil. So said the Prophet Habacuc: *Lord, thine eyes are too pure to bear the sight of evil, and thou canst not give countenance to iniquity* (Hab. i. 13). As we say here on earth, "He cannot bear the sight," to give to understand the abhorrence that one has for a thing, so he says that God cannot bear the sight of evil for the great hatred and abhorrence that He has for it. *Thou art not a God that willest iniquity* (Psalm v. 5). *Thou hast loved justice and hated iniquity* (Psalm xliv. 8). All Holy Writ is full of the abhorrence that God has for sin, and so He cannot be cause or author of it. But apart from this, all other things and all penal evils and afflictions come of the will and ordinance of God. This foundation, also, is quite sure. There is no such thing as fortune in the world; that was a fiction and error of the heathen. The goods that the world calls goods of fortune are not given by fortune—there is no such thing—but by God alone. So says the Holy Spirit by the Wise Man: *Good things and evil things, life and death, poverty and riches, God gives them all* (Ecclus. xi. 14).

And though these things come by means of secondary causes, still it is certain that nothing is done in this great commonwealth of the world but by the will and ordinance of that sovereign Emperor Who governs it. Nothing comes by chance in respect of God; all is registered and sorted out by His hand. He counts all the bones of your body and all the hairs of your head; not one of them shall fall but by His ordinance and will. Why do I speak of men? Not a sparrow falls into the net, says Christ our Redeemer, but by the dispensation and will of God. *Are not two sparrows sold for a penny? and not one of them shall fall to the ground without the providence of your Father* (Matt. x. 29). There is not a leaf that stirs on a tree but by His will. So the Wise Man says of lots: *Lots are thrown into the urn, but God it is that directs them* (Prov. xvi. 33). Although the lots are drawn from the caddy or urn, think not that they come out by chance; they come out only by the ordinance of divine providence, which disposes and wills it so. *The lot fell upon Matthias* (Acts i. 26). It was not by chance that the lot fell on Matthias, but by a particular case and providence of God Who was pleased to choose him for His apostle by that way.

Good philosophers attained to this truth even by the sole light of nature and said that, although in respect of natural causes many things happen by chance, yet in respect of the First Cause they are not by chance, but intended quite on purpose. They give this example. A master sends a servant in some direction on business and sends another servant by a different way to the same place on other business, without the knowledge of either of them, but meaning them to meet there. The meeting of the servants is by chance in respect of themselves, but in respect of their master, who intended it, it is not by chance, but thought out and intended of set purpose. So here, though in respect of men some things fall out by chance because they neither intended nor thought of them; yet in respect of God it is not by chance, but by His knowledge and will, He having so ordained it for secret and hidden ends known to Himself.

What we have to draw from these two fundamental principles is the conclusion and thesis which we proposed—that since all that befalls us comes from the hand of God and all our perfection lies in conforming ourselves to His will, we should take all things as coming from His hand and conform ourselves therein to His most holy and divine will. You must not take anything as coming by chance or by the industry and contrivance of men, for that is what generally gives so much pain and annoyance. You must not think that this or that came upon you because So-and-So managed it, and if it had not been for this or that thing, things would have gone otherwise. You must make no account of that, but take all things as coming from the hand of God, by whatsoever way or whatsoever roundabout process they come, since it is He Who sends them by those means. One of those famous Fathers of the Desert used to say that a man could not find true repose or satisfaction in this life unless he reckoned that there is only God and himself in the world. And St. Dorotheus says that those ancient Fathers made a great point of taking all things as coming from the hand of God, however small they were and in whatever manner they came about, and thereby kept themselves in great peace and quiet and lived a heavenly life.

CHAPTER II

Further Explanation of the Second Fundamental Principle

IT is a truth so settled in Holy Writ that all afflictions and penal evils come from the hand of God, that it would not be necessary for us to take time in proving it, were it not for the obscurity which the devil with his cunning tries to throw over it. From the other also certain truth which we stated, which is that God is not cause or author of sin, the devil draws a false and lying conclusion, making some people believe that, though the evils that come to us by means of natural causes and irrational creatures, as sickness, hunger, and barrenness, come from the hand of God, because there there is no sin nor can be in such creatures, since they are not capable of it; yet the evil and affliction which come about by the fault of a man who wounds me, robs me, dishonors me, does not come from the hand of God nor is guided by the ordinance of His providence, but by the malice and damnable will of another man. This is a very great error. St. Dorotheus says very well, rebuking this error in those who do not take these things as coming from the hand of God: "There are those who, when another person says a word against them or does them any other ill turn, forget God and turn all their rage against their neighbor, imitating dogs who bite the stone and neither look at nor take account of the hand that threw it."

To banish this erroneous action and secure a firm foundation in Catholic truth, theologians observe that two elements there are combined in a sin that man commits; the one is the movement and exterior act, the other, the disorder of the will wandering away from what God commands. God is author of the former; man, of the latter. Let us take the case of a man quarreling with another and killing him. To kill him he must needs put his hand to his sword, draw it and brandish his arm, and deal the blow, and do other natural movements which may be considered by themselves apart from the disorder of the will of the man who does them to kill another. Of all these movements, considered by themselves, God is cause and He produces them as He produces likewise the effects of the action of irrational creatures. For, as these creatures cannot stir nor act without God, so neither can man. He cannot stir his arm nor put his hand to his sword. Besides that, these natural acts are not evil of themselves, for, if a man practises them in necessary self-defense or in a just war or as a minister of justice, and so kills another, he would not sin. But of the fault, which is the defect and disorder of the will, whereby the wicked man does the injury, of that deviation from reason and perversion of the same, God is not cause, although He permits it where He might hinder it; but hinder it He does not, in fulfilment of just judgments of His own. They illustrate this by a comparison. A man has a wound on his foot and goes limping. The cause of his foot's going is the virtue and motive power of his soul; but of his limping, the cause is the wound and not the virtues of the soul. So of the sinful action that man does, the cause of the action is God, but the cause of the fault and sin that there is in the act is the free will of man. Thus, though God is not nor can be cause or author of sin, yet we must hold for certain that all penal evils come from the hand of God and by dispensation of His providence, by whatever way and in whatever manner they come, whether they come by means of natural causes and irrational creatures or by means of rational creatures. God guided the hand of him that hurt you and the tongue of him who gave you the opprobrious name. *Shall there be evil in the city that the Lord hath not done?* says the Prophet Amos (iii. 6). Holy Writ is full of this truth, attributing to God the evil that one man does to another and saying that it is God Who did it.

In the Second Book of Kings, in the account of the chastisement wherewith God chastised David by means of his son Absalom for the sin of adultery and murder that he had committed, God says that it was Himself that was to do it. *So I will raise up over against thee evil from thine own house* (II Kings xii. 11). Hence it is also that the impious kings, who in their pride and cruelty inflicted most atrocious chastisements on the people of God, are called by Scripture instruments of the divine justice. *Ah, for Assur, the rod of my indignation!* (Isaias x. 5). And of Cyrus, King of the Persians, by whom the Lord intended to chastise the Chaldeans, He says: *Whose right hand I have grasped* (Isaias xlv. 1). On which St. Augustine has this excellent remark: "God deals with us as an earthly father is wont to do. When the father is angry with his son, he takes a stick which he finds hard by and chastises his son with it. Then the stick he casts into the fire, and keeps for the son the inheritance. In this way God is wont to take wicked men for an instrument and scourge to chastise the good." We read in ecclesiastical history how, at the destruction of Jerusalem, Titus, general of the Romans, going round the city, saw the ditches (moats) full of corpses and dead bodies and all the neighborhood infected by the stench. Whereupon he raised his eyes to heaven and with a loud voice called God to witness that it was none of his doing that so great slaughter had taken place. And when that barbarian Celaric was going to sack and destroy Rome, a venerable monk met him and begged him not to be the cause of so many evil deeds as were likely to be committed on that expedition. And he replied: "I am not going to Rome of my own accord, but some person assails me every day and torments me, saying: 'Go to Rome and destroy the city.'" Thus all things come from the hand of God and by His ordinance and will. So the Royal Prophet David, when Semei reviled him and flung stones and dirt at him, said to those who would have had him take vengeance on the fellow: *The Lord hath commanded him to curse David; and who shall dare to say, Why has thou commanded it?* (II Kings xvi. 10). He means to say: "The Lord hath taken him for the instrument of my affliction and punishment."

But what great thing is it to recognize men as instruments of the divine justice and providence, since the same is true even of the devils themselves, obstinate and hardened as they are in their malice and anxious for our perdition? St. Gregory observes this marvelously in that saying of Scripture: *An evil spirit of the Lord tormented Saul* (I Kings xvi. 23). The same spirit is called "spirit of the Lord" and "evil spirit"—"evil" by desire of his evil will;

and "of the Lord" to give us to understand that he was sent by God to give that torment to Saul, and God worked by him. And this the text itself there declares, saying: *An evil spirit, sent by the Lord, tormented him (Spiritus nequam a Domino)* (I Kings xvi. 14). And for the same reason, says the saint, the devils, who afflict and persecute the just, are called in Scripture "God's robbers": "robbers" for the evil will that they have to do us harm; and yet "of God" to give us to understand that the power they have to do us harm they have from God. So St. Augustine makes this excellent reflection: "Job did not say 'The Lord hath given, and the devil has taken away,' but he referred all to God: *The Lord hath given, and the Lord hath taken away* (Job i. 21); for he knew well that the devil could do no evil but what God permitted him to do." And the saint goes on to say: "Let no one say, 'The devil has done me this ill turn;' but attribute your affliction and scourge to God, since the devil could do nothing against you nor touch even a hair of your head unless God gave him permission thereto." Thus the devils could not enter into the swine of the Gerasenes, without first asking permission of Christ our Redeemer (Matt. viii. 31). How could they touch you, how could they tempt you, without God's leave? He who could not touch the swine, how shall he touch the children?

CHAPTER III

Of the Great Benefits and Advantages Contained in This Conformity to the Will of God

THE blessed St. Basil says that the height of sanctity and perfection in Christian life consists in attributing the causes of all things, great and small, to God and conforming ourselves therein to His most holy will. But that we may better understand the perfection and importance of this and so be more given to it and more careful to secure it, we will proceed to set forth in particular the benefits and great advantages contained in this conformity to the will of God.

In the first place, this is that true and perfect resignation which the saints and all the masters of spiritual life so greatly extol, and say that it is the root and principle of all our peace and quiet, since in this way a man submits and places himself in the hands of God, like a little clay in the hands of a workman, that He may work in him His entire will, not seeking any longer to be his own, or to live for himself, nor to eat, nor sleep, nor labor for himself, but all for God and for the sake of God. Now this is what this conformity effects, since by it a man entrusts himself entirely to the will of God, so as not to desire to seek anything else than that the divine will may be entirely accomplished in him alike in all that the man himself does and in all that may happen to him, alike in prosperity and consolation and in adversity and affliction. This is so pleasing to God that for it King David was called by God a man according to His own heart. *I have found David, a man according to my own heart, who will accomplish all my wishes* (I Kings xiii. 14). He kept his heart in as much abandonment and subjection to the heart of the Lord, and as prompt and ready for anything that God might please to imprint thereon in the way of affliction or relief, as a piece of soft wax to receive any figure or form that men chose to give it. Therefore he said again and again: *My heart is ready, O God, my heart is ready* (Psalm lvi. 8; cvii. 2).

Secondly, he who shall have attained this entire and perfect conformity to the will of God, will have gained an entire and perfect mortification and mastery of all his passions and evil inclinations. We well know how necessary this mortification is and how highly it is praised and commended by saints and Holy Scripture. Now this mortification is a means necessarily to be presupposed to come to attain to this conformity to the will of God. That is the end, and mortification the means to arrive at that end. Now the ultimate end must always be higher and more perfect than the means. How necessary a means mortification is to come to attain to this entire and perfect conformity to the will of God is easy to see, for what hinders this union and conformity is our own self-will and disorderly appetite. Thus the more a man denies and mortifies his will and appetite, the more easily will he unite and conform himself to the will of God. To unite and adjust a rough piece of wood to another well wrought and polished, it is necessary first to tool it and remove the roughness, otherwise the one will never fit into the other. Now this is what mortification does; it removes our roughness, planing and tooling us, that so we may be able to be united and adjusted to God, conforming ourselves in all to His divine will. Thus the more mortified a man is, the better will he succeed in uniting and adjusting himself to the will of God; and when he shall be perfectly mortified, then will he arrive at this perfect union and conformity.

Hence follows another thing, which may be our number three. This entire resignation and conformity to the will of God is the greatest and most acceptable and agreeable sacrifice that a man can offer of himself to God. In other sacrifices he offers his goods, but in this he offers himself. In other sacrifices and mortifications he mortifies himself in part—as in temperance or modesty, in silence or in patience, he offers a part of himself to God; but this is a holocaust in which a man offers himself entirely and wholly to God to do with all that He wills and as He wills and when He wills, without exception of anything or reservation of anything for himself. Thus, as man is worth more than the property of man and the whole is worth more than the part, so this sacrifice is worth more than all other sacrifices and mortifications. And God sets such store by it that it is this that He requires and asks of us. *Son, give me thy heart* (Prov. xxiii. 26). Thus as the royal hawk feeds only on hearts, so does God feed on that which is most precious and valuable, which is the heart. If you give Him not this, with nothing else can you content or satisfy Him. And this is not asking much of us; for if to us, who are a little heap of dust and ashes, all that God has created is not enough to satisfy or content us, and our tiny little heart will never be satisfied with anything less than God, how can you think to content and satisfy God by giving Him not your whole heart, but part of it, and reserving the rest for yourself? You are much mistaken, since our heart does not admit of being divided or parted in this manner. A little and narrow bed is the heart, says the Prophet Isaias (xxviii. 20); there is no room in it for more than God. Therefore the spouse calls it a *little bed* (Cant. iii. 1), because she kept her heart narrowed in such as way as to leave no room for any other than her Beloved. And whoever shall seek to dilate and widen his heart to make room in it for another, will cast God out of it, and of this His Divine Majesty complains by Isaias (lvii. 8): *Thou hast committed adultery, receiving in the bed of thy heart another than thy Beloved, and to cover the adulterer thou hast uncovered and cast out God.* Had we a thousand hearts, we should offer them all to God, and all should seem to us little compared to what we owe to so great a Lord.

Fourthly, as we said at the beginning, whoever shall reach this conformity, will reach perfect charity and love of God; and the more he shall grow in it, the more will he grow in love of God and consequently in perfection, which consists in this charity and love. This faith, apart from what we said before, is well gathered from what we have said just now, since the love of God consists not in words, but in deeds. "The proof of love is the display of work done," says St. Gregory. And the more difficult the works are and the more they cost us, the more manifest is the love that prompts them. So St. John, to show the love that God bore the world, says: *God hath so loved the world as to give his only-begotten Son to suffer and die for us* (John

iii. 16). And to manifest the love that He bore His Father, Christ our Redeemer says: *That the world may know that I love the Father, arise, let us go hence* (John xiv. 31); and the errand on which He went was to suffer death on the Cross. So He gave testimony to the world that He loved His Father, in accomplishing a commandment so rigorous. Thus it is in works that love is shown; and the greater and more laborious the works are, the greater is the display of love. This entire conformity to the will of God, as we have said, is the greatest sacrifice that we can offer of ourselves to God because it presupposes a perfect mortification and resignation, whereby one offers oneself to God and places oneself entirely in His hands, that He may do therewith what He pleases. And so there is nothing in which a man better shows the love that he bears to God than in this, since he gives and offers Him all that he has and all that he possibly could have and desire; and if he could have more and could give more, he would give it all.

CHAPTER IV

That This Perfect Conformity to the Will of God Is Happiness and Bliss on Earth

HE who shall attain to this entire conformity to the will of God, taking all that happens as coming from His hand and conforming himself therein to His most holy and divine will, will have gained happiness and bliss here on earth, will enjoy very great peace and tranquillity, will ever have perpetual joy and gladness in his soul, which is the happiness and bliss of the blessed enjoyed here by the great servants of God: *The kingdom of God is not eating and drinking, but righteousness and peace and joy in the Holy Ghost* (Rom. xiv. 17). This is the kingdom of God on earth and the paradise of delights which we are able to enjoy here. And rightly is it called bliss, because it makes us in some sort like to the blessed. For as there in heaven there are no changes nor fluctuations, but the blessed ever remain in one frame of mind, rejoicing in God, so here on earth those who have attained to such entire and perfect conformity that all their satisfaction is the satisfaction and will of God, are not disturbed or troubled by the changes of this life or by the various ways in which things turn out. Their will and heart are so united and conformed to the divine will that their seeing that all comes from His hand and that the will and satisfaction of God is accomplished therein, changes afflictions into joys and discomforts into mirth, since they seek and will rather the will of their Beloved than their own. Thus there is nothing that can disturb such people: if anything could disturb them and give them pain, it would be afflictions, adversities, and contumelies; but such things they take for a special delight and consolation, since they come from the hand of God and such is His will. Thus there is nothing left that can possibly disturb or banish the peace and restfulness of their soul.

This is the cause of that unbroken peace and cheerfulness in which we read that those saints of old always lived—a St. Anthony, a St. Dominic, a St. Francis, and others like them. The same we read of our blessed Father Ignatius and we see it ordinarily in the great servants of God. Do you think those saints had not their troubles? Had they no temptations or infirmities such as we have? Did they not pass through various and diversified changes of fortune? Certainly they did, and through much more trying circumstances than we encounter, since it is the greatest saints that God usually exercises and tries with such things. How, then, did they keep ever in the same frame of mind, with the same countenance and deportment, with an interior and exterior serenity and cheerfulness as if it were always Easter with them? The cause thereof was what we are saying, that they had come to attain to an entire conformity to the will of God and placed all their joy in the accomplishment thereof; thus everything turned out to their satisfaction. *To them that love God all things work together unto good* (Rom. viii. 28). *The just shall not be saddened by anything that happens to him* (Prov. xii. 21). Labor, temptation, mortification, all was converted for them into joy because they understood that such was the will of God, in which all their satisfaction lay. They had gained already that happiness and bliss which can be tasted in this life and so they walked as if in glory. St. Catherine of Siena says very well on this point that the just are like Christ our Redeemer, Who never lost the blessedness of His soul for all His many griefs and pains. There the just never lose that blessedness which consists in conformity to the will of God, for all their many afflictions. There ever lasts and remains in them that joy and satisfaction, which consists in the will and good pleasure of God being accomplished in them.

This is a peace so exalted and so extraordinary that St. Paul says of it: *The peace of God, which surpasseth all understanding, keep your hearts and intelligences in Christ Jesus* (Phil. iv. 7). He says that this peace surpasses all understanding, because it is so high and supernatural a gift that human understanding cannot of itself comprehend how it is possible for a heart of flesh to be quiet, peaceful, and full of consolation in the midst of the whirlwinds and storms of temptation and affliction there are in this life. This appears in the marvel of the bush that burned and was not consumed, and in the miracle of the three youths in the Babylonian furnace, who in the midst of the fire remained whole and entire, praising God. This it is that holy Job said, speaking to God: *Lord, thou tormentest me marvelously* (Job x. 16), giving us to understand on the one hand the great affliction and pain that he was suffering and on the other hand the great content and satisfaction that he had in suffering, since such was the will and good pleasure of God.

Cassian relates that an old man of Alexandria, being surrounded by a great multitude of unbelievers uttering curses against him, stood in the midst of them like a lamb, suffering in silence with great peacefulness of heart. They mocked him, gave him buffets and blows, and did him other grievous injuries. Among other things, they said to him with scorn: "What miracles has Jesus Christ wrought?" He answered: "The miracles that He has wrought are that, suffering the injuries that you are doing me, even if they were greater, still I feel no indignation nor anger against you nor any trouble of passion." This is a great marvel and a very high and extraordinary perfection.

Of that mountain of Macedonia called Olympus the ancients say, and St. Augustine refers to it in many places, that it is so high that there is no experience up there of winds or rains or clouds. Even birds cannot harbor there, since it is so high as to rise above the first region of the air and reach to the second; and so the air there is so pure and refined that clouds cannot form and float in it, as they require a more dense atmosphere. And for the same reason birds cannot hold on their way there nor can men live there either, the air being too subtle and refined for respiration. Information of this was given by certain climbers who went up there year after year to offer certain sacrifices. They carried with them moist sponges to put to their nostrils, and so condense the air as to make it breathable. These people wrote up there in the dust certain alphabetic characters, which they found next year as clean-cut and entire as they had left them, which could not be if there were winds and rains. Now this is the state of perfection to which they have mounted up and attained, who have this entire conformity to the will of God. They have mounted and risen so high, they have gained by this time such a perfect peace, that there are no clouds nor winds nor rains to reach them there, nor birds of prey to attack and rob them of the peace and joy of their heart.

St. Augustine on those words: *Blessed are the peacemakers, for they shall be called the children of God* (Matt. v. 9), says that Christ our Redeemer calls peacemakers blessed and children of God because there is nothing in them that contradicts or resists the will of God, but in all things they are conformable like good sons, who in everything seek to be like their father, having no other will this way or that but what their father has this way or that.

This is one of the most spiritual and essential points of spiritual life. He that shall arrive at the pitch of taking all things that befall him, great and small, as coming from the hand of God and so conforming himself to the divine will therein as that all his satisfaction is the satisfaction of God and the fulfilment of His most holy will—such a one has found a paradise on earth. *His abode is in peace and his dwelling on Mount Sion* (Psalm lxxv. 3). Such a one, says St. Bernard, may in all security and confidence sing the canticle of the Wise Man: *In all things I have sought rest, and shall dwell in the inheritance of the Lord* (Ecclus. xxiv. 11) because I have found the true repose and full and complete joy that no one can take away: *that your joy be full, and your joy no man shall take away from you* (John xvi. 22, 24). Oh, if we could succeed in placing all our satisfaction in the fulfilment of the will of God, so that our will should be ever His will and our satisfaction His satisfaction! Oh, that I were minded, O Lord, never to will or will not except as Thou willest and willest not, and that that were my consolation in all things! *It is good for me to cleave unto God, and put my hope in the Lord God* (Psalm lxxii. 28). Oh, what a good thing it would be for my soul to be thus united to God! Oh, how well off should we be, if we were always so united with Him as in all that we did and suffered to regard nothing but the accomplishment of the will of God, and that was all our satisfaction and delight! This is what that holy man, Thomas à Kempis, said: "He to whom all things are one and all lead to one and all things are seen in one, can be steady in heart and rest peacefully on God."

CHAPTER V

That in God Alone Satisfaction Is to Be Found, and He Who Shall Set Up His Rest in Anything Else Shall Never Find True Satisfaction

THEY who place their satisfaction in God and His divine will, enjoy unbroken satisfaction and content, for, being built into that firm pillar, the will of God, they share in the immutability of the divine will and so are always firm and immovable and of one mind. But those who are attached to the things of the world and have set their heart and satisfaction in them, cannot have true and lasting content, for they go as things go and depend on things and are subject to the changes of things. The glorious St. Augustine declares this very well on that saying of the prophet: *He hath conceived sorrow and borne iniquity* (Psalm vii. 15). "Hold for certain," he says, "that you will always be liable to pain and disappointment so long as you do not set up your rest in that which none can take away from you without your will"—*Non enim potest labor finiri nisi hoc quisque diligat quod invito non possit auferri.*

We read of our Father Francis Borgia that, when he came to Granada with the body of the empress and the time came to deliver over his charge, on opening the leaden coffin in which she lay and uncovering her face, it was found to be so changed, so hideous and disfigured, as to strike the beholders with horror. This made such an impression on him, and God touched his heart with such a sense of disillusionment of the things of the world, that he made a firm purpose, saying: "I resolve, my God, never more to serve a master who can die." Let us, then, take this resolution, which is a very good one: "I purpose, Lord, never more to set my heart on anything that can be taken from me by death, on anything that can come to an end, on anything that another can take from me without my will," since in no other way can we find true contentment.

For, says St. Augustine, if you set your heart on that which they can take away from you without your will, it is clear that, when they do take it away, you must feel it. This is natural: a well-loved possession is not given up without grief; and the greater the love, the greater will be the grief. And in confirmation of this he says in another place: "He who shall wish to find satisfaction in himself shall be sad." If you set up your rest in such and such an office or in such an occupation or in being in such a place or anything like that, such a satisfaction can easily be taken from you by the superior, and so you will never live in contentment. If you set up your rest in exterior things or in the fulfilment of your own will, those things easily change: and when they do not change, you yourself change: for what pleases you and satisfies you today, tomorrow displeases and dissatisfies you. If you do not believe it, see it in that people of Israel, who, having the manna, grew weary and asked for other food; and seeing themselves free, at once turned their desire upon their old state of subjection and sighed after Egypt and the garlic and onions they ate there and longed many times to return there. You will never find satisfaction if you set up your rest in those things. But he who shall place all his satisfaction in God and in the fulfilment of His holy will, shall always live content, for God is everlasting, never changes, always remains such as He once for all is. "Would you attain to perpetual and everlasting joy and contentment," says the saint, "set up your rest in God, Who is everlasting."

Holy Writ marks this difference between the fool and the wise and holy man. *The fool changeth like the moon: the holy man remaineth in his wisdom unchanged like the sun* (Ecclus. xxvii. 12). The fool changes as the moon, today waxing and tomorrow waning; today you will see him cheerful and tomorrow sad; now in one mood, now in another because he has placed his love and satisfaction in the changeable and perishable things of the world; and so he dances to the tune of such things and changes with their vicissitudes; like the sea, he goes with the moon—he is moon-struck. But the just and holy man endures like the sun; he keeps ever the same demeanor and is ever of the same mind; there is no waxing and waning in him; he is always cheerful and content because his contentment is in God and in the fulfilment of His most holy will, which none can alter.

Of that holy abbot called Deicola it is told that he always had a smile on his face. And when someone asked him why, he said: "Be what may be and come what may come, no one can take God away from me." *Christum a me tollere nemo potest.* This man had found true contentment because he had set up his rest in what could not fail, and none could take from him. Let us do the like. *Rejoice, ye just, in the Lord* (Psalm xxxii. 1). On these words St. Basil says: Observe that the prophet does not say: Rejoice in the abundance of earthly things, nor in your great ability, learning, and talents, nor in your vigorous health and great bodily strength, nor in the high name and reputation that you enjoy amongst men; but rejoice in the Lord; put all your satisfaction in God and in the fulfilment of His holy will, for that alone is sufficient, and all the rest together cannot satisfy nor afford true contentment.

St. Bernard, in a sermon which he preached on those words of St. Peter: *See, Lord, how we have left all things* (Matt. xix. 27), illustrates and proves this very well. All other things, he says, away from God may occupy the soul and heart of man, but they cannot satisfy it—*occupare potest, replere non potest. The covetous man will never have his fill of money,* says the Wise Man (Eccles. v. 9). He is hungry after pounds, shillings, and pence; but however much he gets, he will never be satisfied. And so of all the things of the world—they cannot satisfy our soul. And this is St. Bernard's reason: Do you know why riches and all the things of the world cannot satisfy? It is because they are not the natural food of the soul—*quia non sunt naturales cibi animae*—nor proportional to its wants. Thus, as air and wind are not the natural food of our body nor proportional to it, and you would laugh if you saw a man starving to death open his mouth to the air like a chameleon, thinking thereby to satisfy and sustain himself, and you would take him for mad; so it is no less madness, says the saint, to think that man's rational soul, which is a spirit, is to be satisfied with temporal and sensible things. It may be puffed out, like the other with air, but it cannot be satisfied, for that is not its food. *Inflari potest, satiari non potest.* Give to every creature the sustenance that is proportional to it—to the body, bodily food; to the spirit, spiritual food. Thus they only shall be blessed who hunger and thirst after justice, for they shall have their fill.

The blessed St. Augustine further explains this reason in his "Soliloquies," speaking of the rational soul. He says: "Thou hast made the rational soul, O Lord, capable of Thy majesty, in such a way that nothing else can satisfy or sate it but Thyself." When the cavity and hollow of a ring is made to the measure of some definite precious stone, nothing else that you can put there can fit or completely fill that void, but only that particular precious stone to the measure of which it was made. If the cavity is triangular, no round thing can fill it. Now our soul is created to the image and likeness of the most Holy Trinity, leaving a vacancy and a cavity and a hollow in our heart capable of God and proportioned to receive God Himself. It is impossible for any other thing to bulk out and fill that vacant place but God Himself. All the round world will not suffice to fill it. "Thou hast made us, O Lord, for Thyself, and our heart is restless till it rests in Thee"—*Fecisti nos, Domine, ad te, et inquietum est cor nostrum donec in te requiescat* (St. Augustine, "Confessions," i. 1).

A very good comparison, and one which illustrates this matter very well, is that common comparison which is drawn from the needle of the mariner's compass. The nature of that needle, after it has been touched by the magnet, is to point to the north, God having given it that natural inclination; and you will see how restless that needle is and how many times it turns and turns back again until it takes its direction to the north; and, that done, it is at once quiet. Now in this way God has created man, with this natural inclination in respect of Himself, as to his north star and last end; and so, until we fix our heart on God, we shall be always like that needle, restless and troubled. To whatever point of the revolving heavens that needle looks, it cannot be quiet; but when it looks to that one point of the heavens, the polar star, which does not revolve, there it fixes itself and is immovable. So as long as you set the eyes of your heart on the things of the world, changeable and perishable, you will not be able to find rest or content; set them on God, and you will find it.

This ought to be a great motive for us to seek after God, even though it were only in our own interest, since we all desire to find satisfaction. St. Augustine says: "We know, brethren, that every man desires joy, but not all seek joy where it is to be found. We cannot live without enjoyment; but whether men hit their mark or miss it all depends on this, whether they aim at and fix their eyes and heart on true satisfaction or on satisfactions apparent and false." The miser, the wrong-doer, the proud man, the ambitious, the glutton, all desire to attain satisfaction; but one puts his satisfaction in heaping up riches, another in gaining high honors and dignities, a third in eating and junketing, another in impure delights. They have not hit the mark in setting up their rest where they ought to have set it and so they will never find it; for all these things, and all that there is in the world, is insufficient to satisfy the soul and give it true content. So the saint says: "Why, then, dost thou range far and wide, poor man, seeking good things for thy soul and body! Love that one Good wherein are all good things, and it suffices; desire that simple Good Which is all good, and it is enough. *Bless the Lord, O my soul, who fillest thy desire with good things* (Psalm cii. 5). Blessed and praised and glorified may He be for ever and ever. Amen."

CHAPTER VI

Another Way of Showing How Conforming Ourselves to the Will of God Is the Way to Find Contentment

THE glorious St. Augustine on those words of our Savior: *Whatever ye shall ask the Father in my name shall be granted you* (John xiv. 13), says that a man should not seek peace and quiet by means of doing his own will and gaining what he has a craving for, because that is not what is good for him or suits him—on the contrary, it may be a bad thing for him—but by acquiescing in the good or better lot that God offers him, and this it is that he ought to ask of God. *Quando nos delectant mala, et non delectant bona, rogare debemus potius Deum ut delectent bona quam ut concedantur mala.* If you find no relish in the accomplishment of the will of God, which is good, but your taste and appetite is bent on the accomplishment of your own will, you ought to beg and entreat of God, not that He would grant you what you wish for, but that He would grant you the grace to relish the accomplishment of His will, which is the good that suits you. He quotes to this effect that passage in Numbers (xi. 4) when the children of Israel grew weary of the manna from heaven which God sent them and desired and asked for flesh meat. God fulfilled their desire, but greatly to their cost, for *while the meat was still in their mouths, the anger of God came upon them, and slew the strongest and overthrew the flower of Israel* (Psalm lxxvii. 31). God in chastisement made a great slaughter amongst them. It is clear that the manna from heaven which God sent them was better than the flesh meat which they sought and the onions and garlic of Egypt which they sighed after. Thus, says the saint, they should not have asked these things of God, but that He would heal their palate to relish the manna from heaven and find a taste in it; and in this way they would have had no temptation to desire other food, for they would have found all things in the manna and all the tastes that they could wish. In the same way, when you are under a fit of temptation or passion and your taste is unhealthy and so you have no relish for virtue and goodness, but like a sick man you crave after evil and noxious food, you must not let yourself be governed by your appetite nor seek for the fulfilment of your desire; for that would not be a means to find contentment, but rather to feel afterwards greater dissatisfaction and more restlessness and trouble. What you should desire and beg of God is that He would heal your palate and give you a taste for the accomplishment of His most holy will, since that is the good that is suited to you, and in this way you will come to gain true peace and true contentment.

St. Dorotheus has drawn this conclusion in another way or, rather, explains the same truth in another manner. He says that he who entirely conforms his will to the will of God so as to have no will one way or another but what God wills this way or that, comes by this means always to do his own will and always remain in great peace and quiet. Let us take an example from obedience, and thereby what we wish to say will be explained, and we shall arrive by one road at two virtues. We commonly say to those who are thinking of being religious and following the way of obedience: "See that here in religion you must not do your own will in anything." St. Dorotheus says: "Go along, you may quite well do it; and I will give you method by which you may do your own will all day long, not only lawfully, but holily and with great perfection. Do you know how? The religious who is thoroughly obedient and has no will of his own, always does his own will because he makes another's will his; and thus, without seeking to do our own will, we always find it in what we are doing." Contrive that your own will shall be no other than the will of the superior, and so all day long you will go about doing your own will, and that with much perfection and merit. In this way I sleep as much as I wish, because I have no wish to sleep more than obedience ordains. I eat what I wish, since I have no wish to eat more than they give me. I pray as I wish, and read and work and do penance as I wish, because in all this I have no wish but to do what obedience has meted out for me and ordained, and so of all the rest. Thus a good religious, by not seeking to do his own will, comes to be always doing his own will. This is how good religious are so cheerful and content; it is the making of the will of obedience their own that keeps them cheerful and content.

Herein lies the whole issue of the ease or hardship of religious life, and hereon depend the cheerfulness and contentment of the religious. If you make up your mind to give up your own will and take the superior's will for yours, you will find religious life very easy and pleasant and you will live in great contentment and cheerfulness; but if you keep another will apart from that of your superior, you cannot live in religion; two different wills are incompatible one with the other. Even with the fact that we have in ourselves one will only, yet because we have a sensitive appetite that contradicts the will and reason, we can hardly get on with it, although this appetite is inferior and subordinate to our will; what would it be with two wills, each claiming the mastership! *No man can serve two masters* (Matt. vi. 24). The difficulty of religious life is not so much in the things themselves and the hardships that there are in it, as is the repugnance of our will and the fancies of our imagination: it is that which makes things to us grievous and difficult. This is easily understood by the difference that we experience in ourselves when we are under temptation and when we are not. When we are free from temptations, we see that things become light and easy to us; but when temptation comes, and sadness and melancholy press upon us, that which used to be easy becomes very difficult, and we fancy that the very sky would fall were we to try it. The difficulty is not in the thing, since that is the same as it was yesterday, but in our bad disposition. When a sick man loathes his food, it is not the fault of the food, which is good and well cooked, but of the peccant humor of the patient, which makes the food seem bad and disagreeable; so it is here.

This is the favor which God does to those whom He calls to religious life; He gives them a relish and a liking for following the will of another. This is the grace of vocation with which God has favored us beyond our brethren who have stayed behind there in the world. Who has given you this facility which you find in giving up your own will and following that of another? Who has given you a new heart, wherewith you have abhorred the things of the world and found a taste for recollection and prayer and mortification? You were not born with it; no, certainly, but rather with the contrary, *for the feelings and thoughts of the human heart are inclined to evil from his youth* (Gen. viii. 21). It has been the grace of the Holy Ghost; it is that which like a good mother has put aloes on the breasts of the world, that that might become bitter to you which was before sweet, and sweetest honey on the things of virtue and religion in order to make that tasty and sweet to you which before seemed bitter and disagreeable. That saint said [St. Agatha]: "I give Thee infinite thanks, O Lord, for having guarded me and chosen me from childhood and for having rid my heart of the things of the world." It is no great thing that we have done in becoming religious; but great and very grand is the favor that the Lord has done us in drawing us to religion and giving us a taste of the manna of heaven while other men are tasting and enjoying themselves on the garlic and onions of Egypt.

Sometimes I set myself to consider how people in the world give up their will and do the will of another in view of their temporal gains and interests, from the grandee by the side of the king to the lackey and stable-boy. They eat, as they say, to another man's hunger and sleep to another man's inclination for sleep; and they are so thoroughly trained to this and have so thoroughly made another's will their own that by this time they have got a liking for this style of life and take it for a pastime. *And this they do to gain a corruptible crown, but we an incorruptible* (I Cor. ix. 25). Is it much for us to get a taste for this style of life so well laid out as that of religion, and make our own the will of the superior, which is better than ours? If they for a little honor and temporal interest make another's will so thoroughly their own that now it is to them a delight and pastime to follow it, turning nights into days and days into nights, is it a great thing for us to do the same for the love of God and for the gaining of life everlasting? Let us, then, resolve to make the superior's will our own, and in this manner we shall always do our own will and live very contented and happy lives in religion, and very spiritual will be our cheerfulness and joy.

Let us now turn this to our purpose and apply it to the matter in hand. Let us make the will of God ours by conforming ourselves to it in all things and not otherwise willing or willing not than as God wills and wills not; in this manner we shall come to do always our own will and to live in great contentment and cheerfulness. It is clear that, if you will only what God wills, your will will be accomplished, and that is what you will and desire. Even the pagan Seneca hit the mark in saying this. "The most exalted and perfect thing in man," he says, "is to know how to suffer with cheerfulness adversities and hardships, and bear all that happens as though it happened of his own will, for so man is obliged to will, knowing that this is the divine will." Oh, in what contentment should we live if we succeeded in making the will of God ours and in never willing aught but what He wills—not merely because in that way our will would always be accomplished, but chiefly for seeing that the will of God, Whom we love so much, is always accomplished and done! For although we ought to help ourselves by what has been said, yet we ought to come to dwell on this and on this we ought to found all our satisfaction, I mean in the contentment of God and the fulfilment of His most holy and divine will. *All things whatsoever he hath willed, the Lord hath done, in heaven, on earth, on the sea, and in all the depths* (Psalm cxxxiv. 6). All things that the Lord has willed, He has done; and He will do all the things that He shall will; and He can do as much as He can will, according to the saying of the Wise Man: *Power waiteth upon thy will* (Wisdom xii. 18). *All things are put in subjection to thee, and there is none that can resist thy will* (Esther xiii. 9; Rom. ix. 19).

CHAPTER VII

Of Other Benefits and Advantages That There Are in This Conformity to the Will of God

ANOTHER great benefit and advantage that there is in this practice is that this entire conformity and resignation to the will of God is one of the best and principal dispositions that we can bring on our part for the Lord to do us favors and fill us with good things. Thus, when God our Lord chose to make of St. Paul, who had been a persecutor of Christians, a preacher of the Gospel, he first disposed him and brought him over to this disposition. He sent a great light from heaven, which threw him from his horse, and opened the eyes of his soul and made him say: *Lord, what wilt thou have me to do?* (Acts ix. 6). See me, O Lord, like a little clay in Thy hands, that Thou mayest make of me what Thou wilt. And so God made of him a chosen vessel, to carry and spread His name all the world over.

Of the holy virgin Gertrude we read that God told her: "Whoever desires that I should come to dwell in him without reserve, must hand over to Me the key of his own will and never ask it back again." For this our Father sets down this resignation and indifference as the principal disposition to receive great favors from God, and wishes everyone to have it who enters on the Exercises; and this is the foundation which he lays at the commencement of them, that we should be indifferent and detached from all things of the world, not desiring rather this than that, but desiring in all that the will of God may be accomplished and done in us. And in the rules and annotations which he puts to help as well him who gives the Exercises as him who makes them, he says: "It will be a very great help for him who makes the Exercises to entrust and offer himself freely and in all to the hands of God, that God may make of him and his whatsoever shall please Him." And the reason of this being such a great disposition and means for the Lord to do us favors, is that on the one hand our way is thereby made clear of the lets and hindrances that may arise out of our evil affections and desires; and on the other hand the more a man trusts in God, putting himself entirely in His hands and not seeking anything except what He wills, the more God is obliged to look after him and all that concerns him.

In another way also this conformity to the will of God is a very effectual means for acquiring and gaining all virtues, since these are acquired by the exercise of their acts. This is the natural way to acquire habits, and in this manner God wills to give us virtue, for He wishes works of grace to be done in accordance with works of nature. Exercise yourself, then, in this resignation and conformity to the will of God, and in this manner you will exercise yourself in all virtues and so you will come to gain them all. Sometimes you will be offered occasions of humility, at other times of obedience, at others of poverty, at others of patience, and so of the rest of the virtues. And the more you exercise yourself in this resignation and conformity to the will of God and the more you grow and perfect yourself in it, the more will you grow and become perfect in all virtues. *Unite thyself with God and endure, that as time goeth on thou mayest grow and thrive in thy life* (Ecclus. ii. 3). Unite thyself to God, conform thyself in all to His will. *Fasten thyself upon God (conglutinare Deo),* says another version, and in this way you will grow and improve much.

To this end the masters of spiritual life advise us—and it is marvelous good advice—to fix our eyes on some higher virtue which includes in itself the rest, and aim at that chiefly in meditation, and direct our examen and all our exercises thereto; for by fixing our eyes on one thing, it is easier to compass it; and, that gained, all is gained. Now one of the chief things upon which we can fix our eyes for this purpose is this entire resignation and conformity to the will of God. Thus meditation and examen will be employed upon it even though we spend on it many years, aye, and our whole life. On those words of the Apostle St. Paul, *Lord, what wilt thou have me to do?* (Acts ix. 6), St. Bernard cries: "O short speech, but full; it embraces all, it leaves nothing out: *Lord, what wilt thou have me to do?* Brief speech, but compendious; living, effectual, and worthy of all admiration." If, then, you are seeking a brief and compendious lesson in the gaining of perfection, here it is: *Lord, what wilt thou have me to do?* And with the prophet: *My heart is ready, O Lord, my heart is ready, disposed and prepared for all that thou requirest of me* (Psalm lvi. 8). Keep this ever in your mouth and in your heart; and in proportion as you grow in it, you will grow in perfection.

There is also another good point and advantage in this exercise; it is that we may draw from it an excellent remedy against a certain sort and manner of temptations which often occur. The devil contrives at times to disturb us with temptations of conditional suppositions and questions. "If the other fellow said this, what would you reply?" "If that were to happen, what would you do?" "How would you behave in such and such a case?" And, being the subtle opponent that he is, he puts things in such a way that, whichever side we take, we seem to find ourselves in a hole, and we cannot hit upon a way out, finding a snare set wherever we turn. Nor does the devil care whether the allegation he uses to catch us be true or mere camouflage and fiction. His trick being to draw a man into some evil consent, it is all one to him what instrument he uses. In these temptations they commonly say that one is not obliged to answer either Yes or No; rather it is better not to answer at all. This advice is especially suitable for scrupulous people, since once they begin to bandy words with the devil and go into question and answer with him, they are doing just what he wants, for he will be never at a loss for something to answer back; and the best to be expected for men coming out of the skirmish is that they shall come out with a broken head.

But there is an answer that I find good and profitable for these temptations, and I think it is better to give this answer than not to answer at all. It is what we have just been saying. To any one of these posers one may answer with eyes shut: "If that is the will of God, I want it;" "I should wish in that case to do what God might wish;" "I refer myself in all to the will of God;" "I would do therein whatever might be my duty;" "The Lord would give me grace not to offend Him in that matter, but that I might do what was His will." This is a general answer, meeting every requirement; and there is no difficulty, but much facility, in thus sticking to generalities. "If it is the will of

God, it is good;" "If it is the will of God, it is the better thing;" "If it is the will of God, it is that which better suits me." I may in all security plant my feet on the will of God and say all these things; and thereby the devil will be handsomely made game of and put to shame, and we shall be well satisfied and encouraged by the victory. As in temptations against faith we are advised—scrupulous people in particular—not to answer in detail, but to say in general: "I hold and believe all that Holy Mother Church holds and believes," so in these temptations it is a good remedy not to answer in detail, but to betake ourselves to the will of God, which is sovereignly just and perfect.

CHAPTER VIII

In Which It Is Confirmed by Examples How Pleasing to God Is This Exercise of Conformity to His Will, and the Great Perfection There Is in It

CAESARIUS relates how there dwelt in a monastery a monk to whom God had given such a grace of working miracles that by the mere touch of his clothes or of the cincture which he wore, he healed the sick. His abbot, attentively considering this and not seeing in that monk any special effulgence of sanctity, called him apart and asked him to tell the reason why God worked such miracles through him. He answered that he did not know; "For," said he, "I do not fast more than the others or take more disciplines or penances, nor spend more time in prayer nor watch more. All I can say is that prosperity does not elate nor adversity discourage me; nothing that happens troubles or disturbs me; my soul is in the same peace and quiet under all circumstances, how various soever they be, whether they touch me or my neighbor." The abbot said to him: "Were you not somewhat troubled and upset that other day, when that knight our enemy set fire to our granary and burned it?" "No," he said, "I felt no trouble in my soul, since I have already left all that in the hands of God, as well prosperity as adversity, as well little as great; I take all with equal thanksgiving as coming from His hand." Then the abbot understood what was the cause of this power of working miracles.

Blosius relates that a poor beggarman of very perfect life, being asked by a theologian how he had attained to perfection, answered in this manner. "I have determined to give myself over to God's will alone, to which I have so conformed my own that whatever God wills, I will also. When hunger exhausts me, when cold pinches me, I praise God. Be the weather fair, or foul and stormy, I likewise praise God. Whatever lot He gives me or permits to come upon me—be it prosperous or unfortunate; be it sweet, or bitter and disagreeable—I receive it at His hand with great alacrity as a very good thing, resigning myself to it in all humility. Never have I been able to find repose in anything that was not God; and now I have found unto myself God, in Whom I enjoy repose and peace everlasting."

The same author tells of a holy virgin who, being asked how she had attained perfection, replied: "All troubles and mishaps I took with great conformity as coming from the hand of God; and anyone who did me any wrong or gave me any annoyance, I took care to pay off by doing him some special service. I never complained to anyone of my troubles, but had recourse only to God, of Whom I received new strength and consolation." Of another virgin of great sanctity he says that, being asked on what practices she had gained such great perfection, she answered with much humility: "I never had pains and afflictions so great but that I desired to suffer more for love of God, taking them for great gifts of His and judging myself unworthy of them."

Tauler tells of a servant of God, wholly resigned into His hands, whom different persons asked to pray for certain affairs. She said she would, and sometimes forgot, yet all that they commended to her succeeded just as they had asked. They came back to return thanks to her, considering that the success was due to her prayers, and she was ashamed and told them to thank God, as she had had no part in the matter. Many came to her on this errand. She made a loving complaint to God, that all the intentions which they commended to her He accomplished in such sort that they came to her to return thanks to her when she had had nothing to do with it. The Lord answered: "See, daughter, the day that thou gavest thy will to Me, I gave thee Mine; and, though thou asked Me nothing in particular, as I understand what thy wishes are, I accomplish them as thou desirest."

In the lives of the Fathers there is told of a farmer whose fields and vineyards always bore better crops than those of his neighbors. His neighbors asking him how that was, he answered that he was not astonished at having better crops than they had, seeing that he had always the weather he wanted. At that they were still more surprised and asked how that could be. He replied: "I never wish for any other weather but what God wishes; and as I wish what God wishes, He gives me crops as I wish."

Sulpicius Severus relates in his Life of the blessed St. Martin, bishop, that in all his intercourse with him he never saw him out of humor or sad, but always in great peace and cheerfulness. And the reason of that he says was because, whatever happened to him, he took it as sent from the hand of God and so conformed himself in all things to God's will with great equanimity and alacrity.

CHAPTER IX

Of Some Facts That Will Render This Exercise of Conformity with the Will of God Easy and Pleasant

THAT this exercise of conformity to the will of God may be made to us easy and pleasant, it is necessary ever to bear in mind the foundation that we laid at the beginning, to the effect that no adversity or affliction can come to us that does not pass through the hands of God and is not checked and registered by His will. Christ our Redeemer taught us this truth, not only in word, but also by His example. When on the night of His Passion He bade St. Peter sheathe his sword, He added: *The chalice that my Father hath given me, shall I not drink it?* (John xviii. 11). He did not say "the chalice that Judas and the scribes and Pharisees have contrived for me," for He knew well that all these were nothing but creatures who waited upon the Father; and what they did in malice and envy, the eternal Father in His infinite wisdom and goodness ordained for the healing of mankind. So he said also to Pilate, who said that he had power to crucify Him or to set Him free: *Thou shouldst not have any power over me, were it not given thee from on high* (John xix. 11); which means, as the saints explain, "were it not done by the counsel and ordinance of God." Thus all comes from on high by the arrangement and order of God.

The Apostle St. Peter says this marvelously well in the fourth chapter of the Acts, explaining that saying of the prophet: *Why have the nations raged, and peoples devised vain plans, against the Lord and against his Christ?* (Psalm ii. 1). He says in explanation: *Truly in this city Herod and Pontius Pilate allied themselves with the Gentiles and with the people of Israel to carry out that which thy power and counsel had determined should be done* (Acts iv. 27). The princes and powers of the earth allied themselves together against Christ our Redeemer to execute and carry into effect what had been decreed and determined in the consistory of the most holy Trinity; they could not go beyond that. And we see that, when God did not will it, all the power of Herod was insufficient to deprive Him of life as a child; and, though Herod massacred all the babes in the neighborhood from two years and under, he could do nothing with Him Whom he sought because He did not will to die then. And the Jews and Pharisees many times sought to lay hands on Christ and put Him to death. On one occasion they took Him to the top of a mountain on which their city was built, to cast Him headlong; and, says the holy Gospel, *He passing through the midst of them went his way* (Luke iv. 30)—in great peace, because He had not chosen that manner of death, and so they could not put Him to it. Another time they sought to stone Him and already had their hands lifted up on high with their stones to throw at Him; and Christ our Redeemer very quietly set Himself to reason with them and ask them: *Many good deeds have I done you: for which of them seek ye to stone me?* (John x. 32). He did not permit nor give them leave to stir their hands, *because his hour was not yet come* (John vii. 30). But when the hour was come at which He had determined to die, then they were able to do what He had determined to suffer because He chose it and gave them leave then to do it. *This is your hour, and the power of darkness* (Luke xxii. 53), as He said to them when they came to take Him. *Every day I was with you in the Temple, and ye did not lay hands on me,* because the hour was not come; now it is come, and so you see me here, *I am he* (John xviii. 8).

What did Saul do there, a figure of Christ's persecutors; what diligence and contrivance did he use to get David into his hands, a king of Israel against a private man, *persecuting one flea,* as David himself says (I Kings xxiv. 15; xxvi. 20). And for all that he could do nothing, for the reason that *God had not given him into his hands* (I Kings xxiii.

14). And therein lies the whole point. St. Cyprian observes very well on those words, *Lead us not into temptation* (Matt. vi. 13), that all our fear and all our devotion and attention in temptations and distresses should be set on God, because neither the devil nor anyone else can do us any harm if God does not first give him power to do it.

In the second place, although this truth, well established, is sufficient and of great efficacy to conform us in all things to the will of God, nevertheless we must not stop there, but pass on to another truth that follows from this and is noted by the saints. It is this, that along with the fact that all things come from the hand of God we are further to understand that they come for our good and improvement. The pains of the damned come from the hand of God, but not for their improvement and correction, but for their chastisement. But as for the pains and labors that God sends men in this life, whether they be just or sinners, we must always so trust in His infinite goodness and mercy as to believe that He sends them for our good and because that is what makes better for our salvation. So said holy Judith to her townsmen when they were in that affliction and so grave crisis, surrounded by their enemies: *Let us believe that God hath sent us these troubles, not for our ruin, but for our amendment and profit* (Judith viii. 27). Of a will so good as that of God, a will that loves us so much, we may rest assured that He seeks only what is good, and what is better and more suited to our condition.

Thirdly, to profit more by this truth (and this is a most efficacious means of attaining conformity to the will of God), we must not be content with understanding speculatively and in the abstract that all things come from the hand of God, take it mechanically and at the word of command, like soldiers firing a volley, simply because faith tells us so or because so we have read or heard, but we must actuate and quicken that faith, bringing ourselves to understand and feel it practically. So we must come to take all things that happen to us as if we saw visibly and sensibly Christ our Lord saying to us: "Take, son, this that I send you: My will is that you do or suffer just now this and this." In this way it will be very easy and pleasant to conform ourselves in all things to the will of God. Surely, if Jesus Christ Himself in person were to appear to you and say: "See, son, this is what I want of thee; I want thee to suffer for Me just now this hardship or infirmity; I want thee to serve Me in this office or ministry"—though it were the hardest thing in the world, you would do it with hearty good will all the days of your life and count yourself very lucky in that God was pleased to make use of you in that way; and by His commanding it you would understand that that was the better thing and more proper for your salvation and you would not doubt of it, nor even at first thoughts would you ever turn against it.

In the fourth place, it is needful that at meditation we should exercise ourselves, and put our strength into this exercise, digging and going deep into this rich mine of the providence, so paternal and so particular, that God has over us, because that is the way to strike on the treasure, as we shall further declare in the following chapters.

CHAPTER X

Of the Paternal and Particular Providence That God Has over Us, and of the Filial Confidence That We Should Have in Him

ONE of the greatest riches and treasures that we enjoy who have the faith, is the providence so particular and so paternal that God exercises over us, so that we are certain that nothing can befall or happen to us but what is checked and registered by the hand of God. So says the Prophet David: *Thou hast compassed us about and guarded us, O Lord, by thy good will as by a strong shield* (Psalm v. 13). We are surrounded on all sides by the good will of God, so that nothing can come in upon us without it and so there is nothing to fear, for God will not allow anything to gain entrance or reach us except it be for our greater good and profit. *For God hath gathered me into his tabernacle, he hath hidden me in the most secret part thereof in the day of trouble,* says the Royal Prophet (Psalm xxvi. 5). In the most secret part of His tabernacle and in the innermost of His secret chamber, God keeps us hidden; He guards us under the shadow of His wings. And more than this, he says: *Thou wilt hide them in the most hidden and secret part of thy face* (Psalm xxx. 21), which are the eyes. In the pupils of His eyes He hides us, and so another reading says, *in the eyes of thy face (in oculis faciei tuae).* God makes us as the pupils of His eyes, that so that may be well fulfilled which is said in another place: *Guard me, O Lord, as the apple of thine eye* (Psalm xvi. 8). As the pupils of His eyes, so are we guarded under His shelter and protection. *Whoever shall touch you,* God says, *toucheth me in the apple of mine eye* (Zach. ii. 8). Nothing can be imagined more sumptuous, more estimable and desirable, than that.

Oh, if we could thoroughly know this and understand it well! How sheltered and secured should we feel; how confident and consoled should we be in all our necessities and afflictions! If a son on earth had a very rich and powerful father, a great favorite at court, how confident and assured would he feel in all transactions and occurrences that the favor and protection of his father would never fail him! How much greater reason, then, have we to feel this confidence and security, considering that we have Him for our Father in Whose hands is all power in heaven and on earth and that nothing can happen to us but what passes first by His hand! If this is the sort of confidence which such a son has in his father, and therewith he sleeps secure, how much more should we have it in Him Who is more of a father than all fathers and in comparison with Whom the others do not deserve the name of fathers! There are no tendernesses of love to compare with what God feels for us, infinitely surpassing all the loves that all the fathers on earth can feel. Of such a Father and Lord we may well feel confident and secure that all He sends us will be for our greater good and profit because the love that He bears us in His only-begotten Son will not let Him do anything else but seek the good of one for whose sake He delivered over that Son to the torments of the Cross. *He who spared not his own Son, but delivered him up for us all, how can it be that with him he hath not given us all things?* says the Apostle St. Paul (Rom. viii. 32). He Who has given us the greater, how shall He fail to give us the less?

And if all men ought to have this confidence in God, how much more religious, whom He has specially adopted for His own and given them the spirit and heart of sons and caused them to renounce and leave their parents according to the flesh and take Him for their Father! What heart and love of a Father and what care and providence will God have over such! *For my father and mother have left me, but the Lord hath taken me to his keeping* (Psalm xxvi. 10). Oh, what a good Father you have taken in exchange for him whom you have left! With all the more reason and all the more confidence may you say: *The Lord is my shepherd, and nothing will be wanting to me* (Psalm xxii. 1). God has taken upon Himself the charge and care of all my affairs; nothing will be wanting to me. *I am a beggar and needy man, but the Lord hath care of me* (Psalm xxxix. 18). God has care of me; God is solicitous about me: who will not take comfort at this and melt away in love of God! Why, Lord, Thou hast charge of me and takest as much care of me as though Thou hadst no other creature to govern but me alone! Oh, that we could dig down and go right deep into this love and providence and protection, so paternal and particular, that God has over us!

Hence springs in the true servants of God a very familiar and filial confidence in Him, which in some cases is so great that there is no son in the world who in all his affairs has such confidence in the protection of his father as they have in that of God. For they know that He has for them more than the heart of a father and more than that of a mother, which is usually the more tender. So He says by Isaias: *What mother is there that forgetteth her infant son, and hath not a heart of pity for him that came forth from her womb? But if it were possible that there should be any mother in whom this forgetfulness found place, it shall never find place in me, saith the Lord: for I bear thee written in my hands, and thy walls are ever before me* (Isaias xlix. 15-16). As though He would say: "I carry thee in my hands and I keep thee ever before my eyes to shelter thee and defend thee." And through the same prophet He declares this by another comparison, very comforting: *I bear thee within my womb* (Isaias xlvi. 3). As the woman who is with child carries her babe within her womb, and that serves for house, litter, wall, support, and all things, in the same way God says that He carries us in His womb. Hereby the servants of God live in such confidence and hold themselves so succored and provided for in all things that they are never troubled or disturbed by the various happenings of this life. *In the season of drought he shall not be solicitous* (Jerem. xvii. 8). The heart of the just, says the Prophet Jeremy, feels no anxiety, nor loses its tranquillity and repose under the variety of events and occurrences because they know that nothing can occur without the will of their Father. They rest in full assurance and confidence on His great love and goodness, believing that all will be for their greater good and that all that they lose on the one side will come back to them on the other in the shape of something of greater worth and value.

From this so familiar and filial confidence that the just have in God there arises in their soul that great peace, tranquillity, and sense of security which they enjoy, according to the word of Isaias: *My people shall sit down in the beauty of peace and in tabernacles of confidence, and in a resting-place well furnished in all sufficiency of good things* (Isaias xxxii. 18). The prophet joins peace and confidence together. And in reality peace of mind is but a necessary effect of confidence; and he who confides in God fears nothing, nor troubles himself at whatever occurs, since he knows God is his protector. *I will repose and sleep in peace,* says the psalmist, *because it is you, O Lord, who out of your singular goodness have confirmed me in hope* (Psalm iv. 9-10). And this filial confidence causes not only great peace, but great joy and gladness, as says St. Paul: *The God of hope fill you with all joy and peace in believing, that ye may abound in hope and the power of the Holy Ghost* (Rom xv. 13). This belief that God knows what He is doing and that He does it for our good, makes us insensible to those disturbances and disappointments and distresses that they feel who look at things with eyes of flesh; nay, further, it makes us feel great joy and gladness on all occasions. And the more this confidence abounds, the more will abound also this joy and spiritual gladness, because the more a soul trusts and loves, the calmer and more assured she is that all must turn to good; she cannot believe or hope anything less of the infinite goodness and love of God.

This it is that made the saints so quiet and unconcerned in the midst of labors and dangers that they feared neither men nor devils nor wild beasts nor any other irrational creatures, because they knew that they could not touch them without the permission and will of God. St. Athanasius relates of the blessed St. Anthony that one time the devils appeared to him in various fearful shapes, in the form of wild beasts, lions, tigers, bulls, serpents, and scorpions, surrounding and threatening him with their claws, teeth, and dreadful roarings and hissings, so that it looked as though they were going to eat him up. The saint mocked them and said to them: "If you had any strength, one alone of you would be a match for one man; but because you are weak and God has taken away your strength, you contrive to band together in a great rout to frighten me. If the Lord has given you any power over me, you see me here—eat me up; but if you have no power or permission from God, why do you labor in vain?" Here we see well the great peace and fortitude that was due in that saint to his conviction that they could do nothing without the will of God, and his perfect conformity to that will. Of this we have many examples in ecclesiastical history.

Of our blessed Father Ignatius we read a similar example in the fifth book of his Life; and in the second book it is told of him how on a voyage he once made to Rome there arose a frightful tempest which broke the mast by the force of the wind and caused the loss of much tackle. All were afraid and prepared for death, thinking that their last hour had come. In this so dangerous plight, when all were struck with terror of death, it is said that he felt no fear; the only thing that grieved him was the thought that he had not served God so well as he should have done. But for the rest he found nothing to be afraid of, *because the winds and the sea obey him* (Matt. viii. 27); they obey God, and without His leave and will waves and storms do not arise and can do no harm to anyone. This is the familiar and filial confidence in God, this is the tranquillity and sense of security to which we should endeavor to arrive by the grace of the Lord through this practice of conformity with the will of God. We must dig down and go deep by means of meditation and consideration in this most rich mine of the providence, so paternal and particular, that God exercises over us. I am certain that nothing can do anything to me, neither men, nor devils, nor any creature whatsoever, beyond what God wishes and gives leave for; let it be done, then, in God's name, since I refuse nothing nor seek anything else but the will of God.

We read of St. Gertrude that nothing could ever drive away or darken in her the constant and secure confidence which she ever had in the most bounteous mercy of God—no danger, no tribulation, no loss of goods, or other impediments, not even her own sins and defects; because she kept the most assured confidence that all things, prosperity and adversity alike, were turned by Divine Providence to her good. On one occasion the Lord said to this holy virgin: "This absolute confidence which a man has in Me, believing that I really can, know now, and will faithfully help him in all things, captivates My heart and appeals so strongly to My mercy that in dealing with such a man, so to speak, I can neither show him favor, for the satisfaction that I take in seeing him so attached to Me notwithstanding and for the increase of his merit; nor yet can I leave him in the lurch and favor him not, considering Who I am and the great love that I bear him." He speaks in human style like one who is held in suspense by love.

Of St. Mechtildis it is related that the Lord said to her: "It gives Me much pleasure when men trust in My goodness and rely upon Me; for whoever shall humbly confide in Me, and trust Me well, I will do him favors in this life and in the next I will reward him beyond his deserts. The more a man shall trust and count upon My goodness, the more he shall obtain; for it is impossible for a man not to obtain that which he piously believes and hopes that he shall obtain, when I have promised it; and for this reason it is advantageous for a man to expect of Me great things and trust Me well." And when the same Mechtildis asked the Lord what it was that it was right for her chiefly to believe of His unspeakable goodness, He replied: "Believe with certain faith that I will receive thee after thy death as a father receives his long-sought son; and that never did father so faithfully divide his estate with his only son as I will impart to thee all My goods and myself. Whoever shall firmly and with humble charity believe this of My goodness, shall attain to bliss."

CHAPTER XI

Of Some Passages and Examples of Holy Scripture to Aid Us in Gaining This Familiar and Filial Confidence in God

FOR the first point it will be well to see the great habit which those ancient Fathers had of attributing all events to God, by whatever channel they came. Holy Scripture relates (Gen. xlii.) how Joseph's brethren were coming home with wheat brought from Egypt. Now Joseph had instructed his steward to put tied up at the mouth of each one's sack the money that they had paid for the wheat, just as they had brought it with them. On their journey they came to stop at a house and they had a mind each one to give his beast a feed of wheat. The first to open his sack saw at once his purse with the money in it and told the others. Each one addressed himself to his sack and they found there the money. The narrative says then that they said in trouble to one another: *What is this that God hath done us?* (Gen. xlii. 28). It is to be well taken note of that they did not say: "This is a trap that they have set for us; there is some fraud here." Nor did they say: "The steward by carelessness has left each one's money in his sack." Nor did they say: "Perhaps he wanted to make a present to us of the money in alms." But they attributed it to God and said: "What can this mean that God hath done to us?"—confessing that, as not a leaf stirs on a tree but by His will, so neither has this happened but by His will. And when Jacob came into Egypt, Joseph went to visit him with his sons, and the old man asked, "What children are these?" and he replied: *These are my sons that God hath given me in this land of Egypt* (Gen. xlviii. 9). Jacob made the same answer on meeting his brother Esau, when the latter asked him what children were those he brought with him; he replied: *These are the sons whom the Lord hath given me* (Gen. xxxiii. 5). And, offering him a present, he said to him: *Receive this present*—he calls it a *blessing* of God, with Whom to bless is to do good—*which,* he says, *God hath done for me, who is he who giveth all things—Suscipe benedictionem quam attuli tibi, et quam donavit mihi Deus tribuens omnia* (Gen. xxxiii. 11).

Likewise, when David in great anger was going to destroy the house of Nabal, and Abigail his wife came out to meet him with a present to appease him, David said: *Blessed be the Lord God of Israel, who hath sent thee today to me, that I might not go on to shed the blood of the house of Nabal* (I Kings xxv. 32). As though he would say: "Thou hast not come of thyself, but God has sent thee that I might not sin; to Him I owe this favor—may He be praised for it." This was the common language of those saints, and should also be ours.

But coming more to the point, the history of holy Joseph, which we have already touched upon, makes marvelously well to our purpose. His brethren out of envy, that he might not come to be in command over them and be their lord, as he had dreamed, sold him for a slave to some traders of Egypt. This means, which they took for his undoing and that he might not come into command, God took to fulfil the designs of His divine providence and bring him to be lord over them and over all the land of Egypt. So said Joseph himself to his brethren when he discovered himself to them, and they were amazed and bewildered at the event. *Be not afraid or alarmed at having sold me into these parts: it was for your good that God sent me here that ye might have food, and the people of Israel might not perish and come to an end. God sent me: it was no design of yours: they were the counsels of God. Can we possibly resist the will of God?* (Gen. xlv. 5-8). Now who will not hereupon trust God? Who will fear the contrivances of men and the reverses of the world, since we see that they are directed to a sure end by God and that the means which men take to persecute us and do us harm, are the very means that God takes for our good and increase? *My counsel shall stand, and all my will be done* (Isaias xlvi. 10). Go here and go there, go where you will, but in the end the will of God must be accomplished, and He will direct the means thereto.

St. Chrysostom dwells to this effect upon another particular of this history, how Pharaoh's cupbearer, after being restored to his office, forgot his interpreter Joseph for two whole years, though he had enjoined upon him so earnestly to remember him and intercede for him with Pharaoh. Think you, says the saint, that it was by chance that he forgot? It was no chance; it was the resolution and plan of God, Who wished to wait for the nick of time and a happy conjuncture to draw Joseph out of prison with greater glory and honor. For, if he had remembered him, possibly his influence might have availed to deliver him immediately from prison in some obscure manner, without his being either heard or seen. But as God our Lord did not intend him to go out in this manner, but with high honor and authority, He allowed the other to forget him for two years, that so might come the time of Pharaoh's dreams, and then at the instance of the king under stress of necessity he might come out with the majesty and glory wherewith he did come out to be lord of the whole land of Egypt. God knew very well, says St. Chrysostom, as a most wise worker in metals, the time for the gold to be in the fire and the time to draw it out.

In the First Book of Kings we have another history in which the providence of God shines clearly out in many particular details. God had told the Prophet Samuel that He would mark out for him the man who was to be king of Israel, that he might anoint him: *Tomorrow at this hour I will send thee him whom thou shalt anoint as King* (I Kings ix. 16). That man was Saul, and the way in which He sent him was this. His father's asses were lost, and his father told him to go and seek them. He took with him a stout young servant, and they ranged hill and dale, but could not discover them nor find any trace of them. Saul was minded to return, since he thought that they were getting late and that his father would be anxious about them. The boy said to him: "We must not go back home without them: but there is in this town a man of God (it was the Prophet Samuel); let us go there for him to tell us about them." On this account they went to Samuel; and when they came, God said to him: *This is the man whom I said I would send thee: him thou must anoint for king* (I Kings ix. 17). Oh, the secret judgments of God! His father sent him to find the she-asses, but God sent him to Samuel to be anointed king. How different are the designs of men from the designs of God! How far were Saul and his father from thinking that he was going to be anointed king! Oh, how far are you many times, and your father and your superior, from what God intends! From the quarter where you least think it, from there does God draw what He wants. It was not without the will of God that the asses were lost; it was not by chance that his father sent Saul after them, nor was it by chance that he could not find them, nor the advice that the boy gave that they should go to consult the prophet about them; but all this was the ordinance and arrangement of God, Who took these means to send Saul to Samuel to anoint him king, as He had said. Your father thought that he was sending you to study at Seville or Salamanca that you might become a great doctor and afterwards might hold some preferment in which you might live like a gentleman; and it was not that, but God was sending you there to receive you into His house and make you a religious. St. Augustine thought, when he went from Rome to Milan—and the prefect of the city, Symmachus, thought the same—that he was going to lecture on rhetoric; and it was not that, but God was sending him to St. Ambrose to be converted.

Let us set ourselves to consider the variety of vocations and the various means whereby God has drawn to religion this person and that, which is certainly matter of admiration. Had it not been for I know not what little thing or trifling incident, you would never have been a religious—and all these were contrivances and inventions of God to draw you to religion. Let this be observed, by the way, for the benefit of some who sometimes have a recurring temptation to think that their vocation cannot be of God because it came by means of trifling things like those. That is a delusion of the devil your enemy, envious of the state and condition in which you are; for it is the usual way of God to make use of these means for the end which He intends; namely, His own greater glory and your good advantage. We have many examples of this in the lives of the saints. *Hath God care of oxen?* (I Cor. ix. 9) or of she-asses? But He uses these means for you to come to reign like Saul: for "to serve God is to reign."

When afterwards the Prophet Samuel went on the part of God to reprove Saul for that disobedience which he had committed in not destroying Amalec as God had commanded him, Samuel after having reproved him turned his back to go away. Saul seized his mantle, that he might not go, but might intercede for him with God. The text says that a piece of Samuel's mantle remained in Saul's hand, the garment being torn. Who would not but think that this tearing and dividing of the prophet's mantle happened by chance, because Saul pulled hard, and the mantle was old and rotten? Yet it did not happen without a particular disposition of God, to make it understood that this signified that Saul was set aside and deprived of the kingdom for his sin. So Samuel, seeing what was done, said to Saul: By this division of my mantle understand that *the Lord hath set thee aside and removed thee from the kingdom of Israel, and hath given it over to thy neighbor, who is a better man than thou* (I Kings xv. 28).

In the same First Book of Kings we read that one time Saul had surrounded David and his followers as in a circle (I Kings xxiii. 26), in such sort that now David despaired of being able to make his escape. In this hard pressure there came a courier in haste to tell Saul that the Philistines had entered into the country and were pillaging and destroying all before them. Saul had to raise the blockade and go off to meet the greater need, and so David escaped. This raid of the Philistines was not by chance, but a contrivance of God thereby to set David free.

Another time the satraps of the Philistines cast David out of their army and induced King Achis to bid him return home, and that though the king kept him in his company with great good will and had great confidence in him. *But,* as he said, *you do not please the satraps* (I Kings xxix. 6). It looked as though this action of the satraps was a mere piece of chance, but it was not chance nor for the end that they thought it, but by the special providence of God, for David on his return found that the Amalekites had set fire to his town of Siceleg and taken captive all his women and children, even David's own wives. He went after them and destroyed them and recovered all the booty and prisoners without exception, which would not have happened if the satraps had not cast him out of their army; and to this God directed their design, though they directed it to something else (I Kings xxx.).

In the history of Esther this particular providence of God shines out clearly in many minute details. What out-of-the-way means did not God use to deliver the people of the Jews from the cruel sentence of King Ashuerus! By what means did He displace Vashti and choose Esther for queen, who was of the people of the Jews, that she might afterwards intercede for them! It looks like chance that Mardochee got wind of the treason that some were plotting against King Ashuerus, and that he came to reveal it, and that the king was lying awake that night and could not sleep, and that he made them bring him the chronicles of his times to entertain him, and that in the reading they hit upon that good deed of Mardochee; yet nothing of this happened by chance, but by the high counsel of God and His special providence, who wished by these means to deliver His people. And so Mardochee sent a message to Esther, when she shrank from entering to speak to the king and excused herself on the plea of not having been called. "Who knoweth but that the reason of thy having been made queen was that thou mightest be able to help us at this time?"

Holy Scripure and ecclesiastical histories are full of like examples, that we may learn to attribute all events to God and take them as coming from His hand for our greater good and profit. In the book of the memoirs of St. Clement there is recounted a notable thing to this purpose. When Simon Magus was being tracked out by St. Peter, St. Barnabas had converted St. Clement at Rome. The latter went to St. Peter, told him of his conversion, and begged to be instructed in the things of the faith. St. Peter said to him: "You have come at an opportune moment, for tomorrow there is arranged to be a public disputation between me and Simon Magus; we will go there and you shall hear what you ask." At this moment there came in two disciples, and told St. Peter how Simon Magus sent them to say how some business had turned up, and beg that the disputation should be put off for three days; and St. Peter said, "Let it be so." When he came out, St. Clement was much distressed; and St. Peter, seeing him sad, asked him: "What is the matter, son, that I see you sad?" St. Clement answered: "I would have you know, father, that I am much distressed at seeing the disputation put off, which I could have wished to have been tomorrow." Here is a thing much to note: in a matter of so small weight St. Peter took his hand, and preached him a great sermon. "See, son," he said, "among the heathen, when things are not done as they wish, they are much put out; but we who know that God guides and governs all, must hold on in great consolation and peace. Know, son, that it has been for your greater good that this has happened, since now you will understand better. Had the disputation come off immediately, you would not have understood so well; since it has been put off, you will understand it better, for between now and then I will instruct you, and you will relish and profit much by it."

I wish to conclude with an example that we have in the Life of our blessed Father Ignatius, in which also this same truth comes out in strong colors; it is the going of Father Francis Xavier to the East Indies. It is a thing worthy of consideration, the way this holy man came to go to the Indies. Our Father Ignatius had named for this mission Fathers Simon Rodriguez and Nicholas de Bobadilla. Father Simon at the time was ill with a quartan ague; nevertheless, he embarked immediately for Portugal. He wrote to Father Bobadilla to come from Calabria to Rome. He came, but so emaciated by the privations and labors of the journey and so weak and injured in one leg when he arrived in Rome—and at the same time the ambassador Don Pedro Mascarenas was on the point of returning to Portugal and could not wait for Bobadilla to get well, nor did he wish to set out without the second Father that had to go to India—that in place of Master Bobadilla there was substituted Father Master Francis Xavier, with the happiest result, and he set out at once with the ambassador for Portugal. That Father Francis Xavier had not been named, but Father Bobadilla, and that they substituted another in Bobadilla's place because the departure was in haste, seems to have been a chance. And yet it was no chance, but by the high counsel of God, Who had determined to make him the apostle of those parts. Further, when they came to Portugal, seeing the great fruit that they produced here, there was an idea of detaining them; and finally it was determined that one of the two should stay there and the other go on to the Indies. You see here another turn of affairs, going to make the issue contingent. But with God there is no contingency; in the end it had to be Father Francis Xavier who went to the Indies, for that was the will of God and so He had determined, since this it was that made for the good of those souls and for His glory. Let men plan as they like and carry it by the way they command; God will take this way as a means to accomplish His plans and do that which is most suitable for you and for His greater glory.

From these and other like examples, as well from Holy Scripture as from our daily witness and experience, as well in others as in ourselves, we must go on planting and imprinting in our heart this confidence by means of meditation and consideration; and we must not stop in this exercise until we feel in our heart a very familiar and filial confidence in God. And take it for certain that the greater the confidence with which you throw yourself upon God, the safer will you be; and on the other hand, until you come to have this filial confidence, you will never enjoy true peace and repose of heart, for without it all things will trouble and alarm you. Let us, then, once for all throw ourselves and cast ourselves altogether into the hands of God and trust in Him as the Apostle St. Peter advises: *Throw all your solicitude upon God, because He hath care of you* (I Pet. v. 7); and the prophet: *Cast thy care upon the Lord, and he will nourish thee* (Psalm liv. 23). Thou, O Lord, hast loved me so much that for me Thou didst deliver Thyself over entirely into the hands of cruel executioners: *and Jesus he delivered over to their will* (Luke xxiii. 25). Is it much that I should place and deliver over my whole self into hands that are not cruel, but so compassionate as Thine, that Thou mayest do with me what Thou wilt, since I am sure that it will not be for anything else than what is better and more appropriate for me?

Let us accept that division and agreement which Christ our Redeemer made with St. Catherine of Siena. The Lord did many comforting favors to this saint, and among them one in particular. He appeared to her one day and said: "Daughter, forget thyself to remember Me; and I will think of thee and take care of thee"—*Cogita tu de me, et ego cogitabo continenter de te.* Oh, what a good agreement and what a good exchange! What a great gain this would be for our souls! Now the Lord is ready to come to this agreement with each one of us: forget yourself and give over scheming; and the more you forget yourself to remember and trust in God, the greater care will God take of you. Who, then, will not accept this division, so advantageous and so consoling, being that which the spouse says she had made with her Beloved: *I to my Beloved, and he in turn commits himself to me* (Cant. vii. 10). And elsewhere: *My beloved to me, and I to him* (Cant. ii. 16).

CHAPTER XII

How Profitable and Perfect a Thing It Would Be to Apply Meditation to This Exercise of Conformity to the Will of God; and How We Should Descend to Particulars Until We Reach the Third Degree of Conformity

JOHN RUYSBROECK, a most learned and spiritual man, relates of a holy virgin that, giving an account of her prayer to her confessor and spiritual father, who must have been a great servant of God and far advanced in prayer, and seeking direction from him, she told him that her exercise in prayer was on the life and Passion of Christ our Redeemer, and that what she drew from thence was a knowledge of herself and of her vices and passions, and grief and compassion for the pains and afflictions of Christ. The confessor said that that was good, but that without much virtue one could elicit a sentiment of tender compassion for the Passion of Christ, as here on earth for mere love and natural affection for a friend one may elicit compassion for his afflictions. The virgin asked: "Would it be a true devotion for a person every day to bewail her sins?" He answered: "That is good too, but not the most excellent of all, since evil is a thing naturally to grieve over." She asked again: "Would it be true devotion to think of the pains of hell and the glory of the blessed?" He answered: "That is not the most sublime either, since Nature herself abhors and refuses what gives pain and loves and seeks after what may afford happiness and glory; thus, if they were to paint a town full of places of pleasure and recreation, Nature would desire it." Hereupon the holy virgin was much distressed and mournful for not knowing to what subject to apply her prayer, the better to please God. A little way from that she perceived a very beautiful child, to whom she told her distress and inconsolable situation. The child told her not to talk that way, because he himself could and would console her. "Go," he said, "to thy spiritual father and say to him that true devotion consists in abnegation and contempt of oneself and entire resignation into the hands of God, as well in adversity as in prosperity, uniting oneself firmly to God by love and conforming entirely one's own will to His will." She was much cheered and told this to her spiritual father, who replied: "There is the point, and to that should meditation be applied, since therein consists perfect charity and love of God, and consequently our advancement and perfection."

Of another holy woman it is told that she was taught by God, in reciting the Our Father to dwell much on these words, *Thy will be done on earth as it is in heaven.* And of the holy virgin, Gertrude, it is related that, inspired by God, she once repeated three hundred and sixty-five times those words of Christ, *Not my will, but thine be done—Non quod ego volo, sed quod tu* (Luke xxii. 42), and she understood that thereby she had greatly pleased God. Let us, then, imitate these examples and apply thereto our meditation and dwell much on this exercise.

That we may be able to do this better and to greater advantages, it is necessary to observe and presuppose two things. The first is that the need of this exercise is principally for the time of adversities, when difficulties come in our way, and things trying to our flesh. It is for these occasions that virtue is most necessary, and then is better seen the love that each one has for God. As in time of peace the king shows his good will to his soldiers by the bounties that he bestows on them, and they in time of war show the love and regard they have for him by fighting and dying in his cause; so in time of consolation and favor the King of heaven gives us marks of the good will He bears us, and we in tribulation show our devotedness to Him more than in the time of prosperity and consolation. Father Master Avila well says that to give thanks to God in time of consolation is the part of all; but to give thanks in time of tribulations and adversities is proper to the good and the perfect; and so it is a music that sounds very sweet and pleasant in the ears of God. Better is one "Thanks be to God!" he says, in adversities than "Blessed be God!" a thousand times repeated in time of prosperity. And so Holy Writ compares the just man to a certain precious stone of deep red color like a ruby, and of great brilliance: *gemmula carbunculi in ornamento auri* (Ecclus. xxxii 7); for, as this stone shines brighter in the night than in the day, so the just man and true servant of God is more brilliant and shows better what he is in tribulations and troubles than in prosperity. This is what Holy Writ praises so much in holy Toby, for that when the Lord permitted that after so many troubles he should also lose his eyesight, he did not on that account fall into any sullen discontent with God nor abate one jot of the fidelity and obedience that he paid Him before, but stood his ground unflinchingly, rendering thanks to God all the days of his life, as well for his blindness as for his eyesight, as also did holy Job in his troubles (Tob. ii. 14; Job i. 21). This, says St.

Augustine, is what we should endeavor to imitate, being the same in adversity as in prosperity and remaining as cheerful and unruffled. As the hand is the same when you close your fist as when you hold your fingers open, so the servant of God in the interior of his soul ought to remain the same, although on the exterior and outside he seems oppressed and pained. So they say of Socrates that no one ever saw him unusually joyful or unusually sad; throughout so many varying phases of fortune he remained always equable even to the end of his life. Will it be too much for us, Christians and religious, to arrive at a perfection which this gentile attained?

The second thing necessary to observe is that it is not enough for us to have in general this conformity to the will of God, for what is in general is easy. Who is there that will not say that he wishes the will of God to be accomplished in him in all things? Bad and good, all say every day in the Pater Noster: *Thy will be done on earth as it is in heaven.* More is necessary than that; it is necessary to break the matter up, descending in particular to those things which seem capable of giving us some pain if they were to occur. And we must not stop until we overcome and smooth down all these difficulties, so that there shall not remain, as they say, so much as a spearman standing; finally, until there is nothing left to stand in the way of our union and conformity in all things to the will of God, but we can face any obstacle that may offer.

We must not rest content with this, but aim at passing on and not stopping until we find in ourselves a disposition to give a hearty, glad, and joyous welcome to the accomplishment of God's will in us, even though it be with troubles, pains, and affronts; and this is the third degree of conformity. But even in this there are different degrees, one above another, which may be reduced to three principal degrees in the way in which the saints speak of the virtue of patience. The first is when on the occurrence of painful events the man does not desire them nor love them, but rather shuns them; still he would rather suffer them than commit any sin to avoid them. This is the lowest degree and is matter of precept. Thus, though the man feels pain, grief, and sadness at the evils that befall him, and though the sick person groans and cries out at the vehemence of his pains, and though the bereaved survivor weeps over the death of the members of his family, yet for all that he holds steadily to his conformity with the will of God.

The second degree is when, though the man does not desire the evils that befall him nor choose them, still, when they come, he accepts them and suffers with a good grace because such is the will and good pleasure of God. What this degree adds to the first is a certain good will and a certain love of the pain for God's sake and a desire to suffer it, not only so long as there is an obligation under precept to suffer it, but further so long as the suffering of it will be agreeable to God. The first degree takes things with patience; the second, beyond that, takes them with promptitude and readiness.

The third degree is when the servant of God, for the great love that he bears to the Lord, not only suffers and accepts with a good grace the pains and afflictions that are sent him, but desires them and rejoices much in them, such being the will of God, as St. Luke says of the apostles when they had been scourged and exposed to public infamy: *They went away rejoicing from the sight of the council, because they had been counted worthy to suffer ignominy for the name of Jesus* (Acts v. 41). And St. Paul: *I am filled with consolation, I superabound in joy in all our tribulation* (II Cor. vii. 4). And again, writing to the Hebrews, he praises them: *Ye have undergone with joy the plundering of your goods, knowing that ye have a better and abiding estate* (Heb. x. 34). This is what we should aim at coming to with the grace of the Lord, that we should bear with joy and gladness all the tribulations and adversities that befall us, as St. James tells us in his canonical epistle: *Count it all joy, my brethren, when ye fall into various trials* (James i. 2). The will and good pleasure of God should be to us a thing so pleasant and sweet, that with this sauce we are able to sweeten all the bitterness that comes upon us; all the troubles and disappointments of life become to us sweet and savory, such being the will and good pleasure of God. And this is what St. Gregory says: "When a soul is strongly bent on God, whatever bitterness she meets with in this life she counts for sweetness; all affliction she reckons to be rest; she desires to die in order to have a fuller enjoyment of life."

St. Catherine of Siena, in a dialogue which she wrote on the consummation of Christian perfection, says that among other things which her sweet Spouse Jesus Christ taught her there was this, that everyone should make to himself a sort of chamber, arched over with a strong arch, which is the divine will, and shut himself up; and stay there perpetually and never stir from thence so much as eye or foot or hand, but be ever sheltered therein like the bee when she is in her hive or the pearl in its shell. Though at the beginning, perhaps, this chamber may appear strait and narrow, she would afterwards find it ample and spacious, and without going out of it would pass to the *everlasting dwellings* (Luke xvi. 12), and would gain in a short time what without it she could not have gained in a long period. Let us, then, do this and let it be our continual exercise. *My beloved to me, and I to him* (Cant. ii. 16). In these two phrases there is exercise for a whole lifetime, and so we should keep them ever in our mouth and in our heart.

CHAPTER XIII

Of the Indifference and Conformity Which a Religious Should Have for Being in Any Part of the World Whither Obedience May Send Him

THAT we may make better profit of this exercise of conformity to the will of God and put in practice what we have said, we will go on to specify some chief things in which we should exercise it. Then we will descend to other general matters which concern all. At present we will begin with some particulars that there are in our Constitutions, since it is right that a religious should show his virtue and religious spirit chiefly in these; and each one may apply the doctrine to other things which there are in his religious order and state of life.

In the seventh part of our Constitutions our Father, speaking of missions, which is one of the principal undertakings of our institute, says that those of the Society must be indifferent to going and residing in any part of the world where obedience sends them, whether among believers or unbelievers, to the Indies or among heretics. And of this the professed make a fourth solemn vow of special obedience to the sovereign pontiff, that they will go readily and generously, without any excuse, to any part of the world whither His Holiness shall send them, without asking for any temporal thing whether for themselves or for another person, whether for the expenses of their journey or for their sustenance there; but that they will go on foot or on horseback, with money or without money, begging alms, as His Holiness shall think best. And our Father says that the end and intention of this vow was to make sure of doing the will of God. For as those first Fathers of the Society were of different provinces and kingdoms, and did not know in what quarters of the world they would best please God, whether among believers or unbelievers, to make sure of the will of God they made this vow to the vicar of Christ, that he might distribute them for this world where he judged it would be best for the greater glory of God. But in the Society, he says, a man ought nowise to meddle or contrive to be in or go to one place rather than another, but should be quite indifferent, leaving the disposition of himself freely and entirely in the hands of his superior, who in God's place will guide him to what shall be for His greater service and glory.

That we may see how indifferent and ready our Father wishes us to be to go to any part of the world to which obedience shall send us, we read in his Life that one time Father James Laynez said to him that he had a desire to go to the Indies, to work for the salvation of those blind heathens, who seemed in peril for want of evangelical laborers. Our Father answered: "I desire nothing of the sort." Being asked his reason he said: "Because we, having made a vow of obedience to the sovereign pontiff, that at his will he may send us to any part of the world on the Lord's service, ought to be indifferent in such a way as not to be inclined to one part rather than to another. Rather," he said, "if I saw myself inclined as you to go to the Indies, I would endeavor to incline myself to the contrary, so to hold hard by that even balance and indifference which is necessary to attain to the perfection of obedience."

We do not mean hereby to say that these desires of the Indies are bad or imperfect, for doubtless they are very good and holy, and also it is well to propose them and lay them before the superior when our Lord gives them. So our Father says there: "Let superiors rejoice that their subjects lay before them these desires, for they are generally a sign that God calls them that way, and so things are done with sweetness." But what we say is this, that it may be seen what indifference and promptitude our Father wishes us to have to go and be in any part of the world, since he would not have us affectioned even to a thing so laborious and so much for the service of the Lord, that this particular affection and desire may be no let or hindrance to stand in the way of that indifference and readiness in which we ought to be for any other thing and any other part of the world whither obedience may choose to send us.

Hence there follow sundry corollaries which will help to the better understanding of this point. The first is that, if those desires of the Indies were to make a man lose any of that indifference and readiness for other things which obedience might order, they would not be good but imperfect desires. If I find such a keenness of desire to go to the Indies or to any other place as to upset me and be the cause of my not being contented here or in any other place where obedience would have me be, or of my not taking the present duties that occupy me here and now with such hearty good will and diligence as before, because I have set my eyes and my heart on something else, that is a clear sign that those desires cannot be good or of God, since they hinder His will, and God cannot be contrary to Himself—especially since the desires and inspirations of the Holy Spirit do not usually bring with them restlessness and agitation of mind, but great peace and tranquillity; and this is one of the signs which the masters of spiritual life lay down to know whether inspirations and desires are of God or no.

The second corollary is that he who is in an all-round readiness, prompt and indifferent to go to any part of the world and to do anything that obedience shall ordain, even though he has no particular desires or inclination to go to the Indies or to other out-of-the-way places, such as others have, need not be distressed at that, for that does not make him be in any worse condition, but rather in a better. For this is the state of mind in which our Father wishes us all to be, so that on our part we should not desire or have any particular affection for this rather than for that, but that we should be rather as the needle of the balance, not inclining one way rather than another. And of this mind are many and, I believe, most of us.

Our Father was once thinking of sending Father Master Nadal on a certain mission; and to do the thing more gently, he wished first to know how his inclination lay. Father Nadal answered in writing that he had no inclination or disinclination to anything. This our Father takes to be the best and most perfect attitude of mind, and with reason; for the other seems to be tied to one thing only, but this in its perfect indifference embraces all things that can possibly be commanded and is equally disposed and pledged to all; and as God sees the heart and will of every man and takes the will for the deed, it is before Him as if already all had been put into execution.

To bring our explanations to a close, I say that, if it is from cowardice and pusillanimity and want of mortification that one has not any of these desires of the Indies, not having pluck and courage to leave the conveniences which he has or thinks he might have here at home, or to suffer the great hardships that are to be endured out there, this would be imperfection and self-love. But take the case where it is not from cowardice or for lack of desires and courage to suffer these or greater hardships for the love of God and for the salvation of souls that a man has nothing of this desire, but because he does not know that that is the will of God or that God does not ask something else of him; but he on his part is so prompt and ready for this and for anything else that he comes to understand to be the will of God that, if they sent him to the Indies or to England* or to any other place whatever, he would go as willingly as if he had desired and asked for it—and even, perhaps, more willingly, as being better assured that he is not doing his own will in the matter, but purely the will of God—there is no doubt but that this is a much better and

*These words were written in 1610.

more perfect frame of mind. And it is men of this frame of mind and this indifference that superiors willingly send also to the Indies.

But, coming back to our principal point, our Father requires of us such indifference and resignation and readiness to be as willingly in one place as in another, in one province as in another, that not even the consideration of bodily health should divert us from this indifference. He says in the third part of the Constitutions that it is proper to our vocation and institute to go about from one part of the world to another and to be where there is greater hope of the service of God and greater aid of souls; yet, if it is found by experience that the climate of some country disagrees with somebody and he is seen to be continually ill there, then it is for the superior to consider the advisability of his going elsewhere where he may enjoy better health and employ himself to better effect in the service of God and of souls. But, he says, the invalid must not ask for this change nor show any inclination that way, but leave himself entirely to the care of the superior. These are his words: *Non tamen erit ipsius infirmi mutationem postulare, nec animi propensionem ad eam ostendere, sed superioris curae id relinquetur.* Our Father here is asking not a little but much of us; for a man must be very indifferent and mortified not only not to ask for, but even not to show any inclination for, a change when his health is going continually from bad to worse.

Thus in what regards going to the Indies or to the countries of heretics a man may well represent his inclination and desire, as we have said, albeit with indifference and resignation; but in this case our Father does not give leave either to ask for a change or to show an inclination and desire thereof, which is much more. The only permission he gives is that, if a man finds himself ill, he should represent to the superior his illness and the indisposition and incapacity which he feels for the work of the ministry, and of that we have a rule that we should represent it. But, once the representation is made, the subject has nothing further to do; the superior will see whether on this supposition it will be better to send him to some other place where he may have better health and do more or whether it would be more to the glory of God that he should stay there where he is, doing less or even doing nothing. However, it is not for the subject to judge; let everyone abandon himself to the guidance of the superior, who governs him in place of God, and take that for better and more for the divine service which he shall ordain. How many are there in these lands, and in others more contrary to their health, to earn their bread there! How many cross the sea and go to the Indies, to Rome, and to Constantinople, for a little property, and risk not only their health but their life! It will not, then, be much for us, being religious, to do for God what people in the world do for money. And, though it occurs to you that elsewhere you might do something or even much, while here where you are, you are so ill that you can do nothing, remember that, all the same, it is better to be here where you are by the will of God doing nothing than to be at the head of things anywhere else, doing your own will, although you did much. Conform yourself to the will of God, Who requires this of you at present for a purpose that He knows and which it is not necessary for you to know.

In the chronicles of the order of St. Francis it is related of the holy brother Giles that, the blessed St. Francis having licensed him to go where he would and live in any province and house that was most to his taste, leaving that to his choice for the greatness of his virtue and holiness, he had scarcely passed four days in the enjoyment of this license when he found his former tranquillity and rest of mind impaired and became a prey to anxiety and trouble. So he went to St. Francis, begging him with much earnestness to designate the place and house where he was to live, and not leave it to his choice, declaring that in that free and large obedience he could find no peace or rest. Good religious do not find peace and contentment in the fulfilment of their own will and do not hanker after this house and place or that; all they wish is that obedience should lead them by the hand and place them where it wills, because they take that to be the will of God, in which alone they find rest and contentment.

CHAPTER XIV

Of the Indifference and Conformity to the Will of God Which a Religious Should Have for Any Office and Occupation in Which Obedience May Place Him

THE indifference and resignation of which we have been speaking ought to be shown also in point of any office or occupation in which obedience shall choose to place us. We see well how many and how various are the offices and occupations that there are in religion; let everyone, then, run his mind through them until he finds that he is equally ready to face any of them. Our Father says in his Constitutions, and we have it in the Rules: "In the exercise of lowly and humble offices, each one should take up those more willingly which are more repugnant to sense, if he be ordered to make that his occupation." Indifference and resignation are more necessary toward lowly and humble offices, because of the repugnance that nature has for them; and so one does more and shows more virtue and perfection in offering himself to God for these offices than in offering himself for others more elevated and honorable. If one so much desired to serve a great lord as to offer himself to serve him all his life long as a running footman and dustman, if needful, it is clear that such a one does more and shows more good will to serve than if he said: "My lord, I will serve you as butler or major-domo;" that would rather be a bid for a salary than an offer of service. And this offer would be all the more considerable, the better parts he had for high offices who offers himself for lowly ones. In the same way, then, if you offer yourself to God, saying: "Lord, I will serve Thee in the office of preacher, or lecturer in theology," you do not do much in that, because high and honorable offices are in themselves desirable; you have little scope for showing in them the desire that you have of serving God. But when you offer yourself to serve in the house of God all the days of your life in lowly and humble offices, offices repugnant to your natural feelings and sensuality, then do you much more show the desire you have of serving God. This is a far more appreciable and valuable service, and all the more so, the better parts you have for higher offices. This should be enough to make us desire lowly and humble offices and to be always more inclined to them, especially since in the house of God no office is low. They even say this on earth of the house of a king, because to serve the king in any office whatsoever is made great account of; how much more will it be to serve God, to serve Whom is to reign.

St. Basil, to give us an affection for lowly and humble offices, quotes the example of Christ, of Whom we read in the holy Gospel that He occupied Himself in such offices, washing the feet of His disciples; and not only that, but serving for a long time His most holy Mother and St. Joseph and being subject and obedient to them in all that they commanded. *And he was subject to them* (Luke ii. 51). From the age of twelve to thirty the holy Gospel tells us nothing of Him but this; whereon the saints well reflect that He must have served and helped them in many lowly offices, especially seeing that they were such poor people as they were. "Let not, then, the Christian"—and much less the religious—"disdain to do what Christ did," says St. Augustine. Since the Son of God did not disdain to busy Himself in these lowly offices for love of us, let us not disdain either to busy ourselves in them either for His love, although it be for all the days of our life.

But, coming more to our point, one of the chief reasons and motives there are to make us take up with hearty good will any office and occupation that obedience may put upon us, should be our being convinced that such is the will of God; for, as we said above, this should be always our consolation and satisfaction in all our occupations, that we are therein doing the will of God. It is this that sates and satisfies the soul: "God wills that I should be doing this now;" "This is the will of God;" "There is nothing more to desire, since there is nothing better or higher than the will of God." Such as live in this way do not care whether they are ordered this or that, or put in a high or low office, since it is all one to them.

The blessed St. Jerome relates an example very pat to this purpose. He says that, in visiting those holy monks of the desert, he saw one of whom the superior, desirous of his spiritual advancement and also to give an example of obedience to the rest of the youthful community, had ordered to drag up hill twice a day a very large stone for the space of three miles, that is, a league, there being no other necessity for it, nor utility either, except for him to obey and mortify his judgment, and he had been at it for eight years. And as this, says St. Jerome, to those who do not understand this virtue of obedience, nor have attained to the purity and simplicity thereof in their spirit of haughtiness and pride, might possibly appear a childish game or an idle act, they asked him how he bore that obedience. And I myself, says St. Jerome, asked the same question, being desirous to know what movements passed in his soul while he was doing this. The monk replied: "I am as full of content and joy when I have done this as if I had done the highest and most important thing that they could have commanded me." St. Jerome says that this reply made such an impression on him that from that date he began to live like a monk. This it is to be a monk and to live like a true religious, not to stop at the exterior work, but to consider that we are fulfilling the will and good pleasure of God. These are they who advance and grow great in virtue and perfection, since the doing of the will of God is their continual nourishment, a nourishment like that of the finest wheaten flour. *Et adipe frumenti satiat te* (Psalm cxlvii. 14).

But someone will say: "I see well that it is great perfection to do the will of God in all things and that in any exercise they command me I can be doing the will of God; but I could wish them to occupy me in some bigger thing and let me do the will of God there." This is an error in first principles; it is, in plain English, wanting God to do your will. I have no mind to draw plans for God; I have no mind to ask that He should fall in with my views and with my likings; I am minded to follow the plans of God and fall in with what He wants of me. St. Augustine says very well: "He is Thy good servant, Lord, who makes no account of Thy command falling in with his will, but of his willing that which Thou commandest"—*Optimus minister tuus est, qui non magis intuetur hoc a te audire quod ipse voluerit, sed potius hoc velle quod a te audierit.* And the holy Abbot Nilus says: "Do not ask of God to do what you want done, but what Christ teaches us to ask for, that His will may be done in me."

Let note be taken of this point, which is very profitable and has a general application to all the hardships and contingencies that can befall us. It is not for us to choose in what and how we are to suffer, but for God. It is not for you to choose the temptations that you are to undergo, or to say: "If it were any other temptation, I should not mind; but this I can't stand." Our pains would not be pains if they were such as we ourselves chose. If you are in earnest in your wish to please God, you should ask Him to take you on the side that He knows best and wishes to take you on, not on the side that you wish. And when the Lord sends you what is most disagreeable to you and what you have the greatest reluctance to suffer, and you fall in with and adapt yourself to that, then you will be a better imitator of Christ our Redeemer, Who said: *Not my will, but thine be done* (Luke xxii. 42). This it is to have an entire conformity to the will of God, offering ourselves in all things to Him that He may do with us what He wills, and after what manner He wills, without exception or contradiction and without reserve of anything to ourselves.

Louis of Blois relates that the holy virgin Gertrude, moved by pity and compassion, prayed to God on behalf of a certain person, who she had heard was complaining impatiently that God was sending her sundry afflictions, infirmities, or temptations which seemed to her not suitable for her. But the Lord replied to the holy virgin: "Tell that person for whom you ask, that since the kingdom of heaven cannot be gained without some affliction and annoyance, she should choose what she thinks will be profitable to her and, when it comes, be patient." From these words and the tone in which the Lord said them, the holy virgin understood that it is a very dangerous kind of impatience, when a man wishes to choose what he has to suffer, saying that such and such things are not proper for his salvation and that he cannot bear what God sends him. Everyone should persuade himself and trust that what God our Lord sends him is what is proper for him, and so take it in patience, conforming therein his will to that of God. Now, as you are not to choose the afflictions and temptations that you are to suffer, but take as from the hand of God what He sends you and understand that that is what befits you best; so neither are you to choose the office and function which you are to discharge, but take as from the hand of God that in which obedience shall place you and understand that that is what suits you best.

They add here another point of high spirituality, and say that a man should be so resigned to the will of God and rest so securely in it as not to desire to know what God intends to do with him and how He will dispose of him. As here on earth, when a nobleman has such confidence in his steward as to know nothing of his property or of what he has in his house—which is a mark of great confidence, as holy Joseph says that his master behaved to him: *Lo, my lord hath handed over to me all things, and knoweth not what he hath in his house* (Gen. xxxix. 8)—so does a man show great confidence in God when he does not seek to know what God means to do with him. "I am in good hands, that is enough for me! *My destinies, O Lord, are in thy hands* (Psalm xxx. 16)." With this I live content and secure, and have no need to know more.

For those who desire posts and offices and ecclesiastical functions of the higher sort, thinking that in them they will gain greater fruit of souls and render greater service to God, I say that they are much mistaken in thinking that this is zeal for the greater service of God and the greater good of souls. No, it is not that; it is jealousy and desire of honor and reputation and of your own comforts. It is because this office and function is more honorable or more in accordance with their own taste and inclination that men desire it. That is clearly seen by this consideration. If you were out there in the world, or by yourself, with some show of reason you might have said: "This is better than that and productive of fruit in souls; I mean to leave this to do that, because one cannot do everything." But here in religion you cannot leave this for that without someone or other having to take up and do what you leave. The only difficulty is that, if you take the alto part, the other man must take the bass. If I were humble, I should rather wish the other man to take the high office because I am apt to believe that he would do it better than I and with greater fruit and with less danger of vanity.

For this and for other like reasons, that is an excellent doctrine of our blessed Father Ignatius which he lays down as a foundation for the election of a state of life. He marks three degrees or modes of humility; and the third and most perfect is, in a choice of two alternatives, each equally making for the glory and service of God, to choose that in which there is most disparagement and abasement of myself, the better therein to resemble and imitate Christ our Redeemer and Lord, Who chose to be disparaged and abased for our sake. And there is therein this other great advantage, that in these things there is less of self-interest; the man has no opportunity for seeking himself therein and escapes the danger of growing vain over them which there is in high and honorable offices. In lowly offices, humility and charity are exercised together, and in them humility is well preserved, doing the acts that are proper to herself; but in those high offices charity is exercised to the risk of humility, and that should be enough to make us not only not desire such preferments, but even to dread them.

CHAPTER XV

Of the Conformity That We Should Have to the Will of God in the Distribution of Natural Gifts and Talents

EVERY individual should be quite content with what God has imparted to him in point of talent, intellect, and genius, and the ability and parts that God has given him, and not be pained or saddened at not having as much ability or talent as his neighbor, nor going for so much as he does. This is a thing that we all have need of; for although men may shine and stand in a more advantageous light in certain things, yet there are always other counterpoises to humble them, wherein they stand in need of this conformity. So it is necessary to be forearmed, since it is the way of the devil to assail many on this side. You are in your studies and, seeing that a fellow-student of yours shows remarkable ability, arguing and answering right well in disputations, there may perhaps come over you some shadow of envy. It does not go so far as to make you sad at the good of your brother, which is properly the sin of envy; but, after all, seeing your companions strong in capacity and going ahead with their talents, while you hang back and cannot get on nor make head at all, you experience some sadness and melancholy and feel abashed and out of countenance in company, and thence there comes over you a feeling of drooping and discouragement and a temptation to abandon your studies and sometimes even religious life. This temptation against vocation has taken hold of some because they were not well grounded in humility. There was one who thought to be a star, conspicuous among all, and that his fame would go out all over the province, of which he was the best student in the course; and, when his dream turned out quite the other way, he became quite abashed and crestfallen: whereupon the devil, seeing such an excellent opportunity, represented to him that he could never recover from this disgrace and disappointment otherwise than by leaving his order. And this is no new temptation, but a very old one.

In the chronicles of the order of St. Dominic there is related an example to this purpose of Albertus Magnus, who was master of St. Thomas Aquinas. Albertus Magnus, when a child, was very devout to our lady, reciting daily certain devotions in her honor, and by her means and intercession entered the order of St. Dominic at the age of sixteen. They say in the chronicles that as a youth he had not much understanding, but was untrained and of little capacity for study; and, seeing his fellow students to be of great and very subtle intellects, he quite lost heart. Thereupon temptation came to press him hard and throw him into danger, so much so that he was on the point of quitting the habit. In this hard press of conflicting thoughts he was succored by a marvelous vision. Sleeping one night, he fancied that he was setting a ladder to the wall of the monastery to get out and leave the place; and, as he was mounting it, he saw on the top four venerable matrons, one of whom seemed to be mistress of the others. When he came near them, one of them laid hold of him and threw him from the ladder, forbidding his going out from the monastery. He persisted in trying to mount a second time, and the second matron behaved to him as the first had done. He wanted to mount a third time, and the third matron asked him the reason why he wanted to leave the monastery. With a blush on his face he replied: "I am going, my lady, because I see others of my class improving in the study of philosophy, while I labor in vain. The shame I suffer on that account is making me leave the order." The matron said to him: "This lady whom you see"—pointing to the fourth—"is the Mother of God and Queen of Heaven whose servants we three are; commend yourself to her; and we will help you and we will entreat her to be your intercessor with her most blessed Son to give you a docile mind that you may make progress in that study." Hearing this, Fra Albert rejoiced much, and the matron taking him to our Lady, he was well received by her, and she asked him what it was that he desired and asked. He answered: "To know philosophy, which I am studying, and do not understand." The Queen of Heaven answered: "Be of good heart and go on studying, for thou shalt be a great man in this faculty. But that thou mayest know," she went on to say, "that this comest to thee from me and not from thy own genius and ability, some days before thy death, while lecturing publicly, thou shalt forget all that thou knowest." With this vision he remained comforted. And from that time he improved much in the study, not only of philosophy, but also of theology and Holy Scripture, as the works that he has left behind him in writing testify. But three years before his death, while he was lecturing at Cologne, he lost his memory entirely for all that concerned the sciences, as though for all his life he had never learned anything at study; and perhaps this was in penance for the little confidence he had had in the talent and ability that God had given him. And, remembering the vision that he had had when he tried to leave his vocation, he recounted publicly to his hearers all that had passed; and so took leave of them, shut himself up in his convent, and spent all his time in prayer and contemplation.

Now, that we may not come into the like dangers, we must needs be fortified beforehand. And the needful fortification for this purpose is great humility; for all this difficulty arises for want of that, because you cannot bear being reckoned the poorest scholar in the class. If they come to tell you that you are not fit to go on further in your studies, and you see your classmates turning into theologians and afterward graduates and preachers, there is need of much humility and much conformity to stand that. And the same will be necessary for the time after your studies, for temptation will occur to you at the thought: "I am not rated so high as the rest; I have not the talent to preach, shine, and speak in public like my neighbor, nor to have business entrusted to me and account taken of me." And I say the same of those who are not students. There will come to you thoughts and temptations: "Oh, that I were a student!" "Oh, that I were a priest!" "Oh, that I were a learned man to be able to gather fruit of souls!" And sometimes the temptation may press you so hard as to endanger your vocation, and even your salvation.

This is a general doctrine that each one may apply to himself according to his state. It is necessary that all be quite conformable to the will of God, each one content with the talent that God has given him and the state in which God has placed him, and that none should want to be more than God wants him to be. The blessed St. Augustine on those words of the psalmist: *Incline my heart to keep thy commandments, and not to avarice* (Psalm cxviii. 36), says that this was the beginning and root of all our evil, that our first parents sought to be more than God had made them; for this they fell from the state that they enjoyed and lost what God had given them. The devil set for them this bait: *Ye shall be as Gods* (Gen. iii. 5); by that he deceived and ruined them. We inherit this inheritance from them, that we have a craving after Godhead and a madness and frenzy for seeking to be more than we are. And, as the devil succeeded so well herein with our first parents, he endeavors to make war on us also by this means, inciting us to desire to be more than God wishes us to be and not be content with the talent that He has given us nor with the state in which He has placed us. And on this account, St. Augustine says, the prophet asks of God: "Lord, give me a heart disinterested and inclined faithfully to follow Thy good pleasure and will, and not my own interests and conveniences." By "avarice" he says is to be there understood all manner of self-interest, and not the mere covetousness of money; and this is what St. Paul says is the root of all evils: *The root of all evils is covetousness* (I Tim. vi. 10).

But, that we may all have this disposition of indifference, conforming ourselves and contenting ourselves with the talent which the Lord has given us and with the state or degree in which He has placed us, it is enough to know that such is the will of God. *All these gifts are the working of one and the same Holy Spirit, distributing to each in particular according to his good pleasure,* says the Apostle St. Paul (I Cor. xii. 11). The Apostle puts here the metaphor, which we have applied above to another purpose, of the human body; and says that, as God has placed the members of the body, giving to each one as He chose, and the feet do not complain that they do not act as the head, nor the hands that they do not act as the eyes, so also in the

Church—and the same in the body of a religious order—God has given each one the post and office that it has pleased Him, and that not by chance, but by a particular resolution and providence of His own. If, then, God wishes you to be feet, it is not reasonable that you should wish to be head; and if God wishes you to be hands, it is not reasonable that you should wish to be eyes. Oh, how right high and right deep are the judgments of God! Who shall be able to comprehend them? *Who of men shall be able to know the counsels of God?* (Wisdom ix. 13). All things, Lord, proceed from Thee, and for that in all things be Thou praised. Thou knowest what it is fit to give to each; and why one has more, and others less, it is not for us to discern. Who knows what would have become of you if you had had great genius and ability? Who knows, if you had had a great talent for preaching and had been much listened to and thought a great deal of, but that that would have been your ruin, as it has been the ruin of others by their running into pride and vanity? "The learned," says that holy man À Kempis, "love to be seen and made account of as such." If with two penn'orth of genius that you have and three ha'porth of letters that you know, and with mediocrity and perhaps less than mediocrity of brains, you are so vain and arrogant that you value yourself, and compare and perhaps prefer yourself to others, and make it a grievance that they do not lay hands on you for this and that post, where would you be if you were really a first-rate man, a man of rare and extraordinary parts? Wings grow on the ant to its evil, and perhaps they would so grow on you.

Truly, if we had not goggles, but eyes, we should rather render infinite thanks to God for having put us in a lowly and humble position and for having given us but poor parts and abilities, and say with that holy man: "I take it for a great blessing, O Lord, not to have many things for which there could follow me in the world outside praise and honor before men." The saints knew very well the great danger there is in these advantages and excellences, and they did not only not desire them, but dreaded them—*Ab altitudine diei timebo*—"I will dread the noonday light" (Psalm lv. 4) —for the great danger there is in them of vanity and perdition; and therefore they pleased God the more, Who would have His servants humble rather than great.

Oh, if we could once for all make up our minds that all is a mockery and a farce but doing the will of God! Oh, if we could finally place all our contentment in the contentment and satisfaction of God! If without learning, or with the smattering of learning and poor abilities that you have, you please God the more, why do you aspire after learning? Why want more learning, more ability, more talents? If you had any reason for wanting them, it would be to please and serve God the better therewith. But if God is more pleased with your having no learning or not getting any more learning, more talent, more ability—as He certainly is pleased, since it is He that has made this distribution—what have you to complain of? What reason have you to wish to be what God does not wish you to be and what it is not fitting that you should be? The great sacrifices that Saul wished to offer were not pleasing to God because they were not according to His will (I Kings xiii. 10; xv. 21); neither will those high and lofty desires of yours be pleasing to God. Our good and our advancement in perfection do not lie in our being learned, nor being preachers, nor in having great parts and talents, nor in understanding high and subtle things, but in doing the will of God and in giving a good account of what He has committed to us and employing well the talent that He has given us. On this we should fix our eyes and on nothing else, because it is this that God requires of us.

A very good comparison to explain this is that of the actors who represent comedies. Their credit and reward does not go by the personage that they represent, but by the good rendering that each one gives of his part. If he who represents the clown does it better than he who represents the emperor, he comes out more appreciated and praised by the audience and better rewarded by the judges. In like manner, what God regards and sets store by in us in this life—which is all like a theatrical representation and a comedy, and God grant that it may not be a tragedy that is soon over!—is not the personage that we represent, one of superior, one of preacher, one of sacristan, one of porter—but the good rendering that each one gives of his part. Thus, if the lay brother does his office well and represents his character better than the preacher or superior does his, he will be held in greater credit with God and be better rewarded and honored. One perhaps that would not have succeeded in the character of the king, gains honor and carries the palm in the character of the page or the shepherd boy. So you also might possibly not have succeeded in playing the preacher or superior, and you may play well the part of the spiritual father or of the lay brother. God knows how to distribute the parts well and assign to each one the character that suits him, *to each one according to his capacity* (Matt. xxv. 15). According to the capability and strength of each, so did the master distribute his talents. Let none, then, desire to play another part or have another talent, but let each one make it his endeavor to play well the part assigned him, to lay out well the talent he has received and give a good account thereof; for in that way he will please God better and receive a greater reward.

CHAPTER XVI

Of the Conformity That We Should Have to the Will of God in Times of Sickness

AS health is a gift of God, so also is sickness. God sends us sickness for our probation, amendment, and correction, and for many other good things and advantages that are apt to flow from it—as knowledge of our own weakness; dissipation of the illusions of our vanity; detachment from the things of earth and the appetites of sensuality; abatement of the impetuosity and strength of our greatest enemy, the flesh; a reminder that this is not our native city, but a sort of inn where we are in exile; and other like things. Wherefore the Wise Man says: *A grave illness maketh the soul temperate and strong* (Ecclus. xxxi. 2). Thus we ought to be as conformable to the will of God in sickness as in health, taking it as coming from the hand of God our Lord when He is pleased to send it. One of those ancient Fathers said to a disciple of his that was sick: "Son, grieve not over thy sickness, but rather render great thanks to God for it; for, if thou art iron, the fire will consume thy rust; and if thou art gold, thou wilt be proved in the fire. It is a great virtue and a great act of religion to render thanks to God in sickness."

Of the blessed St. Clare, Surius relates in her Life that for twenty-eight years she was ill of grievous infirmities, and her patience was so great that in all that time they never noticed her complaining or murmuring at her great affliction, but rather she was continually giving thanks to the Lord. And in her last sickness, when she was so worn out that for seventeen days she was not able to eat a morsel, and her confessor Friar Reginald was consoling her and exhorting her to patience in such a long martyrdom, she answered: "From the time that I came to know the grace of my Lord Jesus Christ through His holy servant

Francis, no sickness has been hard to me, no pain troublesome, and no penance severe." Admirable also in this way and a very rare example, which should give much courage and consolation to the sick, is the life of St. Lidwina, virgin. For thirty-eight years she endured continual and most severe infirmities and pains; and for thirty years she was unable to rise from her poor bed or put her foot on the ground, and there the Lord did her very great favors.

But because certain particular reasons are apt to occur to us to hinder this indifference and conformity under color and appearance of greater good, we will proceed to reply to them and meet them. In the first place, one may say: "For myself I should not mind being sick any more than being in health, but what I do feel is seeming to be a burden to the order and giving trouble in the house." To this I say that this is a rash judgment on superiors and on the community, condemning them of want of charity and want of conformity to the will of God. Your superiors also profess to aim at perfection and to take all things as coming from the hand of the Lord and to conform themselves therein to the divine will; and thus, if God wishes you to be sick and them to be busy waiting on you and comforting you, they also must wish the same; and as you bear the cross which God gives you, they also will take up with great conformity that which He wishes them to bear.

But you will say: "Herein I quite see the great charity that is practised in the Society; the only thing that troubles me is the good that I might be doing in studying, preaching, and hearing confessions, and the lapse of that through my being sick." To this St. Augustine answers very well. He says that we should consider that we do not know whether it will be better to put into execution what we have a mind to or leave it undone; and so we are forced to plan and arrange things according to our capacity; and if afterwards we are able to carry them out as we had planned, we should not rejoice because that has been done which we thought of and desired, but because the Lord has been pleased to have it done so. And if what we thought and planned has not eventually been carried into effect, not on that account should we be troubled and lose our peace. "It is fairer," St. Augustine says, "that we should follow His will than that He should follow ours"—*Aequius est ut nos eius quam ut ille nostram sequatur voluntatem.* And he concludes with an admirable sentence: "He is better at laying out and planning things who is disposed and prepared not to do what God would not have him do, than he who is all anxiety and desire to carry into act what he has thought of"—*Nemo melius ordinat quod agat, nisi qui paratior est non agere quod divina potestate prohibetur quam cupidior agere quod humana cogitatione meditatur.*

In this manner, then, and with this indifference we should plan and arrange what we have to do, being ever quite prepared to conform ourselves to the will of God if so it happens that our plans come not to effect. Thus we shall not be troubled or saddened when through sickness or any other like cause we have not been able to do what we intended and had ready planned out, even though the things intended were in themselves of great benefit to souls. Father Master Avila says very well, writing to a sick priest: "Do not reckon up what you would have done if you had been well, but how much you will please the Lord by acquiescing in being ill. If you seek, as I believe you do seek, purely the will of God, why should you mind being ill rather than well, since His will is all our good?"

St. Chrysostom says that holy Job merited and pleased God more in that saying: *As it hath pleased the Lord, so hath it been done: may the name of the Lord be blessed* (Job i. 21), conforming his will to those afflictions and leprosy that God sent him, than by any amount of almsdeeds and benefactions that he did while he was healthy and rich. In like manner you will please God more by conforming yourself to His will in your sickness than by all that you could have done in health. St. Bonaventure says the same: "There is more perfection in bearing with patience and conformity afflictions and adversities than in being hard at work on excellent good works"—*Perfectius est adversa tolerare patienter quam bonis operibus insudare.* For God has no need of me nor of you to do the good that He wants done in His Church. *I have said to the Lord, Thou art my God, Thou hast no need of my good deeds* (Psalm xv. 2). For the present He wishes to preach to you with this sickness, that you may learn to practise patience and humility; let God act, for He knows what is better, and you don't. If we had any reason for desiring health and strength, it would be to employ them in serving and pleasing God more; but if the Lord is pleased rather and takes it better that I should be occupied in being ill and in bearing with patience the troubles of sickness, His will be done, for that is what is better and more suitable for me. The Apostle St. Paul, preacher to the Gentiles, was left by the Lord in prison two years (Acts xxiv. 27) just at the time that he was so necessary to the primitive Church. There is not much done for you to complain of, if God keeps you in the prison of sickness two months, two years, even your whole life, if He pleases. You are not so necessary in the Church of God as was St. Paul.

To some it is apt to be a difficulty, when they have long and protracted illnesses and indispositions, not to be able to follow the community and to have to be singular in many things, and they are disconsolate over this, thinking that they are not as much religious as the rest, or at least that others may be disedified seeing their singularities and comforts; especially since sometimes the sickness and necessity they are in is not so apparent in the exterior, but only God and the sick man know what he suffers, whereas these singularities and exemptions strike the eye. To this I say that it is a good consideration and a very just sentiment, and he who feels it is to be praised; still he must not give up conformity to the will of God in his infirmity, but double his merit. This is done, on the one hand, by your conforming yourself entirely to the will of God in all your indispositions and ailments, since He wishes you to suffer them; and, on the other, by having a great desire, so far as it rests with you, to follow all the exercises of religion with much punctuality and exactness and feeling in your heart regret at not being able to do what the others do. In this way, besides the merit that you gain by bearing your sickness with patience and conformity, you may merit also under the second head as much as the rest, who are in sound health and fulfil all the exercises.

St. Augustine in his sixty-second sermon *de Tempore,* treating of the obligation that all have to fast at that time under pain of mortal sin, and coming to deal with the case of the invalid who cannot fast, says that for him it is sufficient that he cannot fast, but eats with grief of heart, groaning and sighing because he cannot fast while others are fasting. As the valiant soldier who is brought into camp wounded, feels more his inability to fight any longer or to signalize himself in the service of his king than the pain of his wounds and the rigorous treatment he is put under; so it is proper for good religious, when they are on the sick list, to feel more their inability to go with the community and do the exercises of religion than they feel the sickness itself. Still, after all, neither this nor anything else should rob us of our conformity to the will of God in our sickness, but we should accept it as sent by His hand for His greater glory and our greater good and profit.

The blessed St. Jerome tells how a monk once asked the holy Abbot John the Egyptian to heal him of a sickness and high fever that he had, and the saint replied: "You seek riddance of a thing that is very necessary for you; for, as the uncleanness and filth of bodily things is taken away by soap or strong lye and the like, so souls are purified by sickness and afflictions."

CHAPTER XVII

That We Ought Not to Put Our Trust in Doctors or Drugs, but in God; and Conform Ourselves to His Will Not Only in the Sickness Itself, but in All the Incidents of the Same

WHAT has been said of sickness is to be said also of all other things that are apt to occur in time of sickness. St. Basil gives a very good lesson for us when we are sick. He says that in availing ourselves of medical men and medical appliances we should not put all our trust in them. Thereof Holy Scripture makes it a fault in King Asa: *And in his sickness he sought not the Lord, but trusted rather in the skill of the doctor* (II Chron. xvi. 12). We must not attribute to this the whole cause of our getting better or not getting better, but we must put all our trust in God, Who is pleased sometimes to give us health through these medical appliances and sometimes not. And so, when physician and physic alike fail us, St. Basil says that we should not despair of our case on that account either. We read in the holy Gospel that Christ our Redeemer sometimes healed people by His mere will, as, dealing with that leper who petitioned Him: *Lord, if thou wilt thou canst make me clean,* He answered: *I will, be thou made clean* (Matt. viii. 2-3). At other times He used some application, as when He made clay with spittle and anointed the eyes of the blind man and told him to go and wash in the pool of Siloe (John ix. 6). At other times He left the sick in their sicknesses and would not heal them, although they had spent all their substance on doctors and drugs (Mark v. 26; Luke viii. 43). So now also at times God heals without physicians or physic by His only will; at other times, by means of these medical appliances; at other times, though the patient consults many doctors, and they apply to him great remedies, God will not give health, that so we may learn to put our trust not in human remedies, but in God. As King Ezechias did not attribute his cure to the plaster of figs that Isaias put on his wound, but to God (IV Kings xx. 7-8), so, when you recover from your illness, you must not attribute your cure to doctors or drugs, but to God, *who healeth all our infirmities* (Psalm cii. 3). *For it is not herb or plaster, but thy word, O Lord, that healeth all* (Wisdom xvi. 12). And when you are not cured, neither then either must you complain of doctors and medicines, but in that case also you must attribute all to God, Who does not wish to restore you to health, but that you should remain ill.

In the same way, when the physician has not understood the illness and has erred in the treatment of it—which is a thing that happens often enough even with great doctors and in the case of great personages—you must take that error as a stroke of Providence, as also any neglect or fault which the infirmarian may commit in the care of you. And you must not say that the fever returned because they made such and such a mistake in your treatment, but take it all as coming from the hand of God and say: "It has pleased the Lord that my fever has increased and that such an accident has befallen me;" because it is certain that, though on the part of those who are looking after you there has been a mistake, yet on the part of God it has not been without a set aim and purpose, since on the part of God nothing happens by chance. Think you that the flight of the swallows and their blinding holy Toby with their dung was by chance? It was not without a high decree and a particular will of God, to leave us an example in his person as in that of holy Job. And this the Holy Scripture says: *The Lord permitted that this trial should come upon him, to give to posterity an example of patience as in holy Job* (Tob. ii. 12). And the angel of the Lord said afterwards: *Because thou wert acceptable to God, it was needful that temptation should prove thee* (Tob. xii. 13). To prove thee, God permitted this temptation.

In the lives of the Fathers it is related of the Abbot Stephen that once, when he was sick, his companion was fain to make him a little cake; and, thinking that he was making it with good oil, he made it with linseed oil, which is very bitter, and gave it him. Stephen, as he noticed it, ate a little and said nothing. Another time he made him another in the same way; and, when he had tasted it and had no mind to go on eating, the brother said to him: "Eat, father, it is very good." And he made trial of it to incite him to eat it; and when he felt the bitterness, he began to fret and cry out: "I'm a murderer." And Stephen said to him: "Do not fret, son; for, if God had willed that you should not make a mistake in taking one oil for another, this would not have happened." And of many other holy men we read that they took with great conformity and patience the remedies given them, though they were contrary to what their illness required. So in this manner we ought to take all the mistakes and negligences, as well of the doctor as of the nurses, without complaining of the one, or throwing the fault on the other.

This is a thing in which a man's virtue is revealed and well shown. Great is the edification that a sick religious gives who takes all that is offered him with equanimity and cheerfulness as coming from the hand of God, and lets himself be guided and governed by superiors and infirmarians, forgetting himself and casting off all care of himself. St. Basil says: "You have entrusted your soul to the superior; why not entrust your body also? You have put in his hands your eternal salvation; why not also your temporal well-being?" And since the rule permits us then wholly to give up the care of our body and bids us do so, we should greatly esteem and profit by so advantageous a permission. On the other hand, a sick religious gives great disedification when he takes much care of himself, and keeps a close reckoning what they are to give him and how they are to give it and whether they keep their appointments with him exactly; and if not, he is master of complaints and murmurs.

Cassian says very well that sickness is no obstacle to purity of heart if the sick man knows how to take it as he ought; but "beware," he says, "lest the ailment pass from the body to the soul." If a man behaves in that way and takes occasion of his sickness to do his own will and not be obedient and submissive, then the ailment will pass to the soul and make the superior more concerned about the malady of the soul than about that of the body. You must not cease to show yourself a religious for being ill, nor think that rules do not exist for a sick man and that you may concentrate all your care on your health and comfort and forget your spiritual advancement. "Let him that is sick," says our holy Father, "by showing great humility and patience take care to give no less edification in time of sickness than in time of perfect health." St. Chrysostom on those words of the prophet: *Lord, thou hast crowned us with the buckler of thy good will* (Psalm v. 13), shows how, as long as this life lasts, there is always a conflict, and that we must go armed for it. He says: "This applies alike to the sick and to the healthy; for in time of illness there is particular occasion for this conflict, when pains assail the soul on all sides, when fits of sadness beset it, when the devil is there, inciting us to impatient speech and unmeasured complaints." So then is the time to exercise and show virtue. So says Seneca that the brave man must practise his fortitude as well in his bed, suffering illnesses, as on the field of battle, fighting against the enemy, since the chief part of fortitude is to endure rather than to accomplish. And the Wise Man: *Better is a patient than a strong man; and better is he who is master of his own soul than he who taketh cities by storm* (Prov. xvi. 32).

CHAPTER XVIII

In Which What Has Been Said Is Confirmed by Some Examples

WE read of the holy virgin Gertrude that one day Christ our Redeemer appeared to her, carrying in His right hand health and in His left hand sickness, and told her to choose which she wouldst. She answered: "What I desire, Lord, with all my heart is that Thou wilt not regard my will, but that that may be done in me which shall be for Thy greater glory and satisfaction."

It is told of a client of St. Thomas of Canterbury that in an illness he visited the tomb of the saint to beg him ask God to give him health. He obtained his petition, and went back home well. Then he began to think within himself that, if illness were better for his salvation, why should he seek for health? This reason struck him so forcibly that he went back to the tomb and asked the saint to beg of God to give him what was better for his salvation. God let the illness return, and he lived much consoled under it, understanding that that was what was better for him.

Surius in the Life of St. Vedastus, bishop, relates another like example of a blind man who, on the day of the translation of the body of that holy bishop, greatly desired to see his holy relics and consequently to have sight to see them. He obtained it of our Lord and saw what he desired. And, going about with sight, he turned to prayer that, if that sight did not make for the salvation of his soul, his blindness might return. After making that prayer he remained blind as before.

St. Jerome relates how, when St. Anthony, abbot, was summoned by St. Athanasius, bishop, to the city of Alexandria to help him in confuting and extirpating the heresies that were there, Didymus, who was a most learned man, but blind of the eyes of his body, discussed with St.

Anthony many passages of Holy Scripture in such a manner that the saint was in admiration of his genius and learning. After having discussed these passages, he asked him if he felt sad at being blind. He was loth to reply for shame. After being asked a second and a third time, he in the end openly confessed that he did feel sad thereat. Then the saint said to him: "It is a marvel to me how a man so wise as you can be sad and grieved at not possessing what flies and ants possess and the very earthworms, instead of rejoicing in the possession of what only saints and apostles have merited to obtain." Hence is seen, says St. Jerome, that it is a much greater thing to have spiritual than bodily eyes.

In the history of the order of St. Dominic, Father Hernando del Castillo relates how St. Dominic, while he lived at Rome, used to visit an afflicted sick woman, cloistered and a great servant of God, who had taken up her lodging in a tower hard by the gate of St. John Lateran; and the good father used oftentime to hear her confession and administer to her to the most Holy Sacrament. The woman was called Bona, and her life so well answered to her name that God taught her, like a good woman, to preserve cheerfulness in trials and find repose in death. She suffered a most severe infirmity in her breasts, which were so eaten away by cancer and so full of worms as would have been for any other person an insufferable torment, but not for her, who suffered it with admirable patience and giving of thanks. St. Dominic loved her much, seeing her so suffering and so advanced in virtue. One day, after having confessed and communicated her, he desired to see that cruel and terrible wound, and gained his point, though with some difficulty. When Bona uncovered herself, and the saint saw the putrid mass of the cancer, swarming with worms, and her patience and cheerfulness, he was moved to compassion, but had a greater desire of her wounds than of the treasures of earth and begged her to give one of those worms as a relic. That the servant of God would not do unless he promised to restore it; for she had come to that pitch of joy in seeing herself thus devoured alive that, if any of the worms fell on the ground, she took it back to restore it to its place. So on his word of honor she gave him one, which was well-grown and had a black head. Scarcely had the saint taken it into his hand when it turned into a most beautiful pearl, and the friars in admiration told their father not to return it; but the sick woman asked for her worm and bade them give her back her pearl. But in the act of being given back it returned to its original form of a worm, and the woman put it in her breasts where it had been engendered and grown. St. Dominic prayed for her, made the sign of the cross over her, and left her. But as he was going down the tower-stairs the woman's cancer-eaten breasts fell off from her, worms and all; and little by little the flesh grew in its place, and in a few days she was altogether cured, telling to all who came near her the marvels that God wrought through His servant.

In the same history it is related how, when Friar Reginald was in communication with St. Dominic about taking the habit of his order and had now made up his mind to do so, he took to his bed with a fever which the doctors thought mortal. Father St. Dominic took greatly to heart his recovery and made continual prayer to God our Lord for that intention; and the sick man also along with him called our Lady to his aid with great devotion and earnestness. While the two of them were at this prayer, the most holy Queen of Heaven, our Lady, came into Reginald's room, surrounded with a brightness and splendor quite heavenly and marvelous. She was accompanied by other two holy virgins, whom he took to be St. Cecily and St. Catherine, martyrs. They went up with their sovereign Lady to the sick man's bed. She, as Queen and Mother of Mercy, comforted him and said: "What wouldst thou have me to do for thee? I come to see what thou askest; tell me, and it shall be given thee." Reginald was overpowered and dumfounded with so heavenly a vision and doubted what it became him to do or to say; but one of the saints who accompanied our Lady soon drew him out of this perplexity, saying: "Brother, do not ask for anything, but leave all in her hands, for she knows better what to give than thou what to ask." The sick man followed this counsel, so discreet and well-advised, and so answered the Virgin: "Lady, I ask for nothing; I have no will beyond thine; in it and in thy hands I place myself." The Blessed Virgin then reached out and took some oil which her attendants brought with them for this purpose, and anointed Reginald in the way that it is customary to give extreme unction. So great was the efficacy of the touch of those holy hands that suddenly he found himself well of the fever and as restored in bodily strength as if he had never been ill. And what is more, along with that sovereign favor there was conferred on him another still higher in virtue of the soul, for from that moment he never felt any sensual or impure motion in his person all the days of his life, at no time, no place, and in no occasion.

In "Ecclesiastical History" it is related that among the men who flourished at that time there was a very distinguished man named Benjamin, who had of God the gift of healing the sick without any medicine by the mere touch of his hands, and anointing them with a little oil and saying a prayer over them. Along with this grace of healing others, he himself suffered from dropsy in a very grievous form and became so swollen that he could not come out by the door of his cell without displacing the doorposts. So he remained inside for eight months until he died, sitting in a very large chair, where he cured many ailments, never complaining nor grieving that he could find no remedy for himself. And those who pitied him he consoled, saying: "Pray God for my soul and never mind about my body, for when it was well it served me to no good purpose."

In the "Spiritual Meadow" there is a story of a monk named Barnaby, who on a journey ran a splinter into his foot, and would not have it removed for some days nor have the wound attended to, that he might have something to suffer for the love of God; and it is said that he used to say to those who visited him: "The more the outer man suffers and is mortified, the more the inner man is quickened and strengthened."

In the "Life of St. Pacomius," Surius tells of a monk named Zacheus, who, suffering from epilepsy, would not on that account abate the rigor of his customary abstinence, which consisted in living on bread and salt, nor again cease to repeat the prayers that the other monks were accustomed to say in health, attending matins and the other canonical hours. The rest of the time, in the intervals of prayer, he occupied in making mats, baskets, and ropes; and from the roughness of the esparto grass with which he wove them, his hands were so badly hurt that the blood ran from the cracks in the skin; this he did not to be idle. At night, before sleeping, his custom was to meditate on some passages of Holy Scripture; then he made the sign of the cross all over his body; that done, he retired to rest till the hour of matins, at which, as has been said, he arose and remained at psalmody and prayer until it was daylight. This was the division of his time that this holy invalid made, and these were his ordinary occupations. There happened to come at one time a monk to visit him. He, seeing his hands in such a pitiable state, told him to anoint them with oil and he would not feel such pains in the openings. Zacheus did so; and not only was the pain not mitigated, but it was much increased. He went afterwards to see St. Pacomius and told him what he had done. The saint said to him: "Did you think, son, that God does not see all our infirmities and that He could not heal them if He pleased? Now as to His not doing so, but permitting us to suffer pains so long as He pleases, do you think that He does that for any other purpose but that we may leave the whole care of ourselves to Him and put all our confidence in Him alone; and also for the good and advancement of our souls, so that He may be able afterwards to increase the remuneration and everlasting reward for these short afflictions which He sends us?" Zacheus at that was filled with compunction and said: "Pardon me, father, and pray God for me that He may forgive me this sin of want of confidence and conformity to His will, and desire to get better." At parting with Pacomius, in penance for so light a fault he fasted a whole year a fast so rigorous that he only ate once in two days, and then very little and weeping over it. The great Pacomius used afterwards to recount this notable example to his monks, to urge them to perseverance in work, confidence in God, and zeal to make up for small faults.

CHAPTER XIX

Of the Conformity We Should Have to the Will of God in Death as in Life

WE must also be conformable to the will of God as well for death as for life. And, though this dying is of itself a very difficult thing because, as the philosopher Aristotle says: "Death is the most fearful thing of all," yet in the case of religious this difficulty is in great part smoothed down and taken away, since we are already half-way on our journey to it, and in a manner the whole way. As for the first point, one of the reasons why dying is apt to be a difficult thing to the people in the world, and the approach of that hour gives them pain, is because they are leaving riches, honors, pleasures, amusements, and comforts that they had in this life, as also friends and relations, and in one case a man is leaving his wife, in another his children, who are apt to give great anxiety at that hour, especially when they are left ill-provided for. All this the religious has already left in time, and so it gives him no pain or grief.

When a back tooth is already clear of flesh and loosened from the gums, it is easily drawn; but, if you go about to draw it without loosening it from the flesh, it is apt to cause you much pain. So the religious who is already loosened from the flesh and detached from all those things of the world, is not pained at the hour of death at leaving them, because he has left them already of his own will and with great merit when he entered religion, and not waited for the hour of death to leave them, as those in the world do, when they are forced to leave them although they have no mind so to do, and leave them with great grief and pain and often without any merit at all because it is rather the things that leave the owners than the owners the things. And this is one of the fruits, among many others, of leaving the world and entering religion. St. Chrysostom well observes that they who are in the world, wedded to their property, to the amusements and comforts of this life, find death very painful, according to the saying of the Wise Man: *O death, how bitter is thy memory to the man that hath peace in his riches!* (Ecclus. xli. 1). Even the memory of death is very bitter; what shall be the presence of it! If the thought is bitter, what shall be the taste! But to the religious, who has already left all these things, death is not bitter, but rather very joyful and comfortable, as being the end of all his labors, and an assurance that he is going to receive the recompense and reward of all that he has left for God.

Another chief thing that usually gives pain to people in the world and makes death to them frightful and horrible, as St. Ambrose says, is their bad conscience and want of due dispositions. This again should find no room in the religious, for all his life has been one continual preparation and disposing of himself to die well. It is told of one holy religious how, when the doctor told him to prepare for death, he answered: "Ever since I took the habit, I have done nothing but to prepare for it." This is the daily exercise of the religious. And the state of religion itself is an instruction to us in the disposition which Christ our Redeemer wishes should be ours at His coming. *Let your loins be girt, and lamps burning in your hands* (Luke xii. 35). St. Gregory says that the girding of the loins denotes chastity, and the lamps burning in the hands denote the practice of good works; which two things do mainly shine forth in the state of religion. And so the good religious has nothing to fear in death. And here may be noted a thing that will aid much to our purpose—we have touched upon it above (Treatise II, Chapter 5)—that one of the best signs of having a good conscience and standing well with God, is being well conformed to the divine will in all that regards the hour of death, and looking forward to it with great gladness, as the spouse looks forward to celebrating with her Beloved her heavenly nuptials and espousals. And, contrariwise, it is not a good sign to make a trouble over death and not be in this state of conformity.

There are some good comparisons usually brought to explain this. See you not with what peace and quietness the sheep goes to the butchery, without once bleating or making any resistance, which is the example that Holy Scripture brings of Christ our Redeemer? *He was led like a sheep to the slaughter* (Isaias liii. 7). But the unclean animal, what grunting it sets up and what resistance when they want to kill it! This, then, is the difference between good people, who are represented by the sheep, and evil and carnal people, who are represented by those other animals. The felon under sentence of death, every time he hears the prison door open is saddened, thinking that they mean now to take him out and hang him; but the innocent man, who is marked for discharge, every time he hears the prison opened, rejoices, thinking that they are coming to give him his liberty. So the wicked man, when he hears the passing-bell ring or when sickness holds him in its grip, is very afraid and downcast because, being conscience-stricken, he fancies it is to cast him into the infernal bonfire for ever and ever. Let us, then, do what we ought to do as good religious, and not only shall we feel no difficulty in conforming ourselves to the will of God at the hour of death, but we shall rejoice and pray to God with the prophet to draw us out of this prison. *Draw out my soul from prison* (Psalm cxli. 8). St. Gregory on that text of Job: *Thou shalt not fear the beasts of the earth* (Job v. 22), says: "The feeling of this gladness and of this peace and ease of conscience at the hour of death is the beginning of the recompense of the righteous." Now they are beginning to enjoy one little drop of that peace which as a river in flood will soon enter their souls; they are beginning now to feel their eternal blessedness. On the contrary, the wicked are beginning to experience their torment and their hell in that fear and remorse which comes upon them at that hour.

Thus to desire death and rejoice in the thought of it is a very good sign. St. John Climacus says: "He is much to be praised who every day looks for death; but he is a saint who desires it every hour." So we see that those holy ancient patriarchs nourished this desire, *confessing that they are strangers and pilgrims upon earth* (Heb. xi. 13), not resident proprietors; which is well noted by St. Paul: *They who say this, signify that they are looking for home and country* (Heb. xi. 14), as being in exile here. And so the Royal Prophet sighed: *Woe is me that my sojourning is prolonged* (Psalm cxix. 5). And if those ancient Fathers said and desired this while the gate of heaven was closed and they could not go straight there, what should our desire be now that the gate is open, and as soon as the soul is purified it passes straight to the enjoyment of God!

CHAPTER XX

Of Sundry Reasons and Motives for Which We May Lawfully and Holily Desire Death

THAT we may better and more perfectly conform ourselves to the will of God in death as in life, we will set down here sundry motives and reasons why we may desire death, that out of them we may choose the best. The first reason why one may desire death is to escape the labors and troubles that this life carries with it, for as the Wise Man says: *Better is death than a bitter life* (Ecclus. xxx. 17). In this manner we see that men of the world often desire death and beg it of God; and this they may do without sin, for, after all, the troubles of this life are so many and so oppressive that it is lawful to desire death to escape them. One of the reasons given by the saints why God allowed so many troubles to befall men, was that we should not be so wedded to the world, nor so much in love with this life, but that we might fix our heart and our love on that other world, where *there shall be no weeping nor pain* (Apoc. xxi. 4). St. Augustine says that God our Lord in His infinite goodness and mercy has wished that this life should be short and quickly come to an end, because it is laborious; and that the other, which we hope for, should be everlasting, so that the labor should last only for a short time, but the joy and the rest forever. St. Ambrose says this life is so full of evils and hardships that, if God had not given us death as a punishment, we might have begged for it as a mercy and remedy, to put an end to so many evils and hardships. It is true that men of the world often sin by the impatience with which they take their troubles and by the way in which they beg death of God with complaints and outbursts of impatience. But if they asked peacefully and submissively: "Lord, if it please Thee, draw me out of these troubles; enough for me is the time I have already lived," there would be no sin in that.

In the second place, death may be desired with greater perfection, in order not to see the troubles of the Church and the continual offenses committed against God. So we see that the Prophet Elias desired it. Seeing the persecution of Achab and Jezabel, how they had destroyed the altars and put to death the prophets of God, and that they were seeking for him to do the like to him—on fire with zeal for the honor of God, and seeing that he could not mend matters, he went into the deserts and sat down under a tree, *and desired to die, and said: Lord, if it please thee, take me out of this life,* that I may not see so many evils and offenses against Thee, *for I am no better than my fathers* (III Kings xix. 4). And that valiant captain of the people of God, Judas Maccabeus, said: *It is better to die than to see so many evils and offenses against God* (I Macc. iii. 59); and therewith he encouraged his men to fight.

Of the blessed St. Augustine we read in his Life that, when the Vandals had passed over from Spain into Africa and were laying waste everything, sparing neither man nor woman, nor clergy nor laity, nor children nor old men, they came to the city of Hippo, where he was bishop, and surrounded it in great numbers. St. Augustine, seeing such great tribulation—churches without clergy, cities without inhabitants, all destroyed—wept bitterly in his old age and, calling together his clergy, said to them: "I have asked the Lord either to deliver us from these dangers, or to give us patience, or to take me out of this life that I may not see so many evils; and the Lord has granted me the third request." Forthwith he fell sick in the third month of the siege and died of that sickness. And of our blessed Father Ignatius we read in his Life another like example. This is a perfection proper to saints, to feel so keenly the afflictions of the Church and the offenses committed against the majesty of God as to be unable to suffer them, and so desire death, not to see such evil.

There is also another cause and reason, very good and involving great perfection, for desiring and begging death of God, which is to see ourselves free and safe from the danger of offending Him. For certain it is that, while we are in this life, there is no security that we may not possibly fall into mortal sin; and we know that others have fallen who were more advanced than ourselves and had received great gifts of God and were truly holy and very holy. This is one of the things that more particularly strikes fear into the servants of God and makes them desire to go out of this life. To purchase immunity from sin, one may desire even never to have been born and never to have had existence; how much more to die, since sin is a greater evil than non-existence, and it were better not to be at all than to have sinned. *It were better for that man never to have been born* (Matt. xxvi. 24).

St. Ambrose explains to this purpose the saying of Ecclesiastes (iv. 2): *And I praised the dead rather than the living, and I judged him happier than either who hath never been born.* The dead is preferred to the living because he has now ceased to sin, and he that has never been born is preferred to the dead because he has never been capable of sin. And so it will be a very good practice to elicit often these acts in prayer: "Lord, never permit me to be separated from Thee;" "Lord, if I am ever to offend Thee, take me off straightway before I offend Thee, because I have no will to live except to serve Thee; and if my life is not to be to Thy service, I would have it no longer." This is a practice very agreeable to God and very profitable to ourselves, since it contains an act of sorrow and detestation of sin, it contains an act of humility, it contains an act of love of God, it contains a petition one of the most agreeable that we can offer to God. It is related of St. Louis, King of France, that sometimes his holy mother Queen Doña Blanca (Blanche of Aragon) would say to him: "My son, I would rather see you dead before my eyes than in mortal sin."

And so pleasing to God was this desire and this blessing which she uttered over him, that they say that all his life long he never committed a mortal sin. This desire and petition may work the same effect on you.

And, further, not only for the avoiding of mortal sins, but for the avoiding of venial sins, of which we are full in this life, it is good to desire death. The servant of God should be resolved to die rather than tell a lie, which is a venial sin; and anyone who should die on that score would be a martyr (St. Thomas, 2a 2æ, q. 124, art. 5, ad 2). But it is certain that, if we live, we are sure to commit many venial sins. *Seven times shall the just man fall* (Prov. xxiv. 10), that is, many times; and the longer he lives, the oftener will he fall. And not only for the avoidance of venial sins do the servants of God desire now to go out of this life, but to be free from so many faults and imperfections and the many temptations and miseries of our daily experience.

That holy man (Thomas à Kempis) says very well: "O Lord, how I suffer when I set my mind to think of heavenly things, and at once a crowd of carnal thoughts rush in upon me! Ah, what a life is this, where tribulations and miseries never fail, where all things are full of snares and enemies! When one tribulation goes, another comes; and even while the former conflict is going on, sundry others supervene unexpectedly. How can a life be loved that is full of so many bitternesses, liable to so many calamities and miseries? How is it even called a life, engendering as it does so many deaths and plagues?" (Imitation iii. 48 and 20). We read of a very holy woman that she used to say that, if she had the choice of anything, she would choose nothing else but death, since by that means the soul is removed from all fear of ever doing anything that could be a hindrance to pure love. And it seems a more perfect thing to desire to quit this life in order to avoid venial sins and faults and imperfections than for the avoidance of mortal sins; since the avoidance of mortal sins may be more for fear of hell and for love of self and of one's own advancement than for love of God; but to have such a love of God as to desire death in order to avoid venial sins and faults and imperfections, means great purity of intention and is a thing of high perfection.

But someone will say: "It is to make satisfaction for my faults and defects that I desire to live." To this I say that, if by living longer we always cleared ourselves of the past and did not add new faults, that would be a good pretext; but if you do not clear yourself, but make additions, and the longer you live, the more account you have to render to God, that pretext breaks down. St. Bernard says very well: "Why do we so much desire this life, in which the longer we live, the more we sin?" And St. Jerome: "What difference, think you, is there between him who dies young and him who dies old, except that the old man is more heavily laden with sin than the young man and has a longer account to render to God?" And so St. Bernard comes to a further conclusion herein and uses language in his great humility that we can use with greater truth: "I blush to live because I profit little; I fear to die because I am not prepared. On the whole, however, I prefer to die and commit myself to the mercy of God, because He is bountiful and merciful, than to go on giving scandal to my brethren by my tepid and imperfect life." This is a good conclusion. And Father Master Avila used to say that whoever found himself but indifferently disposed to good, ought to desire death rather than life, by reason of the danger in which he lives, which all ceases with death. St. Ambrose says: "What is death but the burial of vices and the resurrection of virtues?"

All these reasons and motives form good ground for desiring death, but the most perfect motive was that which St. Paul had, to be with Christ Whom he loved so much. *I desire to be loosened and to be with Christ* (Phil. i. 23).

What sayest thou, St. Paul? Why dost thou desire to be loosened from the body? Is it haply to escape sufferings? No, certainly not; for rather *we glory in tribulations* (Rom. v. 3); that is my glory. Then what is it for? To avoid sin? Not that either, *for I am certain that neither death nor life shall be able to separate us from the love of God* (Rom. viii. 38). He was confirmed in grace and knew that he could not lose it, and so he was not concerned to fear that. Why, then, desirest thou death? To be with Christ. He desired it out of pure love—*Because I languish with love* (Cant. ii. 5). He was sick with love, and so sighed after his Beloved, and any delay seemed long to come to enjoy His presence. St. Bonaventure puts this for the first and highest degree of love of God of the three which he assigns. The first is to love God above all things in the world, so that we would not commit a mortal sin for any of them, nor break any commandment of God so binding. This is what Christ our Redeemer said to that young man in the Gospel: *If thou wilt enter into life, keep the commandments* (Matt. xix. 17). That applies to all. The second degree of charity is not to be content with keeping the commandments, but go on to the counsels, which is proper to religious, who aim not only at what is good, but what is better and more perfect, according to the saying of St. Paul: *Be ye renewed interiorly, to know by experience what is the will of God, good and well-pleasing and perfect* (Rom. xii. 2). The third degree of charity, says St. Bonaventure, is when a man is all aglow and on fire with the love of God, so that he feels that he cannot live without Him; and accordingly he desires to see himself free and loose from the prison of this body, to be with Christ. His desire is that this exile may be repealed, and this wall of flesh broken and fall down that stands in his way and hinders his seeing God. Life to such is a matter of patience, or rather of weariness, and death an object of ardent desire.

Of our blessed Father Ignatius we read in his Life that he had the most ardent desire to go out of this prison and bondage of the body. So much did his soul sigh to be with his God that at the thought of death he could not restrain his tears, and his eyes were moistened with pure joy. But it is said in that Life that this ardent desire was not so much for the attainment of the Sovereign Good and the enjoyment of that glorious vision, but rather for seeing the glory and supreme felicity of the most sacred humanity of his Lord, Whom he loved so much; and, as the Royal Prophet said, *to see the delight of the Lord* (Psalm xxvi. 4). As here on earth a friend is apt to rejoice at the sight of the glory and honor of one whom he loves heart and soul, so did our blessed Father desire to be with Christ, forgetful of his own interest and enjoyment and actuated by pure love. He desired to rejoice and be glad for the glory of Christ, congratulating Him on the same, which is the highest and most perfect act of love that we can make. In this way the memory of death, far from being bitter to us, will afford us much satisfaction and joy. Pass on a little further and consider that a few days hence you shall be in heaven, in that joy which *eye hath not seen, nor ear heard, nor can it enter into the heart of man to conceive it* (I Cor. ii. 9), and everything for you shall be converted into joy and gladness. Who would not rejoice at the termination of his exile and the end of his labor! Who would not rejoice at gaining and securing his last end for which he was created! Who would not rejoice at entering into possession of his inheritance, and such an inheritance! Now it is by means of death that we enter into the inheritance of heaven. *When the Lord shall send sleep,* the sleep of death, *to his beloved* (Psalm cxxvi. 2), then shall they awake to the inheritance of the Lord. We cannot enter into the possession of these everlasting good things otherwise than by means of death; and so says the Wise Man: *The just hath hope in his death* (Prov. xiv. 32), for that is the ladder by means of which we mount up to heaven, and this is our comfort in this land of exile. *I will sing to thee, O Lord, and make it my aim to live a pure life without stain of sin: when wilt thou come to me?* (Psalm c. 2). So St. Augustine explains this text: "My thought and desire, O Lord, is to keep myself without stain all my life long, and with that care I will ever go singing, and the burden of my song shall be: When shall this exile, O Lord, be repealed? When wilt Thou come for me? When shall I go, Lord, to Thee?" *When shall I come and appear before the face of God?* (Psalm xli. 2). When shall I be with Thee, O Lord? Oh, how that hour hangs back! Oh, what gladness and joy for me, when they tell me that it is now nigh! *I have rejoiced in the thing that is said to me: We will go into the house of the Lord. Our feet shall be standing in thy courts, O Jerusalem* (Psalm cxxi. 1-2). I imagine myself already standing there in company of the angels and the blessed, rejoicing in Thee, O Lord, for ever and ever."

CHAPTER XXI

What Has Been Said in the Preceding Chapter, Confirmed by Examples

SIMON METAPHRASTES in his Life of St. John the Almoner, Archbishop of Alexandria, relates how a rich man had a son whom he loved very much, and to obtain of God the preservation of his life and health he asked the saint to pray for him, and gave him a great quantity of gold to distribute in alms to the poor for that intention. The saint did so, and at the end of thirty days the son died. The father was smitten with great grief, thinking that the prayer and alms that had been offered for him had gone for nothing. The patriarch, knowing his sadness, offered prayer for him, asking God to console him. God heard his prayer and sent one night a holy angel from heaven, who appeared to the man and told him that he should know that the prayer made for his son had been heard by God;

and that his son was alive and well in heaven and that his death at that time was the right thing for him in view of his salvation; for, if he had lived, he would have turned out badly and made himself unworthy of the glory of God. He said further that he should know that none of the things that happen to us in this life happen otherwise than by the just judgment of God, although the grounds of His judgments are hidden from men; and that man therefore should not give way to excessive sadness, but receive with patient and grateful mind the things that God ordains. With this warning from heaven the father of the deceased boy remained comforted and animated to serve God.

In the history of the Theban Legion there is recounted a singular favor which St. Maurice, captain of that legion, did to a lady very devout to him. She had an only son whom, to the end that he might progress betimes in religious ways, she consecrated, as soon as he was out of his tender age, in the Monastery of St. Maurice, under the care and government of the monks, as was the custom of those times, and as the fathers of Maurus, Placidus, and other noble Romans did with their children in the time of St. Benedict; and, many years later, St. Thomas Aquinas' mother, Theodora, and his brothers, counts of Aquino, did the like with him in the Monastery of Monte Cassino. In the monastery, this only son grew in letters and good customs and monastic discipline right well and in choir with the monks he had begun to sing very sweetly. But a little fever came upon him, whereof he died. The disconsolate mother came to the church and with infinite tears accompanied the dead body to the tomb. But many tears did not suffice to allay the mother's grief nor to make her cease going every day to the grave, there to weep, without measure; and much more at the time when the divine office was said, did she remember how she was deprived of hearing the voice of her son. The lady persevered in this sad exercise, not only in the daytime in the church, but at nights as well in her house, without being able to rest. One time, overcome by weariness, she fell asleep; and in her sleep there appeared to her the holy Captain Maurice, and said: "Woman, why art thou continually weeping over the death of thy son, without being able to put a stop to such a flood of tears?" She answered: "I cannot stop this lamentation all the days of my life; and therefore, as long as I live, I shall always bewail my only son, nor shall my eyes cease to shed tears till death close them and my disconsolate soul leave this body." The saint replied: "I tell thee, woman, not to afflict thyself, nor weep over thy dead son any more as though he were dead, since he is not dead but alive, and is rejoicing with us in everlasting life. As a sign of the truth that I tell thee, rise in the morning for matins, and thou shalt hear the voice of thy son among the voices of the monks, singing the divine office; and not only tomorrow shalt thou have that joy, but every time thou art present at the canonical hours in the church. Cease, then, and put an end to thy tears, since thou hast more occasion for great rejoicing than for sadness." The woman arose, and waited with longing desire for the hour of matins to assure herself of the truth, having still in her mind the while some doubt of its being all a dream. The hour came; and, entering the church, the mother recognized at the intoning of the antiphon the most sweet voice of her blessed son, secure now of his glory in heaven. Throwing off all grief, she gave infinite thanks to God. Every day she had the joy of hearing that voice in the divine office of that church. So did God comfort her on this occasion and bestow on her this rich favor.

An author relates how one day a knight was out hunting, and there came out a wild animal which he chased by himself, without a servant, his company being taken up with killing other game. He followed the chase with great eagerness far apart till he came to a thicket, whence he heard a human voice of ravishing sweetness. He wondered at hearing such a voice in a lonely place, because he thought it could not be any of his servants nor any of the people of that countryside. Desiring to look into the matter, he went into the thicket and found there a leper, hideous to behold and exceedingly filthy, whose flesh was in such a state that it was falling to pieces in every limb and part of his body. At such a sight the knight was greatly amazed and horrified; but, plucking up his courage, he went up to him, saluted him in kind words, and asked if it was he that was singing, and from him that that sweet voice came forth. The leper answered: "Yes, sir, it was I that was singing, and that is my own voice." "How could you be glad," asked the knight, "in the midst of such sufferings?" The poor man answered: "Between God my Lord and me there is no other barrier but this wall of clay, which is my body; when that obstacle is broken through and removed, I shall go to enjoy the vision of His eternal majesty; and as I see it every day falling to pieces, I rejoice and sing with inward gladness of my heart, waiting as I do wait for my departure from this body; for till I leave it I cannot go to the enjoyment of my God, the living fountain, where are found the streams of bliss that flow forever."

St. Cyprian tells of a bishop who was very ill of a grave sickness and reduced to the last extremity, very worried and anxious about death, that was close upon him. He entreated our Lord to prolong his life. Then there appeared to him an angel in the form of a very beautiful and shining youth, who said to him in a grave and severe voice: "On the one hand thou shrinkest from suffering in this life, and on the other, thou hast no mind to go out of it. What wouldst thou have me do with thee?"—giving him to understand that his unwillingness to depart this life was not pleasing to God. The saint declares that the angel said these words to him that in his agony he might tell them and repeat them to others.

Simon Metaphrastes, as quoted by Surius, relates of the holy Abbot Theodosius that, knowing how profitable is the remembrance of death, he sought to give occasion thereof to his disciples for their improvement. Wherefore he had a grave dug, and when it was open, he placed himself with them around it and said: "There is the grave open; for which of you shall we first celebrate the funeral obsequies?" One of his disciples, named Basil, who was a priest, a man of great virtue and so quite disposed and prepared to choose death very gladly, took up the word. Kneeling down, he said: "Bless me, father, for I shall be the first for whom you will have to celebrate the office of requiem." The holy abbot ordered that in his lifetime there should be celebrated for him all the offices that usually are celebrated for the dead, the first day, the third, the ninth, and lastly other funeral honors on the fortieth day. Wonderful to relate, at the end of the office of the fortieth day the monk Basil, being sound and well, without fever or headache or any other malady, like one who falls into a sweet sleep, passed to the Lord to receive the reward of his virtue and of the promptitude and joy wherewith he had desired to be with Christ. Another miracle followed. For during the space of forty days after his death the Abbot Theodosius saw him coming every day to vespers and singing in choir with the rest of the community. Of the rest, none saw him nor heard him sing but one only, a monk of signal virtue, named Aetius, who did hear him sing, but did not see him. He went to Abbot Theodosius and said to him: "Father, don't you hear our brother Basil singing with us?" The abbot answered: "I hear him and see him and will get you to see him as well." They being another day together at office in choir, the abbot saw the holy monk Basil singing in choir with the rest as usual, and pointed him out with his finger to Aetius, praying God at the same time to open his eyes that he might see him. When Aetius saw and recognized him, he went straight running up to embrace him, but could not grasp him, and the vision disappeared at once, saying in a voice that all heard: "Good-bye, my fathers and brothers, good-bye; for henceforth you shall see me no more."

In the chronicles of the order of St. Augustine it is related of St. Columbanus the Younger, cousin and disciple of the holy Abbot Columbanus, that, being in a high fever and near to death and full of a great hope to die, there appeared to him a shining youth and said to him: "Thine abbot's prayers and tears for thy recovery prevent thy going out of this life." Whereupon the saint made loving complaint to his abbot and said to him weeping: "Why do you force me to live so sad a life as this and hinder my entrance into life everlasting?" Then the abbot ceased to weep and pray for him; and so, assembling the religious and receiving the holy sacraments and embracing them all, he died in the Lord.

St. Ambrose relates of the people of Thrace that when men were born they wept, and when they died they made a great feast. They wept at births and made high festival on the day of a death, reckoning very reasonably, as he says, that people coming into this wretched world, replete with so many woes, deserved to be wept over; and when they quitted this place of exile, it was a rational thing to keep feasts and rejoicings for their deliverance from so many miseries. Now if they did so, being gentiles and pagans and having no knowledge of the glory that we hope for, what will it be reasonable for us to feel and do, we who are enlightened by the light of faith and know the good things that they go to enjoy who die in the Lord? So with much more reason does the Wise Man say: *Better is the day of death than the day of birth* (Eccles. vii. 2). St. Jerome says that for this reason Christ our Redeemer, being about to depart from this world to His Father, said to His disciples, who were sad thereat: *If ye loved me, ye would indeed rejoice, because I go to the Father* (John xiv. 28).

And, contrariwise, when He determined to raise Lazarus, He wept (John xi. 35). He did not weep, says St. Jerome, because he was dead, seeing that He was about immediately to raise him up, but He wept because he had to return to this miserable life; He wept because one whom He had loved and still loved so much had to return to the afflictions of this exile.

CHAPTER XXII

Of the Conformity Which We Should Have to the Will of God in the General Afflictions and Calamities Which He Sends Us

WE must not only practise conformity to the will of God in the troubles and mishaps that particularly concern ourselves, but also in those general calamities, famines, wars, sicknesses, deaths, pestilences, and the like, which the Lord sends to His Church. For this it is necessary to take for granted that, though on the one hand we feel these calamities and chastisements and are touched by the misfortunes and troubles of our neighbor, as is right; yet on the other hand, considering them inasmuch as they are the will of God, ordained by His just judgments to bring blessings and advantages which he knows to be to His greater glory, we are able on this consideration to conform ourselves therein to His most holy will. In the same way we see here on earth how, when a judge sentences a man to death, while he feels and regrets the necessity that this man shall die, for natural compassion or because he is his friend, yet he does pass the sentence and will his death, because it makes for the common good of the whole community.

And while it is true that God has not been pleased to oblige us to conform ourselves to His will in all these things so as positively to will them and love them, but is satisfied with our suffering them in patience, without contradiction or repugnance to the divine justice, or murmuring thereat; yet theologians and saints say that it would be a work of greater perfection and merit and of a more perfect and entire resignation, if a man were not only to bear those things and suffer them in patience, but were actually to love them and wish them as being the will and good pleasure of God and the order of His divine justice and subservient to His greater glory, as do the blessed in heaven, who in all things fall in with the will of God. So says St. Thomas, and St. Anselm illustrates it by this comparison. He says that in the glory of heaven our will and the will of God shall go as perfectly together as here on earth do the two eyes of one and the same body, so that one cannot look at a thing without the other also looking at it; and thus, though the thing is seen by both eyes, yet it is always seen as one and the same thing. But as the saints there in heaven fall in with the will of God in all things, seeing in them all the order of His justice and the end of His greater glory to which they are directed, so it will be great perfection for us to imitate the blessed therein, wishing the will of God to be done here on earth as it is in heaven. To will what God wills, for the same reason and end that God wills it, can never cease to be a very good thing.

Posidonius relates of St. Augustine in his Life that when the city of Bona [then called Hippo, near the modern Cape Bona], where he resided, was besieged by the Vandals, looking out upon that scene of ruin and mortality, he comforted himself with that saying of a sage: "He will not be a great man who shall take it for a great thing that stones and buildings fall and mortals die"—*Non erit magnus magnum putans quod cadunt ligna et lapides, et mortales moriuntur.* We have more reason to find comfort in the consideration that all these things come from the hand of God and that such is His will; and though the reason why He sends these afflictions and calamities be hidden, yet it cannot be unjust.

The judgments of God are very profound. They are *a deep abyss,* as the prophet says (Psalm xxxv. 7); and we must not wish to scrutinize and investigate them with our mean and limited understanding, which would be great rashness. *For who hath known the mind of the Lord, and who hath been his counselor?* (Rom. xi. 34; Isaias xl. 13). Who has given you a seat at His council board, that you should wish to meddle in this matter? We can only reverence in humility and believe that from infinite Wisdom nothing can come but what is well calculated to its end, and so well calculated that in the end it will prove to be to our greater good and profit. We must always go on this principle, believing that God of His infinite goodness and mercy would never send or permit the like evils and afflictions were it not to draw from them other greater goods. It is the purpose of God to take to heaven by this road many who would otherwise be lost. How many there are who under these afflictions return with all their heart to God and die in true repentance for their sins and are saved, and in any other way would have been damned! Thus what appears a chastisement and a scourge is a mercy and great benefit.

In the Second Book of Maccabees, after having related that horrible and most cruel persecution of the most impious King Antiochus and the blood that he shed without sparing child or man, married or unmarried woman, and how he plundered and profaned the Temple and the abominations that were committed in it by his orders, the author goes on to say: *I beseech those who shall read this book not to be dismayed at these adverse events, but believe that God has permitted and sent all these afflictions, not for the destruction, but for the amendment and correction of our race* (II Macc. vi. 12). St. Gregory says very well to this effect: The leech sucks the blood of the sick man and all his aim is to satisfy himself and drink all he can; but the aim of the physician is to draw off the bad blood and give health to the patient. This is what God aims at through the affliction and tribulation which He sends us. It would be unwise of the sick man not to let the bad blood be drawn off, looking rather at the lust of the leech than at the intention of the physician. So in our case, whatever trouble comes upon us, whether through the instrumentality of men or through that of any other creature, we should not look at them, but at that most wise physician, who is God; for they all serve Him as leeches and means to draw off the bad blood and give us entire health and salvation. Thus we should understand and believe that He sends us all things for our greater good and profit; and though the Lord had nothing more in view in the matter than to *chastise us* in this life *as sons* (Heb. xii. 7-8), and not keep the chastisement for the next, it would be a great blessing and benefit.

It is related of St. Catherine of Siena that she was once much afflicted by a false witness that they had set up against her, impugning her virtue, when there appeared to her Christ our Redeemer, holding in His right hand a crown of gold, adorned with many pearls and precious stones, and in His left a crown of thorns, and said to her: "My beloved daughter, know that it is necessary to be crowned with these two crowns on different occasions and at different times; this being so, do thou choose which thou preferrest, either to be crowned with this crown of thorns in this life which thou now livest, and to have that other, the precious crown, kept for thee until that life that must last forever; or to have that precious crown given thee in this life, and have kept for thee the crown of thorns till after thy death." The holy virgin answered: "Lord, I have already for a long time denied my own will to follow Thine; therefore it is not for me to choose. But if Thou, O Lord, willest that I should give an answer, I say that I always in this life choose to be conformed to Thy holy Passion, and for love of Thee I wish always to embrace pains for my refreshment." So saying, with her own hands she took the crown of thorns from the hand of the Savior and put it with all her might on her own head with such force that the thorns pierced her all round; and from that time onwards, on many days she felt an actual pain in her head from the thorns entering in there.

CHAPTER XXIII

Of a Means That Will Help Us Much to Bear Well and with Conformity the Afflictions That the Lord Sends Us, As Well Particular As General, Which Is the Knowledge and Inward Consciousness of Our Own Sins

IT is the common doctrine of the saints that, ordinarily speaking, God is wont to send those public calamities and chastisements for sins committed, as we are told in Holy Scripture, which is full of such narratives. *It is for our sins, O Lord, that thou hast sent us these afflictions, because we sin and do evil and obey not thy commandments: therefore whatever thou hast sent upon us, and all that thou hast done us, in strict justice hast thou done it* (Dan. iii. 28). Thus we see that God chastised His people and gave them over into the hands of their enemies when they offended Him and delivered them when they repented of their sins, did penance, and returned to Him. On this account Achior, captain and chief of the sons of Ammon, declared to Holofernes how God protected the people of Israel and how He chastised them when they departed from His obedience. "Therefore," he said, "before attacking them, contrive to find out if at this period they have offended God. If that is the case, you may make sure of the victory; but if not, you had better give up this enterprise. For it will not go well and nothing will come of it but disgrace and confusion, for God will fight for His people, against Whom none can fight and prevail" (Judith v. 5-24).

The saints take special note of this on those words which Christ our Redeemer, after He had healed him, addressed to the man at the Sheep Pool who had been ailing for thirty-eight years. *Now thou art healed: take care henceforth to sin no more, lest something worse befall thee* (John v. 14). Accordingly, one of the means that will help us much in calamities and tribulations, as well general as particular, to fall in with the will of God and bear them in great patience, will be to enter forthwith into ourselves and consider our sins and how we deserve this chastisement, for in this way, whatever adversity befalls us, we shall bear it well and judge it to be less than what would be in proportion to our faults.

St. Bernard and St. Gregory handle this point well. St. Bernard says: "If the fault is felt inwardly, as it ought to be felt, the outward punishment will be felt little or not at all." Thus the holy King David did not feel the curses which Semei launched out against him, seeing the war which his own son was making upon him. *Thou seest that my own son, the fruit of my body, is seeking my life: how much more now a son of Jemini!* (II Kings xvi. 11). St. Gregory on that saying (Job xi. 6): *Thou shalt know that God chastiseth thee less than thy wickedness deserveth,* illustrates this by a good comparison. When a sick man feels his ulcer inflamed or his flesh putrid, he gives himself with good grace over into the hands of the surgeon, to open and cut where he pleases; and the more inflamed and the more putrid the wound, the more willingly does he suffer the knife and the cautery. So when a man really feels the wound and infirmity that sin has caused in his soul, he willingly submits to the cautery of affliction and humiliation and mortification with which God goes about to cure this wound and draw off the putrid matter from it. "The pain of the scourge," he says, "is mitigated when the fault is owned"—*Dolor flagelli temperatur cum culpa cognoscitur.* If you do not take in good part the mortification and affliction that is offered you, it is because you do not know the malady of your faults nor feel the rottenness that is in you, and so you cannot bear to suffer the cautery and the lancet.

Holy men and true servants of God not only take their punishment willingly, but they desire it and earnestly ask it of God. *Who will grant that my petition may come about, and that he who hath begun will even crush me outright, let loose his hand upon me, and cut me down, and this be my consolation, that afflicting me with pain he spare me not* (Job vi. 8). *Prove me, O Lord, and try me,* says the psalmist, *for I am prepared for scourges* (Psalm xxv. 2; xxxvii. 18)—*Bonum mihi, quia humiliasti me.* The servants of God, says St. Gregory, desire that His Majesty may chastise and humble them in this life; and they are rather out of heart when they consider their faults on the one hand, and on the other see that God has not chastised them for them; for then they suspect and fear that He means to defer their chastisement to the next life, when it will be done with rigor. And this is what Job goes on to say: *And this be my consolation, that in afflicting me with sorrows he spare me not.* It is as though they would say: Since God pardons some in this life to chastise them forever in the next, let Him not pardon me in that way in this life, that afterwards He may pardon me forever. Let God chastise me as a loving Father, that He may not afterwards chastise me as a rigorous judge. I will not murmur nor complain of His scourges; *I will not contradict the utterances of the Holy One* (Job vi. 10). This is also what St. Augustine says: "Here burn, here cut, here spare me nothing, that Thou mayest spare me for eternity."

It is part of our ignorance and blindness to feel bodily afflictions so acutely and to take spiritual afflictions so lightly. It is not afflictions that we should feel so much as sins. If we knew and pondered well the gravity of our faults, all punishment would seem to us little and we should say with Job (xxxiii. 27): *I have sinned and indeed done wrong, and have not received as I deserved*—words that we ought to carry ever in our heart and repeat often with our mouth. I have sinned, O Lord, and indeed have done wrong and offended Thy Divine Majesty, and I have not been chastised as I deserved; for all that we can suffer in this life is nothing in comparison with what one single [mortal] sin deserves. *Would that thou couldst come to understand that God punisheth thee much less than thy wickedness deserveth* (Job xi. 6). Whoever will consider that he has offended God and deserved to be in hell for ever and ever, what ignominies, what injuries, what insults will he not take with good will in recompense and satisfaction for the offenses that he has committed against the majesty of God! *Let him curse, for perchance the Lord will be pleased to regard my affliction, and will render me blessings for the curses of this day* (II Kings xvi. 12), said David when Semei cursed and insulted him. Let him alone, let him insult me, let him load me with injuries and insults; perchance the Lord will be satisfied with that and will hold Himself compensated and satisfied thereby for my sins and have mercy on me; and that will be a great piece of luck for me. This is the way in which we should embrace the insults and hardships that meet us. They are welcome, for haply the Lord will be pleased to take them in discount and satisfaction for our sins and will have mercy on us, and that will be great good luck. If the time that we wasted in complaining and resenting our afflictions, we spent in turning in this manner upon ourselves, we should please God more and mend matters better.

The saints used this means on the like occasions and made a practice of it. Thus we read of some of them, as St. Catherine of Siena and others, that they attributed to their sins the afflictions and scourges that God sent His Church, and said: "I am the cause of these wars; my sins are the cause of this pestilence and these troubles that God sends us." They thought that their sins deserved all that and more. And it makes in confirmation of this, that God has often punished a whole people for the sin of one individual, as for the sin of David He sent a pestilence upon all the people of Israel, and Scripture says that there died seventy thousand men in three days (II Kings xxiv. 15). But you will say, he was a king, and for the sins of the head God chastises the people. But for the sin of Achan, a private man, who had stolen certain little things at Jericho, God punished the whole people, so that three thousand soldiers of the most valiant in the army turned their backs on the enemy and were forced to fly on his account. Not only for the sin of the head, but also for the sin of an individual God is wont to punish the rest. In this way the saints explain what Holy Scripture so often repeats, that God visits the sins of the fathers on the children even to the third and fourth generation. The *fault* of the father, Scripture says, shall not pass on to the son, nor that of the son on to the father. *The soul that sinneth, the same shall die: the son shall not bear the fault of the father, nor the father the fault of the son* (Exod. xx. 5; xxxiv. 7: Num. xiv. 18; Ezech. xviii. 20). But as regards *punishment,* God is wont to punish some for the sins of others; and so perhaps for my sins, or yours, God will punish the whole house and the whole order.

Let us, then, keep before our eyes on the one hand this consideration, and on the other the good pleasure of God, and so we shall easily fall in with His will and with the afflictions which He sends us, and shall say with the priest Heli: *He is the Lord, let him do what is good in his eyes* (I Kings iii. 18); and those holy Maccabees: *As it shall be the will of God in heaven, so let it be done* (I Macc. iii. 60); and with the Prophet David: *I was dumb, O Lord, and opened not my mouth, because thou didst it* (Psalm xxxviii. 10). I complained not, O Lord, of the troubles Thou hast sent me; rather, as if I were dumb, I was silent and bore them with much patience and conformity because

I knew, Lord, that Thou didst send them. This should be always our consolation in all things. God wills it, God does it, God commands it; it is He that sends it; it is welcome. There is no other reason required for bearing all things well.

On those words of the psalm: *My beloved is as the son of the unicorn* (Psalm xxviii. 7), the saints observe that God is compared to the unicorn because the unicorn has its horn below its eyes, that it may see right well where it strikes, not as the bull, which has its horns above and does not see where it deals its blow; and, further, the unicorn heals with that very horn wherewith it strikes; so God heals with that wherewith He strikes.

So pleasing to God is this conformity and humble submission to punishment that sometimes it is a means to appease the Lord and make Him give over the punishment. In the ecclesiastical histories it is told of Attila, King of the Goths, who laid waste so many provinces and called himself the Terror of the World and the Scourge of God, that, when he was besieging the city of Troyes in Champagne, in France, there went out to meet him St. Lupus, bishop of that city, clad in his pontifical robes, with all his clergy, and said to him: "Who art thou, that troublest and disturbest the earth?" He replied: "I am the Scourge of God." Then the holy bishop bade them open the gates, saying: "Welcome to the Scourge of God." And the soldiers coming into the city, the Lord blinded them in such a way that they went through without doing any harm. For though Attila was a scourge, the Lord would not have him be such to those who received him as His scourge with so great submission.

CHAPTER XXIV

Of the Conformity That We Ought to Have with the Will of God in Dryness and Desolation in Prayer

NOT only ought we to conform ourselves to the will of God in exterior, natural, and human things, but also in that which many think it is a point of sanctity to desire more and more; I mean, in spiritual and supernatural goods, as divine consolations, even virtues, even the gift of prayer, peace, restfulness, and inward tranquillity of soul. But someone will ask: Is it possible to have in these things a will of one's own and an inordinate love, so that it should become necessary to check oneself in these things? Yes, I say, it is; and here we shall see the malice of self-love, since it shrinks not from intermingling its baleful poison in such good things. Consolations and spiritual delights are good, because with them the soul easily puts aside and abhors all pleasure and delight in the things of earth, which are the food and nourishment of vices, and animates and bestirs herself to go on nimbly in the service of God, as the prophet says: *I ran in the way of thy commandments when thou didst enlarge my heart* (Psalm cxviii. 32). The heart is dilated and enlarged by spiritual consolation, as it is straitened and narrowed by sadness. Hence the Prophet David said that, when God sent him consolations, they were as wings that made him run and fly in the way of virtue and God's commandments.

Spiritual consolations are besides a great aid to a man to break his will and conquer his appetites and mortify his flesh and more vigorously take up the crosses and afflictions that occur. And therefore God usually sends consolations and delights to those to whom He intends to send troubles and tribulations, that so they may make ready and be disposed to bear them well and profitably. Thus Christ consoled His disciples on Mount Thabor with His glorious Transfiguration, that afterwards they might not be shocked at seeing Him suffering and dying on a cross. So we see that God is ordinarily wont to give these spiritual consolations to beginners, to make them effectually abandon the delights of earth for those of heaven; and afterwards, when He has smitten them with His love and they have struck deep roots in virtue, He usually exercises them with aridities, that they may gain more patience and humility and merit an increase of grace and glory by serving God for pure love, without consolations. And that is why some, at the beginning, at their first entrance into religion, or haply out in the world when they had their first desires of religious life, felt more consolation and taste for spiritual things than they experienced afterwards. For God treated them according to their age, giving them the milk of babes to uproot and detach them from the world and make them abhor and reject its offers; but afterwards, when they became able to eat their bread, crust and all, then He gives them the food of grown-up men. That is why the saints advise us, in time of consolation, to prepare for temptation, as in time of peace men make ready for war, because consolations are usually the first vespers of temptations and tribulations.

As spiritual consolations are very good and very profitable if we know how to use them, so, when the Lord gives them, they are to be received with thankfulness. But if we were to dwell upon these consolations and desire them solely for our own satisfaction, that would be a piece of vicious and disorderly self-love. As in things necessary for life, like eating, drinking, sleeping, and the rest, it would be a fault if a man were to take for an end in these actions the pleasure which they give, so it is with consolations in prayer—to take them for an end in themselves would be a fault of spiritual gluttony. We are not to desire or take these things for our own pleasure and satisfaction, but as a means to the ends already prescribed. As the sick man who has a disgust for the food necessary to his sustenance, rejoices to find some taste in it, not for the taste, but for the awakening of the appetite to be able to eat and preserve life, so the servant of God should not seek spiritual consolation to rest therein, but because by this spiritual refreshment the soul is animated and nourished to labor in the way of virtue and hold fast thereto. In this way delights are not desired as delights, but for the greater glory of God and inasmuch as they redound to His greater honor and glory.

But I further say that, though one does desire these spiritual consolations in this manner and for the ends stated, which are good and holy, there may nevertheless be excess in such desires, and an admixture of disorderly self-love, in case they are desired without restraint and with unmeasured eagerness and greed, so that, if they fail you, you are not so content or conformed to the will of God, but rather restless, complaining, and in pain. This is a disorderly affection and spiritual greediness. One should not be attached so ardently and without measure to spiritual consolations that, if God be not pleased to give them, the soul loses its peace and repose and conformity to the will of God; for better is the will of God than all those consolations, and more important it is to live in conformity and satisfaction with what God is pleased to give.

What I say of spiritual delights and consolations, I understand also of the gift of prayer and the ready entry into it which we desire to have, and of peace and tranquillity and interior repose of the soul, and of all other spiritual advantages. Here also there may be a disorderly affection and greediness when such things are desired with such impetuosity and greed that, in case of failure to attain all that is desired, there arise complaint and discontent and lack of conformity to the will of God. And by "spiritual delights and consolations" we here understand, not only devotion and sensible delights and comforts, but also the very substance and gift of prayer, and entering upon it and remaining in it with that quiet and calm we should like to have. Or, rather, of this we shall now principally treat, showing how we are to conform ourselves in the matter to the will of God and not indulge in unmeasured greed and impetuous cravings therein.

As for delights and consolations and sensible movements of devotion, a man would readily forego all that if what is substantial in prayer were given him and he felt in himself the fruit thereof; for all know well enough that prayer does not consist in these smacks of fervor and fits of tender devotion; and therefore but little virtue is needed to go without them. But to go to meditation and be then turned into stone, with an aridity so great that you have started it only to find God locking you out and hiding Himself, as though there had come upon you that curse wherewith He threatened His people: *I will make the heavens as of iron and the earth of brass* (Levit. xxvi. 19; Deut. xxviii. 23)—for that, more virtue is required and more fortitude. Heaven to such persons seems of iron and earth of brass, forasmuch as there never falls on them one drop of rain to soften their heart and yield a harvest to maintain them. There is nothing but barrenness and dryness without end. And not only is there dryness, but sometimes such a great distraction and wandering of thoughts—aye, and sometimes such foul and evil thoughts—that it seems you have come there only to be tempted and molested with all kinds of temptations. Tell such people that it is a good remedy to think of death and Christ crucified, and they will say: "I know that already myself; if I could only do it, what would be wanting to me?" Sometimes you are in such a state at meditation that you cannot think of that; or if you do think of it and contrive to bring it to mind, it does not move you nor pick you up at all; it makes no impression. This is what we call desolation, dryness, and spiritual dereliction; and in this also it is necessary to conform ourselves to the will of God.

This is a point of great importance because it is one of the commonest complaints and severest struggles that those meet with who take to meditation, and all groan and lament when they find themselves in this condition. Hearing tell of the praises of meditation, how as your meditation goes, so goes all the day and all your life; and how meditation is one of the principal means that we have for our own advancement and the good of our neighbor; and all the while seeing themselves, as they think, so far from meditating, they give themselves much pain and fancy that God has abandoned and forgotten them; they come to fear that they have lost His friendship and are in His disgrace, because now they can find no access to Him. And their temptation is increased by seeing other people in a few days making much progress in meditation, as it were without trouble, while they, for all their labor and longing, do not get on at all. Hence spring other and worse temptations: as to complain of God for treating them in that manner, and to be minded to give over the exercise of meditation, as a thing not made for them, since they do so badly in it. The pain of all this is much increased by the devil's putting it into their minds that they themselves are the cause of it all, and it is for their fault that God treats them so. Thus some people live very disconsolate lives and come out from meditation as from a torture, sad and melancholy, a torment to themselves and to all who have to deal with them. We will proceed now, by the grace of the Lord, to answer and meet this temptation and complaint.

CHAPTER XXV

Satisfying the Complaint of Those Who Are Dry and Disconsolate at Meditation

IN the first place, I do not say that a man should not feel glad when God visits him, for it is clear that one cannot but feel gladness at the presence of one's Beloved; nor do I say that one should not feel His absence, when He chastises with aridities and temptations, because I see well that one cannot help feeling what Christ our Redeemer felt, being forsaken by His eternal Father, when on the Cross He cried: *My God, my God, why hast thou forsaken me?* (Matt. xxvii. 46). But what I desire is that we should know how to profit by this affliction and trial wherewith God is often wont to prove His elect—that we should meet it with fortitude, and say: *Not as I will, but as thou* (Matt. xxvi. 39). Holiness and perfection do not consist in these consolations, nor in a high and exalted habit of prayer, nor are such things the measure of our advancement. Our advancement consists in true love of God, in union and entire conformity with the will of God, for bitter and for sweet, for adversity as for prosperity. We ought to take from the hand of God the cross of dereliction as we take the delight of consolation, giving thanks for both the one and the other. "If Thou wouldest have me in darkness, blessed be Thou; and if Thou wouldest have me in light, blessed be Thou; if Thou wishest to console me, blessed be Thou; and if Thou wishest to have me in trouble, blessed be Thou" (Ā Kempis, iii. 17). So St. Paul: *In all things return thanks, for this is the will of God in Christ Jesus for you all* (I Thess. v. 18). If it is the will of God, what more have we to desire? What is there more in life than to please God? If He is conducting my life by this dark and rugged path, I have no mind to yearn after another way, bright and pleasant though it be. God wishes my neighbor to go by that road which I see and have a liking for, and me by this desert, void of all consolation; I would not exchange my barrenness for his fertility. So they say who have eyes opened to reality, and with this they console themselves. Father Master Avila says well: "Oh, if the Lord would open our eyes, how we should see clearer than the light of the sun, that all things in heaven and earth are too mean, too unworthy, for us to desire or delight in apart from the will of God; and there is nothing, however small and bitter it be, that has not its value when joined to that will. It is incomparably better to be in anguishes, desolations, aridities, and temptations, if He would have it so, than to enjoy any amount of sweetnesses, consolations, and contemplations away from His will."

But someone will say: "If I knew that this was God's will and that He was pleased and satisfied therewith, I should easily fall in with it and be satisfied to pass my whole life in this condition, but it seems to me that God wants me to make my meditation better and with more recollection and attention; and this is what gives me pain, that it is through my own fault and negligence and my not doing my part that I am so dry and cannot get at the meditation. If only I understood and were satisfied that I was doing all that rested with me, and that there was no fault on my part, I should not be in pain at all." This complaint is well drawn up; there is nothing more to be said; it sums up all the reasons that can be urged on behalf of those who make the like complaints. Therefore if we can meet this well we shall have made a good thing of it, seeing that it is such a common complaint and that there is no one, however holy and perfect he may be, who does not suffer at times from these aridities and spiritual desolations.

So we read of the blessed St. Francis and of St. Catherine of Siena, for all their being such cherished favorites of God. St. Anthony Abbot enjoyed such a high prayer that nights seemed to him but a passing breath of time and he complained of the sun's rising so early. Yet at times he was so fatigued and overwhelmed with evil and importunate thoughts that he cried out to God: "Lord, I would fain be good, and my thoughts will not let me!" St. Bernard made the same complaint and cried: "My heart is withered, it is clotted like milk, parched like earth without water; it is so hard that it cannot be moved to tears; psalmody is tasteless, I have no mind to read, I have no delight in prayer, and find not my customary meditations. Where is that inebriation of spirit? Where that serenity of mind, and peace and joy in the Holy Ghost?" Thus this doctrine I am delivering is necessary for all, and I trust in the Lord that I shall be able to satisfy all.

To begin, then, I grant that it is all your fault—your distractions and your dryness and your inability to pray. It is well that you should understand and say that for your past sins and present negligences the Lord is minded to chastise you, by giving you no access to meditation, leaving you unable to keep recollected or quiet or attentive, you not deserving otherwise. Still, it does not follow that you have ground of complaint, but only of great conformity to the will of God. Would you see this clearly? Out of your own mouth and from what you yourself have said, I am minded to judge. *Out of thine own mouth I judge thee* (Luke xviii. 23).

[Q. Question. R. Reply.]

Q. Do you not know and say that for your past sins and your present faults and negligences you deserve great chastisement of God?

R. Yes, for sure; I have many times deserved hell, and so no chastisement will be too great for me, but all will be mercy and indulgence in comparison with what I deserve. And if God shall wish to send me some chastisement in this life, I will take that for a particular benefit, holding it for an assurance that God has pardoned my sins and that He does not mean to chastise me in the next life, seeing that He chastises me in this.

Q. Enough, no more is needed; I am content with that. But that it be not all words, let us come to deeds. This is the chastisement that God wishes you to suffer now for your sins—these fits of desolation, these distractions and aridities, this spiritual dereliction, this turning of your heaven into bronze and your earth into brass, this device of God's shutting Himself off and hiding Himself from you and giving you no access to meditation. Hereby God means to chastise you now and purge away your faults. Do you not think that your past sins and your present pieces of carelessness and negligence well deserve this chastisement?

R. Yes, for sure; and this is very little compared with what I deserve, and is full of justice and mercy. Of justice, because I have so often shut the gate of my heart to God and have turned a deaf ear when He rapped at my door with His holy inspirations; and as I have resisted them many times, it is just now that, though I cry out, He turns a deaf ear and answers me not and will not open the door to me, but slams it in my face. This is a most just punishment, but very little for what I deserve. Again it is full of mercy because I deserve much more than I get.

Q. Then conform yourself to the will of God in this chastisement and receive it with thanksgiving, since He chastises you with so much mercy and not according to your deserts. Do you not say that you deserved hell? Then how do you dare to ask of God consolations and comforts at meditation, and to find open access and familiarity with God therein, and the peace and quiet and repose of sons well cherished and entertained? And how do you dare to make complaint of the contrary? Do you not see that that is great impudence and great pride? Let it be enough for you that God keeps you in His house and allows you to stand in His presence; and esteem and recognize that for a great favor and benefit.

If we had humility of heart, we should never open our mouths to complain, whatever way the Lord treated us, and thus this temptation would easily cease.

CHAPTER XXVI

How to Turn Aridity and Desolation into a Good and Profitable Prayer

NOT only should we stop this complaining within ourselves, but we should contrive to draw profit from these aridities and desolations and make out of them a good prayer (Treatise V, Chapter 19). When we feel thus distressed, we should say: "Lord, inasmuch as this is my own fault, I am very sorry for it; but inasmuch as it is Thy will and the just chastisement of my sins, I accept it with hearty good will, not merely now or for a short time, but for all the days of my life, even though they be many. I offer myself to this cross and am ready to bear it with thankfulness." This patience and humility, this resignation and conformity, is much more pleasing to God than complaints and unmeasured fretting. Tell me, who do you think would be more pleasing to his parents—the son who was content with whatever they gave him, or the other who was satisfied with nothing, but was always grumbling and complaining, thinking whatever he got was not good enough? Clearly, the former; and so it is with God. The son who suffers in silence, in content and conformity with the will of his heavenly Father, taking whatever He sends him, though it be a hard and fleshless bone, is more grateful and acceptable to God than the malcontent and the grumbler, who goes about complaining that he gets nothing or that what is given to others is not given to him. Tell me, further, who does better and moves people more to give him alms and show him compassion and pity—the beggar who complains because they do not answer him at once and because they give him nothing, or the beggar who stands perseveringly at the rich man's gate with patience and silence, making no complaint, satisfied with having rung once and made sure that they heard him? The master of the house knows that he is there, waiting with humility and patience. It is clear that this poor man moves men much to pity, while the other, the proud one, rather disgusts them and stirs their indignation. So it is also with God. I ask you, what better meditation could you make and what greater spiritual fruit could you gather than much patience in tribulation, much conformity to the will of God, and much love of Him? Why do we go to meditation except to gain those ends? When God sends us aridities and temptations in meditation, and we conform ourselves to His will, we make one of the greatest acts of patience and love of God that it is possible to make. Love is shown in suffering afflictions; and these aridities are the greatest of afflictions to the servants of God. Spiritual men feel them more than what touches property, health, or temporal advantage. To conform ourselves to the will of God in afflictions like these, is to imitate Christ our Redeemer in the spiritual dereliction which He suffered on the Cross; and to accept this spiritual cross for a whole lifetime, if the Lord be pleased to give it, solely to give satisfaction to God, is a great act of patience and of love of God and a very high and profitable prayer and a thing of great perfection, so much so that some call these afflicted persons excellent martyrs.

Once more I ask: Why do you go to meditation but to gain humility and self-knowledge? How often have you asked God to give you to understand who you are? Now in this manner He has heard your prayer and wishes to give you to understand that He has heard it. Some people will have it that self-knowledge consists in a deep sense of sin and in shedding many tears thereupon. But they are wrong; that is God, not you. To be like a stone, that is being yourself. And if God does not strike the rock, neither water will come forth therefrom nor honey. In this consists self-knowledge, the beginning of all good; and of this you have your hands full when you are in this condition. If you gain this self-knowledge from your meditation, you will have gained great fruit therefrom.

CHAPTER XXVII

Other Reasons to Comfort and Conform Us to the Will of God in Dryness and Desolation at Meditation

ALTHOUGH it is well to think, for our greater confusion and humiliation, that our distress comes through our own fault, nevertheless we should be aware that such distress is not always the chastisement of sin, but an arrangement and deep providence of the Lord, Who distributes His gifts as suits Him. It is not proper for the whole body to be eyes, or feet, or hands, or head, but there must be different members in the Church; and this special and eminent prayer of which we have spoken in the treatise On Prayer (Chapters 4-5) is not suited to be given to all, nor need it be given to them, because they do not merit it. Even though they did merit it, nevertheless they will merit more in another way, and God will do them a greater favor in giving them this than in giving them that. There have been many great saints of whom we do not know that they attained anything else than the ordinary prayer; and if they did attain anything more, still they would say with St. Paul: *Far be it from me to glory except in the cross of our Lord Jesus Christ* (Gal. vi. 14).

Father Master Avila makes hereon a very consoling remark. "There are some," he says, "whom God leaves in desolation for many years and sometimes for the whole of their lives; and theirs, I believe, is the happier lot if they have faith enough not to be disheartened, and patience and fortitude enough to suffer so great a deprivation." Once a man comes to persuade himself that this is the happier condition for him, he will readily fall in with the will of God. Saints and masters of spiritual life give many reasons to explain and prove that this is the happier condition for such people; but for the present we will give only one of the principal reasons, taken from St. Augustine, St. Jerome, St. Gregory, and others. It is that not all are equal to preserving humility at the height of contemplation. Scarce have we shed one little tear when we fancy ourselves spiritual men, men of prayer, and perhaps compare and prefer ourselves to others. Even St. Paul seems to have needed some counterpoise not to be lifted up by these things. *Lest the greatness of revelations should lift me up, there was given me a thorn in the flesh, an angel of satan to buffet me* (II Cor. xii. 7). Though he had been raised up to the third heaven and had received great revelations, yet God permitted temptation to come upon him, to humble him and let him know his weakness. Therefore, though this road seems the higher, that other is the safer. And so the most wise God, Who guides us all to one end, which is Himself, takes each by that path which He knows to be most suitable to him. Haply, if you found great facility in meditation, instead of coming forth from it humbled and improved, you would have come out proud and puffed up; but this other way you are ever humbled and confounded and take yourself for the least of all. This way, then, is for you the more suitable and safe, though you do not understand it. *You know not what you ask* (Matt. xx. 22). St. Gregory teaches a good lesson to our purpose on those words of Job: *If he cometh to me, I shall not see him. If he goeth away, I shall not understand* (Job ix. 11). Man is so blinded by sin, he says, that he does not know when he is approaching God or when he is going away from Him; and oftentimes what he thinks is a grace of God and a means of drawing nearer to God, turns out after all to be divine anger and an occasion of God's retiring from him; while oftentimes what he thinks is divine anger and a cause of God's withdrawing from him and forgetting him, is a grace and a cause why God should not withdraw from him. Who is there that, seeing himself elevated to a lofty height of contemplation and much consoled and favored of God, will not think that he is drawing nearer to God? Yet oftentimes from these favors one comes to a sense of pride and false security and vain confidence, and the devil brings him to fall just by that whereby he thought he was mounting up and approaching nearer to God. And, contrariwise, a man seeing himself disconsolate and afflicted with grave temptations, much harassed with indecent and blasphemous thoughts and thoughts against faith, thinks that God is angry with him and is forsaking him, whereas it is just then that God is nearer him, because thereon he humbles himself more and knows his own weakness and flings himself upon God more heartily and thoroughly, putting in Him all his confidence and seeking never to be separated from Him. Thus that is not the better way which you think is best, but the way by which God chooses to take you.

Further, this very bitterness, pain, and grief that you feel, thinking that you do not practise prayer so well as in reason you should, may be another ground of comfort; it is a particular grace and favor of God and a sign that you love Him, since there is no grief without some love. I cannot be sorry for not serving Him well, without some purpose and will to serve Him well; thus this pain and grief spring from love of God and desire to serve Him better. If you made no account of serving Him badly, of making a bad meditation, of doing your work ill, it would be a bad sign; but to feel pain and grief because you do things badly is a good sign. But this pain is appeased by the consideration that the failure, so far as it is painful, is the will of God, and by conforming yourself to that will and giving Him thanks that He lets you be thus desirous to please Him, although it seem to you that your performances are poor.

And further, though we do nothing else in prayer but assist thereat and stand in presence of His Royal and Divine Majesty, we thereby do great service to God, as we see that it greatly makes to the majesty of kings and princes on earth that the grandees of their court come every day to the palace and assist and stand there in presence. *Blessed is he that watcheth at my gates daily, and keepeth guard at the posts of my door* (Prov. viii. 34). To the glory of the majesty of God, and the lowliness of our condition, and the greatness of the business we have on hand, it belongs that we should be oftentimes in waiting, keeping watch at the gates of His heavenly palace; and when He opens the gates, render Him thanks; and when He opens not, humble ourselves, knowing that we do not deserve it. In this way, your prayer will always be excellent and profitable, saying with Bartholomew of the martyrs: "All hail, thou bitterness, bitter and most bitter, but full of graces and blessings."

CHAPTER XXVIII

That It Is a Great Mistake and Grave Temptation to Give Over Meditation for Finding Ourselves in the Condition Aforesaid

HENCE it follows that it is a great mistake and a grave temptation, when one sees himself in this condition, to give up meditation or not go on with it so steadily, on the idea that one can make nothing of it, and it is sheer waste of time. With this temptation the devil has made many give up meditation, not only many seculars, but also many religious. And when he cannot make them give it up altogether, he gets them to make less effort over it, or spend in it less time than they ought. Many begin to give themselves to meditation, and so long as they have fine weather and devotion they go on and continue very well; but coming to the season of dryness and distraction, they fancy that this is no prayer, but a new sin, being there before God with so much distraction and so little reverence. Thus, little by little, they abandon meditation and fancy they serve God better in other exercises and occupations than in being there making such a poor figure at prayer. The devil, seeing their weakness here, makes the best of his opportunity and attacks them in such force with evil thoughts and distractions at meditation that they take that time for lost. Thus, little by little, he gets them to abandon meditation altogether, and virtue with it. In come cases things go further still; indeed, we know many in which this has been the first step to perdition.

There is a friend who will share thy table and will not stand by thee in the day of thy distress (Ecclus. vi. 10). To rejoice in God—there is none who will not do that; but to labor and suffer for His sake is the sign of true love. When meditation is attended with consolation and devotion, it is not much for you to persevere in it and spend many hours over it. You may do that for your own satisfaction and to suit your own taste. It is a sign that such was your motive, when you cease to persevere the moment that consolation fails. God's true friends are proved when He sends them desolation and dryness and distractions. Then are seen the faithful servants who seek not their own interest, but purely the will and contentment of God. It is then that we must persevere in humility and patience, spending over meditation all the time marked out for it, and even a little more, as our Father advises, thereby to overcome the temptation and show ourselves strong and resolute against the devil.

Palladius relates that, when he was engaged in consideration of the things of God, shut up in a cell, he had a great temptation of aridity and many annoying thoughts; and it came into his head that he should abandon that exercise as doing him no good. He went to the holy Macarius of Alexandria and told him of this temptation and asked his advice. The saint replied: "When these thoughts tell you to go your way and that you are making nothing of it, tell them: 'Here I mean to stay within the walls of this cell for love of Christ.'" Which was telling him to persevere and be satisfied with doing that holy work for love of Christ, even though he gathered no fruit from it but that. That is a very good answer for us when this temptation comes to us. For the principal end which we should have in view in this holy exercise, and the intention with which we should go to it and work at it, is not our own pleasure and satisfaction, but to do a good and holy work, thereby to please God and give Him satisfaction, and pay some part of the great debt we owe Him for being what He is and the innumerable benefits that we have received at His hand. Since He wishes and is pleased at my being here just now, I am satisfied although I seem to be doing nothing.

It is related of St. Catherine of Siena that for several days she was in desolation, deprived of spiritual consolations and not feeling her usual fervor of devotion, and besides much molested with evil thoughts, foul and impure thoughts which she could not shake off. Still she did not on that account give up her prayer, but did it the best way she could, persevering in it very diligently, and she thus addressed herself: "Thou vile sinner, thou dost not deserve any consolation. What, shalt not thou fain be content with not being condemned to hell, even though thou wert to bear these darknesses and torments all thy life long? Surely it was not to get consolations in this life that thou didst betake thyself to the service of God, but to enjoy Him in heaven everlastingly. Get up, then, and go on with thy exercises and persevere in fidelity to thy Lord."

Let us, then, imitate these examples and steady ourselves by these words of a holy man: "Let this be my consolation,

O Lord, willingly to forego all human consolation; and if Thy consolation also fail me, let Thy will and Thy just proving of me be to me in place of the highest consolation" (Ā Kempis). If we attain to this, that the will and satisfaction of God is all our satisfaction, and this very lack of all consolation is our satisfaction for its being the will and satisfaction of God, then shall we have true satisfaction such as nothing can take away from us.

CHAPTER XXIX

What Has Been Said Is Confirmed by Some Examples

IN the chronicles of the order of St. Dominic it is related that a Father of the order, one of the first and most considerable, a man of exemplary life and great purity of soul, never felt any manner of consolation or pleasure in the exercises of religion, neither in prayer, nor in contemplation, nor in reading. And as he was always hearing tell of the dainty cheer God made for others and of the spiritual transports they experienced, he was half in despair. In this state he set himself in prayer one night before a crucifix, weeping bitterly the while, and went so far as to utter these wild words: "Lord, I have always heard that in goodness and gentleness Thou surpassest all Thy creatures. Behold me here, who have served Thee many years and have suffered on Thy account abundant tribulations and with hearty good will have given myself up to Thee alone. If for a quarter of the time I have served Thee I had served a tyrant, he would have shown me some sign of benevolence, were it only one kind word, one kind look, one smile; but Thou, O Lord, hast never given me any good cheer nor have I received of Thee the least favor of those which Thou art wont to do to others. Thou being sweetness itself, why art Thou to me harder than a hundred tyrants? What is this, Lord? Why wishest Thou me to suffer thus?"

At this point there came a crash as if the whole church were coming down, and in the roof there was a fearful din, as though thousands of dogs with their teeth were crunching up the woodwork. He was amazed and troubled with fear, and turning his head to see what was the matter, he saw behind him the most foul and horrible vision in the world, a devil who held a bar of iron in his hand, wherewith he gave him a great blow on the body. Whereupon he fell to the ground and could not rise, but plucked up heart to crawl as far as an altar that was near, unable to manage himself for sheer pain, as though all his bones were out of joint for blows. When the friars rose for prime, they found him as one dead, without knowing the cause of so sudden and fatal an accident. They carried him to the infirmary, where for three whole weeks he lay in severe pain. So great was the stench, so filthy and nauseous, that the religious could nowise come in to attend to him without first stopping their noses, and taking many other precautions. At the end of that time he gathered some strength and was able to stand on his feet, whereupon he sought to cure himself of his foolish presumption and pride. Accordingly, returning to the place where he had committed the fault, he sought there the remedy of it, and with many tears and great humility he made his prayer, very different from the former. He confessed his fault, acknowledging himself unworthy of any good and very deserving of pain and chastisement. And the Lord comforted him with a voice from heaven, which said: "If thou wantest consolation and sweetness, it is right for thee to be humble; acknowledge thy lowliness. and understand that thou art viler than dust and of less value than the worms under thy feet." Thereby he learned a great lesson, and henceforth was a most perfect religious.

Of our blessed Father Ignatius we read a very different story. It is told in his Life that, looking at his faults and bewailing them, he said that he wished that in punishment of them the Lord would some time deprive him of the delight of His consolations, that this check might make him more careful and watchful in His service; but that such was the mercy of the Lord and the abundance of the sweetness and gentleness of His grace in dealing with him that, the more faults he fell into and the more he desired to be treated in this manner, the greater was the kindness of the Lord towards him and the greater the abundance in which He showered down upon him the treasures of His liberality. And so he said that he believed there was not a man in the world in whom these two things met as they did in himself; such unfaithfulness to God in the first place, and on the other side the reception of so many great and continual favors from His hand.

Blosius relates of a servant of God that the Lord did him great favors, consoling and illuminating him and showing him marvelous things in prayer; and he with much humility, and desire still further to please God, asked Him, if that would be to His service and better pleasure, to withdraw from him this grace. God heard his prayer, and withdrew it for five years, leaving him to suffer many temptations, desolations, and anguishes. One day, when he was weeping bitterly, two angels appeared to him and offered to console him; to whom he replied: "I do not ask for consolation; it is consolation enough for me that the will of God is accomplished in me."

The same Blosius relates that Christ our Redeemer said to St. Bridget: "Daughter, why art thou troubled and anxious?" She answered: "Because I am afflicted with useless and evil thoughts and cannot shake them off, and they cause me great anxiety about Thy dreadful judgment." Then the Lord said: "This is true justice, that as thou didst take delight in the vanities of the world against My will, so now thou shouldst be molested with a variety of painful and perverse thoughts against thy will. Nevertheless, thou shouldst fear My judgment with moderation and discretion, confiding firmly and continually in Me that I am thy God; for thou oughtest to hold it for a most certain truth that the evil thoughts which a man resists and rejects are a purgatory, and a crown for his soul. If thou canst not hinder them, suffer them with patience, and protest against them with thy will. And though thou consent not to them, still, for all that, fear lest pride come over thee on that account and bring thee to a fall; because whoever stands, it is only the grace of God that holds him up."

Blosius in his book on "Comfort for the Pusillanimous," quotes from Tauler: "Many, when they are harassed by tribulation, are wont to say to me: 'Father, I am in a bad way, I am not getting on well, I am worn out with various troubles and melancholy.' In reply to him who says this, I tell him that he is going on all right and meriting a great reward. Then they say: 'Sir, it is not so; on the contrary, I believe this comes of my faults.' On that I say to them: 'Whether it comes of your sins or not, believe that God has put upon you this cross, and thank Him for it; suffer and be entirely resigned.' Still they say: 'Interiorly, I am a prey to great dryness and darkness.' I say: 'My dear child, suffer with patience and you will gain more merit thereby than if you were borne along on a flood of sensible devotion.' "

It is related of a great servant of God that he said: "For forty years I have served our Lord and practised meditation, and never have I found in it any relish or consolation; nevertheless, on the day on which I practise it, I find in myself great support for exercises of virtue; but when I fail in it, I feel so weak that I cannot stir a feather to fly to anything good."

CHAPTER XXX

Of Conformity to the Will of God in the Distribution of Virtues and Supernatural Gifts

AS we must be conformable to the will of God in whatever manner He pleases to treat us in prayer, so also in regard of all other virtues and gifts and spiritual advantages. It is a very good thing to desire all virtues and sigh after them and strive to attain them, but in our desire for improvement and growth and progress in virtue we must possess our souls in peace if we do not attain our desire. If God will not give you the chastity of an angel, but you suffer grave temptations in that matter, it is better for you to keep your patience and conformity to the will of God than go about worrying and complaining that you fall short of the purity of the angels. If God is not ready to give you such a meekness as He gave a Moses and a David, or such patience as He gave a Job, but you feel stirrings and promptings to the contrary, it is well for you to be ashamed and humbled, and thence take occasion to set little store by yourself; but it is not well for you to lose your peace of mind and be full of worries and complaints that God has not made you as patient as a Job or as humble as a St. Francis. We needs must conform ourselves to the will of God in these things, for we never shall find peace otherwise. Father Master Avila says very well: "I do not believe that there ever was a saint in this world who did not desire to be better than he was; but that did not rob them of their peace, for their desire was not prompted by selfish greed, which never says, 'Enough,' but by God, with Whose distribution they were content. Although He gave them little, they would have been content even with less, taking it for the part of true love to be content with what was given them rather than desire more, despite all the whisperings of self-love pretending that such desire was for the better service of God."

But someone will say that this is tantamount to saying that we ought not to be fervent in desire to be more and more virtuous and better, but leave all to God, soul as well as body; and so apparently we should give occasion to tepidity and weakness, caring nothing to grow and go forward. Be this point well noted, since it is of great importance. It is a very good reply and objection, so good that beyond this there is nothing else to fear in the matter. *There is no doctrine, however good it be, that may not be abused, if you do not know how to apply it properly.* So this may be abused in its bearing on prayer and on other virtues and spiritual gifts; wherefore a good explanation and right understanding is here necessary.

I do not say that we should not desire to be holier every day, and strive ever to imitate what is better, and be diligent and fervent in doing so; for that is what we came into religion for; and if we do not do that, we shall not be good religious. In exterior things men should be diligent without fretting and complaining. So say the saints, and so Christ our Redeemer lays down His prohibition in the Gospel: *I tell you, be not solicitous for your life, what ye shall eat, nor for your body what ye shall put on* (Matt. vi. 25), reprehending excessive solicitude and anxiety and greediness in these things, but not relieving us of proper care and diligence about them, but rather commanding us to have it and giving it to us for penance: *In the sweat of thy brow thou shalt eat thy bread* (Gen. iii. 19). It is necessary, in fact, that men should labor and be diligent to get their food, and to do otherwise would be tempting God. So in the same way must it be in spiritual things and in the striving after virtues and gifts of God. Bound as we are to be very diligent and careful in this endeavor, still it must be done in such a way as not to part with our peace of soul and conformity to the will of God. Do what is to be done on your part; but if after all you see that you are not so successful as you wished, you must not fall into impatience, which would be worse than the original fault, not even though the failure seems to have been due to your own faint-heartedness, a thing that is apt to discourage many. Take care to make honest efforts; and if they are not all successful and you fall into some faults, do not be amazed at that, nor lose heart; such are we all! I am a man and not an angel; weak, not consummate in sanctity. God knows well our weakness and our misery. *He knoweth the clay of which we are made* (Psalm cii. 13), and wishes us not to be discouraged at our faults, but to repent and humble ourselves, and rise again at once, and ask for more strength of the Lord, and take care to go contented both inwardly and outwardly. It is more to the point that you should rise at once, with cheerfulness which doubles your strength for the service of God, than that, thinking to bewail your sins for God's sake, you should displease that same God by serving Him badly with drooping heart and drooping wings and other evil features that are wont to take rise from thence.

The only thing to fear here is the danger that we have touched upon of tepidity gaining entrance upon us, and our omitting to do what is on our part under color of saying: "God must give it me; all must come from the hand of God; I can do no more." We must be on our guard against the same danger in what we were saying of prayer; we must take care that sloth does not impose upon us here either under this pretense. But once this side door is closed, and you are honestly doing what it rests with you to do, God is more pleased with patience and humility in your weaknesses than with those fits of unmeasured anguish and sadness which some fall into at the thought that they are not growing in virtue and perfection as they would wish, nor find the facility in prayer which they would desire. This business of prayer and perfection is not done by grumblings and fisticuffs, but by God's giving it to whom He will, and as He wills, and in such time as He pleases. It is certain that not all are to be equal who are to go to heaven, nor must we despair because we are none of the best who go there, nor perhaps even of the middling good; but we must fall in with the will of God in all and return thanks to our Lord that He holds out to us hope of finding salvation by His mercy. And if we do not succeed in being without faults, let us give thanks to God that He gives us a knowledge of our shortcomings; and seeing that we are not going to heaven by the high path of virtues, as some go, let us be content to travel by knowledge of our sins and sorrow for them, as many go.

St. Jerome says: "Let others offer in the temple of the Lord, each according to his ability; some gold, silver, and precious stones; others silks, crimson, purple, and embroidery. Enough for me to offer in the temple skins of goats and hides of animals." Let others, then, offer to God their virtues and heroic and excellent acts and their high and lofty contemplations; enough for me to offer to God my lowliness, knowing myself and acknowledging myself a sinner, imperfect and evil, and presenting myself before His Majesty as one poor and needy. And it is well to rejoice for this at heart, and give thanks to God that He does not deprive us of this also which He has given us, as He does to men who have utterly lost His favor.

St. Bonaventure, Gerson, and others add here a remark which goes far to confirm what has been said. They say that many persons serve God better for not having the virtue and recollection that they desire than they would do if they had it. As they are, they live in humility and walk with care and diligence, endeavoring to mount and go forward, and having frequent recourse to God; but the other way they would possibly become proud, negligent, and tepid in the service of God, thinking that they had already got all that they need have, and would have no mind to labor for more. Be this said to the end that we may honestly do what lies in our power, and walk with diligence and care aiming at perfection; and then let us be satisfied with what the Lord gives us and not be disconsolate or in distress about what we cannot gain and what is not in our power. That would be, as Father Master Avila well says, like being in pain because they did not give us wings to fly through the air.

CHAPTER XXXI

Of the Conformity That We Should Have to the Will of God As Regards the Good Things of Heavenly Glory

NOT only in the good things of grace, but also in the good things of heavenly glory, we should conform ourselves to the will of God. The true servant of God should be so detached from his own interests, even in these things, as to rejoice more because the will of God is fulfilled in him than in all else that could interest him. "It is great perfection not to seek one's own interest in anything, either little or great, either in temporal or in eternal, because Thy will, O Lord, and the love of Thy honor ought to overtop all things, and we ought to find more consolation and contentment in that than in all benefits received or receivable" (Ā Kempis). This is the contentment and joy of the blessed. The saints in heaven rejoice more in the fulfilment of the will of God than in the greatness of their own glory. They are so transformed into God and so united to His will, that the glory that they enjoy and the happy lot that has fallen to them they do not welcome so much for the advantage that they bring them and the satisfaction which they receive as because God is pleased thereby and such is the will of God. Hence it comes to be that each of them is so contented and delighted with the degree that he holds as not to desire any more, nor is he in any way pained that another has more; because, seeing God, the soul is so transformed into Him as to cease to will as herself and begin to will as God; and as she sees that this is the satisfaction and good pleasure of God, so it is also her joy and her satisfaction.

This is the perfection that we see shine forth in those great saints, in a Moses, in a St. Paul, who for the salvation of souls and the greater glory of God seemingly forgot themselves and took no account of their own glory. *Lord, pardon this people or blot me out from thy own book,* said Moses to God (Exod. xxxii. 31-32); and St. Paul: *I desired to be anathema from Christ for the sake of my brethren* (Rom. ix. 3). From him afterwards a St. Martin and other saints learned: "If still I am necessary to Thy people, I refuse not labor." They postponed their rest and willingly ceded something of that glorious reward which they were now so near, and offered themselves anew to labor for the greater service and glory of God. This is doing the will of God here on earth as it is done in heaven, wholly to forget our own interest, and place all our satisfaction in doing the will of God, and count and hold the pleasing of God more than our own advancement and the possession of heaven and earth.

Here is well seen the perfection that this exercise of conformity to the will of God asks of us. If we are to withdraw our eyes from our interest in spiritual goods, and even from eternal goods and the glory of heaven itself, to fix them on the satisfaction and will of God, how shall it be with other interests and human considerations? Hence it will be understood how far from this perfection he is who makes a difficulty of conforming himself to the will of God in those things of which we spoke at the beginning; of being in this place or that, in this office or in another, of being in good health or in sickness, of being made little of or much of by others. We were just saying that we must make more account of the will and satisfaction of God than of all the gains that can possibly be made in spiritual and even in eternal goods; and are you boggling over these things that in respect of them are mere ordure! To him who desires so much the satisfaction of God and the fulfilment of His divine will that he willingly cedes his own glory and is content with the lowest place, not because he is wanting in desire of work and doing doughty deeds, but only to seek better the satisfaction and good pleasure of God, all other things will be very easy, since he makes the renunciation and cession of the highest thing that can be renounced for the love of God. This is the utmost renunciation that man can make to conform himself to the will of God, when he says: "If God would have me die this instant and suffer diminution of glory thereby, I would rather have that lot than die twenty or thirty years hence and so obtain much greater glory; and if, on the other hand, by dying now I could make sure of my glory, still, if God would rather have me do and suffer for many years in this place of imprisonment and exile, I prefer that above immediate admission to the glory of the blessed; for my joy and glory is the satisfaction of God and the fulfilment of His will. *Thou art my glory and the lifter up of my head* (Psalm iii. 4)."

Of our blessed Father Ignatius there is related a rare example of this. One day, being in company with Father Master Lainez and others, on some point that was raised he put them this question: "Tell me, Master Lainez, what you would do if God made you this offer and said: 'If you wish to die now, I will draw you out of the prison of this body and give you eternal glory; whereas, if you wish to go on living, I give you no assurance what is to become of you, but leave you to take your chance. If you live and persevere in virtue, I will give you your reward; but if you fall away from good, I will judge you as I find you.' Now, if our Lord said this to you, and you understood that by remaining some time in this life you could render some great and notable service to His Divine Majesty, what would you choose?" Father Lainez answered: "For myself, Father, I acknowledge to your reverence that I would choose to go at once to the enjoyment of God and make sure of my salvation and deliver myself from danger in a matter of such importance." Then said our holy Father: "Well, I certainly should not do so; but if I judged that by remaining in the world I could render some special service to our Lord, I would beg Him to leave me in it till the work was done; I would fix my eyes on that work, and not on myself, taking no account of my own danger or my own security." And he did not think that thereby he was endangering his own salvation, but rather rendering it more certain and more splendid for having trusted God and stayed here on earth in His service. "For what king or prince is there in the world," said he, "who, if he offered his courtier some great emolument, and the courtier declined the present enjoyment of that emolument in order to be able to render some notable service to his master, would not hold himself bound to keep and augment that reward for that courtier, since he was depriving himself of it for his love and to serve him better? Now if men act so, who are ungrateful and thankless, what are we to expect of the Lord, Who so forestalls us with His grace and does us so many favors? How could we fear that He would desert us and let us fall for having put off our own blessedness and given up the enjoyment of it for His sake? That cannot be believed or feared of such a Lord."

CHAPTER XXXII

Of Conformity and Union and Perfect Love for God, and How We Should Practise This Exercise

FOR the better seeing of the perfection and great excellence contained in this exercise of conformity with the will of God, and that we may know how far we can attain to it, by way of conclusion and termination of this treatise we will say a little about a very high exercise of the love of God which the saints and masters of the spiritual life put before us. And it seems to come in very well here, because, as St. Denis the Areopagite says, one of the principal effects of love is to unite the wills of them that love one another so that they concur in willing or not willing the same thing. Thus, the more united one is and the more conformed to the will of God, the greater will be one's love of God; and the greater that love, the greater the union and conformity with the will of God. To explain this it is necessary to mount up in thought to heaven, loving and conforming ourselves to the will of God. Have the same will with Him to take or refuse; for the nearer we approach to this, the more perfect will be our exercise. The glorious Apostle and Evangelist St. John says that the sight of God makes the blessed like unto Him: *When He shall appear, we shall be like him, because we shall see him as he is* (I John iii. 2). In seeing God, the blessed are so transformed into God as to have one will and one wish with Him. Let us see, then, what is the will and wish and love of God, for thereby we shall come to see what is the wish and will of the blessed, and thence we may gather what our wish and love and will should be to be perfect. The wish and will of God, and His highest and most perfect love, is of His own glory and of His own being, supremely perfect and glorious. This, then, is the wish and will and love of the blessed. Thus the love of the saints and blessed is a love and wish whereby they love and wish with all their strength that God should be what He is and be in Himself so good and glorious and worthy of honor as He is. And as they see in God all that they desire, then follows from that in them that *fruit of the Holy Ghost,* which the Apostle says is an unspeakable *joy* (Gal. v. 22), at seeing Him Whom they love so full of good things and treasures in Himself.

By what we see on earth we shall be able to get some inkling of the divine joy which the blessed hereby receive. See how great is the joy and gladness that a good son receives at seeing his dearly-loved father honored and sought after by all; learned, rich and powerful, and highly esteemed and cherished by the king. Certainly there are sons so good that they will say that there is nothing to compare with the joy that they receive at seeing their father made so much of. Now if this joy is so great on earth, where love is so weak and good things so mean, what must be the joy of the saints at seeing their true Lord and Creator and heavenly Father, into Whom they are so transformed by love, so good, so holy, so radiant in beauty, so infinitely powerful that all creation holds its being and its beauty solely of His will, and without that will not a leaf could stir on the tree! And, accordingly, the Apostle St. Paul says it is a joy so great as *eye hath not seen, nor ear heard, nor can it enter into the heart of man* (I Cor. ii. 9). This is that *rushing river* which St. John in the Apocalypse saw *coming forth from the throne of God and the Lamb* (Apoc. xxii. 1), which *giveth joy to the City of God* (Psalm xlv. 5), whereof the blessed in heaven drink and, thereby inebriated with love, sing that everlasting Alleluia, glorifying and blessing God. *Alleluia, praised be the Lord, for now our Lord God omnipotent reigneth, let us rejoice and be glad and give him glory* (Apoc. xix. 6). They are praising and rejoicing at the great glory of God, giving Him congratulations and expressions of satisfaction, with great jubilation and rejoicing. *Blessing and glory and wisdom and thanksgiving, honor and power and strength be to our Lord God for ever and ever* (Apoc. vii. 12).

This is the love which the saints bear to God in heaven and the conformity which they have to His divine will—to speak of such things as we can, considering the poorness of our understanding. This is what we should try to imitate in our way here on earth, that the will of God may be done on earth as it is in heaven. *Look and do according to the pattern that I have shown thee on the mount,* said God to Moses (Exod. xxv. 40), when He bade him construct the Tabernacle. So we should do all things here on earth according to the plan that is carried out there on that high mountain of glory. We must set ourselves to loving and willing that which the blessed in heaven are loving and willing; and that which they are loving and willing is God Himself, Who is His own glory and His own being, sovereignly perfect and glorious.

That each one may be able to do this better for himself, we will set down here briefly the practice of this exercise. When you are at prayer, consider with the understanding the infinite being of God, His eternity, His omnipotence, His infinite wisdom, beauty, glory, and beatitude. Then use your will, rejoicing, delighting, and taking complacency and satisfaction in that God is what He is, that He is God, that the being and infinite good which He holds, He holds of Himself; that He has no need of anybody, and all have need of Him; that He is almighty and so good and so holy and so full of glory as in Himself He is.

St. Thomas and the theologians say that this is the greatest and most perfect act of the love of God. So it is also the highest and most consummate act of conformity to the will of God, because there is no greater nor more perfect love of God than that which God Himself bears to Himself, which is a love of His own glory and of His own sovereignly perfect and glorious being, nor can there be a better will than that. It follows that our love will be greater and more perfect in proportion as it is likened to this love wherewith God loves Himself, and the greater and more perfect will be our union and conformity with His divine will. And, further, philosophers say that to love another is to seek his good; whence it follows that the greater good we desire for another, the more we love him. Now the greatest good that we can seek for God is that which He already has, which is His infinite being, His infinite goodness, wisdom, omnipotence, and glory. When we love any creature, we not only are pleased at any good thing that he has, but we are able to wish for him some other good thing which he has not, since every creature can grow; but coming to God, we cannot wish Him in Himself any good thing which He has not, since He is infinite on every side, and so He cannot have in Himself more power, nor more glory, nor more wisdom, nor more goodness than He has. And so the greatest good that we can wish God, and consequently the greatest love that we can bear Him, is to rejoice and be glad and feel complacency and satisfaction that God has all those good things that He has, and that He is so good as He is, so rich, so powerful, so infinite, and so glorious.

The saints who are in heaven, and the most sacred humanity of Christ our Redeemer, and the most glorious Virgin our Lady, and all the choirs of angels rejoice to see God so fair and beautiful and so laden with all fulness of good things. So great is the joy and gladness that they feel thereat that nothing will satisfy them but to break out into praises of this Lord, and they never have enough of praising and blessing Him for ever and ever, as the prophet says: *Blessed are they who dwell in thy house, O Lord, they shall praise thee world without end* (Psalm lxxxiii. 5). In like manner we should unite our hearts and lift up our voices with theirs, as Mother Church teaches us: "Deign, O Lord, to admit our voices also, along with those of all the angels and blessed, crying out to Thee in suppliant acknowledgment, 'Holy, holy, holy, Lord God of hosts; the heavens and earth are full of Thy glory.'" Always, or as continually as is in our power, we ought to occupy ourselves in praising and glorifying God, exulting and rejoicing in the good and glory and sovereignty that He enjoys, and giving Him congratulations and felicitations thereupon. In this manner we shall liken ourselves here, in our poor way, to the blessed in heaven and even to God Himself, and we

shall exercise the highest love and the most perfect conformity to the will of God that we possibly can exercise.

CHAPTER XXXIII

How Much This Exercise Is Recommended and Repeated in Holy Scripture

BY the extent to which Holy Scripture recommends and repeats this exercise, we may well understand its value, excellence, and how pleasing it is to God, and at the same time we can take thence matter to practise it and occupy ourselves further therein. The Royal Prophet in the Psalms at every step invites us to this exercise, saying: *Be glad and exult, ye just, in the Lord, and glory all ye right of heart. Exult, ye just, in the Lord. Delight in the Lord, and he will give thee thy heart's desires* (Psalm xxxi. 11; xxxii. 1; xxxvi. 4), or, to say better, what thou desirest and hast need of. This is a prayer in which you ask without asking, and God hears the desires of your heart. The Apostle St. Paul, writing to the Philippians, says: *Rejoice in the Lord always.* And thinking that this was not an advice to be given once only, he repeats it: *Again I say, rejoice* (Phil. iv. 4). This is the joy with which the most holy Virgin rejoiced, when she said: *And my spirit hath exulted in God my Savior* (Luke i. 47). With this joy also Christ our Redeemer rejoiced, as the Gospel says: *He exulted in the Holy Ghost* (Luke x. 21). And the Prophet David says that so great was the joy and gladness which his soul experienced in considering the greatness of the excellence and glory of God, and what fit matter it furnishes to all for rejoicing in the infinite good that God enjoys, that the joy redounded abundantly even upon his body, and his very flesh was kindled with love of God: *My heart and my flesh have exulted in the living God* (Psalm lxxxiii. 2). And elsewhere he says: *My soul shall*

exult in the Lord, and take delight in God her Savior: all my bones shall say, Lord, who is like unto thee? (Psalm xxxiv. 9-10). And because this love is a thing so divine and heavenly, the Church, guided by the Holy Spirit, at the beginning of the canonical hours, commencing matins, invites us in the invitatory to love the Lord in this manner, being glad and rejoicing in His infinite excellences, taking it from Psalm xciv. 1, 3-4: *Come let us rejoice in the Lord, let us utter a cry of joy before God our Savior: let us come before His face with praise, and make to Him a joyful sound of psalms: for the Lord is a great God, and a great king above all gods: for the sea is His, and He made it, and His hands planted the dry land.* And for the same reason and to the same effect the Church puts at the end of all the psalms *Gloria Patri.* This is that entry into the joy of God which Christ our Redeemer speaks of in the Gospel: *Enter thou into the joy of thy Lord* (Matt. xxv. 21)—to share in the infinite joy of God, and be taken up with rejoicing and exulting along with God Himself in His glory and beauty and infinite riches.

To incite us more to this exercise and cause us constantly to advance in this joy and exultation, it will aid us much to consider how good and beautiful and glorious God is. So beautiful is He that the bare sight of Him renders those who see Him blessed; and if those who are in hell were to come to see God, all their pains would cease and they would pass from hell to paradise. *This is life everlasting, to know thee, the one true God* (John xvii. 3). In this consists the glory of the saints, in seeing God. This is what makes them blessed, and that, not for one day or one year, but forever, because never can they be sated or weary with looking upon God, but they shall always find new joy therein, as the Apocalypse (xiv. 3) says: *And they sang as it were a new song.* Herein it seems that the goodness, beauty, and infinite perfection of God are sufficiently declared; but there is more still that may be added, and plenty more still. God is so beautiful and glorious that, in seeing Himself, God finds His happiness. The glory and beatitude of God is in seeing and loving Himself. See if we are not right in delighting and rejoicing in a goodness and beauty so great as to make glad the whole of that City of God, and render all its citizens blessed, and God Himself also blessed in knowing and loving Himself.

CHAPTER XXXIV

How We May Further Extend This Exercise

WE may also familiarize ourselves with this exercise and extend it further by exercising this love on the sacred humanity of Christ our Lord, considering its dignity and great perfection, and taking complacency and delight in it, being glad and rejoicing within ourselves that this most blessed humanity is so elevated and united with the Divine Person, so full of grace and glory, as to be the instrument of the Divinity in working such excellent works as are the sanctification and glorification of all the elect, and all supernatural gifts and graces that are communicated to men; and finally being glad and rejoicing at all that belongs to the perfection and glory of that most glorious soul and that most holy body of Christ our Redeemer, dwelling thereon with affectionate love and gladness in the way that saints consider the most holy Queen of Angels rejoiced on the day of the Resurrection, when she saw her most blessed Son so triumphant and glorious; and as Holy Writ tells us of the patriarch Joseph when he heard tell that his son was alive and was lord of all the land of Egypt. So great was his joy that his spirit revived, and he said: *Enough for me that my son Joseph liveth:* I want no more *than to see him, and with that I shall die content* (Gen. xlv. 28).

We may make this same exercise on the glory of our Lady and of other saints. It will be an excellent devotion on their feast days to spend some part of our meditation on this exercise. It will be one of the best homages that we can pay them, since the greatest love of which we are capable is to desire for them the greatest good of which they are capable, rejoicing and being glad at their so great glory and offering them our congratulations on the same. The Church assigns this exercise for the Feast of the Assumption of our Lady: "Today the Virgin Mary ascends to heaven: let us rejoice because she reigns with Christ forever." And at the commencement of Mass on this feast and many others she invites us to this exercise, animating us by the example of the angels who take part in it. "Let us all rejoice in the Lord, celebrating this feast in honor of the Blessed Virgin Mary, at whose Assumption the angels rejoice and unite in praising the Son of God." There is another gain and advantage in this exercise regarding the saints, and particularly regarding the most holy humanity of Christ our Lord, and it is that hence we come little by little to rise in our exercises and gain access to the Divinity; for, as Christ Himself says, He is the way and gate whereby to enter in to the Father (John x. 7; xiv. 6).

In this exercise also, which concerns itself with God as God, there are degrees, and we may familiarize ourselves more with it by coming down to things of earth. For though it is true that God cannot be augmented in Himself, seeing that He is infinite, and so we cannot wish Him in Himself any good that He has not got; yet God may be augmented externally in His creatures; that is, He may be more known and loved and glorified by them. When our soul considers at meditation how worthy God is to be loved and served by His creatures, we may occupy ourselves in wishing and desiring that all souls, created and to be created, should know Him, love Him, praise and glorify Him in all things. Would, O Lord, that we could convert all the infidels and sinners that there are in the world, and bring it about that none should offend Thee and all should obey and employ themselves in Thy service now and for ever and ever! *Hallowed be thy name: let all the earth adore thee, and celebrate thee, and sing canticles to thy name* (Matt. vi. 9; Psalm lxv. 4). And thus we may go on to think of a thousand sorts of service that creatures might pay God, and desire them to be so paid.

Hence each one should descend to desiring and endeavoring to do the will of God and work for His greater glory in what relates to himself, contriving ever to do that which he takes to be the will of God and His greater glory, ascending to what Christ our Redeemer says of Himself in the Gospel: *I ever do what is pleasing to my Father* (John viii. 29). For, as the Evangelist St. John says: *He who sayeth that he knoweth him, and keepeth not his commandments, is a liar: but whoever keepeth his word, in him the charity of God is perfect* (I John ii. 4-5). He who says that he knows and loves God, but does not do His will, is not telling the truth; he lies. But he who keeps the commandments and does the will of God, he has perfect charity and love of God. Hence, to love God and live in entire conformity to His will, it is not enough for a man to take complacency in the perfections of God and to wish all the rest of creation to love and glorify God, but the man himself must offer and dedicate himself entirely to fulfilling the will of God. For how can anyone say with truth that he desires the greater glory of God when in what he can, and in what lies in his power, he does not seek to procure it? This is the love that the soul exercises herself in when at meditation she forms resolutions and true desires to accomplish the will of God in this thing and in that thing and in all the rest that offers. This is the exercise which we are ordinarily wont to go through at meditation.

Hereby we have opened out a great field where we can occupy ourselves for a long time at meditation in this exercise, and we have set forth the great profit and perfection there is in it. It only remains now for us to set to work and begin to make trial here upon earth of that which we are to practise afterwards to such good effect in heaven. *The fire of God burneth in Sion, and the furnace thereof is forever kindled in Jerusalem* (Isaias xxxi. 9). Here there must begin to be enkindled in our hearts this fire of the love of God; but the flames, the height and perfection, shall be in the heavenly Jerusalem, which is glory.